Frommer's®
Cape Cod, Nantucket & Martha's Vineyard

My Cape Cod, Nantucket & Martha's Vineyard
by Laura M. Reckford

MOST PEOPLE VISIT CAPE COD, NANTUCKET, AND MARTHA'S VINEYARD

for the beaches. That's understandable. The beaches are wonderful: from the warm waters of Buzzards Bay to the sandy stretches along Cape Cod Bay, where low tide unveils miles of shells and sea life for beachcombers. The calm waters of Nantucket Sound are most popular with families, and the pristine National Seashore beaches, along the rough, unpredictable Atlantic Ocean, are beloved by surfers.

The Cape and Islands have much more to offer, though—centuries of history, for example. Places like the Dexter Grist Mill, in Sandwich, remind us what life was like for Colonial-era Cape residents. And Aquinnah, on Martha's Vineyard, is the ancestral home of Wampanoag, the Native American tribe that first called this region home.

As for outdoor activities, the bike paths, golf courses, and kayaking routes are among the best in New England. But what I like best about the Cape and Islands is the fact that on the busiest, hottest day in August, you can find a secluded place—a favorite walking path, a bike trail, a waterway. You'll stroll, pedal, or paddle a short distance, and miraculously, you'll be the only one there. The following photos offer just a glimpse of why those of us who live on the Cape and the Islands wouldn't live anywhere else.

DOCK ST.
Coffee
Shop

No trip to Nantucket Island is complete without a stroll around **NANTUCKET HARBOR (left)**. I like to start at the north end of the harbor at the Ropewalk, where yachters meet at the island's only outdoor raw bar—a lively summer scene. Then I wander around the edge of the harbor, gawking at the yachts, until reaching Old South Wharf, where a row of art galleries awaits.

BIKE SHOPS (above) are ubiquitous on Martha's Vineyard, where getting around on two wheels is a great option. My favorite route is an all-day circle-the-island tour that begins in Edgartown, loops through the up-island towns of West Tisbury, Chilmark, and Aquinnah, and passes through Vineyard Haven and Oak Buffs. You can stop along the way for shopping, sight-seeing, picnicking and, of course, relaxing on some of the island's prettiest beaches.

On the Cape and Islands, getting outside is what it's all about. Most people grab a blanket and head for the beach. Whether it's a secluded beach in **BREWSTER (left)**, accessed only by a narrow path over the dunes, or a family stroll on a lovely stretch of beach on **NANTUCKET (below)**, you'll find a beach for every mood. For more vigorous activity, head for the links. My favorite golf course for scenery is **HIGHLAND LINKS (above right)** in Truro. Playing in the shadow of Highland Lighthouse, on a 50-foot bluff overlooking the Atlantic Ocean, is an undeniable pleasure. If biking is more your speed, the **CAPE COD RAIL TRAIL (below right)** winds past scenic Nauset Marsh, in Orleans. And if you're riding your bike to the nearest ice cream shop, even better.

An overflowing portion of steaming **CHERRYSTONE CLAMS (left)**, some cold beverages, a group of friends—the ingredients of a perfect Cape Cod cocktail hour. The wonderful thing about eating shellfish on the Cape is that the fisherman who hauled it in could very well be sitting at the next table. It's easy to find fresh off-the-boat seafood on the Cape and Islands; it's a specialty of the region.

The colors of the clay **CLIFFS OF AQUINNAH (below)**, on Martha's Vineyard, change depending on the time of day. In the first light of morning, the colors are subdued, but they seem to grow more intense as the sun rises. By sunset, the cliffs appear to glow from within. Making the trek to the far side of the island to see these cliffs is a must.

DEXTER'S GRIST MILL (above), on Shawme Pond in Sandwich, is one of the Cape's historic treasures. The Colonial-era building has survived for 3½ centuries and is just one of the many historic sites on the Cape and Islands, from lighthouses to windmills to historic houses, that are open to visitors. The mill still grinds corn, which you can take home with you. It's a bargain—a 2-pound bag costs a few dollars.

Best Cape clam shack? That's a tricky one. For authentic Cape Cod atmosphere, you can't beat **CAP'T CASS ROCK HARBOR SEAFOOD (right),** in Orleans, where the colorful buoys on one exterior wall serve as a beacon to fried-fish aficionados. It's casual here. You just belly up to the counter and order a big plate of fried clams—with bellies, of course.

Of the many places to watch the sunset on the Cape and Islands, nothing comes close to **ROCK HARBOR (left)**, in Orleans, where the ebbing glow of the sunset lights up the trees that were placed in the harbor as channel markers. Rock Harbor is also where to find the Cape's biggest sport fishing fleet—18 boats wait to take you out to snag bluefish, striped bass, tuna, and other big-game fish.

I never get tired of wandering through the Camp Meeting Grounds, in Oak Bluffs on Martha's Vineyard, to see the whimsical **"GINGERBREAD" COTTAGES (above)**. These homes are a prime example of the Victorian architectural style known as Carpenter Gothic, in which craftsmen used their tools to construct intricate scrollwork and other ornamental flourishes. The campgrounds were built for Methodist revival meetings; in the center is the magnificent Trinity Park Tabernacle, an open-sided iron chapel.

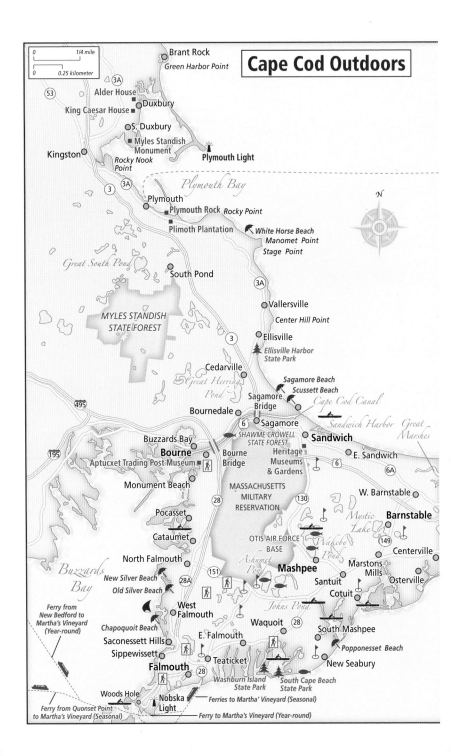

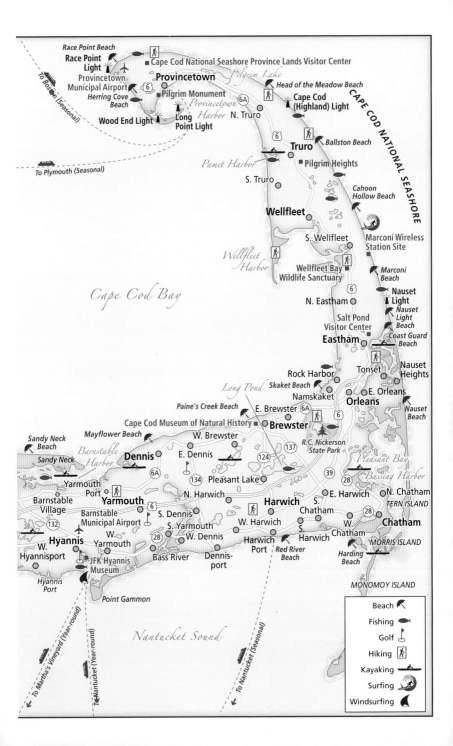

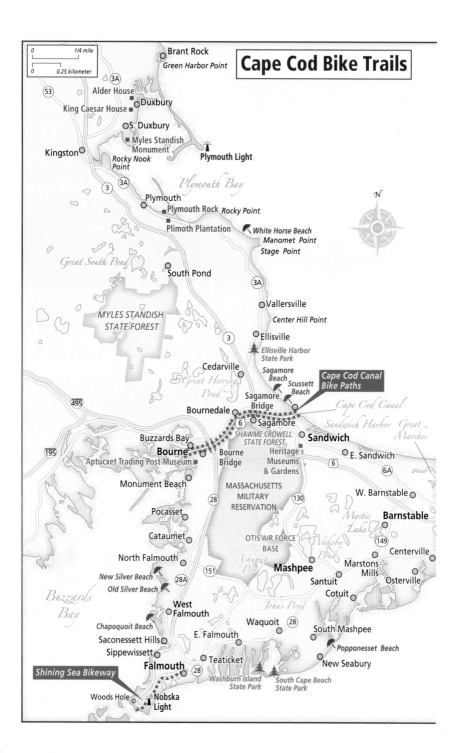

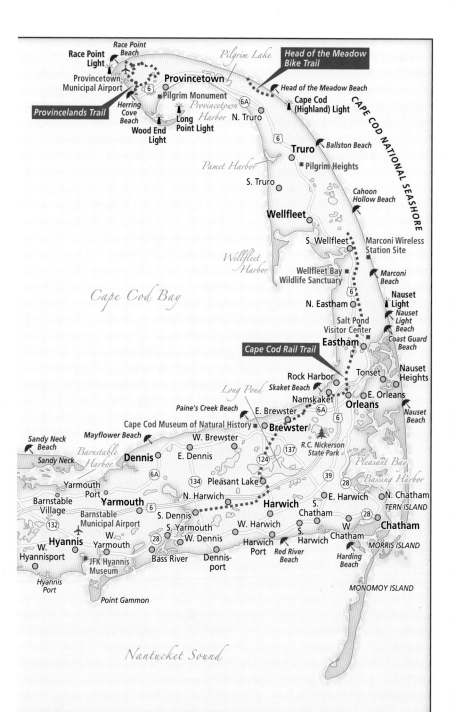

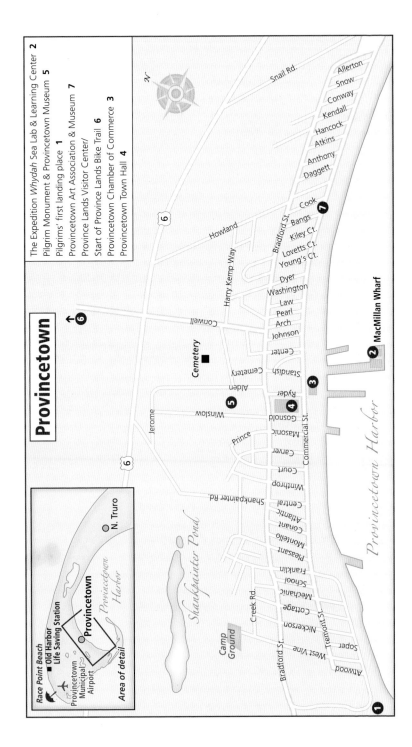

Provincetown

The Expedition *Whydah* Sea Lab & Learning Center **2**
Pilgrim Monument & Provincetown Museum **5**
Pilgrims' first landing place **1**
Provincetown Art Association & Museum **7**
Province Lands Visitor Center/
Start of Province Lands Bike Trail **6**
Provincetown Chamber of Commerce **3**
Provincetown Town Hall **4**

Provincetown Harbor

MacMillan Wharf **2**

Shankpainter Pond

Cemetery

Camp Ground

N

Area of detail

Race Point Beach
Old Harbor Life Saving Station
Provincetown Municipal Airport
Provincetown
Provincetown Harbor
N. Truro

Provincetown

Snail Rd.

Allerton
Snow
Conway
Kendall
Hancock
Atkins
Anthony
Daggett

Cook
Bangs
Kiley Ct.
Lovetts Ct.
Young's Ct.
Bradford St.
Howland
Harry Kemp Way
Dyer
Washington
Law
Pearl
Arch
Johnson
Center
Conwell
Standish
Cemetery
Alden
Ryder
Gosnold
Masonic
Commercial St.
Carver
Prince
Winslow
Jerome
Court
Winthrop
Shankpainter Rd.
Central
Atlantic
Conant
Montello
Pleasant
Franklin
School
Mechanic
Cottage
Nickerson
Creek Rd.
Bradford St.
West Vine
Tremont St.
Soper
Atwood

6

6

6

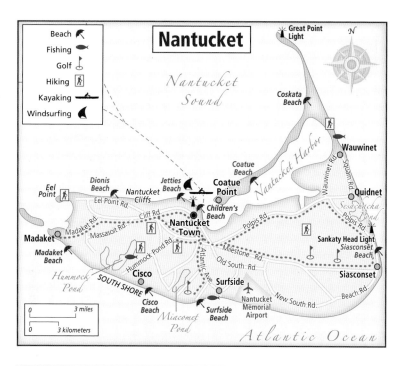

Nantucket

Legend
- Beach
- Fishing
- Golf
- Hiking
- Kayaking
- Windsurfing

Nantucket Sound

Great Point Light

Coskata Beach

Wauwinet

Quidnet

Coatue Beach

Nantucket Harbor

Coatue Point

Jetties Beach

Children's Beach

Eel Point

Dionis Beach

Nantucket Cliffs

Eel Point Rd.

Cliff Rd.

Nantucket Town

Madaket Rd.

Massasoit Rd.

Madaket

Madaket Beach

Hummock Pond Rd.

Cisco

Hummock Pond

SOUTH SHORE

Cisco Beach

Miacomet Pond

Atlantic Ave.

Milestone Rd.

Old South Rd.

Polpis Rd.

Sankaty Head Light

Siasconset Beach

Siasconset

Sesachacha Pond

Polpis Rd.

Squam Rd.

Wauwinet Rd.

Surfside

Surfside Beach

Nantucket Memorial Airport

New South Rd.

Beach Rd.

Atlantic Ocean

0 — 3 miles
0 — 3 kilometers

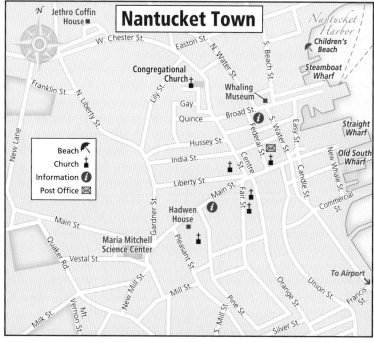

Nantucket Town

Jethro Coffin House

Nantucket Harbor

W. Chester St.

Easton St.

Children's Beach

Steamboat Wharf

Congregational Church

N. Water St.

S. Beach St.

Whaling Museum

Franklin St.

N. Liberty St.

Lily St.

Gay

Quince

Broad St.

Federal St.

Straight Wharf

Easy St.

Old South Wharf

New Whale St.

Hussey St.

India St.

Liberty St.

Centre St.

S. Water St.

Candle St.

Commercial St.

New Lane

Main St.

Fair St.

Hadwen House

Legend
- Beach
- Church
- Information
- Post Office

Gardner St.

Maria Mitchell Science Center

Quaker Rd.

Vestal St.

Pleasant St.

New Mill St.

Mt. Vernon St.

Mill St.

S. Mill St.

Pine St.

Orange St.

Union St.

To Airport

Francis St.

Silver St.

Milk St.

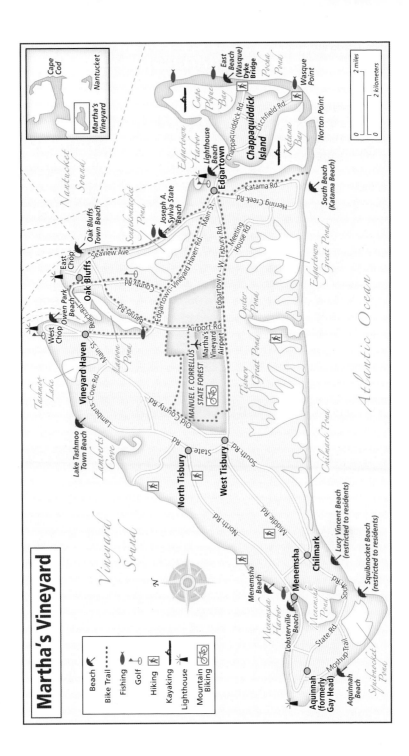

Martha's Vineyard

Legend:
- Beach
- Bike Trail
- Fishing
- Golf
- Hiking
- Kayaking
- Lighthouse
- Mountain Biking

Cape Cod

Nantucket

Martha's Vineyard

2 miles

2 kilometers

Chappaquiddick Island

East Beach (Wasque)
Dyke Bridge
Wasque Point
Pocha Pond
Cape Poge Bay
Katama Bay
Norton Point
Litchfield Rd.
Chappaquiddick Rd.

Edgartown Harbor
Lighthouse Beach
Edgartown

Katama Rd.
South Beach (Katama Beach)
Herring Creek Rd.

Joseph A. Sylvia State Beach
Oak Bluffs Town Beach
Seaview Ave.
Main St.
Edgartown-Vineyard Haven Rd.
Meeting House Rd.
Edgartown-W. Tisbury Rd.

Seatontacket Pond
County Rd.
Barnes Rd.
Airport Rd.
Martha's Vineyard Airport
MANUEL F. CORRELLUS STATE FOREST
Old County Rd.

Edgartown Great Pond
Oyster Pond
Tisbury Great Pond

East Chop
Oak Bluffs
West Chop
Owen Park Beach
Vineyard Haven
Beach Rd.
Lambert's Cove Rd.
Main St.
Lagoon Pond

Nantucket Sound

Vineyard Sound

Tashmoo Lake
Lake Tashmoo Town Beach
Lambert's Cove

State Rd.
North Tisbury
West Tisbury
South Rd.
North Rd.
Middle Rd.

Atlantic Ocean

Chilmark Pond
Chilmark
Menemsha
Menemsha Beach
Menemsha Harbor
Menemsha Pond
Lobsterville Beach

Lucy Vincent Beach (restricted to residents)
Squibnocket Beach (restricted to residents)

South Rd.
State Rd.
Moshup Trail

Aquinnah (formerly Gay Head)
Aquinnah Beach
Squibnocket Pond

Frommer's®
Cape Cod, Nantucket & Martha's Vineyard 2009

by Laura M. Reckford

Here's what the critics say about Frommer's:

"Amazingly easy to use. Very portable, very complete."
—BOOKLIST

"Detailed, accurate, and easy-to-read information
for all price ranges."
—GLAMOUR MAGAZINE

"Hotel information is close to encyclopedic."
—DES MOINES SUNDAY REGISTER

"Frommer's Guides have a way of giving you
a real feel for a place."
—KNIGHT RIDDER NEWSPAPERS

WILEY
Wiley Publishing, Inc.

ABOUT THE AUTHOR

Laura M. Reckford is the managing editor of *The Falmouth Enterprise* newspaper in
Falmouth on Cape Cod. Formerly the managing editor of *Cape Cod Life* magazine, she has
also been on the editorial staffs of *Good Housekeeping* magazine and *Entertainment Weekly*. She
co-authored the first edition of *France For Dummies* (published by Wiley Publishing, Inc).

Published by:

WILEY PUBLISHING, INC.

111 River St.
Hoboken, NJ 07030-5774

ISBN 978-0-470-38515-9
Editor: Jennifer Polland
Production Editor: Katie Robinson
Cartographer: Andy Dolan
Photo Editor: Richard H. Fox
Production by Wiley Indianapolis Composition Services

Front cover photo: Martha's Vineyard: Woman in summer dress on the beach
Back cover photo: Pleasant Lake General Store, located along the Cape Cod bike trail

For information on our other products and services or to obtain technical support, please
contact our Customer Care Department within the U.S. at 800/762-2974, outside the
U.S. at 317/572-3993 or fax 317/572-4002.

Wiley also publishes its books in a variety of electronic formats. Some content that
appears in print may not be available in electronic formats.

Manufactured in the United States of America

5   4   3   2   1

CONTENTS

10 MARTHA'S VINEYARD 252

FAST FACTS, TOLL-FREE NUMBERS & WEBSITES 288

INDEX 299

LIST OF MAPS

AN INVITATION TO THE READER

In researching this book, we discovered many wonderful places—hotels, restaurants, shops, and more. We're sure you'll find others. Please tell us about them, so we can share the information with your fellow travelers in upcoming editions. If you were disappointed with a recommendation, we'd love to know that, too. Please write to:

Frommer's Cape Cod, Nantucket & Martha's Vineyard 2009
Wiley Publishing, Inc. • 111 River St. • Hoboken, NJ 07030-5774

AN ADDITIONAL NOTE

Please be advised that travel information is subject to change at any time—and this is especially true of prices. We therefore suggest that you write or call ahead for confirmation when making your travel plans. The authors, editors, and publisher cannot be held responsible for the experiences of readers while traveling. Your safety is important to us, however, so we encourage you to stay alert and be aware of your surroundings. Keep a close eye on cameras, purses, and wallets, all favorite targets of thieves and pickpockets.

FROMMER'S STAR RATINGS, ICONS & ABBREVIATIONS

Every hotel, restaurant, and attraction listing in this guide has been ranked for quality, value, service, amenities, and special features using a star-rating system. In country, state, and regional guides, we also rate towns and regions to help you narrow down your choices and budget your time accordingly. Hotels and restaurants are rated on a scale of zero (recommended) to three stars (exceptional). Attractions, shopping, nightlife, towns, and regions are rated according to the following scale: zero stars (recommended), one star (highly recommended), two stars (very highly recommended), and three stars (must-see).

In addition to the star-rating system, we also use seven feature icons that point you to the great deals, in-the-know advice, and unique experiences that separate travelers from tourists. Throughout the book, look for:

Finds	Special finds—those places only insiders know about
Fun Facts	Fun facts—details that make travelers more informed and their trips more fun
Kids	Best bets for kids and advice for the whole family
Moments	Special moments—those experiences that memories are made of
Overrated	Places or experiences not worth your time or money
Tips	Insider tips—great ways to save time and money
Value	Great values—where to get the best deals

The following **abbreviations** are used for credit cards:

AE	American Express	**DISC**	Discover	**V**	Visa
DC	Diners Club	**MC**	MasterCard		

FROMMERS.COM

Now that you have this guidebook to help you plan a great trip, visit our website at www.frommers.com for additional travel information on more than 4,000 destinations. We update features regularly to give you instant access to the most current trip-planning information available. At Frommers.com, you'll find scoops on the best airfares, lodging rates, and car rental bargains. You can even book your travel online through our reliable travel booking partners. Other popular features include:

- Online updates of our most popular guidebooks
- Vacation sweepstakes and contest giveaways
- Newsletters highlighting the hottest travel trends
- Podcasts, interactive maps, and up-to-the-minute events listings
- Opinionated blog entries by Arthur Frommer himself
- Online travel message boards with featured travel discussions

What's New in Cape Cod, Nantucket & Martha's Vineyard

The following are highlights of what's new on the Cape and islands.

THE UPPER CAPE In Falmouth, the long-awaited completion of the **Shining Sea Bikeway,** a bike path along a former rail line that will stretch from Woods Hole all the way to North Falmouth—about 12 miles—is nearly here. It has taken more than 10 years for the idea of the extension to come to fruition; construction began in the summer of 2008 and is expected to be completed in the late spring of 2009. This will make the Shining Sea Bikeway one of the longest and most scenic bike paths on the Cape, only shorter than the 25-mile Cape Cod Rail Trail. The new terminus of the path will be on County Road in North Falmouth, which is the extension to Route 151. There will be parking at this end of the path, as well as on Depot Avenue and on Locust Street.

The **Woods Hole Inn** (6 Luscombe Ave., Woods Hole; ℂ 508/495-0248), which has operated as a sort of lodging house for decades, is now a spruced up bed-and-breakfast in a very central location, with views of Vineyard Sound and Martha's Vineyard. Guest rooms are reasonably priced and the innkeepers are maintaining an eco-friendly theme with recycling, composting, and other energy saving techniques. The new restaurant at the Woods Hole Inn is **Quick's Hole** (ℂ 508/540-4848), a hip fast food den that specializes in burritos.

Falmouth Raw Bar (56 Scranton Ave., Falmouth; ℂ **508/548-7RAW** [508/548-7729]), on Falmouth Inner Harbor, offers fresh steamers, oysters, littlenecks, and shrimp. Their specialty is the giant lobster roll at $25. The drinks menu is twice as long as the food menu, with specialties including frozen concoctions like Jamaican Jelly Bean, a modified piña colada.

The venerable **Fishmonger's Cafe** (56 Water St., Woods Hole; ℂ **508/540-5376**), a Woods Hole institution since the 1970s, has new owners who are working on updating the menu.

THE MID CAPE On Main Street in Hyannis is **Columbo's Café** (544 Main St., Hyannis; ℂ **508/790-5700**), the newest restaurant by Dave Columbo, the owner of the nearby Roadhouse Café. Columbo's concentrates on such classics as pasta and pizza and intends to stay open year-round.

In Yarmouth, one of the Cape's best restaurants, **902 Main,** has closed. The chef, the very talented Gilbert Pepin, is now at **Belfry Bistro** in Sandwich (8 Jarves St., Sandwich; ℂ **508/888-8550**).

THE LOWER CAPE Weekend (217 Main St., East Orleans; ℂ **508/255-9300**) is a new playful shop that has opened in an 1832 building that used to be a general store. The shop's owner, Mari Pocari, a former set decorator, has stocked the store with jewelry, art, women's fashions, children's apparel and spa products.

THE OUTER CAPE The buzz around **Bistro 404** (404 Commercial St., Provincetown; ✆ 508/487-5404), a new restaurant located at the site of the former Chester Restaurant, has been very positive. This is an unabashedly fancy dining option, where diners should expect to spend close to $100 per person, including wine for a soup-to-nuts meal.

On the other end of the spectrum is **Frappo66** (at the Art House, ✆ 508/487-9066), an updated cafeteria where diners can have a quick snack or a complete meal at about half the price of comparable establishments. But the food is very good here and the convenience of a cafeteria-style option is undeniable.

One inn that just keeps getting better and better is **Carpe Diem Guest House** (12-14 Johnson St., Provincetown; ✆ 508/487-4242), which has added a full-service spa with massage rooms, Provincetown's largest steam room, a Finnish dry sauna, and hydrojet spa tub. The innkeepers have also added a new building with four new guest suites, commons rooms, and patios.

Surfside Hotel and Suites (543 Commercial St., Provincetown; ✆ 860/757-8616), has freshened up its decor with new bedding and linens. The two large motel buildings in this complex are on both sides of Commercial Street, so a good number of the 83 rooms have ocean views, making this a comfortable and reasonably priced place to stay.

NANTUCKET The Nantucket Lifesaving Museum has undergone a $3-million renovation and is now the **Nantucket Shipwreck and Lifesaving Museum** (158 Polpis Rd., Nantucket; ✆ 508/228-1885). The museum now offers a child-friendly tour of its many unusual artifacts.

A fun new store in the center of town is **Current Vintage** (4 Easy St., Nantucket; ✆ 508/228-5073), which stocks both upscale vintage clothing and accessories and hard-to-find wines.

A big loss on Main Street was the closing of **Congdon's,** one of two side-by-side pharmacies with soda fountain/lunch counters. The remaining business, **Nantucket Pharmacy** still has great breakfast and lunch sandwiches and the best smoothie on the island.

Provisions, a deli located at Harbor Square, has new owners. Although they still have the popular turkey terrific sandwich on the menu, the word is the old charm has been lost, at least for now.

The most exciting restaurant renovation on Nantucket is the **Galley Beach** (54 Jefferson Ave., Nantucket; ✆ 508/228-9641), the beachfront restaurant at the Cliffside Beach Club. Prices are pretty steep, but you want to at least have a drink and hang out at the bar at this exquisite venue.

The owners of the **Jared Coffin House** (29 Broad St., Nantucket; ✆ 508/228-1894) have still not begun upgrades, though they did replace the inn's atmosphere pub, the Tap Room, with a Chinese restaurant called Harbor Wok. The company also owns The Wauwinet, the White Elephant, and the Wharf Cottages.

MARTHA'S VINEYARD The ownership of the **Harbor View Hotel** (131 N. Water St., Edgartown; ✆ 508/627-7000) is still working on a major renovation, but they have finished renovating the inn's two restaurants, which are now called **Water Street,** a fine-dining venue, and **Henry's,** a clubby bar. A spa and fitness center has also been added.

The **Hob Knob** (128 Main St., Edgartown; ✆ 508/627-9510) is trying to reinvent itself as an eco-friendly boutique hotel. Besides recycling and composting, the inn has installed eco-friendly materials, like LEED-certified carpets, low VOC paints, and non-toxic cleaning products.

The Best of Cape Cod & the Islands

Cape Cod is a curling peninsula only 70 miles long that encompasses hundreds of miles of beaches and more freshwater ponds than there are days in the year. The ocean's many moods rule this thin spit of land, and in summer, it has a very sunny disposition indeed. The "arm" of the Cape has beckoned wayfarers since pre-Colonial times. These days, more than five million visitors flock from around the world each year to enjoy nature's nonstop carnival, a combination of torrid sun, and cool, salty air.

On the Cape, days have a way of unfurling aimlessly but pleasantly, with a round of inviolable rituals. First and foremost is a long, restful stint at the beach (you can opt for either the warmer, gently lapping waters of Cape Cod Bay or the pounding Atlantic surf). The beach is generally followed by a stroll through the shops of the nearest town and an obligatory ice-cream stop. After a desalinating shower and perhaps a nap (the pristine air has a way of inspiring snoozes), it's time for a fabulous dinner. There are few experiences quite so blissful as sitting at a picnic table overlooking a bustling harbor and feasting on a just-caught, butter-dripping, boiled lobster.

Be forewarned, however, that the Cape can be a bit too popular at full swing. European settlers waited nearly 3 centuries to go splashing in the surf, but ever since the Victorians donned their bathing costumes there's been no stopping the waves of sun-, sand-, and sea-worshippers who pour onto this peninsula and the islands beyond every summer.

Experienced travelers are beginning to discover the subtler appeal of the off season, when the population and prices plummet. For some, the prospect of sunbathing with the midsummer crowds on sizzling sand can't hold a candle to the chance to take long, solitary strolls on a windswept beach, with only the gulls as company. Come Labor Day (or Columbus Day, for stragglers) the crowds clear out, and the whole place hibernates until Memorial Day weekend, the official start of "the season." It's in this downtime that you're most likely to experience the "real" Cape. For some, it may take a little resourcefulness to see the beauty in the wintry, shuttered landscape (even the Pilgrims, who forsook this spot for Plymouth, didn't have quite the necessary mettle), but the people who do stick around are an interesting, independent-minded lot worth getting to know.

As alluring as it is on the surface, the region becomes all the more so as you become more intimately acquainted with it. One visit is likely to prompt a follow-up. Although you can see all of the Cape, and the islands as well, in a matter of days, you could spend a lifetime exploring its many facets and still just begin to take it all in. Early Pilgrims saw in this isolated spot the opportunity for religious freedom, whaling merchants the watery road to riches, and artists the path to capturing the brilliance of nature's palette. Whatever the incursions of commercialism and overdevelopment, the land is suffused with spirit, and it attracts seekers still.

PEMBROKE

Marshfield
MARSHFIELD
Brant Rock
Green Harbor
3A

Pembroke

DUXBURY
53
Millbrook
Duxbury
3

Silver L.
South
Duxbury
Guret Pt.

27
North
Plympton
Kingston
Plymouth Harbor
North Plymouth
KINGSTON

Plympton
PLYMPTON
Plymouth

White Horse
Beach

North
Carver
44
Billington Sea
Manomet

Great South Pd.
3A

58
Carver
PLYMOUTH
Vallerville
C A P E

CARVER
Long Pd.
B A

MYLES STANDISH
STATE FOREST
Ellisville

Sampson Pd.
Halfway Pd.

South
Carver
White
Island
Shores
Cedarville

495
White
Island Pd.
Great Herring Pd.

SCUSSET BEACH S.P.

West
Wareham
25
WAREHAM
Sagamore
Town Neck Beach
Sandwich

ROCHESTER
Wareham
Buzzards
Bay
Cape Cod Canal
East
Sandwich
Sandy Neck Beach

Weweantic
Onset
Bourne
MASSACHUSETTS
MIL. RES.
6
Sandy Neck

Rochester
6
Monument
Beach
BOURNE
Forestdale
Lawrence Pd.
6A
West
Barnstable

MARION
Pocasset
130
Mystic L.
149

195
Marion
28
Wakeby Pd.
BARNSTAB

MATTAPOISETT
Wings Neck
Cataumet
OTIS A.N.G.B.
Mashpee
Marstons
Mills
Wequaquet L.
Centerville

Mattapoisett
Scraggy Neck
North Falmouth
28A
Ashumet Pd.
Santuit
North Bay
Craigville
Beach

West I.
Old Silver Beach
Coonamessett Pd.
151
Johns Pd.
Cotuit
Osterville

BUZZARDS BAY
West Falmouth
FALMOUTH
Waquoit
MASHPEE
28

Sippewissett
Teaticket
East
Falmouth
Grews Pond
Great Pd.
South
Mashpee
Popponesset

Falmouth
Surf Drive Beach
Falmouth
Heights
Beach
Menauhaunt
Beach
Waquoit
Bay
New Seabury
SOUTH CAPE BEACH S.P.

Woods Hole
Nobska Pt.

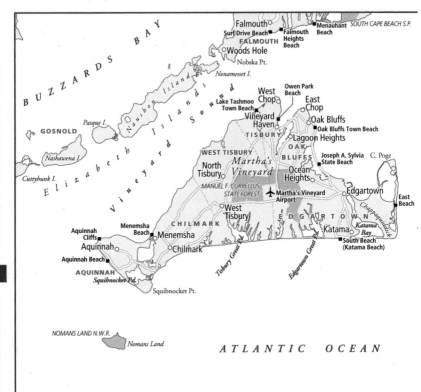

Narrowing down possible "bests" is a tough call, even for a native of the region. The selections in this chapter are intended merely as an introduction to some of the highlights. They're listed from closest in to farthest out along the Cape, followed by the islands. A great many other outstanding resorts, hotels, inns, attractions, and destinations are described in the pages of this book. Once you start wandering, you're sure to discover bests of your own.

Basic contact information is given for the places listed below. You'll find more information by referring to the appropriate chapters of the book.

1 THE BEST BEACHES

It is difficult to identify the best beaches without specifying for whom: fearless surfers or timid toddlers, party types or incurable recluses? At the bayside and sound beaches, for instance, the water tends to be much more placid than it is on the ocean, and thus better for little ones who plan only to splash and muck about.

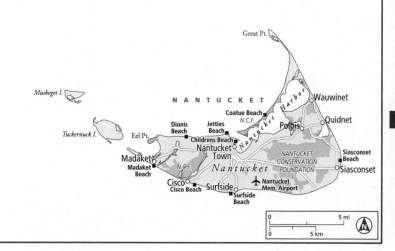

- **Sandy Neck Beach:** This relatively unpopulated, 6-mile barrier beach, extending from the eastern edge of Sandwich to shelter Barnstable Harbor, features pretty little dunes seldom seen on the bayside. Hike in far enough (but avoid the nests of piping plovers), and you're sure to find a secluded spot. Adventurous types can even camp overnight with permission (© **508/ 362-8300**). See p. 79.

- **Falmouth Heights Beach:** On a clear day, you can see Martha's Vineyard from this hip beach in Falmouth's most picturesque neighborhood. The newer motels take in the same view as do grand turn-of-the-20th-century homes, and the beach fills up with families throughout the day. Off season, this beach is virtually deserted, perfect for romantic arm-in-arm strolling. See p. 95.

- **Nauset Beach:** Located along the outer "elbow" of the Cape, this barrier beach descends all the way from East Orleans to a point opposite Chatham—about 9 miles in all, each mile increasingly deserted. The entry point, however, is a body squeeze: It's here that the young crowd convenes to strut their stuff.

Administered by the town of Orleans, but still considered part of the Cape Cod National Seashore, Nauset Beach has paid parking, restrooms, and a snack bar. See p. 174.

- **Cahoon Hollow Beach:** Spectacular Cahoon Hollow Beach on the rough, frigid Atlantic Ocean is your reward at the end of a winding trek down a 75-foot dune. See p. 189.

- **Race Point Beach:** Unlike many of the beaches closer to Provincetown, which are tacitly reserved for gays or lesbians, Race Point—another Cape Cod National Seashore beach at the northernmost tip of the Cape—is strictly nondenominational. Even whales are welcome—they can often be spotted with the bare eye, surging toward Stellwagen Bank. The Province Lands Visitor Center at Race Point (② **508/487-1256**) has particularly good views. See p. 207.

- **Jetties Beach:** Among the region's beaches, Nantucket's have, as a rule, the best amenities; most have restrooms, showers, lifeguards, and food. For families and active types, Jetties Beach (just $^1/_2$ mile from the center of town) can't be beat. Offering boat and windsurfing rentals, tennis courts, volleyball nets, a playground, and great fishing (off the eponymous jetties), it's also scenic (those jetties again) with calm, warm water. See p. 230.

- **Aquinnah Beach** (formerly **Gay Head,** Martha's Vineyard): These landmark bluffs on the western extremity of Martha's Vineyard (call the **Chamber of Commerce** at ② **508/693-0085** for directions) are threatened with erosion, so it's no longer politically correct to engage in multicolored mud baths, as hippies once did. Still, it's an incredibly scenic place to swim—come early to beat the crowds. See p. 262.

2 THE BEST BIKE ROUTES

Blessed with many gently rolling hills, the Cape and islands are custom-made for a bike trek—whether as a way to get to the beach or as an outing unto itself.

- **Cape Cod Canal** (② **508/759-5991**): On this 14-mile loop maintained by the **U.S. Army Corps of Engineers,** you can race alongside the varied craft taking shortcuts through the world's widest sea-level canal. See p. 80.

- **Shining Sea Bikeway** (② **508/548-8500**): Connecting Falmouth to Woods Hole by way of the shore and the picturesque Nobska Lighthouse, this 4-mile path—soon to be increased to 12 miles—lets you dash to the ferry or dally at the beach of your choice. See p. 96.

- **Cape Cod Rail Trail** (② **508/896-3491**): Reclaimed by the Rails-to-Trails Conservancy, this paved railroad bed

currently stretches some 25 miles from South Dennis all the way to Wellfleet, with innumerable detours that beckon en route. Several sections of the bike path have recently been rehabilitated to make for an even smoother ride. See chapters 6 through 8.

- **Province Lands Trail** (② **508/487-1256**): Offering a rigorous workout, this 7-mile network swoops among the dunes and stunted forests at the very tip of the Cape. Take your time enjoying this moonscape. Be sure to stop off at Race Point Beach for a bracing dip, and at the **Province Lands Visitor Center** (② **508/487-1256**) as well. See p. 207.

- **Nantucket Town to Madaket** (② **508/228-1700**): Only 3 miles wide and 14 miles long, Nantucket is a snap to cover by bike. The 6-mile Madaket path crosses undulating moors to reach a beach with boisterous surf. See "Beaches & Recreational Pursuits," in chapter 9.

- **Nantucket Town to Surfside** (© 508/228-1700): An easy, flat few miles from town, Surfside Beach is a perfect mini-excursion for the whole family. There are even benches along the route if you'd like to stop and admire the scrub pine and beach plums. When you return to town, pause at Brant Point to watch the yachts maneuver in and out of Nantucket Harbor. See "Beaches & Recreational Pursuits," in chapter 9.

- **Oak Bluffs to Edgartown** (Martha's Vineyard; © 508/693-0085): All of Martha's Vineyard is easily accessible for two-wheel recreationists. This 6-mile

path hugs the water almost all the way, so you're never far from a refreshing dip. See "Beaches & Recreational Pursuits," in chapter 10.

- **Chilmark to Aquinnah** (Martha's Vineyard; © 508/693-0085): The Vineyard's awe-inspiring vistas of ponds, inlets, and ocean greet you at every turn as you bike along State Road and then turn onto the Moshup Trail, a road that takes you along the coast up to Aquinnah. It's a strenuous ride with perhaps the best views in the region. On the way back, treat yourself to a bike-ferry ride to the fishing village of Menemsha. See "Beaches & Recreational Pursuits," in chapter 10.

3 THE BEST SMALL TOWNS & VILLAGES

The prettier towns of the Cape and islands combine the austere traditionalism of New England—clusters of well-tended historic houses punctuated by modest white steeples—with a whiff of their own salty history.

- **Sandwich:** For a "gateway" town, Sandwich is remarkably composed and peaceful. Not-too-fussy preservation efforts have ensured the survival of many of this first settlement's attractions, such as the pond that feeds the 17th-century **Dexter Grist Mill** (© 508/888-4910). Generous endowments fund an assortment of fascinating museums including the multifaceted **Heritage Museums and Gardens** (© 508/888-3300), famous for its splendid rhododendrons but interesting to all for its many other exhibits. See p. 81.

- **Woods Hole:** Besides being the Cape's main gateway to Martha's Vineyard, Woods Hole is a world-renowned science community, a charming fishing village, and a bohemian mecca. A proper tour of town should include visits to the aquarium and the Woods

Hole Oceanographic Institution, a stroll along the bustling harbor, and a drink at the Captain Kidd bar, the Cape's top tavern. See "Falmouth," in chapter 5.

- **Yarmouth Port:** It may look somewhat staid on the surface (Hallet's, the local soda fountain, hasn't changed much since 1889, except it now rents videos), but there are a number of quirky attractions here. A museum features the works of author/illustrator Edward Gorey, a Yarmouth Port resident who died in 2000. There's also the gloriously jumbled **Parnassus Books,** owned by vintage bookseller Ben Muse. Stop at **Inaho,** 157 Main St. (© 508/362-5522), all but hidden within an ordinary frame house, for the Cape's best sushi. See p. 136.

- **Chatham:** Only Provincetown offers better strolling-and-shopping options, and Chatham's are G-rated. This is perhaps the Cape's quaintest town. In summer, Friday-night band concerts draw multigenerational crowds by the thousands. For a fun natural history lesson, take a boat ride to see the hordes of seals on uninhabited Monomoy Island. See p. 162.

- **Wellfleet:** A magnet for creative souls (literary as well as visual), this otherwise classic New England town is a haven of good taste—from its dozens of shops and galleries to its premier restaurant, Aesop's Tables. All is not prissy, however: certainly not the iconoclastic offerings at the **Wellfleet Harbor Actors' Theatre** (© 508/349-6835) or the goings-on at the Beachcomber, one of the Cape's best nightclubs. See p. 188.

- **Provincetown:** At the far tip of the Cape's curl, in intensely beautiful surroundings, is Provincetown. Its history goes back nearly 400 years, and in the last century, it's been a veritable headquarters of bohemia—more writers and artists have holed up here than you could shake a stick at. It's also, of course, among the world's great gay and lesbian resort areas—people come here for the pleasure of being "out" together in great numbers. If you're uncomfortable with same-sex public displays of affection, this stop might be best left off your itinerary. More open-minded straights will have a great time—Provincetown has savory food, fun shopping, terrific company, and fascinating people-watching. See p. 204.

- **Nantucket Town:** This former whaling town is so well-preserved it looks as though the whalers left their grand houses and cobblestone streets just yesterday. Tourism may be rampant here, but it's without the tackier side effects, thanks to stringent preservation measures. A

gamut of enticing shops offers luxury goods from around the world. Time has not so much stood still here as vanished. So relax and shift into island time, dictated purely by your desires. See chapter 9.

- **Oak Bluffs, Martha's Vineyard:** This harbor town on Martha's Vineyard evolved from a mid-19th-century Methodist campground. Pleased with the scenic and refreshing oceanside setting (and who wouldn't be?), the faithful started replacing their canvas tents with hundreds of tiny, elaborately decorated and gaudily painted "gingerbread" cottages. Still operated primarily as a religious community, the revivalist village is flanked by a commercial zone known for its rocking nightlife. See chapter 10.

- **Edgartown, Martha's Vineyard:** For many visitors, Edgartown *is* Martha's Vineyard. Its regal captains' houses and manicured lawns epitomize a more refined way of life. Roses climb white picket fences, and the tolling of the Whaling Church bell signals dinnertime. By July, a procession of gleaming pleasure boats glides past Edgartown Lighthouse into the harbor, and shops overflow with luxury goods and fine art. Edgartown's old-fashioned Fourth of July parade harkens back to small-town America, as hundreds line Main Street cheering the loudest for the floats with the most heart. It's a picture-perfect little town, a slice of homemade apple pie to go with nearby Oak Bluff's hot-fudge sundae. See p. 259.

4 THE BEST LUXURY HOTELS & INNS

- **Wequassett Resort and Golf Club** (Harwich; © **800/225-7125** or 508/432-5400): This Chatham institution occupies its own little peninsula on Pleasant Bay and offers excellent sailing

and tennis clinics. It is also next to the Cape's premier golf course and guests have members' privileges. You'll be tempted to just relax, though—especially if you score one of the clapboard cottages, done in an upscale country mode, right on the water. The on-site restaurant, **28 Atlantic,** is now one of the Cape's best. See p. 159.

- **Captain's House Inn** (Chatham; ✆ **800/ 315-0728** or 508/945-0127): An elegant country inn that positively drips with good taste, this is among the best small inns in the region. Most rooms have fireplaces, elegant paneling, and antiques throughout; the rooms are sumptuous yet cozy. This may be the ultimate spot to enjoy Chatham's Christmas Stroll festivities, but you may need to book your room a couple of years in advance. See p. 169.

- **Brass Key Guesthouse** (Provincetown; ✆ **800/842-9858** or 508/487-9005): The Brass Key Guesthouse, a compound consisting of five historic buildings, is *the* place to stay in Provincetown. With Ritz-Carlton–style amenities in mind, the owners have created a paean to luxury. These are the kind of innkeepers who think of everything: Pillows are goose down, showers have wall jets, and gratis iced tea is delivered poolside. See p. 213.

- **Cliffside Beach Club** (Nantucket; ✆ **800/932-9645** or 508/228-0618): Right on the beach and within walking distance (about 1 mile) of town, this is the premier lodging on the island. It may not be as fancy as some, but there's a sublime beachy-ness to the whole setup: simply decorated rooms; cheerful, youthful staff; a sea of antique wicker in the clubhouse; and of course, the blue, yellow, and green umbrellas lined up on the beach. Every Fourth of July, guests get a front-row seat for the fireworks show at nearby Jetties Beach. See p. 238.

- **Winnetu Oceanside Resort** (Edgartown, Martha's Vineyard; ✆ **866/335-1133**): This resort on Katama Beach, just outside Edgartown, has seemingly come out of nowhere in the last few years to become one of the best luxury hotels in the region. The Winnetu stands apart from other luxury resorts because it's also a wonderful place for families, with lots of activities to keep kids busy. The resort's restaurant, **Lure** (✆ **508/627-3663**), complete with a distant water view, is one of the island's best fine-dining options. See p. 273.

5 THE BEST HOTEL DEALS

- **Simmons Homestead Inn** (Hyannisport; ✆ **800/637-1649** or 508/778-4999): Bill Putman may be the most personable and hospitable innkeeper on Cape Cod. He is determined that his guests have an excellent vacation, a factor that may make the Simmons Homestead Inn one of the best deals around. A former race-car driver/ad exec, Putman has filled his inn with a merry mishmash of animals (stuffed, sculpted, or painted). But his passion is automobiles, and you'll enjoy touring his "museum" of more than 55 red sports cars. See p. 122.

- **Lamb and Lion Inn** (Barnstable; ✆ **800/909-6923** or 508/362-6823): Part B&B, part motel, this historic Cape cottage has been turned into a comfortable lodging with a pool. Hallways have murals, and rooms are creatively decorated. See p. 124.

- **Old Sea Pines Inn** (Brewster; ✆ **508/ 896-6114**): This reasonably priced, large historic inn is a great spot for families. Accommodations range from small singles with shared bathrooms to family suites. In summer, the dining room is the location for weekly dinner theater performances. See p. 154.

- **The Orleans Inn** (Orleans; ✆ **508/ 255-2222**): Don't miss this inn, perched right on the edge of Town Cove, and make sure to get a room facing the water. Built in 1875, the inn has been restored to its former grandeur. The water view and great location make this a terrific value. See p. 178.

- **The Inn at Duck Creeke** (Wellfleet; ✆ **508/349-9333**): In one of the Cape's most charming towns, this humble and historic complex offers no-frills rooms, some with shared bathrooms, for bargain prices. With grandmotherly touches like chenille bedspreads, it will make you feel right at home. A good restaurant and a tavern are also on the property. See p. 196.

- **Beachside at Nantucket** (Nantucket; ✆ **800/322-4433** or 508/228-2241): Although the in-season rates at Nantucket's only motel are about the same as at other B&Bs in town, the off-season rates are a real bargain. Specials could include rooms for less than $110 a night in May. The property is also one of the only lodgings in town with a pool. See p. 239.

- **Edgartown Inn** (Edgartown, Martha's Vineyard; ✆ **508/627-4794**): This quirky, old-fashioned inn is located in the heart of Edgartown. The smells of freshly baked goodies fill the air, and the staff is friendly and helpful. Most important, prices have stayed reasonable, a rarity on the Vineyard. See p. 274.

- **Wesley Hotel** (Oak Bluffs, Martha's Vineyard; ✆ **800/638-9027** or 508/ 693-6611): This imposing 1879 property, overlooking Oak Bluffs Harbor, is a solid entry in the good-value category, especially with its low off-season rates. It's a no-frills hotel with a great location, just steps from Circuit Avenue, the heart of Oak Bluffs. See p. 276.

6 THE BEST RESTAURANTS

It wasn't long ago that "fancy" food in these parts began and ended with classic French. Now "fancy," when it comes to food, is almost out of style and French food is hard to find. Although one of this year's "bests" is Italian and one is Mexican, most occupy that catchall category of New American, with influences from all over the world. Several aren't even fancy at all, just memorable.

- **Osteria La Civetta** (Falmouth; ✆ **508/ 540-1616**): It hasn't taken long for locals to realize that what's cooking at the little osteria on Main Street is something very special and authentic. This is the kind of place where the owners, who are from Bologna, send the chefs to Italy in the off-season to learn new skills. From the handmade pasta to the specialty desserts, this is a must try. See p. 105.

- **Heather** (Mashpee; ✆ **508/539-0025**): Chef/owner Heather Allen has created the perfect restaurant, a place where ambiance, service and wonderful food come together in the somewhat surprising location of a strip mall in Mashpee. But you'll forget all that once you settle in to what is bound to be a memorable meal. See p. 113.

- **The Regatta of Cotuit at the Crocker House** (Cotuit; ✆ **508/428-5715**): What most distinguishes the Regatta from its competition is the sensational service so rare at local establishments. The Regatta has a quintessential old Cape Cod setting—the building was once a stagecoach inn, and the decor is formal Federal style. Food here is consistently excellent, with fresh ingredients, generous portions, and creative preparations. See p. 128.

- **28 Atlantic** (Harwich; ✆ **508/430-3000**): This superb restaurant at the Wequassett Resort and Golf Club offers the most elegant dining in the region. Floor-to-ceiling plate glass windows give you a panoramic view of Pleasant Bay. The menu is loaded with delicacies from around the world. In this graceful setting, professional waiters will see to your comfort and thorough satisfaction. See p. 160.

- **Bramble Inn and Restaurant** (Brewster; ✆ **508/896-7644**): An elegant entry in the Lower Cape dining scene, the Bramble Inn attracts those who don't mind a rather steeply priced, four-course, fixed-price dinner. The five intimate dining rooms are decorated with antique china and fresh flowers. Chef Ruth Manchester is a local favorite for her extraordinary, evolving cuisine. See p. 153.

- **Devon's** (Provincetown; ✆ **508/487-4773**): The namesake of Devon's is a multitalented restaurateur with a great attitude. That positive vibe permeates every part of this small fine-dining restaurant, a former fishing shack on Provincetown's far East End. Serving New American cuisine with an emphasis on local provender, this is one of Provincetown's most romantic options, but its teensiness means you do need a reservation. See p. 217.

- **Lorraine's** (Provincetown; ✆ **508/487-6074**): This is exciting cuisine, part Mexican, part New American, and all sensational. Even people who don't like

Mexican food should try Lorraine's. Start your meal off with a shot of tequila from the four-page menu and chase it with their special-recipe tomato juice. Now you're off and running. Try something different—you can hardly help it here—like the sea scallops flambéed in tequila and topped with green-chili sauce. See p. 218.

- **Galley Beach** (Nantucket; ✆ **508/228-9641**): Newly redecorated, this exquisite beachfront restaurant next to the Cliffside Beach Club is the place to go if you want to feel like you are in a spread of *Travel + Leisure* magazine. Delicious food too! See p. 243.

- **Straight Wharf** (Nantucket; ✆ **508/228-4499**): Talented chef/owners have made this *the* fine-dining restaurant on Nantucket. Make your reservation for 8pm, so you can sit on the outside deck and watch the sun set over the harbor. Whether you opt for one of their specialty seafood dishes (wild striped bass with gazpacho) or choose a land-based entree (filet of Kobe beef), you will not be disappointed. See p. 244.

- **Atria** (Edgartown, Martha's Vineyard; ✆ **508/627-5850**): This fine-dining venue on Upper Main Street gets rave reviews for its gourmet cuisine and high-caliber service. The menu, featuring produce and meats from local farmers and the daily catch from local fishermen, takes its influences from around the country and around the world. See p. 278.

7 THE BEST CLAM SHACKS

- **The Clam Shack** (Falmouth Harbor; ✆ **508/540-7758**): The ultimate clam shack sits on the edge of the harbor and serves up reasonably priced fried seafood with all the fixings. Order the fried clams (with bellies, please!), and squeeze

into the picnic tables beside the counter to await your feast. See p. 107.

- **Cap't Cass Rock Harbor Seafood** (Orleans; no phone): Take a photo of the family in front of this shack covered with colorful buoys, and then go inside and chow down. Hearty portions of simply prepared fresh fish keep diners coming back year after year. See p. 180.

- **Arnold's Lobster & Clam Bar** (Eastham; ☎ **508/255-2575**): Once you get served a heaping plate of fried seafood here, you won't bother with any other clam shack. No one else gives you so much for such a reasonable price on Cape Cod. See p. 187.

- **Moby Dick's Restaurant** (Wellfleet; ☎ **508/349-9795**): Unfortunately, word has spread about this terrific restaurant, and it can get pretty mobbed here around supper time. Still, it's a terrific place to bring the family, screaming kids and all. The clambake special is a $1^1/_4$-pound lobster, native Monomoy steamed clams, and corn on the cob. Perfect. See p. 197.

- **Sayle's Seafood** (Nantucket; ☎ **508/228-4599**): Take a 10-minute walk from town on Washington Street Extension, and you'll arrive at this fish store-cum-clam shack. Charlie Sayles is a local fisherman, and everything here is deliciously fresh. Get your fried clams to go and eat them at the beach. See p. 237.

- **The Bite** (Menemsha, Martha's Vineyard; ☎ **508/645-9239**): A travel writer once called it the best restaurant on Martha's Vineyard, perhaps in retaliation for a high-priced meal in Edgartown. Nevertheless, this is a top-shelf clam shack, tucked away in a picturesque fishing village. Order your meal to go and stroll over to the beach, which has the best sunset views on the island. The fried clams are delicious; some say the secret is the batter. Of course, the fish, unloaded just steps away, couldn't be fresher. See p. 285.

8 THE BEST SHOPPING

No matter how spectacular the scenery or splendid the weather, certain towns have so many intriguing shops that you'll be lured away from the beach, at least temporarily. The inventory is so carefully culled or created that just browsing can be sufficient entertainment, but slip a credit card into your cutoffs just in case.

- **Chatham:** Old-fashioned, tree-shaded Main Street is packed with inviting storefronts, including the **Chatham Glass Company** (☎ **508/945-5547**), where you can literally look over their shoulders as artisans craft glass treasures.

- **Wellfleet:** The commercial district is 2 blocks long; the art zone is twice that. Pick up a walking map to locate the galleries in town: **Cherrystone Gallery** (☎ **508/349-3026**) tops the don't-miss list. Seekers of low-key chic will want to check out two designers, **Hannah**

(☎ **508/349-9884**) and **Karol Richardson** (☎ **508/349-6378**). See p. 194 and 195. For designer produce and impeccable seafood, peruse the array at the homey **Hatch's Fish & Produce Market** (☎ **508/349-2810** for fish, or 508/349-6734 for produce) behind Town Hall. See p. 198.

- **Provincetown:** Overlooking the import junk that floods the center of town, the 3-mile strip of Commercial Street is a shopaholic's dream. It's all here, seemingly direct from SoHo: sensual, cutting-edge clothing (for every sex and permutation thereof), art, jewelry, antiques, and more. And whatever you really need but didn't know you needed can be found at **Marine Specialties** (☎ **508/487-1730**), a warehouse packed with surplus essentials. See p. 213.

- **Nantucket:** Imagine Martha Stewart cloned a hundredfold, and you'll have some idea of the tenor of shops in this well-preserved 19th-century town. Centre Street—known as "Petticoat Row" in whaling days—still caters to feminine tastes, and the town's many esteemed antiques stores would never deign to present anything less than the genuine article. See the "Shopping" section, p. 236.

- **Oak Bluffs, Martha's Vineyard:** Circuit Avenue, chockablock with fun stores like **Craftworks** (149 Circuit Ave.; © **508/693-7463**) and **Third**

World Trading Co. (52 Circuit Ave.; © **508/693-5550**), has long been a destination for those looking for unique gifts. But now, a short walk away on Dukes County Avenue, there is a new "gallery district," a cluster of six little shops awaiting exploration. From the **Alison Shaw Gallery,** with walls lined by the well-known photographer's vivid works, to **Pik Nik,** a store full of all manner of art, clothing and unusual gifts, there is definitely lots here for the discriminating browser.

9 THE BEST BARS & CLUBS

- **Grumpy's** (Falmouth; © **508/540-3930**): Come to Grumpy's to hear some down and dirty blues or local cover bands rocking out. There's live music weekend nights year-round. It's also a friendly bar scene, attracting people of all ages, locals and tourists alike. See p. 110.
- **Embargo** (Hyannis; © **508/771-9700**): Most consider this the best bar in town and, even better, it's for grown-ups. There is live music nightly in the Back Door Bistro and a sizzling Monday-night Jazz Series popular with locals and those in the know. See p. 129.
- **The Beachcomber** (Wellfleet; © **508/349-6055**): Perched atop the towering dunes of Cahoon Hollow Beach, this bar and dance club is one of the most scenic watering holes on Cape Cod. Although the crowd tends to be on the young and rowdy side, the young at heart are also welcome. See p. 198.
- **Crown & Anchor** (Provincetown; © **508/487-1430**): The specialty bars

at this large complex span leather, disco, comedy, drag shows, and cabaret. See p. 222.
- **The Chicken Box** (Nantucket; © **508/228-9717**): The Box is the rocking spot for the 20-something crowd, but depending on the band or theme (reggae, disco, and so on), it can sometimes seem like the whole island is trying to get through the doors here. Jimmy Buffett makes an appearance late at night at least once every summer to jam with the band. See p. 251.
- **Offshore Ale Company** (Oak Bluffs, Martha's Vineyard; © **508/693-2626**): The Vineyard's first and only brew pub features eight locally made beers on tap and entertainment six nights a week in season. See p. 286.
- **Outerland** (Martha's Vineyard Airport, Martha's Vineyard; © **508/693-1137**): Formerly the Hot Tin Roof, this sprawling club at the airport has been the place to see big names on the Vineyard for decades. See p. 286.

Cape Cod in Depth

Cape Cod still resembles the old Patti Page song "Old Cape Cod," with plenty of "sand dunes and salty air," and even "quaint little villages here and there," but it is also a modern destination. Several towns in the Cape are in the process of installing town-wide Wi-Fi (that's wireless Internet for you Luddites), and a number of the region's hotels have top-shelf amenities, including elaborate spas. Sophisticated restaurants abound, along with chic boutiques and cutting-edge art galleries.

Some visitors are surprised that Cape Cod is not one place but many places—15 towns in all and numerous villages, each with its own personality. The nearby islands of elegant Nantucket and quaint Martha's Vineyard also have unique personalities.

Politically, the Cape and islands struggle with the usual issues of small town America, including trying to stay authentic and preserve their ties to history while still embracing modernization. The difference between other small towns and the Cape is that its history and natural beauty—the fact that this is where the Pilgrims actually landed first and that it is home to miles of pristine beaches, for instance—is also its livelihood. People come to see these quaint New England villages and these famous sand dunes—about 75 feet high in places along the Cape Cod National Seashore—and if they pave paradise and put up a parking lot, no one will come to visit. So, preservation is prized in all of the Cape's 15 towns and you will find fascinating historic sites—windmills, historic houses, and lighthouses, to name a few—throughout the region.

The 15 towns of the Cape and the nearby islands of Martha's Vineyard and Nantucket have managed to maintain their special qualities, and visitors still do come by the millions every summer. They bike, hike, kayak, and bask in the sun. They visit historic sites, dine out at refined restaurants, eat in at clambakes, and shop 'til they drop.

Of course, urban and suburban issues of growth, like traffic, wastewater disposal, water quality, and especially traffic—did I mention traffic?—are omnipresent. Writer Kurt Vonnegut, a former Cape Cod resident, once said of Cape traffic, "Traffic to Hyannis port was backed up through three villages. There were license plates from every state in the republic. The line was moving about 4 miles an hour. I was passed by several groups of 50-mile hikers. My radiator came to a boil four times." The Cape's traffic is notorious, and smart visitors plan their vacations to stay off the roads during prime times and choose a lodging option that is within walking or biking distance from the beach, as well as shops and restaurants (a surprisingly easy option in many of the Cape's towns).

Cape Cod, Martha's Vineyard and Nantucket offer a kind of perfect vacation. There are many unforgettable experiences to be had here, like the time when I saw three minke whales jump out of the water simultaneously, their fluked tails lined up in formation, during a whale watch at Stellwagen Bank, a protected ocean reserve off Provincetown. There are moments of the sublime, like when you chow down on a heaping stack of fried clams (bellies and all) while sitting at a picnic table with a view of the setting sun at Menemsha Harbor on Martha's Vineyard. And there are moments of enrichment, like shooting the breeze with an honest-to-goodness miller while watching him grind corn in a restored 17th-century gristmill in Sandwich. But mostly the Cape and islands are about enjoying a low-key beach vacation, preferably with buckets, shovels, and a trashy novel in tow.

The Cape Cod of today is many things at once: a popular vacationland, a mecca for wealthy second homeowners, a historic fishing village, a hip urban scene, a sleepy retirement community, a suburban subdivision, and even a bedroom community for Boston. Towns wrestle with how to maintain vibrant year-round communities as wealthy second homeowners buy up properties and drive up the cost of living for the average Joe. Towns also struggle to preserve each community's authentic character. As for Martha's Vineyard and Nantucket: the rich are richer, and the struggle is greater. The character of Martha's Vineyard and Nantucket are even more at risk from the dreaded sameness of corporate America, because they are both still so unique.

People on the Cape and islands are talking about the identical issues they are talking about throughout New England, around the country and even around the world: global warming, green energy, water and air quality, drugs and crime, health care, immigrants, education, and affordable housing. In classic New England style, the year-round residents of the Cape's villages and towns—there are about 230,000 of us—turn out for town meetings once or twice a year to decide the major issues and spending of the town. Discussions range from school funding to the Patriot Act and everything in between. What's a town meeting like? Show up and see for yourself. Everyone is welcome.

A big issue for all 15 Cape Cod towns in these tough economic times is the lack of funding for general municipal needs, like schools and sewage. Although school populations are shrinking as working families are allegedly leaving the Cape in droves, expenses, like the cost of energy, continue to rise. That means big cuts: Teachers are being laid off, programs are being eliminated, and in some districts parents are paying for things like music programs, sports programs, and even school bus transportation. Water quality is another hot topic at town hall meetings, since the region has an antiquated sewage system that does not prevent wastewater from leaking into the ground and contaminating the bays and estuaries. Several towns are working on sewer plans—systems that probably should have been installed decades ago—while others are embarking on major plans to clean up coastal ponds. In a place where sailing is a lifestyle and the beaches are vital to the economy, there is far too much murky water.

Cape Cod and the islands are tourist destinations, and naturally, their economy rests heavily on the tourism industry. Therefore, the shortage of workers for the Cape's many seasonal minimum wage jobs presents a problem. Positions for restaurant dishwashers, hotel chamber maids, and landscapers are going unfilled as it gets harder and harder to find people to take these jobs. Many large employers

Fun Facts   Old, but Not Feeble

The Cape has an aging population. We are by percentage older than any other county in the commonwealth of Massachusetts. But we are also active, and many senior citizens on Cape Cod bike, kayak and sail well in to their eighties.

used to bring workers in from overseas, from places like Jamaica, Brazil, and Eastern Europe under the H2B visa program, which is a program that allowed foreign workers sponsored by an employer to work in the U.S. for 6-month periods. Cape Cod businesses would employ these workers during the summer's prime tourist season. However, Federal legislation to extend the program has been mired in the larger national debate about immigration in general, and in the summer of 2008, for the first time in a decade, the foreign workers did not come to Cape Cod. Though the Cape and islands are home to a large population of Brazilian immigrants, the region's employers are already contemplating how to handle the shortage in staff for the summer of 2009 and beyond.

One drive past the large, elaborate seaside homes anywhere along the Cape may give some visitors the impression that the region is wealthy, but that is far from true. While the area does have gorgeous second homes that belong to the uber-wealthy, there are many middle-class neighborhoods and pockets of poverty, and even enclaves of homeless people who sleep in the woods and line up for free meals at the Salvation Army in Hyannis. The Cape's human service agencies struggle to provide services to all the families that need them and housing agencies work to create more affordable units, especially rentals, to house the working poor, disabled, and elderly. Many housing projects run into problems with neighbors who don't want the units, but many Cape Cod residents acknowledge that more housing must be built. The main question is how and where to do it. The concept of re-development (converting unused shops and industrial buildings into affordable housing) is gaining momentum and is also favored by planners at the Cape Cod Commission, the county land use agency.

On the islands of Nantucket and Martha's Vineyard the biggest question is: How can locals afford to stay in a place where millionaires, like Bill Gates of Microsoft, have mansions they visit for one week a year? Keeping the character of the islands—and that means the fishermen, carpenters, and shopkeepers, and not just the cobblestones streets and white picket fences—is critical to islanders of all incomes. The fact that Nantucket still has a character to protect is a tribute to past planners who designated the entire island as a historic district, a legacy that has served it well. Nantucket is the kind of place where the prospect of installing the island's first traffic light can cause an uproar. Residents are right to fight to maintain the island's character, because it is the subtle, incremental growth (a strip mall here, a historic house demolition there) that has altered so much of the character of the Cape's 15 towns. Like Nantucket, Martha's Vineyard also must fight to preserve its history and character. Only here, the problem is mansionization, where bigger and bigger houses are built, replacing cottages and blocking views of the water.

Although the region is fighting to maintain its character, it is also looking to the future. The nation's first off-shore wind

Destination Weddings in Provincetown

In 2003, when the Massachusetts Supreme Judicial Court ruled that marriage between homosexuals is legal, same sex couples flocked to all 15 Cape towns, and particularly to Provincetown, one of the country's top gay resorts, to tie the knot among the sand dunes and salt air.

The Wampanoag Tribe

When the Pilgrims first arrived in Cape Cod in 1620, they were greeted by the **Wampanoag Tribe,** a group of Native Americans who lived in the region. The Wampanoags were only officially recognized by the U.S. Government in 2007—387 years later! Today, the Wampanoags hope to build a casino off-Cape in nearby Middleborough, about 20 miles from the Bourne Bridge. If plans for the casino are accepted, the Wampanoags could use the profits from the casino to fund tribe needs, like housing and education. Those plans are awaiting decisions by the governor and state legislature, who are debating if and how to allow casinos in the state.

The tribe, which has about 1,500 members today, is in the process of organizing some of its cultural artifacts. The **Indian Museum** on Route 130 in Mashpee (© **508/477-0208**) is currently undergoing a renovation.

project—35 wind turbines in Nantucket Sound—is in the planning stages. The project has been through years of permitting with state and federal agencies weighing in. Although some people object to the industrialization of Nantucket Sound, many residents are in favor of the project, relishing the chance for the Cape to lead the nation in the construction of alternative energies. Energy conservation is becoming not just smart on the wallet and good for the environment, but absolutely vital to our future. Throughout the Cape and islands, energy efficient cars, solar panels on buildings, and expanded recycling programs abound. Today, the Cape and islands are a sea of "green" surrounded by oceans of blue.

2 LOOKING BACK AT CAPE COD & THE ISLANDS

THE PILGRIMS MEET SQUANTO: ARRIVING IN THE NEW WORLD IN 1620

In November 1620, a gaunt and exhausted band of Pilgrims traveling on a rickety boat called the *Mayflower* landed on the tip of the Cape in what is now Provincetown. While some people believe that they landed in nearby Plymouth, the Pilgrims actually landed in Provincetown. Plymouth was their second stop. While in Provincetown, they put together a little agreement called the **Mayflower Compact,** which was the first governing document of Plymouth Colony. At the far east end of Commercial Street in Provincetown, a rock marks the spot where the Pilgrims are believed to have landed, and a bas-relief on Bradford Street behind Town Hall pays tribute to the Mayflower Compact.

The Pilgrims were not the first European explorers to discover the region. Cape Cod was named around 1602 by explorer **Bartholomew Gosnold,** after "the great stoare of codfysshes" he saw offshore. He is also said to have named Martha's Vineyard after his daughter and the large number of grapevines he saw. But many say the area had been visited by Europeans long before Gosnold, and some local historians believe they have evidence, in the form of markings on boulders, that the **Vikings** were here as early as A.D. 1,000.

Impressions

With all the known parts of the civilized world behind them, the pilgrims found in this beach not an end but a beginning, whatever it might entail, and that of course is why they went there.

—John Hay, *The Great Beach*, 1963

However, the Cape's cultural history really begins with the **Wampanoag Tribe,** a name that translates as "The People of the First Light." This Native American tribe inhabited the northeast coast and used the area that is now the town of Mashpee on the Upper Cape as one of their bases. The Pilgrims were greeted by members of the Wampanoag Tribe, among them **Squanto,** who is said to have stayed with the newcomers for the 1¹/₂ years that they lived over in Plymouth, teaching them the ways of the New World. The Wampanoags were friendly to the Europeans, offering them food during the cold winter and showing them how to farm crops in the sandy soil. The Pilgrims seem to have repaid them with smallpox and some beaver pelts. The Pilgrims set up one of the first trading posts, at a spot the Native Americans had long been using, at what is now the **Aptucxet Trading Post Museum** (24 Aptucxet Rd., Bourne; © **508/759-8487**).

The Wampanoags were receptive to missionary efforts that led them to be known as "the praying Indians." The 1684 **Indian Meeting House** where they worshiped is one of the oldest churches on Cape Cod and is considered the oldest Indian church in the United States. It is located within an old Indian cemetery on Route 28 in Mashpee, and can be visited by appointment (© **508/477-0208**).

Around 1675 relations between the white man and the Indian soured and **King Phillip's War** was waged by Chief Metacomet (who the Pilgrims called King Phillip). The 2-year war resulted in the deaths of about 600 settlers and 3,000 Indians.

LET'S SETTLE HERE: EARLY TOWNS ON CAPE COD

The Pilgrims continued on to Plymouth, but within a few years other settlers came from Europe and settled on the Cape. The first town to be incorporated, **Sandwich,** was founded in 1637. The early settlers braved the dangerous cross-Atlantic voyage to escape religious persecution in Europe. Here they formed congregations of religious groups, including Quakers, which are still evident in several Cape Cod towns; the Congregational Church in West Barnstable, founded in 1630, has one of the longest uninterrupted congregations of that denomination in the world. One historian, Henry C. Kittredge, described the early Cape Cod settlers as "zealots and idealists."

The first settlements on the Cape in the early 17th century were compact. The idea was that every member of the community was in close proximity to three crucial places: the mill, the market, and the meeting. They used the large marshlands, particularly those north of Sandwich and Barnstable as salt hay for grazing sheep and cattle. Most of the Cape was wooded and the early settlers cleared much of the land to raise livestock and used much of the wood to build homes. The first couple of generations of settlers were farmers who were self-sufficient, growing corn and other crops, and raising sheep, pigs, and cattle. For variety, they would indulge in delicacies from the sea, like clams and lobsters. Corn was the principle crop and each town soon had a miller to grind the corn. The early mills were operated either through water power or wind power, and the miller was considered one of the most distinguished citizens of the town, because of his prized skill. As there were no stores, any item not grown on the property or made locally had to be purchased from England at great expense. It was easier to buy a parcel of land than an hourglass, noted Kittredge.

As the oldest town in the Cape, Sandwich is a good place to explore the Cape's early history. Evidence of 17th-century life can be found at the **Hoxie House,** built in 1675 (Route 130, Sandwich center; ✆ **508/888-1173**), the **Dexter Grist Mill,** built in 1654 on Shawme Pond (Town Hall Square; ✆ **508/888-4910**), the **Sandwich Glass Museum** (109 Main St., Sandwich; ✆ **508/888-0251**), and the **Heritage Museums and Gardens** (67 Grove St.; ✆ **508/888-3300**).

Some fine examples of historic houses are also on the islands of Nantucket and Martha's Vineyard. In Edgartown on Martha's Vineyard, the **Vincent House,** built in 1672, is the oldest house on the island (off Main Street, between Planting Field Way and Church Street; ✆ **508/627-8017**). On Nantucket, the **Jethro Coffin House** (✆ **508/228-1894**), a 1686 salt box home gets the distinction of being the oldest building on the island, though there are countless examples of well-preserved historic structures here, given that the entire island is designated as a historic district.

FROM PIRATES TO WHALERS: THE CAPE'S RICH MARITIME HISTORY

Before the Cape Cod Canal was dug out and the bridges were constructed in the 1930s, the shipping route around the arm of the Cape carried the reputation as "the graveyard of the Atlantic," for all the shipwrecks that took place among the treacherous shoals and currents off the Cape. Lighthouses were built—the first one was Highland Light in 1797 at Truro—in order to help captains navigate the tricky

The *Whydah:* A Pirate's Treasure Trove

One of the most famous ships that fell prey to the ocean was the ***Whydah,*** a pirate ship that wrecked near Wellfleet in 1717. The ship was captained by the notorious pirate Samuel (Black Jack) Bellamy. Bellamy and his pirate crew had captured a couple of other vessels in Nantucket Sound, but then the small fleet, manned by what is said to be crews of drunken pirates, was caught in a gale. The two other ships wrecked first, then the *Whydah,* which still had Bellamy aboard, wrecked a couple miles south of Wellfleet's Cahoon's Hollow Beach. Bellamy and 140 of his men drowned. Two men, both who had been captured from other ships, made it to shore alive. They alerted the locals who set about to haul in whatever they could that washed ashore from the wrecks. The one thing that the plunderers never did find was the chest of pirate's gold. It took almost 270 years for that loot to be found.

In 1984, local adventurer Barry Clifford began to excavate the site. His findings, including thousands of gold and silver coins, can be viewed at the **Expedition Whydah Sea Lab and Learning Center** in Provincetown (MacMillan Wharf; ✆ **508/487-8899**).

coastline that often became enveloped in a dense fog. **Highland Light,** also called Cape Cod Light, and the nearby museum run by the Truro Historical Society can be visited (27 Highland Light Rd., Truro; ✆ **508/487-1121**).

There are many tales of shipwrecks at the **Nantucket Shipwreck and Lifesaving Museum** (158 Polpis Rd., Nantucket; ✆ **508/228-1885**) and at the **Old Harbor Lifesaving Museum** in Provincetown (Race Point Beach; ✆ **508/487-1256**), which both tell the story of the men who risked their lives to save those who would have drowned at sea. Most were lost, but the lifesavers, which later became the **U.S. Coast Guard,** would patrol the coastline ready to assist if need be. A side business, that was quite a bit less noble, was run by those called **"mooncussers,"** who would watch by the full moon for shipwrecks and stand by to pick through any valuable parts of the wreck that came ashore.

Whaling was a prominent and lucrative industry from about 1750 to about 1850, when the industry began to wane. Whalers proved to be some of the most successful seafarers in the Cape's history. In order to make bountiful catches, whalers traveled around the world, and when they returned, they inevitably brought souvenirs home with them. Therefore, the homes of successful sea captains on the Cape and islands became virtual museums containing treasures from across the globe.

Nantucket became an important whaling port, and its wealth was renowned. The **Nantucket Whaling Museum** (13 Broad St.; ✆ **508/228-1894**) houses exhibits that show the history of whaling and the bounty it allowed seafarers to bring home. The museum displays the interior of an actual candle house, where whale blubber was transformed into candles. Other remnants of whaling life displayed at the museum are the **scrimshaw** (elaborate carvings made from tooth and bone) that sailors would carve to pass the time during the months at sea and **sailor's valentines,** the colorful boxes decorated with hearts made of seashells that crew members purchased from Caribbean ports for their sweethearts.

The **Great Fire of 1846** destroyed Nantucket's town center. After the fire razed the town, much of the town center was rebuilt with the riches from whaling journeys. An economic bust period in the late 19th century meant that nothing was changed for decades and the town has been virtually preserved from that mid-19th century period, cobblestoned streets and all.

Edgartown on Martha's Vineyard also thrived during this period, and there are numerous examples of the majestic sea captain's houses—mostly private homes—along North Water Street. There is also a large concentration of sea captains' houses along Route 6A in **Brewster,** nicknamed the sea captain's town. This is a good place to admire widow's walks, those rooftop porches that were said to allow the wives of sea captains to scan the horizon in anticipation of the return of their men. There are many sea captains' homes that you can visit in the region, but exceptional examples are the **Hadwen House** on Nantucket (96 Main St.; ✆ **508/228-1894**), the **Dr. Daniel Fisher House** in Edgartown (99 Main St.; ✆ **508/627-8017**) and the **Julia Wood House** at the **Falmouth Museums on the Green** in Falmouth center (at the Village Green; ✆ **508/548-4857**).

Although the fishing industry has been suffering in recent years from over-fishing, the Cape and islands are still the home of many who make their living by harvesting from the sea. In some families, the profession goes back for generations. Stop by the **Fish Pier** in the town of **Chatham** in the Lower Cape after noon to see fishermen unloading their catches. This too is an important part of the history of the region.

Impressions

I am not the only person who came here to spend two weeks and remained a lifetime.

—Mary Heaton Vorse, *Time and the Town: A Provincetown Chronicle*, 1991

THE FIRST TOURISTS: SPIRITUALISTS & SCIENTISTS

The late 19th century brought the beginnings of the tourism industry to the Cape and islands. The first tourists to these shores were looking toward the heavens but they were not seeking the sun. They came—by the hundreds—for religious retreats.

In Oak Bluffs, on Martha's Vineyard, Methodists would gather in a grove close to the harbor for revivalist camp meetings. The canvas tents they erected for the extended religious revivals were eventually expanded into tiny cottages. Today visitors can stroll around and see these "gingerbread cottages," a name that has been coined after the elaborate Victorian-era scrollwork and brightly-colored details on the houses and also see the **Trinity Park Tabernacle,** the largest wrought iron structure in the country. Open air services and concerts are still held here every summer. The **Cottage Museum** (1 Trinity Park; ✆ **508/693-7784**) tells the history of the camp meeting grounds and has early photographs of the visitors, who dressed in modest Victorian garb.

Across Vineyard Sound in the village of **Woods Hole** in Falmouth, a different kind of summer tourist was discovering the area. Scientists—especially oceanographers—interested in spending their summer vacations surrounded by other scientists were beginning to gather for seminars. Founded as a summer lab in 1888, **Marine Biological Laboratory (MBL)** today is an international center for research, education and training in biology with about 50 Nobel Laureates associated with it. Woods Hole is also home to the **Woods Hole Oceanographic Institution (WHOI),** which was founded in 1930 and is dedicated to ocean research, education and exploration. The institute runs on about $100 million a year in grants, many from the U.S. Navy. Both **MBL** (100 Water St.; ✆ **508/289-7423**) and **WHOI** (15 School St.; ✆ **508/289-2663**) have visitor centers open to the public. Perhaps drawn by the scientists at MBL and WHOI, several other science organizations have sprouted up in Woods Hole. The village is home to a branch of the **National Oceanic and Atmosphere Administration** and a semester-at-sea school called **Sea Education Association.** The village is a hub for scientists, fishermen, artists, and bohemians, particularly in the summer.

From around the 1890s to the 1930s, summer cottage communities began to spring up all over the Cape and islands for those who could afford a small second home. Two particularly picturesque summer cottage communities are **Falmouth Heights,** a village along the south shore of Falmouth where Victorian-era cottages were built on and around a central hill, and **Siasconset**—known as **'Sconset**—on Nantucket, where the tiny cottages are all near the ocean, and are festooned with climbing roses and ringed by white picket fences.

AN ARTIST COLONY FORMS ON THE OUTER CAPE

Around 1900, a group of artists from New York led by **Charles Hawthorne** discovered **Provincetown**, a tiny picturesque

Impressions

fishing village at the tip of the Cape where the native population of fishermen, many of Portuguese descent, had developed a colorful community. The artists, who set up their easels on the piers and the tiny lanes, made it an even more colorful community. Hawthorne taught his students to paint outside—*en plein air,* as the French say—and to give an idea of the figures through broad brush strokes with a palette knife, concentrating on the nuances of shadow and angle and color rather than getting hung up on detail.

Another famous artist who set up a school decades later in the 1950s was **Hans Hofmann,** a German who favored abstraction and whose background in art studies reached back to the Paris school of Henri Matisse. New York artists of the **Art Students League,** where Hofmann also taught, began taking summer homes in Provincetown and the nearby towns of Wellfleet and Truro. Some of them even moved there year-round. Visit the **Provincetown Art Association and Museum** (460 Commercial St.; ✆ **508/487-1750**) to understand the rich art history of the town.

As writers and intellectuals followed, the area became a hotbed of bohemia, a kind of Greenwich Village of the north. The liberal, artsy, open-mindedness of the populace made the area also a popular spot for gays, and Provincetown is now one of the country's top gay resorts.

THE GREAT BEACH IS SAVED: JOHN F. KENNEDY & THE CAPE COD NATIONAL SEASHORE

Cape Cod really became well-known when the second oldest son of a certain family who had been vacationing on the Cape for decades, became president. It was the glamour of seeing John F. Kennedy sailing his boat, the Honeyfitz, off **Hyannisport** that gave Cape Cod worldwide panache in the 1960s. Some say the place has never recovered. Hyannis, which is actually a village in the town of Barnstable, is by far the most built-up part of the Cape. It has a giant mall and numerous plazas surrounded by seas of asphalt. It also has the **John F. Kennedy Hyannis Museum** (397 Main St.; ✆ **508/790-3077**), a large photo display that continues to be one of the Cape's top tourist draws. The Kennedy compound is still in Hyannisport and is considered "home" for many of the Kennedy clan. Vehicles are warned away from the area by signs, but the curious can still get a good look at the compound, which consists of several homes set closely together, by taking a sightseeing boat trip out of Hyannis Harbor. The Kennedy family's favorite pastimes, like sailing in Nantucket Sound, continue through the generations.

JFK also did his part to preserve the Cape. In August 1961, he signed a bill designating 27,000 acres from Chatham to Provincetown as a new national park, the **Cape Cod National Seashore.** Visiting the national seashore can mean a trip to one of its spectacular beaches, along 40 miles of coastline from Nauset Beach in Orleans to Herring Cove in Provincetown, or following a ranger on a nature walk through the endangered habitat of an Atlantic White Cedar Swamp in Wellfleet. There are numerous nature trails offering self-guided tours throughout the seashore,

as well as several historic buildings set up as museums. Maps and information can be found at the **Salt Pond Visitor Center** on Route 6 in Eastham (© **508/255-3421**). Standing on this pristine seashore looking out at the churning Atlantic Ocean, putting all America behind you, to paraphrase Henry David Thoreau, continues to be one of the most cherished experiences for those visiting Cape Cod.

3 ART & ARCHITECTURE

ART

Artists began coming to the Outer Cape—Provincetown, Truro and Wellfleet—in the late 19th century when painter **Charles Hawthorne** started teaching classes about painting *en plein air,* with easels set up outside, making use of the famous Cape Cod light, an atmospheric quality local artists prize. Hawthorne soon opened the **Cape Cod School of Art** and later served as one of the founders of the **Provincetown Art Association,** formed as a gathering spot for local artists. Hawthorne's method stressed getting the crux of an image—colors, shapes and nuance—rather than worrying about detail. His students' paintings of local Portuguese children are called "mud heads," as they show the children virtually without facial features, and instead use well-placed shadows or the tilt of a head to reveal the mood of the child.

Hawthorne's protégé, **Henry Hensch,** continued the school, also stressing the Impressionistic style of using soft colors to paint images like flowers and streetscapes. In the 1950s, **Hans Hofmann,** an intimidating artist who had strong ideas about color and abstraction, came to the Cape. He was known to cut up a student's painting and reorder the pieces as part of his critique. Around the time Hofmann came to the Cape, other abstract expressionist stars of the period, like Franz Kline, Mark

Rothko, and Robert Motherwell, also visited the area and acquired summer homes.

Today, the legacy of Hawthorne, Hensch, and Hofman still lives on in the Cape. **John Grillo** is a Wellfleet artist who paints large colorful murals of the opera, circus, and tango; his murals are on display at Café Heaven on Commercial Street as well as the Cove Gallery in Wellfleet. **The Fine Arts Works Center** (24 Pearl St., Provincetown; © **508/487-9960**), which awards residencies each winter, ensures that a new group of artists and writers are inspired by Provincetown every year. Wellfleet's reputation as an art center is as strong as Provincetown's, and has even been called "the art gallery town," as there are about a dozen interesting galleries along Main Street and Commercial Street. In Falmouth, there are several excellent potters within a few miles of each other along the road to Woods Hole—just look for the signs for "pottery" and pull in to take a look.

The Cape and islands are also a great place to find crafts. On Martha's Vineyard, for example, sculptural iron weather vanes can be found at many local galleries. Historic crafts are also abundant on Martha's Vineyard and Nantucket. Nineteenth-century sailors created crafts to pass the time on their long seafaring trips: **scrimshaw,** elaborate sculptures made of ivory or whale bone; **sailor's valentines,** decorative wood boxes containing colorful shells; and **Nantucket lightship baskets,** handmade reed baskets with mahogany tops and scrimshaw ornamentation, were all popular crafts created by sailors—although sailor's valentines are now thought to have been purchased on Caribbean islands and brought back to New England. Today, some artisans are crafting modern examples of these crafts using the old methods.

To find an artist's studio, pick up the invaluable guide, *Arts & Artisan Trails of Cape Cod, Martha's Vineyard, and Nantucket* from the Cape Cod Chamber of Commerce. It lists about 200 artists, and their studios.

ARCHITECTURE

The Cape's architectural style is best known for its namesake **Cape Cod House,** a simple, wooden, shingled $1^1/_2$ story cottage with a central chimney. The first Cape Cod style homes were built in the 17th century by European settlers. Since then, there have been many adjustments to the classic Cape style over the centuries, but you can see early examples of this style, including charming half cape's, along Route 6A, mostly in the village of Yarmouthport.

A great way to see the history of early American architecture is to drive along the old stagecoach route, Route 6A, formerly known as the Old King's Highway. The narrow road winds along the north side of the Cape from Bourne to Orleans. Here, you will see colonial homes of all styles, many of which belonged to wealthy sea captains. **Georgian Colonial** homes were popular in the 1700s, and tend to be two-story square and symmetrical homes that often have two chimneys, one on each side of the roof. You can find several fine examples of Georgian style homes on Stony Brook Road near the intersection with Route 6A in Brewster. Also look for **Federal** style homes, which have classical elements like columns at the entryway or a

Palladian window (which is shaped like a half oval) above the front door. A good example is the **Julia Wood House,** part of the Falmouth Historical Society Museums on the Green property in Falmouth center. There are more elaborate homes in the **Greek Revival** style, which was popular in the mid-19th century; these two-story houses typically have a gabled roof, a columned veranda, and other "Greek" architecture elements that mimic temples, like doorways bounded by carved columns with friezes above. A fine example of Greek Revival is the **Dr. Daniel Fisher House** on Main Street in Edgartown on Martha's Vineyard. Also look for elaborate homes built in the **Second Empire (Mansard)** style, a fancy style inspired by the French houses with mansard roofs and elaborate carvings. A classic example is the **Captain Penniman House** in Eastham, which is open for tours in the summer. Homes built in the **Carpenter Gothic** style, or "gingerbread" homes, were popular as well; these Victorian homes tend to be painted playfully in bright colors and adorned with elaborate woodwork carvings and cut-outs on the roof and the trim. Examples can be found in the Methodist campground in Oak Bluffs on Martha's Vineyard.

On the Outer Cape and particularly within the bounds of the Cape Cod National Seashore, there is a movement afoot to save **"modern"** 1950s houses from the school of Walter Gropius, one of the leaders of the Bauhaus movement. Think glass boxes and you'll have an idea of what these houses look like. The jury is out on whether this architectural style will be accepted as suitably historic to qualify for preservation, but there is no doubt as to its aesthetic value or its harmony with the land. Set low into the landscape and facing outwards, all windows, on the ocean, these houses are without a doubt classic Cape houses of an entirely different sort.

ONE GIANT SAND BAR

In the beginning, there were the glaciers. The Cape and islands were formed relatively recently, merely 18,000 years ago, during the last episode of global warming, when glaciers receded from the area leaving a sandy substrate. In other words, parts of the Cape and islands—particularly the Outer Cape and Nantucket—are actually just giant sand bars. But what fine sand bars they are.

The best way to explore the geologic and natural essence of Cape Cod is with a visit to the 44,000-acre **Cape Cod National Seashore.** Stretching from Orleans to Provincetown, it covers 40 miles of pristine beach, marsh, kettle ponds and uplands. There are miles of biking and walking trails, including one in Truro that passes by a wild cranberry bog.

In the geologic scheme of things, Cape Cod is sort of a here-today, gone-tomorrow phenomena. Cape Cod's outer beach sees an erosion rate of about four feet per year. So the place is quite a bit different from when Henry David Thoreau walked from Eastham to Provincetown on the Atlantic side of the coast in the mid-19th century. However, a walk along the shore can still be the setting for a range of surprises. A simple stroll along the beach may present a piece of cloudy sea glass, stones and seashells of all shapes and colors, or even a glimpse of a pod of whales offshore. A great beachcombing site is the shoreline of Brewster on Cape Cod Bay where the tide recedes, leaving what seems like miles of ocean floor perfect for exploration.

The terrain of the Outer Cape feels different from the rest of the Cape. Larger trees like oaks and elms are replaced by pitched pine and scrub oak. This is where dune grass, beach plum and rosa rugosa, the hearty beach rose, are sometimes the only thing holding the sandy ground in place. But these fragile and rare habitats, like the **Atlantic White Cedar Swamp Trail** near Marconi Beach in Wellfleet, are where many rare and beautiful species— like the delicate orchid, called lady-slippers—can be found.

The salt marsh habitat, which is found in all parts of the Cape and on both islands is considered one of the keys to the health of estuaries and ponds. It works like a natural filter, cleaning groundwater before it enters estuaries. It was not too long ago that these areas used to be called swamps, and they were filled and paved for construction of things like shopping malls. Now they are protected with some of the toughest environmental regulations in the country.

WILDLIFE

The wetlands of the Cape and islands are part of one of the country's greatest annual wildlife spectacles: the passage of thousands of **migratory birds** in spring and fall. Warblers, herons, terns, and oystercatchers; shorebirds like avocets and the endangered Piping Plover; dozens of species of ducks; huge flocks of snow geese, owls, and hawks—these are just a few of the birds that take a rest stop on the Cape as they pass along the Atlantic Flyway, which for some birds extends from winter homes in South America to breeding grounds in the vast, marshy tundra within the Arctic Circle.

March, April, October, and November are all good months to see migrating waterfowl. August is the month to observe migrating shorebirds, with thousands stopping to feed at places like Monomoy Island, Nauset Marsh, and Sandwich's Great Marsh. Fewer shorebirds stop at the Cape in spring, but those that do will be decked out in the bird equivalent of a tux—their breeding plumage. Songbirds pass through in May, in their brightest

Impressions

Its geography is simple and explicit. It has the odd flung-out shape of a sand bar, with an excellent but boring canal at one end and at its furthest, wildest shore, Provincetown, the haunt of extroverts and practitioners of the half-arts such as soap-carving and sandal-making, where women with mustaches stare stonily at men with earrings.

—writer Paul Theroux

plumage and in full-throated song (both color and voice are muted in the fall migration). If you're birding on the Cape during the height of the summer season, you'll find plenty of herons, egrets, terns, and osprey wherever you find sand and wetlands.

The Piping Plover, a small, sand-colored shore bird, is a threatened species that nests on Cape Cod. Its populations are so small that each pair that nests is watched closely. The Cape Cod National Seashore is considered one of the most important nesting areas for the Piping Plover and beaches in several parts of the Cape, including Nauset Beach in Orleans and Race Point Beach in Provincetown, are closed every year while the Piping Plovers nest. Ignore the bumper stickers that say, "Piping Plovers taste like chicken," and

learn to love these tiny little birds that live on the shore's edge.

The other great wildlife-watching opportunity this region is known for is **whale-watching.** The humpbacks, huge finbacks, and small minkes all cluster to feed around the Stellwagen Bank north of Provincetown from April all the way through November. Monomoy Island is worth a special trip for **seal-watching.** In late winter, thousands of harbor seals take their version of a holiday in the sun, retreating to Monomoy from Maine and points north. Many stay for most of the year. They share the island with thousands of wintering sea ducks, as well as other migrating birds in the spring and fall. For info call the **Cape Cod Museum of Natural History** (© **508/896-3867**).

5 CAPE COD IN POPULAR CULTURE

Over the past 100 years, the Cape and islands have been a very popular place for authors and other creative types. In fact, a selection from authors who have summered here, lived here year-round, or simply enjoyed visiting would fill a weighty tome.

During the 20th century, the Outer Cape was a prime gathering spot for writers and the intelligentsia of the day. Playwright **Eugene O'Neill,** winner of three Pulitzer Prizes and the 1936 Nobel Prize, had his first play, *Bound East for Cardiff,*

performed in a shack on a wharf in Provincetown during the summer of 1916. That was long before he became one of the giants of modern drama. In the 1981 film *Reds,* directed by and starring Warren Beatty, the part of Eugene O'Neill is played by Jack Nicholson and parts of the movie are set in Provincetown. In the 1950s, playwright **Tennessee Williams** was a prominent Provincetown resident, who is rumored to have written parts of *Cat On A Hot Tin Roof* while staying at Captain Jack's Wharf, a bohemian lodging spot on the west end of town. **Norman Mailer** lived in Provincetown for years and filmed his directorial debut, *Tough Guys Don't Dance,* in Provincetown. **Paul Theroux** and **Kurt Vonnegut,** who was a founding member of the still-lively Barnstable Comedy Club, both had houses here and wrote about Cape Cod. **Sebastian Junger,** author of *The Perfect Storm,* has a family home in Truro and is a member of the Provincetown artists club, the Beachcombers.

Any recommended reading list for the Cape and islands starts with the classic *Cape Cod* by Henry David Thoreau. The famous author traveled to Cape Cod from 1849 to 1857, riding the stagecoach from Boston to Orleans and then walking from Eastham to Provincetown. Another classic book of the region is *The Outermost House* by Henry Beston, which tells the story of the author's year living in a cabin on the beach in Eastham, recording the seasonal changes. Perhaps my favorite overview of Cape Cod literature can be found in *Cape Cod Stories,* edited by John Miller and Tim Smith, with selections by 26 top writers from Herman Melville to Norman Mailer.

For good beach reading, *Cape Cod* by William Martin is an entertaining novel with a lot of history thrown in by a bestselling author. There's also *The Great Beach* by John Hay, a naturalist's history of Cape Cod. For history buffs, *Time and the Town: A Provincetown Chronicle* by Mary Heaton Vorse retells the classic history of the town on the Cape's tip in the early part of the 20th century. For two very different takes on Provincetown both released in 2002, read *Land's End: A Walk in Provincetown* by Michael Cunningham, the Pulitzer Prize–winning author of *The Hours,* and *Ptown: Art, Sex and Money on the Outer Cape* by Peter Manso, which provides a bleaker view of Provincetown. *Away Off Shore: Nantucket Island and Its People, 1602–1890* by Nathaniel Philbrick gives a comprehensive and entertaining history of the island. *Mostly on Martha's Vineyard* by Henry Beetle Hough is the entertaining autobiography by the longtime editor of the *Vineyard Gazette.*

True crime novels were practically invented on the Cape with Leo Damore's *In His Garden: The Anatomy of a Murderer,* about a serial murderer in Provincetown and Truro. The tradition of true crime set in the Outer Cape has continued in recent years with *Invisible Eden: A Story of Love and Murder on Cape Cod* by Maria Flook, about the murder of Christa Worthington in Truro in 2002. *The Year We Disappeared* by Cyline Busby and her father John Busby, published in 2008, tells the true story of when John Busby was shot in the face while working as a police officer in Falmouth. In the course of telling the story, the book reveals some dark secrets about that town on the Upper Cape.

Although the Cape doesn't receive the same attention from the media as, say, New York City or Los Angeles, Nantucket did get a lot of publicity from *Wings,* a popular television show that ran for seven years in the 1990s and was set in Nantucket's tiny airport, which, these days, is being expanded to twice the size. Music on Cape Cod must begin and end with Patti Page's classic song, "Old Cape Cod." There's really nothing else that comes close.

6 EATING & DRINKING

Cape Cod's restaurant scene has come a long way from the traditional clam shack, even though those shacks—where you can get lobster with all the fixins' or a steaming, towering plate of fried clams—are still the stuff of which Cape Cod memories are made. Today, there are sophisticated restaurants, expensive places serving a sort of generic fine dining called New American cuisine. Some of these places are quite good, but be prepared to pay for it (on the islands, entrees have hit the $50 mark).

Cape Cod has long been known for its local seafood, and you won't find a restaurant anywhere in the region without seafood on the menu. Fried fish, especially fried clams, are considered the ultimate Cape Cod meal. Another favorite is lobster, broiled with butter sauce. But for more sophisticated fare, look for grilled fish specials, such as striped bass in midsummer. Raw bars serve local oysters—the ones from Wellfleet are world-famous and Cotuit oysters are also notable—as well as "steamers," which are steamed clams. The other type of clam you will see on menus is the quahog (pronounced "ko-hog"), which is often served baked, meaning that the meat is cooked and mixed with bread crumbs and then returned to the shell. Steamed mussels are also popular, and are usually served in a garlicky broth. Scallops are another fixture on local menus; look for scallops from Nantucket, which are especially prized.

If you want boiled lobster but don't like to wrestle with it, you can order "lazy man's lobster," a dish that presents lobster meat that has been removed and placed loosely back in the shell. You can also order a lobster roll, which is cold lobster on a hotdog roll, sometimes served with mayonnaise or lettuce. New England clam chowder is another local specialty; it is a creamy, white broth that is served with clams and potatoes (note that it is different from Manhattan clam chowder, which has a red broth). You will sometimes find clam chowder prepared with bacon or Portuguese spicy sausage, like linguica or chorizo. Portuguese breads also can be found at local markets and on some menus.

Provincetown, Martha's Vineyard, and Nantucket are all considered dining meccas. In Provincetown, the easiest way to decide where to eat is to stroll up and down Commercial Street, checking out the menus. Although there are a number of expensive, fine-dining choices, Provincetown also has great inexpensive "street food," like burritos at the **Aquarium Shops,** burgers at **Mojo's** on Macmillan Wharf, and crepes from **The Outer Crepe** and others that come and go with the seasons. You never know what you'll find along Commercial Street, but there are also choices for cheap eats. On Martha's Vineyard, try **Atria** and **Detente** in Edgartown, or **Balance** and **Sweet Life** in Oak Bluffs for a memorable meal. Trying not to break the bank is the problem on this island. Nantucket is also well-known for having far too many fine-dining establishments, but few choices for the frugal diner. For that special night out, you could go to **Straight Wharf, Company of the Cauldron** or **The Galley Beach.** If you are on a budget, you might want to hit Broad Street and take out food from any of the places along what locals call "the strip." There is some pretty good eating here—my favorite is **Stubby's**—for not too much money.

Impressions

No one can eat enough steamed clams . . . No meal is more delicious than steamed clams dipped in drawn butter, together with cups of clam broth and Portuguese bread.

—Peter Hunt, *Peter Hunt's Cape Cod Cookbook,* 1954

The Local Brew

Both Martha's Vineyard and Nantucket have local breweries. On the Vineyard, **Off-Shore Ale Company** (30 Kennebec Ave., Oak Bluffs; ✆ **508/693-2626**) taps into eight varieties of their own beer. Nantucket's **Cisco Brewers** (5 and 7 Bartlett Farm Rd., Nantucket; ✆ **508/325-5929**) is famous for its brew called Whale's Tale Pale Ale. The brew is also available at many local restaurants.

Falmouth has become the place on the Cape to find ethnic cuisine. Besides the typical Chinese fare, there is Indian, Jamaican, and Thai cuisine. There are also several other excellent restaurants in Falmouth, including two Italian places on Main Street that are worth driving from the mid-Cape for (at least that's what my mid-Cape friends tell me).

Dining trends like tapas and wine bars have hit the Cape, and it looks like they may be here to stay. While you can find tapas options in almost every town, the most promising locales are **Embargo** in Hyannis, **Gracie's Table** in Dennis, and **Cinco** on Nantucket.

Ambience is an important part of any dining experience, and the Cape is endowed with numerous water-side restaurants. Great spots with water views are **Falmouth Raw Bar** on Falmouth Inner Harbor, **Baxter's** in Hyannis, the **Red Inn** in Provincetown, **The Home Port** in Menemsha on Martha's Vineyard, and **Ropewalk** on Nantucket. Just be prepared to pay extra for that spectacular water view.

Dining hours on Cape Cod are earlier than in most cities, as befits the many families and seniors who vacation here and call the area home. Most restaurants open for dinner at 5pm and serve until at least 10pm in season and 9pm off season. Breakfast places are usually open from 7 to 11am and lunch hours are typically 11:30am to 2:30pm. But, there are restaurants in every town that serve food throughout the day with no break.

At most restaurants on the Cape and islands, tips are not included on the bill. But there are some exceptions, particularly among the higher-priced restaurants, and generally when you are dining with a party of six or more people. Always check your bill closely to be sure the tip has not been included. If you are unsure, ask your server. In general, a 15% to 20% tip is expected on meals. If you find fault with any aspect of a restaurant, you should ask to speak with a manager immediately, but keep in mind that when a meal goes awry, it often is not the fault of the server.

CAPE COD IN DEPTH

2

EATING & DRINKING

3

Planning Your Trip

The Cape is really many capes: tony in some places, tacky in others; in patches a nature lover's dream, a living historical treasure, or a hotbed of creativity. This chapter will tell you what you need to plan your trip to Cape Cod, Martha's Vineyard and Nantucket and steer you there smoothly; for international visitors, there is essential information, helpful tips, and advice on the more common problems that you may encounter while vacationing on Cape Cod and the islands. Planning a trip to Cape Cod is a little more complex than packing flip-flops and suntan lotion. But remember, this is a destination that is supposed to be about relaxation, lying on a sun-kissed beach, listening to the lapping surf, or walking along a wildflower-lined path to watch the sun set over the horizon. These simple pleasures are why people have been coming to Cape Cod to vacation for more than a century.

Visiting Cape Cod means traveling over either the Bourne Bridge or the Sagamore Bridge. Most visitors arrive by car, but you can also take a bus or even travel by plane to one of several small airports in the region. You'll need a place to stay in one of the Cape's 15 towns or on one of the islands, and this book is loaded with options. You'll also need a way to get around. Public transportation leaves much to be desired in most Cape Cod towns, although several have good beach shuttles. Public transportation on both Martha's Vineyard and Nantucket, on the other hand, is excellent. There is also the option of bringing or renting a bike, a great way to travel from your rental house or hotel to the beach. There's lots more nitty-gritty information below, from information on passports and dates for festivals to weather predications and tips on dining. To pinpoint where you want to go in the area, and what you want to do, peruse the region-by-region chapters.

For additional help in planning your trip and for more on-the-ground resources on the Cape and islands, please turn to the "Fast Facts, Toll-Free Numbers & Websites" appendix on p. 288.

1 VISITOR INFORMATION

For the free *Getaway Guide,* which covers the whole state, contact the **Massachusetts Office of Travel and Tourism,** 100 Cambridge St., 13th floor, Boston, MA 02202 (© **800/447-MASS** (800/447-6277), ext. 454, or 617/727-3201; www. massvacation.com).

The **Cape Cod Chamber of Commerce,** at the intersection of routes 6 and 132 (accessed from the exit ramp of Exit 6 off Rte. 6), in Hyannis (© **888/332-2732;** fax 508/362-2156; www.capecodchamber. org); **Martha's Vineyard Chamber of Commerce,** Beach Road, Vineyard Haven, MA 02568 (© **508/693-0085;** fax 508/693-7589; www.mvy.com); and **Nantucket Island Chamber of Commerce,** 48 Main St., Nantucket, MA 02554 (© **508/228-1700;** fax 508/325-4925; www.nantucket chamber.org), can provide location-specific information and answer any questions that may arise. On Nantucket, there is also **Nantucket Visitor Services** located on 25 Federal St. (© **508/228-0925**), a visitor information center that keeps a list of lodging availability on the island.

In addition, most towns on the Cape have their own chambers of commerce, which are listed in the relevant chapters that follow. All chamber offices have small town guides that include detailed maps of the town. You can print out your own map before you go from http://world.maporama.com.

The **American Automobile Association** (AAA; ✆ **800/222-8252**) will provide a complimentary map and guide covering the area to its members.

TRAVEL BLOGS & TRAVELOGUES

Several local newspapers and magazines maintain blogs on Cape Cod topics. Visit **Capenews.net** *(The Enterprise),* **Capecodonline.com** *(Cape Cod Times),* and **Capecodtoday.com** *(Best Read Guide).*

Other blogs include

- www.gridskipper.com
- www.travelblog.com
- www.travelblog.org
- www.worldhum.com
- www.writtenroad.com

SPORTS INFORMATION

Cape Cod Chamber of Commerce (✆ **508/862-0700;** fax 508/362-2156; www.capecodchamber.org) offers a list of fishing and sporting contacts. Those interested in outdoor activities will find reams of info through the **Great Outdoor Recreation Pages** (www.gorp.com). Birders should call the **Cape Cod Museum of Natural History** (✆ **508/896-3867**) for info about the Cape Cod Bird Club or call the **Birdwatchers General Store** in Orleans (✆ **508/255-6974**) for top spots and the latest sightings. Many of the Cape's golf clubs are open to the public; for an annotated listing and advice, call ✆ **800/TEE-BALL** (800/833-2255) or check www.golfcapecod.com.

2 ENTRY REQUIREMENTS

PASSPORTS

New regulations issued by the Department of Homeland Security now require virtually every air traveler entering the U.S. to show a passport. As of January 23, 2007, all persons, including U.S. citizens, traveling by air between the United States and Canada, Mexico, Central and South America, the Caribbean, and Bermuda are required to present a valid passport. As of January 31, 2008, U.S. and Canadian citizens entering the U.S. at land and sea ports of entry from within the Western Hemisphere will need to present government-issued proof of citizenship, such as a birth certificate, along with a government issued photo ID, such as a driver's license. A passport is not required for U.S. or Canadian citizens entering by land or sea, but it is highly encouraged to carry one.

For information on how to obtain a passport, go to "**Passports**" in the "**Fast Facts**" appendix (p. 292).

VISAS

The U.S. State Department has a **Visa Waiver Program (VWP)** allowing citizens of the following countries to enter the United States without a visa for stays of up to 90 days: Andorra, Australia, Austria, Belgium, Brunei, Denmark, Finland, France, Germany, Iceland, Ireland, Italy, Japan, Liechtenstein, Luxembourg, Monaco, the Netherlands, New Zealand, Norway, Portugal, San Marino, Singapore, Slovenia, Spain, Sweden, Switzerland, and the United Kingdom. (*Note:* This list was accurate at press time; for the most up-to-date list of countries in the VWP, consult www.travel.state.gov/visa.) Even though a visa isn't necessary, in an effort to help

U.S. officials check travelers against terror watch lists before they arrive at U.S. borders, as of January 12, 2009, visitors from VWP countries must register online before boarding a plane or a boat to the U.S. Travelers will complete an electronic application providing basic personal and travel eligibility information. The Department of Homeland Security recommends filling out the form at least 3 days before traveling. Authorizations will be valid for up to 2 years or until the traveler's passport expires, whichever comes first. Currently, there is no fee for the online application. Canadian citizens may enter the United States without visas; they will need to show passports (if traveling by air) and proof of residence, however. *Note:* Any passport issued on or after October 26, 2006, by a VWP country must be an **e-Passport** for VWP travelers to be eligible to enter the U.S. without a visa. Citizens of these nations also need to present a round-trip air or cruise ticket upon arrival. E-Passports contain computer chips capable of storing biometric information, such as the required digital photograph of the holder. (You can identify an e-Passport by the symbol on the bottom center cover of your passport.) If your passport doesn't have this feature, you can still travel without a visa if it is a valid passport issued before October 26, 2005, and includes a machine-readable zone, or between October 26, 2005, and October 25, 2006, and includes a digital photograph. For more information, go to **www.travel.state.gov/visa**.

Citizens of all other countries must have (1) a valid passport that expires at least 6 months later than the scheduled end of their visit to the U.S., and (2) a tourist visa. To obtain a visa, applicants must schedule an appointment with a U.S. consulate or embassy, fill out the application forms (available from www.travel.state.gov/visa), and pay a $131 fee. Wait times can be lengthy, so it's best to initiate the process as soon as possible.

As of January 2004, many international visitors traveling on visas to the United States will be photographed and fingerprinted on arrival at Customs in airports and on cruise ships in a program created by the Department of Homeland Security called **US-VISIT.** Exempt from the extra scrutiny are visitors entering by land or those (mostly in Europe) who don't require a visa for short-term visits. For more information, go to the Homeland Security website at **www.dhs.gov/dhspublic**.

For specifics on how to get a visa, go to "**Visas**" in the "**Fast Facts**" appendix (p. 295).

MEDICAL REQUIREMENTS

Unless you're arriving from an area known to be suffering from an epidemic (particularly cholera or yellow fever), inoculations or vaccinations are not required for entry into the United States.

CUSTOMS
What You Can Bring into the U.S.

Every visitor more than 21 years of age may bring in, free of duty, the following: (1) 1 liter of wine or hard liquor; (2) 200 cigarettes, 100 cigars (but not from Cuba), or 3 pounds of smoking tobacco; and (3) $100 worth of gifts. These exemptions are offered to travelers who spend at least 72 hours in the United States and who have not claimed them within the preceding 6 months. It is forbidden to bring into the country almost any meat products (including canned, fresh, and dried meat products such as buillion, soup mixes, and so on). Generally, condiments including vinegars, oils, spices, coffee, tea, and some cheeses and baked goods are permitted. Avoid rice products, as rice can often harbor insects. Bringing fruits and vegetables is not advised, though not prohibited. Customs will allow produce depending on where you got it and where you're going after you arrive in the U.S. Foreign tourists may carry in or out up to $10,000 in U.S. or foreign currency with no formalities; larger sums must be declared to U.S. Customs on entering or leaving, which includes filing form CM 4790. For details regarding U.S. Customs and Border Protection, consult your nearest U.S. embassy or consulate, or **U.S. Customs** (www.customs.ustreas.gov).

What You Can Take Home from Cape Cod & the Islands

U.S. Citizens: For specifics on what you can bring back and the corresponding fees, download the invaluable free pamphlet *Know Before You Go* online at www.cbp.gov. (Click on "Travel," and then click on "Know Before You Go! Online Brochure") Or contact the U.S. Customs & Border Protection (CBP), 1300 Pennsylvania Ave., NW, Washington, DC 20229 (© **877/287-8667**) and request the pamphlet.

Canadian Citizens: For a clear summary of Canadian rules, write for the booklet "I Declare," issued by the Canada Border Services Agency (© **800/461-9999** in Canada, or 204/983-3500; www.cbsa-asfc.gc.ca).

U.K. Citizens: For information, contact **HM Customs & Excise** at © **0845/010-9000** (from outside the U.K., 020/8929-0152), or consult their website at www.hmce.gov.uk.

Australian Citizens: A helpful brochure available from Australian consulates or Customs offices is *Know Before You Go.* For more information, call the **Australian Customs Service** at © **1300/363-263,** or log on to www.customs.gov.au.

New Zealand Citizens: Most questions are answered in a free pamphlet available at New Zealand consulates and Customs offices: *New Zealand Customs Guide for Travellers, Notice no. 4.* For more information, contact **New Zealand Customs,** The Customhouse, 17–21 Whitmore St., Box 2218, Wellington (© **04/473-6099** or 0800/428-786; www.customs.govt.nz).

3 WHEN TO GO

Once strictly a warm-weather destination, the Cape and islands traditionally open the season with a splash on Memorial Day weekend and shutter up come Labor Day. The official beginning of summer is heralded by the Figawi sailboat race (see "Calendar of Events," below) on Memorial Day weekend. Traffic all over the Cape is horrendous on this last weekend in May, and ferries are booked solid. It's a rowdy party weekend, but then, strangely, things slow down for a few weeks until late June. The weekend closest to July 4th is another major mob scene, when summer really gets rolling. It's no wonder that July is the second-busiest month of the year and August is by far the most popular month for visiting the region: You are virtually guaranteed good beach weather these two months, and the Atlantic Ocean warms to comfortable swimming temperatures. Summer comes to an end with Labor Day, a heavily trafficked weekend you'll probably want to avoid.

SHOULDER SEASONS

Cape Cod now welcomes more and more tourists to witness the tender blossoms of spring and the fiery foliage of autumn. During these shoulder seasons, lodging tends to cost less, and a fair number of restaurants and attractions remain open. Most important, traffic is manageable. In addition, the natives seem far more accommodating in the off season, and shopping bargains abound.

In the last few years, a number of entertaining town festivals and events have attracted crowds in the spring and fall (see "Calendar of Events," below). Spring

> **Tips** **Shopping Bargains**
>
> Provincetown's October sales are to die for. Discounts often range from 50% to 70% off as merchants clear the shelves before closing for the winter. And remember, Provincetown is not just tacky T-shirt stores. There are excellent men's and women's clothing stores, as well as an abundance of fancy home-accessories stores. See p. 211.

brings daffodil festivals and fall brings cranberry, arts and harvest festivals. Unless your idea of the perfect vacation requires a swim in the ocean, you may be better off with the smaller crowds and better deals of the shoulder months: May, June, September, or October.

OFF SEASON

November and December don't quite qualify as off season on the Cape and islands. In fact, some say the most crowded time on Nantucket is during the Christmas Stroll in early December; it kicks off a month of holiday events. Martha's Vineyard also rolls out the red carpet in December with events in Edgartown and Vineyard Haven, including Santa arriving on the ferry. Many towns on the Cape, such as Sandwich, Osterville, Falmouth, and Chatham, also have big holiday festivals (see "Calendar of Events," below). The holidays are quite popular for family gatherings on the Cape and islands.

Tourist-oriented establishments on the Cape and islands traditionally close during the coldest months, but some tough out the quietest season—January through March. It's a rare treat to enjoy the region's historic towns and pristine landscapes with almost no one but natives stirring about. To avoid disappointment in the off season, however, always be sure to call ahead to check schedules.

CLIMATE

The Gulf Stream renders the Cape and islands generally about 10° warmer in winter than the mainland, and offshore winds keep them about 10° cooler in summer (you'll probably need a sweater most evenings). The only downside of being surrounded by water is the tendency toward fog; typically, it's sunny about 2 days out of 3—not bad odds. And the foggy days can be rather romantic. Pack some good books for when it pours.

SUMMER The first few weeks of June can be a perfect time to visit the region, but be forewarned: You may need to request a room with a fireplace. Weather this time of year, particularly in the Outer Cape, can be unpredictable at best. At worst, it's cold and rainy. Don't count on swimming in the ocean unless you're a member of the Polar Bear Club. Late June weather is usually lovely. July and August can be perfect—sunny and breezy—or damp, foggy, and humid. Usually it's a combination of the two.

AUTUMN On Cape Cod, it usually starts feeling like fall a week or two after Labor Day. September and October are splendid: Leaves start to change color, roads start to unclog, and everyone seems happier. The ocean retains enough heat to make for bearable swimming during the sunny days of Indian summer, and the subtly varied hues of the trees and moors are always changing, always lovely. Day temperatures are perfect for long hikes along the seashore. By October, you'll need a sweater during the day, and evenings can be downright chilly. But this is a lovely time of year on the Cape and islands.

WINTER It's not supposed to snow on Cape Cod, but it does. In recent years, some towns have had more than 100 inches. During a recent winter, the Cape received virtually no snow until a surprise blizzard on April 1. January through March are on the bleak side. This is when a lot of locals head south to sunnier climes.

SPRING April is a cheerful time on the Cape and islands, and daffodil festivals abound. In May and June, the entire Cape blossoms. Gardening goes way beyond hobby in this gentle climate, and blooms are profuse from May right through the summer. But springtime weather can be rainy, and the Atlantic Ocean is bone-chillingly cold.

Hyannis's Average Monthly Temperatures

		Jan	Feb	Mar	Apr	May	June	July	Aug	Sept	Oct	Nov	Dec
High Temps.	(°F)	40	41	42	53	62	71	78	76	70	59	49	40
	(°C)	4	5	6	12	17	22	26	24	21	15	9	4
Low Temps.	(°F)	25	26	28	40	48	56	63	61	56	47	37	26
	(°C)	-4	-3	-2	4	9	13	17	16	13	8	3	-3

CALENDAR OF EVENTS

For an exhaustive list of events beyond those listed here, check http://events.frommers.com, where you'll find a searchable, up-to-the-minute roster of what's happening in cities all over the world.

APRIL

Brewster in Bloom, Brewster. You'll find open houses, a crafts fair and flea market, and hot-air balloons. The Old King's Highway (Rte. 6A) is lined with thousands of daffodils. Call ✆ **508/896-3500.** Late April.

Daffodil Festival, Nantucket. Spring's arrival is heralded with masses of yellow blooms adorning everything in sight, including a cavalcade of antique cars. Call ✆ **508/228-1700.** Late April.

MAY

Chatham Maritime Festival, Chatham. A festival to raise awareness of Chatham's fishing industry with food and events at the Chatham Fish Pier and on Main Street. Call ✆ **508/945-5199.** Early May.

Herb Festival, Sandwich. Activities include exhibits, talks, and garden walks at the Green Briar Nature Center. Call ✆ **508/888-6870.** Mid-May.

Cape Maritime Week, Cape-wide. A multitude of cultural organizations mount special events, such as lighthouse tours, highlighting the region's nautical history. Activities include Coast Guard open houses, lectures, walking tours, and more. The week is sponsored by the Cape Cod Commission. Call ✆ **508/362-3828.** Mid-May.

Nantucket Wine Festival, Nantucket. Vintners from all over converge on Nantucket for wine tastings and cuisine provided by some of the island's top chefs. The Grand Cru is the main event. Call ✆ **508/228-1128.** Late May.

Figawi Sailboat Race, Hyannis to Nantucket. This is the largest—and wildest—race on the East Coast. Intense partying in Hyannis and on Nantucket surrounds this popular event. Call ✆ **508/362-5230.** Late May.

Dexter Rhododendron Festival, Sandwich. Heritage Museums and Gardens—at the peak of bloom—sells offshoots of its incomparable botanical collection. Call ✆ **508/888-3300.** Late May.

Brewster Historical Society Antiques Fair, Brewster. This outdoor extravaganza features 80 top dealers. Call ✆ **508/896-3500.** Early June.

A Taste of the Vineyard, Martha's Vineyard. Island restaurateurs offer samplings of their specialties at Edgartown's Whaling Church to benefit the Martha's Vineyard Preservation Trust. Call ✆ **508/627-8017.** Mid-June.

Harborfest Celebration, Nantucket. It's a chance to sample competing chowders and board tall ships. Call ✆ **508/228-1700.** Mid-June.

Provincetown Film Festival, Provincetown. Focusing on alternative film, this fete has brought out celebrities like John Waters and Lily Tomlin. Call ✆ **508/487-FILM** (508/487-3456). Mid-June.

Nantucket Film Festival, Nantucket. This annual event focuses on storytelling through film and includes showings of short and feature-length films, documentaries, staged readings, panel discussions, and screenplay competitions. Sponsors include *Vanity Fair* magazine, so you may see a celebrity or two. Call ✆ **508/228-1700.** Mid-June.

Arts Alive Festival, Falmouth. Dozens of artists and performers, including painters, musicians, dancers, filmmakers, and storytellers, give demonstrations, show films, sell artwork and put on performances at this weekend-long event that opens with a town dance on the library lawn. Call ✆ **508/548-8500.** Mid-June.

St. Barnabas Strawberry Festival, Falmouth. Indulge in strawberry shortcake, as well as barbecue and lots of children's games on the grounds of St. Barnabas Church next to the Village Green. Call ✆ **508/548-8500.** Mid-June.

Aptucxet Strawberry Festival, Bourne. The Aptucxet Trading Post Museum, a replica of the country's first store, hosts crafts demonstrations, accompanied by fresh strawberry shortcake. Call ✆ **508/759-9487.** Late June.

Provincetown Portuguese Festival, Provincetown. This cultural event celebrates Provincetown's Portuguese heritage with music, dancing, exhibits, food, a parade, fireworks, and the traditional Blessing of the Fleet. Call ✆ **508/487-3424.** Late June.

Rock 'n' Roll Ramble, Sandwich. Vintage cars from the '50s and '60s converge on Heritage Museums and Gardens for a concert and mutual admiration. Call ✆ **508/888-3300.** Late June.

JULY

Edgartown Regatta, Martha's Vineyard. A highly social sailing event. Call ✆ **508/693-0085.** Early July.

Wampanoag Pow Wow, Mashpee. Native American tribes from around the country converge to enjoy traditional dances and games. Call ✆ **508/477-0208.** July 4th weekend.

Independence Day, Falmouth. The fireworks at Falmouth Heights Beach are one of the largest shows in the region. Your best bet is to park in town earlier in the evening and walk over to the Heights. Call ✆ **508/548-8500.** July 4th weekend.

Independence Day, Nantucket. The highlight of the island's busiest weekend is fireworks on Jetties Beach. Call ✆ **508/228-0925.** July 4th weekend.

Independence Day, Edgartown. An old-fashioned, small-town parade and fireworks over Edgartown Harbor are the highlights of this beloved event. Call ✆ **508/693-0085.** July 4th weekend.

Independence Day, Provincetown. Festivities include a spirited parade, entertainment, and fireworks over the harbor. Call ✆ **508/487-3424.** July 4th weekend.

Independence Day, Barnstable. A spectacular fireworks display over either Barnstable Harbor or Hyannis Harbor (depending on the nesting of the Piping Plovers). Call ✆ **800/4-HYNNIS** (800/449-6647). July 4th weekend.

Barnstable County Fair, East Falmouth. This old-fashioned, 10-day agricultural extravaganza is complete with prize produce and livestock and of course rides and a midway. There are concerts nightly. Call ✆ **508/548-8500.** Mid-July.

Woods Hole Film Festival, Falmouth. A festival that spans 2 weeks and numerous venues and features small independent films. Call ✆ **508/548-8500.** Late July.

AUGUST

Jazz by the Sea and Pops by the Sea, Hyannis. Celebrity "conductors"—such as Olympia Dukakis—enliven these two outdoor concerts. Call ✆ **800/4-HYNNIS** (800/449-6647). Early August.

Possible Dreams Auction, Martha's Vineyard. Resident celebrities give—and bid—their all to support the endeavors of Martha's Vineyard Community Services. Call ✆ **508/693-7900.** Early August.

In the Spirit Arts Festival, Martha's Vineyard. Oak Bluffs celebrates its cultural diversity with food, music, and children's fun. Call ✆ **508/693-0085.** Early August.

Mashpee Night at the Pops, Mashpee Commons. A concert by the Cape Cod Symphony Orchestra followed by fireworks. This event attracts about 15,000 pops fans. Call ✆ **508/477-0792.** Early August.

Falmouth Road Race, Falmouth. Joggers and world-class runners turn out in droves—10,000 strong—for this annual sprint race that covers just over 7 miles. Entry registration is by lottery and ends in May. Unregistered runners are not allowed to participate. Call ✆ **508/540-7000** or check out their website, www. falmouthroadrace.com. Mid-August.

Carnival Week, Provincetown. The gay community's annual blowout features performers, parties, and an outrageous costume parade. Call ✆ **508/487-2313.** Mid-August.

Agricultural Society Livestock Show and Fair, Martha's Vineyard. In West Tisbury, you'll find a classic country carnival and a celebration of the Vineyard's agricultural tradition. Call ✆ **508/693-9549.** Mid-August.

Sandcastle and Sculpture Day, Nantucket. This fairly serious but fun contest is categorized by age group, which ups the odds of winning. Call ✆ **508/228-1700.** Mid-August.

Festival Days, Dennis. Six days of events, including fun-for-the-family activities, such as a kite-flying contest, canoe race, crafts fair, and more. Call ✆ **800/243-9920** or 508/398-3568. Late August.

Illumination Night, Martha's Vineyard. The Oak Bluffs campground is lit with hundreds of Japanese lanterns. Campground officials keep this event a secret until the last minute, so it's hard to plan ahead. Call ✆ **508/693-0085.** Late August.

Oak Bluffs Fireworks and Band Concert, Martha's Vineyard. It's the summer's last blast. Call ✆ **508/693-0085.** Late August.

SEPTEMBER

POP Goes the Summer, Barnstable County Fairgrounds, Falmouth. Experience a Cape Cod Symphony Orchestra concert followed by fireworks. Call ✆ **508/548-8500.** Early September.

Bourne Scallop Festival, Bourne. This annual weekend event features food, crafts, rides, musical entertainment, and more. Call ✆ **508/759-6000.** Early September.

Windmill Weekend, Eastham. This jolly community festival includes a sand-art competition, road races, band concerts, an arts-and-crafts show, a tricycle race, and professional entertainment. The highlight of this weekend is the square dance held under the historic windmill. Call ✆ **508/255-3444.** Early September.

Cranberry Festival, Harwich. This is a chance to observe and celebrate the colorful harvest, with 9 days of events ranging from pancake breakfasts to fireworks. Call ✆ **800/441-3199** or 508/432-1600. Mid-September.

Martha's Vineyard Striped Bass and Bluefish Derby, Martha's Vineyard. In its 56th year, the region's premier fishing derby and one of the country's oldest is a month-long classic contest. Call ✆ **508/693-0085.** Mid-September to mid-October.

Sandwich Boardwalk Celebration, Sandwich. This community did some serious bonding years ago when their boardwalk was damaged by a storm, and everyone pitched in to build a new one. This festival, with professional kite flying and entertainment for families, has become an annual tradition. Call ✆ **508/833-9755.** Late September.

Harbor Swim for Life, Provincetown. Stalwart swimmers participate in this event to raise money for local AIDS organizations. The race is followed by a festive Mermaid Brunch and a sunset "Festival of Happiness" on Herring Cove Beach. Call ✆ **508/487-1930.** Late September.

Provincetown Arts Festival, Provincetown. Building up to the Provincetown Art Association and Museum Annual Consignment Auction (✆ **508/487-1750**), this festival, which takes place over 4 weekends, is an extraordinary opportunity to collect works spanning the past century. Local artists hold open studios, actors stage readings of Eugene O'Neill, and galleries hold special exhibits. Call ✆ **508/487-3424.** Late September to mid-October.

OCTOBER

Wellfleet OysterFest, Wellfleet. Spend a weekend learning about and tasting Wellfleet's world-famous oysters at this weekend-long street festival including arts, crafts, and live music. For information, contact the Wellfleet Chamber at ✆ **508/349-2510** or go to **www.wellfleetoysterfest.org**. Always the weekend (beginning on Fri) after Columbus Day.

Trash Fish Banquet, Provincetown. Unsung, or perhaps undersung, species are creatively cooked to benefit the Center for Coastal Studies. Call ✆ **508/487-3622.** Mid-October.

Women's Week, Provincetown. This is a gathering of artists, entertainers, and educators, as well as women who just want to have fun. Call ✆ **508/487-2313.** Mid-October.

Walking Weekend, Cape-wide. Over 45 guided walks (averaging 2 hr. in length) are sponsored by an organization called Cape Pathways to foster appreciation for the Cape's unique ecology and cultural accomplishments. Call ✆ **508/362-3828.** Mid-October.

Nantucket Harvest Festival, Nantucket. This festival features inn tours and a big chowder contest, just when the foliage is at its burnished prime. Call ✆ **508/228-1700.** Mid-October.

Nantucket Arts Festival, Nantucket. This weeklong event includes a wet-paint sale, mini film festival, writers and their works, gallery exhibitions, artist demonstrations, theater, concerts, photography, and more. Call ✆ **508/228-1700.** Mid-October.

Yarmouth Seaside Festival, Yarmouth. Enjoy a parade, fireworks, arts and crafts, contests, and sporting events. Call ✆ **508/778-1008.** Mid-October.

NOVEMBER

Lighting of the Pilgrim Monument, Provincetown. The Italianate tower turns into a monumental holiday ornament, as carolers convene below. Call ✆ **508/487-1310.** Thanksgiving Eve (late Nov).

Harbor Lighting, Hyannis. The boats parade by, atwinkle with lights, and Santa arrives via lobster boat. Call ✆ **508/362-5230.** Late November.

Fall Festival, Edgartown. Family activities at the Felix Neck Wildlife Sanctuary include a treasure hunt, wildlife walks, and wreath making. Call ✆ **508/627-4850.** Late November.

Chatham's Christmas by the Sea, Chatham. A month of townwide events include historic-inn tours, carolers, hayrides, open houses, a dinner dance, and Santa. Call ✆ **508/945-5199.** Late November through December.

DECEMBER

Christmas Stroll, Nantucket. The island briefly stirs from its winter slumber for one last shopping/feasting spree, attended by costumed carolers, Santa in a horse-drawn carriage, and a "talking" Christmas tree. This event is the pinnacle of **Nantucket Noel,** a month of festivities starting in late November.

Ferries and lodging establishments book up months before this event, so you'll need to plan ahead. Call ✆ **508/228-1700.** Early December.

Falmouth Christmas by the Sea, Falmouth. A weekend of caroling, tree lighting, Santa, entertainment, and a parade that centers on the historic and lavishly decorated Falmouth Village Green. Call ✆ **508/548-8500.** Early December.

Christmas in Sandwich, Sandwich. Seasonal open houses, exhibits, community caroling, and merchant promotions take place throughout the town. Call ✆ **508/833-9755.** Early December.

Holly Folly, Provincetown. The annual Gay and Lesbian Holiday Festival has events open to all, including guesthouse tours, holiday parties, the Reindeer Run, concerts, and more. Call ✆ **508/487-2313.** Early December.

Yarmouth Port Christmas Stroll, Yarmouth Port. Stroll along the Old King's Highway for open houses, visits with Santa, and caroling. Call ✆ **508/778-1008.** Early December.

Christmas Weekend in the Harwiches, Harwich. This townwide celebration features entertainment, merchant promotions, hayrides, visits with Santa, and more. Call ✆ **508/432-1600.** Mid-December.

First Night, Chatham. Following Boston's lead, Chatham puts on a festive evening featuring local performers. Call ✆ **508/945-5199.** New Year's Eve.

4 GETTING THERE & GETTING AROUND

GETTING TO CAPE COD & THE ISLANDS
By Plane

Most major carriers offer service to **Boston's Logan Airport,** and from there, it's a quick half-hour commuter flight to **Hyannis** or **Provincetown** (about $195 round-trip), or the islands (to **Martha's Vineyard** or **Nantucket,** about $235 round-trip). It's also easy to shuttle in from New York (from LaGuardia to Hyannis, LaGuardia to Martha's Vineyard, or LaGuardia to Nantucket, all about $500 round-trip). Nonstop flights from either LaGuardia or Newark to Hyannis, Martha's Vineyard, or Nantucket take about 1 hour and 15 minutes. Connections are also available between these airports and to New Bedford, and private charters are easy to arrange. Comparison shopping by phone (or computer) can pay off, since preliminary research will help you find the best deal. For example, Continental offers service to Hyannis from LaGuardia Airport and a seasonal service from Newark Airport to Martha's Vineyard and Nantucket. US Airways services Hyannis from LaGuardia; they also service Martha's Vineyard and Nantucket from both Logan and LaGuardia. Cape Air is the only airline currently offering service from Logan Airport to Provincetown.

Among the larger airlines serving Logan Airport are **American Airlines** (© 800/433-7300; www.aa.com), **Continental** (© 800/525-0280; www.continental. com), **Delta** (© 800/221-1212; www. delta.com), **Northwest** (© 800/225-2525; www.nwa.com), **United** (© 800/241-6522; www.united.com), and **US Airways** (© 800/428-4322; www.usairways.com).

Carriers to the Cape and islands include all of the above, plus **Cape Air/Nantucket Airlines** (© 800/352-0714 or 508/771-6944; www.flycapeair.com), **US Airways/Colgan Air** (© 800/272-5488 or 508/775-7077; www.colganair.com), and **Island Airlines** (© 800/248-7779 or 508/775-6606; www.nantucket.net/trans/islandair).

Flying over to Nantucket from Hyannis takes about 20 minutes, depending on the weather, costs about $109 round-trip, and is a great way to avoid the hectic ferry scene. Island Airlines and Cape Air make the most frequent trips from Hyannis to Nantucket, and between these two air carriers alone, there are over 50 flights per day. Charter flights are offered by both airlines.

The commuter flights have their own little fare wars, so it's worth calling around. And though flights may lessen in frequency during the off season, fares sometimes descend as well.

From Logan Airport in Boston, the Cape is about a 1½- to 2½-hour drive, depending on traffic and how far along it you intend to go. Boston to Hyannis, the Cape's transportation hub, is about a 2-hour drive, or 2½ hours via the Plymouth & Brockton bus line (© 508/771-6191); from there, you can take a ferry ride to either island.

Arriving at the Airport
IMMIGRATION & CUSTOMS CLEARANCE International visitors arriving by air, no matter what the port of entry, should cultivate patience and resignation before setting foot on U.S. soil. U.S. airports have considerably beefed up security clearances in the years since the September 11, 2001, terrorist attacks, and clearing Customs and Immigration can take as long as 2 hours.

Getting into Town from the Airport
Visitors to the Cape and islands who are flying in to Boston's Logan Airport or T.F. Green Airport in Providence, Rhode Island, can rent a car and drive to Cape Cod in about an hour and a half (from Boston) or an hour (from Providence).

Driving maps are generally available at car rental locations.

The major route from Boston's Logan Airport is Route 93 South to Route 3, which ends at the Sagamore Bridge. The Sagamore Bridge is the bridge to use to access all the Cape towns except Falmouth and the island of Martha's Vineyard. For those two destinations, plus parts of Bourne, the best route from Logan Airport is Route 93 to Route 24 to Route 495, which turns in to Route 25 near the Bourne Bridge.

From Providence, Rhode Island, you take Route 195 all the way to Route 25 and the Bourne Bridge.

Though cars are not needed for the average visitor to Martha's Vineyard and Nantucket, some visitors choose to rent a car or even a Jeep so that they can drive on certain beaches. Rental establishments on both islands offer ample Jeep rentals in addition to car rentals.

Long-Haul Flights: How to Stay Comfortable

- Your choice of airline and airplane will definitely affect your leg room. Find more details about U.S. airlines at **www.seatguru.com**. For international airlines, the research firm Skytrax has posted a list of average seat pitches at **www.airlinequality.com**.
- Emergency exit seats and bulkhead seats typically have the most legroom. Emergency exit seats are usually left unassigned until the day of a flight (to ensure that someone able-bodied fills the seats); it's worth checking in online at home (if the airline offers that option) or getting to the ticket counter early to snag one of these spots for a long flight. Many passengers find that bulkhead seating offers more legroom, but keep in mind that bulkhead seats have no storage space on the floor in front of you.
- To have two seats for yourself in a three-seat row, try for an aisle seat in a center section toward the back of coach. If you're traveling with a companion, book an aisle and a window seat. Middle seats are usually booked last, so chances are good you'll end up with three seats to yourselves. And in the event that a third passenger is assigned the middle seat, he or she will probably be more than happy to trade for a window or an aisle.
- To sleep, avoid the last row of any section or the row in front of an emergency exit, as these seats are the least likely to recline. Avoid seats near highly trafficked toilet areas. Avoid seats in the back of many jets—these can be narrower than those in the rest of coach.

Or reserve a window seat so you can rest your head and avoid being bumped in the aisle.
- Get up, walk around, and stretch every 60 to 90 minutes to keep your blood flowing. This helps avoid **deep vein thrombosis.**
- Drink water before, during, and after your flight to combat the lack of humidity in airplane cabins. Avoid caffeine and alcohol, which will dehydrate you.

By Car

Similar to the directions above in "Getting into Town from the Airport," visitors from the south (New York, for example) will approach the Cape Cod Canal via Route I-95 to Route 195 to Route 25 and over the Bourne Bridge. Those coming from Boston can either come that way (reaching Rte. 25 via I-93 to Rte. 24 and I-495) or head directly south from Boston on I-93 to Route 3, leading over the Sagamore Bridge.

The bridges are only 3 miles apart, with connecting roads on both sides of the canal, so either will do. The one you choose will most likely depend on where you're going. If you're planning to head south to Falmouth or take a ferry to Martha's Vineyard, you'll want to take the Bourne Bridge and follow Route 28 about 10 miles to Falmouth.

If you're heading farther east of the Sagamore Bridge to any of the other 14 towns on the Cape or to Nantucket, you'll want to travel over the Sagamore Bridge and take Route 6 or its scenic sidekick, Route 6A, which merges with Route 28 in Orleans. From Orleans, the main road is Route 6 all the way to Provincetown.

Those traveling to Nantucket should take the Sagamore Bridge and drive down Route 6 until reaching Exit 7. From there you can follow signs to one of the two ferry terminals (Steamship Authority or Hy-Line) in Hyannis.

The big challenge, actually, is getting over either bridge, especially on summer

(Tips) A Word about Traffic

Cape Cod traffic is nothing if not predictable. You do not want to be driving over the Bourne or Sagamore bridges to come onto the Cape on a summer Friday between 4 and 8pm. Saturday between 10am and 3pm is an equally bad time to arrive. Most of all, you do not want to try to get off the Cape on a Sunday or a holiday Monday between 2 and 8pm. If you find yourself in one of the infamous Cape Cod traffic jams (on Memorial Day in 2000, traffic was backed up 18 miles east from the Sagamore Bridge), there are options. Here are my personal traffic-beating tips. Don't tell anyone.

1. The Bourne Bridge is almost always a less crowded route than the Sagamore Bridge. You can connect to Route 6 from the Bourne Bridge via the canal road, or see number 3 below.
2. When heading off the Cape on Route 6, turn off at Exit 5. Take Route 149 south to Route 28. At the Mashpee Rotary, take Route 151 to Route 28 in North Falmouth. Take Route 28 to the Bourne Bridge.
3. To get onto the Cape to points east of Yarmouth, follow number 2 in reverse.
4. If you are traveling to Nantucket and plan to park your car in Hyannis, watch the signs on Route 6 to see whether the parking lot at Cape Cod Community College is open. If it is, take Exit 6 and make a right turn onto Route 132. Cape Cod Community College is about a half-mile on the right. A free shuttle will take you to the ferry.
5. If you are heading to Martha's Vineyard, consider taking a passenger ferry from Rhode Island or New Bedford (see chapter 10). Otherwise, be alert to the signs on Route 28 about parking lots. These signs are accurate. If they say the lot is full in Woods Hole, you will not be allowed to park there, so don't bother driving down to check it out. Follow the signs to the open parking lots, and a free shuttle bus will take you to the ferry.

weekends, when upward of 100,000 cars all try to cross at once. Savvy residents avoid at all costs driving onto the Cape on Friday afternoon or joining the mass exodus on Sunday (or Mon, in the case of a holiday weekend), and you'd be wise to follow suit. Call **SmarTraveler** (© **617/ 374-1234** or cellular *1) for up-to-the-minute news on congestion and alternate routes, as well as parking availability in the pay-per-night parking lots that serve the island ferries.

Traffic can throw a major monkey wrench into these projections, but on average, driving time to Hyannis is 5 hours (no traffic) to 7 hours from New

York and $1^1/2$ to 2 hours from Boston. It'll take about 1 to $1^1/2$ hours more to drive all the way to Provincetown.

Traffic can truly be a nightmare on peak weekends. Cars are enough of a bother on the Cape itself: If you're not planning to cover much ground, forego the "convenience" and rent a bike instead (some B&Bs offer "loaners"). On the islands, cars are truly superfluous. Expensive to ferry back and forth ($175 one-way to Nantucket in season, and that's if you manage to make a reservation months, even a year, in advance or are willing to sit in "standby" for many hours), a car will prove a nuisance in the crowded port towns, where urban-style gridlock is not uncommon. Should you change your mind and want to go motoring once you arrive, you can always rent a car on the islands (see "Getting Around Cape Cod & the Islands," below), usually for *less than the cost of bringing your own vehicle over.*

If you do come by car, have a mechanic check it out beforehand. If you're a member of the **American Automobile Association (AAA; ℂ 800/222-4357)** or another national auto club, call beforehand to ask about travel insurance, towing services, free trip planning, and other services that may be available.

For listings of the national car rental agencies with branches on Cape Cod, Martha's Vineyard and Nantucket, please see "Toll-Free Numbers & Websites" in the appendix (p. 295).

TRAVEL TIMES Please note that traffic is very heavy over the bridges onto the Cape on Friday afternoons and going over the bridges off the Cape on Sunday afternoons. Saturday can also have heavy traffic because it is the start and end of the rental cycle at most weekly vacation units. The Bourne Bridge is usually less crowded than the Sagamore Bridge, but unless you are going to Falmouth, you'll have to merge with the Sagamore Bridge traffic on Route 6 anyway. If you are trying to catch a ferry, particularly in Hyannis, always leave plenty of extra time.

By Bus

Greyhound (ℂ 800/231-2222) connects Boston with the rest of the country, and **Bonanza Bus Lines/Peter Pan (ℂ 888/751-8800** or 508/548-7588) covers a good portion of southern New England. Logan Airport to Falmouth costs about $27 each way. Bonanza links Boston's Logan Airport and South Station with Bourne, Falmouth, and Woods Hole; its buses from New York reach the same destinations, plus Hyannis. From New York to Hyannis or Woods Hole, the 6-hour

ride costs about $73 each way. **Plymouth & Brockton (ℂ 508/771-6191;** www.p-b.com) offers service from Logan and South Station to Hyannis by way of Sagamore and Barnstable, and offers connections from there to the towns of Yarmouth, Dennis, Brewster, Orleans, Eastham, Wellfleet, Truro, and Provincetown.

Note: If you plan to catch a ferry, don't count on the bus arriving on time (there's no telling what the traffic may do). Plan to take the second-to-last ferry of the day, so you have a backup; and even so, schedule your arrival with an hour to spare.

By Boat

Arriving by water to Martha's Vineyard, Nantucket, or even Provincetown gives you a chance to decompress from city worries, while taking in glorious views both coming and going. All the ferries are equipped to carry bikes, for about $12 round-trip.

To Provincetown

Bay State Cruise Company (ℂ 617/748-1428; www.provincetownfastferry.com) runs a fast ferry to Provincetown from Boston, in addition to a daily round-trip conventional ferry, both from Commonwealth Pier at Boston's World Trade Center. The fast ferry makes three trips a day from May to early October. The trip, which takes 90 minutes, costs $49 one-way, $79 round-trip adults; $31 one-way, $58 round-trip for children; and $43 one-way, $73 round-trip for seniors. The conventional ferry leaves daily late June through Labor Day, and on weekends late May to late June and mid- to late September. The voyage ($41 round-trip for adults; free for children 4–11) takes about 3 hours each way.

   Boston Harbor Cruises (ℂ 617/227-4321; www.bostonharborcruises.com) runs fast ferries from Long Wharf in Boston to Provincetown's Macmillan's Wharf late June to mid-September. It's a 90-minute trip. In high season, there are two to three

Travel Times to Cape Cod & the Islands

New York to Hyannis	5 to 7 hours, depending on traffic
Boston to Hyannis	1½ hours with no traffic
Sagamore Bridge to Orleans	1 hour; with high-season traffic, 2 to 3 hours
Sagamore Bridge to Provincetown	1½ hours with little traffic
Hyannis to Sagamore Bridge	30 minutes; on Sunday afternoons in season, 3 hours
Bourne Bridge to Woods Hole	35 minutes; Friday afternoons in season, 1¾ hours
Hyannis to Nantucket by plane	12 minutes
Hyannis to Nantucket by Steamship Authority or Hy-Line high-speed catamaran	1 hour
Hyannis to Nantucket by slow Steamship Authority or Hy-Line ferries	2¼ hours
Woods Hole to Martha's Vineyard aboard the Steamship Authority ferries	45 minutes
Falmouth to Edgartown, Martha's Vineyard, aboard the *Pied Piper*	1 hour
Falmouth to Oak Bluffs, Martha's Vineyard, aboard the *Island Queen*	35 minutes

round-trips a day. Ferry tickets cost $49 one-way, $77 round-trip for adults. Tickets for seniors cost $43 one-way, $71 round-trip; and tickets for children cost $37 one-way, $66 round-trip. Bikes cost $5 each way. Reservations are a must on this popular boat.

You can also ferry directly to Provincetown from Plymouth, in season, with **Captain John Boats** (© 508/747-2400; www.provincetownferry.com); the trip takes 1½ hours and costs $37 round-trip for adults, $32 for seniors, $27 for children 12 and under. Bikes cost an extra $5. In July and August, only round-trip tickets are sold. In mid-June to early September, trips leave daily. From late May to mid-June, trips run weekends only.

For detailed information on ferries to the islands, see the "Getting There" sections in chapters 9 and 10.

To Martha's Vineyard

The three "down-island" ports of Martha's Vineyard are hooked up to the Cape and mainland in various ways. **Oak Bluffs** has the busiest harbor in season. It's served by the **Hy-Line** from Hyannis or Nantucket (© 508/778-2600; www.hy-linecruises. com), the *Island Queen* from Falmouth Harbor (© 508/548-4800; www.island queen.com), and the state-run **Steamship Authority** car ferry from Woods Hole (© 508/477-8600; www.steamship authority.com, where you can buy tickets online).

Edgartown is serviced by the **Falmouth Ferry Service,** a passengers-only ferry called the *Pied Piper* (© **508/548-9400;** www.falmouthferry.com), which leaves from the west side of Falmouth Harbor and makes a 1-hour crossing (six crossings a day in season). It costs about twice as much as the other ferries to the Vineyard. **Vineyard Haven** welcomes **Steamship Authority** car and passenger ferries from Woods Hole year-round (over 20 crossings a day on weekends in season). If you want to bring your car, you'll need a reservation (© **508/477-8600** or online at **www. steamshipauthority.com**), although there's limited standby space available for those willing to wait around, except during certain peak-demand stretches in summer. Passengers not planning to bring a car do not need a reservation.

From Falmouth, the *Island Queen* makes the quickest crossing, at about 35 minutes. Round-trip fares on all ferry choices to Martha's Vineyard range from about $15 to $50, depending on the distance, and the round-trip rate for cars in season is $260 to $300. Parking costs $10 to $20 per day, depending on the ferry company. Including all of the ferry services, there are dozens of crossings a day from the Cape to the Vineyard in summer.

Hy-line runs a year-round high-speed ferry to Martha's Vineyard from Hyannis in 55 minutes. In season, there are five trips a day and the round-trip fare is $63 for adults and $45 for children. The traditional ferry makes the trip in season only once per day, takes 1 hour 35 minutes, and costs $39 for adults, $20 for children for round-trip tickets.

From New Bedford, Massachusetts, the fast ferry MV *Whaling City Express* travels to Martha's Vineyard in 1 hour. It makes six trips a day in season and is in service year-round, 7 days a week. A ticket costs $64 round-trip for adults; and $34 round-trip for children 12 and under ; and $56 round-trip for seniors. Contact New England Fast Ferry for details (© **866/453-6800** [toll-free]; www.nefastferry.com).

From **North Kingstown, Rhode Island,** to Oak Bluffs on Martha's Vineyard, the company Vineyard Fast Ferry runs its high-speed catamaran, *Millennium,* two to three round-trips daily from mid-June through October. The trip takes 90 minutes. Rates are $75 round-trip for adults, $52 round-trip for children 4 to 12. The ferry service can also set up shuttle service between Providence Airport or the nearest Amtrak station and the ferry terminal starting at $18 each way. Reservations for the ferry and/or the shuttle can be made by calling © **401/295-4040** or visiting their website at www.vineyardfastferry.com.

To Nantucket

There are two competing high-speed ferries to Nantucket from Hyannis; both take 1 hour. The passengers-only **MV Grey Lady** (© **800/492-8082**), Hy-Line's high-speed catamaran, costs $71 round-trip, $39 one-way for adults; $50 round-trip, $29 one-way for children (© **508/778-2600;** www.hy-linecruises.com).

The Steamship Authority runs its own high-speed catamaran, the *Iyanough,* which costs $65 round-trip for adults and $49 round-trip for children (© **508/477-8600;** www.steamshipauthority.com).

Both the Steamship Authority and Hy-Line also run slow ferries (2¼ hr.) to Nantucket. The Steamship Authority charges $33 round-trip, and Hy-Line charges $39 round-trip. Incidentally, transporting a car costs an astronomical $300 round-trip in season—which makes it pretty silly to bring a car when you consider that the island is only 3 miles wide and 15 miles end to end. A bike (bring your own or rent on-island) will more than suffice.

Ferries also travel to Nantucket from Harwich Port by the **Freedom Cruise Line** (© **508/432-8999;** www.nantucket islandferry.com), which makes three trips a day in season and one trip a day in spring and fall. It costs $68 round-trip for adults, $55 for children.

A certain frenzy usually accompanies the ferry departures, but if you arrive about an hour early, you should have plenty of time to drop off your luggage at the pier beforehand, so you won't have to lug it around. Call **SmarTraveler** (see "By Car," earlier) or listen to radio station 1610 AM to find out what's up and whether traffic is clogged. The Steamship Authority boats offer a luggage trolley, which often fills to capacity half-hour or more before departure, so it pays to get there early. The Hy-Line staff cheerfully attends to all the loading of luggage and bikes. It's a lot less hassle.

Note: See the note on bus-ferry connections under "By Bus," above. The same holds true for return journeys: Ferry arrival times tend to be more reliable, but give yourself plenty of time, and don't take a chance on the last bus of the day.

GETTING AROUND CAPE COD & THE ISLANDS
By Car

Once you've made it over one of the bridges guarding the Cape Cod Canal—or bypassed the bridges by flying or boating in—getting around is relatively easy. Traveling by car does offer the greatest degree of flexibility, although you'll probably wish no one else knew that. While traffic can often be frustrating, parking is another problem. In densely packed towns like Provincetown, finding a free, legal space is like winning the lottery. Parking is also problematic at many beaches. Some are closed to all but residents, and visitors will almost always have to pay a day rate of about $10 to $20. Renters staying a week or longer can arrange for a discounted weeklong or month-long sticker through the local town hall (you'll probably need to show your lease, as well as your car registration). You can usually squeeze into the Cape Cod National Seashore lots if you show up early (by 9am); here the fee is only $15 a day, or $45 per season.

Further complicating the heavy car traffic on the Cape is the seemingly disproportionate number of bad drivers. A few key traffic rules: A right turn is allowed at a red light after stopping, unless otherwise posted. In a rotary (think traffic circle with Boston drivers), cars within the circle have the right of way until they manage to get out. Four-way stops call for extreme caution or extreme courtesy, and sometimes both.

Rental cars are available at the Hyannis Airport and at branch offices of major chains in several towns. The usual maze of rental offers prevails. Almost every rental firm tries to pad its profits by selling Loss-Damage Waiver (LDW) insurance at a cost of $8 to $15 extra per day. Before succumbing to the hard sell, check with your insurance carrier and credit card companies; chances are, you're already covered. If not, the LDW may prove a wise investment. Exorbitant charges for gasoline are another ploy to look out for; be sure to top off the tank just before bringing the car in.

Certain car-rental agencies have also set maximum ages or may refuse to rent to those with bad driving records. If such restrictions might affect you, ask about requirements when you book to avoid problems later.

It's worthwhile to call around to the various rental companies to compare prices and to inquire about any discounts available (members of AAA or AARP, for instance, may be eligible for reduced rates). The national companies represented on the Cape and islands include **Avis** (© 800/331-1212), **Budget** (© 800/527-0700), **Hertz** (© 800/654-3131), **National** (© 800/227-7368), and **Thrifty** (© 800/367-2277).

Internet resources can make comparison-shopping easier. **Travelocity** (www.travelocity.com) and **Expedia** (www.expedia.com) help you compare prices and locate car-rental bargains from various companies nationwide. They will even make your reservation for you once you've found the best deal. Also check out **BreezeNet.com,** which offers domestic car-rental discounts with some of the most competitive rates around.

If you're visiting from abroad and plan to rent a car in the United States, keep in mind that foreign driver's licenses are usually recognized in the U.S., but you should get an international one if your home license is not in English.

For additional car rental agencies, see the "Toll-Free Numbers & Websites Appendix," p. 288.

By Bus

To discourage congestion and provide a pleasant experience, a growing number of towns offer free or low-cost in-town shuttles in season. You'll find such services in Falmouth, Woods Hole, Mashpee, Hyannis, Dennis, Yarmouth, Harwich, Martha's Vineyard, and Nantucket. Each town's chamber of commerce can fill you in, or call the **Cape Cod Regional Transit Authority** (© 800/352-7155 or 508/385-8326). For commercial bus service between towns, see "Getting to Cape Cod & the Islands," earlier in this chapter.

By Boat

For ferries linking the Cape and islands, see "Getting There" in chapters 9 and 10. Other local water-taxi services and cruise opportunities are listed by town in the appropriate chapters.

By Bike

The bicycle is the perfect conveyance for the Cape and islands, for distances great and small. The Cape has some extremely

scenic bike paths, including the glorious Cape Cod Rail Trail, which meanders through seven towns for over 25 miles. Two wheels are the best way to explore Nantucket's flat terrain, and there are scenic bike routes through all six towns on Martha's Vineyard. You'll find a rental shop in just about every town (see the listings under "Bicycling," in subsequent chapters), or better yet, bring your own.

By Moped

They're legal on the islands and can be rented at many bicycle-rental shops, but locals loathe them: They're noisy, polluting, traffic-clogging, and a menace both to their riders and to innocent bystanders. In other words, *caveat renter,* and expect some dirty looks.

By Taxi

You'll find taxi stands at most airports and ferry terminals. The islands also offer jitney services with set rates, such as **Adam Cab** on Martha's Vineyard (© 800/281-4462 or 508/693-3332) and **A-1 Taxi** on Nantucket (© 508/228-3330). Several offer bike racks or can arrange for bike transportation with advance notice—call around until you find what you need. Some companies offer sight-seeing tours. Among the larger taxi fleets on the Cape are **Falmouth Taxi** (© 800/618-8294 or 508/548-4100), **Hyannis Taxi Service** (© 800/773-0600 or 508/775-0400), and Provincetown's **Mercedes Cab** (© 508/487-3333), which delivers elegance at no extra charge. Other cab companies are listed in the Yellow Pages, as are limousine liveries.

5 MONEY & COSTS

It's always advisable to bring money in a variety of forms on a vacation: a mix of cash, credit cards, and traveler's checks. You should also exchange enough petty

cash to cover airport incidentals, tipping, and transportation to your hotel before you leave home, or withdraw money upon arrival at an airport ATM.

Though the Cape and islands—especially the islands—might seem pricey compared to nontourist areas, visitors used to city prices will find costs quite reasonable. Basically, you can get by on very little if you don't need luxury (rooms in older motels off season go for as little as $95 a night). Then again, you could spend $1,000 or more on a room—per night. Most of the nicer rooms fall between $250 and $350 a night in summer, half that in off season.

Restaurant prices offer just as wide a range. You could dine on clam rolls, for instance, at less than $14 a head, or blow that much or more on a mere appetizer. With such a great variety of dining styles available everywhere, the choice is yours.

CURRENCY

The most common bills are the $1 (a "buck"), $5, $10, and $20 denominations. There are also $2 bills (seldom encountered), $50 bills, and $100 bills (the last two are usually not welcome as payment for small purchases).

Coins come in seven denominations: 1¢ (1 cent, or a penny); 5¢ (5 cents, or a nickel); 10¢ (10 cents, or a dime); 25¢ (25 cents, or a quarter); 50¢ (50 cents, or a half dollar); the gold-colored Sacagawea and presidential coins, worth $1; and the rare silver dollar.

ATMS

Every town on the Cape has multiple ATMs (automated teller machines), sometimes referred to as "cash machines," or "cashpoints." These are the easiest and best source of cash when you're away from home.

The **Cirrus** (© **800/424-7787;** www. mastercard.com) and **PLUS** (© **800/843-7587;** www.visa.com) networks span the country; you can find them even in remote regions. Look at the back of your bank card to see which network you're on, and then call or check online for ATM locations on Cape Cod and the islands. Be sure you know your personal identification number (PIN) and daily withdrawal limit before you depart. ***Note:*** Remember that many banks impose a fee every time you use a card at another bank's ATM. In addition, the bank from which you withdraw cash may charge its own fee. To compare banks' ATM fees within the U.S., use **www.bankrate.com**.

CREDIT CARDS & DEBIT CARDS

Credit cards are the most widely used form of payment in the United States: **Visa** (Barclaycard in Britain), **MasterCard** (EuroCard in Europe, Access in Britain, Chargex in Canada), **American Express, Diners Club,** and **Discover.** They also provide a convenient record of all your expenses, and they generally offer relatively good exchange rates. You can withdraw cash advances from your credit cards at banks or ATMs, provided you know your PIN.

Visitors from outside the U.S. should inquire whether their bank assesses a 1% to 3% fee on charges incurred abroad.

It's highly recommended that you travel with at least one major credit card. You must have one to rent a car, and hotels and airlines usually require a credit card imprint as a deposit against expenses.

ATM cards with major credit card backing, known as **"debit cards,"** are now a commonly acceptable form of payment in most stores and restaurants. Debit cards draw money directly from your checking account. Some stores enable you to receive "cash back" on your debit card purchases as well. The same is true at most U.S. post offices.

TRAVELER'S CHECKS

Traveler's checks are widely accepted on Cape Cod and the islands, as they are throughout the U.S., but foreign visitors should make sure that they're denominated in U.S. dollars; foreign-currency checks are often difficult to exchange.

You can buy traveler's checks at most banks. Most are offered in denominations of $20, $50, $100, $500, and sometimes $1,000. Generally, you'll pay a service charge ranging from 1% to 4%.

The most popular traveler's checks are offered by **American Express** (© **800/807-6233,** or 800/221-7282 for cardholders—this number accepts collect calls, offers service in several foreign languages, and exempts AmEx gold and platinum cardholders from the 1% fee) and **Visa** (© **800/732-1322**)—AAA members can obtain Visa checks for a $9.95 fee (for checks up to $1,500) at most AAA offices or by calling © **866/339-3378.** Call © **800/223-9920** for information on MasterCard traveler's checks.

If you do choose to carry traveler's checks, keep a record of their serial numbers separate from your checks in the event that they are stolen or lost. You'll get a refund faster if you know the numbers.

Another option is the new **prepaid traveler's check cards,** reloadable cards that work much like debit cards but aren't linked to your checking account. The **American Express Travelers Cheque Card,** for example, requires a minimum deposit ($300), sets a maximum balance ($2,750), and has a one-time issuance fee of $14. You can withdraw money from an ATM ($2.50 per transaction, not including bank fees), and the funds can be purchased in dollars, euros, or pounds. If you lose the card, your available funds will be refunded within 24 hours.

6 HEALTH

STAYING HEALTHY

The water is drinkable throughout the Cape and islands, though residents tend to prefer bottled water available in all grocery stores and convenience stores. Most menus contain a warning to beware of uncooked fish because it can carry diseases. However, considering the amount of fish consumed in the region (fish is a staple in local restaurants), food illness is extremely rare on the Cape and islands. Many restaurants, including fine-dining establishments, include a vegetarian main course on the menu, but kosher foods are difficult to find. When in doubt, it's best to ask.

General Availability of Health Care

You'll find numerous large chain pharmacies on Cape Cod. There's a CVS and Brooks Drugstore in almost every town; a CVS in Hyannis is open 24 hours (see the "Fast Facts" appendix). In the Outer Cape towns of Wellfleet and Truro and in some of the towns up-island on Martha's

Vineyard, you might be a half-hour drive from a pharmacy, so it's best to come prepared with everything you need.

Common Ailments

SUN Even in this northerly clime, **sunburn** is a real hazard—as is, increasingly, **sun exposure,** whatever the latitude. For most skin types, it's safest to start with a lotion with a high SPF and work your way down. Be sure to reapply often, according to the directions; and no matter how thoroughly you slather on lotion, try to stay in the shade during prime frying time—11am to 2pm. Kids should always wear sunscreen with a high SPF number, or a cover-up such as a T-shirt, if they're going to be playing outside for long periods of time (and just try to stop them!). Sunglasses with UVP (ultraviolet protection) lenses will help shield your eyes.

INSECTS The sea breezes keep most **mosquitoes** on the move, but not always (said Thoreau: "I have never been so much troubled by mosquitoes as in such localities"), so pack some bug spray. Birds on the Cape have been diagnosed with **West Nile disease,** so it's a good idea not to let a mosquito bite you if at all possible. Mosquitoes are the carrier of this disease, which just reached the United States a few years ago. However, the chances of catching West Nile are very low.

The most dangerous insect you're likely to encounter may not be so easily dissuaded. Unfortunately, pinhead-size **deer ticks,** which transmit **Lyme disease** (named for the Connecticut community where the malady was diagnosed), are widespread along the Massachusetts coast, and they're especially active just when you're apt to be there: April through October. Nantucket has the dubious distinction of having the highest concentration of Lyme disease in the country. A vaccine tested there is now on the market. Ask your doctor if you should consider the vaccine. If caught in its early stages—symptoms include a ring-shaped rash and flulike achiness—the disease is easily countered with antibiotics; if it's left untreated, however, the effects could eventually prove fatal.

The best protection, so far, is prevention. Avoid walking in brush or high grass—it's bad for the dunes, anyway. If you insist on bushwhacking, cover up in light-colored clothing (the better to spot any clinging ticks), consisting of a long-sleeved shirt and long pants tucked into high white socks. Camping stores such as EMS sell bush pants that are perfect for this purpose—they're actually comfortable in warm weather. For double protection, spray your clothes and hands (but not face) with a DEET-based insect repellent. Check your clothes before removing them, and then check your body; it helps to use a mirror, or call upon a significant other. Showering after such an outing is a good safeguard. If, despite your best precautions, you find you've brought home a

parasite, remove it with tweezers by pulling directly outward, if you can manage to do so without squeezing the body (that would serve only to inject more bacteria into your bloodstream). Dab the bite with alcohol to help disinfect it, and save the tick in a closed jar. If you're within a few minutes of a medical facility, have a doctor deal with the extraction; if you do it yourself, go for testing and treatment as soon as you can and take the tick with you.

The **Lyme Disease Foundation** (© 860/ 525-2000) distributes brochures to tourist areas and is also able to field questions. Other good sources of information are the **Centers for Disease Control** (© 888/ 232-3228 or 404/332-4555) and the **Massachusetts Department of Public Health** (© 866/627-7968).

PLANTS There's one other very good reason not to go in for splendor in the grass: **poison ivy.** The shiny, purplish, three-leafed clusters are ubiquitous and potent; if you so much as brush past a frond, the plant's oil is likely to raise an itchy welt. Clothing that has been in contact with the plant can spread the harmless but irritating toxin to your skin; it's even transmitted by smoke. If you think you've been exposed, your best bet is to wash with soap immediately (otherwise the oil may spread elsewhere on your body). Calamine lotion—available without prescription at all drugstores—should help soothe the itching. You won't spread the rash by scratching, since it's the oil that does the spreading, but scratches could get infected, so resist the temptation.

BICYCLING HAZARDS There's one key health precaution you can take if you plan to do any bicycling while on the Cape and islands: **a helmet.** In Massachusetts, children 12 and under are required to wear one. All the good bike shops rent helmets as well, and those few extra bucks could save your life.

WHAT TO DO IF YOU GET SICK AWAY FROM HOME

In a medical emergency, the Falmouth Hospital and Cape Cod Hospital **emergency rooms** are your best bets, but you will be billed for any services performed. There is also the **Cape Cod Free Clinic and Health Center** (𝓒 508/477-7079) in Mashpee Commons, a walk-in clinic that treats even people without insurance. We list **hospitals** and **emergency numbers** under "Fast Facts," p. 288.

If you suffer from a chronic illness, consult your doctor before your departure from home. Pack **prescription medications** in your carry-on luggage, and carry them in their original containers, with pharmacy labels—otherwise they won't make it through airport security. Visitors from outside the U.S. should carry generic names of prescription drugs. For U.S. travelers, most reliable health-care plans provide coverage if you get sick away from home. Foreign visitors may have to pay all medical costs upfront and be reimbursed later.

We list **additional emergency numbers** in the "Fast Facts" appendix, p. 288.

---

7 SAFETY

Tourist areas in the United States are generally safe, and the Cape and islands are safer than most. Although a number of towns, particularly the larger ones, suffer their share of crime (much of it drug- and alcohol-related), there's no such thing as a "bad neighborhood" here, per se. However, with crime on the increase everywhere, you need to stay alert and take the usual precautions. Avoid carrying valuables with you on the street or at the beach, and be discreet with expensive cameras and electronic equipment. When milling in crowds (in Hyannis or Provincetown, for example), place your billfold in an inside pocket, and hang on to your purse; anything kept in a backpack should be buried beyond reach. In closely packed places, such as restaurants, theaters, and ferries, keep your possessions in sight, and never sling a bag over the back of your chair: It's too easy a target. Alas, anything left visible in a car, locked or unlocked, is an open invitation, even in secluded Nantucket.

It would be rare in this region to find security staff screening all those who enter a hotel, especially if there's a restaurant on the premises, so don't relax your guard until your door is securely locked. Many areas are still so countrified that homeowners don't even lock their doors, and you'll find that most B&Bs are fairly laissez-faire; a few lack bedroom door locks altogether. If you're traveling light, it shouldn't matter, but if you're the cautious type, inquire about security measures before setting out.

Women, unfortunately, are no safer here than anywhere else, so avoid visiting deserted areas alone, even during the day. Hyannis can get a bit rowdy when its dance clubs are in full swing, and even more so when they let out. For the most part, though, this is a peaceful place, more like the 1950s, and as long as you keep your wits about you, you should be able to relax, relatively speaking.

DRIVING SAFETY Though Massachusetts is quite strict, drunk driving is a definite hazard: The police logs are full of offenses, from foolish to fatal. The best tactic is to avoid the offenders as much as possible, primarily by staying off the roads late at night. It's probably not a good idea to cover long distances at night, in any case, since there are no 24-hour gas stations to help out in case of emergency. In the event of a breakdown, drivers are usually advised to stay in the car with the doors locked until the police arrive. This is a small and friendly enough place, though, that it would probably be all right to take a chance on the kindness of strangers. Use your judgment, and err, if at all, on the side of caution.

Carjacking has yet to make an appearance on the Cape, but car theft runs high in Massachusetts as a whole, so lock your doors even if the natives never bother.

8 SPECIALIZED TRAVEL RESOURCES

TRAVELERS WITH DISABILITIES

Most disabilities shouldn't stop anyone from traveling in the U.S. Thanks to provisions in the Americans with Disabilities Act, most public places are required to comply with disability-friendly regulations. Almost all public establishments (including hotels, restaurants, museums, and so on, but not including certain National Historic Landmarks), and at least some modes of public transportation provide accessible entrances and other facilities for those with disabilities.

Unfortunately, on Cape Cod and the islands many of the historic buildings are not ADA-compliant (accessible for travelers with disabilities). Modern construction, however, is generally equipped with such amenities as ramps, and most inns and restaurants have accessible bathrooms.

For more on organizations that offer resources to disabled travelers, go to www.frommers.com/planning.

GAY & LESBIAN TRAVELERS

Gay and lesbian travelers, singly or in pairs, will feel right at home in Provincetown, a world-renowned gay vacation capital. They should also feel comfortable wandering farther afield. This is a sophisticated, semiurban population, and you'll rarely encounter an overtly bigoted innkeeper, shopkeeper, or restaurateur. If you do, report them to the **Massachusetts Commission Against Discrimination,** 1 Ashburton Place, Room 601, Boston, MA 02108 (© **617/727-3990**).

To avoid unpleasant situations, read between the lines of promotional literature ("fun for the whole family" may mean not much fun for you), or be blunt in stating your expectations (for example, "It will be for myself and my partner, [name goes here], and we'd like a queen bed, if possible"). The descriptions of each establishment listed in this book should give some idea of their suitability and compatibility.

For more gay and lesbian travel resources visit www.frommers.com/planning.

SENIOR TRAVEL

With relatively mild winters and splendid summers, Cape Cod and the islands are popular retirement spots. In fact, as of the 2000 U.S. Census, more than a third of the population was 55 or older. Businesses from museums to B&Bs cater to this clientele with attractive discounts, and many restaurants offer early-bird specials (smaller portions at lower prices, offered before the ordinary dinner hour).

Members of **AARP,** 601 E St. NW, Washington, DC 20049 (© **888/687-2277;** www.aarp.org), get discounts on hotels, airfares, and car rentals. AARP offers members a wide range of benefits, including *AARP The Magazine* and a monthly newsletter. Anyone older than 50 can join.

For more information and resources on travel for seniors, see www.frommers.com/planning.

FAMILY TRAVEL

Basically a giant sandbox with a fringe of waves, the Cape and islands are ideal family vacation spots. A number of the larger hotels and motels offer deals whereby kids can share their parent's room for free. But beware of the fancier B&Bs: Although it's illegal for them to do so, some actively discriminate against children (see "Tips on Accommodations," later in this chapter). The kind that do are apt to be the kind that children dislike, so it's no great loss. For the most part, the local tourism industry is big on serving family needs, so there's not much you'll need to do by way of advance preparation.

A Frommer's guide that provides in-depth info for families visiting the region is *Frommer's Family Vacations in the National Parks* (Wiley Publishing, Inc.), which has a large section on the Cape Cod National Seashore.

To locate accommodations, restaurants, and attractions that are particularly kid-friendly, refer to the "Kids" icon throughout this guide.

For a list of more family-friendly travel resources, visit www.frommers.com/planning.

STUDENT TRAVEL

Check out the **International Student Travel Confederation (ISTC)** (www.istc.org) website for comprehensive travel services information and details on how to get an **International Student Identity Card (ISIC),** which qualifies students for substantial savings on rail passes, plane tickets, entrance fees, and more. It also provides students with basic health and life insurance and a 24-hour helpline. The card is valid for a maximum of 18 months. You can apply for the card online or in person at **STA Travel** (© **800/781-4040** in North America; © 132-782 in Australia; © 087/1230-0040 in the U.K.; www.statravel.com), the biggest student travel agency in the world; check out the website to locate STA Travel offices worldwide. If you're no longer a student but are still under 26, you can get an **International Youth Travel Card (IYTC)** from the same people, which entitles you to some

discounts. **Travel CUTS** (© **800/592-2887;** www.travelcuts.com) offers similar services for both Canadians and U.S. residents. Irish students may prefer to turn to **USIT** (© **01/602-1904;** www.usit.ie), an Ireland-based specialist in student, youth, and independent travel.

TRAVELING WITH PETS

Families love to bring their pets to Cape Cod. Usually they bring dogs, but one pet-friendly cottage colony owner told me about a guest who showed up with two horses. A number of inexpensive motels on the Cape welcome dogs or set aside a few rooms for guests who bring their dog. Some of these charge a pet fee.

The most deluxe pet accommodations in the region are surely the Woof Cottages, also known as the Wharf Cottages, at Nantucket's **The Cottages at the Boat Basin** (© **866/838-9253;** www.thecottagesnantucket.com). You can stay with your dog or cat in specially designated units that come with plush pet beds, toys, and treats, plus a bandanna to make your dog as stylish as a Nantucket native.

In Provincetown, perhaps the Cape's dog-friendliest community, dozens of people walk their dogs down Commercial Street every day. Many motels allow pets, and dogs are welcome at several outdoor cafes.

Every town has good hiking trails where people exercise their dogs—sometimes off-leash, even though the law forbids it. Most towns don't permit dogs on the beach in peak daytime hours and/or in summer, but you can take your dog onto many beaches in early morning and evening and/or off season. Check with the local chamber of commerce for the local rules.

Dogs are not allowed on many trails in Cape Cod National Seashore, though you may walk your dog on-leash on some of its beaches; look for signs posted with the dog rules.

Wherever you go with your pet, don't forget to clean up. Some beaches and trails have plastic bag dispensers and trash cans for that use.

For more resources about traveling with pets, go to www.frommers.com/planning.

9 SUSTAINABLE TOURISM/ECOTOURISM

Nature's beauty is one of the great assets of Cape Cod and the islands. Besides Cape Cod National Seashore, there are numerous protected areas run by state and local authorities—that's why sustainable tourism is so important to this area.

Sustainable tourism is conscientious travel. It means being careful with the environments you explore, and respecting the communities you visit. Two overlapping components of sustainable travel are **ecotourism** and **ethical tourism.** The **International Ecotourism Society (TIES)** defines ecotourism as responsible travel to natural areas that conserves the environment and improves the well-being of local people. TIES suggests that ecotourists follow these principles:

- Minimize environmental impact.
- Build environmental and cultural awareness and respect.
- Provide positive experiences for both visitors and hosts.
- Provide direct financial benefits for conservation and for local people.
- Raise sensitivity to host countries' political, environmental, and social climates.
- Support international human rights and labor agreements.

You can find some eco-friendly travel tips and statistics, as well as touring companies and associations—listed by destination under "Travel Choice"—at the **TIES** website, www.ecotourism.org. Also check out **Ecotravel.com,** which lets you search for sustainable touring companies in several categories (water-based, land-based, spiritually oriented, and so on).

While much of the focus of eco-tourism is about reducing impacts on the natural environment, ethical tourism concentrates on ways to preserve and enhance local economies and communities, regardless of location. You can embrace ethical tourism by staying at a locally owned hotel or shopping at a store that employs local workers and sells locally produced goods.

Responsible Travel (www.responsible travel.com) is a great source of sustainable travel ideas; the site is run by a spokesperson for ethical tourism in the travel industry. **Sustainable Travel International** (www.sustainabletravelinternational.org) promotes ethical tourism practices, and manages an extensive directory of sustainable properties and tour operators around the world.

In the U.K., **Tourism Concern** (www.tourismconcern.org.uk) works to reduce social and environmental problems connected to tourism. The **Association of Independent Tour Operators (AITO)** (www.aito.co.uk) is a group of specialist operators leading the field in making holidays sustainable.

Volunteer travel has become increasingly popular among those who want to venture beyond the standard group-tour experience to learn languages, interact with locals, and make a positive difference while on vacation. Volunteer travel usually doesn't require special skills—just a willingness to work hard—and programs vary in length from a few days to a number of weeks. Some programs provide free housing and food, but many require volunteers to pay for travel expenses, which can add up quickly.

For general info on volunteer travel, visit **www.volunteerabroad.org** and **www.idealist.org.**

10 PACKAGES FOR THE INDEPENDENT TRAVELER

Package tours are simply a way to buy the airfare, accommodations, and other elements of your trip (such as car rentals, airport transfers, and sometimes even activities) at the same time and often at discounted prices.

One good source of package deals is the airlines themselves. Most major airlines offer air/land packages, including **American Airlines Vacations** (© 800/321-2121; www.aavacations.com), **Delta Vacations** (© 800/654-6559; www.deltavacations.com), **Continental Airlines Vacations** (© 800/301-3800; www.covacations.com), and **United Vacations** (© 888/854-3899;

www.unitedvacations.com). Several big **online travel agencies**—Expedia, Travelocity, Orbitz, Site59, and Lastminute.com—also do a brisk business in packages.

Travel packages are also listed in the travel section of your local Sunday newspaper. Or check ads in the national travel magazines such as *Arthur Frommer's Budget Travel Magazine, Travel + Leisure, National Geographic Traveler,* and *Condé Nast Traveler.*

For more information on Package Tours and for tips on booking your trip, see www.frommers.com/planning.

11 SPECIAL-INTEREST TRIPS

A number of organizations, outfitters, and tour companies offer special trips to Cape Cod, Nantucket, and Martha's Vineyard.

BIKING
Several biking tour companies offer bike trips on Cape Cod and the islands. My favorite, **Bike Riders** (© 800/473-7040; www.bikeriderstours.com), offers a 6-day "island-hopping" trip to Martha's Vineyard and Nantucket in which you stay at top hotels on the islands and eat at terrific restaurants. After biking all day, you've earned the pampering! Trips are in June, July, and August and cost about $2,500.

FISHING
Orvis Fly-Fishing School, based at the Chatham Bars Inn in Chatham (© 800/235-9763; www.orvis.com), offers 2-day fly-fishing seminars on the Cape for about $430.

HIKING
Every town on Cape Cod has open space with excellent hiking trails. The local

chapter of Audubon, at **Wellfleet Bay Wildlife Sanctuary** in South Wellfleet (© 508/349-2615; www.massaudubon.org), offers hikes of all lengths, including a half-day trip to Monomoy, an island and bird sanctuary off Chatham.

KAYAKING
Kayaking has become almost as popular as biking on the Cape and islands. Depending on your skill level, there are dozens of estuaries and inlets to explore, as well as more challenging waterways to conquer. For example, you might enjoy a meandering paddle trip through the estuaries of Nauset Marsh or a trip across Vineyard Sound from Woods Hole to Martha's Vineyard, which is a 4-mile trip through sometimes choppy waters. You'll need a sea kayak for that trip. A number of outfits based on Cape Cod offer kayaking trips and lessons. **Eric Gustafson** runs guided kayak tours (© 508/349-1429; www.funseekers.org) of kettle ponds and tidal rivers from Chatham to Truro. **Cape Cod**

Kayak (© 508/563-9377; www.capecod kayak.com) offers eco-tours on waterways mainly on the Upper Cape. **Eastern Mountain Sports** in Hyannis (© 508/362-8690; www.ems.com) sponsors trips mainly in the mid-Cape area. **Goose Hummuck** in Orleans (© 508/255-2620; www.goose.com) runs kayak trips mainly in the Lower Cape. **Cape Outback Adventures** in Wellfleet (© 508/349-1617; capeoutback.com) runs kayak trips in the Lower and Outer Cape. Daylong trips cost anywhere from $40 to $70.

12 STAYING CONNECTED

TELEPHONES

Generally, hotel surcharges on long-distance and local calls are astronomical, so you're better off using your **cellphone** or a **public pay telephone.** Many convenience groceries and packaging services sell **prepaid calling cards** in denominations up to $50; for international visitors these can be the least expensive way to call home. Many public pay phones at airports now accept American Express, MasterCard, and Visa credit cards. **Local calls** made from pay phones in most locales cost either 25¢ or 35¢ (no pennies, please).

Most long-distance and international calls can be dialed directly from any phone. **For calls within the United States and to Canada,** dial © 1 followed by the area code and the seven-digit number. **For other international calls,** dial © 011 followed by the country code, city code, and the number you are calling.

Calls to area codes **800, 888, 877,** and **866** are toll-free. However, calls to area codes **700** and **900** (chat lines, bulletin boards, "dating" services, and so on) can be very expensive—usually a charge of 95¢ to $3 or more per minute, and they sometimes have minimum charges that can run as high as $15 or more.

For **reversed-charge or collect calls,** and for person-to-person calls, dial the number 0, then the area code and number; an operator will come on the line, and you should specify whether you are calling collect, person-to-person, or both. If your operator-assisted call is international, ask for the overseas operator.

For **local directory assistance** ("information"), dial © 411; for long-distance information, dial © 1, then the appropriate area code and 555-1212.

CELLPHONES

Just because your cellphone works at home doesn't mean it'll work everywhere in the U.S. (thanks to our nation's fragmented cellphone system). It's a good bet that your phone will work in major cities, but take a look at your wireless company's coverage map on its website before heading out; T-Mobile, Sprint, and Nextel are particularly weak in rural areas. If you need to stay in touch at a destination where you know your phone won't work, **rent** a phone that does from **InTouch USA** (© 800/872-7626; www.intouchglobal. com) or a rental car location, but beware that you'll pay $1 a minute or more for airtime.

If you're not from the U.S., you'll be appalled at the poor reach of the **GSM (Global System for Mobile Communications) wireless network,** which is used by much of the rest of the world. Your phone will probably work in most major U.S. cities; it definitely won't work in many rural areas. To see where GSM phones work in the U.S., check out www.t-mobile. com/coverage. And you may or may not be able to send SMS (text messaging) home.

Online Traveler's Toolbox

Veteran travelers usually carry some essential items to make their trips easier. Following is a selection of handy online tools to bookmark and use:

- **Airplane Food** (www.airlinemeals.net)
- **Airplane Seating** (www.seatguru.com and www.airlinequality.com)
- **Cape-wide Restaurants** (www.capecoddining.com)
- **Foreign Languages for Travelers** (www.travlang.com)
- **Maps** (www.mapquest.com)
- **Provincetown Restaurants and Attractions** (www.provincetown.com)
- **Time and Date** (www.timeanddate.com)
- **Universal Currency Converter** (www.xe.com/ucc)
- **Upper Cape Restaurants and Attractions** (www.capenews.net)
- **Visa ATM Locator** (www.visa.com), **MasterCard ATM Locator** (www.mastercard.com)
- **Weather** (www.intellicast.com and www.weather.com)

VOICE-OVER INTERNET PROTOCOL (VOIP)

If you have web access while traveling, consider a broadband-based telephone service (in technical terms, **Voice-over Internet protocol,** or **VoIP**) such as Skype (www.skype.com) or Vonage (www.vonage.com), which allow you to make free international calls from your laptop or in a cybercafe. Neither service requires the people you're calling to also have that service (though there are fees if they do not). Check the websites for details.

INTERNET/E-MAIL
With Your Own Computer

More and more hotels, resorts, airports, cafes, and retailers are going Wi-Fi (wireless fidelity), becoming "hotspots" that offer free high-speed Wi-Fi access or charge a small fee for usage. Wi-Fi is even found in campgrounds, RV parks, and even entire towns. Most laptops sold today have built-in wireless capability. To find public Wi-Fi hotspots at your destination, go to **www.jiwire.com;** its Hotspot Finder

holds the world's largest directory of public wireless hotspots.

For dial-up access, most business-class hotels in the U.S. offer dataports for laptop modems, and a few thousand hotels in the U.S. and Europe now offer free high-speed Internet access.

Wherever you go, bring a **connection kit** of the right power and phone adapters, a spare phone cord, and a spare Ethernet network cable—or find out whether your hotel supplies them to guests.

For information on electrical currency conversions, see "Electricity," in the "Fast Facts" appendix (p. 289).

Without Your Own Computer

To find cybercafes, check www.cybercaptive.com and www.cybercafe.com. Though they are rare on the Cape and islands, you will find good ones in Provincetown and on Nantucket. In addition, almost every library on the Cape has free Internet access.

Most major airports have **Internet kiosks** that provide basic Web access for a per-minute fee that's usually higher than cybercafe prices. Check out copy shops like **Kinko's** (FedEx Kinkos), which offers computer stations with fully loaded software (as well as Wi-Fi).

For help locating cybercafes and other establishments where you can go for Internet access, please see "Internet Access" in the "Fast Facts" appendix (p. 291).

13 TIPS ON ACCOMMODATIONS

The listings in this book feature a range of summer rates for a room with double occupancy. Keep in mind that this figure does not take into account the state and local tax, which is 9.7%. Prices off season are typically discounted by about 20% to 30%, sometimes more.

Virtually every town on the Cape has lodgings to suit every taste and budget. The essential trick is to secure reservations months in advance for the peak season of July through August (June and Sept are getting crowded, too). You can't count on luck; in fact, unless you're just planning a day trip, you probably shouldn't even visit at the height of summer unless you've prearranged a place to stay.

Accommodations range from sprawling, full-facility resorts to cozy little B&Bs with room for only a handful of guests. The price differential, surprisingly enough, may not be that great. A room at a particularly exquisite inn might run more than a modern hotel room with every imaginable amenity.

Because there are hundreds of lodging establishments of every stripe throughout the Cape and islands, I've focused only on those with special qualities: superb facilities, for example, or especially friendly and helpful hosts. I've personally visited every place listed in this guide, but worthy new inns—as well as resurrected old ones—are constantly popping up.

For tips on surfing for hotel deals online, visit www.frommers.com/planning.

RESERVATIONS SERVICES Several reservations services cover the region, but the only one I can personally vouch for—their standards being as exacting as mine—is **Destinnations** (© 800/333-4667 or 508/790-0566). Representing hundreds of top inns throughout New England, Destinnations can also design custom tours that cater to special interests, such as golf or antiquing.

Otherwise, it's buyer beware when it comes to such promotional terms as "water view" or "beachfront" (Provincetown's in-town beach, for instance, is quite scenic for strolls, but a bit too close to an active harbor to make for pleasant swimming). To spare yourself disappointment, always call ahead to request a brochure. Some inns and hotels offer special packages, which they may or may not list, so always inquire. Most require a 2-night minimum on weekends, 3 or even 5 if it's a holiday weekend. All provide free parking, although in a congested area such as Provincetown, you may have to play musical spaces.

FAMILY-FRIENDLY CHOICES Although all lodgings in the state are prohibited by law from discriminating on the basis of age, a lot of the fancier, fussier B&Bs will be none too happy if you show up with a young child or infant in tow. You might not be too happy either, spending your entire vacation attending to damage control. It can't hurt to inquire—perhaps anonymously, before calling to book—about an establishment's attitude toward children and its suitability for their needs. If you get the impression that your child won't be welcome, there's no point in pushing it: The child, sensing correctly that he/she is not wanted, is likely to exceed your worst expectations. If, on the other hand, you know your child to be a reliable model of "company behavior," you might want to risk an unannounced arrival.

It's probably easier from the outset, though, to seek out places that like having kids around. Motels are always a safe bet (it's what they're designed for), and the descriptions provided in this book should indicate other likely spots.

A popular family option—but again, you must make plans as much as a year in advance—is to rent a cottage or house by the week, or even month (see below).

RENTING A COTTAGE OR HOUSE

Families planning a Cape Cod vacation, especially families with young children, should consider renting a cottage or house rather than choosing an inn or hotel. The trick to finding a great rental can be summed up in two words: *Book early.* Start calling Realtors in January and February (if not sooner—some vacationers who return every summer book a year in advance). If you can visit earlier in the year to check out a few places, that helps, but if not, you may be able to view choices on a Realtor's website or see photos that the Realtor can mail to you.

Believe it or not, there are parts of Cape Cod that are not close to a beach. When talking to a Realtor, ask specifically for rentals on the water, with views of the water, or within a half-mile of a beach. You'll have a better Cape Cod vacation if you are within walking distance of a beach.

Prices on rentals vary, but they are always much lower off season. Depending on the rental, off season could mean late June or even late August, so ask what the cutoff dates are for high-season prices. Location is the single biggest factor in determining price: A two-bedroom cottage could cost $800 a week in Dennis or $8,000 a week on Nantucket. Tell your Realtor your price range and what you are looking for, and he or she will select appropriate listings for you to choose from.

Each town's chamber of commerce can put you in touch with local Realtors. You can also call the **Cape Cod & Islands Association of Realtors** (© 508/957-4300; www.cciaor.com) for a complete list of Realtors in the area.

Here is a list of good Realtors with rentals in different regions of the Cape and on the islands: **Real Estate Associates** in North Falmouth (© 508/563-7173), **Kinlin/Grover Realtors** in Sandwich (© 508/888-1555), **Bay Village Realty** in Brewster (© 800/833-4958), **Duarte/Downey Real Estate** in Truro (© 508/349-7588), **Linda R. Bassett Vacation Rentals** on Martha's Vineyard (© 800/338-9201), and **Nantucket Real Estate Co.** on Nantucket (© 508/228-3131).

CAMPING A number of state parks and recreation areas maintain campgrounds; for a full listing for the state, contact the **Department of Conservation and Recreation,** Division of Forests and Parks (© 617/727-3180).

The largest such area on the Cape is the 2,000-acre **Nickerson State Park** (© 508/896-3491), offering over 400 campsites. The Massachusetts Audubon Society offers limited tenting at its 1,000-acre **Wellfleet Bay Wildlife Sanctuary** (© 508/349-2615).

Note: Camping is expressly forbidden within the Cape Cod National Seashore (with the exception of a few "grandfathered" commercial campgrounds) and on Nantucket. Seashore camping is not allowed on Martha's Vineyard either. The Vineyard has one campground, called **Martha's Vineyard Family Campground** on Vineyard Haven–Edgartown Road (© 508/693-3772), which is in the middle of the island and far from a beach.

A partial list of private campgrounds that belong to the **Massachusetts Association of Campground Owners** appears in the Massachusetts Office of Travel and Tourism's free *Getaway Guide* (© 800/447-6277, ext. 454).

In addition to the online travel booking sites **Travelocity, Expedia, Orbitz, Priceline,** and **Hotwire,** you can book hotels through **Hotels.com, Quikbook** (www.quikbook.com), and **Travelaxe** (www.travelaxe.net).

HotelChatter.com is a daily webzine offering smart coverage and critiques of hotels worldwide. Go to **TripAdvisor.com** or **HotelShark.com** for helpful independent consumer reviews of hotels and resort properties.

It's a good idea to **get a confirmation number** and **make a printout** of any online booking transaction.

SAVING ON YOUR HOTEL ROOM

The **rack rate** is the maximum rate that a hotel charges for a room. Hardly anybody pays this price, however, except in high season or on holidays. To lower the cost of your room:

- **Ask about special rates or other discounts.** You may qualify for corporate, student, military, senior, frequent-flier, trade union, or other discounts.
- **Dial direct.** When booking a room in a chain hotel, you'll often get a better deal by calling the individual hotel's reservation desk rather than the chain's main number.
- **Book online.** Many hotels offer Internet-only discounts, or supply rooms to Priceline, Hotwire, or Expedia at rates much lower than the ones you can get through the hotel itself.
- **Remember the law of supply and demand.** Resort hotels are most crowded and therefore most expensive on weekends, so discounts are usually available for midweek stays. Business hotels in downtown locations are busiest during the week, so you can expect big discounts over the weekend.
- **Look into group or long-stay discounts.** If you come as part of a large

group, you should be able to negotiate a bargain rate. Likewise, if you're planning a long stay (at least 5 days), you might qualify for a discount. As a general rule, expect 1 night free after a 7-night stay.

- **Sidestep excess surcharges and hidden costs.** Many hotels have the unpleasant practice of nickel-and-diming its guests with opaque surcharges. When you book a room, ask what is included in the room rate, and what is extra. Avoid dialing direct from hotel phones, which can have exorbitant rates. And don't be tempted by the room's minibar offerings. Finally, ask about local taxes and service charges, which can increase the cost of a room by 15% or more.
- **Carefully consider your hotel's meal plan.** If you enjoy eating out and sampling the local cuisine, it makes sense to choose a **Continental Plan (CP),** which includes breakfast only, or a **European Plan (EP),** which doesn't include any meals and allows you maximum flexibility. If you're more interested in saving money, opt for a **Modified American Plan (MAP),** which includes breakfast and one meal, or the **American Plan (AP),** which includes three meals. If you must choose a MAP, see if you can get a free lunch at your hotel if you decide to do dinner out.
- **Book an efficiency.** A room with a kitchenette allows you to shop for groceries and cook your own meals. This is a big money saver, especially for families on long stays.
- **Consider enrolling in hotel "frequent-stay" programs,** which are upping the ante lately to win the loyalty of repeat customers. Frequent guests can now accumulate points or credits to earn free hotel nights, airline miles, in-room amenities, merchandise, tickets to concerts and events, and discounts on sporting facilities. Perks are awarded

House-Swapping

House-swapping is becoming a more popular and viable means of travel; you stay in their place, they stay in yours, and you both get an authentic and personal view of the area, the opposite of the escapist retreat that many hotels offer. Try **HomeLink International** (www.homelink.org), the largest and oldest home-swapping organization, founded in 1952, with over 11,000 listings worldwide ($75 for a yearly membership). **HomeExchange.com** ($50 for 6,000 listings) and **InterVac.com** ($70 for over 10,000 listings) are also reliable.

not only by many chain hotels and motels (Hilton HHonors, Marriott Rewards, Wyndham ByRequest, to name a few), but some individual inns and B&Bs.

LANDING THE BEST ROOM

Somebody has to get the best room in the house. It might as well be you. You can start by joining the hotel's frequent-guest program, which may make you eligible for upgrades. Always ask about a corner room. They're often larger and quieter, with more windows and light, and they often cost the same as standard rooms. When you make your reservation, ask if the hotel is renovating; if it is, request a room away from the construction. If you're a light sleeper, request a quiet room away from vending or ice machines, elevators, restaurants, bars, and discos. Ask for a room that has most recently been renovated or redecorated.

If you aren't happy with your room when you arrive, ask for another one. Most lodgings will be willing to accommodate you.

In resort areas, particularly in warm climates, ask the following questions before you book a room:

- What's the view like? Cost-conscious travelers may be willing to pay less for a back room facing the parking lot, especially if they don't plan to spend much time in their room.

- Does the room have air-conditioning or ceiling fans? Do the windows open? If they do, and the nighttime entertainment takes place alfresco, you may want to find out when show time is over.
- What's included in the price? Your room may be moderately priced, but if you're charged for beach chairs, towels, sports equipment, and other amenities, you could end up spending more than you bargained for.
- How far is the room from the beach and other amenities? If it's far, is there transportation to and from the beach, and is it free?

HOSTEL INFORMATION

Hostelling International/American Youth Hostels (✆ 202/783-6161; www.hihostels.com) offers low-cost dorm accommodations at four sites on the Cape and islands. Rates vary but average around $25 per person per night for nonmembers; members pay $22. Membership is $28 a year for adults, $18 for adults 55 and over, free for children 17 and under. Note that there's a "lockout" period (typically 10am–5pm daily), and, likely, a limit on the length of stay. HI/AYH properties are located in Eastham, just off the bike trail; in a former Coast Guard station overlooking Ballston Beach in Truro; adjoining the 4,000-acre Manuel F. Correllus State Forest in West Tisbury on Martha's Vineyard; and in an 1874 lifesaving station on Surfside Beach on Nantucket.

PLANNING YOUR TRIP

3

TIPS ON ACCOMMODATIONS

Suggested Itineraries

You can easily see a sampling of the highlights on the Cape and islands in a week, and you'll still have many hours for lounging around on the beach, a don't-miss activity. Two weeks will enable you to see all the most interesting attractions in the region plus have even more time to spend with your family. It's best to plan a leisurely visit that allows plenty of opportunities to try a different beach every day, to poke around antiques shops, or to explore marshes by kayak.

Cape Cod does not have a very convenient public transportation system, so you will have to drive your own car to see the sites. Take traffic into account when planning your itineraries. Getting an early start on the road is critical if you are staying in Falmouth, say, and want to drive to the Outer Cape to check out the Cape Cod National Seashore. Avoid midday drives on roads such as Route 28 from Falmouth to Dennis; it tends to be loaded with traffic.

Both Martha's Vineyard and Nantucket have excellent public transportation systems, and when you visit the islands you can leave your car behind. On both islands, and occasionally on Cape Cod, you can explore on bicycle; I'll include the must-ride bike paths.

Staying in a central area on the Cape is a good strategy for exploring the peninsula. Spending a couple of nights in Provincetown or on the islands of Nantucket and Martha's Vineyard is also a real treat.

There are 15 towns on Cape Cod, six towns on Martha's Vineyard, and one main town on Nantucket. The itineraries below do not include visits to every town, but you may find yourself stopping between recommended attractions for, say, refreshment at a quaint ice-cream parlor. The Cape is full of discoveries for those who wander off the beaten track.

No matter which itinerary you choose, you'll want to include some unstructured time on the beach or at one of the Cape's many freshwater ponds, because enjoying the outdoors is really what the Cape is all about.

1 THE REGIONS IN BRIEF

Newcomers—known locally as "wash-ashores"—invariably struggle with the terms "Upper" and "Lower," used to describe, respectively, the westernmost and easternmost sections of the Cape. The distinction is thought to allude to the longitude, which decreases as you head east.

Many find it helpful to use the analogy of the "arm" of Cape Cod, with the Upper Cape towns of Sandwich, Falmouth, Bourne, and Mashpee forming the upper arm; Chatham the elbow of the Lower Cape; and Provincetown the "fist." On Martha's Vineyard, similar confusion reigns over what's meant by "up-island" and "down-island." Down-island consists of the touristy port towns of Vineyard Haven, Oak Bluffs, and Edgartown. In the summer months, locals try to stay up-island, avoiding down-island at all costs.

Even the term "land" may be a bit misleading; the Cape and islands are actually just heaps of sand, without bedrock. Described geologically as "terminal moraine," they're

The Outer Cape

PROVINCETOWN

TRURO

WELLFLEET

EASTHAM

The Upper Cape

The Lower Cape

ORLEANS

BREWSTER

DENNIS

BOURNE SANDWICH

BARNSTABLE YARMOUTH

HARWICH CHATHAM

MASHPEE

FALMOUTH

The Mid Cape

SUGGESTED ITINERARIES

4

THE REGIONS IN BRIEF

what remains of the grit heaved and dumped by the motion of massive glaciers that finally receded some 12,000 years ago, leaving a legacy of "kettle ponds"—steep-sided freshwater pools formed when sharp fragments of the glacier were left to melt in place. Under the relentless onslaught of storms and tides, the landmass's outlines are still subject to constant change and eventual erasure.

The modern landscape is vastly different from what was visible a century ago. Virtually all the trees represent new growth. The settlers, in their rush to build houses and ships and to fuel hearths and factories, plundered all the lumber. Were it not for the recession during the late 19th century, you'd be looking at turnip fields and "poverty grass"—so called because it will grow anywhere, needing next to nothing to survive. Instead, the Lower Cape and Mid Cape are now lushly forested, and if the tree cover gets spindly along the Outer Cape, it's the result of battery by salt winds rather than human depredation.

The islands also show the effects of the ocean winds—predominantly those out of the southwest. Harbor towns and down-island areas enjoy a canopy of trees, and the more exposed portions consist primarily of grassy sand plains and moors.

The shoreline has eroded about a full mile since Colonial times, and current scientific predictions give the Cape and islands a projected life span of as much as 5,000 more years—or as little as 500. Not to make light of the situation, but this is all the more reason to enjoy them while you can!

The 15 towns on Cape Cod have quite distinct personalities to match the varied landscape. Few similarities exist, for instance, among rural Truro, rowdy Hyannis, and historic Sandwich Village.

Most frequent vacationers to Cape Cod return to the same village every year, rarely venturing beyond their chosen town's lines. But the resourceful visitor who explores the region, perhaps driving the Old King's Highway (Rte. 6A), shopping in Chatham, beaching it at the National Seashore, and checking out an island or two, will get an eyeful of the area's diversity.

Visitors may be confused by the similar names of towns on the Cape, particularly in the Mid Cape area. When you book a room, it may be helpful to understand these distinctions. Barnstable County consists of the 15 towns on Cape Cod, all of which are made up of individual villages. The largest town on Cape Cod is called Barnstable, and it is made up of eight villages: Cotuit, Osterville, Marstons Mills, Centerville, Hyannis, Hyannisport, West Barnstable, and (is there an echo in here?) Barnstable Village.

Despite the similar names, towns and even villages on the Cape retain their distinct characters. For instance, picturesque little Barnstable Village (along Rte. 6A, the historic Old King's Hwy.) couldn't be more different from Hyannis (off Rte. 28), transportation hub and home of the mall. Both are villages in the town of Barnstable. In the same vein, the sleepy, rural village of West Barnstable (off Rte. 6A) doesn't have much in common with wealthy, preppy Osterville (off Rte. 28 on the coast). Other notable villages in Barnstable include Cotuit (off Rte. 28; historic and quaint), Marstons Mills (off Rte. 28 but inland; mainly residential), Centerville (off Rte. 28; beachy, yet with some commercial sprawl), and Hyannisport (off Rte. 28 on the coast; a residential neighborhood made famous by the Kennedys).

A number of other villages and towns are notable for their unique characteristics. Woods Hole—where bohemians and scientists coexist in a bustling ferry port—is a village in the town of Falmouth, whose downtown has a pleasant Main Street and picture-postcard town green. Chatham and Osterville both have main streets that are destinations for shoppers seeking expensive, quality wares. Gay-friendly Provincetown has a colorful main street with great people-watching opportunities. Sandwich may well be the quaintest town; Wellfleet, the most artsy. West Barnstable, Barnstable, Yarmouth Port, Dennis, and Brewster are all prototypical New England villages along the historic Old King's Highway. Of these, Dennis Village has the most going on, with a museum, cinema, and playhouse all in one historic complex. The Outer Cape towns (Eastham, Wellfleet, Truro, and Provincetown) have the National Seashore beaches, but many families prefer the accessibility of the villages on Nantucket Sound: West Dennis and Harwich Port offer pretty beaches with calm surf and warmer waters.

On the islands, location is also an important factor. Most visitors to Nantucket choose lodging in town, where everything is within walking distance. On Martha's Vineyard, down-island towns (Vineyard Haven, Oak Bluffs, and Edgartown) host the majority of the action—shops, restaurants, and multitudes of tourists. If a serene escape from the grind is what you seek, you may want to be up-island (West Tisbury; Chilmark, including the village of Menemsha; or Aquinnah), but you'll need a car—or a passion for biking—to enjoy these locations.

Socially, the towns of the Cape and islands have their differences, too. Older, more protected communities like Sandwich, Falmouth, and Edgartown appeal to traditionalists, while 20-somethings and adventurous types of all ages seem to feel more at home in open-minded, forward-thinking settings such as Wellfleet or Provincetown. Families are sure to have a fabulous time everywhere on the Cape and islands, because splashing surf and expanses of sand are ubiquitous.

Route 28 east of Hyannis, an eyesore of tacky strip-mall development, represents a warning of what the future holds unless residents continue to clamp down on zoning. Though the pressures of development are unrelenting, Cape lovers have done a pretty good job, so far, of fending off more egregious offenders. The Cape Cod National Seashore—though hotly protested when it was instituted in 1961—serves as a living reminder of the glory that could have been lost, or perhaps reserved solely for the enjoyment of the ultrarich.

Today, it is the unspoiled natural beauty and historical charm of the area that attracts visitors. Cape Cod's yearly haul of 17 million visitors infuses the region with more than $700 million in revenues. Tourism has been the leading business sector since the late 19th century and is likely to remain so for centuries to come.

2 CAPE COD & THE ISLANDS IN 1 WEEK

This route gives you an overview of the highlights of the Cape, Nantucket, and Martha's Vineyard. You'll see the major attractions, like the Heritage Museums and Gardens in Sandwich, the Shining Sea Bikeway in Falmouth and Commercial Street in Provincetown, plus the islands. It's a whirlwind tour, but builds in some downtime for relaxing. See p. 68 for a map of this itinerary.

Day ❶: Arrive in Falmouth

After arriving in **Falmouth ★★★**, the second largest of Cape Cod's 15 towns, take a bike ride down the 4-mile **Shining Sea Bikeway ★★★** (p. 96) from Falmouth center to the village of Woods Hole to get a feel for the coastline. The bike path offers views of Martha's Vineyard and passes saltwater ponds and marshland. **Woods Hole ★★★** (p. 99) is the home of several world-renowned science institutions, including **Woods Hole Oceanographic Institution.** Check out the fishing fleet on the Woods Hole dock, the houseboats in Great Harbor, and the free **aquarium ★**, where you can watch seals being fed.

Day ❷: Day Trip to Martha's Vineyard

Hop a ferry from Woods Hole or Falmouth Inner Harbor for the 30- to 45-minute trip to Vineyard Haven or Oak Bluffs on **Martha's Vineyard.** While on the Vineyard, you can take a quick stroll around the three down-island towns of **Oak Bluffs ★★★**, **Edgartown ★★★**, and **Vineyard Haven ★★**, which are connected by frequent shuttle buses. In Oak Bluffs, you'll want to see the **gingerbread houses ★★★** (p. 252), which are Carpenter Gothic-style homes built in the late 19th century when the area was the site of frequent revival meetings. The cottages

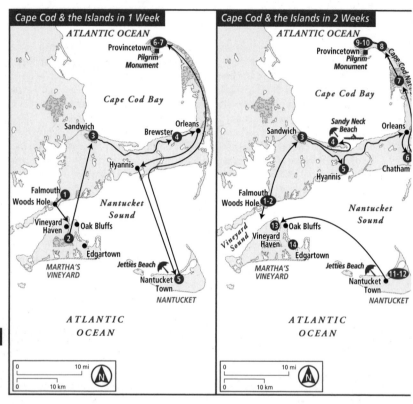

Cape Cod & the Islands in 1 Week

ATLANTIC OCEAN

Provincetown 6-7
Pilgrim Monument

Cape Cod Bay

Sandwich 3
Brewster 4
Orleans

Hyannis

Falmouth 1
Woods Hole

Nantucket Sound

Vineyard Haven
Oak Bluffs 2

Edgartown

Jetties Beach
Nantucket Town 5
NANTUCKET

MARTHA'S VINEYARD

ATLANTIC OCEAN

0   10 mi
0   10 km
N

Cape Cod & the Islands in 2 Weeks

ATLANTIC OCEAN

Provincetown 9-10 8
Pilgrim Monument
Cape Cod Nat'l 7

Cape Cod Bay

Sandy Neck Beach
Sandwich 3
4
Orleans
5 6
Chatham
Hyannis

Falmouth 1-2
Woods Hole

Nantucket Sound

Vineyard Sound
Oak Bluffs 13
Vineyard Haven
14
Edgartown

Jetties Beach
Nantucket Town 11-12
NANTUCKET

MARTHA'S VINEYARD

ATLANTIC OCEAN

0   10 mi
0   10 km
N

surround the **Trinity Park Tabernacle** ★★ (p. 267), an elegant open-air church.

Day ❸: Sandwich ★★★

You'll need a full day to explore the town of **Sandwich,** and you'll need an early start. In the morning, visit the **Heritage Museums and Gardens** ★★★ (p. 81) near **Shawme Pond,** a short drive from the center of town. After taking a few hours to enjoy Heritage'sa unique collections and extensive gardens, stop at the **Sandwich Glass Museum** ★★ (p. 82), in the center of town, to learn about this fascinating industry and to watch glass artisans in action. End your day at **Sandy Neck Beach** ★★★ (p. 79), one of the Cape's most beautiful beaches.

Day ❹: The Old King's Highway (Rte. 6A), Brewster & Orleans

Drive up the **Old King's Highway/Route 6A** from Sandwich to Brewster, checking out interesting stores along the way, particularly the fine antiques shops. Spend the rest of the morning visiting one of Brewster's bay beaches, like **Breakwater Beach** ★★ (p. 148), during low tide and explore the flats, the miles of exposed beach left when the tide recedes. In the afternoon, head out from **Rock Harbor** in **Orleans** ★★ on an afternoon charter fishing trip (p. 174).

Day ❺: A Day Trip to Nantucket

Take the 1-hour fast ferry from Hyannis, either the Hy-Line or the Steamship

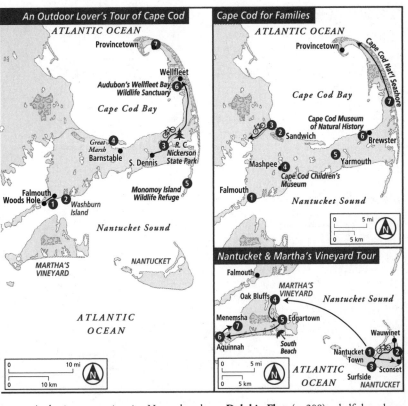

An Outdoor Lover's Tour of Cape Cod

ATLANTIC OCEAN
Provincetown 7
Wellfleet 6
Audubon's Wellfleet Bay
Wildlife Sanctuary
Cape Cod Bay
Great 4
Marsh
Barnstable
S. Dennis
R. C.
Nickerson
3 State Park
Monomoy Island
Wildlife Refuge 5
Falmouth 1
Woods Hole 2
Washburn
Island
Nantucket Sound
MARTHA'S
VINEYARD
NANTUCKET
ATLANTIC
OCEAN
0   10 mi
0   10 km

Cape Cod for Families

ATLANTIC OCEAN
Provincetown
Cape Cod Nat'l Seashore
7
Cape Cod Bay
Cape Cod Museum
of Natural History
3
2 Sandwich
6 Brewster
5 Yarmouth
Mashpee
4
Cape Cod Children's
Museum
Falmouth 1
Nantucket Sound
0   5 mi
0   5 km

Nantucket & Martha's Vineyard Tour

Falmouth
MARTHA'S
VINEYARD
Oak Bluffs 4
Nantucket Sound
Menemsha
7
6
5 Edgartown
Aquinnah
South
Beach
Wauwinet
Nantucket 1 2
Town
3 Sconset
Surfside
ATLANTIC
OCEAN
NANTUCKET
0   5 mi
0   5 km

Authority, to arrive in Nantucket by lunchtime. Buy sandwiches in town and bike to **Jetties Beach ★★★** (p. 230) for a picnic lunch. Explore several historic sites on foot. The **Whaling Museum ★★★** (p. 234) is a must. Other interesting sites are the **Jethro Coffin House ★★** (p. 233), Nantucket's oldest house, and the **Hadwen House ★★** (p. 232), an example of the town's 19th-century prosperity.

Day ⑥: Whale-Watching

It's tough to take in everything **Provincetown ★★★** has to offer in 1 day, so I've given it 2. Staying overnight for a couple of nights will give you enough time to take in this multifaceted and unique town. One must is a **whale-watch** on the

Dolphin Fleet (p. 209), a half-day adventure out to **Stellwagen Bank** to see the magnificent ritual of whales feeding in their natural habitat. You'll be tired and hungry after the boat ride. Wander down **Commercial Street,** stopping at shops along the way, to choose a restaurant for dinner, preferably one on the water with a sunset view.

Day ⑦: Provincetown ★★★

Your second day in Provincetown should include a trip to the **Pilgrim Monument & Provincetown Museum ★★** (p. 210). Climb the 116 steps of the monument to get a bird's-eye view of the tip of the Cape, the curling spit of sand bordered by marshes and massive dunes. The museum gives a great overview of the history of the town. Adventurous bike riders will want to take a couple of hours to bike the **Province Lands Trail ★★**, which winds its way past marshland and over dunes. Take a sunset sail on the ***Bay Lady II*** ★ (p. 208), a handsome schooner, before settling in for another good meal at one of Provincetown's fine restaurants.

---

3 CAPE COD & THE ISLANDS IN 2 WEEKS

Two weeks on the Cape and islands gives you ample time for a relaxing family vacation that takes in a number of the sites. You'll get to take a leisurely drive down the Old King's Highway, explore art galleries in Provincetown, listen to a town band concert in Chatham, and even take a kayak trip in Barnstable's Great Marsh. See p. 68 for a map of this itinerary.

Day ❶: Falmouth ★★★

Start your tour of the Cape and islands in **Falmouth** where you'll need a couple of days to see all the sites. Bike down the **Shining Sea Bikeway ★★★** (p. 96) to the village of **Woods Hole ★★★**, a fishing village and world-renowned science center. Visit the aquarium and take a 90-minute discovery cruise aboard **OceanQuest ★★** (p. 89), a fun science-filled boat cruise. Wander through the free **Spohr Gardens** (p. 98) in Quissett near Woods Hole.

Day ❷: Sailing in Vineyard Sound

Spend the morning at **Falmouth Heights Beach ★★★** (p. 95), and then head to **Grew's Pond ★★** (p. 95), a freshwater pond in **Goodwill Park,** for swimming and a picnic lunch. Take a sunset cruise around Vineyard Sound on the ***Liberte*** ★★ (p. 97), a 74-foot, three-masted schooner out of **Falmouth Inner Harbor.**

Day ❸: Sandwich ★★★

Spend several hours exploring the **Heritage Museums and Gardens ★★★** (p. 81) in Sandwich. Check out **Sandy Neck Beach ★★★** (p. 79), one of the Cape's best beaches. On the way home, stop for ice cream at **Twin Acres Ice Cream Shoppe** (p. 87), an ice-cream shop out of another century.

Day ❹: Kayak Trip to Sandy Neck

Exploring estuaries of the Cape by kayak is a great way to get away from the crowds. A trip around the **Great Marsh** in Barnstable and over to **Sandy Neck** (p. 79), the 7-mile peninsula that extends from Sandwich, can take a couple of hours or most of a day, depending on how much you want to do. Experienced kayakers will want to paddle out to the tip of Sandy Neck where there's an isolated 19th-century summer community, complete with lighthouse and a couple dozen simple cottages.

Day ❺: A Drive up Route 6A, a Trip to Hyannis

The **John F. Kennedy Hyannis Museum** (p. 120) is one of the most popular attractions on the Cape. Visit it first thing in the morning, and then walk around **Hyannis Harbor,** which, as part of a new renovation, has a number of small crafts shacks where artists demonstrate and sell their wares. Drive over to the north side of the Cape to explore the **Old King's Highway/ Route 6A,** which stretches from Sandwich to Orleans. The road hasn't changed much since the 19th century when it was a stage-coach route. There's great shopping, especially antiquing, on Route 6A, as well as restaurants in all price ranges.

Day ❻: Chatham ★★★

Spend the day in **Chatham,** one of the Cape's most charming towns. Stroll down **Main Street** to check out the shops. Stop at the **Chatham Fish Pier** (p. 164) to watch the fishermen bring in the daily catch. Drive to **Morris Island,** part of the **Monomoy National Wildlife Refuge** ★★ (p. 165), to hike trails and do some bird-watching. Have a drink on the porch of the Chatham Bars Inn and then head over for a band concert (every Fri night in summer) at Kate Gould Park.

Day ❼: Cape Cod National Seashore

A visit to **Cape Cod National Seashore** (p. 190) is not just a day on the beach. There are visitor centers, numerous trails, and several historic sites. The first stop is **Fort Hill,** which has one of the best scenic vistas on the Cape. Your next stop is the **Salt Pond Visitor Center** ★★ (p. 185) in Eastham. In Truro, you can visit the **Highland House Museum and Highland Lighthouse** (p. 201). A climb to the top of the lighthouse will give you a great view of the coastline. Continue on to **Provincetown** ★★★ for a visit to the **Province Lands Visitor Center** (p. 210) and the **Old Harbor Life-Saving Museum** ★ (p. 210).

Day ❽: Whale-Watching Off Provincetown

You'll need several days in **Provincetown** to take in all that this unique place has to offer. A trip to **Stellwagen Bank** on a **whale-watch** takes half a day, but it's an experience you'll always remember. See p. 209.

Day ❾: Provincetown History & Arts

The **Pilgrim Monument & Provincetown Museum** ★★ (p. 210) are musts for an overview of the history of the town and a bird's-eye view of the geography from the top of the monument. You'll want to leave

yourself plenty of time for strolling along Commercial Street and stopping at galleries, especially the **Provincetown Art Association & Museum** ★★ (p. 210). For those who enjoy biking, pedaling through the Provincetown dunes on the Province Lands trail is heaven.

Day ❿: A Sail Off the Coast of Provincetown

A hike along the **West End breakwater** ★★ is a temptation for most visitors, but only the truly hearty hike all the way out to Long Point at the tip of the Cape Cod peninsula. A less vigorous way to get there is by boat; Flyer's Boatyard runs frequent shuttles. End your day with a sunset sail on the *Bay Lady II* ★ (p. 208), a 73-foot schooner.

Day ⓫: Exploring Nantucket

It's worth it to spend a couple of nights on **Nantucket** to see the whole island and to have time to try out some of the fabulous fine-dining restaurants. The island is perfect for casual bikers. You can crisscross the entire island on well-maintained bike paths. You may want to try all the major paths, to 'Sconset, to **Madaket,** and to **Surfside Beach.** For history buffs, the first stop is the **Whaling Museum** ★★★ (p. 234). A Nantucket Historical Association ticket will get you into several other interesting historic sites. Leave plenty of time to wander the cobbled streets of Nantucket for shopping.

Day ⓬: Nantucket Tours

Two terrific tours on Nantucket will give you special insight on the island: around the **harbor** and out to **Great Point.** Several companies offer a cruise around the harbor, including **Endeavor Sailing Excursions** (p. 234), or you can rent your own motorboat to check it out. The Trustees of Reservations offers tours through the **Coskata-Coatue Wildlife Refuge** and out to **Great Point Lighthouse.**

Day ⓭: Arrive on Martha's Vineyard

Whether you decide to explore by shuttle bus, by guided bus tour, or by bicycle, you'll have time to see the major sites on the island of **Martha's Vineyard** in a couple of days. Start your visit in **Vineyard Haven,** which has, arguably, the best shopping on the island. With your gift shopping completed, you can head over to **Oak Bluffs** to check out the "gingerbread houses," the turn-of-the-20th-century Victorian cottages clustered around the **Trinity Park Tabernacle** (p. 267). Before

leaving Oak Bluffs, take a ride on the **Flying Horses Carousel** (p. 267).

Day ⓮: Edgartown & Aquinnah

Next head to **Edgartown,** a quintessential New England town of sea captains' houses and white picket fences. Take the 5-minute ferry over to **Chappaquiddick** to stroll through **Mytoi,** a 14-acre Japanese garden. Head "up-island," by bike or shuttle bus, to **West Tisbury,** to check out the interesting art galleries. In **Chilmark,** you'll want to stop in **Menemsha,** a traditional, weathered fishing village. In **Aquinnah,** you'll visit the red-clay **Gay Head Cliffs.**

4 AN OUTDOOR LOVER'S TOUR OF CAPE COD

Many people visit Cape Cod because of its natural beauty. If you are one of those who enjoy getting outside, whether to hike, bike, or kayak, this itinerary is for you. You'll bike along the coastline, paddle through marshes, and watch seals and whales frolic offshore. This is the real Cape Cod, far from the traffic and T-shirt shops. See p. 68 for a map of this itinerary.

Day ❶: A Bike Ride & a Sail

One of the Cape's best bike trails is the **Shining Sea Bikeway** in **Falmouth.** Rent a bike at Corner Cycle on the Queen's Byway and ride 4 miles on the beachfront path, all the way to **Woods Hole.** In Woods Hole, have lunch at an outdoor table at one of the fine restaurants. After exploring the village of Woods Hole, bike back to Falmouth. On the way, you can check out the osprey nest on **Oyster Pond,** near Surf Drive Beach. In the afternoon or early evening, take a 2-hour sailboat ride on the three-masted *Liberte,* a custom schooner. The sunset cruise is the most popular.

Day ❷: Washburn Island in Falmouth

A 40-minute paddle by canoe or kayak will land you on **Washburn Island** (p. 98), a state-owned sanctuary in **Waquoit Bay**

containing nature trails and pristine beaches. There are 10 primitive campsites on the island, most located close to the beach. The island feels wonderfully isolated, though you are only a stone's throw from densely populated summer communities in Falmouth.

Day ❸: Biking the Rail Trail ★★★

Biking the 25-mile **Cape Cod Rail Trail** (p. 138) from **Dennis** to **Wellfleet** is a great way to take in the Cape's diverse ecosystems, past woods, dunes, ponds, marshes, and cranberry bogs. Most people bike just a section of the trail. The portion within **Nickerson State Park** in **Brewster** is a popular spur. You'll pass places to purchase snacks, drinks, and sandwiches along the way, so it's possible to make a day of it, stopping for a picnic at the halfway point.

Day ❹: Kayaking Barnstable's Great Marsh

One of the best all-day kayak trips on the Cape is through **Barnstable's Great Marsh** and out to the tip of **Sandy Neck.** After launching in **Barnstable Harbor,** you can spend hours exploring the marsh, paddling deep up into **Scorton Creek** at high tide. Paddle out of the marsh before low tide, and then parallel the shore of Sandy Neck all the way out to the little summer colony on the tip. You can check out the lighthouse and picnic on the beach before paddling back to Barnstable Harbor.

Day ❺: The Seals of Monomoy

Several companies run boat tours out to the island of **South Monomoy** off the coast of Chatham to view the enormous **gray seal colony.** Boats leave out of Stage Harbor. Both islands of North Monomoy and South Monomoy together make up a 2,750-acre **wildlife sanctuary** favored by

migrating birds. Audubon runs bird-watching tours to the islands in season.

Day ❻: Audubon Sanctuary in Wellfleet

You could spend all day (and the night if you're an Audubon member) exploring the trails at **Audubon's Wellfleet Bay Wildlife Sanctuary** (p. 165). The 1,000-acre refuge features a butterfly garden and numerous trails in addition to a visitor center whose design is on the cutting edge of environmentally friendly architecture.

Day ❼: Watching Whales in Stellwagen Bank

Whale-watching (p. 209) is an activity the whole family can enjoy. It takes a couple of hours for the boat to get out to **Stellwagen Bank,** the prime fishing ground for whales in the area. Once there, you're bound to see several different types. The onboard naturalist will help you identify them.

---

5 CAPE COD FOR FAMILIES

Cape Cod really is perfect for families. Numerous attractions are designed to entertain, and tire out, the little ones. Want to do more than build sand castles at the beach? This tour contains a number of fun and educational activities all over the Cape. See p. 68 for a map of this itinerary.

Day ❶: A Day at the Beach

Ease your way into the laid-back Cape Cod lifestyle by spending the morning at the beach. Beaches most suitable for children include **Old Silver Beach** ★★★ (p. 96) in **Falmouth.** Spend the afternoon at one of the Cape's pristine ponds, like **Grew's Pond** ★★ in Falmouth.

Day ❷: Sandwich ★★★

Sandwich offers several attractions that are big hits with children and that adults will also enjoy. **Heritage Museums and Gardens** ★★★ (p. 81) contains several buildings containing collections as diverse as antique cars and baseball memorabilia.

Dexter Grist Mill ★ (p. 81) offers a fascinating history lesson at a gristmill that still functions. **Green Briar Nature Center** ★ (p. 80) has walking trails and a jam kitchen.

Day ❸: Cartwheels 2 & Cape Cod Canal Bike Path

Spend the morning riding the **Cape Cod Canal Bike Path** ★★★ (p. 88), a flat, easy trail. Another way to see the canal is by boat. **Cape Cod Canal Cruises** offers an inexpensive family cruise. In the afternoon, head to **Cartwheels 2** (p. 91). Kids can't resist the go-carts, bumper boats, and minigolf.

Day ❹: A Museum for Kids

Spend the morning at the **Cape Cod Children's Museum** ★ (p. 112) in **Mashpee,** which is particularly good for younger kids. The perfect afternoon activity is a discovery cruise organized by **OceanQuest** (p. 89), which leaves from Great Harbor in **Woods Hole** and treats your kids like miniscientists. End the day in **Falmouth** with a **free outdoor concert** at Peg Noonan Park (Fri) or at **Bigelow Marine Park** (Thurs) or a free outdoor children's movie (Wed).

Day ❺: Kids Stuff in Yarmouth

There are several children's activity sites in Yarmouth along Route 28. If the **trampolines, go-carts,** and **minigolf** (p. 133) don't tire them out, you can take them to the **ZooQuarium** ★ (p. 133) to hang out at the petting zoo and catch a sea lion show.

Day ❻: Cape Cod Museum of Natural History

Your kids will be having so much fun they might not realize they are learning something at the **Cape Cod Museum of Natural History** ★★★ (p. 150) in Brewster. Don't forget to explore the paths behind the beach, especially the **John Wing Trail,** which leads all the way out to Cape Cod Bay. Look closely as you walk. You may spot a turtle or even a rare bird. The museum keeps lists of all the birds spotted in recent days.

Day ❼: Cape Cod National Seashore

Kids love the huge dunes and big waves at the **Cape Cod National Seashore.** Just be sure you stay near the lifeguards and keep an eye on the little ones. There are a number of terrific walking trails from **Eastham** to **Provincetown** within the national seashore that are fun to explore, especially the **Pilgrim Spring Trail** in Truro (p. 201). After a morning at the beach, don't forget to stop at **Ben & Jerry's Scoop Shop** (p. 188) in Eastham. Spend the afternoon on a **whale-watch** (p. 209) out of **Provincetown** ★★★.

6 NANTUCKET & MARTHA'S VINEYARD

The islands of Nantucket and Martha's Vineyard are as distinct as two neighboring islands can be. This tour lets you explore both of them in a week. You'll see the highlights of both islands—the beaches and historic sites of Nantucket and the scenic landscapes and quaint towns on the Vineyard. See p. 68 for a map of this itinerary.

Day ❶: Arrive on Nantucket

Explore the cobbled streets of historic **Nantucket,** which has some of the best shopping in the region. Walk, bike, taxi, or take a shuttle bus down to **Jetties Beach** ★★★ (p. 230), a beautiful expanse of sand that has the added benefit of numerous amenities, including tennis courts, volleyball nets, a playground, and a skate park. After the beach, bike or drive out to **Madaket Beach** ★★★ on the west side of the island to watch the sunset.

Day ❷: Biking the Island

Spend your second day on the island taking a bike tour. From town take the **Milestone Road path** out to '**Sconset** ★★, where you can marvel at the tiny rose-covered cottages. Bike back to town on the **Polpis Road bike path,** passing the red-striped **Sankaty Head Lighthouse** along the way. On the Polpis path, you can take a side trip to **Wauwinet,** where it's possible to hike or four-wheel-drive out to **Great Point Lighthouse.**

Day ❸: Beaching & Boating

In the morning, bike to **Surfside Beach** ★★★, just 3 miles south of town. In the afternoon, take a cruise around **Nantucket Harbor,** checking out the multimillion-dollar yachts and the workaday fishing boats.

Day ❹: Arrive on Martha's Vineyard

Take the seasonal ferry from Nantucket to **Oak Bluffs,** the most boisterous town on **Martha's Vineyard.** Wander through the camp meeting grounds to see the elaborate 19th-century **"gingerbread cottages,"** in the island's first summer community. Ride the **Flying Horses Carousel** (p. 267) and duck into **Mad Martha's Ice Cream Parlor** ★★ to buy a cone, which you can eat while watching the world go by on **Circuit Avenue.** At night, head to **Vineyard Haven** to see a play at the **Vineyard Playhouse** (p. 286), or go out to the airport to hear live music at the island's top club, **Outerland** (p. 286).

Day ❺: Edgartown

Bike or drive to **Edgartown,** where you can wander past white picket fences in front of grand sea captains' houses. Numerous gift shops, clothing stores, and art galleries are in the center of town. Take a bike ride to **Katama** ★★★, also called South Beach (p. 263), which fronts the Atlantic Ocean.

Day ❻: Aquinnah

Drive, bike, or take the shuttle bus out to **Aquinnah,** the homeland of the Vineyard's Native American community. Walk out to the viewing spot where you can see both the majestic red-clay **Gay Head Cliffs** and the picturesque red brick **Gay Head Lighthouse** (p. 287). A long path leads down to the beach itself, a pristine beauty.

Day ❼: An Arboretum & a Fishing Village

Visit Chilmark's **Polly Hill Arboretum** (p. 266) in the morning. It's a delight to wander past stone walls, through the dogwood alley and the "tunnel of love," an arbor of bleached hornbeam. Spend the afternoon in the tiny fishing village of **Menemsha,** part of the town of **Chilmark.** Wander down the dock to watch the fishing boats unloading the catch of the day, which will be served in the island's restaurants that night. The waters of **Menemsha Beach** ★★ (p. 262) in Vineyard Sound are surprisingly warm in the summer. Watching the sunset over a picnic dinner in Menemsha is a Vineyard tradition.

5

The Upper Cape

Just over an hour from Boston by car, the Upper Cape towns have become bedroom as well as summer communities. They may not have the let-the-good-times-roll feel of towns farther east, but they're spared the seasonal changeability of the more resorty towns. Shops and restaurants—many catering to an older, affluent crowd—tend to stay open year-round.

The four Upper Cape towns are all quite different. Bourne straddles the Cape Cod Canal; a few of its villages (Bournedale, Buzzards Bay, and Sagamore Beach) are on the mainland side, and the others (Cataumet, Pocasset, Bourne, Monument Beach, and Sagamore) are on the Cape side. The Canal provides this area with most of its recreational opportunities: biking, fishing, canal cruises, and the herring run.

Sandwich is the Cape's oldest town. At its core sits a lovely historic village, offering lots of unique shops and charming inns. Still, the town is primarily a pastoral place, with several working farms. In East Sandwich, miles of conservation land lead out to Sandy Neck, a barrier beach extending into Barnstable. The Old King's Highway (Rte. 6A) winds its way through Sandwich past a number of fine gift shops, galleries, and specialty stores.

Falmouth, the site of Cape Cod's first summer colony, is one of the larger towns on the Cape; it has a year-round population of 32,000. Main Street—with a number of high-quality boutiques, restaurants, and galleries, in addition to the usual touristy T-shirt shops—offers prime strolling and shopping. Falmouth's Village Green is quintessential New England, with two imposing historic churches: St. Barnabas, a sturdy reddish stone building; and the First Congregational, a white-clapboard, steepled church boasting a Paul Revere bell. Just north of Falmouth center, along Route 28A, lies West Falmouth; it has several good antiques stores, a fine general store, and a picture-perfect little harbor.

The most scenic drive in Falmouth leads to the beach at Falmouth Heights, a bluff covered with grand, shingled Victorians built during the first wave of tourist fever in the late 1800s. Falmouth's southernmost village is Woods Hole, which is the main ferry port for Martha's Vineyard. Home at any given time to several thousand research scientists, it has a certain neo-Bohemian panache, lively bars, and an air of vigorous intellectual inquiry. It's also a working fishing village and one of the most picturesque spots on the Cape.

Mashpee is the ancestral home of the Cape's Native American tribe, the Wampanoags. Much of the town's coastline is occupied by a huge resort called New Seabury; inland, the Mashpee National Wildlife Refuge offers frequent walking tours through its thousands of woodland acres.

1 SANDWICH ★★★

3 miles E of Sagamore; 16 miles NW of Hyannis

Sandwich is both the oldest town on the Cape and, arguably, the quaintest. Towering oak trees and historic houses line its winding Main Street. Two early-19th-century churches and the columned Greek Revival Town Hall, in service since 1834, surround the town

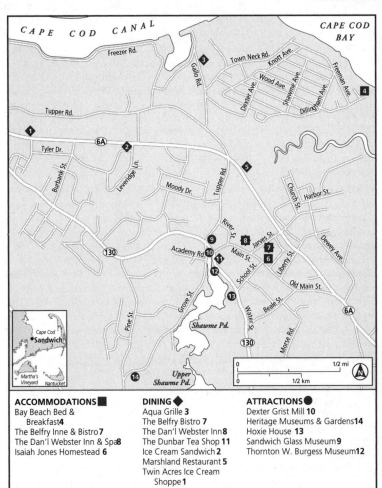

ACCOMMODATIONS ■
Bay Beach Bed & Breakfast **4**
The Belfry Inne & Bistro **7**
The Dan'l Webster Inn & Spa **8**
Isaiah Jones Homestead **6**

DINING ◆
Aqua Grille **3**
The Belfry Bistro **7**
The Dan'l Webster Inn **8**
The Dunbar Tea Shop **11**
Ice Cream Sandwich **2**
Marshland Restaurant **5**
Twin Acres Ice Cream Shoppe **1**

ATTRACTIONS ●
Dexter Grist Mill **10**
Heritage Museums & Gardens **14**
Hoxie House **13**
Sandwich Glass Museum **9**
Thornton W. Burgess Museum **12**

square. A 1640 gristmill still grinds corn beside bucolic Shawme Pond, which is frequented by swans, geese, ducks, and canoeists. To the north, villagers have built a boardwalk over the extensive salt marsh. Farther east, Sandy Neck, one of the Cape's most beautiful beaches, reaches into Cape Cod Bay.

Sandwich was founded in 1637 by a contingent of Puritans looking for a quiet place to worship. There is still an element of peacefulness in this little town located just a few miles from the Sagamore Bridge.

Sandwich's claim to fame is its prominence as the home to the nation's first glass factories in the early to mid-19th century. The famous Boston and Sandwich Glass Company and others employed more than 500 craftspeople in town. In fact, the town still supports a number of highly skilled glassmakers. Sandwich is fortunate to have two very well-endowed museums—the **Heritage Museums and Gardens ★★★** and the **Sandwich Glass Museum ★★**—as well as quirkier sites, like the **Green Briar Nature Center & Jam Kitchen ★** and the **Thornton W. Burgess Museum ★**.

Many historic homesteads have been converted into charming bed-and-breakfasts that welcome guests year-round. There are also excellent antiques shops in the area. The town is a convenient base for exploring other parts of the Cape that may offer more lively activities, like the nightlife of Hyannis or the ocean beaches of Wellfleet.

ESSENTIALS

GETTING THERE   If you're driving, take Route 6A east toward Sandwich after crossing either the Bourne Bridge or the Sagamore Bridge. The Sagamore Bridge will get you closer to your destination. You can also fly into Hyannis (see "Getting There & Getting Around," in chapter 3).

VISITOR INFORMATION   Contact the **Cape Cod Chamber of Commerce,** routes 6 and 132, Hyannis, MA 02601 (© **888/332-2732;** fax 508/362-2156; www.capecodchamber.org), open year-round, mid-April to mid-November daily 9am to 5pm; mid-November to mid-April Monday to Saturday 10am to 4pm. Stop in at the **Route 25 Visitor's Center** (© **508/759-3814;** fax 508/759-2146), open daily, year-round, Saturday to Thursday 9am to 6pm and Friday 9am to 8pm. The **Sandwich Chamber of Commerce** (© **508/833-9755;** www.sandwichchamber.com) and **Sandwich Visitor Services Board** (www.sandwichmass.org) put out a handy Sandwich booklet. The **Sandwich Information Center** (© **508/833-1632**) is on Route 130 (Exit 2 off Rte. 6, the Mid-Cape Hwy.). The **Cape Cod Canal Region Chamber of Commerce,** 70 Main St., Buzzards Bay (© **508/759-6000;** fax 508/759-6965; www.capecodcanalchamber.org), open year-round, Monday to Friday 9am to 5pm, can provide literature on both Sandwich and Bourne. A consortium of Sandwich businesses has put together an excellent walking guide (with map) available at most inns in town.

A GET-ACQUAINTED STROLL

This walk starts at the Sandwich Glass Museum, ends at the Dunbar Tea Shop, and takes 2 to 4 hours, depending on the number of stops you make; you'll cover about 1$^1/_4$ miles. Your best bet is to explore the village on any midsummer day between 10am and 4pm, except Sunday, when some spots are closed.

You may park (free with admission) at the **Sandwich Glass Museum,** 129 Main St. (© **508/888-0251**), a well-curated collection tracing the town's history with an emphasis on glass made in Sandwich from 1825 to 1888.

Farther down Grove Street is **Old Cemetery Point,** overlooking peaceful Shawme Pond, about $^1/_3$ mile down the road. Read the historic headstones and keep an eye out for box turtles. Head back through the center of town and observe the exterior of **Old Town Hall,** on Main Street—a magnificent Greek Revival edifice, complete with Doric columns. It still houses some town offices. Continue down Main Street, past the **First Church of Christ,** which is topped by an impressive spire. Built by a colleague of renowned Boston architect Charles Bulfinch in 1847, it was reportedly modeled on Sir Christopher Wren's St. Mary-le-Bow, in London. The next church you'll pass, to your left, is an **1833 meetinghouse,** now privately owned, which has been used in years past as a doll museum and a bed-and-breakfast.

Continue down Main Street and take a left on Jarves Street to admire the **Belfry Inne and Bistro** (© 800/844-4542 or 508/888-8550), a church and rectory converted into a very smart inn and restaurant. The restaurant, with its soaring ceilings and stained glass, is one of the prettiest and most unique dining spaces on Cape Cod.

Retracing your steps along Jarves Street, make a left-right zigzag along Main and School streets to reach Water Street, which skirts the eastern edge of Shawme Pond. Directly opposite, on the shore side of Water Street, you'll spot the **Hoxie House** ★ at 18 Water St. (© 508/888-1173), one of the oldest houses on the Cape. The interior is spare—not out of any aesthetic ideal but because resources were so hard to come by in Colonial New England. The settlers didn't even have closets because they were taxed as an additional room, windows were tiny to avoid the tax on glass, and pockets were considered a waste of good material. Docents explain all the details in frequent tours.

After the Hoxie House tour, head northward along Water Street, passing (on the same side) the **Thornton W. Burgess Museum,** 4 Water St. (© 508/888-4668), which celebrates the life and work of native son Burgess (1874–1965). He was a highly successful author of children's books and creator of such still-beloved characters as Jimmy Skunk and Grandfather Frog. Just past the Burgess Museum is the **Dexter Grist Mill** ★ (© 508/888-4910), a lovingly restored water mill (ca. 1640). The millstones still grind corn; buy a bag of meal to go, but only if you'll have a chance to whip up something later in the day (it doesn't keep well). Now that you're back at the center of town, this is a good time to pause for a spot of tea. The **Dunbar Tea Shop,** 1 Water St. (© 508/833-2485), serves hearty lunches, teas, and breakfasts. The attached shop features British imports and antiques, including vintage books. It's a pleasant place to while away a good portion of the afternoon.

BEACHES & RECREATIONAL PURSUITS

BEACHES   For the Sandwich beaches listed below, nonresident parking stickers—$40 for the length of your stay—are available at **Sandwich Town Hall Annex,** 145 Main St. (© 508/833-8012). *Note:* No swimming is allowed within the Cape Cod Canal because the currents are much too swift and dangerous.

- **Sandy Neck Beach** ★★★, off Sandy Neck Road in East Sandwich: This 6-mile stretch of silken barrier beach with low, rounded dunes is one of the Cape's prettiest and most unspoiled. It is somewhat isolated, with no commercial businesses or accommodations on the beach. Because it is a Cape Cod Bay beach, the water tends to be warmer than the open ocean, and the waves are never too high. That makes it popular with families. The fact that the beach stretches out for miles makes it popular with endangered Piping Plovers—and their nemesis, off-road vehicles (ORV). That means that the ORV trails are closed for much of the summer while the Piping Plover chicks hatch. ORV permits ($140 per season for nonresidents) can be purchased at the gatehouse (© 508/362-8300). ORV drivers must be equipped with supplies like a spare tire, jack, shovel, and tire-pressure gauge. Parking for the beach in the upper parking lot costs $15 per day in season. Up to 3 days of camping in self-contained vehicles is permitted at $10 per night plus an ORV permit.
- **Town Neck Beach,** off Town Neck Road in Sandwich: A bit rocky but ruggedly pretty, this narrow beach offers a busy view of passing ships, plus restrooms and a snack bar. Parking costs $10 per day, or you could hike from town (about 1½ miles) via the community-built boardwalk spanning the salt marsh.

- **Wakeby Pond,** Ryder Conservation Area, John Ewer Road (off South Sandwich Rd. on the Mashpee border): The beach, on the Cape's largest freshwater pond, has life-guards, restrooms, and parking ($10 per day).

BICYCLING The **U.S. Army Corps of Engineers** (recreation hot line: ✆ 508/759-5991) maintains a flat, 14-mile loop along the **Cape Cod Canal ★★★**, equally suited to bicyclists, skaters, runners, and strollers. The most convenient place to park (free) is at the Bourne Recreation Area, north of the Bourne Bridge, on the Cape side. You can also park at the Sandcatcher Recreation Area at the end of Freezer Road in Sandwich.

BOATING If you want to explore under power of your own paddle, you can rent canoes and kayaks in Falmouth and float around Old Sandwich Harbor, out to Sandy Neck, or through the salt-marsh maze of Scorton Creek, which leads out to Talbot Point, a wooded spit of conservation land.

FISHING Sandwich has eight fishable ponds; for details and a license, inquire at **Town Hall** in the center of town (✆ 508/888-0340). Permits cost nonresidents $39 for the season, $25 for a 3-day pass. Children, seniors, and Massachusetts residents receive discounts. No permit is required to fish from the banks of the Cape Cod Canal. Here your catch might include striped bass, bluefish, cod, pollock, flounder, or fluke. Call the **U.S. Army Corps of Engineers** (✆ 508/759-5991) for Canal tide and fishing information.

FITNESS The local fitness center is the **Sportsite Health Club** at 315 Cotuit Rd. in Sandwich (✆ 508/888-7900). It offers 15,000 square feet of Nautilus and other fitness equipment, along with steam baths, saunas, racquetball, classes, and free child care. A 1-day pass costs $12.

GOLF The **Sandwich Hollows Golf Club,** on Service Road in East Sandwich (✆ 508/888-3384), is a 6,200-yard, par-71 town-owned course. In season, a round costs $30 to $62, depending on the day and time. The 18-hole, par-3 **Holly Ridge Golf Course,** on Country Club Road in South Sandwich (✆ 508/428-5577), is, at 2,900 yards, shorter and easier. A round costs $34 in season, with afternoon discounts.

NATURE & WILDLIFE AREAS The **Shawme-Crowell State Forest,** off Route 130 in Sandwich (✆ 508/888-0351), offers 298 campsites and 742 acres to roam. Entrance is free; parking costs $2. Camping costs $12 for Massachusetts residents, $14 for nonresidents.

The **Sandwich Boardwalk ★**, which the community rebuilt in 1991 after Hurricane Bob blew away the 1874 original, links the town and Town Neck Beach by way of salt marshes that attract many birds, including great blue herons.

As if to signify how oddly enchanted this little corner of the world is, there's a sweet little (57-acre) nature center here—and within it is an even sweeter kitchen, where local ladies have been cooking up jams and jellies since 1903. The **Green Briar Nature Center & Jam Kitchen ★** is at 6 Discovery Hill (off Rte. 6A, about 1½ miles east of town center; ✆ 508/888-6870); once you've caught a whiff of the jam, you'll want to take some home. (Try the local delicacy, beach-plum jelly.) Jam-making workshops are offered for adults and children in the summer and fall. Prices are $38 per person for adult classes (members of the Thornton Burgess Society pay $28); the same price covers one adult and one child for family workshops. Children will be intrigued by the expansive kitchen, as well as some old-fashioned nature exhibits on such animals as rabbits, turtles, iguanas, and snakes. The center is open mid-April to December, Monday through Saturday 10am to 4pm, Sunday 1 to 4pm; January to mid-April Tuesday through Saturday 10am to

4pm. Admission is by donation; the suggested donation is $1 per child and $5 for families. Summer story time is at 10:30am on Monday, Wednesday, and Saturday, costing $2 per person.

TENNIS   Sandwich has public courts at the Wing School, Oak Ridge School, Forestdale School, and Sandwich High School. Contact the **Sandwich Recreation Department** (© 508/888-4361) for details.

SANDWICH HISTORICAL SIGHTS

Dexter Grist Mill ★ (Kids)   This charmingly weathered building has survived some 350 years and at least as many lives. At present, it serves its original purpose, grinding corn with turbine power; you can watch the wooden gears in action and buy a bag to take home and cook up into Colonial "johnnycakes" (short for "cakes for the journey") or trendy polenta. Fresh corn meal costs $3.50 for a 2-pound bag, $9 for three bags. During the glassmaking boom of the 1800s, this mill was but one of many pressed into service to keep the factory workers well fed. When the laborers dispersed, the mill sat useless until a local entrepreneur thought to convert it into a tearoom to serve the new tide of tourists arriving by motorcar. The mill was fully restored in 1961 and will probably be good for a few more centuries of stalwart service.

Water St. (on Shawme Pond, behind Town Hall). © **508/888-4910.** Admission $3 adults, $2 children 6–12; combination ticket for Dexter Mill and Hoxie House ($5 adults, $3 children) available from the Hoxie House (see below). July–Aug daily 10am–4:45pm; call for off-season hours. Closed mid-Oct to mid-June.

Heritage Museums and Gardens ★★★ (Finds) (Kids)   This is one of those rare museums that appeals equally to adults and the children they drag along: The latter will leave clamoring for another visit. All ages have the run of 76 beautifully landscaped acres, crisscrossed with walking paths and riotous with color in late spring, when the towering rhododendrons burst forth in blooms that range from soft pink to gaudy orange. Scattered buildings house a wide variety of collections, from Native American artifacts to Cape Cod Baseball League memorabilia. The art holdings, especially the primitive portraits, are outstanding. The high point for most children will be a ride on the 1912 carousel (safely preserved indoors). Also sure to dazzle is the replica Shaker round barn packed with gleaming antique automobiles, including some once owned by celebrities (don't miss Gary Cooper's Duesenberg). Next door is the Carousel Cafe, good for a restorative snack, including soups, sandwiches, and salads. The gift shop at the gatehouse is also worth checking out. Call ahead for a schedule of the outdoor summer concerts usually held Sundays around 2pm, free with admission.

Grove and Pine sts. (about ½ mile southwest of the town center). © **508/888-3300.** www.heritage museumsandgardens.org. Admission $12 adults, $10 seniors (60 and over), $6 children 4–16, free for children 3 and under. Apr–Oct daily 10am–5pm. No tickets sold after 4:15pm. Closed Nov–Mar.

Hoxie House ★   Once a contender for the title of the Cape's oldest house (a couple of privately owned Provincetown houses appear to have a stronger claim), this saltbox (ca. 1680) is nonetheless a noteworthy beauty, with its diamond-pane windows and broad interior planking—made of "king's wood," so called because England's king had, under pain of severe penalty, reserved the larger trees for his warships. The house was occupied, pretty much as is, with neither electricity nor plumbing, into the 1950s, which explains how it remained so remarkably intact. Even so, it had to be taken apart and reassembled to serve as the model Colonial home you see today. Fortunately, restorers opted not for the cluttered Colonial Revival look but a stark austerity that's much more historically accurate and shows off to advantage a handful of antiques on semipermanent loan from Boston's Museum of Fine Arts.

18 Water St. (on Shawme Pond, about ¹/₄ mile south of the town center). ℂ **508/888-1173.** Admission $3 adults, $2 children 12–16, free for children 11 and under; combination ticket ($5 adults, $3 children) available here for Hoxie House and Dexter Grist Mill (see above). Mid-June to mid-Oct Mon–Sat 10am–5pm; Sun 1–5pm. Closed mid-Oct to mid-June.

Sandwich Glass Museum ★★ (Finds) Even if you don't consider yourself a glass fan, make an exception for this fascinating museum, which captures the history of the town. A 20-minute video introduces Deming Jarves's brilliant endeavor, which flourished from 1828 to 1888, bringing glassware—a rare commodity available only to the rich—within reach of the middle classes. Jarves picked the perfect spot, surrounded by old-growth forest, to fuel the furnaces, with a harbor handy for shipping in fine sand from farther up the coast and salt-marsh hay with which to pack outgoing orders. All went well until Midwestern glass factories started using coal; unable to keep up with their level of mass production, he switched back to handblown techniques.

A multimillion-dollar renovation and expansion has freshened up the entire museum, and glass is displayed in light and airy rooms. Highlights of the renovation include a furnace, where glass-blowing demonstrations are featured, and a multimedia theater. Since the museum is run by the Sandwich Historical Society, one room is given over to changing exhibits highlighting other eras in the town's history, such as its stellar seafaring days. An excellent gift shop stocks Sandwich-glass replicas, as well as original glassworks by area artisans.

Note: Arrive by 3:30pm to allow yourself time to see glass-blowing demonstrations and presentations in the theater.

129 Main St. (in the center of town). ℂ **508/888-0251.** www.sandwichglassmuseum.org. Admission $5 adults, $1.25 children 6–14, free for children 5 and under. Apr–Dec daily 9:30am–5pm; Feb–Mar Wed–Sun 9:30am–4pm. Closed Jan, Thanksgiving, and Christmas.

Thornton W. Burgess Museum ★ (Kids) Prominent in the early half of the 20th century, this locally bred children's book author racked up 170 tomes to his credit, as well as 15,000 stories. His somewhat simple texts, featuring anthropomorphic animals prone to preaching, may seem a bit dated, but they still go over big with little listeners, especially at the summer-morning story hours. The gift shop carries reissues of his work, should they desire a memento. It's also worth a peek inside to see Harrison Cady's spirited illustrations and exhibits attesting to Burgess's other life work, conservation. He may have inherited this interest from his aunt (the original inhabitant of this 1756 cottage), who gained a certain notoriety for claiming that she could communicate directly with the animal and plant worlds. The museum offers walking tours of Victorian Sandwich on Thursday mornings in June, July, and August. Tours start on the museum grounds at 10:30am. Animal story times take place Monday, Thursday, and Saturday mornings at 10:30am in July and August, weather permitting.

4 Water St. (on Shawme Pond, near the center of town). ℂ **508/888-4668.** www.thorntonburgess.org. Suggested donation $2 adults, $1 children. Mid-Apr to Oct Mon–Sat 10am–4pm; Sun 1–4pm. Closed Nov to mid-Apr.

KID STUFF

The venerable 18-hole **Sandwich Minigolf** (ℂ **508/833-1905**), 159 Rte. 6A, at the corner of Main Street, is a grassy 1950s classic that encapsulates Cape Cod history. Built on a former cranberry bog, it boasts an unusual floating green. Hours are Monday to

SHOPPING

Small as it is, Sandwich has a handful of appealing shops—some with items you're unlikely to find anywhere else. Most of the shops are concentrated in the center of town. Several of the museums listed above (see "Sandwich Historical Sights," above) also have worthwhile gift shops.

ANTIQUES & COLLECTIBLES The **Sandwich Antiques Center,** 131 Rte. 6A, at Jarves Street (📞 **508/833-3600**), showcases wares from over 100 dealers in 6,000 square feet of rooms. It's headed by a congenial auctioneer and offers virtual one-stop shopping for the likes of Sandwich glass, primitives, country furnishings—you name it. The center is open daily year-round.

ARTS & CRAFTS The **Giving Tree Gallery,** 550 Rte. 6A, East Sandwich, about 4 miles east of the town center (📞 **508/888-5446**), is an art and fine-crafts gallery with something extra: a nature walk through bamboo trails. Intriguing sculptures are placed strategically around the property. The path through a bamboo forest is for those who appreciate a Far Eastern aesthetic. In fact, there's something very Zen about the whole Giving Tree experience. It's closed January to late May.

For the finest in art glass and the perfect souvenir of your Sandwich vacation, visit **The Glass Studio,** 470 Rte. 6A, East Sandwich (📞 **508/888-6681**), where master glass blower Michael Magyar crafts one-of-a-kind pieces like his "sea bubbles" series and Venetian-style goblets. Watch glass blowing Thursday through Sunday from 10am to 5pm.

At **McDermott Glass Studio & Gallery,** 272 Cotuit Rd., Sandwich (📞 **508/477-0705**), Dave McDermott creates exquisite handblown art glass, from vases to stemware. Glass blowing takes place Wednesday to Saturday from 10am to 5pm.

BOOKS **Titcomb's Book Shop,** 432 Rte. 6A, East Sandwich, about 4 miles east of the town center (📞 **508/888-2331**), has a terrific selection of books (both new and used) relating to Cape Cod and much more. Look for the life-size statue of Ben Franklin out front.

FOOD & WINE **Crow Farm,** 192 Rte. 6A, ¼ mile east of the town center (📞 **508/888-0690**), is a picture-perfect farm stand purveying superb local produce like sweet corn, tomatoes, peaches, and apples, as well as flowers. It's closed Sunday in summer but open daily in spring and fall. It's closed late December through April. **The Brown Jug,** 155 Main St. in Sandwich (📞 **508/888-4669**), is stocked with delicacies from around the corner and around the world, from fine cheeses and olive oils to rich baked goods and hearty homemade breads.

GIFTS/HOME DECOR **The Weather Store,** 146 Main St. (📞 **508/888-1200**), has a fascinating collection of meteorological paraphernalia, old and new, ranging from antique instruments to coffee-table books. Although technically open year-round, from January through April it's open by chance or appointment. At **Wicked Goods,** 153 Main St., Sandwich (📞 **508/888-8800**), you'll find a wide range of beach-inspired gifts and just plain fun accents for the home.

SEAFOOD **Joe's Lobster & Fish Market,** off Coast Guard Road, near Sandwich Marina (📞 **800/491-2971** or 508/888-2971), is where to go for the freshest fish and shellfish to prepare at your cottage rental.

Sandwich has a number of motels along Route 6A, but the one with the best location is **Sandy Neck Motel** at 669 Rte. 6A, East Sandwich (© **800/564-3992** or 508/362-3992; www.sandyneck.com), which sits at the entrance to the road leading to Sandy Neck, the best beach in these parts. Rates are $129 double and $150 to $299 for one- and two-room efficiencies. It's closed November to mid-April.

Expensive

Bay Beach Bed & Breakfast ★★   Each of the three rooms in this luxurious beach-front home, overlooking Town Neck Beach with a view of the Sagamore Bridge and the boat traffic along the Canal, has amenities to add to a romantic interlude, like a fireplace, double Jacuzzi, and CD player. This is Sandwich's only on-beach lodging option.

3 Bay Beach Lane (on Town Beach), Sandwich, MA 02563. © **508/888-8813.** Fax 508/888-5416. www. baybeach.com. 3 units. Summer $285–$325 double. Rates include continental breakfast. MC, V. Closed Nov–Apr. No children under 16. *In room:* A/C, TV/DVD, fridge, hair dryer, iron.

The Dan'l Webster Inn and Spa ★★   This large lodging and dining spot in the center of Sandwich village is a dependable bet for a comfortable stay or a hearty meal. The inn encompasses a modern main building, designed to look historic, as well as several historic homes nearby that have been outfitted with modern amenities. The main building sits on the site of a Colonial tavern favored by Daniel Webster, the famous orator who enjoyed fishing on the Cape. The suites located in nearby historic houses are especially appealing; they feature fireplaces and canopy beds. There are also eight deluxe one-room suites in the main building with amenities like balconies, gas fireplaces, oversize whirlpool baths, and heated tile floors in the bathrooms. The inn's common spaces are bustling; sometimes tour buses stop here. The restaurant is quite good, especially considering the high volume of customers (see "Where to Dine," below). An on-site spa offers massages, facials, and other body treatments.

149 Main St. (in the center of town), Sandwich, MA 02563. © **800/444-3566** or 508/888-3622. Fax 508/888-5156. www.danlwebsterinn.com. 46 units. Summer $289–$249 double; $339–$399 suite. Rates include full breakfast weekdays and off season only. AE, DC, DISC, MC, V. **Amenities:** Restaurant; tavern/ bar; small outdoor heated pool; access to health club (2 miles away); spa; room service. *In room:* A/C, TV, hair dryer, iron.

Moderate

The Belfry Inne & Bistro ★★ Finds   This lodging option consists of three historic buildings in the center of Sandwich village. The turreted 1879 **rectory** has romantic rooms with queen-size retrofitted antique beds, a claw-foot tub (or Jacuzzi) for every room, and a scattering of fireplaces and private balconies. Next door is **the Abbey,** a former church that owner Chris Wilson has converted into six unique deluxe guest rooms, several with fireplaces and whirlpool baths, and a very fine restaurant (see "Where to Dine," below). The abbey rooms are painted vivid colors and tucked cleverly into sections of this old church. One room features a stained-glass window; another has angel windows. All of the Abbey rooms have Jacuzzis. Mr. Wilson also owns the **Village House,** located next door, with six rooms decorated in a French country style within an 1860 Federal-style house.

8 Jarves St. (in the center of town), Sandwich, MA 02563. © **800/844-4542** or 508/888-8550. Fax 508/888-3922. www.belfryinn.com. 20 units (in 3 properties). Summer $165–$310 double. Rates include full breakfast. AE, MC, V. **Amenities:** Restaurant (see review, below). *In room:* AC, TV, Wi-Fi, hair dryer, iron.

Isaiah Jones Homestead Bed & Breakfast ★ ⓥ Value   Of the many B&Bs in Sandwich Center, this one is a particularly good value. The innkeepers have appointed this courtly 1849 Victorian with fine antiques and reproductions. Many rooms have additional romantic touches like fireplaces and oversize whirlpool baths. Two minisuites in the carriage house have sitting alcoves with sleeper sofas. The three-course breakfast, served with fine china and crystal, is highly refined.

165 Main St. (in the center of town), Sandwich, MA 02563. ⓒ **800/526-1625** or 508/888-9115. Fax 508/888-9648. www.isaiahjones.com. 7 units. Summer $175–$275 double. Rates include full breakfast. AE, DISC, MC, V. No children under 12. *In room:* A/C, TV/DVD, hair dryer, no phone.

Wingscorton Farm Inn ★★ ⓕ Finds ⓚ Kids   This 7-acre farmhouse inn, located a 5-minute walk from a small and quiet bay beach, will delight youngsters and animal lovers of all ages. It's been a working farm since 1758 and still houses a cheerful brood of sheep, goats, dogs, cats, chickens, a pet turkey, and a potbellied pig on its tree-shaded grounds. The main house is a classic Colonial with a "keeping room" boasting a 9-foot-long hearth. Upstairs are two paneled bedrooms with canopy beds, working fireplaces, braided rugs, and antiques. The carriage house has a loft bedroom, kitchen and private deck.

11 Wing Blvd. (off Rte. 6A, about 5 miles east of the town center), East Sandwich, MA 02537. ⓒ **508/888-0534.** Fax 508/888-0545. 4 units, carriage house, cottage. Summer $225 suite; $250 carriage house; $1,100 weekly cottage. Rates for suites and carriage house include full breakfast. AE, MC, V. Pets welcome. *In room:* A/C, TV, fridge, no phone.

Inexpensive
Spring Garden Inn ★ ⓥ Value ⓚ Kids   This well-maintained, beautifully landscaped motel overlooks acres of conservation land known as the Great Sandwich Salt Marsh. Every room comes with a south-oriented patio or porch that takes in the lush view. Barbecue grills and picnic tables are available outside on the mahogany deck. With its spacious, tree-shaded backyard and pool, the reasonably priced motel is understandably popular with families. Guests will also appreciate the complimentary homemade continental breakfasts.

578 Rte. 6A (P.O. Box 867; about 5 miles east of the town center), East Sandwich, MA 02537. ⓒ **866/345-5641** or 508/888-0710. Fax 508/833-2849. www.springgarden.com. 11 units, 9 with tub/shower, 2 with shower only. Summer $105–$115 double; $130 efficiency. Rates include continental breakfast. DISC, MC, V. Closed Dec–Mar. **Amenities:** Outdoor pool. *In room:* A/C, TV/DVD, fridge, coffeemaker, iron.

Spring Hill Motor Lodge ★   This motel boasts all sorts of amenities, like an outdoor heated pool and a night-lit tennis court, and the owners keep it in top condition. The interiors are cheerfully contemporary, the grounds verdant. In addition to the motel rooms, there are three cottages that are light, airy, and comfortable. The cottages have full kitchens (microwave ovens instead of standard ovens) as well as two televisions and a VCR.

351 Rte. 6A (about 2¹⁄₂ miles east of the town center), East Sandwich, MA 02537. ⓒ **800/647-2514** or 508/888-1456. Fax 508/833-1556. www.springhillmotorlodge.com. 24 units, 20 with tub/shower; 4 cottages with shower only. Summer $135–$185 double; $225–$275 1-bedroom cottage; $330–$350 2-bedroom cottage. AE, DC, DISC, MC, V. **Amenities:** Elegantly landscaped heated outdoor pool; night-lit tennis court. *In room:* A/C, TV, fridge, coffeemaker.

WHERE TO DINE
Expensive
The Belfry Bistro ★★ ⓕ Finds   NEW AMERICAN   Sandwich's most romantic dining option is located in a renovated abbey. Portions are generous. The menu changes seasonally, but among the appetizers you might find a Thai-crab-and-baby-shrimp cake or mini

barbecue pork empanadas, which are braised and wrapped in pastry. The entrees run the gamut from the unusual black grouper roasted in a banana leaf to the traditional grilled filet of beef over whipped potatoes with green beans. Because this restaurant hosts many weddings and other events, it is sometimes closed to the public, so be sure to call ahead. While the Belfry Bistro serves dinner only, the more casual **Painted Lady Café** next door serves lighter, less expensive ($8–$25) fare, like brie cheeseburgers and chicken potpie, from 11:30am to 3pm and 4 to 8:30pm. The Painted Lady serves lunch only on Sunday and is closed Monday.

8 Jarves St. (in the center of town). ☎ **508/888-8550.** Reservations recommended. Main courses $20–$32. AE, MC, V. Feb–Dec Tues–Sun 5–10pm (last seating at 8:30pm). Closed Jan.

The Dan'l Webster Inn ★★ AMERICAN   You have a choice of four main dining rooms—from a casual, Colonial-motif tavern to a skylight-topped conservatory fronting a splendid garden. The atmospheric Tavern at the Inn, with its own pub-style menu, is perhaps the most popular. All of the dining rooms are served by the same kitchen. Appealing high-season specials are the sugar cane-skewered shrimp and the sesame-encrusted striped bass. For lighter appetites, half-portions are available. There is also a children's menu.

149 Main St. (in the center of town). ☎ **508/888-3622.** Reservations recommended. Main courses $18–$29; tavern menu $7–$14. AE, DC, DISC, MC, V. June–Aug daily 7:30–11am, 11:30am–3pm, and 4:30–9pm; call for off-season hours. Open year-round.

Moderate

Aqua Grille ★ SEAFOOD   Overlooking Sandwich's picturesque marina and not-so-picturesque power plant, this dining spot, owned by the respected Zartarian family of The Paddock Restaurant in Hyannis, wants to be the premier place for fish in Sandwich. All the elements are in place: a spacious, attractive dining room decorated in pleasing aqua shades; a glass-enclosed harbor-view deck; and a long, curving bar. The food is delicious and plentiful, with fish (grilled or fried) the obvious choice, plus lots of pasta dishes. The towering lobster salad with green string beans, tomato, avocado, chives, and crème fraîche is the perfect antidote to a steamy summer night. Try to get a table that doesn't face the power plant.

14 Gallo Rd. (next to Sandwich Marina). ☎ **508/888-8889.** www.aquagrille.com. Reservations recommended. Main courses $8–$24. AE, DC, MC, V. Late Apr to Oct Mon–Fri 11:30am–8:30pm, Sat–Sun noon–9pm. Closed Nov to late Apr.

Inexpensive

The Bee-Hive Tavern ★ AMERICAN   A cut above the rather characterless restaurants clustered along this stretch of road, this modern-day tavern offers atmospheric old-time touches without going overboard. Green-shaded banker's lamps, for example, illuminate the dark wooden booths, and vintage prints and paintings convey a clubby feel. The food is good if not spectacular, and well priced for what it is. The menu features steaks, chops, and fresh-caught fish among the pricier choices; burgers, sandwiches, and salads cater to lighter appetites (and wallets). This is a great option for lunch, when you should try one of the Cape's best lobster rolls.

406 Rte. 6A (about 1/2 mile east of the town center), East Sandwich. ☎ **508/833-1184.** Main courses $7–$16. MC, V. Mon–Sat 11:30am–3pm and 5–9pm; Sun 9–11:30am, noon–4pm, and 5–9pm. Open year-round.

The Dunbar Tea Shop (Finds) BRITISH Whether you choose the cozy confines of the Tea Room on a crisp autumn day or the shady outside grove in summer, you'll enjoy the hearty English classics served here. Lunch beginning at 11am features homemade soups, salads, and sandwiches like the Farmer's Lunch (crusty warm bread, roast beef, horseradish sauce, and English mustard). The Tea Room also serves tea, of course, with all the traditional fixings and accompaniments you'd expect. A tea-themed gift shop is attached.

1 Water St. (in the center of town). (C) **508/833-2485.** www.dunbarteashop.com. Main courses under $10. DISC, MC, V. June–Sept daily 11am–4:30pm; Oct–May Wed–Mon 11am–4:30pm.

Marshland Restaurant on 6A (Value) (Kids) DINER Locals have been digging this diner for 2 decades. This is home-cooked grub, slung fast and cheap. You'll gobble up the hearty breakfast and be back in time for dinner, when fried seafood plates are a specialty.

109 Rte. 6A. (C) **508/888-9824.** Most items under $10. No credit cards. Daily 5am–9pm. Open year-round.

Sweets

Sweet tooth acting up? Stop by Sandwich's appropriately named **Ice Cream Sandwich** ★ at 66 Rte. 6A, across from the Stop & Shop ((C) **508/888-7237**), for a couple of scoops of the best local ice cream. Try the Cape Cod chocolate chunk. It's closed November through March. Sandwich's most classic ice-cream shop is **Twin Acres Ice Cream Shoppe,** 23 Rte. 6A, Sandwich ((C) **508/888-0566**), which specializes in soft serve. With its red, white, and blue bunting, this place is right out of a Norman Rockwell illustration.

OTHER ACTIVITIES

Hemisphere This beachfront restaurant and club with views of Cape Cod Bay is fine for a drink or a bite to eat. Head out to the second-floor deck and grab one of the tables along the railing, where the views are sensational. Closed Nov–Mar. 98 Town Neck Rd. (Rte. 6A to Tupper Rd.; 1/2 mile to Town Neck Rd.) (C) **508/888-6166.**

Sandwich Auction House Do you have the guts—not to mention the funds—to be a player? You'll find out soon enough as the bidding grows heated over an ever-changing parade of antique goods, from chests to portraits to spinning wheels. Antique-rug auctions take place once a month. Sit on your hands if you must. Auctions are held the first and third Saturday of every month, year-round; previews start at 2pm the same day. MasterCard and Visa are accepted. 15 Tupper Rd. (at Rte. 6A). (C) **508/888-1926.** www.sandwichauction.com. Free admission.

---

2 BOURNE

4 miles W of Sagamore; 16 miles NW of Hyannis

Bourne, with seven villages, hugs Buzzards Bay on both sides of the Cape Cod Canal. The town has changed quite a bit since President Grover Cleveland moved to Bourne more than 100 years ago. Evidently attracted by the trout, he decided to set up his summer White House at Monument Beach in the 1890s. That house is long gone, but one vestige—his personal train station—is on view at the Aptucxet Trading Post Museum, a reconstructed version of this country's first place of commerce, where Pilgrims traded with Native Americans and the Dutch. Also visible from here—and from the Cape Cod Canal bike path, which runs right past the post—is the intriguing **Vertical Lift Railroad Bridge** (built in 1935); its track moves up or down to permit the passage, respectively, of ships or trains. Cataumet, with its winding roads, is the most upscale village in Bourne. The village of Buzzards Bay, its somewhat dingy Main Street paralleling the canal, has most of the shops.

ESSENTIALS

GETTING THERE   The villages in the town of Bourne are on both sides of the Cape Cod Canal. To get to Buzzards Bay, take Exit 1 off Route 25 before crossing the Bourne Bridge. To get to Cataumet, Pocasset, Monument Beach, and Bourne Village cross the Bourne Bridge. Follow Route 28 south, a limited access highway, and watch the signs for the appropriate exit. You can also fly into Hyannis (see "Getting There & Getting Around," in chapter 3).

VISITOR INFORMATION   Contact the **Cape Cod Chamber of Commerce** (see "Visitor Information," in the "Sandwich" section, earlier in this chapter) or stop at the **Route 25 Visitor's Center.** The **Cape Cod Canal Region Chamber of Commerce,** 70 Main St., Buzzards Bay (© 508/759-6000), can provide literature on Bourne.

BEACHES & RECREATIONAL PURSUITS

BEACHES   Bourne has only one public beach: **Monument Beach ★**, off Shore Road. Half the parking lot is free (this fills up fast), and the other half requires a sticker from **Bourne Town Hall** at 24 Perry Ave. in Buzzards Bay (© 508/759-0623). Though the beach is small and pebbly, it's picturesque. Full public-beach facilities accompany the relatively warm waters of Buzzards Bay.

BICYCLING   See "Bicycling," under "Sandwich," earlier in this chapter. The **Cape Cod Canal bike path ★★★**, 14 miles on both sides of the Canal, is one of the best on the Cape. On the mainland side of the Canal, on Main Street in Buzzards Bay, access is at the far end of Buzzards Bay Park. On the Cape side of the Canal, access is at the Bourne Recreation Area, just north of the Bourne Bridge, along Canal Road.

BOATING   If you have your own canoe or kayak or want to rent one in Falmouth, you'll enjoy exploring Back River and Phinney's Harbor at Monument Beach. **Cape Cod Kayak** (© 508/563-9377; www.capecodkayak.com) rents kayaks (free delivery) by the day or week and offers lessons and ecotours on local waterways. Canoe and kayak rentals are $35 to $60 for a full day. Lessons are $49 per hour. Two- or 3-hour trips are $45 to $65.

FISHING   So plentiful are the herring making their spring migration up the **Bournedale Herring Run ★★** (Army Corps of Engineers © 508/759-5991; Rte. 6 in Bournedale, about 1 mile southwest of the Sagamore Bridge rotary) that you can net them once they've reached their destination, Great Herring Pond. You can obtain a shellfish permit from **Bourne Town Hall** at 24 Perry Ave., Buzzards Bay (© 508/759-0613). Also plentiful here are pickerel, white perch, walleye, and bass. For freshwater fishing at Flax Pond and Red Brook Pond in Pocasset, you'll need a license from the Bourne Town Hall (see above). You can also obtain a freshwater fishing license at **Red Top Sporting Goods** at 265 Main St. in Buzzards Bay (© 508/759-3371). Surf casting along the Cape Cod Canal requires no permit.

Kids OceanQuest

No visit to the Cape would be complete without some type of seafaring excursion on the Atlantic. If you're not a sailor or if you don't have the time or budget for an all-day boat trip, consider a unique, hands-on discovery cruise with **OceanQuest ★★**, Water Street (in the center of town), Woods Hole (✆ **800/376-2326** or 508/385-7656; www.oceanquestonline.org). Departing from Woods Hole, these 1½-hour harbor cruises are perfect for families, as real marine research is conducted with passengers serving as bona fide data collectors.

Here's how it works. Participants are split into two teams. Up in the bow, company founder Kathy Mullin, or a scientist borrowed from one of the revered local institutes, trains the new crew in the niceties of reading water temperature, assessing turbidity, and taking other key measurements. In the stern, passengers get to examine the specimens hauled up by the dredger. Midway into the trip, the teams switch stations, so that everyone gets to contemplate topics such as the sex life of a spider crab or why the water looks a particular shade of blue or green. Kids get a real kick out of being addressed as "Doctor," and even adults who think they know it all will probably come away much better informed.

The 90-minute cruise costs $22 for adults, $17 for children 4 to 12, $5 for children 3 and under; boats shove off four times a day Monday through Friday from mid-June to early September. Trips depart at 10am, noon, 2pm, and 4pm. Reservations are strongly recommended.

ICE-SKATING The **John Gallo Ice Arena,** 231 Sandwich Rd. in Bourne (✆ **508/759-8904;** www.galloarena.com), is open to the public daily from September to March with reduced hours in the summer. Rates are $3 for adults, $2 for children.

NATURE & WILDLIFE AREAS The Bourne Conservation Trust has managed to get hold of a handful of small plots; for information, contact the town **Conservation Commission** (✆ **508/759-0625**). The largest tract is the **Four Ponds Conservation Area/Town Forest,** which consists of 280 acres off Barlows Landing Road in Pocasset. The 40-acre **Nivling-Alexander Reserve** (off Shore Rd. at Thaxter Rd.) has three walking trails and flanks Red Brook Pond, where fishing is permitted (see above); it offers a half-mile wooded walk past several cranberry bogs. The **U.S. Army Corps of Engineers** (✆ **508/759-5991**), which is in charge of the **Cape Cod Canal,** gives free naturalist-guided nature walks and slide shows about the Canal. Visit the **Cape Cod Canal Visitor Center,** 60 Ed Moffitt Dr. (at the northeast corner of the canal; take Rte. 130 to Tupper Rd. to Town Neck Rd. to Coast Guard Rd.), Sandwich (✆ **508/833-9678**), for more details about this interesting waterway. There are several exhibits, as well as free public programs and canal guide booklets. Open daily 10am to 5pm in season.

TENNIS In the Bourne area, public courts are located near the old schoolhouse on County Road in Cataumet, and in Chester Park, opposite the railroad station in Monument Beach. For information, call the **Bourne Memorial Community Center** on Main Street in Buzzards Bay (✆ **508/759-0650**), which also has courts.

Aptucxet Trading Post Museum   Long before the Canal was a twinkle in Myles Standish's (and later, George Washington's) eye, Native Americans had been portaging goods between two rivers, the Manomet and Scusset, that once almost met at this site; its name in Algonquian means "little trap in the river." The Pilgrims were quick to notice that Aptucxet made an ideal trading spot, especially since, as Gov. William Bradford pointed out, it would allow them to trade with the Dutch to the south without "the compassing of Cape-Codd and those dangerous shoulds [shoals]." In 1627, the Pilgrims built an outpost here, hoping to cash in as conduits for native-caught pelts. The present building is a replica, built after a pair of local archaeologists, using ancient maps, uncovered the original foundation in 1926. The other detritus they dug up (arrowheads, pottery shards, and so on) is displayed in a roomful of rather dim, crowded display cases. Also be sure to have a look at the **Bournedale Stone,** which was discovered serving as a threshold for a Native American church built in the late 17th century. Overturned, it revealed strange, runelike inscriptions—fueling the legend (unsubstantiated as yet) that Vikings roamed the Cape around A.D. 1000.

Even though the building is not authentic, the curator does a very good job of conjuring up the hard, lonely life led by the pair of sentinels assigned here. Several other odd artifacts are scattered about the grounds, such as **President Grover Cleveland's personal train station** from his estate at Gray Gables.

The **Cape Cod Canal bike path** ★★★ runs right behind the museum. This is a good spot from which to observe the **Vertical Lift Railroad Bridge** ★, which represented state-of-the-art technology for its time (1935, when it cost $1.5 million). Rush hour, between 5 and 6pm, is your best chance to catch the bridge lowering its trestle (for the garbage cars headed off-Cape). In the off season, you might get a colorful sunset thrown in for good measure.

24 Aptucxet Rd., off Perry Ave. (about ¹/₂ mile west of the town center), Bourne Village. © **508/759-9487.** Admission $4 adults, $3.50 seniors, $2 children 6–18, free for children 5 and under. Families do not pay more than $10 in total. July–Aug Tues–Sat 10am–4pm, Sun 3–5pm; June and Sept Tues–Sat 10am–5pm. Closed Oct–May.

TAKE A CRUISE

Cape Cod Canal Cruises ★★ (Value) (Kids)   Get an underbelly view of the Cape's two swooping car bridges and its unusual railroad bridge as you wend your way among a wide array of interesting craft and a narrator fills you in on the Canal's history. Basically, it was the brainchild of New York financial wizard Augustus Perry Belmont, who completed it in 1914 at a cost of $16 million and never saw a penny of profit. Found to be too narrow and perilous (the current reverses with the tides, roughly every 6 hr.), the ambitious waterway was handed over to the U.S. Army Corps of Engineers for expansion in 1928 at the discount price of $11.5 million. It continues to serve as a vital shortcut, sparing some 30,000 boats yearly the long, dangerous circuit of the Outer Cape.

The 4pm **family cruise,** offered Monday to Saturday, is a real bargain, at $12 per adult and free for children 12 and under. The Sunday-afternoon trip is accompanied by New Orleans–style jazz, and the sunset-entertainment cruises on Friday and Saturday (adults over 21 only) feature live bands.

Onset Bay Town Pier (on the northern side of the Canal, about 2 miles west of the Bourne Bridge), Onset. © **508/295-3883.** www.hy-linecruises.com. Tickets $12–$18 adults, children 12 and under free. Mid-June to Sept departures Mon 10am, 2pm, and 4:30pm; Tues–Thurs 10am, 2pm, 4:30pm, and 7pm; Fri–Sat 10am, 2pm, 4:30pm, and 8pm; Sun 10am and 2pm. Call for off-season schedule. Closed mid-Oct to Apr.

Sports fans of all ages will enjoy taking in nine innings of the Grand Old Game. Part of the elite-amateur **Cape Cod Baseball League** (© 508/432-6909; www.capecodbaseball. org), the Bourne Braves play at Coady School Field, in Buzzards Bay, in July and August. Games are free. Call the **Cape Cod Canal Region Chamber of Commerce** (© 508/759-6000) to check the schedule.

KID STUFF

Stuck with a gray day? Pack the family off to **Cartwheels 2** at 343 Macarthur Blvd. (Route 28), about 2 miles south of the Bourne Bridge (© 508/743-9930). As far as entertaining kids goes, this place is probably the best bargain on the Cape. Older kids will like the go-carts and wiffle ball cages. Little kids have a moonwalk, bumper boats, and minigolf. It's $6 per ride, but you'll definitely want to buy an unlimited-rides pass for $20 for a couple hours to save money.

SHOPPING

Instead of the usual cutesy Cape Cod shops, Bourne is known for its factory outlets. **Cape Cod Factory Outlet Mall,** just off Route 6, Exit 1, Sagamore (© 508/888-8417), has 20 stores including Van Heusen, L'Eggs/Hanes/Playtex/Bali, Osh Kosh B'Gosh, Bass Shoe, and Samsonite.

GIFTS You can observe artisans continuing the tradition of the Boston & Sandwich Glass Company at **Pairpoint Glass Works,** 851 Sandwich Rd. (Rte. 6A, near the foot of the Sagamore Bridge), Sagamore (© 800/899-0953 or 508/888-2344). Thomas J. Pairpoint was a leading designer in the 1880s. The output includes skillful replicas. Glass blowing takes place Monday to Friday from 9am to 4pm. Bargain-lovers flock to the **Christmas Tree Shops** at the Sagamore Bridge, Sagamore (© 508/888-7010). The stock here is not just holiday-related. Housed in an oversize thatch-roofed Tudor cottage, complete with spinning windmill (you can't miss it), the array is Woolworthian in scope. There are six more branches of Christmas Tree Shops in other towns on the Cape.

SEAFOOD You couldn't hope for a fresher catch than what you'll find at **Cataumet Fish,** 1360 Rte. 28A, Cataumet (© 508/564-5956). Buy a whole fish or cart home a couple of lobsters.

WHERE TO STAY

The Beachmoor ★ (Value) Quite a bit off the beaten track, this property located right at the mouth of the Cape Cod Canal next to the Massachusetts Military Academy offers bargain rates and a pleasant ambience. There are views of the Cape Cod Canal from the suite, the commons room, and the superb casual restaurant on the first floor (see "Where to Dine," below). Rooms are decorated individually and with flair, and there's loving attention to detail throughout. For instance, iron bedsteads are romantically draped with gauzy fabric, and curtains are handmade with lacy netting. A tiny private beach in front of the hotel is perfect for sunning.

11 Buttermilk Way (south on Main St., left on Academy Dr., right on Tower Lane), Buzzards Bay, MA 02532. © 508/759-7522. www.beachmoor.com. 6 units. Summer $85–$95 double; $125 suite. Rates include continental breakfast. AE, DC, DISC, MC, V. Closed Jan to mid-Feb. **Amenities:** Restaurant (see below). *In room:* TV/VCR, no phone.

Expensive

The Beachmoor ★★ NEW AMERICAN If you happen to be anywhere near the Bourne Bridge and in need of dinner, you'll want to head over to the Beachmoor in Buzzards Bay. They serve up terrific food along with a wonderful view of the Cape Cod Canal. Specialties at dinner include Beachmoor Stew (shrimp, clams, scallops, lobster, and fish in a saffron broth) and the daily trilogy, which might include poached salmon with béarnaise sauce, grilled swordfish with basil butter, and broiled scallops in lemon butter. Save room for dessert, and if baked pear is on the menu, don't hesitate. It's a heavenly concoction of crisp-on-the-outside, doughy-on-the-inside pastry surrounding delicate baked pears, served with vanilla ice cream and raspberry sauce. Evening entertainment is offered on Friday (Nick Lombardo singalong) and Saturday (Al "Fingers" Russo at the piano bar). On Sunday, there's a brunch buffet for $15.

11 Buttermilk Way, Buzzards Bay. ⓒ **508/759-7522.** Reservations recommended. Main courses $16–$30. AE, DC, DISC, MC, V. Apr–Sept Wed–Sat 5–10pm, Sun 11:30am–8pm; Oct–Dec Thurs–Sat 5–10pm, Sun 11:30am–8pm. Closed Jan–Mar.

Moderate

The Chart Room ★★ SEAFOOD Great sunset views over Red Brook Harbor and fresh fish are reason enough to visit this dockside restaurant, housed in a former railroad barge at a busy marina. A piano bar lends a bit of elegance, as does the well-heeled clientele. The only downside is due to this restaurant's ongoing popularity; it can get very loud here. The younger crowd likes to gather at the bar for the mudslides, said to be the best in the region.

1 Shipyard Lane (in the Kingman Yacht Center, off Shore Rd.), Cataumet. ⓒ **508/563-5350.** Dinner reservations required. Main courses $12–$25. AE, MC, V. Mid-June to early Sept daily 11:30am–10pm; mid-May to mid-June and early Sept to mid-Oct Thurs–Sat 11:30am–10pm, Sun 11:30am–3pm. Closed mid-Oct to mid-May.

Mashnee Island Grill and Beach Bar ★ (Finds) SEAFOOD You'll impress all your friends if you can actually find this classic Cape Cod restaurant, surrounded on three sides by water. Sitting on the large deck of this restaurant is the quintessential summer experience. What started out as a run-down beach bar is now a terrific place for lunch on a sunny summer day. The house favorite is the fish and chips, made with a large piece of fresh cod encased in crunchy batter. Perhaps even more popular are the burgers, either the Mashnee Island burger with pineapple, bacon, cheese, and shrimp or the Aussie with bacon, cheese, and a fried egg on top. There's live entertainment Sunday from 4 to 7pm in season.

162 Leeward Rd., Bourne. (At the Bourne Bridge rotary, take the first right onto Trowbridge Rd. At the VFW Post stay right and follow signs to Mashnee Island; cross causeway to Mashnee Island and take 1st left for Grill.) ⓒ **508/759-9390.** Reservations not accepted. Main courses $6–$19. MC, V. June–Aug daily 11:30am–10pm; Sept–Dec and May Thurs 4–10pm, Fri–Sat 11:30am–10pm, Sun 4pm–sunset. Closed Jan–Apr.

The Parrot Bar and Grill NEW AMERICAN This upbeat casual family restaurant specializes in seafood and pasta. Try the lobster pie or the blackened swordfish with Southwestern salsa. Local bands entertain Thursday to Saturday with no cover charge.

1356 Rte. 28A, Cataumet. ⓒ **508/563-2117.** Reservations recommended in season. Main courses $10–$15. MC, V. Daily 11:30am–10pm.

An Internet Cafe

The best Web cafe on the Cape is **The Daily Brew Coffee Bar and Cafe,** Cataumet Square, Cataumet (1370 Rte. 28A, Cataumet; C **508/564-4755**), where you can get awesome espressos, cappuccinos, and baked goods, as well as soups, salads, and sandwiches. Several computers are located upstairs if you want to log on. There is outside seating on a covered patio in back. The cafe is open 5am to 3pm year-round.

BOURNE AFTER DARK

On weekends, local bands draw a crowd of young adults to the **Courtyard Restaurant and Bar,** Cataumet Square, Cataumet (C **508/563-1818**). Cover charge varies. From here you can barhop to **The Parrot Bar and Grill,** 1356 Rte. 28A (see "Where to Dine," above), which has live music Thursday to Saturday in season.

3 FALMOUTH ★★★

18 miles S of Sagamore; 20 miles SW of Hyannis

Falmouth is a classic New England town, complete with historic churches alongside the Village Green and a bustling Main Street. The town offers a variety of activities and summer events for vacationers, from beautiful beaches and bike paths to weekly outdoor band concerts and summer theater. Founded in 1660 by Quakers from Sandwich, Falmouth proved remarkably arable territory: By the 19th century, it reigned as the strawberry capital of the world. Today, with over 32,000 year-round residents, it's the second-largest town on the Cape, after Barnstable.

With more than a century of catering to summertime guests (it was the first "fashionable" Cape resort, served by trains from Boston starting in the 1870s), Falmouth residents have hospitality down to an art. The area around the historic **Village Green ★★** (used for military exercises in the pre-Revolutionary days) is a veritable hotbed of B&Bs, with each vying to provide the most elaborate breakfasts and solicitous advice. Listen to your hosts, and you'll soon feel like a native.

Officially a village within Falmouth (one of eight), tiny **Woods Hole ★★★** has been a world-renowned oceanic research center since 1871, when the U.S. Commission of Fish and Fisheries set up a primitive seasonal collection station. Today the various scientific institutes crowded around the harbor—principally, the National Marine Fisheries Service, the Marine Biological Laboratory (founded in 1888), and the Woods Hole Oceanographic Institute (a newcomer as of 1930)—have research budgets in the tens of millions of dollars and employ thousands of scientists. Woods Hole's scientific institutions offer a unique opportunity to get in-depth—and often hands-on—exposure to marine biology.

Belying the stereotype of the nerdy scientist, the Woods Hole community is far from uptight; in fact, it's one of the hipper communities on the Cape. In the past few decades, a number of agreeable restaurants and shops have cropped up, making the small, crowded gauntlet of Water Street (don't even think of parking here in summer) a very pleasant place to stroll.

West Falmouth ★★ (which is really more north of town, stretched alongside Buzzards Bay) has held on to its bucolic character and makes a lovely drive, with perhaps an occasional stop for the more alluring antiques stores. **Falmouth Heights ★★★**, a cluster of shingled Victorian summer houses on a bluff east of Falmouth's harbor, is as popular as it is picturesque; its narrow ribbon of beach is a magnet for all, especially families. The **Waquoit Bay** area ★, a few miles east of town, has thus far eluded the over-commercialization that blights most of Route 28, and with luck and foresight will continue to do so. Several thousand acres of this vital estuarine ecosystem are now under federal custody.

ESSENTIALS

GETTING THERE   After crossing either the Bourne or Sagamore bridge, take Route 28 or 28A south. Crossing the Bourne Bridge will get you closer to your destination. Or fly into Hyannis (see "Getting There & Getting Around," in chapter 3).

Falmouth's bus station near the center of town is serviced by **Peter Pan Bus Lines** (59 Depot Ave.; ✆ **888/751-8800** or 508/548-7588; www.peterpanbus.com). Daily express buses run to and from Boston's Logan Airport ($30 one-way, $55 round-trip), as well as Boston's South Station train and bus terminal ($26 one-way, $50 round-trip). There are also daily buses to Providence, Rhode Island ($56 round-trip); T. F. Green Airport in Providence ($58 round-trip); and New York City ($121 round-trip). Off-season, there are discounts for 7- and 14-day advance purchases.

To get around Falmouth and Woods Hole (where parking in summer is impossible due to ferry traffic to Martha's Vineyard), use the seasonal (late June to Labor Day) **Whoosh Trolley** (✆ **800/352-7155;** www.thebreeze.info), which makes a circuit every 20 minutes down Falmouth's Main Street to Woods Hole from 9:30am to 7:10pm Monday to Friday and until 9:30pm on weekends from late May to late September and later in midsummer. You can pick up the trolley at the Falmouth Mall on Route 28, where there is plenty of parking. You can also flag down the trolley anywhere along the route. The trolley fare is $1 per trip or $3 for a 1-day pass.

Tip: The **Whoosh Trolley**'s extended hours (until 10:30pm Fri–Sat in July and Aug) means you can use it to go down to Woods Hole in the summer for dinner. Otherwise, parking in Woods Hole in high season can be a major challenge.

The **Sea Line Shuttle** (✆ **800/352-7155**) connects Woods Hole, Falmouth, and Mashpee with Hyannis year-round (except holidays). The fare ranges from $1 to $4, depending on distance; children under 5 ride free.

VISITOR INFORMATION   Contact the **Falmouth Chamber of Commerce,** Academy Lane, Falmouth, MA 02541 (✆ **800/526-8532** or 508/548-8500; fax 508/548-8521; www.falmouth-capecod.com), which is open year-round Monday to Friday 9am to 5pm and Saturday 9am to 4pm, or the **Cape Cod Chamber of Commerce** (see "Visitor Information," in the "Sandwich" section, earlier in this chapter).

WINDING DOWN   For a well-earned pick-me-up, take a biscotti break at **Coffee Obsession** ★ (✆ **508/540-2233**), a hip and friendly coffee bar in the Queens Buyway at the corner of North Main and Palmer Avenue.

BEACHES & RECREATIONAL PURSUITS

BEACHES   Although Old Silver Beach, Surf Drive Beach, and Menauhant Beach will sell a 1-day pass, most other Falmouth public beaches require a parking sticker. Day passes to Old Silver are $20 and day passes to Surf Drive and Menauhant are $10. Renters can obtain temporary beach parking stickers, for $50 per week or $80 per month, at **Falmouth Town Hall,** 59 Town Hall Sq. (✆ **508/548-7611**), or at the **Surf Drive Beach Bathhouse** in season (✆ **508/548-8623**). The town beaches for which a parking fee is charged all have lifeguards, restrooms, and concession stands. Some of Falmouth's more notable public shores are as follows:

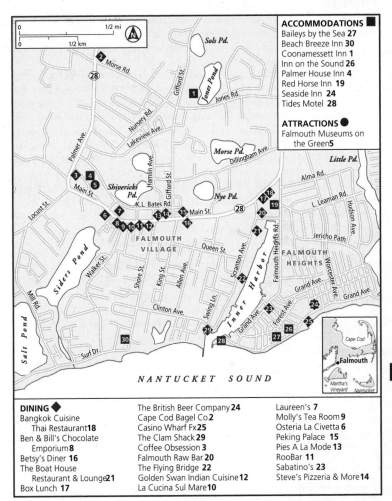

- **Falmouth Heights Beach ★★★**, off Grand Avenue in Falmouth Heights: Once a rowdy spot, this is primarily a family beach these days. Parking is sticker-only and some local inns will provide stickers to guests. This neighborhood supported the Cape's first summer colony; the grand Victorian mansions still overlook the beach. The beach has lifeguards and bathroom facilities.
- **Grew's Pond ★★**, in Goodwill Park off Palmer Avenue in Falmouth: This freshwater pond in a large town forest stays fairly uncrowded, even in the middle of summer. While everyone else is experiencing beach rage, trying to find parking at Falmouth's popular saltwater beaches, here you park for free and can wander shady paths around

the pond. Here you'll find picnic tables, a playground, barbecue grills, a lifeguard, and restrooms.

- **Menauhant Beach** ★, off Central Avenue in East Falmouth: A bit off the beaten track, Menauhant is a little less mobbed than Falmouth Heights Beach and better protected from the winds. There are lifeguards, bathroom facilities, and a bathhouse. A 1-day parking pass costs $10.
- **Old Silver Beach** ★★★, off Route 28A in North Falmouth: Western-facing (great for sunsets) and relatively calm, this warm Buzzards Bay beach is a popular, often crowded, choice. This is the chosen spot for the college crowd and other rowdy young folk. Mothers and their charges cluster on the opposite side of the street where a shallow pool formed by a sandbar is perfect for toddlers. The beach boasts several amenities, including a bathhouse with showers and bathrooms, food concessions, and lifeguards. Windsurfers are available to rent in season. A 1-day parking pass costs $20.
- **Surf Drive Beach** ★★★, off Shore Street in Falmouth: About a half-mile from downtown, and appealing to families, this is an easy-to-get-to choice (it's a 10-min. walk from Main St.) but with limited parking. The area between the jetties is a shallow, calm area called "the kiddie pool." You'll find an outdoor shower, bathrooms, a food concession, and lifeguards. A 1-day parking pass costs $10.

BICYCLING   The **Shining Sea Bikeway** ★★★ (© 508/548-8500) is a 4-mile beauty skirting Vineyard Sound from Falmouth to Woods Hole; it connects with a 23-mile scenic-road loop through pretty Sippewissett. This is one of the Cape's most scenic bike paths and one of the few that travels alongside the shoreline. There is free parking at the trailhead on Locust Street, on Depot Avenue, and in numerous parking lots behind Main Street. The Falmouth Chamber of Commerce offers a map and brochure about the Shining Sea Bikeway. Biking along this former railroad track that follows prehistoric Wampanoag Indian trails, the bike path passes 21 acres of woodlands, marsh, swamp, salt ponds, and seascape.

Construction is scheduled to be completed by the summer of 2009 on an 8-mile extension of the Shining Sea Bikeway, all the way to North Falmouth. That will make the bikeway a total of about 12 miles from North Falmouth to Woods Hole.

The path's name is a nod to Falmouth's own Katharine Lee Bates, who wrote the lyrics to "America the Beautiful" with its verse, "And crown thy good with brotherhood, from sea to shining sea!"

The closest bike shop—convenient to the main cluster of B&Bs, some of which offer "loaners"—is **Corner Cycle** at Palmer Avenue and North Main Street (© 508/540-4195). A half-day bike rental is $17 ($12 for children), a 24-hour rental $26 ($15 for children). For a broad selection of vehicles—from six-speed cruisers to six-passenger "surreys"—and good advice on routes, visit **Holiday Cycles** at 465 Grand Ave. in Falmouth Heights (© 508/540-3549), where a half-day bike rental is $20, a 24-hour rental $25, a week rental $65. The surreys rent for $20 to $30 an hour. Holiday Cycles does not accept credit cards.

BIRD-WATCHING   The **Shining Sea Bikeway** (see above) is a great spot to bird-watch, especially near Oyster Pond where there's an osprey nest. Keep an eye out for yellow-breasted chats and orange-crowned warblers, as well as waterfowl like mallards and buffleheads. You may also see herons and egrets.

BOATING   **Patriot Party Boats,** 227 Clinton Ave. (at Scranton Ave. on the harbor), Falmouth (© **800/734-0088** or 508/548-2626; www.patriotpartyboats.com or www.theliberte.com), offers one-stop shopping for would-be boaters. The Patriot fleet includes a poky fishing vessel, the *Patriot Too;* and a 74-foot, three-masted schooner, the *Liberte* ★★ (2-hr. sails; $20–$30 adults, $15–$20 children 11 and under). On the *Liberte,* Chris Tieje hauls up the sails and regales passengers about his custom-made schooner, while the impressive vessel cruises the sound. The most expensive trip and the most popular is the sunset sail at 6:30pm. Other trips leave at 10:30am and 2pm. For info on fishing trips, see "Fishing," below.

   Cape Cod Kayak (© **508/563-9377;** www.capecodkayak.com) rents kayaks (free delivery) by the day or week, and offers lessons and ecotours on local waterways. Canoe and kayak rentals are $35 to $60 for 8 hours. Lessons are $49 per hour. Four-hour trips are $45 to $65.

   If you want to explore on your own, a great area for exploring is Waquoit Bay (see "Nature & Wildlife Areas," below). **Washburn Island** ★★★, a protected reserve with wooded trails and pristine beaches, is about a 45-minute paddle from the town boat ramp near Edward's Boat Yard on Route 28 in East Falmouth.

FISHING   Falmouth has six fishable ponds. A complimentary fishing map and guide are available from the Falmouth Chamber of Commerce. Freshwater fishing and shell-fishing licenses can be obtained at **Falmouth Town Hall,** 59 Town Hall Sq. (© **508/548-7611,** ext. 219). Freshwater fishing licenses can also be obtained at **Eastman's Sport & Tackle,** 150 Main St. (© **508/548-6900**).

   Surf Drive Beach is a great spot for surf casting, once the crowds have dispersed. Other good locations are the jetties off Nobska Point in Woods Hole and Bristol Beach on Menauhant Road in East Falmouth.

   To go after bigger prey, head out with a group on one of the **Patriot Party Boats** based in Falmouth's Inner Harbor (© **800/734-0088** or 508/548-2626). Boats leave twice daily, at 8am and 1pm, in season. The *Patriot Too,* with an enclosed deck, is ideal for family-style "bottom fishing" (4-hr. trips $40 adults, $25 children 11 and under; sport-fishing trips $70 adults, $40 children; equipment and instruction provided).

   For deep-sea fishing enthusiasts, there are about a half-dozen sportfishing outfits that operate out of Falmouth Inner Harbor, cruising around Nantucket Sound, Vineyard Sound, and the Elizabeth Islands for bass, blues, tuna, and shark. Trips cost about $500 for a half-day, $700 for a full day. Call the chamber (© **508/548-8500**) for info.

FITNESS   If you're jonesing for time in the gym, the **Falmouth Sports Center** at 33 Highfield Dr. (© **508/548-7433**) offers weight-training facilities for $9 per day. Rac-quetball costs an extra $12 per person per hour. Tennis is $26 per person per hour.

GOLF   Falmouth abounds in golf courses—six public ones at last count. Among the more notable is the challenging 18-hole championship course at **Ballymeade Country Club,** 125 Falmouth Woods Rd. (© **508/540-4005**). Greens fees are $71 (weekdays) and $81 (weekends) and include carts.

ICE-SKATING   Public skating ($4 per person) is offered year-round at the **Falmouth Ice Arena,** 9 Skating Lane off Palmer Avenue (© **508/548-7080;** www.falmouthicearena. com), the home rink of Colleen Coyne, who was part of the gold-medal 1998 Olympic hockey team; call for information and hours.

NATURE & WILDLIFE AREAS   **Ashumet Holly and Wildlife Sanctuary** ★★, oper-ated by the Massachusetts Audubon Society at 186 Ashumet Rd., off Route 151

(© **508/362-1426**), is an intriguing 49-acre collection of more than 1,000 holly trees spanning 65 species and culled worldwide. Preserved by the state's first commissioner of agriculture, who was concerned that commercial harvesting might wipe out native species, they flourish here, along with over 130 species of birds and a carpet of Oriental lotus blossoms, which covers a kettle pond come summer. The trail fee is $3 for adults and $2 for seniors and children 15 and under.

Close to the center of Falmouth (just follow Depot Rd. to the end) is the 650-acre **Beebe Woods** ★★, a treasure for hikers and dog walkers. From here, you can wend your way to the **Peterson Farm** ★★ (entrance off Woods Hole Rd.; take a right at the Quissett farm stand), purchased by the town of Falmouth in 1997. The 90-acre farm has paths through woods and fields, as well as a flock of sheep grazing in a meadow near historic farm buildings. Bluebird boxes (special birdhouses for bluebirds) line the path on the way to a quiet pond. There is no charge to walk in Beebe Woods.

Tiny but dazzling, the privately owned **Spohr Gardens** ★ on Fells Road, off Oyster Pond Road in Woods Hole, invites visitors to explore 6 magical acres beside Oyster Pond. In the spring, thousands of daffodils bloom, followed by rhododendrons and day lilies. Paths wind past a collection of nautical treasures, like huge anchors and millstones. Remarkably, this private garden is free and open to the public. Donations for garden maintenance are accepted.

Named for its round shape that sticks out into the harbor, **The Knob** ★★, 13 acres of trails at Quissett Harbor at the end of Quissett Road, provides a perfect short walk and lovely views of Buzzards Bay. There's very limited parking at this small, secluded harbor, so try it early or late in the day. The Knob is owned by the nonprofit group Salt Pond Areas Bird Sanctuaries and is free and open to the public.

The 2,250-acre **Waquoit Bay National Estuarine Research Reserve (WBNERR),** at 149 Waquoit Hwy. in East Falmouth (© **508/457-0495;** www.waquoitbayreserve.org), maintains a 1-mile, self-guided nature trail. The reserve also offers a number of walks and interpretive programs, including the popular "Evenings on the Bluff" on Tuesday nights at 6:30pm that is geared toward families. The visitor center is open Monday to Friday from 10am to 4pm. You'll find several interesting exhibits especially appropriate for children. On Saturday in season WBNERR hosts a free 20-minute cruise over to **Washburn Island** ★★. Once on the island visitors can explore its wooded trails or relax on its pristine beaches. The 12-passenger motorboat leaves at 9am and returns by 12:30pm. The reserve also manages 11 primitive campsites on Washburn Island. Permits cost a mere $10 a night. Advance reservations for the cruise and camping are required and can be made by calling © **877/422-6762.** (The campsites book up 6 months in advance for summer weekends, but you'll have better luck with a late spring or early fall booking.)

TENNIS   Among the courts open to the public are those at the **Falmouth High School,** 874 Gifford Rd., Falmouth Recreation Department; and at the **Lawrence School** on Lakeview Avenue, a few blocks from the center of town. Call the Falmouth Chamber of Commerce (© **508/548-8500**) for information. Both are first-come, first-served. Among the commercial enterprises offering outdoor courts—clay, Har-Tru, and hard— are **Ballymeade Country Club** (see "Golf," above) and the **Falmouth Sports Center** (see "Fitness," above), which has six indoor courts in addition to three outside. Rates are $52 an hour for singles.

WATERSPORTS   Falmouth is something of a sailboarding mecca, prized for its unflagging southwesterly winds. Although Old Silver Beach in North Falmouth is the most popular spot for windsurfing, the sport is allowed there only prior to 9am and after 5pm.

The Trunk River area on the west end of Falmouth's Surf Drive Beach and a portion of Chapoquoit Beach are the only public beaches where windsurfers are allowed during the day. Concessions rent windsurfing equipment at Surf Drive Beach. Windsurfing races are held at Trunk River Beach, about a mile west from Surf Drive Beach, Saturday mornings in the summer.

SEA SCIENCE IN WOODS HOLE

Marine Biological Laboratory   The small Robert W. Pierce Visitors Center and Gift Shop offers visitors who are short on time a chance to gain some insight into the goings-on at this preeminent scientific facility, part of which is housed in an 1836 candle factory. Visitors can peer into a microscope, like the scientists on staff here, to observe marine organisms. A guided tour requires a little more forethought—the MBL prefers that reservations be made a week in advance—but will definitely reward the curious. After a slide presentation, a retired scientist leads visitors through the holding tanks and then to the lab to observe actual research in progress. The MBL's area of inquiry is not limited to the aquatic but encompasses the "biological process common to all life forms."

100 Water St. (at MBL St., in the center of town). *C* **508/289-7423** or 289-7623 (to schedule tours). www. mbl.edu. Free admission. Visitors Center July–Aug Mon–Sat 10am–5pm, Sun noon–4:30pm; call for off-season hours. Closed Jan–Apr. 1-hr. tours by reservation (no children under 10) late June through Aug Mon–Fri 1, 2, and 3pm.

Woods Hole Oceanographic Institution Exhibit Center and Gift Shop   This world-class research organization—locally referred to by its acronym, WHOI (pronounced *hoo-ey*)—is dedicated to the study of marine science. And with some $80 million in annual funding at stake, there's serious science going on here. This is a small but interactive exhibit center. Kids might enjoy looking through microscopes at organisms or listening to sounds of marine animals on a computer. *Titanic* fans will enjoy the brief video, displays, and a life-size model of the submersible that discovered the wreck. You can climb into the model and flick switches if you like. One-hour walking tours of WHOI are offered twice a day on weekdays in July and August; reservations are required and can be made by calling *C* **508/289-2252.**

15 School St. (off Water St.). *C* **508/289-2663.** www.whoi.edu. $2 donation requested. Late May to early Sept Mon–Sat 10am–4:30pm; call for off-season hours. Closed Jan–Mar.

Woods Hole Science Aquarium ★ **(Kids)**   A little beat up after 1¼ centuries of service and endless streams of eager schoolchildren, this aquarium—the first such institution in the country—may not be state of the art, but it's a treasure nonetheless. The highlight is the recently renovated state-of-the-art seal tank out front that houses LuSeal and Bumper, grey seals that are too injured to be released in the wild. The displays, focusing on local waters, might make you think twice before taking a dip. Children show no hesitation, though, in getting up to their elbows in the "touch tanks"; adults are also welcome to dabble. A key exhibit that everyone should see concerns the effect of plastic trash on the marine environment.

Albatross St. (off the western end of Water St.). *C* **508/495-2001.** Free admission; donations accepted. Mid-June to early Sept Tues–Sat 11am–4pm; early Sept to mid-June Mon–Fri 10am–4pm. Adults need a picture ID to enter.

FALMOUTH HISTORICAL SIGHTS

Falmouth Museums on the Green ★★   Knowledgeable volunteers will lead you through three buildings that contain fascinating vestiges of Falmouth's colorful history.

Tours begin at the 1790 Julia Wood House, built by Revolutionary physician Dr. Francis Wicks; a simulacrum of his office, complete with terrifying tools, is not for the faint of heart. Next door, past an authentic Colonial garden, is the mid-18th-century **Conant House,** which evolved from a half-Cape built to accommodate the town's minister; it now houses nautical collections, including intricate "sailor's valentines" made of shells, and whaling exhibits. A china hutch in the dining room displays romantic Staffordshire china. A special room chronicles the life of Katharine Lee Bates, Falmouth-born author of "America the Beautiful." Also on the grounds is the **Dudley Hallett Barn,** which contains vintage farm tools and the sleigh that Dr. Wicks used for house calls.

In the summer, the museum sponsors guided strolls, gallery talks, trolley tours, and afternoon teas. The free 90-minute guided strolls take place every Tuesday in July, August, and September. Groups meet at 10am at the Hallett Barn. Trolley tours take place every Wednesday at 10am in September and October. The $15-per-person cost includes museum admission. Teas take place Thursdays mid-July through August from 1 to 3pm, weather permitting. The $12-per-person fee includes museum admission.

55–65 Palmer Ave. (at the Village Green). ⓒ **508/548-4857.** www.falmouthhistoricalsociety.org. Admission $5 adults, free for children 12 and under. Late June to early Oct Tues–Fri 10am–4pm, Sat 10am–1pm. Open early Oct to late June by appointment.

Woods Hole Historical Museum ★   Exhibits change at this small but charming museum. The permanent 1895 diorama of the town should give you the former flavor of this combination seaport/scientific community and tourist destination. The neighboring barn shelters a Small Boat Museum including an Old Town canoe, a Cape Cod "knockabout," a Herreshoff 12^{1}/$_{2}$, and a fine example of a "spritsail" boat. There's also the reconstructed 1893 hobby workshop of a local doctor. To delve into town lore in more detail, reserve a place on one of the free walking tours offered Tuesdays at 4pm in July and August.

579 Woods Hole Rd. (on the eastern edge of town), Woods Hole. ⓒ **508/548-7270.** Free admission; donations welcome. Mid-June to mid-Sept Tues–Sat 10am–4pm; off season by appointment.

BASEBALL

Part of the elite-amateur **Cape Cod Baseball League** (ⓒ **508/432-6909;** www.capecod baseball.org), the Falmouth Commodores play at Guv Fuller Field behind the Gus Canty Community Center, off East Main Street, in July and August. Admission is free, though a donation of $5 is requested. Call the **Falmouth Chamber of Commerce** (ⓒ **508/548-8500**) to check the schedule, or pick one up at the **Gus Canty Community Center,** 790 E. Main St. (ⓒ **508/457-2567**).

SHOPPING

Falmouth's spiffy Main Street has a number of good clothing, home-goods, and gift stores. There are also several good arts-and-crafts galleries in West Falmouth and Woods Hole.

ANTIQUES   **Good & White,** at 635 W. Falmouth Hwy. in West Falmouth (ⓒ **508/548-2772**), is an antiques store that has been featured in several home magazines.

ARTS & CRAFTS   **Jan Collins Selman Fine Art,** 317 Main St., Falmouth (ⓒ **508/457-5533**), not only shows the fine pastels and paintings of Ms. Selman, but also features artwork from many other established and emerging artists from the area. Joan Lederman creates and sells her one-of-a-kind ceramics at **The Soft Earth ★**, in Woods Hole (ⓒ **508/540-5237;** www.thesoftearth.com). Lederman glazes her pottery with sediment found on ocean floors all over the world. She obtains much of her material from the oceanographic scientists based in Woods Hole. The colors and patterns created by the sediment make each of her practical pieces—which include bowls, platters, mugs, vases, and the like—utterly unique works of art. Her studio/gallery is open to visitors from 11am to 1pm weekdays or by appointment.

BOOKS **Booksmith,** 7 Davis Straits (in Falmouth Plaza), Falmouth (© **508/540-6064**), is a terrific all-around bookstore, with a good selection of novels and nonfiction paperbacks for beach reading. The very appealing **Eight Cousins Children's Books,** 189 Main St., Falmouth (© **508/548-5548**), offers books, games, and toys for children of all ages. The town's largest repository of books is **Inkwell Bookstore** at 199 Main St., Falmouth (© **508/540-0039**), where you'll find a good mix of beach reading and nonfiction, plus the town's biggest magazine rack.

FASHION Don't be too intimidated to browse in **Maxwell & Co.,** 200 Main St. (in the center of town), Falmouth (© **508/540-8752**), which may be the highest-end clothier on the Cape. Comfortable Italian fashions are displayed here in an elegant setting. Their end-of-summer sale in mid-August offers up to 70% off the prices of these exquisite goods.

The clothing at **Caline for Kids,** 149 Main St. (in the center of town), Falmouth (© **508/548-2533**), ranges from practical to elegant, and sometimes manages to be both. Sizes from newborn to 14 are available.

Europa, 628 Rte. 28A, West Falmouth (© **508/540-7814**), features interesting and stylish international clothes and gifts. They add up to a sophisticated look, liberated from cookie-cutter predictability. There's also a small but adorable selection of clothes for very young children.

FOOD & WINE People drive from all over the region for the wine selection (and prices) at **Kappy's,** 21 Spring Bars Rd., off Route 28 (© **508/548-2600**), the Cape's largest liquor, beer, and wine store. "Pick your own" is the password at the long-established **Tony Andrews Farm and Produce Stand,** 394 Old Meeting House Rd. (about 1½ miles north of Rte. 28), East Falmouth (© **508/548-4717;** www.tonyandrewsfarmstand.com), where it's strawberries early in the summer, and tomatoes, sweet corn, and more as the season progresses. Of course, you can just buy them here without picking, though the Puritans wouldn't have approved. **Coonamessett Farm,** 277 Hatchville Rd. (about 1 mile east of Sandwich Rd.), Hatchville (© **508/563-2560;** www.coonamessettfarm. com), has a full farm stand of vegetables grown in the fields out back. You can pick your own vegetables, look at the farm animals (including two cute llamas), or rent a canoe for a paddle in the pond out back. A **Vegetarian Buffet Dinner** is served Friday nights in season (5–8pm; $17 adults, $8.95 children, free for ages 5 and under) at the farm's cafe. The popular **Jamaican Buffet Dinner** on Wednesday nights in summer (5–8pm; same price as above) features jerk chicken and live reggae music.

GIFTS **Bojangles,** 239 Main St. (© **508/548-9888**), is a high-end gift shop/women's clothing boutique. Stop here for fun gifts and fine crafts, including exceptional hand-painted glassware. **Oolala** at 45 N. Main St. (© **508/495-3888**) is still funky, but with glassware, kitchen accessories, rugs, and lighting.

SPA **Bellezza Day Spa,** 221 Main St. (© **508/299-8300**), is perhaps the most luxurious beauty shop on Cape Cod. Set in a high-ceilinged storefront on Falmouth's Main Street, the spa offers all manner of facials, waxings, massages, manicures, hair cuts, and other services.

For a basic motel with a great location, try the **Tides Motel** (© 508/548-3126; www.tidesmotelcapecod.com) on Clinton Avenue at the far west end of Grand Avenue in Falmouth Heights. The 1950s-style no-frills (no air-conditioning, no phone) motel sits on the beach at the head of Falmouth Harbor facing Vineyard Sound. Rates in season are $165 to $170 double, $215 suite. It's closed late October to mid-May.

The **Red Horse Inn** ★ at 28 Falmouth Heights Rd., Falmouth (© 508/548-0053; www.redhorseinn.com), is a family-friendly option just a short walk from Falmouth Inner Harbor. The 22 rooms are priced from $180 to $225, and kids will love the large outdoor pool. Open year-round.

The **Seaside Inn** at 263 Grand Ave., Falmouth Heights (© 800/827-1976 or 508/540-4120; www.seasideinnfalmouth.com), is a reasonably priced motel in a superb location, across the street from Falmouth Heights Beach and next to the British Beer Company, a family-style restaurant. The 23 rooms with air-conditioning, TVs, phones with free calls, and some with kitchenettes, are priced at $189 to $229 for a double, $259 to $304 for a deluxe room. Open year-round.

Expensive

Inn on the Sound ★★ (Finds)   The ambience here is as breezy as the setting, high on a bluff beside Falmouth's premier sunning beach, with a sweeping view of Vineyard Sound from the large front deck. There's none of the usual frilly/cutesy stuff in these well-appointed guest rooms, most of which have ocean views, several with their own private decks. Many of the bathrooms have been renovated with large, luxurious tiled showers. The deluxe suite ideal for families has two bedrooms, a living room, a kitchenette, and a private entrance. The focal point of the inn's living room is a handsome boulder hearth (nice for those nippy nights). Most guests enjoy having their breakfast, which features lots of home-baked goodies, served on the front deck.

313 Grand Ave., Falmouth Heights, MA 02540. © 800/564-9668 or 508/457-9666. Fax 508/457-9631. www.innonthesound.com. 10 units, 8 with tub/shower, 2 with shower only. Summer $195–$325 double. Rates include continental breakfast. AE, DISC, MC, V. Open year-round. No children under 18 (except in suite). *In room:* TV, hair dryer, no phone.

Moderate

Baileys By the Sea ★ (Finds)   If you love the beach, the location of this charming bed-and-breakfast a few steps from Falmouth Heights Beach is liable to make you swoon. Bailey's has a casual feel, with whitewashed walls and views of Vineyard Sound from all seven of the inn's rooms. Everything about this inn feels very summer-y, from the sheer curtains, full with breezes; the rocking chairs; even the waffle robes provided in each room. Falmouth Heights, one of the Cape's first summery communities, is a wonderful place to stroll and gaze at Victorian homes, or simply walk for miles along the beach, with views of Martha's Vineyard in the distance. Besides the beach just out the door, there are also two restaurants, a family-style tavern and a fine-dining establishment, both a short walk away.

321 Grand Ave., Falmouth Heights, MA 02540. © 866/548-5748 or 508/495-4900. Fax 508/548-6974. www.baileysbythesea.com. 7 units. Summer $195–$290 double. Rates include full breakfast. MC, V. Open year-round. *In room:* A/C, TV, hair dryer.

Beach Breeze Inn ★   This inn has a great location, just steps from Surf Drive Beach and a short and pleasant stroll to Main Street with its many shops and restaurants. Guests here beat the summer traffic blues, because with beach and town within walking distance, you never need to use your car! Rooms are sunny and spacious with motel-style privacy; many of them have separate entrances. The inn was built in 1858, and spent many years as a run-down boardinghouse. It has been thoroughly freshened up and is now a terrific lodging option, particularly for families.

321 Shore St. (about ¼ mile south of Main St.), Falmouth, MA 02540. ℂ **800/828-3255** or 508/548-1765. www.beachbreezeinn.com. 20 units. Summer $179–$289 double; $1,500–$1,700 weekly efficiencies. MC, V. **Amenities:** Unheated pool. *In room:* TV, fridge.

Coonamessett Inn ★★   A gracious inn built around the core of a 1796 homestead, the Coonamessett Inn is Falmouth's most traditional lodging choice. The original inn was a few miles away and flanked the namesake river. Set on 7 lushly landscaped acres overlooking a pond, it has the feel of an attractive country club. Some of the rooms, decorated in reproduction antiques, can be a bit somber, so try to get one with good light (rooms nos. 1–6, plus the "village rooms" that face the pond). Most have a separate sitting room attached. On-site is a restaurant featuring a very comfortable tavern room as well as a more formal dining room. The extensive buffet brunch here on Sundays brings out people from all over town.

Jones Rd. and Gifford St. (about ½ mile north of Main St.), Falmouth, MA 02540. ℂ **508/548-2300.** Fax 508/540-9831. www.capecodrestaurants.org. 27 units, 1 cottage. Summer $170–$250 double; $220 2-bedroom suite; $280 cottage. Rates include continental breakfast. AE, MC, V. **Amenities:** Restaurant. *In room:* A/C, TV, coffeemaker, hair dryer.

Palmer House Inn ★   Located just steps from the historic Falmouth Village Green and a bike-rental shop, and a short stroll to Main Street's shops and restaurants, the Palmer House Inn, a vintage Queen Anne Victorian, has a terrific location. Innkeepers Bill and Pat O'Connell are most welcoming. Rooms are decorated to highlight the inn's 19th-century heritage with pretty floral wallpaper, curtains, and bedding. Rooms feature majestic beds, including a canopied mahogany beauty in a turret room. The Henry James Room on the third floor has a romantically draped four-poster bed and a whirlpool bath under a skylit cathedral ceiling. The living room is a fine place to curl up with a book in front of the fireplace or to gather before dinner with a glass of wine, provided by your hosts. Breakfasts in the sunny dining room are elaborate, with options like Swiss eggs in puff pastry or chocolate-stuffed French toast.

81 Palmer Ave. (on Falmouth Village Green), Falmouth, MA 02540. ℂ **800/472-2632** or 508/548-1230. Fax 508/540-1878. www.palmerhouseinn.com. 17 units. Summer $199–$300 double. Rates include full breakfast. AE, MC, V. *In room:* A/C, TV, hair dryer, iron.

Sands of Time Motor Inn & Harbor House ★★   This property, which is across the street from the Woods Hole ferry terminal, consists of two buildings: a two-story motel in front of a shingled 1879 Victorian mansion. The motel rooms feature crisp, above-average decor, plus private porches overlooking the harbor. The rooms in the Harbor House are more lavish and romantic—some with four-posters, working fireplaces, wicker furnishings, and harbor views. There is a small heated pool on the grounds. All rooms are equipped with computer jacks.

549 Woods Hole Rd., Woods Hole, MA 02543. ℂ **800/841-0114** or 508/548-6300. Fax 508/457-0160. www.sandsoftime.com. 36 units, 2 with shared bathroom. Summer $179–$199 double. Rates include continental breakfast. AE, DC, DISC, MC, V. Closed Nov–Mar. **Amenities:** Small heated pool; 2 tennis courts. *In room:* A/C, TV.

Woods Hole Inn ★★   This newly opened inn in the heart of Woods Hole is the place to stay for people who want to be in the thick of it. The ferry terminal is just steps from the back door, so expect to hear the horn announcing its departure beginning at the crack of dawn. But in addition to the noise and hurly burly of this urban setting, there are the beautiful views of Vineyard Sound and Martha's Vineyard from the rooms and the unique charm of this seafaring port at every turn. Rooms are beautifully decorated with high-end amenities and the innkeepers live up to a commitment to stay "green" in a range of ways.

6 Luscombe Ave., Woods Hole, MA 02540. (©) **508/495-0248.** www.visitwoodsholeinn.com. 5 units. Summer $150–$225 double. Rates include continental breakfast. MC, V. Open year-round. Pet-friendly. **Amenities:** Bikes. *In room:* TV/DVD, Wi-Fi.

WHERE TO DINE
Expensive
The Boat House Restaurant and Lounge ★ NEW AMERICAN/SEAFOOD   Set harborside, the large plate-glass windows of this casual restaurant overlook mainly powerboats stacked high in a marina on Falmouth Inner Harbor. Service is very friendly here and the atmosphere, especially from the large bar area, tends to be quite jovial. The food, though pricey, is very good. Standouts are bouillabaisse and garlic-oil-rubbed sirloin. There are also a number of pasta and fried-fish choices on the menu. This place turns into a rowdy club with live music on summer evenings (see "Falmouth After Dark" later in this chapter). It's particularly appealing at lunchtime when prices are lower and the bar scene is quieter.

88 Scranton Ave. (on Falmouth Inner Harbor), Falmouth. (©) **508/548-7800.** Reservations accepted. Main courses $18–$26. AE, MC, V. Mid-June to mid-Sept daily 11:30am–10pm; call for off-season hours. Closed mid-Oct to mid-May.

Casino Wharf Fx ★ SEAFOOD   This new high-end two-story restaurant replaced the infamous Casino, a rowdy nightclub with legendary wet T-shirt contests. Although it's beachfront location is sublime, the Marriott-style decor is better suited to a Boston hotel than a Cape restaurant. Both levels of the restaurant have soaring ceilings and large outdoor decks set above the beach. The top-level deck is open to the weather (and rather high up at the equivalent of three floors above the beach). Both floors also have large bars positioned for beach views out the restaurant's floor-to-ceiling windows. I recommend coming here for lunch and ordering either the delicious Cape Cod Reuben—a fried cod sandwich with cheese—or yummy swordfish kabobs. Dinner is somewhat pricey, with traditional grilled seafood and steak entrees.

286 Grand Ave. (next to Falmouth Heights Beach), Falmouth Heights. (©) **508/540-6120.** Reservations accepted. Main courses $18–$40. AE, MC, V. Daily Mon–Fri 11:30am–3pm and 5:30–10pm; call for off-season hours. Open year-round.

Falmouth Raw Bar ★ SHELLFISH   If what you crave is a giant lobster roll, which consists of chunks of lobster and mayo on a big hotdog roll, this stylish bar overlooking Falmouth Inner Harbor is the place to get it—for $25. There are also steamed lobster dinners, Wellfleet oysters, local steamers, local little necks, and shrimp, and that's about it. The drinks menu is about twice as long as the food menu, with frozen drinks a specialty.

56 Scranton Ave. (at the corner of Robbins Rd, next to Falmouth Inner Harbor), Falmouth. (©) **508/548-7RAW** (508/548-7729). Reservations not accepted. Main courses $17–$45. AE, MC, V. Daily 11:30am–10pm; call for off-season hours. Closed mid-Oct through April.

Fishmonger's Cafe ★ VEGETARIAN/NATURAL FOODS   A cherished carry-over from the early 1970s, this sunny, casual cafe attracts local young people and scientists, as well as Bermuda-shorted tourists, with an ever-changing array of imaginatively prepared dishes. Prices have risen substantially over the past couple of years, making dinner in this casual setting feel like a splurge. The eclectic dinner menu changes every few days with some exotic fare, like Thai entrees. Regulars sit at the counter to enjoy a bowl of the Fisherman's Stew while schmoozing with staff bustling about the open kitchen. Newcomers usually go for the tables by the window, where you can watch boats come and go from Eel Pond. The menu ranges widely (lunch could be a tempeh burger made with fermented soybeans, or ordinary beef), and longtime customers look to the blackboard for the latest innovations, which invariably include delectable desserts like pumpkin-pecan pie.

56 Water St. (at the Eel Pond drawbridge), Woods Hole. (𝓒 **508/540-5376.** Reservations not accepted. Main courses $15–$25. AE, MC, V. Mid-June to Oct daily 7am–10pm; call for off-season hours. Closed mid-Dec to mid-Feb.

La Cucina Sul Mare ★★ (Finds) ITALIAN   Locals and tourists alike line up outside this popular Main Street restaurant, one of Falmouth's best, craving its hearty Italian fare. The interior features cheerful murals and a tin ceiling, and large picture windows overlook Main Street. A new outside deck in the back is a setting on warm nights. Chef/owner Mark Ciflone's signature dishes include classic Italian specialties like lasagna, braised lamb shanks, *osso buco,* lobster *fra diavlo* over linguine, chicken Parmesan, and veal piccata, among others. The desserts here are homemade and delicious. Service is often excellent.

237 Main St. (in the center of town), Falmouth. (𝓒 **508/548-5600.** Reservations not accepted (but you can call ahead a ¹/₂ hour before arriving to put your name on the list). Main courses $15–$25. AE, MC, V. Daily 11:30am–2pm and 5–10pm; call for off-season hours. Open year-round.

Osteria La Civetta ★★★ (Finds) NORTHERN ITALIAN   This authentic and intimate restaurant is run by the Toselli family of Bologna, Italy. This is European style dining and service: Courses are ordered a la carte, meat is not served on the same plate as pasta, and even vegetables are ordered separately. Because diners are expected to have multiple courses, servings are smaller than at the average American restaurant. But diners can share courses for a moderately priced fine dining experience. The food here is exquisite. With homemade pasta, the *lasagna alla Bolognese* is a great choice. Another favorite is the handmade *tagliatelle al funghi e tartufo nero,* which has porcini mushrooms and black truffle oil. Desserts are also made on site: My favorite is the chocolate salami; don't ask, just order and eat.

133 Main St. (across from the post office), Falmouth. (𝓒 **508/540-1616.** Reservations recommended. Main courses $15–$25. MC, V. Wed–Sun 11:30am–2pm and 6–10pm. Open year-round.

Phusion Grille ★★ NEW AMERICAN   This restaurant has a terrific location on Eel Pond in Woods Hole. The interior is all blond wood and Asian screens, but nothing blocks the views of the wraparound floor-to-ceiling windows. The food can be inconsistent here, though it is frequently very good and served by skilled waitstaff. Favorites are filet mignon on a wild-mushroom risotto cake, and diver scallops with fresh herbed pasta. The dessert menu features a very special fresh-fruit strudel. There is live music at Sunday brunch and weekend evenings in summer.

71 Water St., Woods Hole. (𝓒 **508/457-3100.** Reservations not accepted. Main courses $21–$27. AE, MC, V. Tues–Sat 11:30am–2pm; Sun 9am–2pm; daily 5–10pm. Closed mid-Oct to mid-May.

RooBar ★★★ NEW AMERICAN   RooBar is the top restaurant in town for service, food, and atmosphere. With handblown glass lamps over the bar and metal sconce sculptures on the walls, it's an arty and hip setting. The food is exceptionally yummy, if pricey. Creative appetizers include Thai wontons with ginger chicken and a crispy tuna stick with a spicy dipping sauce. Good main-course choices include the snapper pie, which is a braised snapper in a puff pastry, and coriander-crusted day-boat cod with fried coconut polenta. Pizzas ($11–$15) from the wood-fired oven come with unusual toppings like scallops, prosciutto, and beef satay. For dessert, go for the crème brûlée. They don't take reservations, but if you call a half-hour ahead, you can put your name on the waiting list. Two other RooBars in Hyannis and Chatham are under different management but are also worth a visit.

285 Main St. (at Cahoon Court, in the center of town), Falmouth. ✆ **508/548-8600.** Reservations not accepted (but you can call ahead a ¹/₂ hour before arriving to put your name on the list). Main courses $11–$26. AE, MC, V. Wed–Sun 11:30am–3pm; daily 5–10pm; call for off-season hours. Open year-round.

Moderate

The Captain Kidd Bar ★★ (Finds) SEAFOOD/PUB FARE   This atmospheric pub is a good place to come for a drink and a pizza, appetizers, or a light meal. The semiofficial heart of Woods Hole, Captain Kidd really comes into its own once the tourist hordes subside. It's then that the year-round scientists and fishing crews can huddle around the fireplace, congregate on the glassed porch overlooking Eel Pond, or belly up to the hand-carved mahogany bar (thought to date from the early 1800s) and drink to their heart's content. Although the Kidd shares a kitchen with a fancier and more expensive seasonal restaurant next door called **The Waterfront,** the fare at the Kidd is pub grub and some seafood. Homemade clam chowder is thick as paste, with large chunks of potato and clam; stuffed quahogs are piled high, and french fries are the real deal, thickly sliced. Another attraction here is wireless Internet access along with several computers, set up for free Internet use.

77 Water St. (west of the Eel Pond drawbridge), Woods Hole. ✆ **508/548-9206.** www.thecaptainkidd. com. Reservations not accepted. Main courses $15–$20; pizzas $7–$11. AE, MC, V. Daily 11am–4pm and 5–9pm. Pizza served to 11pm in summer. Open year-round.

Chapoquoit Grill ★★ NEW AMERICAN   One of the few worthwhile dining spots in sleepy West Falmouth, this little roadside bistro has Californian aspirations: wood-grilled slabs of fish accompanied by trendy salsas and crispy personal pizzas delivered straight from the brick oven. People drive here from miles around for the flavorful food. A no-reservations policy means long waits nightly in season and weekends year-round.

410 Rte. 28A, West Falmouth. ✆ **508/540-7794.** Reservations not accepted, but patrons can call ahead to be put on a wait list. Main courses $10–$18. MC, V. Daily 5–10pm.

The Flying Bridge ★ (Kids) AMERICAN/CONTINENTAL   Seafood, appropriately enough, predominates at this shipshape harborside megarestaurant (capacity: nearly 600). With three bars tossed into the mix and live music upstairs on weekends, things can get a bit crazy; you'll find comparative peace and quiet—as well as tiptop nautical views—out on the deck. In addition to basic bar food (Buffalo chicken wings and the like), you'll find hefty hunks of protein and fish in many guises, from fish and chips—with optional malt vinegar—to appealing blackboard specials. This is a great place to bring the kids because they'll enjoy wandering onto the attached dock to watch the ducks in the harbor.

220 Scranton Ave. (about ¹/₂ mile south of Main St., on Falmouth Inner Harbor). ✆ **508/548-2700.** www. capecodrestaurants.org. Reservations not accepted. Main courses $8–$20. AE, MC, V. Mid-Apr to mid-Oct daily 11:30am–10pm. Closed mid-Oct to mid-Apr.

Landfall ★★ (Kids) AMERICAN   A terrific harbor setting, Cape Cod-y cuisine, and good service make this Woods Hole seafood restaurant stand out. This is the type of place where you'll see the owner busing tables on busy nights. Besides the usual fish and pasta dishes, there's "lite fare" like burgers and fish and chips for under $15. This is a great place to bring the kids; a children's menu comes with games and crayons. Or come for a drink at the half-dory bar to enjoy this massive wooden building constructed of salvage, both marine and terrestrial. The "ship's knees" on the ceiling are the ribs of an old schooner that broke up on the shores of Cuttyhunk Island; the big stained-glass window came from a mansion on nearby Penzance Point. A large bank of windows looks out onto the harbor, and the Martha's Vineyard ferry, when docking, appears to be making a beeline straight for your table.

2 Luscombe Ave. (¹/₂ block south of Water St.), Woods Hole. © **508/548-1758.** Reservations recommended. Main courses $7–$26. AE, MC, V. Mid-May to Sept daily 11:30am–9:30pm; call for off-season hours. Closed late Nov to mid-Apr.

Laureen's ★ MIDDLE EASTERN/NEW AMERICAN   This attractive cafe, with indoor and outdoor tables in the center of town, is ideal for a quick bite or sip. It specializes in vegetarian and Middle Eastern fare. Try one of the feta pizzas. Everything is available to go, or you can eat here. Service is a little on the leisurely side, so relax into a lengthy and entirely enjoyable meal.

170 Main St. (in the center of town). © **508/540-9104.** Reservations accepted. Main courses $12–$23. AE, MC, V. Daily 8:30am–3pm; Thurs–Sun 5:30–9pm. Open year-round.

Inexpensive

Betsy's Diner ★ (Finds) (Kids) AMERICAN   I once had the best piece of baked scrod ever at this vintage 1950s diner. It was breaded with cornflakes. This is hearty food like your mother used to make, if your mother was a variation of June Cleaver. The menu features turkey dinner, breakfast all day, and homemade soups. Some say the fried clams here are the best in town. Many people come for the large selection of scrumptious homemade pies, which may be the best on Cape Cod. Each red vinyl booth is equipped with its own jukebox with retro hits.

457 Main St. (a couple blocks east of the center of town), Falmouth. © **508/540-0060.** No reservations accepted. All items under $11. AE, MC, V. Mon–Sat 6am–8pm; Sun 6am–2pm; call for off-season hours. Open year-round.

The British Beer Company ★ PUB FARE/PIZZA   The view is great at this faux British pub across the street from Falmouth Heights beach. The food quality, though, is inconsistent. Stick with the fish and chips, and you'll be fine. The lobster bisque is also good and has won local awards. Of course, there is beer, 23 drafts available, like Guinness and John Courage, as well as bottled selections.

263 Grand Ave. (across from the beach), Falmouth Heights. © **508/540-9600.** Reservations not accepted. All items under $15. AE, DC, DISC, MC, V. Daily noon–11:30pm. Open year-round.

The Clam Shack (Kids) SEAFOOD   This classic clam shack sits at the head of Falmouth harbor and offers steaming plates of fried seafood that you carry to a picnic table inside, outside, or up on the roof deck with the best view in town. The food is basic clam-shack fare, but the fish is fresh and you can't beat the view. Kids will love the casual atmosphere and the outdoor dining on the roof deck. Do note that prices are a little higher here than at clam shacks in town without the harbor view.

227 Clinton Ave. (off Scranton Ave. on Falmouth Inner Harbor, about 1 mile south of Main St.), Falmouth. ✆ **508/540-7758.** Reservations not accepted. Main courses $5–$25. No credit cards. Daily 11:30am–7:30pm. Closed early Sept to late May.

Peking Palace ★★ CHINESE/JAPANESE/THAI   This popular, well-kept Chinese restaurant has an extensive menu that includes Japanese and Thai food. There are also three regional Chinese cuisines (Cantonese, Mandarin, and Szechuan), as well as Polynesian. The decor is modern and sophisticated. Sip a fancy drink to give yourself time to take in the menu, and be sure to solicit your server's opinion: That's how I encountered some heavenly spicy chilled squid. This is the only place in town that serves dinner until midnight.

452 Main St. (a few blocks east of the center of town), Falmouth. ✆ **508/540-8204.** Reservations for parties of 6 or more only. Main courses $5–$15. AE, MC, V. Daily 11:30am–midnight. Open year-round.

Quick's Hole ★ SANDWICHES/BURRITOS   Just steps from the Woods Hole ferry terminal, this is a great place for a quick sandwich. Named after a nautical landmark off the Elizabeth Islands nearby, this is high quality fast food—especially the burritos, which are spicy enough to have one patron report, "my eyes are sweating."

Luscombe Ave., Woods Hole. ✆ **508/540-4848.** Reservations not accepted. Main courses $5–$15. Cash only. Daily 11:30am–6:30pm. Closed mid-Oct to April.

Multicultural Dining in Falmouth

Several year-round ethnic restaurants in Falmouth have made choosing where to eat even more fun. **Iriecorna Jamaican Restaurant** ★, 420 E. Falmouth Hwy. (at the corner of Meetinghouse Rd., in the Town and Country Shoppes Plaza), East Falmouth (✆ **508/457-7774**), is a tiny but ambitious Jamaican restaurant. Owner Leroy Lewin welcomes you and aims to please. The food is delicious and well priced. There's jerk chicken and dumplings, whole flounder in a brown stew, and even curried goat. For vegetarians, there's Rasta Pasta with stir-fried veggies and tofu. Main courses range from $11 to $18, and it's open daily from 11am to 9pm. Credit cards are accepted.

If you crave authentic spicy Indian food, head to **Golden Swan Indian Cuisine** ★, 323 Main St. (in the center of town), Falmouth (✆ **508/540-6580**). For better or for worse, this place kept the name, the waitstaff, and most of the decor (including the pilgrim plates on the bathroom doors) of the old Golden Swan, which served 50s-style "Continental cuisine" since the 1970s. But don't be fooled. This is the real thing: curries, lamb stews, and mouthwatering fried breads. A number of delicious vegetarian entrees are also available. You can choose from several different levels of heat; choose the hottest and have a hose ready. Main courses are $9 to $18. Open daily 11:30am to 9pm; reservations and credit cards are accepted.

Bangkok Cuisine Thai Restaurant, 809 Main St. (at the east end of Main St. just west of Falmouth Heights Rd.; ✆ **508/495-3760**), serves delicious Thai cuisine, including all the traditional dishes, like pad thai, mee siam, and various curries. Wash your meal down with a frothy and sweet Thai-style iced tea. Main courses are $9 to $14. Open Monday to Saturday 11am to 3pm and 4 to 9:30pm, Sunday 4 to 9pm. Reservations and credit cards accepted.

Take-Out & Picnic Fare

Cape Cod Bagel Co., 419 Palmer Ave., Falmouth (✆ **508/548-8485**), carries the usual bagel sandwiches, soups, coffee, and other beverages, but the bagels here, made on the premises, are definitely the best in town. Open 6am to 5:30pm. **Box Lunch,** 781 Main St., Falmouth (✆ **508/457-7657**), is one of a number of franchises on the Cape that carry the pita "rollwiches." These are excellent sandwiches (over 50 selections) made fast, and they're perfect for picnics. Open 8am to 6pm. **Steve's Pizzeria & More,** 374 Main St., Falmouth (© **508/457-9454**), has good pizza and subs, and quick service. Open 11am to 11pm.

Coffee & Tea

Coffee Obsession, 110 Palmer Ave. in the Queen's Buyway Shops (© **508/540-2233**), is a hip coffee bar where everyone goes for a cuppa joe. It's open from 6am to 7pm Monday through Saturday and 7am to 6:30pm on Sunday. You'll see slackers, suits, and surfers all lined up for the best coffee in town. **Coffee O.,** as it's known to locals, has a branch in **Woods Hole,** at 38 Water St. (© **508/540-8130**). The Woods Hole location has several computers with Internet access and a play area for children; it's open daily 6:30am to 9pm.

    Molly's Tea Room, 227 Main St. (© **508/457-1666**), is the place to get an authentic cup of tea and a light meal, perhaps a sandwich or a salad. A full case of baked goodies beckons. It's open year-round, daily 11:30am to 8pm.

Sweets

Locals know to get to **Pie in the Sky Dessert Café and Bake Shop,** 10 Water St., Woods Hole (© **508/540-5475**), by 9am for sticky buns, the best anywhere. Those bound for Martha's Vineyard stop at this small bakery near the ferry terminal for treats before hopping on the boat.

    Falmouth residents are the beneficiaries of a struggle for ice-cream bragging rights: **Ben & Bill's Chocolate Emporium** ★, at 209 Main St., in the center of town (© **508/548-7878**), draws crowds even in winter, late into the evening. They come for the homemade ice cream, not to mention the hand-dipped candies showcased in a wraparound display—a chocoholic's nightmare or dream come true, depending. Those who can trust themselves not to go hog-wild might enjoy watching the ice cream being made. Open 9am to 11pm.

    Pies A La Mode, 352 Main St., unit 4, Falmouth (© **508/540-8777**), has delicious homemade ice cream and gelato, a lighter blend than ice cream, as well as wonderful baked goods, including homemade quiches. Open Monday to Saturday 10am to 10pm and Sunday noon to 9pm in season; call for off-season hours.

    There's also **Smitty's Homemade Ice Cream** ★, at 326 E. Falmouth Hwy. (© **508/457-1060**), whose proprietor, the cheerful blond Smitty, is an ice-cream man from central casting.

FALMOUTH AFTER DARK

DRINKS Ever since the close of the famous nightclub The Casino-By-The-Sea in Falmouth Heights, those looking for a fun waterfront drinking establishment have frequented **The Boathouse** (© **508/548-7800**) at 88 Scranton Ave. on Falmouth Inner Harbor. The Boathouse features live bands in season, from classic rock to jazz, and dancing is popular here. Cover for live shows varies; the place is closed September to mid-May.

    Grab a stool at **The British Beer Company** ★, 263 Grand Ave., Falmouth Heights (© **508/540-9600**), and choose from a revolving selection of over 18 drafts from the British Isles as you ponder views of the beach across the street.

    God knows whom you'll meet in the rough-and-tumble old **The Captain Kidd Bar** ★, 77 Water St., in Woods Hole (© **508/548-9206**): maybe a lobsterwoman, maybe a Nobel Prize winner. Good grub, too—see "Where to Dine," earlier.

Everyone heads to **Liam Maguire's Irish Pub** ★, at 273 Main St. in Falmouth (© **508/548-0285**), for a taste of the Emerald Isle. Live music on weekends year-round, often by Liam himself. No cover.

Grumpy's, at 29 Locust St. (© **508/540-3930**), is a good old bar/shack with live music (rock, blues, and jazz) Thursday to Saturday nights. Cover is $2 to $10. Look for free passes on the counter at Coffee Obsession nearby.

The great menu with lots of intriguing appetizers at **RooBar,** 285 Main St., in Falmouth (© **508/548-8600**), draws a hip crowd.

FILM The Upper Cape's only year-round art-house cinema is **Nickelodeon Cinemas,** 742 Rte. 151, East Falmouth (© **508/563-6510**). With six small screens, this is a great alternative to the usual mall movies.

PERFORMANCE Off season, **The Woods Hole Folk Music Society** ★ (© **508/540-0320**) mounts biweekly concerts October through May (first and third Sun of each month), attracting a real grassroots crowd to Community Hall on Water Street, by the Eel Pond drawbridge. General admission is $8; discounts are available for members, seniors, and children.

The **Cape Cod Theatre Project** (© **508/457-4242;** www.capecodtheatreproject.org) is a playwrights' workshop open to the public. These staged play readings are performed for just a few weeks in July, usually at the Woods Hole Community Hall. The play choices tend to be provocative and elicit strong opinions. The rest of the year the talent behind these productions is most likely strutting the boards in New York City. Call for a schedule. Admission is $20.

Starting at about 7:30pm on Thursday evenings in July and August, the spirited volunteers of the **Falmouth Town Band** swing through big-band numbers as small fries (and some oldsters) dance about. Concerts are held at the Band Shell, on Scranton Avenue next to Falmouth Inner Harbor, and are free. On Friday nights in summer **free concerts are held in Peg Noonan Park** on Main Street; you might hear anything from a jazz quartet to a folk singer. On Wednesday nights in summer, also in Peg Noonan Park, there are **free children's movies** shown on a big screen at dusk. Call the Falmouth Chamber of Commerce at © **508/548-8500** for details.

The top talent from college drama departments across the country form the **College Light Opera Company** ★ (© **508/548-0668;** www.collegelightopera.com), which puts on a fast-paced summer repertory from late June through August. So winning is the work of these 32 young actors and 17 musicians (some of them ultimately Broadway-bound) that the house is usually booked solid, so call well ahead or keep your fingers crossed for a scattering of singles. Its venue, the Highfield Theatre, on the Depot Avenue Extension off North Main Street in Falmouth, is a former horse barn and for the past half-century has been a terrific straw-hat theater. Performances are held Tuesday to Saturday at 8pm; there's also a Thursday matinee at 2pm. Tickets are $30.

4 MASHPEE

11 miles SE of Sagamore; 12 miles W of Hyannis

Mashpee is a study in contrasts. This is the location of South Cape Beach State Park, a beautiful stretch of unspoiled coastline on Nantucket South, but the major portion of Mashpee's shoreline has been claimed by the New Seabury Resort development. Further housing developments are rapidly carving up the inland woods, leaving less and less room for the region's original residents, the Mashpee Wampanoags, whose nomadic ancestors began convening in summer camps by these shores millennia ago. In 1660, concerned by the natives' rapid disenfranchisement and heartened by their willingness to convert, missionary Richard Bourne got the Plymouth General Court to grant his "praying Indians" a 10,500-acre "plantation" in perpetuity. The provision proved far from perpetual, as settlers—and much later, developers—began chipping away at the holdings.

After lengthy litigation in the 1970s and early 1980s, the Mashpee Wampanoags—whose tribal roster now numbers about 1,000—were denied tribal status (unlike the Gay Head Wampanoags of Martha's Vineyard) and were stymied in their efforts to preserve the land. It was only in 1995, with the backing of local legislators, that the sizable—5,871 acres—Mashpee National Wildlife Refuge was carved out of the disputed territory.

ESSENTIALS

GETTING THERE   After crossing the Sagamore Bridge, take Route 6 to Exit 2, and Route 130 south. Or you can cross the Bourne Bridge and take Route 28 south about 6 miles to Route 151, which leads to Mashpee. You can also fly into Hyannis (see "Getting There & Getting Around," in chapter 3).

VISITOR INFORMATION   Contact the **Mashpee Chamber of Commerce** at the Cape Cod Five Cent Savings Bank, Mashpee Commons, P.O. Box 1245, Mashpee, MA 02649 (© **508/477-0792;** fax 508/477-5541; www.mashpeechamber.com); or the **Cape Cod Chamber of Commerce.** (See "Visitor Information," in the "Sandwich" section, earlier in this chapter.)

BEACHES & RECREATIONAL PURSUITS

BEACHES   The small part of the shoreline not reserved for the New Seabury Resort is an under-sung sleeper: **South Cape Beach** ★★★, off Great Oak Road (5 miles south of the Mashpee rotary). Mashpee is set amid the 450-acre **South Cape Beach State Park** (© **508/457-0495**). This lengthy stretch of beach has miles of hiking trails. Parking costs $7 per day.

BOATING   Cape Cod Kayak (© **508/563-9377;** www.capecodkayak.com) rents kayaks (free delivery) by the day or week and offers lessons and ecotours on local waterways. Call for a schedule and more information, or see "Beaches & Recreational Pursuits," in the "Falmouth" section, earlier in this chapter.

If you'd rather explore on your own, you can rent a canoe in Falmouth (see the "Falmouth" section, earlier in this chapter) and paddle around the Mashpee River, Popponesset Bay, and Mashpee/Wakeby Pond.

FISHING   **Mashpee/Wakeby Pond** (boat landing off Rte. 130, Fisherman's Dr.) is considered one of the top 10 bass-fishing lakes in the country. Saltwater fishing licenses can be obtained at Sandwich, Falmouth, or Barnstable town halls. South Cape Beach in Mashpee (see "Beaches," above) is a prime spot for surf casting.

NATURE TRAILS   The **Mashpee Conservation Commission** (© **508/539-1414**, ext. 540) sponsors free naturalist-guided nature tours throughout Mashpee from May through December. Call for a schedule. A shady peninsula jutting into the Cape's largest body of fresh water (the adjoining Wakeby/Mashpee Pond), the 135-acre **Lowell Holly Reservation** off South Sandwich Road in the northern corner of the township harbors some 500 holly trees and a number of magnificent centennial beeches. The stewards of this enchanted place, the **Trustees of the Reservation** (© **978/921-1944**), charge $6 per day for the 2-mile trail loop on summer weekends; weekday admission is free. **South Cape Beach State Park** (see "Beaches," above) also offers a network of sandy trails.

WATERSPORTS   The town of Mashpee offers swimming lessons at **Attaquin Park** at Mashpee/Wakeby Pond off Route 130, and also at South Cape Beach; call the **town leisure services department** (© 508/539-1400, ext. 519) for details.

FOR KIDS   The Cape Cod Children's Museum ★, 577 Great Neck Rd. S. (© 508/539-8788; www.capecodchildrensmuseum.org), has a toddler castle and a 30-foot pirate ship, among other kid pleasers. It also sponsors many special events. The museum is open Monday through Saturday 10am to 5pm and Sunday noon to 5pm. Admission is $6 for ages 1 to 59, $5 for seniors.

SHOPPING

Shopping in Mashpee is pretty much limited to the **Mashpee Commons,** at the Mashpee rotary, routes 151 and 28 (© 508/477-5400). Designed to resemble an ideal New England village (right down to the sidewalk measurements, modeled on Woodstock, Vermont), Mashpee Commons is a gussied-up shopping complex with a facadelike feel. This is where you'll find chains like **Gap, Talbots, Banana Republic,** and **Starbucks.** There's also **M. Brann** for retro accessories and the **Signature Gallery** for superb American crafts. For book hounds, there's **Market Street Bookshop,** 20 Steeple St. (© 508/539-6985), a fine independent bookstore. For **movies** playing at Mashpee Commons 6, call © 800/FANDANGO (800/326-3264).

WHERE TO STAY

New Seabury Resort ★★ (Kids)   Only a mere 26 of the 1,600 condos in this 2,300-acre resort are available for vacationers to rent by the night. Those lucky enough to get one of them can enjoy a 3¹/₂-mile private beach on Vineyard Sound. The tastefully decorated condos are clustered into "villages" of varying personalities: Maushop, for instance, with its crushed-shell walkways and clambering roses, is meant to mimic Nantucket. The Popponesset Marketplace with restaurants and gift shops on the premises also sponsors concerts and other family events.

Great Neck Rd. S. (about 4 miles south of the Mashpee rotary), New Seabury, MA 02649. © **800/999-9033** or 508/477-9111. Fax 508/477-9790. www.newseabury.com. 29 units. Summer $330 1-bedroom villa; $498 2-bedroom villa. AE, DC, MC, V. **Amenities:** 5 restaurants (including the Popponesset Inn, an upscale venue popular for weddings; and the congenial Raw Bar with fresh seafood); 2 outdoor pools; 2 18-hole golf courses; 16 all-weather tennis courts; health club; bike trails (w/rentals); miniature golf; scheduled children's activities. *In room:* TV.

WHERE TO DINE
Expensive

Bleu ★★ FRENCH BISTRO   A sophisticated menu awaits diners at Bleu, the funky French bistro at bustling Mashpee Commons. Chef Frederic Feufeu (no kidding) brings a delicacy to dishes such as white-truffle honey-glazed duck breast with mission figs and roasted filet mignon on sautéed potatoes. There are also fish and vegetarian choices. A bistro menu, available all evening, lists less expensive, lighter choices. The wine list offers numerous vintages by the glass and many well-priced choices. As you would expect for a French restaurant, the desserts are especially appealing.

7 Market St., Mashpee Commons (at the intersection of rtes 151 and 28). © **508/539-7907.** www.bleurestaurant.com. Reservations recommended. Main courses $16–$29. AE, MC, V. Mon–Sat 11:30am–4pm and 5–10pm; Sun noon–10pm. Open year-round.

Restaurant Heather ★★★ NEW AMERICAN This first-class restaurant owned and operated by Heather Allen is a contender for the best dining establishment on the Cape. The first surprise is the space, all curving walls and cozy sitting areas. The second surprise is the excellent service, something unusual to find on the Cape. The third and perhaps best surprise is the food: Every dish is a triumph of creativity. The menu varies with the seasons. On the appetizer list in the fall, for example, you might find a creamy and curried pumpkin bisque or a cracked spinach ravioli that gets its melt-in-your mouth flavor from lobster, scallops and boursin cheese. As for main courses, there could be a crispy duckling with a ginger glaze, or a roasted salmon with potato gnocchi. Desserts like the cinnamon and apple cake are all house-made. For those on a budget, Heather does a fabulous $21 three-course prix-fixe menu every night, and on Saturdays from 5 to 6pm.

20 Joy St. (off Rt. 28, in South Cape Village plaza across from Mashpee Commons), Mashpee. **508/539-0025.** Reservations recommended. Main courses $18–$34. AE, MC, V. Tues–Sun 5am–9:30pm. Open year-round.

Trevi Café and Wine Bar MEDITERRANEAN This restaurant brings a dash of European style to the Mashpee Commons open-air mall. The lunch menu features wonderful paninis and salads; dinner offerings, besides salads and sandwiches, come mainly from an interesting *tapas* menu, offering small servings of such delectables as grilled asparagus or homemade buttery pasta in a white-wine and garlic sauce. A few regular-size entrees are available nightly as specials. This is a terrific place to come for either a light bite, perhaps something quick before a movie, or a big meal. The main seating area is a large sunny patio. Inside is taken up mostly by a large bar area where patrons can choose from the extensive wine list or cocktail menu.

25 Market St., Mashpee Commons. **508/477-0055.** Reservations accepted. Main courses $11–$32. MC, V. Daily 11:30am–10pm. Open year-round.

Moderate

Siena Italian Bar and Grill NORTHERN ITALIAN This large, loud, and popular restaurant serves tasty Italian fare next to the movie theater in Mashpee Commons. Specialties include the brick-oven pizzas and the creative pasta dishes. Some find the portions on the small side, but the quality is usually quite good.

11A Steeple St., Mashpee Commons. **508/477-5929.** Reservations accepted. Main courses $9–$26. MC, V. Mon–Sat 11:30am–3:30pm and 5–10pm; Sun noon–9pm. Open year-round.

The Mid Cape

If the Cape had a capital, Hyannis would be it. The Kennedy mystique, peaking with the 1960s Camelot era of John and Jackie, triggered development that over the decades has created a sprawling concrete jungle and has nearly doubled the Cape's year-round population. At over 200,000, the number of people living here year-round is still climbing. The summer population is about three times that, and you'd swear every single person had daily errands to run in Hyannis. That said, this teeming town still has pockets of charm. The waterfront area, where the islands' ferries dock, has been spruced up by the Walkway to the Sea, a path and park area. Main Street in Hyannis, long eclipsed by the megastores along Route 132, is a pleasant place to stroll.

The town of Barnstable, the seat of Cape Cod's Barnstable County government, is made up of eight villages: Hyannis, Hyannisport, Barnstable Village, West Barnstable, Osterville, Centerville, Cotuit, and Marstons Mills. Along the north side of the Cape on Route 6A (the Old King's Hwy.) is Barnstable Village, its compact Main Street anchored by an imposing granite county courthouse. West Barnstable, also on 6A, has a handful of delightful specialty stores and views of acres of salt marsh leading out to Cape Cod Bay. Along the Mid Cape's south coast (off Rte. 28) are Cotuit, Marstons Mills, Osterville, and Centerville, all with gracious residential sections. Osterville has a charming strollable Main Street, and Centerville has Barnstable's best public beach, at Craigville.

While Barnstable is an ideal base from which to explore the rest of the Cape and the islands, there's also fun to be had

nearby. If you are staying in the vicinity of Hyannis, you'll certainly want to head over to the north side of the Cape for a drive along the Old King's Highway, but you'll also want to stroll around Hyannis Harbor, stopping for lunch at Tugboat's or Baxter's, where seagulls will compete for a bite of your lobster roll. You'll find a number of interesting shops and galleries on Main Street in Hyannis (see "Shopping," below), as well as cafes and bars (see "Hyannis & Environs After Dark," later in this chapter).

Some of the finest seaside mansions on the Cape are in the old-money villages of Cotuit, Osterville, Centerville, and Hyannisport. To explore this "Gold Coast" by car, take some detours off Route 28, driving south toward Nantucket Sound. These winding country roads are also good for biking (see "Bicycling," below).

The towns of Yarmouth and Dennis straddle the Mid Cape from north to south, with the northside villages along the historic Old King's Highway and the southside villages along commercialized and overdeveloped Route 28. That's not to say there aren't some very nice enclaves along the south shore. Some of the beaches along this stretch of Nantucket Sound (West Dennis Beach and Parker's River Beach in South Yarmouth) are popular with families, but the villages themselves (Dennisport and South and West Yarmouth) have definitely seen better days. Developers in the last 30 years have gotten carried away. In stark contrast, Yarmouth Port and Dennis Village on the north side are perfect little time capsules, loaded with old-fashioned New England charm, an encyclopedic array of historic homes, galleries, and terrific small shops.

15 miles E of Sagamore; 44 miles S of Provincetown

As the commercial center and transportation hub of the Cape, hyperdeveloped Hyannis—officially a "village"—grossly overshadows the actual seat of town government in the bucolic community of Barnstable. The two locales couldn't be more dissimilar. As peaceful as Hyannis is hectic, the bay area along historic Route 6A unfolds in a blur of greenery and well-kept Colonial houses. It's no wonder many visitors experience "post-Camelot letdown" the first time they venture southward to Hyannis. The downtown area, sapped by the strip development that proliferated at the edges of town after the Cape Cod Mall was built in 1970, is making a valiant comeback, with attractive banners and a pretty public park flanking the wharf where frequent ferries depart for the islands. If you were to confine your visit to this one town, however, you'd get a warped view of the Cape. Along routes 132 and 28, you could be visiting Anywhere, USA: They're lined with the standard chain stores, restaurants, and hotels, and mired with maddening traffic.

Hyannis has more beds and better room rates than anywhere else on the Cape, but there's little rationale for staying right in town or along the highways—unless you happen to have missed the last ferry out to Nantucket. Even elaborate resort facilities can't begin to compensate for the lack of local color.

The best strategy is to stay somewhere peaceful near the edge of town, in one of the moneyed villages, like Hyannisport or Centerville, to the west, or in one of the bayside villages of Barnstable and West Barnstable due north, and just go into Hyannis to sample the restaurants and nightlife. Hyannis and environs can offer plenty of both to suit every palate and personality.

ESSENTIALS

GETTING THERE   After crossing either the Bourne or Sagamore bridge, head east on Route 6 or 6A. The Sagamore Bridge will get you closer to your destination. Route 6A passes through West Barnstable and Barnstable Village; Exit 6 (Rte. 132) off Route 6 leads to Hyannis.

You can fly into Hyannis, and there is good bus service from Boston and New York (see "Getting There & Getting Around," in chapter 3, for more information).

The **Sea Line** (© **800/352-7155**) makes a circuit of Barnstable, Mashpee, and Falmouth, Monday through Saturday, and the fare is a reasonable $1 to $4 (depending on the distance); children 5 and under ride free. The **Hyannis Area Trolley** (© **800/352-7155** or 508/385-1430) covers two loops—the Route 132 malls and the Main Street/waterfront area—every half-hour from 10am to 9pm from late June to early September. Rates are $1 for adults, 50¢ for seniors, and free for children under 6.

VISITOR INFORMATION   For information, contact the **Hyannis Area Chamber of Commerce,** 1481 Rte. 132, Hyannis, MA 02601 (© **877/492-6647** or 508/362-5230; fax 508/362-9499; www.hyannis.com), which is open Monday through Saturday 9am to 5pm, Sunday 10am to 2pm; or the **Cape Cod Chamber of Commerce,** routes 6 and 132 (just off the Exit 6 eastbound ramp), Hyannis, MA 02601 (© **888/332-2732;** fax 508/362-2156; www.capecodchamber.org), open year-round, mid-April to mid-November daily 9am to 5pm; mid-November to mid-April Monday through Saturday 10am to 4pm.

BEACHES   Barnstable's primary bay beach is Sandy Neck Beach, accessed through East Sandwich (see "Beaches & Recreational Pursuits," under "Sandwich," in chapter 5). Most of the Nantucket Sound beaches are fairly protected and thus not big in terms of surf. Beach parking costs $15 a day, usually payable at the lot; for a weeklong parking sticker ($40), visit the Recreation Department at 141 Bassett Lane, at the **Kennedy Memorial Skating Rink** (© 508/790-6345).

- **Craigville Beach ★★★**, off Craigville Beach Road in Centerville: Once a magnet for Methodist "camp" meetings (conference centers still line the shore), this broad expanse of sand boasts lifeguards and restrooms. A destination for the bronzed and buffed, it's known as "Muscle Beach."

- **Kalmus Beach ★★**, off Gosnold Street in Hyannisport: This 800-foot spit of sand stretching toward the mouth of the harbor makes an ideal launching site for windsurfing enthusiasts, who sometimes seem to play chicken with the steady parade of ferries. The surf is tame, the slope shallow, and the conditions ideal for little kids. There are lifeguards, a snack bar, and restrooms.

- **Orrin Keyes Beach ★★** (also known as Sea Beach), at the end of Sea Street in Hyannis: This little beach at the end of a residential road is popular with families.

- **Veterans Beach,** off Ocean Street in Hyannis: A small stretch of harborside sand adjoining the John F. Kennedy Memorial (a moving tribute from the town), this spot is not tops for swimming, unless you're very young and easily wowed. Parking is usually easy, though, and it's walkable from town. The snack bar, restrooms, and playground will see to a family's needs.

BICYCLING   Although there are no paved bike paths in Barnstable (the Rail Trail in Dennis is the closest), the winding roads in Marstons Mills and Osterville make for pleasant scenic rides. There's free public parking at the Marstons Mills millpond at the intersection of routes 28 and 149 or behind the stores in Osterville Center. From the intersection of routes 28 and 149, bear right on Route 149 where it turns into Main Street. Main Street soon intersects with Route 28; cross Route 28 (carefully), and then cruise down South County Road into Osterville. Several roads here afford wonderful bay views, not to mention views of some of the finest homes on Cape Cod. For the best views, bike to the ends of Bay Street, West Bay Road, and Eel River Road to Sea View Avenue. A leisurely bike ride through this area is perhaps the best way to see some of the most impressive seaside mansions on the Cape.

BOATING   You can rent a kayak from Eastern Mountain Sports (see "Watersports," below) for $50 a day or $100 for 3 days and paddle around **Scorton Creek, Sandy Neck,** and **Barnstable Harbor** on the north side of the Cape. On the south side of the Cape, paddlers enjoy the waters around **Great Island** in Osterville. In Centerville, you can navigate the **Centerville River.** For experienced paddlers, **Barnstable's Great Marsh**— one of the largest in New England—offers beautiful waterways out to Sandy Neck.

FISHING   The township of Barnstable has 11 ponds for freshwater fishing; for information and permits, visit **Town Hall** at 367 Main St., Hyannis (© 508/862-4044); or **Sports Port,** 149 W. Main St., Hyannis (© 508/775-3096). Shellfishing permits are available from the **Department of Natural Resources** at 1189 Phinneys Lane, Centerville (© 508/790-6272). Surf-casting, sans license, is permitted on Sandy Neck (see "Beaches & Recreational Pursuits," under "Sandwich," in chapter 5).

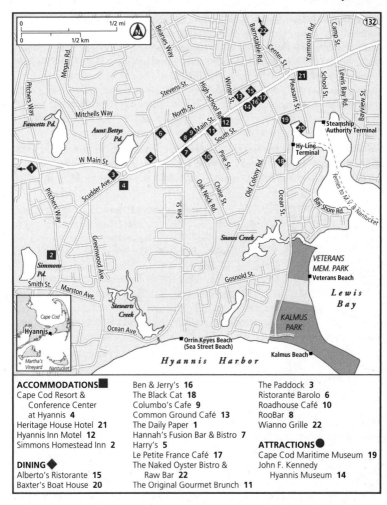

ACCOMMODATIONS
Cape Cod Resort &
    Conference Center
    at Hyannis **4**
Heritage House Hotel **21**
Hyannis Inn Motel **12**
Simmons Homestead Inn **2**

DINING
Alberto's Ristorante **15**
Baxter's Boat House **20**

Ben & Jerry's **16**
The Black Cat **18**
Columbo's Cafe **9**
Common Ground Café **13**
The Daily Paper **1**
Hannah's Fusion Bar & Bistro **7**
Harry's **5**
Le Petite France Café **17**
The Naked Oyster Bistro &
    Raw Bar **22**
The Original Gourmet Brunch **11**

The Paddock **3**
Ristorante Barolo **6**
Roadhouse Café **10**
RooBar **8**
Wianno Grille **22**

ATTRACTIONS
Cape Cod Maritime Museum **19**
John F. Kennedy
    Hyannis Museum **14**

Among the charter boats berthed in **Barnstable Harbor** is the *Drifter* (© 508/398-2061), a 36-foot boat offering half- and full-day trips costing $550 to $775, depending on the length of the trip and the number of people. **Hy-Line Cruises** offers seasonal sonar-aided "bottom" or blues fishing from its Ocean Street dock in Hyannis (© 508/790-0696). The cost for a half-day trip is $31 to $38 per adult, $23 to $33 for kids. **Helen H Deep-Sea Fishing** at 137 Pleasant St., Hyannis (© 508/790-0660), offers year-round expeditions aboard a 100-foot boat with a heated cabin and full galley. Adults pay $34, children $22.

GOLF   Open year-round, the **Hyannis Golf Club,** Route 132 (© 508/362-2606), offers a 46-station driving range, as well as an 18-hole championship course. High-season greens fees are $60. Smaller but scenic, the 9-hole **Cotuit High Ground Country Club** is at 31 Crockers Neck Rd., Cotuit (© **508/428-9863**). An 18-hole round costs $20.

HARBOR CRUISES   For a fun and informative introduction to the harbor and its residents, take a leisurely, 1-hour, narrated tour aboard one of Hy-Line Cruises' 1911 steamer replicas, **MV *Patience*** or **MV *Prudence*.** There are five 1-hour family cruises a day in season, but for a real treat take the Sunday 3pm "Ice Cream Float," which includes a design-your-own Ben & Jerry's ice-cream sundae. Hy-Line Cruises depart from the Ocean Street Dock (© **508/790-0696**; www.hy-linecruises.com), and you should call for a reservation and schedule. Tickets are $16 for adults and free to $8.50 for children 12 and under; 16 departures daily from late June to September; closed November to mid-April. Credit cards are accepted. Parking is $3 per car.

WATERSPORTS   **Eastern Mountain Sports,** 1513 Iyannough Rd./Rte. 132 (© **508/362-8690**; www.ems.com), offers rental kayaks—tents and sleeping bags, too—and sponsors free clinics and walks, like a full-moon hike. Kayaks rent for $50 a day, $100 for 3 days.

WHALE-WATCHING   Although Provincetown is about an hour closer to the whales' preferred feeding grounds, it would take you at least an hour (possibly hours on a summer weekend) to drive all the way down-Cape. If your time and itinerary are limited, hop aboard **Hyannis Whale Watcher Cruises,** Barnstable Harbor (about ¹/₂ mile north of Rte. 6A on Mill Way), Barnstable (© **888/942-5392** or 508/362-6088; fax 508/362-9739; www.whales.net), for a 4-hour voyage on a 100-foot high-speed cruiser. Naturalists provide the narration, and should you fail to spot a whale, your next trek is free. Tickets cost $45 for adults, $40 for seniors (62 and older), and $26 for children 4 to 12 from April through mid-October; call for a schedule and off-season rates. No trips mid-October through March.

BASEBALL

The two locally based Cape Cod Baseball League elite amateur teams are the **Hyannis Mets** (who play at McKeon Field on Old Colony Blvd.) and the **Cotuit Kettleers** (Lowell Park). For a schedule, contact the **Hyannis Area Chamber of Commerce** (© **508/362-5230**) or the **Barnstable Recreation Department** (© **508/790-6345**).

KID STUFF

The **Lightning Falls** minigolf course, 455 W. Main St. (© **508/771-3194**), offers a nice diversion for young children or for the young at heart. A round costs $6.50 for adults, $5.50 for children. Open in season 10am to 11pm. About a mile north, off Route 132, the **Cape Cod Potato Chips factory** on Breed's Hill Road at Independence Drive (© **508/775-7253**) offers free quickie tours that end with a tasting. Tours are held in July and August, Monday to Friday from 9am to 5pm. Call for off-season hours. On Wednesday mornings in summer, the **Cape Cod Melody Tent** at the West End rotary (© **508/775-5630**; www.melodytent.com) offers children's theater productions. Tickets are $8 and can be ordered from **Ticketmaster** (© **800/347-0808**; www.ticketmaster.com).

SHOPPING

Although Hyannis is undoubtedly the commercial center of the Cape, the stores you'll find there are fairly standard for the most part; you could probably find their ilk anywhere else in the country. It's in the wealthy enclaves west of Hyannis, and along the antiquated Old King's Highway (Rte. 6A) to the north, that you're likely to find the real gems. On weekends from late May to mid June, and daily from mid-June through September, arts enthusiasts may want to visit **Harbor Your Arts** ★, Ocean Street (along Hyannis Harbor; www.harboryourarts.com). In its seven artists' shacks, you can watch the artists at work and buy directly from them.

ANTIQUES/COLLECTIBLES Of the hundreds of antiques shops scattered through the region, perhaps a dozen qualify as destinations for well-schooled collectors. **Harden Studios,** 3264 Rte. 6A (in the center of town), Barnstable Village (© **508/362-7711**), is one. Owner Charles M. Harden used to supply to-the-trade-only dealers in the Boston Design Center. An architect by training, he renovated this antique house, built around 1720, to display his finds. Some items, such as primitive portraits and mourning embroidery, are all but extinct outside of museums. Other sturdy, serviceable pieces, such as Colonial corner cabinets and slant-top desks, are competitively priced, as are the antique Oriental carpets underfoot. An adjoining barn gallery features nature-centered works by area artists, including Harden's son, an accomplished etcher.

ARTS & CRAFTS The caliber of the shows at the **Cape Cod Art Association (CCAA),** 3480 Rte. 6A (about ⅓ mile west of Hyannis Rd.), Barnstable (© **508/362-2909**), may vary—this is, after all, a nonprofit community venture—but it's worth visiting just to see the skylit studios, designed by CCAA member Richard Sears Gallagher in 1972. Everyone raves about "Cape light," and here you'll see it used to optimal advantage. If the setting fires up artistic yearnings, inquire about classes and workshops, which are held year-round.

Ex-Nantucketer Bob Marks fashions the only authentic Nantucket lightship baskets crafted off-island; and as aficionados know, they don't come cheap (a mere handbag typically runs in the thousands). The other handmade furnishings found at **Oak and Ivory,** 1112 Main St. (about 1 mile south of Rte. 28), Osterville (© **508/428-9425**), from woven throw rugs to pared-down neo-shaker furniture, fit the country-chic mode at more approachable prices.

At 374 Main St. in Hyannis, **Red Fish, Blue Fish** (© **508/775-8700**) wins the funky-gallery award, hands down. Owner Jane Walsh makes jewelry in the front window, but inside this closetlike space, every inch is covered with something unusual and handmade. There is usually a teenager or two hanging out here.

Tao Water Art Gallery, 1989 Rte. 6A, West Barnstable (© **508/375-0428**), is a former garage converted into a very Zen-like space. It features paintings by Chinese artists as well as museum reproductions of Chinese antiques and jade.

Richard Kiusalas and Steven Whittlesey salvage antique lumber and turn it into cupboards, tables, and chairs, among other things; old windows are retrofitted as mirrors. Most of the stock at **West Barnstable Tables,** 2454 Meetinghouse Way (off Rte. 149 near the intersection of Rte. 6A), West Barnstable (© **508/362-2676**), looks freshly made, albeit with wood of unusually high quality. Pieces are priced accordingly: A dining-room set—pine trestle table with six bow-back chairs—runs more than $4,000. When the wood still bears interesting traces of its former life, it's turned into folk-art furniture.

BOOKS & EPHEMERA Named for the revolutionary printer who helped foment the War of Independence, **Isaiah Thomas Books & Prints,** 4632 Falmouth Rd. (Rte. 28, near Rte. 130), Cotuit (© **508/428-2752**), has a 60,000-volume collection, housed in an 1850 home. The shop is full of treasures, clustered by topic. Owner/expert James S.

Camelot on Cape Cod: The Kennedys in Hyannisport

It's been more than 40 years since those days of Camelot, when JFK was in the White House and America seemed rejuvenated by the Kennedy style, but the Kennedy sites on Cape Cod still attract record numbers of visitors every summer. In July 1999, when John Jr.'s plane crashed into Vineyard Sound, thousands visited the Kennedy Hyannis Museum to mourn the loss by viewing classic photos of the family in Hyannisport.

Images of Jack Kennedy sailing his jaunty *Wianno Senior* on Nantucket Sound off Hyannisport form part of this nation's collective memory. The vacationing JFK was all tousled hair, toothy grin, earthy charisma, and attractive *joie de vivre*. Remember Jackie sitting beside him, wearing a patterned silk scarf around her head and looking like she'd rather be in Newport, where no one had ever heard of touch football?

The Kennedys always knew how to have fun, and they had it in Hyannisport. And ever since Hyannisport became JFK's summer White House, Cape Cod has been inextricably linked to the Kennedy clan. Although the Kennedys spend time elsewhere—working in Washington or wintering in Palm Beach—when they go home, they go to Cape Cod. Generations of Kennedys have sailed these waters, sunned on these beaches, patronized local businesses, and generally had a high old time.

Meanwhile, much has changed since the early 1960s on Cape Cod, especially in the Mid Cape area. In those 40-plus years, the mall was built in Hyannis, and urban sprawl infested routes 132 and 28. Yet much, thankfully, remains the same. The Kennedy compound, with its large, gabled Dutch Colonial houses, still commands the end of Scudder Avenue in Hyannisport. Nearby is the private Hyannisport Golf Club, where Rose loved to play a short round on the foggy oceanfront course. The beaches here are still pristine.

To bask in the Kennedys' Cape Cod experience, visit the **John F. Kennedy Hyannis Museum,** 397 Main St., Hyannis (© **508/790-3077**). Admission is $5

Visbeck is happy to show off his first editions, rare miniatures, and maps; you get the sense that sales are secondary to sheer bibliophilic pleasure.

You should be able to find just about any book you're looking for at the big chain bookstores, **Borders,** 990 Iyannough Rd. (Rte. 132), Hyannis (© **508/862-6363**); and **Barnes & Noble,** 769 Iyannough Rd. (at the Cape Cod Mall on Rte. 132), Hyannis (© **508/862-6310**).

FOOD   Cape Cod Potato Chips, Breed's Hill Road (at Independence Way, off Rte. 132), Hyannis (© **508/775-7253**), really are the world's best. Long a local favorite—they're chunkier than the norm—they originate right here. Free factory tours are offered Monday to Friday from 9am to 5pm in July and August. Call for off-season hours.

HOME DECOR   As a Nantucket innkeeper whiling away the winter, Claire Murray took up hooking rugs and turned her knack into an international business. At **Claire**

for adults, $2.50 for children 10 to 16, and $3 for seniors, and hours are from mid-April through October Monday to Saturday 9am to 5pm and Sunday and holidays from noon to 5pm. Last admission is at 3:30pm. Call for off-season hours. The museum shows a documentary on Kennedy narrated by Walter Cronkite and contains several rooms' worth of photos of the Kennedys on Cape Cod. The candid shots included in this permanent display capture some of the quieter moments, as well as JFK's legendary charm. Most of us have seen some of these photos before, but here they are all blown up, mounted, and neatly labeled; if you get confused about lineage, consult the family tree on the wall at the end of the exhibit. The last 3 years of JFK's life were a bit chaotic (some 25,000 well-wishers thronged the roads when the senator and president-to-be returned from the 1960 Democratic Convention), but he continued to treasure the Cape as "the one place I can think and be alone."

Busloads of tourists visit the **Kennedy Memorial** just above Veterans Beach on Ocean Avenue; it's a moving tribute, beautifully maintained by the town, but crowds in season can be distracting. Finally, you may want to drive by the simple white clapboard church, St. Francis Xavier, on South Street; Rose attended Mass daily, and Caroline Kennedy and several other cousins got married here.

Spend your day in the Mid Cape recreating like a privileged Kennedy scion. Rent a windsurfer at Kalmus Beach. Play a round of golf at the **Hyannis Golf Club** (© **508/362-2606**), a public course on Route 132. **Four Seas Ice Cream** (© **508/775-1394**), at 360 S. Main St. in Centerville, is a must. For lodging right in Hyannisport, stay at **Simmons Homestead Inn,** 288 Scudder Ave., Hyannisport (© **800/637-1649** or 508/778-4999).

Rose Kennedy once told a reporter, "Our family would rather be in Hyannisport in the summer than anyplace else in the world." And yours?

Murray, 867 Main St. (in the center of town), Osterville (© **508/420-3562**), and at her store at 770 Rte. 6A in West Barnstable (© **508/375-0331**), hobbyists can find all the fixings for various needle crafts, including kits, and advice as needed. Those of us with little time on our hands can just buy the finished goods, from sweaters and quilts to the signature folk-motif rugs.

Flowery pastels are the hallmark of **Joan Peters,** 885 Main St. (in the center of town), Osterville (© **508/428-3418**), favored by the *Town & Country* set. She designs a wide array of compatible fabrics and ceramics—right down to the bathroom sink, if need be—so that it's easy to achieve a pervasive, light-splashed look that doesn't look too overtly matched and mixed.

SEAFOOD   The best place to buy fresh seafood in the vicinity of Hyannis is **Cape Fish & Lobster** at 406 W. Main St. in Centerville (© **508/771-1122**). This is where the top restaurateurs in Hyannis get their seafood. The prices are reasonable, and the catch is the freshest in town.

A MARITIME MUSEUM

The **Cape Cod Maritime Museum** at 135 South St. in Hyannis, on the eastern end of Aselton Park (© **508/775-1723;** www.capecodmaritimemuseum.org) is small but interesting. The museum displays artifacts from ships that wrecked off the shore of Cape Cod and exhibits a collection of items from the United States Lifesaving Service, the precursor to the Coast Guard. The museum is open Monday through Saturday 10am to 4pm, Sunday noon to 4pm. Admission is $5 for adults, $4 for students and seniors, free for children 6 and under.

WHERE TO STAY
In Hyannis, Hyannisport & Craigville

There are a variety of large, generic but convenient hotels and motels in Hyannis.

Heritage House Hotel, 259 Main St. (in the center of town), Hyannis (© **800/352-7189** or 508/775-7000; www.heritagehousehotel.com), is ideally located on Main Street, walking distance from restaurants, shops, and the ferries to Nantucket and Martha's Vineyard. There is an indoor and an outdoor pool, hot tub and saunas, and a restaurant/lounge on-site. During the high season, the 143 rooms are priced at $139 on weekdays and $209 on weekends for double occupancy.

Also centrally located on Main Street within strolling distance of restaurants, shopping, and the ferries is the 77-room **Hyannis Inn Motel,** 473 Main St., Hyannis (© **800/922-8993** or 508/775-0255; www.hyannisinn.com). Summer rates are $147 to $154 double—a real value. During the Kennedy administration, this motel served as the press headquarters. It has an indoor pool, a breakfast restaurant (not included with room rates), and a cocktail lounge. Closed late October to mid-March.

If you prefer more amenities, there's the **Cape Cod Resort and Conference Center at Hyannis** at the West End Circle just off Main Street (© **508/775-7775;** www.capecod resortandconference.com). Summer rates are $200 to $230 double. Out the back door is an 18-hole, par-3 executive golf course. There are also an indoor and an outdoor pool, two restaurants, and a fitness center.

A great choice for families is the **Cape Codder Resort & Spa,** 1225 Iyannough Rd./Rte. 132 (at the intersection of Bearse's Way), Hyannis (© **888/297-2200** or 508/771-3000; www.capecodderresort.com). It features two restaurants (Grand Cru Wine Bar and Hearth 'n Kettle for families), and a spa (massage and other body treatments). Kids love the indoor wave pool with two water slides. Summer rates in the 261 rooms are $199 to $247 double, $369 to $382 suite. Rooms have all the usual amenities, plus high-speed Internet access and Nintendo.

Moderate
Simmons Homestead Inn ★★ (Finds) The first things passers-by notice are all the classic red sports cars: 56 at last count. A former ad exec and race-car driver, innkeeper Bill Putman likes to collect. He's made his sports-car collection into a small museum open to the public (admission: $8 adults, $4 children 10 to 16; free for inn guests) called **Toad Hall,** from *The Wind in the Willows.* Inside the inn is his animal collection. The stuffed toys, sculptures, needlepoint, and wallpaper differentiate the rather traditional rooms in this rambling 1820s captain's manse. This is an inn where you'll find everyone around the hearth sipping complimentary wine (served at "6-ish") while they compare

notes and nail down dinner plans. To help his guests plan their days and evenings, Putman **123**
has typed up extensive notes on day trips (including the islands), bike routes (he supplies
the bikes), and his own quirky restaurant reviews. Guests who prefer privacy may book the
spiffily updated "servants' quarters," a spacious, airy wing with its own private deck. Rooms
vary in size, but all are decorated with comfort and a sense of humor in mind. Four ham-
mocks swing from trees in the shady backyard of this homey establishment.

288 Scudder Ave. (about 1/4 mile west of the West End rotary), Hyannisport, MA 02647. © **800/637-1649**
or 508/778-4999. Fax 508/790-1342. www.simmonshomesteadinn.com. 14 units. Summer $210–$260
double; $350 2-bedroom suite. Rates include full breakfast. AE, DISC, MC, V. Dogs welcome. **Amenities:**
Bikes; billiards parlor. In room: AC ($10/night charge), hair dryer, iron, no phone.

In Barnstable & West Barnstable

To check on availability at 17 bed-and-breakfasts along Route 6A, check out www.historic
capecodbay.com.

Moderate

The Acworth Inn   Anyone looking to avoid the excess of Victorian furnishings in
many B&Bs will delight in the simple, fresh, immaculate decor here. A couple of rooms
have extra amenities like TVs, minifridges, and whirlpool baths. Two rooms in the carriage house have been combined into a romantic luxury suite with whirlpool bath, TV/
VCR, working fireplace, air-conditioning, and minifridge. The three-course breakfasts
include such favorites as cranberry pie, quiches, and stuffed French toast. The inn is close
to Barnstable Village and popular Cape Cod Bay beaches, so the complimentary bikes
may be all you need in the way of wheels.

4352 Rte. 6A/Old King's Hwy. (near the Yarmouth Port border), Cummaquid, MA 02637. © **800/362-
6363** or 508/362-3330. Fax 508/375-0304. www.acworthinn.com. 5 units. Summer $145–$165 double;
$210 suite. Rates include full breakfast. AE, DISC, MC, V. Open year-round. **Amenities:** Bikes. In room: A/C,
hair dryer, iron, no phone.

Ashley Manor Inn   A lovely country inn along the Old King's Highway, this house
is a much-modified 1699 Colonial mansion that retains many of its original features,
including a hearth with beehive oven, built-in corner cupboards in the wainscoted dining
room, and wide-board floors, many of them brightened with Nantucket-style splatter
paint. The rooms, all but one of which boast a working fireplace, are spacious and inviting: true retreats. A deluxe room in its own wing has a separate entrance, whirlpool bath,
glass-enclosed shower, canopy bed, and fireplace. All bathrooms are supplied with luxury
towels of 100% Egyptian cotton. The 2-acre property itself is shielded from the road by
an enormous privet hedge, and fragrant boxwood camouflages a Har-Tru tennis court.
(You'll find loaner bikes beside it, ready to roll.) Romantics can sequester themselves in
the flower-fringed gazebo. Breakfast on the brick patio is worth waking up for.

3660 Rte. 6A (just east of Hyannis Rd.), Barnstable, MA 02630. © **888/535-2246** or 508/362-8044. Fax
508/362-9927. www.ashleymanor.net. 6 units. Summer $175 double; $235 suite. Rates include full breakfast. AE, DISC, MC, V. No children under 14. **Amenities:** Har-Tru tennis court; bikes. In room: A/C, TV, coffeemaker, hair dryer.

Beechwood Inn ★★ (Finds)   Look for a butterscotch-colored 1853 Queen Anne
Victorian all but enshrouded in weeping beech trees. Admirers of late-19th-century decor
are in for a treat: The interior remains dark and rich, with a red-velvet parlor and tin
ceilings in the dining room where innkeeper Debbie Traugot serves a three-course breakfast featuring home-baked delights such as applesauce pancakes and raspberry bread. Two
of the upstairs bedrooms embody distinctive period styles: The Cottage Room contains

furniture painted in an 1860s mode, and the Eastlake Room is modeled on the aesthetic precepts of William Morris that flourished in the 1880s. Each affords a distant view of the sparkling bay. All rooms have Sealy Posturepedic Plush mattresses. Rooms range from quite spacious (Lilac) to romantically snug (Garret); some have a fireplace and TV/VCR. The Traugots breed golden retrievers and guests are free to play with puppies, if they so desire.

2839 Rte. 6A (about 1½ miles east of Rte. 132), Barnstable, MA 02630. ✆ **800/609-6618** or 508/362-6618. Fax 508/362-0298. www.beechwoodinn.com. 6 units, 4 with tub/shower, 2 with shower only. Summer $185–$210 double. Rates include full breakfast. AE, DISC, MC, V. No children under 12. *In room:* A/C, TV/VCR, Wi-Fi, fridge, hair dryer, no phone.

Lamb and Lion Inn ★ This is an unusual property: part B&B, part motel. From the roadside, it's one of those charming old Cape Cod cottages (ca. 1740) along the Old King's Highway (where charming "Capes" are ubiquitous), set up on a knoll with a sloping lawn full of colorful flowers. Inside, it's a motel-like space with units encircling a pool and hot tub. The rooms are all individually decorated, and six rooms have kitchenettes. All rooms in the main inn building are air-conditioned. The multilevel barn suite, with three loft-type bedrooms, is a funky historic space (built in 1740), filled with rustic nooks and crannies. There's also an outdoor shower, a true Cape Cod tradition.

2504 Main St. (Rte. 6A), Barnstable, MA 02630. ✆ **800/909-6923** or 508/362-6823. Fax 508/362-0227. www.lambandlion.com. 10 units, 6 with tub/shower, 4 with shower only. Summer $189–$275 double. Rates include continental breakfast. MC, V. Well-behaved pets allowed (40-lb. limit). **Amenities:** Pool; hot tub. *In room:* A/C, TV.

WHERE TO DINE
In Hyannis
Expensive
Alberto's Ristorante ★★ ITALIAN Alberto's explores the full range of Italian cuisine, with a classicist's attention to components and composition. Owner/chef Felisberto Barreiro's most popular dishes are his treatments of lobster, rack of lamb, and beef tenderloin. Hand-cut pasta is also a specialty, including the ultrarich seafood ravioli cloaked in saffron-cream sauce. Though the atmosphere is elegant, with sconces shedding a warm glow over well-spaced, linen-draped tables, it is not one of hushed reverence: People clearly come here to have a good time, and the friendly service and fabulous food ensure that they do. Locals who appreciate a bargain know to come between 3 and 6pm, when a full dinner, with soup, salad, and dessert, costs as little as $10 to $15. There's live jazz or piano music daily year-round.

360 Main St., Hyannis. ✆ **508/778-1770.** Reservations recommended. Main courses $11–$27. AE, DC, DISC, MC, V. Daily 11:30am–11pm. Open year-round.

The Black Cat ★ NEW AMERICAN Conveniently located on Hyannis Harbor less than a block from the Hy-Line ferries, this is a fine place to catch a quick bite or full meal while you wait for your boat to come in. The menu is pretty basic—steak, pasta, and, of course, fish—but attention is paid to the details; the onion rings, for instance, are made fresh. The dining room, with its bar of gleaming mahogany and brass, will appeal to chilled travelers on a blustery day; in fine weather, you might prefer the porch. There's live jazz on the weekends in season.

165 Ocean St. (opposite the Ocean St. Dock), Hyannis. ✆ **508/778-1233.** Reservations not accepted. Main courses $15–$29. AE, DC, DISC, MC, V. Apr–Oct daily 11:30am–9pm; call for off-season hours. Closed Jan.

Hannah's Fusion Bar and Bistro ★ INTERNATIONAL/ASIAN   After serving as chef at the RooBar and starting the restaurant Phusion, both in Falmouth, Chef Binh Phu has created a following for his innovative cuisine. A labor of love for this Vietnamese native, Hannah's is a showcase for his genius at blending ingredients. For example, main courses might include Mongolian coffee–encrusted pork tenderloin or pan-seared ginger and lemon grass-marinated Atlantic salmon. There's also a special sushi menu. His all-chocolate dessert menu features delicacies like Key lime pie with a chocolate trellis. Those who catch the early-bird menu (5–6:30pm) get a choice of soup or appetizer, choice of main course, plus dessert for $20.

615 Main St., Hyannis (the west end of town). ✆ 508/778-5565. Reservations recommended. Main courses $18–$30. AE, DC, DISC, MC, V. Apr–Oct daily 5–10pm; call for off-season hours. Open year-round.

The Naked Oyster Bistro and Raw Bar ★ NEW AMERICAN   Overlook the fact that this fun bistro restaurant is located in an office complex and enjoy the experience. The specialty here is fresh local seafood, and oyster fans will be fascinated by the selection of "dressed oysters," from the traditional Rockefeller to a more exotic baked *oishi* with wasabi and soy. The main courses feature spicy options like sautéed Thai shrimp and blackened Cajun swordfish, as well as hearty dishes like grilled filet mignon with garlic mashed potatoes. Portions are large and service is professional and cheerful. In the evenings, there is a young-professionals bar scene here, and some say the bartenders serve the best martinis in town.

20 Independence Dr. (just off Rte. 132 at Park Place), Hyannis. ✆ 508/778-6500. Reservations accepted. Main courses $14–$24. AE, MC, V. June–Aug daily 4–9:30pm; Sept–May Mon–Fri 11:30am–3pm, daily 4–9:30pm. Open year-round.

The Paddock ★★ CONTINENTAL   In the more than 3 decades The Paddock has been open, it has maintained a solid reputation in the community with consistently good food and service. The dining room is candlelit and romantic; on clear nights, you can sit on the plant-filled summer porch. The menu combines creative options with traditional choices (you can still order extra béarnaise sauce on the side). For appetizers, there's chicken-liver pâté, but also polenta crab cakes with chipotle-chili cream and sweet mango salsa. Main courses include filet mignon—yes, this is the place to come for steak in the Mid Cape—and sesame-encrusted yellowfin tuna served rare with Asian greens. The 300-bottle wine list has received awards from *Wine Spectator* for years. There is free valet parking, and a pianist entertains nightly in the pub area. Because the Cape Cod Melody Tent is right next door, you'll need to go early or after 9pm to avoid the crowds if an act is playing. *Note:* Those attending a Melody Tent performance can leave their car in The Paddock lot during the performance if they eat here first.

West End rotary (at the intersection of W. Main and Main sts.), Hyannis. ✆ 508/775-7677. www.paddockcapecod.com. Reservations recommended. Main courses lunch $7–$13, dinner $17–$28. AE, DC, DISC, MC, V. Apr to mid-Nov Mon–Sat 11:30am–2:30pm and 5–10pm, Sun noon–8:45pm. Closed mid-Nov to Mar.

Ristorante Barolo ★★ NORTHERN ITALIAN   This is the best Italian restaurant in town. Part of a smart-looking brick office complex, this thoroughly up-to-date establishment does everything right, from offering extra-virgin olive oil in which to dunk its crusty bread to getting those pastas perfectly al dente. Appetizers perfect for sharing are *Polpette Gartinate alla Romana* (homemade meatballs in a tomato-and-basil sauce) and *Gamberi al Martini* (shrimp sautéed with fresh scallions and martini-wine sauce). Entrees include a number of tempting veal choices, like *Vitello alla Sorrentina* (Provimi-brand veal, mozzarella, and basil with plum-tomato sauce), as well as such favorites as *Linguine al Frutti di Mare,* with littlenecks, mussels, shrimp, and calamari. The desserts are brought in daily from Boston's famed North End.

1 Financial Place (297 North St., just off the West End rotary), Hyannis. © 508/778-2878. Reservations recommended. Main courses $10–$27. AE, DC, MC, V. June–Sept Sun–Thurs 4:30–10:30pm, Fri–Sat 4:30–11pm; call for off-season hours. Open year-round.

Roadhouse Café ★★ AMERICAN/NORTHERN ITALIAN This is neither a roadhouse nor a cafe, but it is a solid entry in the Hyannis dining scene. The extensive menu is pretty much split between American standards such as steak (not to mention oysters Rockefeller or casino) and real Italian cooking, unstinting on the garlic. A less expensive, lighter-fare menu, including what some have called "the best burger in the world," is served in the snazzy bistro in back. Among the appetizers are such delicacies as beef carpaccio with fresh-shaved Parmesan, and vine-ripened tomatoes and buffalo mozzarella drizzled with balsamic vinaigrette. The vinaigrette also makes a tasty marinade for native swordfish headed for the grill. The signature dessert, a distinctly non-Italian cheesecake infused with Baileys Irish Cream, is a must-try. Music lovers know to come on Monday nights for the live jazz in the bistro (see "Hyannis & Environs After Dark," below).

488 South St. (off Main St., near the West End rotary), Hyannis. © 508/775-2386. Reservations recommended. Main courses $15–$26. AE, DC, DISC, MC, V. Daily 4–9:30pm. Open year-round.

RooBar ★ BISTRO This stylish bistro is one of the few truly hip spots in Hyannis. You may want to sit at the bar and have a few appetizers like the chicken pot sticker (pan-seared wonton wrappers filled with an Asian chicken-and-vegetable stuffing with an orange marmalade dipping sauce) or a simple plate of oysters on the half-shell. There's also a selection of delicious gourmet pizzas (see "Hyannis & Environs After Dark," below).

586 Main St., Hyannis. © 508/778-6515. Reservations recommended. Main courses $9–$25. AE, DC, MC, V. Daily 5–10pm. Open year-round.

Wianno Grille ★ PUB/SEAFOOD When you're in the mood for a nothing-fancy meal in sleek surroundings, this new restaurant near the Barnstable Airport may be just the ticket. Calling itself an "upscale pub," the Wianno Grille offers straightforward fare like fish and chips, burgers, sandwiches, and salads, as well as heartier dishes such as barbecue ribs, sirloin, and lamb chops. The main floor has an almost-room-length bar and cozy booths. Downstairs you'll find larger tables more suitable for families. Sunday brunch is popular here.

380 Barnstable Rd., Hyannis (Staples Plaza, just off the airport rotary). © 508/778-5587. Reservations accepted. Main courses $8–$25. AE, MC, V. Daily 11:30am–10pm. Open year-round.

Moderate

Columbo's Café ★ ITALIAN This traditional Italian café was opened in recent years by Dave Columbo, who owns the Roadhouse Café nearby. The place to go for old-fashioned Italian food like you would find in Boston's Old North End, this restaurant fills a gap for a style of cuisine that is not found too often in these parts. Forget nouvelle cuisine and twirl some of this hearty pasta around a fork and dig in.

544 Main St. (on the west end of town), Hyannis. © 508/790-5700. Reservations not accepted. Main courses $12–$22. MC, V. Daily 5–10pm. Open year-round.

Harry's ★ CAJUN Seemingly transported from the French Quarter, this small restaurant/bar—park benches serve as booths—has added some Italian and French options to its menu, but it's the authentic Cajun cooking that keeps customers coming back: baby back ribs, jambalaya, hoppin' johns, red beans, and rice. On the weekends, get set for a heaping serving of R&B (see "Hyannis & Environs After Dark," below). This place hops until 1am. *Tip:* Arrive for a late dinner around 8:30pm and you'll have yourself a great table once the music starts.

700 Main St. (at Stevens St., near the West End rotary), Hyannis. (C) **508/778-4188.** Reservations not accepted. Main courses $10–$19. MC, V. Daily for food service 11:30am–10pm, bar until 1am. Open year-round.

Inexpensive

Baxter's Boat House ★ (Value) (Kids) SEAFOOD   A shingled shack on a jetty jutting out into the harbor, Baxter's has catered to the boating crowd since the mid-1950s with Cape classics such as fried clams and fish virtually any way you like it, from baked to blackened, served on paper plates at picnic tables. This is a good place to bring a brood of kids. If you sit out on the deck, be wary of swooping seagulls looking to spirit away your lunch.

177 Pleasant St. (near the Steamship Authority ferry), Hyannis. (C) **508/775-7040.** Main courses $8–$14. AE, MC, V. Late May to early Sept daily 11:30am–9pm; hours may vary at the beginning and end of the season. Closed mid-Oct to early Apr.

Common Ground Cafe ★ (Value) AMERICAN   Talk about an out-of-body experience: Step off Main Street Hyannis into this New Age-y sandwich shop run by a commune. The barn-board walls and wide-plank floors surround alcoves with private booths containing amorphous tree-stump tables. You can see straight up to the second-floor juice-and-smoothie bar, where they also sell some health and beauty products. But enough about atmosphere; this place makes the best iced tea on Cape Cod (the house blend is a mixture of mint teas and lemon). Everything is made from scratch here. The sandwiches and salads are, as you'd expect, wholesome and delicious. They also have some south-of-the-border choices: The burrito with turkey is a winner. If I understand correctly from their literature (available at the door), the "Common Ground" is love. Count me in.

420 Main St., Hyannis. (C) **508/778-8390.** Most items under $6. AE, DC, DISC, MC, V. Mon–Thurs 10am–9pm; Fri and Sun 10am–3pm. Closed Sat. Open year-round.

The Daily Paper ★ (Value) DINER   The newest diner in town has all the expected accoutrements, like red banquets and a long diner counter with plenty of swivel stools, but there is also excellent grub here, including what one diner called, "the best toast I've ever had." Breakfast is served until 11:30am Monday through Saturday and all day on Sunday. There is also a kids menu.

644 West Main St., Hyannis. (C) **508/790-8800.** Most items under $10. MC, V. Mon–Sat 6am–2pm; Sun 7am–1pm.

The Original Gourmet Brunch ★ (Finds) AMERICAN   Though the name feels very 1970s, this classic breakfast joint hearkens back to the 1950s, when small, quirky family-owned restaurants were all that Cape Cod had to offer. When you travel the narrow red brick path off Main Street into this humble low-ceilinged establishment, you may first notice the oddly slanted floors. Next you'll see the walls covered with autographed photos of celebrities that have rubbed elbows with owner Joe Cotellessa, the man who probably seated you. The menu offers over 100 combinations of omelets, from peanut butter and jelly to bacon and asparagus. There are also Belgian waffles, quiche, and award-winning chili.

517 Main St., Hyannis. (C) **508/771-2558.** Reservations not accepted. All items under $11. MC, V. Daily 7am–2pm. Open year-round.

La Petite France Cafe, 349 Main St., Hyannis, in the center of town (© **508/775-1067**), serves scrumptious croissants, breads, and pastries, all baked on-site. For lunch, there are homemade soups, quiches, and crepes, as well as sandwiches and salads. Open Monday to Saturday 8am to 3pm. Closed January to mid-March.

Vermont's favorite sons, **Ben & Jerry,** have one of their playful ice-cream parlors at 352 Main St., Hyannis (© **508/790-0910**). Open daily from 10:30am to midnight.

A modest luncheonette may make an unlikely shrine, but since 1934, several generations of summer-goers—including enthusiastic Kennedys—have fed their ice-cream cravings at **Four Seas,** 360 S. Main St., at Main Street, in the center of Centerville (© **508/775-1394**). Founder Richard Warren was into exotic flavors long before they became the norm. His specialties include rum-butter toffee, cantaloupe, and—at the height of the season—Cape Cod beach plum. Closed early September to late May.

Takeout & Picnic Fare

Another branch of the popular **Box Lunch** (© **508/790-5855**), serving pita "roll-wiches," is right on Main Street (no. 357) in Hyannis. These are the best—and fastest—sandwiches in town. Open Monday to Wednesday 9am to 6pm, Thursday to Saturday 9am to 8pm, Sunday 9am to 5pm.

In Barnstable Village, Osterville & Cotuit

Very Expensive

The Regatta of Cotuit ★★★ NEW AMERICAN   The Regatta continues to be one of the best fine-dining spots on Cape Cod. This 1790 Cape was once a stagecoach inn and some may find the Federal-era atmosphere a tad formal, but the food and service are always top-notch. Nightly specials might include such hearty offerings as roasted buffalo tenderloin with blackberry Madeira sauce served with braised fresh greens and a Stilton sage bread pudding; or sautéed filet of halibut with a citrus beurre blanc, lobster mashed potatoes, and a marinated vegetable salad. The cuisine is exquisitely prepared and presented, fortified by herbs and vegetables plucked fresh from the kitchen garden, and the mood is invariably festive. A pianist plays 5 to 7 nights a week, year-round.

4631 Rte. 28 (near the intersection of Rte. 130), Cotuit. © **508/428-5715.** www.regattarestaurant.com. Reservations recommended. Main courses $19–$36. AE, MC, V. Apr–Dec daily 5–9pm; Jan–Mar Wed–Sun 5–9pm.

Expensive

The Barnstable Restaurant and Tavern ★★ NEW AMERICAN/PUB   Located in a 200-year-old stagecoach stop on the Old King's Highway, Barnstable Tavern has long been a sought-after destination. In recent years, chef/owner Rob Calderone has put together a menu of sophisticated options such as roast lamb with mustard sauce, roast duck with orange liqueur sauce, and sole piccata. A raw bar spotlights local oysters and clams. Families looking for a reasonably priced meal will be pleased by the pub fare—burgers, sandwiches, pasta, fried seafood—that's still served amid the atmosphere of the olden days. The wine list is notable for its large number of well-priced bottles.

3176 Main St./Rte. 6A (in the center of Barnstable Village). © **508/362-2355.** Reservations accepted. Main courses $9–$25. AC, DC, MC, V. Daily 11:30am–9pm. Open year-round.

Dolphin Restaurant ★ NEW AMERICAN   It looks like just another run-of-the-mill roadside eatery, so it's easy to miss from the road. Never mind the corny decor (pine paneling and clunky captains' chairs) or the little plate of crackers and cheese dip that greets you at the table, both carry-overs from the restaurant's 1953 debut. The finesse is to be found in the menu, where amid the more typical fried fish you'll find such delicacies as Chilean sea bass with roasted corn salsa and lime vinaigrette, roast duck with mango glaze and toasted coconut, or arctic char with caramelized onions and citrus butter. The signature dessert is amaretto bread pudding.

3250 Rte. 6A (in the center of town), Barnstable. ✆ 508/362-6610. Reservations not accepted. Main courses $17–$23. AE, MC, V. May–Oct daily 5–9:30pm, Mon–Sat 11:30am–3pm; call for off-season hours. Open year-round.

Keepers Restaurant ★ NEW AMERICAN   You'll really feel like an insider as you wind your way through the fancy neighborhoods of Osterville to this small, fine-dining restaurant set in the old Crosby boatyard. In the mid–19th century, the Crosby brothers invented a new kind of sailboat that came about "quick like a cat." You can still see wooden Crosby Cat sailboats in the boatyard, as well as million-dollar yachts. The catch of the day reigns at this restaurant specializing in creative fish dishes.

72 Crosby Circle (at the end of West Bay Rd., on the harbor at the Crosby Boat Yard), Osterville. ✆ 508/428-6719. Reservations highly recommended. Main courses $17–$25. MC, V. June–Aug daily 11:30am–2:30pm and 5–9pm; call for off-season hours. Closed late Sept to mid-May.

Mattakeese Wharf ★ SEAFOOD   This water-view fish house, with broad decks jutting out into the Barnstable harbor, gets packed in season; don't even bother on summer weekends. The outdoor seating fills up first, and no wonder, with Sandy Neck sunsets to marvel over and fish so fresh it could have flopped on deck. There's a Mediterranean subtext to the extensive menu. The bouillabaisse is worthy of the name, and the varied combinations of pasta, seafood, and sauce—from Alfredo to *fra diavolo*—invite return visits. There's live piano music most nights in season.

271 Mill Way (about 1/2 mile north of Rte. 6A), Barnstable. ✆ 508/362-4511. Reservations recommended. Main courses $14–$28. AE, DC, DISC, MC, V. June to mid-Oct daily 11:30am–9pm; call for off-season hours. Closed mid-Oct to Apr.

HYANNIS & ENVIRONS AFTER DARK
Low-Key Evenings
Baxter's Boat House   This congenial little lounge, with map-topped tables and low-key blues piano, draws an attractive crowd, including the occasional vacationing celebrity. See "Where to Dine," earlier. 177 Pleasant St. ✆ 508/775-7040.

Embargo   Attracting a hip crowd of singles in the 30 to 50 age group, this hip and upbeat Spanish themed bar is well worth a stop for some tapas and a drink—make mine sangria!—before dinner. 453 Main St. ✆ 508/771-9700.

The Island Merchant   This hip little cafe on Main Street in Hyannis has great Greenwich Village atmosphere. Readings and acoustic performances are held on weekends. Great sandwiches and baked goods are offered for lunch. Besides coffee and tea, there's beer and wine. 302 Main St. ✆ 508/771-1337; www.theislandmerchant.com.

Roadhouse Café   Duck into this dark-paneled bar, decorated like an English gentlemen's club in burgundy leather, if you're looking for sophisticated entertainment and company. The bar stocks 48 boutique beers, in addition to all the usual hard, soft, and sweet liquors, and you won't go hoarse trying to converse over the soft jazz. The bistro area next to the bar has live jazz piano nightly. See "Where to Dine," earlier. Insiders know to show up Monday nights to hear local jazz great Dave McKenna. 488 South St. ✆ 508/775-2386.

RooBar   This bistro feels very Manhattan, with ultracool servers; a long, sleek bar area; and lots of attitude. The food is good, too. See "Where to Dine," earlier. 586 Main St. ✆ 508/778-6515.

Live & Loud

Asa's Grille at the Asa Bearse House   Live bands late-night are the draw at this place, centrally located on Hyannis's Main Street and attracting a mostly young crowd. 415 Main St. ✆ 508/775-9600.

Harry's   There's hardly room to eat here, let alone rock out, but the cramped dance floor makes for instant camaraderie. The classic blues music heard here, like Rick Russell and the Cadillac Horns, really demands to be absorbed in such an intimate space. Live performance reigns nightly in season and about 5 nights a week year-round. See "Where to Dine," earlier. 700 Mains St. (at Stevens St.) ✆ 508/778-4188. Thurs–Sat cover $10 or less.

Performances, Movies, Readings & Lectures

The Barnstable Comedy Club   A local favorite since 1922, the oldest amateur theater group in the country offers a mix of old chestnuts and original farces off season. Call for schedule. 3171 Rte. 6A (in the center of town), Barnstable. ✆ 508/362-6333. Tickets $12–$15, students and seniors $10–$14.

The Cape Cod Melody Tent ★   Built as a summer theater in 1950, this billowy blue big-top proved even better suited to variety shows. A nonprofit venture since 1990 (proceeds fund other cultural initiatives Cape-wide), the Melody Tent has hosted the major performers of the past half-century, from jazz greats to comedians, crooners to rockers. Every seat is a winner in this grand oval, only 20 banked aisles deep. Curtain 8pm nightly July to early September. There's also a children's theater program Wednesday mornings at 11am; tickets are $8. Call for schedule. West End rotary. ✆ 508/775-5630 or Ticketmaster ✆ 800/347-0808. www.melodytent.org. Tickets $18–$45.

2 YARMOUTH ★

19 miles E of Sandwich; 38 miles S of Provincetown

This cross section represents the Cape at its best—and worst. Yarmouth Port, on Cape Cod Bay, is an enchanting town, clustered with interesting shops and architectural pearls, whereas the sound-side "villages" of West to South Yarmouth are an object lesson in unbridled development run amok. This section of Route 28 is a nightmarish gauntlet of tacky accommodations and "attractions." Yet even here, you'll find several spots of interest.

Legend has it that Leif Eriksson found the region very attractive indeed, and set up what was meant to be a permanent camp by the Bass River around A.D. 1000. No trace has yet been found—other than the puzzling "Bournedale stone," with its vaguely runic inscriptions, now housed at the Aptucxet Trading Post Museum in Bourne. Why Eriksson left—and whether, in fact, he came to Cape Cod at all, and not some similar spot— are mysteries still unanswered. We do know that Yarmouth, most likely named for an English port, was the second Cape town to incorporate, following closely on the heels of Sandwich, and that at the height of the shipping boom, Yarmouth Port boasted a "Captain's Row" of 50 fine houses, most of which remain showpieces to this day.

So, you've got the north shore for culture and refinement, and the south shore for kitsch. Take your pick or enjoy the best of both worlds.

ESSENTIALS

GETTING THERE After crossing either the Bourne or Sagamore bridge, head east on Route 6 or 6A. The section of Route 6A north of Route 6's Exit 7 passes through the village of Yarmouth Port. The villages of West Yarmouth, Bass River, and South Yarmouth are located along Route 28, east of Hyannis; to reach them from Route 6, take Exit 7 south (Yarmouth Rd.) or Exit 8 south (Station St.); or fly into Hyannis (see "Getting There," in chapter 3).

If you need to get around the area without a car, the Yarmouth Easy Shuttle circles Route 28 from Hyannis's bus terminal; for details, contact the Yarmouth Area Chamber of Commerce (see below).

GETTING AROUND The **H2O Line** (Cape Cod Regional Transit Authority, ✆ **800/ 352-7155**) runs from Hyannis to Orleans, making stops in Yarmouth on six round-trips daily. Trips from Dennisport to Hyannis cost $2.50. The **Yarmouth Shuttle,** also called **The Breeze** (www.thebreeze.info) and also run by the Cape Cod Regional Transit Authority, travels down Route 28 (from Hyannis to the Bass River) and down Old Main Road in South Yarmouth, and makes stops at Seagull and Bass River beaches. Flag it down anywhere along the route. Fares start at $1 and increase depending on the length of your ride.

VISITOR INFORMATION Contact the **Yarmouth Area Chamber of Commerce,** 657 Rte. 28, West Yarmouth, MA 02673 (✆ **800/732-1008** or 508/778-1008; fax 508/778-5114; www.yarmouthcapecod.com); or the **Cape Cod Chamber of Commerce** (see "Visitor Information," in the "Hyannis, Barnstable, Neighboring Villages & Environs" section, earlier in this chapter). The Yarmouth chamber is open Monday through Friday 9am to 5pm, Sunday 10am to 3pm, in season. Off season, the hours are Monday through Friday 9am to 5pm.

BEACHES & RECREATIONAL PURSUITS

BEACHES Yarmouth boasts 11 saltwater and 2 pond beaches open to the public. The body-per-square-yard ratio can be pretty intense along the sound, but so is the social scene, so no one seems to mind. The beachside parking lots charge $12 to $15 a day and sell weeklong stickers ($50).

- **Bass River Beach** ★, off South Shore Drive in Bass River (South Yarmouth): Located at the mouth of the largest tidal river on the eastern seaboard, this sound beach offers restroom facilities and a snack bar, plus a wheelchair-accessible fishing pier. The beaches along the south shore (Nantucket Sound) tend to be clean and sandy with comfortable water temps (kids will want to stay in all day), but they can also be crowded during peak times. You'll need a beach sticker or a day pass to park here.
- **Gray's Beach,** off Center Street in Yarmouth Port: This isn't much of a beach, but tame waters make this tiny spit of dark sand good for young children; it adjoins the Callery-Darling Conservation Area (see "Nature & Wildlife Areas," below). The Bass Hole boardwalk offers one of the Mid Cape's most scenic walks. Parking is free here, and there's a picnic area with grills.
- **Parker's River Beach,** off South Shore Drive in Bass River: The usual amenities are available, like restrooms and a snack bar, plus a 20-foot gazebo for the sun-shy. A beach sticker or day pass is required.
- **Seagull Beach** ★, off South Sea Avenue in West Yarmouth: Rolling dunes, a boardwalk, and all the necessary facilities, like restrooms and a snack bar, attract a young crowd. Bring bug spray, though: Greenhead flies get the munchies in July. You'll need a beach sticker or day pass to park here.

6

BICYCLING   The **Cape Cod Rail Trail ★★★** (📞 508/896-3491) is a few miles away on Route 134 (near the entrance to Rte. 6) in South Dennis. Rent a bike at the trail head, and if you are feeling Olympian, bike all the way to Wellfleet (25 miles).

BOATING   You can rent a canoe or kayak at **Cape Cod Waterways,** 16 Rte. 28, Dennisport (📞 508/398-0080), and paddle along the Bass River, which flows between South Yarmouth and West Dennis on the south side of the Cape. Canoe or kayak rental for 1¹/₂ hours costs $24 to $32.

FISHING   Of the five fishing ponds in the Yarmouth area, Long Pond near South Yarmouth is known for its largemouth bass and pickerel; for details and a license (shell-fishing is another option), visit **Town Hall** at 1146 Rte. 28 in South Yarmouth (📞 508/398-2231), or **Riverview Bait and Tackle** at 1273 Rte. 28 in South Yarmouth (📞 508/394-1036). Full-season licenses for Massachusetts residents cost $28; for out-of-staters, $38. You can cast for striped bass and bluefish off the pier at Bass River Beach (see "Beaches," above).

FITNESS   The **Mid-Cape Racquet Club** (see "Tennis," below) doubles as a fitness center.

GOLF   The township maintains two 18-hole courses: the seasonal **Bayberry Hills,** off West Yarmouth Road in West Yarmouth (📞 508/394-5597), and the **Bass River Golf Course,** off High Bank Road in South Yarmouth (📞 508/398-9079), founded in 1900 and open year-round. A round at Bayberry costs $85; at Bass River it costs $58. Prices are reduced in the afternoon. Another 18-holer open to the public is the par-54 **Blue Rock Golf Course** off High Bank Road in South Yarmouth (📞 508/398-9295), open year-round, where a round costs $49.

NATURE & WILDLIFE AREAS   For a pleasant stroll, follow the 2 miles of trails maintained by the **Historical Society of Old Yarmouth** on 53 acres. Park behind the post office and check in at the gatehouse, whose herb garden displays a "Wheel of Thyme." The in-season trail fee (50¢ adults, 25¢ children) includes a keyed trail guide: Look for—but do not pick—the endangered pink lady slipper, a local orchid. Your path will cross the transplanted 1873 Kelley Chapel, said to have been built by a Quaker grandfather to comfort his daughter after the death of her child.

In Yarmouth Port, follow Centre Street about a mile north and bear northeast on Homers Dock Road; from here a 2.5-mile trail through the Callery-Darling Conservation Area leads to Gray's Beach, where you can continue across the Bass Hole Boardwalk for a lovely view of the marsh.

TENNIS   There are four public courts at Flax Pond, off North Main Street in South Yarmouth; four more at Sandy Pond, on Buck Island Road off Higgins Crowell Road; plus 10 at Dennis-Yarmouth High School at Station Avenue in South Yarmouth. For details, contact the **Yarmouth Recreation Department** (📞 508/398-2231). **The Mid-Cape Racquet Club,** 193 Whites Path, South Yarmouth (📞 508/394-3511), has nine indoor courts ($22 per person, per hr.), plus racquetball and squash courts (one each, $15 per person) and health-club facilities ($15 per day).

BASEBALL & SOCCER

The **Dennis-Yarmouth Red Sox,** part of the Cape Cod Baseball League, play at Dennis-Yarmouth Regional High School's Red Wilson Field off Station Avenue in South Yarmouth. For a schedule, contact the **Yarmouth Chamber of Commerce** (📞 508/778-1008),

The **Cape Cod Crusaders** soccer team takes on a dozen other Atlantic-coast teams mid-May to early August, also at the Dennis-Yarmouth Regional High School. For details, contact the **Yarmouth Chamber of Commerce** (☏ 508/778-1008).

KID STUFF

Children tend to crave the "junk" we adults condemn, so they're likely to be enthralled by the rainy-day enticements of Route 28, which include trampolines, batting cages, pitch and putt, and bumper cars. Among the more enduringly appealing miniature-golf courses clamoring for attention is **Pirate's Cove**, at 728 Main St./Rte. 28, South Yarmouth (☏ 508/394-6200; open daily 10am–10pm in season; closed Nov to mid-Apr), where the trap decor is strong on macabre humor and there are two 18-hole courses. A round is $7.95 for those aged 13 years and older, $6.95 for children aged 12 and under.

ZooQuarium ★ (Kids) This slightly scruffy wildlife museum has made great strides in recent years toward blending entertainment with education. It's a little easier to enjoy the seal and sea lion show once you've been assured that the stars do, in fact, like performing. They have been trained with positive reinforcement only and arrived with injuries that precluded their survival in the wild. The aquarium is arranged in realistic habitats, and the "zoo" consists primarily of indigenous fauna, both domesticated and wild (the pacing bobcat is liable to give you pause). Children will be entranced by the Zoorific theater (a live-animal education program) and the children's discovery center with hands-on activities. The exhibit, "A Walk Through the Cape Cod Woods," features some of the little creatures that inhabit the woodland floor. A very creditable effort is made to convey the need for ecological preservation.

674 Rte. 28 (midway between West Yarmouth and Bass River), West Yarmouth. ☏ **508/775-8883.** www. zooquariumcapecod.net. Admission $9.75 adults, $6.75 children 2–9. June to August daily 9:30am–5pm; Sept to Nov 9:30am–4pm, closed Tuesdays; Dec to Feb weekends only 9:30am–3pm. Closed March to May.

SHOPPING

Driving Route 6A, the Old King's Highway, in Yarmouth Port, you'll pass a number of antiques stores and fine shops for the home. Unless you have children in tow, you may want to bypass Route 28 entirely and stay on the pretty north side of Yarmouth.

ANTIQUES/COLLECTIBLES Check out **Town Crier Antiques,** 153 Rte. 6A (in the center of town), Yarmouth Port (☏ 508/362-3138), for fun stuff such as well-priced quilts, glassware, and attendant paraphernalia. Closed November to mid-May.

BOOKS The most colorful bookshop on the Cape (if not the whole East Coast) is **Parnassus Books,** 220 Rte. 6A (about ¹/₄ mile east of the town center), Yarmouth Port (☏ 508/362-6420). This jam-packed repository—housed in an 1858 Swedenborgian church—is the creation of Ben Muse, who has been collecting and selling vintage tomes since the 1960s. Relevant new stock, including the Cape-related reissues published by Parnassus Imprints, is offered alongside the older treasures. Don't expect much hand-holding on the part of the gruff proprietor. You'll earn his respect by knowing what you're looking for or, better yet, being willing to browse until it finds you. The outdoor racks, maintained on an honor system, are open 24 hours a day, for those who suffer from abibliophobia—fear of lacking for reading material.

To emulate that Cape look—breezy chic—study the key ingredients artfully assembled at **Design Works,** 159 Rte. 6A (in the center of town), Yarmouth Port (© **508/362-9698**): stripped-pine antiques, crisp linens, and colorful majolica.

The design approach at **Peach Tree Designs,** 173 Rte. 6A (in the center of town), Yarmouth Port (© **508/362-8317**), is much more adventurous and eclectic. A bold hand is evident in the juxtaposition of disparate elements, from hunting prints to beribboned hats, model ships to hand-woven throws. The gift pickings are superlative as well—especially if you're shopping for yourself.

MUSEUMS

Captain Bangs Hallet House Museum ★

Typical of the sumptuous tastes of the time, this 1840 Greek Revival house is named for the China trade seafarer who lived here from 1863 to 1893. The Historical Society of Old Yarmouth, which oversees the property, has filled its beautifully proportioned rooms with the finest furnishings of the day, from Hitchcock chairs to a Hepplewhite sofa. The rustic kitchen in back belongs to the 1740 core around which this showy edifice was erected. Note the nearly 200-year-old weeping beech tree and the herb garden beyond, which lead to a scenic 2-mile walking trail (see "Nature & Wildlife Areas," above).

11 Strawberry Lane (off Rte. 6A, about ½ mile east of the town center; park behind the post office at 231 Rte. 6A), Yarmouth Port. © 508/362-3021. www.hsoy.org. Admission $3 adults, 50¢ children 12 and under. June–Oct Thurs–Sun tours at 1, 2, and 3pm. Groups by appointment. Closed Nov–May.

The Edward Gorey House ★★

At this museum devoted to the life and works of Edward Gorey, you can peek into the artist's whimsically mischievous world. Perhaps most widely known for the animated opening to the television series *Mystery!* on PBS, Gorey died in 2000, and his home on the Yarmouth Port Common has been converted into an intimate museum. On display are original artworks, photographs, and first editions from his career as an author, playwright, illustrator, and costume and set designer. Gorey's passion for animals is also a focus of the collection.

8 Strawberry Lane (off Rte. 6A, on the Common), Yarmouth Port. © 508/362-3909. www.edwardgorey house.org. Admission $5 adults, $3 students and seniors, $2 children 6–12, free for children 5 and under. Wed–Sat 11am–4pm; Sun noon–4pm. Closed Feb.

Winslow Crocker House ★★

The only property on the Cape currently preserved by the prestigious Society for the Preservation of New England Antiquities, this house, built around 1780, deserves every honor. Not only is it a lovely example of the shingled Georgian style, it's packed with outstanding antiques—Jacobean to Chippendale—collected in the 1930s by Mary Thacher, a descendant of the town's first land grantee. Anthony Thacher and his family had a rougher crossing than most: Their ship foundered off Cape Ann in 1635 (near an island that now bears their name), and though their four children drowned, Thacher and his wife were able to make it to shore, clinging to the family cradle. You'll come across a 1690 replica in the parlor. Thacher's son, John, a colonel, built the house next door around 1680, and—with the help of two successive wives—raised a total of 21 children. All the museum-worthy objects in the Winslow Crocker House would seem to have similar stories to tell. For antiques lovers, as well as anyone interested in local lore, this is a valuable cache and a very worthwhile stop.

250 Rte. 6A (about ½ mile east of the town center), Yarmouth Port. © 617/227-3957, ext. 256. www. historicnewengland.org. Admission $4, free to Yarmouth Port residents and SPNEA members. June–Oct 1st Sat of each month, tours hourly 11am–5pm (last tour at 4pm). Closed Nov–May.

So many hotels and motels line Route 28 and the shore in West and South Yarmouth that it may be hard to make sense of the choices. The following are some that offer clean rooms and cater to families looking for a reasonably priced beach vacation. All are within a few miles of the beach or right on the beach. For those staying on Route 28, the town runs frequent beach shuttles in season.

The **Tidewater Inn,** 135 Main St./Rte. 28, West Yarmouth (© **800/338-6322** or 508/775-6322; www.tidewater-capecod.com), is a short walk ($^1/_2$ mile) from a small beach on Lewis Bay, and a not-so-short walk (about a mile) from Hyannis's Main Street and the ferries to Nantucket. Summer rates are $140 to $160 for double occupancy. One of the more attractive motels along this strip, it's a white clapboard double-decker motel with green shutters and doors. The Tidewater also has an indoor pool, an outdoor pool, and a breakfast restaurant.

All Seasons Motor Inn, 1199 Main St./Rte. 28, South Yarmouth (© **800/527-0359** or 508/394-7600; www.allseasons.com), is popular with families. The summer rate is $165 double. It has indoor and outdoor heated pools, a breakfast restaurant, and exercise and game rooms.

Ocean Mist ★, 97 S. Shore Dr., South Yarmouth (© **800/248-6478** or 508/398-2633; www.innseasonresorts.com), is a large motel right on the beach. There's also an indoor pool, just in case it rains. Summer rates are $209 double, $259 suite. A good choice if you have kids.

Very Expensive

Red Jacket Resort ★★ (Kids) Of the huge resort motels lining Nantucket Sound in South Yarmouth, Red Jacket has the best location and activities. Some of the activities include kayaking, paddleboat and sailboat rentals, catamaran cruises, a daily summertime children's program of supervised sports and activities (which may take advantage of the playground), minigolf, shuffleboard, horseshoes, badminton, and basketball and volley-ball (one court of each). All rooms have a balcony or private porch; you'll want one overlooking the private beach on Nantucket Sound or looking out toward Parker's River.

1 S. Shore Dr. (P.O. Box 88), South Yarmouth, MA 02664. © **800/672-0500** or 508/398-6941. Fax 508/398-1214. www.redjacketresorts.com. 170 units, 14 cottages. Summer $285–$430 double; $495–$950 cottages. A $15 resort fee per day is added to all bills. MC, V. Closed Nov to mid-Apr. **Amenities:** Restaurant; bar/lounge; indoor and outdoor heated pools; putting green; tennis court; exercise room; whirlpool; sauna; concierge, ice-cream shop. *In room:* A/C, TV/VCR, fridge, hair dryer.

Expensive

Captain Farris House ★★ Sumptuous is the only way to describe this 1845 inn, improbably set amid a peaceful garden, a block off bustling Route 28. A skilled interior decorator has combined fine antiques and striking contemporary touches to lift this inn's interiors way above the average homey B&B decor. Some suites are apartment-size, containing sitting rooms equipped with a fireplace and whirlpool-tub bathrooms bigger than the average bedroom. Next door, the 1825 Elisha Jenkins House contains an additional large suite with its own sundeck.

308 Old Main St. (just west of the Bass River Bridge), Bass River, MA 02664-4530. © **800/350-9477** or 508/760-2818. Fax 508/398-1262. www.captainfarris.com. 10 units, 9 with tub/shower, 1 with shower only. Summer $170–$215 double; $215–$280 suite. Rates include full breakfast. AE, DISC, MC, V. Open year-round. *In room:* A/C, TV/VCR, hair dryer, iron.

The Inn at Cape Cod ★ You can't miss this captain's house/bed-and-breakfast; it's the one that looks like a tall, thin southern plantation manor with four towering Ionic columns. Upon entering the elegant foyer with its grandly curving staircase, you are led into a comfortable common seating-and-breakfast area. My favorite guest room is the very romantic front room with a sitting room and large private balcony overlooking the scenic Old King's Highway. Behind the inn are miles of wooded walking trails.

4 Summer St. (P.O. Box 96), Yarmouth Port, MA 02675. ℂ 800/850-7301 or 508/375-0590. www.innat capecod.com. 9 units, 2 with tub/shower, 7 with shower only. Summer $160–$250 double; $295 suite. Rates include full breakfast. MC, V. Closed Dec–Feb. No children under 8. *In room:* A/C, TV/DVD, Wi-Fi, iron.

Liberty Hill Inn ★ This 1825 Greek Revival captain's house is set high on a knoll in charming Yarmouth Port, just off Route 6A, the Old King's Highway, which, with its majestic captains' houses and century-old elm trees, hasn't changed much in the last 100 years. Rooms in the main house, with its narrow stairways, have Colonial antiques and wicker furniture. The carriage house with four rooms is suitable for families with children. The inn stands out for its breakfasts with such delectables as baked blueberry French toast and crab scramble. One room is accessible for visitors with disabilities.

77 Main St. (Rte. 6A, 1 mile from the village center), Yarmouth Port, MA 02675. ℂ 800/821-3977 or 508/362-3976. Fax 508/362-6485. www.libertyhillinn.com. 9 units. Summer $140–$225 double. Rates include full breakfast and afternoon tea. AE, MC, V. Open year-round. *In room:* A/C, TV/DVD, Wi-Fi, hair dryer, iron, no phone.

WHERE TO DINE
Expensive

abbicci ★★★ MEDITERRANEAN After a renovation that added a bar and an even more sophisticated ambiance, abbicci, which means "the basics" in Italian, continues to draw accolades. Look for the mustard-yellow Cape Cod cottage and let a valet park your car. You enter into a sleek bar area where you can eat dinner, or wait for a seat in the dining rooms. This restaurant is very popular in the summer, so choose an off-time for dinner if you want to get seated promptly. On the menu, you'll find seafood dishes, as well as veal, lamb, and, of course, pasta, all in a delicate Northern Italian style. You'll relish the luxurious flavors, like those found in the herb-crusted lamb with polenta or the halibut with truffle emulsion. The *tapas* menu, served in the afternoons, features small dishes priced from $6 to $10.

43 Main St./Rte. 6A (near the Cummaquid border), Yarmouth Port. ℂ 508/362-3501. www.abbicci.com. Reservations recommended. Main courses $17–$38. AE, MC, V. Fri, Sat and Mon noon–3pm; Sun 11am–3pm; daily 5–10pm. Open year-round.

Moderate

Inaho ★★ Finds JAPANESE What better application of the Cape's oceanic bounty than fresh-off-the-boat sushi? You can sit in awe at the sushi bar and watch chef/owner Yuji Watanabe perform his legerdemain, or enjoy the privacy afforded by a gleaming wooden booth. From the front, Inaho is a typical Cape Cod cottage, but park in the back so you can enter through the Japanese garden. The decor is minimalist with traditional shoji screens and crisp navy-and-white banners softened by tranquil music and service.

157 Main St./Rte. 6A (in the village center), Yarmouth Port. ℂ 508/362-5522. Reservations recommended. Main courses $13–$23; sushi rolls $3–$7. MC, V. Mon–Sat 4:30–10pm. Open year-round.

you're looking for, you can't do much better than this. It's an old stagecoach inn, serving Yankee basics like prime rib and baked scrod. The food is fresh, hearty, and tasty. People are catching on that this is good food at reasonable prices, so it can be crowded on weekends in season. One of the most requested dishes is the deluxe lobster roll, with huge chunks of fresh lobster. The Sunday brunch, a combination buffet and a la carte meal, is popular. A lighter-fare menu is also available.

223 Rte. 6A (in the center of Yarmouth Port). ✆ **508/362-9962.** Reservations recommended. Main courses $14–$25. AE, DC, DISC, MC, V. June–Oct Tues–Sat 11:30am–2pm, Sun 10am–1pm, daily 4:30–9pm; call for off-season hours. Open year-round.

3 DENNIS ★

20 miles E of Sandwich; 36 miles S of Provincetown

If Dennis looks like a jigsaw puzzle piece snapped around Yarmouth, that's because it didn't break away until 1793, when the community adopted the name of Rev. Josiah Dennis, who had ministered to Yarmouth's "East Parish" for close to 4 decades. His 1736 home has been restored and now serves as a local-history museum.

In Dennis, as in Yarmouth, virtually all the good stuff—pretty drives, inviting shops, and restaurants with real personality—are in the north, along Route 6A. Route 28 is chockablock with more typical tourist attractions, RV parks, and family-oriented motels—some with fairly sophisticated facilities but nonetheless undistinguished enough not to warrant even a drive-by (the few exceptions are noted below). In budgeting your time, be sure to allocate the lion's share to Dennis Village and not its southern offshoots. It's as stimulating and unspoiled today as it was when it welcomed the Cape Playhouse, the country's oldest surviving straw-hat theater, during the anything-goes 1920s.

ESSENTIALS

GETTING THERE   After crossing either the Bourne Bridge or the Sagamore Bridge, head east on Route 6 or 6A. The Sagamore Bridge will get you closer to your destination. Route 6A passes through the villages of Dennis and East Dennis (which can also be reached via northbound Rte. 134 from Rte. 6's Exit 9). Route 134 South leads to the village of South Dennis; if you follow Route 134 all the way to Route 28, the village of West Dennis will be a couple of miles to your west, and Dennisport a couple of miles east. Or fly into Hyannis (see "Getting There," in chapter 3).

GETTING AROUND   The **H2O Line** (Cape Cod Regional Transit Authority, ✆ **800/352-7155**) runs from Hyannis to Orleans, making stops in Dennis on six round-trips daily. Trips from Dennisport to Hyannis cost $2.50.

VISITOR INFORMATION   Contact the **Dennis Chamber of Commerce,** 242 Swan River Rd., West Dennis, MA 02670 (✆ **508/398-3568;** www.dennischamber.com), or the **Cape Cod Chamber of Commerce** (see "Visitor Information," in the "Hyannis, Barnstable, Neighboring Villages & Environs" section, earlier in this chapter). The Dennis chamber is open May to October Monday through Friday 10am to 4pm; November to April Monday through Friday 10am to 2pm.

BEACHES   Dennis harbors more than a dozen saltwater and two freshwater beaches open to nonresidents. The bay beaches are charming and a big hit with families, who prize the easygoing surf, so soft it won't bring toddlers to their knees. The beaches on the sound tend to attract wall-to-wall families, but the parking lots are usually not too crowded, since so many beachgoers stay within walking distance. The lots charge $15 per day; for a weeklong permit ($55), visit **Town Hall** on Main Street in South Dennis (© **508/394-8300**).

- **Chapin Beach ★★**, off Route 6A in Dennis: This is a nice, long bay beach pocked with occasional boulders and surrounded by dunes. There is no lifeguard, but there are restrooms.

- **Corporation Beach ★★**, off Route 6A in Dennis: Before it filled in with sand, this bay beach—with wheelchair-accessible boardwalk, lifeguards, snack bar, restrooms, and a children's play area—was once a packet landing owned by a shipbuilding corporation comprised of area residents.

- **Mayflower Beach ★★**, off Route 6A in Dennis: This 1,200-foot bay beach has the necessary amenities, plus an accessible boardwalk. The tide pools attract lots of children.

- **Scargo Lake** in Dennis: This large kettle-hole pond (formed by a melting fragment of a glacier) has two pleasant beaches: Scargo Beach, accessible right off Route 6A, and Princess Beach, off Scargo Hill Road, where there are restrooms and a picnic area.

- **West Dennis Beach ★**, off Route 28 in West Dennis: This long (¹/₂-mile) but narrow beach along the sound has lifeguards, a playground, a snack bar, restrooms, and a special kite-flying area. The eastern end is reserved for residents; the western end tends, in any case, to be less packed.

BICYCLING   The 25-mile **Cape Cod Rail Trail ★★★** (© **508/896-3491**) starts—or, depending on your perspective, ends—here, on Route 134, a half-mile south of Route 6's Exit 9. Once a Penn Central track, this 8-foot-wide paved bikeway extends all the way to Wellfleet (with a few on-road lapses), passing through woods, marshes, and dunes. Sustenance is never too far off-trail, and plenty of bike shops dot the course. At the trail head is **Bob's Bike Shop,** 430 Rte. 134, South Dennis (© **508/760-4723**), which rents bikes and in-line skates and does repairs. Rates are $12 for 2 hours and up to $24 for the full day. Another paved bike path runs along Old Bass Road, 3¹/₂ miles north to Route 6A.

BOATING   Located on the small and placid Swan River, **Cape Cod Waterways,** 16 Rte. 28, Dennisport (© **508/398-0080**), rents canoes, kayaks, and paddleboats for exploring 200-acre Swan Pond (less than a mile north) or Nantucket Sound (2 miles south). A full-day kayak rental costs $58 for a single, $74 for a tandem.

  Bass River Cruises, located at Bass River Bridge (at Rte. 28) in West Dennis (© **508/362-5555;** www.capecodrivercruise.com), explores the Bass and Weir rivers the way Leif Eriksson might have—by boat. This one, a poky but stable custom minibarge, the MV *Starfish,* is motorized, so the whole circuit takes only 1¹/₂ hours. If some of the tales strike you as rather tall, there's still plenty of wildlife and prime real estate to ogle. Trips are offered four times a day mid-May through mid-October; tickets are $18 for adults and $7 for children ages 1 to 11. Call for the schedule.

FISHING   Fishing is allowed in Fresh Pond and Scargo Lake, where the catch includes trout and smallmouth bass; for a license (shellfishing is also permitted), visit **Town Hall**

on Main Street in South Dennis (© **508/394-8300**), or **Riverview Bait and Tackle** at 1273 Rte. 28 in South Yarmouth (© **508/394-1036**). Plenty of people drop a line off the Bass River Bridge along Route 28 in West Dennis. Several charter boats operate out of the Northside Marina in East Dennis's Sesuit Harbor, including the *Albatross* (© **508/385-3244**), which charges $32 for adults, $28 for children 11 and under and seniors. It makes two 4-hour trips per day.

FITNESS/JOGGING   For joggers, and fitness freaks in general, the 1.5-mile **Life-course trail,** located at Old Bass River and Access roads in South Dennis, features 20 exercise stations along its tree-shaded path.

GOLF   The public is welcome to use two 18-hole championship courses: the hilly, par-71 **Dennis Highlands** on Old Bass River Road in Dennis and the even more challenging par-72 **Dennis Pines** on Golf Course Road in East Dennis. For information on either course, call © **508/385-8347.** Both charge $60 for a round, less in the afternoons.

NATURE & WILDLIFE AREAS   Behind the town hall parking lot on Main Street in South Dennis, a half-mile walk along the **Indian Lands Conservation Trail** leads to the Bass River, where blue herons and kingfishers often take shelter. Dirt roads off South Street in East Dennis, beyond the Quivet Cemetery, lead to **Crow's Pasture,** a patchwork of marshes and dunes bordering the bay; this circular trail is about 2.5 miles round-trip.

TENNIS   Public courts are located at the Dennis-Yarmouth Regional High School in South Yarmouth and at Wixon Middle School on Route 134 in South Dennis; for details, contact the **Dennis Recreation Department** (© **508/394-8300**). Or you may be able to book time at the **Mashantum Tennis Club** off Nobscusset Road in Dennis Village (© **508/385-7043**), which has clay courts for $10 per person. Also try **Sesuit Tennis Centre** at 1389 Rte. 6A in East Dennis (© **508/385-2200**). At Sesuit, singles and doubles are $25 per person.

MUSEUMS

Cape Cod Museum of Art ★★   Part of the prettily landscaped Cape Playhouse complex, this museum has done a great job of acquiring hundreds of works by representative area artists dating back to the turn of the 20th century. The large galleries upstairs display special exhibits, sometimes a single artist, sometimes groups. The rooms downstairs show works from the permanent collection, including many works from Provincetown artists going back to the early years of the 20th century. There's also an outdoor sculpture garden. Call ahead for a schedule of special shows, lectures, concerts, and classes. *Note:* Admission is free (donation requested) on Thursday from 10am to 8pm.

60 Hope Lane (off Rte. 6A in the center of the village; from Rte. 6, take Exit 9B and make a left on Rte. 6A; museum is two miles down Rte. 6A), Dennis Village. © **508/385-4477.** www.cmfa.org. Admission $8 adults, free for children 17 and under. Tues–Sat 10am–5pm; Thurs 10am–8pm; Sun noon–5pm. Open year-round.

Josiah Dennis Manse and Old West Schoolhouse (Kids   This compact 1736 saltbox housed Rev. Josiah Dennis, the town's first minister. Though not necessarily original, the furnishings are fascinating, as is a diorama of the Shiverick Shipyard, which was the source in the mid-1800s of the world's swiftest ships. Costumed guides lead guests through a maritime room and a children's room. There is also a Native American exhibit. Don't miss the 1770 schoolhouse, where a comprehensive (if strict) approach to learning is beautifully preserved.

77 Nobscusset Rd. (north of Rte. 6A, about 1/2 mile west of the town center). (**©** **508/385-2232.** Donations accepted. Late June to mid-Sept Tues 10am–noon; Thurs 2–4pm. Closed mid-Sept to late June.

Scargo Tower (Moments) All that remains of the grand Nobscusset Hotel, this 28-foot stone observatory looks out from its 160-foot perch over the entire Outer Cape, including the tightly furled tip that is Provincetown. In the foreground is Scargo Lake—the legacy, native legend has it, of either the giant god Maushop or perhaps a princess who bid her handmaidens to scoop it out with clamshells.

Scargo Hill Rd. (off Old Bass River Rd., south of Rte. 6A in the center of town). No phone. Free admission. Daily 6am–10pm.

BASEBALL

The Dennis-Yarmouth Red Sox, part of the Cape Cod Baseball League, play at Dennis-Yarmouth High School's Red Wilson Field off Station Avenue in South Yarmouth. For a schedule, contact the **Yarmouth Area Chamber of Commerce,** 657 Rte. 28, West Yarmouth, MA 02673 (**©** **508/778-1008**); the **Yarmouth Recreation Department** (**©** **508/398-2231,** ext. 284); or the **League** (**©** **508/432-6909**).

KID STUFF

If kids get sick of all the miscellaneous go-carts and minigolf concessions on Route 28, they can take in a show. On Thursday and Friday mornings in season, at 9:30 and 11:30am, the **Cape Playhouse** at 820 Rte. 6A in Dennis (**©** **508/385-3911;** www.capeplayhouse.com) hosts various visiting companies that mount children's theater geared toward kids ages 4 and up; at only $8 to $9, tickets go fast.

SHOPPING

You can pretty much ignore Route 28. There's a growing cluster of antiques shops in Dennisport, but the stock is flea-market level and requires more patience than most mere browsers—as opposed to avid collectors—may be able to muster. Save your time and money for the better shops along Route 6A, where you'll also find fine contemporary crafts.

ANTIQUES/COLLECTIBLES More than 136 dealers stock the co-op **Antiques Center of Cape Cod,** 243 Rte. 6A (about 1 mile south of Dennis Village center), Dennis (**©** **508/385-6400**); it's the largest such enterprise on the Cape. You'll find all the usual "smalls" on the first floor; the big stuff—from blanket chests to copper bathtubs—beckons above.

Eldred's, 1483 Rte. 6A (about 1/4 mile west of Dennis Village center), East Dennis (**©** **508/385-3116;** www.eldreds.com), where the gavel has been wielded for more than 40 years, is the Cape's most prestigious auction house. Specialties include Asian art, American and European paintings, marine art, and Americana. Call for a schedule.

The premier place for antique wicker furniture on the Cape is **Leslie Curtis Design and Antiques** at two locations in Dennis Village, 776 Main St./Rte. 6A and 838 Main St./Rte. 6A (**©** **508/385-2921**). Her wicker selection includes Victorian pieces and Bar Harbor wicker of the 1920s. She also specializes in French Quimper pottery and American 19th-century furniture.

ARTS & CRAFTS The creations of **Ross Coppelman Goldsmith,** 1439 Rte. 6A (about 1/4 mile west of the town center), East Dennis (**©** **508/385-7900**)—mostly fashioned of lustrous 22-karat gold—have an iconic drama to them: They seem to draw on the aesthetics of some grand, lost civilization.

Scargo Stoneware Pottery and Art Gallery, 30 Dr. Lord's Rd. S. (off Rte. 6A, about 1 mile east of the town center), Dennis (📞 508/385-3894), is a magical place. Harry Holl set up his glass-ceilinged studio here in 1952; today his work, and the output of his four grown daughters, fills a sylvan glade overlooking Scargo Lake. Much of it—such as the signature birdhouses shaped like fanciful castles—is meant to reside outside. The other wares deserve a place of honor on the dining-room table or perhaps over a mantle. Hand-painted tiles by Sarah Holl are particularly enchanting.

BOOKS Bookstore junkies (you know who you are) will love **Armchair Bookshop,** 619 Rte. 6A, Dennis Village (📞 508/385-0900), one of those quaint little bookshops that does everything right. This one seems to specialize (unofficially) in books about dogs, in tribute to the friendly golden retrievers in residence. But you'll find everything here, from bestsellers to books of local interest to children's books and more. There is also a large selection of cards and gift items. It's all very well organized and a delight for browsers.

WHERE TO STAY
Very Expensive
Lighthouse Inn ★★ (Kids) Set on placid West Dennis Beach on Nantucket Sound, this popular resort has been welcoming families for more than 60 years. In 1938, Everett Stone acquired a decommissioned 1855 lighthouse and built a charming inn and a 9-acre cottage colony around it. Today his grandsons run the show, pretty much as he envisioned it; the lighthouse has even been resuscitated. As they have for at least two generations, families gather at group tables in the summer-camp-scale dining room to plot their day over breakfast and recap over dinner. Many coordinate their vacations so that they can catch up with the same group of friends year after year. With a private beach, heated outdoor pool, tennis courts, and motley amusements such as miniature golf and shuffleboard right on the premises, there's plenty to do. The rooms aren't what you'd call fancy, but some have great Nantucket Sound views. Four rooms are fully accessible to travelers with disabilities.

The dining room—with state flags rippling from the rafters—is open to the general public and serves breakfast, lunch, and dinner. The prices are reasonable, and the menu isn't half as stuffy as you might expect: Lunch is served under umbrellas on the deck overlooking Nantucket Sound, a delightful setting in which to enjoy a club sandwich. This is one of the few places left on the Cape where you can be on the "American Plan," in which both breakfast and dinner are included in your bill. Down the road, at the entrance to the complex, The Sand Bar, a classic bar with cabaret-style entertainment, serves as an on-site nightspot (see "Dennis After Dark," later).

1 Lighthouse Inn Rd. (off Lower County Rd., ¹/₂ mile south of Rte. 28), West Dennis, MA 02670. 📞 508/398-2244. Fax 508/398-5658. www.lighthouseinn.com. 44 units, 24 cottages. Summer $248–$280 double; $298–$322 1-bedroom cottage; $483–$564 2-bedroom cottage; $543–$624 3-bedroom cottage. Rates include full breakfast and all gratuities. MC, V. Closed mid-Oct to mid-May. **Amenities:** 2 restaurants (large dining room, pool snack bar); bar w/entertainment; outdoor heated pool w/ample sunning deck, chairs, umbrellas, and pool house/changing rooms; outdoor tennis court; shuffleboard; volleyball; minigolf; InnKids, a free supervised play program (ages 3–11) offered July–Aug; game room. *In room:* A/C, TV, fridge, hair dryer, iron, safe.

Expensive
Corsair & Cross Rip Resort Motels ★ (Kids) Of the many family-oriented motels lining this part of Nantucket Sound, these two neighbors are among the nicest, with fresh

contemporary decor, two beach-view pools, and their own chunk of sand, a 200-foot long private beach. As a rainy-day backup, there's an indoor pool, a game room, and a toddler playroom equipped with toys. Some rooms have kitchenettes. All rooms have access to barbecue grills.

41 Chase Ave. (off Depot St., 1 mile southeast of Rte. 28), Dennisport, MA 02639. ✆ **800/201-1072** or 508/398-2279. Fax 508/760-6681. www.corsaircrossrip.com. 47 units. Summer $195–$355 double. Special packages and family weekly rates available. AE, MC, V. Closed mid-Oct to Apr. **Amenities:** 2 outdoor pools and 1 indoor pool; outdoor Jacuzzi; toddler playroom and kids' playground; game room; coin-op washers and dryers. *In room:* A/C, TV, fax, fridge, coffeemaker, hair dryer, iron.

Moderate
Isaiah Hall B&B Inn ★★   So keyed-in is this Greek Revival farmhouse to the doings at the nearby Cape Playhouse that you might as well be backstage. Many stars have stayed here over the past half-century, and, if you're lucky, you'll find a few sharing the space. The "great room" in the carriage-house annex seems to foment late-night discussions, to be continued over home-baked breakfasts at the long plank table that dominates the 1857 country kitchen. Room styles range from 1940s knotty pine to spacious and spiffy. They are quaint, countrified, and spotlessly clean. Four have balconies or decks. Two of the rooms have minifridges, and one has a fireplace. The inn's location on a quiet side street in a residential neighborhood bodes well for a good night's sleep, but it's also just a short walk to restaurants, entertainment options, and Corporation Beach on Cape Cod Bay.

152 Whig St. (1 block northwest of the Cape Playhouse), Dennis, MA 02638. ✆ **800/736-0160** or 508/385-9928. Fax 508/385-5879. www.isaiahhallinn.com. 12 units, 6 with tub/shower, 6 with shower only. Summer $185–$225 double; $220 suite. Rates include full breakfast. AE, DISC, MC, V. Open year-round. No children 7 and under. *In room:* A/C, TV/VCR, hair dryer, iron.

WHERE TO DINE
Expensive
Blue Moon Bistro ★★ MEDITERRANEAN   Beautiful presentations of innovative cuisine are the hallmarks at this Dennis Village venue, one of the newer entries in the Cape's fine-dining roster. The restaurant's deep blue ceiling and dark wood floors contribute to the warm and inviting atmosphere; crisp white tablecloths hint at the elegant dining to come. Chef/owner Peter Hyde, who was trained in Europe, gives a twist to traditional recipes. Instead of a crab cake, his is a crab-and-cod cake with spicy red peppers. His Mediterranean fish soup includes the Portuguese sausage, chorizo, for added pizzazz. There are always a couple of vegetarian options on the menu in addition to fish and meat, including the luscious grilled beef tenderloin wrapped in house-smoked bacon. Don't miss the homemade desserts.

605 Main St./Rte. 6A (in the center of Dennis Village), Dennis Village. ✆ **508/385-7100.** Reservations suggested. Main courses $16–$30. AE, MC, V. June to late Aug Wed–Sat 5–10pm, Tues and Sun 5–9:30pm; Apr–May and late Aug to Nov Wed–Sun 4–11pm. Closed Dec–Mar.

Gracie's Table ★ (Finds) SPANISH TAPAS   Just steps from the Cape Playhouse and Cape Cinema, Gracie's Table offers something different on Cape Cod: Spanish-style dining. Preparations by chef/owner Ann Austin are inspired by cuisine from the Basque region, as well as southwest France. Although there are plenty of full meals to choose from, the specialty here is *tapas,* small unusual dishes. The best way to enjoy tapas is for each diner to choose several smaller dishes and share the different tastes with their dining companions. Tapas choices include hot lobster roll, potato-and-chorizo tortilla, and tuna carpaccio with horseradish sorbet. The dining room is sleek and sophisticated, and is staffed by professional servers who are always willing to recommend their favorite tapas.

800 Main St./Rte. 6A (at Theatre Marketplace in front of the Cape Playhouse complex), Dennis Village. *(C)* **508/385-5600.** Reservations recommended. Tapas $5–$15; main courses $18–$30. AE, MC, V. Wed–Mon 5–9pm; call for off-season hours. Open year-round.

The Ocean House New American Bistro and Bar ★★★ (Finds) NEW AMERI-
CAN This restaurant set on the beach overlooking Nantucket Sound has long had a stellar reputation, and under Chef Anthony Sylvestri and a menu of fusion cuisine, it's better than ever. There's a buzz around this creative cuisine, making this oceanfront restaurant a must-go location. One appealing thing about the Ocean House is that you can come for a multicourse fine-dining meal or just some appetizers. Favorites here are the lemon grass-battered gray sole and the grilled beef tenderloin with Maytag blue cheese. With the dining room's large arches framing the beach beyond, this is a wonderful place to spend the evening.

3 Chase Ave. (at Depot St., on the beach), Dennisport. *(C)* **508/394-0700.** Reservations strongly recommended. Main courses $18–$34. MC, V. June–Sept Tues–Sun 5–10pm; call for off-season hours. Open year-round.

The Red Pheasant Inn ★★★ NEW AMERICAN An enduring Cape favorite
since 1977, this handsome space—an 18th-century barn turned chandlery—has managed not only to keep pace with trends but to remain a front-runner. Favorites from chef/owner Bill Atwood include roast rack of lamb, boneless roast duckling, and sole meunière. In the fall, expect game specials like venison and ostrich. His signature cherrystone-and-scallop chowder gets its zip from fresh-plucked thyme. Two massive brick fireplaces tend to be the focal point in the off season, drawing in the weary—and delighted—wanderer. In fine weather, you'll want to sit out in the garden room.

905 Main St. (about ¹/₂ mile east of the town center), East Dennis. *(C)* **508/385-2133.** Reservations required. Main courses $18–$30. DISC, MC, V. Jan–Mar Wed–Sun 5–9:30pm; Apr–Dec daily 5–9pm.

Scargo Cafe ★ INTERNATIONAL A richly paneled captain's house given a mod-
ernist reworking, this lively bistro—named for Dennis's scenic lake—deftly spans old and new with a menu neatly split into "traditional" and "adventurous" categories. Traditionalists will find surf and turf, and the popular grilled lamb loins served with mint jelly (talk about traditional!); adventurous dishes include the likes of "wildcat chicken" (a sauté of sausage, mushrooms, and raisins, flambéed with apricot brandy). The menu here is pricey, but lighter and less expensive nibbles ($11–$14), such as burgers or "Scallop Harpoon"—a bacon-wrapped skewerful, served over rice—are available throughout the day, a boon for beachgoers who tend to return ravenous. Serving food until 11pm makes this an option after a show at the Cape Playhouse across the street.

799 Main St./Rte. 6A (opposite the Cape Playhouse), Dennis Village. *(C)* **508/385-8200.** www.scargocafe. com. Reservations accepted for parties of 6 or more. Main courses $19–$31. AE, DISC, MC, V. Mid-June to mid-Sept daily 11am–4pm and 4:30–11pm; mid-Sept to mid-June daily 11am–10pm.

Moderate
Center Stage Café & Backstage Pub ★ NEW AMERICAN Located in the same
complex as the Cape Playhouse and Cape Cinema, this place could get away with nothing-special food and service. Instead, the Center Stage has become a destination in itself, in addition to being *the* place to go after a show. The beauty of this place is you can get anything from a burger or sandwich to a multicourse meal. Hours are extended

for convenient bites before or after a show. From fresh lobster roll to barbecue chicken pizza to Delmonico steak, it's all here. This is also a great place to grab a drink before or after a show; the bar is cozy and convivial.

36 Hope Lane (on the grounds of the Cape Playhouse), Dennis Village. © **508/385-7737.** Reservations suggested. Main courses $8–$22. AE, MC, V. June to late Aug Mon–Sat 4:30–10pm; Apr–May and late Aug to Nov Wed–Sun 4–11pm. Closed Dec–Mar.

Clancy's of Dennisport ★ SEAFOOD   Every Cape Cod town has its own version of the "fish place with a fantastic view." Here, the vista is relatively low-key: the eatery overlooks the placid Swan River. When they're looking for a not-too-fancy meal, this is a place where both families and couples can go for consistently good inexpensive food. The menu features homemade meatloaf, turkey dinners, sandwiches, salads, burgers, and pasta, in addition to fish, chicken, and steak. Clancy's is also a good choice for Sunday brunch, and it has a kids' menu.

8 Upper County Rd. (east of Rte. 134), Dennisport. © **508/394-6661.** Reservations accepted. Main courses $7–$24. AE, DISC, MC, V. June–Aug daily 11:30am–10pm; call for off-season hours. Open year-round.

Gina's by the Sea ★★ ITALIAN   A landmark amid Dennis's "Little Italy" beach community since 1938, this intimate little restaurant has a few tricks up its sleeve, such as homemade ravioli stuffed with smoked mozzarella. Most of the fare here is the traditional Italian food of our youth, but nonetheless tasty: The ultra-garlicky shrimp scampi, for instance, needs no updating. Save room for Mrs. Riley's Chocolate Rum Cake, made daily by owner Larry Riley's mother; it's scrumptious. This popular place fills up fast, so if you want to eat before 8:30pm, arrive before 5:30pm. Take a sunset or moonlight walk on the beach (just over the dune) to round out the evening.

134 Taunton Ave. (about 1½ miles northwest of Rte. 6A; turn north across from the Dennis Public Market and follow the signs). © **508/385-3213.** Reservations not accepted. Main courses $10–$23. AE, MC, V. Apr–Nov Thurs–Sun 5–10pm. Closed Dec–Mar.

Inexpensive
Captain Frosty's ★ (Kids) SEAFOOD   Here you won't find the typical, tasteless, deep-fried seafood seemingly dipped in greasy cement. The breading is light (thanks to healthy canola oil), and the fish itself is the finest available—fresh off the local day boats and hooked rather than netted (the maritime equivalent of clear-cutting a forest). You won't find a more luscious lobster roll anywhere, and the clam-cake fritters seem to fly out the door.

219 Rte. 6A (about 1 mile west of the town center). © **508/385-8548.** Most items under $15. No credit cards. June–Aug daily 11am–9pm; call for off-season hours. Closed late Sept to early Apr.

The Dog House ★ (Finds) HOT DOG STAND   This just might be the ultimate hot-dog stand, housed in a tiny peaked-roofed hut about a half-mile from Nantucket Sound. Hot dogs, cheese dogs, and chili dogs with all the fixings are the specialty here, but there's also chili and hamburgers. For non-carnivores there's the Surf Burger (salmon). French fries are thickly cut, and onion rings are hand-battered. Fresh lemonade is on hand to wash it all down. Down your dog at one of the dozen picnic tables in this pine glade.

189 Lower County Rd., Dennisport. © **508/398-7774.** All items under $10. No credit cards. Mid-May to mid-Sept daily 11am–8:30pm; call for off-season hours. Closed mid-Oct to mid-May.

Joey's Pizzeria ★ (Finds) PIZZA   Joey says he tried dozens of recipes before perfecting his pizza dough—and it shows. These flavorful old-style Italian thin-crust pies may just be the best pizza on Cape Cod. The menu also has subs and pasta dishes.

197 Lower County Rd., Dennisport. ✆ **508/398-7437.** All pizzas under $17. MC, V. Mid-May to mid-Sept
daily 11:30am–10pm; call for off-season hours. Closed mid-Oct to mid-May.

Marathon Seafood SEAFOOD   Family-owned and operated for over 15 years, this
place holds its own among the Route 28 fast-food/clam-shack competition. You should
order a heaping, steaming platter of fried fish, clams, scallops, or shrimp, or a combo
served with french fries and onion rings. Wash it down with a chocolate milkshake. It's
hard on the heart but easy on the wallet.

231 Rte. 28, West Dennis. ✆ **508/394-3379.** Main courses $7–$15. MC, V. June–Sept daily 11am–11pm;
call for off-season hours. Closed Dec–Feb.

Sesuit Harbor Cafe ★ SEAFOOD   Right on the beach in a busy boatyard, this clam
shack promises one of those authentic Cape Cod experiences that are becoming harder
and harder to find. It's worth seeking out the family-owned establishment for its picture-
postcard views and tasty food. Specialties include clam chowder, lobster rolls, and fried
clams. Good breakfasts, too. Order from the counter and find a seat at one of the picnic
tables outside.

357 Sesuit Neck Rd. (Rte. 6A to Bridge St.; take a right on Sesuit Neck and follow to the harbor), East Dennis. ✆ **508/385-6134.** Reservations not accepted. Main courses $7–$17. MC, V. June–Sept daily 7am–
8:30pm; call for off-season hours. Closed mid-Oct to late Apr.

Sweets
Ice Cream Smuggler ★   A noteworthy stop on any Cape-wide ice-cream crusade,
this cheerful parlor dispenses terrific custom homemade flavors, as well as seductive
sundae concoctions and fudge-bottom pies.

716 Rte. 6A (in Dennis Village center). ✆ **508/385-5307.** July–Aug daily 11am–10:30pm; Apr–June and
Sept to mid-Oct noon–9pm. Closed mid-Oct to Mar.

Stage Stop Candy ★   Considered by some to be Cape Cod's best chocolates, this is
a must-visit for candy fanatics.

411 Main St./Rte. 28, Dennisport. ✆ **508/394-1791.** July–Aug Mon–Sat 9am–8:30pm, Sun 10:30am–
8:30pm; call for off-season hours. Closed for 2 weeks in Jan.

Sundae School ★   For a time-travel treat, visit this spacious barn retrofitted with a
turn-of-the-20th-century marble soda fountain and other artifacts from the golden age
of ice cream. Homemade flavors include Milky Way, Kahlúa Chip, and Grapenut. Local
berries and real whipped cream make for especially tasty toppings.

381 Lower County Rd. (at Sea St., about ¹/₃ mile south of Rte. 28), Dennisport. ✆ **508/394-9122.** Summer
daily 11am–11pm; weekends only in spring and fall. Closed mid-Sept to mid-Apr.

DENNIS AFTER DARK
Performances
Cape Playhouse   The oldest continuously active straw-hat theater in the country and
still one of the best, this way-off-Broadway enterprise was the 1927 brainstorm of Raymond Moore, who'd spent a few summers as a playwright in Provincetown and quickly
tired of the strictures of "little theater." Salvaging an 1838 meetinghouse, he plunked it
amid a meadow and got his New York buddy, designer Cleon Throckmorton, to turn it
into a proper theater. Even with a roof that leaked, it was an immediate success, and a
parade of stars—both established and budding—have trod the boards in the decades
since, from Ginger Rogers to Jane Fonda (her dad spent his salad days there, too, playing
opposite Bette Davis in her stage debut), Humphrey Bogart to Tab Hunter. Not all of

today's headliners are quite as impressive (many hail from the netherworld of TV reruns), but the theater can be counted on for a varied season of polished work. Performances are held mid-June to early September, Monday to Saturday at 8pm; matinees take place Wednesday to Thursday at 2pm. On Friday mornings, performances of children's theater are at 9:30 and 11:30am. 820 Rte. 6A (in the center of town), Dennis Village. © 877/385-3911 or 508/385-3911. www.capeplayhouse.com. Tickets $25–$50, children's theater $8–$9.

Live Music & Entertainment

Compass Rose Summer Shanty   This small bar and restaurant in the middle of a marina is a great little place to have a drink overlooking the harbor. Food is just so-so, though they do make a delicious lobster roll, which is big enough to split between two people. Seating is outside on the deck overlooking the Bass River or inside where a pianist entertains nightly except Tuesdays in season. One of the musicians plays Jimmy Buffett-style tunes, which seems about right for the atmosphere at this place. Bass River Marina (off Rt. 28), West Dennis. © 508/394-0400.

O'Shea's Olde Inne (Finds)   You'd probably drive right by this Irish pub/roadhouse if we didn't tell you about it. A walk through the doors of the modest old Cape cottage is a step back in time. Late in the evenings, someone is bound to take out a guitar or a fiddle, and everyone will sing along. There's live music 'til midnight 7 nights a week in season. 348 Main St. (Rt. 28), West Dennis. © 508/398-8887.

The Sand Bar   This homey cabana was built in 1949, the very year Dennis went "wet." Rock King, a combination boogie-woogie pianist and comedian, still rules the evening and wows the crowd on Thursdays and Saturdays. At the Lighthouse Inn (see "Where to Stay," above), West Dennis. © 508/398-7586. Tues–Sun, opens at 8pm. Cover varies. Free admission for guests of the Lighthouse Inn. Closed mid-Sept to mid-June.

A Retro Movie Theater

Cape Cinema (Moments)   In 1930, Raymond Moore—perceiving of motion pictures as a complement rather than a threat to live theater—added a movie house, modeled on Centerville's Congregational Church, to the Cape Playhouse complex. The interior decoration is an Art Deco surprise, with a Prometheus-themed ceiling mural and folding curtain designed by artist Rockwell Kent and Broadway set designer Jo Mielziner. The art-house programming makes this one of the few places on Cape Cod where you can see movies that are not standard mall fare. That, plus the setting and seating—black leather armchairs—may spoil you forever for what passes for cinemas today. Open year-round with three shows daily. Purists will love that this movie theater is commercial-free. 36 Hope Lane (off Rte. 6A, in the center of town). © 508/385-2503 (recording) or 385-5644. www. capecinema.com. Tickets $8.50.

7

The Lower Cape

The four towns on the Lower Cape are primarily family-oriented summer communities. In the quaint village of Harwich Port, the beach is a mere block off Main Street, so the eternal summertime pastime of a barefoot stroll capped off by an ice-cream cone can still be easily observed. To get to Chatham at the Cape's elbow requires an intentional detour, which may have helped preserve that town as a charming and more upscale locale than some of the other towns along the Nantucket Sound. With its Main Street a gamut of appealing shops and eateries, Chatham approaches an all-American, small-town ideal—complemented nicely by a scenic lighthouse and plentiful beaches nearby.

Occupying the easternmost portion of historic Route 6A, Brewster still enjoys much the same cachet that it boasted as a high roller in the maritime trade. But for a relatively recent incursion of condos and, of course, the cars, it looks much as it might have in the late 19th century; its general store still serves as a social center. For some reason—perhaps because excellence breeds competition—Brewster has spawned several fine restaurants and has become something of a magnet for gourmands.

As the gateway to the Outer Cape, where all roads merge, Orleans offers more variety in the way of shops and entertainment than some of its neighbors. Its nearby cousin, East Orleans, is in itself a destination, offering a couple of fun restaurants and—best of all—a chunk of magnificent, unspoiled Cape Cod National Seashore.

1 BREWSTER ★★

25 miles E of Sandwich; 31 miles S of Provincetown

One of the "youngest" of the Cape towns, Brewster—named for the Pilgrim leader William Brewster—dissociated itself from Harwich in 1803, the better to enjoy its newfound riches as a hotbed of the shipping industry. All along the winding curves of the Old King's Highway (now Rte. 6A), successful captains erected scores of proud houses—99 in all, according to the local lore. When Henry David Thoreau passed through in the mid-1850s, he remarked: "This town has more mates and masters of vessels than any other town in the country."

The Greek/Gothic Revival First Parish Church, built in 1834, embodies many of those mates' and masters' stories. Among the more dramatic tales conjured by the gravestones in back is that of Capt. David Nickerson, who is said to have rescued an infant during the French Revolution—possibly the son of Louis XVI and Marie Antoinette. Whatever his origins, "René Rousseau" followed in his adoptive father's footsteps, ultimately drowning at sea. His name was incised on the back of Nickerson's headstone, according to the custom of the day. Nickerson's name also appears on a pew in the white clapboard church.

Brewster still gives the impression of setting itself apart, mostly free of the commercial encroachments that have plagued the Cape's southern shore. The 380-acre condo-and-golf complex known as Ocean Edge, on what was once a huge private estate, is a premier resort destination. Brewster also welcomes the tens of thousands of transient campers and day-trippers who arrive each summer to enjoy the nearly 2,000 wooded acres of Nickerson State Park.

ESSENTIALS

GETTING THERE After crossing either the Sagamore Bridge or the Bourne Bridge (see "Getting There & Getting Around," in chapter 3), head east on Route 6 or 6A. Crossing the Sagamore Bridge will get you closer to your destination. Route 6A on the north side of the Cape passes through the villages of West Brewster, Brewster, and East Brewster. You can also reach Brewster by taking Route 6's Exit 10 north, along Route 124. Or fly into Hyannis (see "Getting There," in chapter 3).

VISITOR INFORMATION Contact the **Brewster Chamber of Commerce Visitor Center** behind Brewster Town Hall, 2198 Main St./Rte. 6A, Brewster (© **508/896-3500;** fax 508/896-1086; www.brewstercapecod.org); or the **Cape Cod Chamber of Commerce,** routes 6 and 132, Hyannis, MA 02601 (© **888/332-2732;** www.capecod chamber.org). The Brewster Visitor Center is open from mid-June to early September daily from 9am to 3pm and is closed from mid-October to late April. The Cape Cod Chamber of Commerce visitor center is open year-round Monday to Saturday from 9am to 5pm and Sundays and holidays from 10am to 4pm.

BEACHES & RECREATIONAL PURSUITS

BEACHES Brewster's eight lovely bay beaches have minimal facilities. When the tide is out, the "beach" enlarges to as much as 2 miles, leaving behind tide pools to splash in and explore, and vast stretches of rippled, reddish "garnet" sand. On a clear day, you can see the whole curve of the Cape, from Sandwich to Provincetown. That hulking wreck midway, incidentally, is the USS *James Longstreet,* pressed into service for target practice in 1943, and used for that purpose right up until 1970; it's now a popular dive site. You can purchase a beach parking sticker ($15 per day, $50 per week) at the **Visitor Center** behind Town Hall at 2198 Main St. (Rte. 6A, ¹/₂ mile east of the General Store; © **508/896-4511**).

- **Breakwater Beach ★★**, off Breakwater Road, Brewster: A brief walk from the center of town, this calm, shallow beach (the only one with restrooms) is ideal for young children. This was once a packet landing, where packet boats would unload tourists and load up produce—a system that worked until the railroads came along.
- **Flax Pond ★★** in Nickerson State Park (see "Nature & Wildlife Areas," below): This large freshwater pond, surrounded by pines, has a bathhouse and offers watersports rentals. The park contains two more ponds with beaches—Cliff and Little Cliff. Access and parking are free.
- **Linnells Landing Beach ★**, on Linnell Road in East Brewster: This is a ¹/₂-mile, wheelchair-accessible bay beach.
- **Paines Creek Beach ★**, off Paines Creek Road, West Brewster: With 1¹/₂ miles in which to stretch out, this bay beach has something to offer sun lovers and nature lovers alike. Your kids will love it if you arrive when the tide's coming in—the current will give an air mattress a nice little ride.

BICYCLING The **Cape Cod Rail Trail ★★★** intersects with the 8-mile **Nickerson State Park** trail system at the park entrance, where there's plenty of free parking; you could follow the Rail Trail back to Dennis (about 12 miles) or onward toward Wellfleet

(13 miles). **Idle Times** (© **508/255-8281**) provides rentals within the park in season. Another good place to hop on the trail is Underpass Road, about a half-mile south of Route 6A. Here you'll find **Brewster Bicycle Rental,** 442 Underpass Rd. (© **508/896-8149**), and Brewster Express, which makes sandwiches to go. Both shops offer free parking. Bicycle rentals start at around $14 for 4 hours and go up to about $25 for 24 hours.

BOATING   You can rent a canoe at **Jack's Boat Rentals** (© **508/896-8556**), located on either Cliff Pond or Flax Pond within Nickerson State Park. Canoes cost $25 a half-hour and $15 for each additional half-hour. There are also kayaks, paddleboats, surf bikes, and Sunfish sailboats to rent. You can rent a kayak by the day or the week from **Goose Hummock** on Town Cove in Orleans (© **508/255-2620**) and paddle around Paines and Quivett creeks, as well as Upper and Lower Mill ponds. Renting a kayak to paddle around Town Cove for 3 hours will cost you $25 to $45. A 24-hour kayak rental costs $50 to $75.

FISHING   Brewster offers more ponds for fishing than any other town: 14 in all. Among the most popular are Cliff and Higgins ponds (within Nickerson State Park), which are regularly stocked. For a license, visit the town clerk at **Town Hall** at 2198 Rte. 6A (© **508/896-3701**). Brewster lacks a deep harbor, so would-be deep-sea fishers will have to head to Barnstable or, better yet, Orleans.

GOLF   One of the most challenging courses in Brewster is **Captain's Golf Course** at 1000 Freemans Way (© **508/896-5100**). In season, a round at Captain's course is $64, with discounted afternoon rates.

NATURE & WILDLIFE AREAS   Admission is free to the three trails maintained by the **Cape Cod Museum of Natural History** (see below). The **South Trail,** covering a .75 mile round-trip south of Route 6A, crosses a natural cranberry bog beside Paines Creek to reach a hardwood forest of beeches and tupelos; toward the end of the loop, you'll come upon a "glacial erratic," a huge boulder dropped by a receding glacier. Before heading out on the .25-mile **North Trail,** stop in at the museum for a free guide describing the local flora, including wild roses, cattails, and sumacs. Also accessible from the museum parking lot is the **John Wing Trail,** a 1.5-mile network traversing 140 acres of preservation land, including upland, salt marsh, and beach. (*Note:* This can be a soggy trip. Be sure to heed the posted warnings about high tides, especially in spring, or you might very well find yourself stranded.) Keep an eye out for marsh hawks and blue herons.

As it crosses Route 6A, Paines Creek Road becomes Run Hill Road. Follow it to the end to reach **Punkhorn Park Lands,** an undeveloped 800-acre tract popular with mountain bikers; it features several kettle ponds, a "quaking bog," and 45 miles of dirt paths composing three marked trails (you'll find trail guides at the trail heads).

Though short, the .25-mile jaunt around the **Stony Brook Grist Mill** (see below) is especially scenic. In spring, you can watch the alewives (freshwater herring) vaulting upstream to spawn, and in the summer, the millpond is surrounded and scented by honeysuckle. Also relatively small, at only 25 acres, the **Spruce Hill Conservation Area** behind the Brewster Historical Society Museum (see below) includes a 600-foot stretch of beach, reached by a former carriage road reportedly favored by Prohibition bootleggers.

Just east of the museum is the 1,955-acre **Nickerson State Park** at Route 6 and Crosby Lane (© **508/896-3491**), the legacy of a vast, self-sustaining private estate that once generated its own electricity (with a horse-powered plant) and attracted notable guests, such as President Grover Cleveland, with its own golf course and game preserve.

Today it's a nature preserve encompassing 420 campsites (reservations pour in a year in advance to Reserve America at ✆ **877/422-6762,** which charges $15 for Massachusetts residents, $17 for out-of-staters), eight kettle ponds (stocked year-round with trout), and 8 miles of bicycle paths. The rest is trees—some 88,000 evergreens, planted by the Civilian Conservation Corps. This is land that has been through a lot but, thanks to careful management, is bouncing back.

TENNIS   Five public courts are located behind the police station; for details, contact the **Brewster Recreation Department** (✆ **508/896-9430**).

WATERSPORTS   Various small sailboats, kayaks, canoes, and even aqua bikes (also known as sea cycles) are available seasonally at **Jack's Boat Rentals** (✆ **508/896-8556**), located on Flax Pond within Nickerson State Park (see "Boating," above). Canoe or kayak rentals for a couple of hours cost $40.

BREWSTER HISTORIC SIGHTS & MUSEUMS

Brewster Historical Society Museum   This somewhat scattershot collection offers glimpses of Brewster's past. It includes a model of the town's first house (built in 1660), vestiges of an old post office and barbershop, and various relics of the China trade—the import business that made the town's fortune.

3341 Rte. 6A (about 1 mile east of the town center). ✆ **508/896-9521.** Free admission; donations accepted. July–Aug Thurs–Sat 1–4pm; call for off-season hours. Closed early Oct–May.

Brewster Ladies' Library   So inviting is the buttercup-yellow facade of this Victorian library, built in 1868, that curiosity will undoubtedly draw you inside. The two young ladies who started up this enterprise in 1852 with a shelf full of books had the right idea. The original pair of reading rooms remains intact, with facing fireplaces and comfy armchairs. A major addition houses meeting rooms, an auditorium, and a Brewster history room. The library hosts special exhibits, lectures, and concerts.

1822 Rte. 6A (about ⅛ mile southwest of the Brewster Store). ✆ **508/896-3913.** www.brewster ladieslibrary.org. Free admission. Tues and Thurs 10am–8pm; Wed, Fri–Sat 10am–5pm. Closed Sun–Mon.

Cape Cod Museum of Natural History ★★★ **Kids**   Long before "ecology" had become a buzzword, noted naturalist writer John Hay helped found a museum that celebrates—and helps preserve—Cape Cod's unique landscape. Open since 1954, the museum was also prescient in presenting interactive exhibits. The display on whales, for instance, invites the viewer to press a button to hear eerie whale songs; the children's exhibits include an animal-puppet theater. All ages are invariably intrigued by the "live hive"—like an ant farm, only with busy bees. Four marine-room tanks (one 125-gal. tank and three 55-gal. tanks) contain freshwater and saltwater fish, turtles, frogs, crabs, lobsters, starfish, and a variety of mollusks. The bulk of the museum, naturally, is outdoors, where 85 acres invite exploration (see "Nature & Wildlife Areas," above). Visitors are encouraged to log their bird and animal sightings upon their return. A true force in fostering environmental appreciation, the museum sponsors all sorts of activities, like lectures, concerts, marsh cruises, bike tours, and "eco-treks"—including a sleepover on uninhabited Monomoy Island off Chatham. Other activities include evening astronomy cruises, seal cruises, and Pleasant Bay excursions. Call for a schedule.

869 Rte. 6A (about 2 miles west of the town center). ✆ **800/479-3867** (eastern Mass. only) or 508/896-3867. www.ccmnh.org. Admission $8 adults, $7 seniors 65 and over, $3.50 children 3–12. June–Sept daily 9:30am–4pm; Oct–Mar Wed–Sun 11am–3pm; Apr–May Wed–Sun 10am–4pm. Closed major holidays.

Harris-Black House and Higgins Farm Windmill   Most Cape towns can still boast a windmill or two, with a few of them even functioning, but this no-longer-working model is especially handsome. Built in 1795 in the "smock" style that can be traced back to Colonial days, it boasts an unusual cap shaped like a boat's hull. A few steps away is a classic half-Cape house, built that same year, consisting of one square room, 16 feet to a side. Here, one of the poorer members of the community—a blacksmith who doubled as barber—lived simply, yet apparently happily, with his wife and 10 children.

785 Rte. 6A (about 2 miles west of the town center on the Drummer Boy grounds), West Brewster. ✆ **508/896-9521.** Free admission. July–Aug Thurs–Sat 1–4pm; call for off-season hours. Closed Nov–Apr.

Stony Brook Grist Mill and Museum ★ (**Kids**)   It may be hard to believe, but this rustic mill beside a stream was once one of the most active manufacturing communities in New England, cranking out cloth, boots, and ironwork for over a century, starting with the American Revolution. The one remaining structure was built in 1873, toward the end of West Brewster's commercial run, near the site of a 1663 water-powered mill, America's first. After decades of producing overalls and, later, ice cream (with ice dredged from the adjoining pond), the factory was bought by the town and fitted out as a corn mill, with period millstones. Volunteers now demonstrate and urge onlookers to get in on the action in the restored gristmill. A bag of cornmeal costs $2. The second story serves as a repository for all sorts of Brewster memorabilia, including some ancient arrowheads. Archaeological excavations in this vicinity, sponsored by the Cape Cod Museum of Natural History, have unearthed artifacts dating back some 10,000 years. As you stroll about the millpond (see "Nature & Wildlife Areas," above), be on the lookout—who knows what you'll stumble across?

830 Stony Brook Rd. (at the intersection of Satucket Rd.). ✆ **508/896-6745.** Free admission. July–Aug Sat 10am–2pm; call for off-season hours. Closed Sept–Apr.

BASEBALL

The Brewster Whitecaps of the **Cape Cod Baseball League** play at the Cape Cod Tech field off Route 6's Exit 11. For a schedule, contact the **Brewster Chamber of Commerce** (✆ **508/896-3500**), the **Brewster Recreation Department** (✆ **508/896-9430**), or the **League** (✆ **508/432-6909**).

KID STUFF

For an educational experience that's also fun, take the kids to the **Cape Cod Museum of Natural History** ★★★ and the **Stony Brook Grist Mill** ★ (see above for both). Both have walking trails, and the museum has extensive exhibits geared toward children, including a number of interactive exhibits.

SHOPPING

ANTIQUES/COLLECTIBLES   Brewster's stretch of Route 6A offers the best antiquing on the entire Cape. Die-hards would do well to stop at every intriguing shop; you never know what you might find. There are several consistent standouts.

Deborah Rita, proprietor of **Countryside Antiques,** 2052 Main St./Rte. 6A (✆ **508/896-1444**), roams the world in search of stylish furnishings, mostly old, though age—and price—are evidently no object.

ARTS & CRAFTS   Clayton Calderwood's **Clayworks,** 3820 Main St. (Rte. 6A), Brewster (✆ **508/255-4937**), is always worth a stop, if only to marvel at the famous mammoth urns. There's also a world of functional ware here like bowls, pots, and lamps, in porcelain, stoneware, and terra cotta.

At **The Spectrum,** 369 Rte. 6A, about 1 mile east of the Dennis border (© **800/221-2472** or 508/385-3322), you'll find the kind of crafts that gave crafts a good name: fun stuff, with a certain irony to it, but unmistakably chic. In 1966, two young RISD (Rhode Island School of Design) grads opened shop in a rural schoolhouse. Bob Libby and Addison Pratt now oversee six stores: three on the Cape and islands (the other branches are in Hyannis and on Nantucket), and one each in Newport, Troy (Mich.), and Palm Beach. Their taste is top-of-the-line, as you'll see in a quick tour of this split-level, country-modern shop.

Collectors from around the world converge at **Sydenstricker Glass,** 420 Main St., Brewster (© **508/385-3272;** www.sydenstricker.com), in which a kiln-fired process developed in the mid-1960s that uses concepts from the art of enameling yields unique glassware, especially dishes and stemware.

GIFTS/HOME DECOR   Though quite a bit spiffier than a "real" general store, **The Brewster Store,** 1935 Main St./Rte. 6A, in the center of town (© 508/896-3744), an 1866 survivor that was fashioned from an 1852 Universalist church is a fun place to shop for sundries and catch up on local gossip. The wares are mostly tourist-oriented these days but include some handy kitchen gear (cobalt glassware, for example) and beach paraphernalia. Give the kids a couple of dimes to feed the Nickelodeon piano machine, and relax on a sunny church pew out front as you pore over the local paper.

You don't have to be a foodie—though it helps—to go gaga over the exhaustive collection of culinary paraphernalia, from esoteric instruments to foodstuffs, at **The Cook Shop,** 1091 Rte. 6A, about 1¹/₂ miles west of the town center (© **508/896-7698**). If you're stuck cooking up a practical yet unusual house gift, look no further.

SEAFOOD   Breakwater Fish and Lobster at 235 Underpass Rd. in Brewster (© 508/896-7080) stocks the freshest fish in town and also sells smoked fish.

AN INTERNET CAFE & HERB SHOP

Stop at **Great Cape Herbs,** 2624 Main St./Rte. 6A (about 2 miles east of town center) in Brewster (© **508/896-5900**), to pick up all manner of herbs or to use the Internet. This is one of the few places on the Cape that provides computers and Internet access on Sundays. The store is open daily in summer.

WHERE TO STAY
Very Expensive
Ocean Edge Resort & Club ★   Simultaneously evocative of a camp, a country club, and a private seaside estate, Ocean Edge offers something for everyone. Replete with New England–style charm—lovely quilts, sliding glass doors that lead to patios or balconies—hotel rooms off the mansion are extremely large and comfortable. Spread out across the 400-acre property, one- to three-bedroom villas offer the freedom of a private residence (full kitchens, washer/dryers, and fireplaces in some) and the convenience of not having to drive anywhere if you don't want to (shuttle buses run all over the property). However, you might want to go out for groceries or to a local restaurant once in a while; the food served here is fine but not impressive. Whether you go for a getaway with your family or friends, or even for a romantic escape, you won't lack for things to do. A few of your many options: Relax on the private 700-foot beach, complete with complimentary towels and chairs; go swimming (take your pick from one of the four pools here); play golf

or tennis; rent a bike and ride the 26-mile Rail Trail; eat fresh seafood at a clambake; or roast marshmallows over a bonfire on the beach and make s'mores.

2907 Main St., Brewster, MA 02631. ✆ **508/896-9000.** Fax 508/896-9123. www.oceanedge.com. 335 units. Summer $335–$525 hotel room (double); $405–$550 1-bedroom villa; $800–$1,800/night or $2,400–$7,500/week 2- to 3-bedroom villa. Minimum-nights' stay restrictions may apply during peak time periods. AE, DISC, MC, V. Open year-round. **Amenities:** 4 restaurants; 6 pools (2 indoor, 4 outdoor) and 2 toddler pools; 18-hole championship golf course; 11 tennis courts; fitness center; bike trail and bike rentals; children's program for ages 4–12; concierge; business center; babysitting; laundry and dry-cleaning services; conference/banqueting facilities; housekeeping service. *In room:* A/C, TV, Wi-Fi, full kitchen or kitchenette (in villas), coffeemaker, hair dryer, iron, safe (in hotel rooms).

Expensive

Captain Freeman Inn ★★ Donna and Peter Amadeo are the owners of this mint-green 1866 Victorian, one of the best B&Bs in the area. The "luxury rooms" each have a fireplace and private porch with a two-person hot tub. Delectable yet healthy breakfasts are served in the elegant parlor or on a screened porch overlooking the outdoor pool and a lush lawn set up for badminton and croquet. A wine-and-beer bar stands at your service for an afternoon or evening refreshment. Breakwater Beach is a 5-minute walk away.

15 Breakwater Rd. (off Rte. 6A, in the town center), Brewster, MA 02631. ✆ **800/843-4664** or 508/896-8837. Fax 508/896-5618. www.captainfreemaninn.com. 12 units, all with tub/shower. Summer $200–$240 double. Rates include full breakfast and afternoon tea. MC, V. No children under age 10. **Amenities:** Outdoor heated pool; loaner bikes. *In room:* A/C, hair dryer.

Moderate

The Bramble Inn and Restaurant ★★ ⓥⓐⓛⓤⓔ Cliff and Ruth Manchester oversee this rambling mid-19th-century home, decorated in a breezy, country-casual manner. The inn building, constructed in 1861, houses one of the Cape's best restaurants (see "Where to Dine," below) on the first floor. The rooms are small and spare, but quaint, with antique touches like canopy beds with crocheted bedspreads. Cliff makes creative breakfasts, such as mixed-fruit Swedish pancakes, which are served outside in the court-yard garden. The inn is about a half-mile from calm beaches on Cape Cod Bay.

2019 Rte. 6A (about ¹/₃ mile east of the town center), Brewster, MA 02631. ✆ **508/896-7644.** Fax 508/896-9332. www.brambleinn.com. 5 units, 2 with tub/shower, 3 with shower only. Summer $158–$178 double. Rates include full breakfast. AE, DISC, MC, V. Closed Dec 31–Apr 1. **Amenities:** Restaurant. *In room:* A/C, TV, hair dryer, iron.

Candleberry Inn ★ Innkeepers Stuart and Charlotte Fyfe graciously welcome guests to their restored 18th-century Federal-style home. These spacious accommodations feature wide-board floors, wainscoting, and windows with original glass. The decor is country but not cutesy. Some rooms have working fireplaces and canopy beds. Extras include terry-cloth robes in every room as well as down pillows and feather beds. Three rooms in the carriage house are decorated in a more contemporary style; two share an outside deck, one is a deluxe suite, and all have TVs. In season, the three-course full breakfast is frequently served on the sunny porch overlooking the 2 acres of landscaped grounds—which have colorful flower beds throughout. Guests love the view of Main Street from the "glider" rocking benches on the lawn. Breakwater Beach is about a mile north.

1882 Main St./Rte. 6A (from Rte. 6, take Exit 9B; take a right on 6A, inn is 4¹/₂ miles on left), Brewster, MA 02631. ✆ **800/573-4769** or 508/896-3300. Fax 508/896-4016. www.candleberryinn.com. 8 units, 1 with tub/shower, 7 with shower only. Summer $145–$160 double; $195 suite. Rates include full breakfast and afternoon tea. AE, DISC, MC, V. Open year-round. Children 10 and over welcome. *In room:* A/C, hair dryer.

Michael's Cottages and Bed & Breakfast ★ ⓥValue   These cottages on an immaculately groomed compound are small yet centrally located. Across the street is Brewster's Drummer Boy park, which has a playground, historic windmill, and antique house; Brewster's summer band concerts are held there as well. The closest beach is Paines Creek, about 1 mile away. There are three one-bedroom cottages, one small two-bedroom cottage, one efficiency, and two B&B rooms. The cottages have screened porches, fireplaces, and microwaves. The two-bedroom cottage also has a dishwasher and washer/dryer. In July and August, rentals are available by the week only.

618 Main St./Rte. 6A, Brewster, MA 02631. ⓒ **800/399-2967** or 508/896-4025. Fax 508/896-3158. www.michaelsinbrewster.com. 7 units, 2 with tub/shower, 5 with shower only. Summer $150–$160 double; $775–$890 double weekly; $1,445 2-bedroom weekly. B&B rooms include continental breakfast. AE, DISC, MC, V. Open year-round. *In room:* A/C, TV, fridge, coffeemaker, hair dryer.

Inexpensive
Old Sea Pines Inn ★★ ⓥValue ⓚKids   This reasonably priced, large historic inn is a great spot for families. In the main house, the parlor, the expansive porch lined with rockers, and a handful of rather minuscule boarding-school-scale rooms on the second floor recall the inn's days as the Sea Pines School of Charm and Personality for Young Women. (These bargain rooms with shared bathrooms are the only ones in the house without air-conditioning, but at $85 per night in season, who cares?) This is one of the few places on the Cape where solo travelers can find a single room for substantially less than a double. There are two other buildings, one of which is fully wheelchair-accessible (another rarity among historic inns). Whereas the main house has an air of exuberance muted by gentility, the annex rooms are downright playful, with colorful accouterments, including pink TVs. Sunday evenings from mid-June through mid-September, Old Sea Pines is the site of a dinner/theater performance by the Cape Cod Repertory Theatre Company (see "Brewster After Dark," below).

2553 Main St. (about 1 mile east of the town center), Brewster, MA 02631. ⓒ **508/896-6114.** Fax 508/632-0084. www.oldseapinesinn.com. 24 units, 5 with shared bathroom. Summer $85 shared bathroom; $110–$165 double; $160–$190 suite. Rates include full breakfast and afternoon tea. AE, DC, DISC, MC, V. Closed Jan–Mar. *In room:* TV, hair dryer, iron.

WHERE TO DINE
Very Expensive
The Bramble Inn and Restaurant ★★★ CONTINENTAL   Often named among the best restaurants on Cape Cod, there's an impromptu feel to this intimate restaurant, an enclave of five small rooms each imbued with its own personality, from sporting (the Tack Room) to best-Sunday-behavior (the Elegant Parlor). One-of-a-kind antique table settings add to the charm. Such niceties fade to mere backdrop, though, beside Ruth Manchester's extraordinary cuisine. A four-course (eight- to 10-option) menu that evolves every few weeks gives her free rein to follow fresh enthusiasms, as well as seasonal delicacies. Any specifics are quickly history, but she has a solid grounding in Mediterranean cuisines and a gift for improvising exotic influences. Her assorted seafood curry (with lobster, cod, scallops, and shrimp in a light curry sauce with grilled banana, toasted almonds, coconut, and chutney) and her rack of lamb (with deep-fried beet-and-fontina polenta, pan-seared zucchini, and mustard port cream) have been written up in *The New York Times.* An a la carte bistro menu is now available Sunday to Thursday in the Hunt Room bar and in the courtyard garden.

2019 Main St./Rte. 6A (about 1/3 mile east of Rte. 124), Brewster. ✆ **508/896-7644.** Reservations required for fine dining, but not accepted for bistro. Fixed-price dinner $40–$70. AE, DISC, MC, V. June to early Sept daily 6–9pm; call for off-season hours. Closed Jan–Mar.

Chillingsworth ★★★ FRENCH   This longtime contender for the title of fanciest restaurant on the Cape now has two dining options: the formal dining room with jackets recommended for men, and the more casual bistro. The fancy dining room boasts antique appointments reaching back several centuries and a seven-course table *d'hôte* menu that will challenge the most shameless gourmands. Focus on the taste sensations, which are indeed sensational. Specialties include steamed lobster over spinach and fennel with sea beans and lobster-basil butter sauce; and seared and roasted boneless rib-eye of veal with fresh morels, mushroom torte, and asparagus. Finish it off with warm chocolate cake with pistachio ice cream and chocolate drizzle. Or try the moderately priced a la carte bistro, which operates from a separate kitchen and serves lunch and dinner daily in season in the adjoining greenhouse or under huge umbrellas on the shady lawn. There are also three deluxe inn rooms ($110–$150, double occupancy) on the premises.

2449 Main St./Rte. 6A (from Rte. 6, take Exit 10; take a right on 6A, 1 1/2 miles on left), Brewster. ✆ **800/ 430-3640** or 508/896-3640. Reservations required for fine dining at dinner, but recommended for bistro and lunch. Jackets recommended for men in formal dining room. Fixed-price meals $70; bistro $17–$28. AE, DC, MC, V. Mid-June to Aug Thurs–Sun 11:30am–2:30pm, Mon–Sun 6–9:30pm (bistro opens for dinner at 5:30pm; on Mon one seating only for fine-dining 7–7:30pm); call for off-season hours. Closed Dec to mid-May.

Expensive

The Brewster Fish House ★★ NEW AMERICAN   Many locals and visitors alike swear this small, intimate eatery humbly occupying an old house on the side of Route 6A is the Cape's best restaurant. The approach to seafood is nothing if not inspired. Consider, for instance, an appetizer: day-boat sea scallop ceviche with bell pepper, jalapeño, and basil; or the main course: crisp-skin wild striped bass with Stony Island mussels. These are two examples of summer menu items devised to take advantage of the latest haul. Besides seafood, there are always beef and vegetarian dishes on the menu. No wonder the place is packed. Better get here early (before 7pm) if you want to get in.

2208 Main St./Rte. 6A (from Rte. 6, take Exit 12 toward Brewster), Brewster. ✆ **508/896-7867.** Reservations not accepted. Main courses $17–$29. MC, V. May–Aug Mon–Sat 11:30am–3pm and 5–9:30pm, Sun noon–3pm and 5–9:30pm; call for off-season hours. Closed Dec–Apr.

Moderate

Brewster Inn & Chowder House ★ ECLECTIC   To really get the gist of the expression "chow down," just observe the early-evening crowd happily doing so at this plain century-old restaurant known mostly by word of mouth. The draw is hearty, predictable staples—the homemade chowder; various fried, broiled, or baked fish—at prices geared to ordinary people rather than splurging tourists. Check the blackboard for interesting variations—maybe mussels steamed in cream and curry. If you like to indulge in a martini before your meal, this place makes the best ones in town. There's also a good old bar, The Woodshed (see "Brewster After Dark," below), out back.

1993 Rte. 6A (in the center of town). ✆ **508/896-7771.** Reservations not accepted. Main courses $12–$18. AE, DISC, MC, V. Late May to mid-Oct daily 11:30am–3pm and 5–10pm; call for off-season hours. Open year-round.

Cobie's ★ (Kids) AMERICAN   Accessible to cars whizzing along Route 6A and within collapsing distance for cyclists exploring the Rail Trail, this picture-perfect clam shack has been dishing out exemplary fried clams, lobster rolls, foot-long hot dogs, black-and-white frappés, and all the other beloved staples of summer since 1948.

3260 Rte. 6A (about 2 miles east of Brewster center). (C) **508/896-7021.** Most items under $15. No credit cards. Late May to early Sept daily 10:30am–9pm. Closed early Sept to late May.

Sweets

How unusual to find a bake shop tucked away in a sweet little country gift shop. **Hopkins House Bakery,** 2727 Main St. ((C) **508/896-3450**), is an especially good one, with hermit cookies (molasses, raisins, and nuts) a standout. Heather Baxter also bakes breads and terrific muffins, including what she calls "the best corn muffin ever." Homemade fruit pies and sticky buns are also a specialty. Open Thursdays through Sundays 8am to 5pm in July and August, weekends only in June and September. Closed October to May.

BREWSTER AFTER DARK

Performances at the **Cape Cod Repertory Theatre,** 3299 Rte. 6A, East Brewster, about 2¹/₂ miles east of Brewster center ((C) **866/811-4111** or 508/896-1888; www.caperep.org or www.capetix.com), are given Tuesday to Saturday at 8pm from early July to early September. In summer, this shoestring troupe tackles the Bard, as well as serious contemporary fare, at a 200-seat outdoor theater on the old Crosby estate (now state-owned and undergoing restoration). Tickets for outdoor performances are $28. In season, they also put on a Broadway musical-dinner revue Sunday and Monday nights at the **Old Sea Pines Inn** ($55 fixed price; see "Where to Stay," above). Off season they perform at various locales. Call for off-season hours.

Hot local bands take the tiny stage seasonally at **The Woodshed,** at the Brewster Inn & Chowder House, 1993 Rte. 6A ((C) **508/896-7771**), a far cry from the glitzy discos on the southern shore. If your tastes run more to Raitt and Buffett than techno, you'll feel right at home in this dark, friendly dive. Cover charge $5.

---

2 HARWICH ★

---

24 miles E of Sandwich; 32 miles S of Provincetown

Harwich Port, the village in the town of Harwich where most vacationers find themselves, is the quintessential sleepy seaside village, not too mucked up—as yet—by the creeping commercialization of Route 28. The town's main claim to fame is as the birthplace, in 1846, of commercial cranberry cultivation: The "bitter berry," as the Narragansetts called it, is now Massachusetts's leading agricultural product. The curious can find elucidating displays on this and other local distinctions at the Brooks Academy Museum in the inland town of Harwich. The incurious, or merely vacation-minded, can loll on the beach.

ESSENTIALS

GETTING THERE   After crossing the Sagamore Bridge (see "Getting There," in chapter 3), head east on Route 6 and take Exit 10 south along Route 124. Harwich is located at the intersection of Route 39, where the two routes converge. Head southwest to Harwich Port and West Harwich, both located on Route 28. East Harwich (more easily reached from Rte. 6's Exit 11) is inland, a few miles northeast. Or fly into Hyannis (see "Getting There," in chapter 3).

VISITOR INFORMATION   Contact the **Harwich Chamber of Commerce,** Route 28,
Harwich Port, MA 02646 (📞 **800/441-3199** or 508/432-1600; fax 508/430-2105;
www.harwichcc.com), open late May to late September daily from 9am to 5pm; call for
off-season hours. You can also contact the **Cape Cod Chamber of Commerce** (see
"Visitor Information," in the "Brewster" section, earlier in this chapter).

BEACHES & RECREATIONAL PURSUITS

BEACHES   The Harwich coast is basically one continuous beach punctuated by the
occasional harbor. Harwich Port is so close to the sound that it's a snap to walk the block
or two to the water—provided you find a parking place in town (try the lot near the
chamber of commerce booth in the center of town). Parking right at the beach is pretty
much limited to residents and renters, who can obtain a weekly sticker for $55 at the
Community Center, 100 Oak St., Harwich (📞 **508/430-7552**).

- **Bank Street Beach** ★★, at the end of Bank Street in Harwich Port: This is one of
  the few sound beaches in Harwich Port that has parking, but you will need a sticker.
  The sound beaches are generally warm and calm and very good beaches for swimming.
  This is a pretty (and popular) stretch where you'll see lots of families as well as the
  self-conscious college crowd. As for amenities, there are lifeguards and restrooms.
- **Hinckleys Pond** ★ and **Seymours Pond** ★, west of Route 124 and right off the Rail
  Trail, and **Bucks Pond** ★★, off Depot Road at Route 39 northeast of Harwich:
  Although Hinckleys and Bucks have limited parking, no parking sticker is required.
  At Seymours, however, you will need a sticker. Lifeguards are on staff in season, but
  you won't find any restrooms here.
- **Red River Beach** ★, off Uncle Venies Road south of Route 28 in South Harwich:
  This is the only sound beach in town offering parking for day-trippers (they still have
  to get here early to nab a spot); the daily fee is $10. Marked off with stone jetties, this
  narrow, 2,700-foot beach has full facilities with bathrooms. It also has lifeguards.
- **Sand Pond** ★, off Great Western Road near Depot Street: This beach honors the
  weekly beach sticker, as do the two parking lots at Long Pond (between routes 137
  and 124). The beach has restrooms and lifeguards.

BICYCLING   Transecting Harwich for about 5 miles, the Cape Cod Rail Trail skirts
some pretty ponds in the western part before veering north and zigzagging toward
Brewster along Route 124. For rentals and information, contact **The Bike Depot,** 500
Depot Rd., North Harwich (📞 **508/430-4375**), which is on the bike trail. A 24-hour
bike rental costs $30.

BOATING   You can rent a canoe by the day or the week at **Goose Hummock** in
Orleans (📞 **508/255-2620**) and paddle down the Herring River in West Harwich.
Meandering from a reservoir south to the sound, the river is a natural herring run framed
by a cattail marsh.

FISHING   There are six ponds available for fishing in the Harwich area, as well as
extensive shellfishing in season; for details and a license, visit **Town Hall** at 732 Main St.
in Harwich (📞 **508/430-7516**). For supplies and instruction, visit **Fishing the Cape,** at
the Harwich Commons, routes 137 and 39 (📞 **508/432-1200**); it's the official Cape
headquarters for the **Orvis Saltwater Fly-Fishing School and Guides** (📞 **800/235-9763;** www.orvis.com). Instruction for 2 days costs $470. Several deep-sea fishing boats

operate out of Saquatucket Harbor (off Rte. 28, about ¹/₂ mile east of Harwich Port), including the 33-footer *Fish Tale* (© 508/432-3783), which charges $650 for 6 hours and $800 (includes lunch) for 8 hours. The 65-foot *Yankee* (© 508/432-2520) is a party boat out of Saquatucket Harbor offering two 4-hour trips per day (8am–noon, 12:30–4:30pm) Monday through Saturday and one trip on Sunday in season. Off season, there's one trip per day. Trips cost $35 for adults and $33 for seniors and children 9 and under.

GOLF   Both the championship 18-hole **Cranberry Valley Golf Course** at 183 Oak St. in Harwich (© 508/430-5234), which wends its way among cranberry bogs, and the 9-hole **Harwich Port Golf Club** on Forest and South streets in Harwich Port (© 508/432-0250) are open to the public. Cranberry Valley charges $62 for a round, and Harwich Port Golf Club charges $30 for 18 holes.

NATURE & WILDLIFE AREAS   The largest preserve in Harwich is the 245-acre **Bells Neck Conservation Area** north of Route 28 near the Dennis border. It encompasses the Herring River, ideal for birding and canoeing (see "Boating," above).

TENNIS   Public courts are available on a first-come, first-served basis at the Cape Cod Technical High School on Route 124 and Brooks Park on Oak Street, about ¹/₄ mile east of Harwich center off Route 39; for details, contact the **Harwich Recreation Department** (© 508/430-7553). Open late May through September, the **Wychmere Harbor Tennis Club** at 792 Main St. in Harwich Port (© 508/430-7012) comprises nine Har-Tru courts and two hard courts; lessons can be scheduled. Court time is $50 for the day.

HISTORICAL HARWICH

Brooks Academy Museum ★   Gathered in an 1844 Greek Revival academy that offered the country's first courses in navigation, the collections of the Harwich Historical Society are good for a rainy afternoon's worth of wonderment. On permanent display is an extensive exhibition chronicling the early days of the cranberry industry, when harvesting was a backbreaking chore performed on hands and knees with a wooden scoop, mostly by migrant workers. (It simplified matters enormously once someone figured out that the bogs could be flooded and threshed so that the berries bob to the surface.) Other holdings include Native American tools, paintings by local artist C. D. Cahoon, nautical items of historical interest, and extensive textiles, imaginatively presented. The complex also includes a Revolutionary powder house and—kids might get a kick out of this—a nicely restored 1872 outhouse.

80 Parallel St. (at the intersection of Sisson Rd. and Main St., about 1 mile north of Harwich Port center). © **508/432-8089.** Free admission, but donations accepted. Mid-June to mid-Oct Wed and Fri 1–4pm, Thurs 1–7pm. Closed mid-Oct to mid-June.

BASEBALL

The Harwich Mariners, part of the **Cape Cod Baseball League,** play at Whithouse Field behind the high school in Harwich. For a schedule, contact the **Harwich Chamber of Commerce** (© 508/432-1600), the **Harwich Recreation & Youth Department** (© 508/430-7553), or the **League** (© 508/432-6909).

KID STUFF

West Harwich gets some spillover from Dennis's overdevelopment, including such junior-tourist attractions as **Harbor Glen Miniature Golf** at 168 Rte. 28 (© 508/432-8240), which costs $6 for those 13 and over, $4 for those 6 to 12, and $2 for those 5 and under; the **Trampoline Center** at 296 Rte. 28 (© **508/432-8717**), which costs $5 for 10 minutes; and **Bud's Go-Karts** at the intersection of routes 28 and 39 (© **508/432-4964**), which welcomes hot rodders as young as 8, provided they meet the height requirement (54 in.). The go-carts are $6 per ride. All three are open until 10 or 11pm in summer. For free self-entertainment, visit **Castle in the Clouds,** a community-built playground behind the Harwich Elementary School on South Street in Harwich. Young culture mavens might want to take in a performance at the **Harwich Junior Theatre** at 105 Division St. in West Harwich (© **508/432-2002;** www.hjtcapecod.org), which has been satisfying summer customers since 1952; if you plan to stick around for a while, your youngsters could even take classes and possibly work their way onstage. Tickets cost $12 to $22 adults, $16 seniors 65 and over, $12 youths 20 and under.

SHOPPING

Route 28 harbors lots of minimalls and shops, big on gifts (on the trite side) and unsensational art. With a few exceptions, save your power shopping for Chatham.

ANTIQUES/COLLECTIBLES **The Barn at Windsong,** 245 Bank St., a half-mile north of Harwich Port center, midway between routes 28 and 39 (© **508/432-8281**), is the kind of archetypal shop antiquers crave: a lovely old barn in the country, packed with premium goods. Offerings include furniture, glass, china, and rugs. Closed November through April.

WHERE TO STAY

There are several above-average motels in Harwich. **The Tern Inn,** 91 Chase St., West Harwich (© **800/432-3718** or 508/432-3714; www.theterninn.com), is in a quiet residential neighborhood. Summer rates are $149 to $159 for a double, and $975 per week for a one-bedroom cottage, $1,200 for a three-bedroom cottage. The Tern has a small, unheated pool. Rooms do not have phones, but all have TVs, minifridges, and air-conditioning. Just 75 yards from a wide Nantucket Sound beach, **The Commodore Inn ★**, 30 Earle Rd., West Harwich (© **800/368-1180** or 508/432-1180; www.commodore inn.com), has 27 lovely rooms resembling upscale condos with cathedral ceilings and an outdoor heated pool. It's a short walk to the beach. Rates are $215 to $245 double and include a full buffet breakfast in season. All rooms have microwave ovens and minifridges, as well as air-conditioning, TVs, and phones with dataports. Some have Jacuzzis and fireplaces. Closed mid-October to March. **Sandpiper Beach Inn ★★**, 16 Bank St., Harwich Port (© **800/433-2234** or 508/432-0485; www.sandpiperbeachinn.com), is plunked right on a lovely Nantucket Sound beach. All rooms have air-conditioning, phones, TVs, hair dryers, and fridges. Summer rates (including continental breakfast) are $220 to $440 double, $370 to $440 for suites. Closed November to mid-April.

Very Expensive

Wequassett Resort and Golf Club ★★★   This 22-acre resort set on Pleasant Bay has been the place to go for vacationing tennis, golf and sailing enthusiasts, with all three close at hand. Inn guests enjoy exclusive nonmember privileges to Cape Cod National Golf Club. The restaurant on-site, 28 Atlantic, is one of the Cape's top dining spots (see below). Rooms are spread out in a half-dozen buildings and are spacious and comfortable, with 15 beachfront units. All rooms have either a balcony or a patio, and rooms for guests with disabilities are available. The calm private bay beach just steps from the rooms is called Clam Point. Chatham's North Beach is a 15-minute ride via the inn's Power Skiff (cost $12 adults, $5 children).

2173 Rte. 28 (about 5 miles northeast of Chatham center, on Pleasant Bay), Harwich, MA 02633. © **800/225-7125** or 508/432-5400. Fax 508/432-5032. www.wequassett.com. 104 units. Summer $475–$825 double; $795–$1,450 suites. AE, DC, DISC, MC, V. Closed Dec–Mar. **Amenities:** 2 restaurants (28 Atlantic for fine dining, see review below, and Outer Bar and Grille for casual fare, both open to the public); pear-shaped heated outdoor pool; golf course next door ($105 a round plus $20 for a cart); 4 all-weather Plexipave tennis courts ($15 an hr. per person) plus a pro shop; fitness room; watersports equipment (sailboards, Sunfish, Daysailers, and Hobie Cats for about $40 an hr.); bike rentals ($20–$40 per day); Children's Fun Club ($25 for half-day, $45 for full day); concierge; secretarial services; room service; in-room massage; babysitting; van service; yoga and pilates classes ($15); horseshoes, basketball, and volleyball equipment. *In room:* A/C, TV, minibar, coffeemaker, hair dryer, iron.

Winstead Inn and Beach Resort ★★   This property is composed of two buildings set about a mile apart: the 14-room Beach House Inn on a private Nantucket Sound beach and a short walk from Harwich Port, and the remodeled seven-room Winstead Inn near Harwich center. The Beach House is an antiques-filled 1920s inn. The Winstead, is a handsome Colonial-style building with a pool. Both inn buildings are within walking distance of shops and restaurants, so you don't have to contend with summer traffic. Those staying at the Winstead can take a free shuttle to the beach in a 1949 Pontiac Woody.

4 Braddock Lane, Harwich, MA 02646. © **800/870-4405** or 508/432-4444. Fax 508/432-9152. www. winsteadinn.com. 21 units. Summer $295–$485 double. Rates include continental breakfast. MC, V. Open year-round. **Amenities:** Outdoor heated pool at Winstead property. *In room:* A/C, TV, fridge, hair dryer.

WHERE TO DINE
Very Expensive

L'Alouette Bistro ★★   CONTEMPORARY FRENCH   If you're looking for a romantic spot with candlelit dining, you'll find it at this cozy old Cape cottage, where owners Alan and Gretchen Champney give classic French cuisine a shot in the arm. Choices like escargot and seared foie gras are authentically presented, but there are also surprises, such as pistachio-crusted lamb with Bordeaux sauce. The pasta with poached lobster and truffled cognac and tarragon sauce is a pleasing twist on a traditional favorite.

787 Rte. 28 (about ½ mile east of the town center), Harwich Port. © **508/430-0405.** Reservations recommended. Main courses $22–$34. AE, DISC, MC, V. Late May to mid-Oct daily 5–9pm (last reservation at 8:30pm); mid-Oct to late May Tues–Sun 5–9pm.

28 Atlantic ★★★   NEW AMERICAN   This restaurant on the grounds of the Wequassett Resort and Golf Club is one of the top places to eat on Cape Cod. The elegant spacious dining room overlooks Pleasant Bay through immense floor-to-ceiling glass panels. Service is professional and stylish. And the food stands out as superb, from the *amuse bouche* (a little taste teaser) offered at the start of the meal, to the exceptional desserts served at the end. Menu items use local provender as much as possible, but there are also delicacies from around the world. You might start with the Cape lobster and roasted corn bisque with sherried Devonshire cream; move on to the composed salad of mâche, melon, prosciutto, grapes, goat-cheese mousse, and tawny port syrup; and then get to your main course, perhaps skillet-seared local bluefish with saffron-smoked mussel risotto, wilted Swiss chard, and lobster oil. You're in for a treat here; it's all exquisite. For more casual dining, the Wequassett has just completed a multimillion-dollar renovation of its poolside cafe, called the **Outer Bar** ★★. Open to the public from 11:30am to 10pm, this is a stylish place to grab a drink or a light meal while listening to live jazz and basking in views of Pleasant Bay.

2173 Rte. 28 (at the Wequassett Resort and Golf Club, about 5 miles northwest of Chatham center, on Pleasant Bay). 🕻 **508/430-3000.** www.wequassett.com. Reservations recommended. Main courses $21–$44. AE, DC, DISC, MC, V. May–Nov daily 7–11am and 6–10pm; call for off-season hours. Closed Dec to mid-Apr.

Expensive

Buca's Tuscan Roadhouse ★★ (Finds) NORTHERN ITALIAN   No wonder this place is so popular: an atmosphere that's somehow romantic and festive at the same time, wonderful food, and superior service. The only problem is getting a reservation, even in January. But once you do land a table you can relax into this most enjoyable dining experience. Homemade pastas, off-the-boat fish, tender cuts of meat—it doesn't get much better than this. From basics like eggplant parmigiana to *cacciucco,* a mélange of seafood in a garlicky broth, the food is delicious. Wines by the glass are also exceptional.

4 Depot Rd. (on the corner of Rt. 28, close to the Chatham border), Harwich. 🕻 **508/432-6900.** Reservations recommended. Main courses $18–$25. AE, MC, V. June–Aug daily 5–9:30pm; call for off-season hours. Open year-round.

The Cape Sea Grille ★★ NEW AMERICAN   Chef/owner Doug Ramler is the new power behind the stove at this upscale enterprise occupying a peach-toned 19th-century beach house, a former sea captain's home. The dining rooms tend toward the impersonal side, perhaps the restaurant's only weak link. The food is excellent. The specialty of the house is the pan-seared lobster with pancetta, potatoes, grilled asparagus, and a Calvados-saffron reduction, but other enticing choices on the menu include seafood *tapas* and duck confit. City sophisticates who insist on creativity and innovation will find this the most consistently rewarding source in town. The restaurant is also a short walk to a neighborhood beach, the perfect place for an after-dinner moonlight stroll.

31 Sea St. (south of Rte. 28 in the center of town), Harwich Port. 🕻 **508/432-4745.** Reservations recommended. Main courses $19–$33. AE, MC, V. June–Aug daily 5–10pm; call for off-season hours. Closed mid-Nov to early Apr.

Circadia Bistro at the Country Inn ★★ NEW AMERICAN   Whether you sit in the rustic tavern or the more formal dining room of this antique Cape inn, you'll probably be near one of the nine fireplaces. The menu changes nightly, but you'll always find unusual combinations beautifully presented. For example, a salad of beet carpaccio and shaved fennel is the perfect start to a dinner of pan-fried flounder with seafood-wonton ravioli. Besides wonderful fish and shellfish selections, there are also beef, lamb, duck, and vegetarian items on the menu. The tavern also offers a lighter-fare menu ($8–$17).

86 Sisson Rd. (north of Rte. 28 in the center of town), Harwich Port. 🕻 **508/432-2769.** Reservations recommended. Main courses $19–$32. AE, MC, V. June–Oct daily 5–10pm; Nov–May Thurs–Sun 5–10pm.

Moderate

Villa Roma ★ (Finds) ITALIAN   If you didn't know about this perfect little roadhouse, you'd drive right by. Walk into the dimly lit bar area and then to one of the comfortably snug dining rooms. This old house retains the charm of Olde Cape Cod, something that is becoming harder and harder to find. On the menu is classic Italian fare, nothing fancy. There's lasagna with homemade meatballs, shrimp scampi, and a wonderfully light veal piccata. The prices are very reasonable, even cheap, considering your meal comes with a salad or soup. But the best thing about this place is the atmosphere and the friendly staff.

278 Rte. 28, West Harwich. 🕻 **508/432-6868.** Reservations for 6 or more only. Main courses $10–$20. AE, MC, V. Daily 5–9:30pm. Open year-round.

Seafood Sam's (Kids) SEAFOOD   Strategically located within a big bounce of the Trampoline Center, this McDonald's-style clam shack—part of a Cape-wide chain—dishes out deep-fried seafood, fast.

302 Rte. 28 (about ¹/₂ mile east of the town center), Harwich Port. ✆ **508/432-1422.** Most items under $12. DISC, MC, V. Mid-Feb to late Nov daily 11am–9pm. Closed late Nov to mid-Feb.

Sweets

Sundae School ★ ICE CREAM   Another branch of the local chain (also in Dennis Port and East Orleans), this is homemade ice cream and a sure crowd pleaser with the kids. Real whipped cream and real cherries will keep the parents happy, too. Fresh-fruit sundaes are a popular choice here, and everyone likes to admire the 1938 ice-cream truck.

606 Main St. (in the center of town), Harwich Port. ✆ **508/430-2444.** Mid-May to early Oct daily 11am–10:30pm. Closed early Oct to mid-May.

HARWICH AFTER DARK

The Irish Pub ★   For years, this has been the premier Irish bar on the Cape. It feels authentic because it is. A variety of live entertainment (it could be Irish music, karaoke, or anything in between) Thursday to Saturday in season is usually rollicking good fun. 126 Main St. (Rte. 28), West Harwich. ✆ **508/432-8808.** Cover under $5.

3 CHATHAM ★★★

32 miles E of Sandwich; 24 miles S of Provincetown

Sticking out like a sore elbow (and out of the way of much of the Cape's tourist flow), Chatham was one of the first spots to attract early explorers. Samuel de Champlain stopped by in 1606 but got into a tussle with the prior occupants over some copper cooking pots; he ended up leaving in a hurry. The first colonist to stick around was William Nickerson of Yarmouth, who befriended a local sachem (tribal leader) and built a house beside his wigwam in 1656. One prospered; the other—for obvious reasons—didn't. To this day, listings for Nickersons still occupy a half-page in the Cape Cod phone book.

Chatham, along with Provincetown, is the only area on the Cape to support a sizeable commercial fishing fleet—against increasing odds. Overfishing has resulted in closely monitored limits to give the stock time to bounce back. Boats must now go out as far as 100 miles to catch their fill. Despite the difficulties, it's a way of life few locals would willingly relinquish. As in Provincetown, there's surprisingly little animosity between the hardworking residents and the summer vacationers at play, perhaps because it's clear that discerning tourist dollars are helping to preserve this lovely town for all.

ESSENTIALS

GETTING THERE   After crossing the Sagamore Bridge (see "Getting There," in chapter 3), head east on Route 6 and take Exit 11 south (Rte. 137) to Route 28. From this intersection, the village of South Chatham is about a half-mile west, and West Chatham is about 1¹/₂ miles east. Chatham itself is about 2 miles farther east on Route 28. To fly to Chatham, take a commercial flight into Hyannis (see "Getting There," in chapter 3).

VISITOR INFORMATION   Visit the **Cape Cod Chamber of Commerce** (see "Visitor Information," in the "Brewster" section, earlier in this chapter); the **Chatham Chamber of Commerce,** 533 Main St., Chatham, MA 02633 (© **800/715-5567** or 508/945-5199; www.chathaminfo.com); or the **Chatham Chamber booth** (no phone) at the intersection of routes 137 and 28. Hours for both the Chatham chamber and the booth are July and August Monday to Saturday 10am to 6pm, Sunday noon to 6pm; closed late October to April. Call for off-season hours.

A STROLL AROUND CHATHAM

A stroll around Chatham, taking you from one end of Main Street to the other and to interesting sites nearby, can give you a great feel for this picturesque town. The walk covers a distance of approximately 2¹/₂ miles and takes 2 to 3 hours, depending on how many stops you make along the way. Parking on Main Street can be a challenge at the height of summer, so pretend you're a turn-of-the-20th-century traveler and start out at the **Chatham Railroad Museum** ★ on 153 Depot St. (closed mid-Sept to mid-June), 1 block north of Main Street at the western end of town. You can't miss it: It's a gaudy 1887 Victorian station in the "Railroad Gothic" style, painted yellow with fanciful russet ornamentation. The building itself is full of railroading memorabilia, and the big exhibits—antique passenger cars—are out back.

If you've got children along, they'll surely want to stretch their legs (and imaginations) at the **Play-a-Round Park** ★★, opposite the Railroad Museum. Dreamed up by prominent playground designer Robert Leathers, it's a marvelous maze of tubes, rope ladders, slides, and swings. The only way you'll get going again is to promise to come back.

Head west to the end of Depot Street and right on Old Harbor Road, which, if followed past Main Street, becomes State Harbor Road. About a mile farther along, past Oyster Pond, you'll encounter the **Atwood House Museum** ★ at 347 Stage Harbor Rd. (© **508/945-2493;** www.chathamhistoricalsociety.org; closed Oct to mid-June). The 1752 house itself shelters the odds and ends collected by the Chatham Historical Society over the past 7 decades; piece by piece, they tell the story of the town. The Society even managed to save an entire 1947 "fishing camp," a run-down cottage that looks as if the occupant just stepped out to check a line.

Heading back toward Main Street, bear right on Cross Street and look for **Chase Park and Bowling Green,** presided over by the Old Grist Mill, built in the late 18th century. You might actually try some lawn bowling along the lovingly tended greens before returning to Main Street, where the shops are too prolific and special to pass up. Then head eastward toward the shore, but be sure to duck into the **Mayo House** at 540 Main St. (© **508/945-4084**), a sweet little three-quarter Cape built in 1818. Entrance is free, and—if you've studiously avoided lengthy historical house tours so far—it can give you, in just a couple of minutes, a good sense of what life might have been like here in centuries past.

Main Street veers right when it reaches the shore. Continue along for about ¹/₄ mile to view the **Chatham Light** ★★, an 1876 beacon not open to the public, but still in operation: Its light shines 15 miles out to sea. This is a good vantage point from which to marvel over the "break" that burst through Chatham's barrier beach in 1987. In the years since, the newly created island, South Beach, has already glommed onto the coastline, becoming a peninsula. This is one landscape that rarely stays put for long.

Retrace your steps northward along the shore. In about ³/₄ mile, you'll pass the grand **Chatham Bars Inn** ★★★ at Shore Road and Seaview Street (© **800/527-4884** or

508/945-0096), which started out as a private hunting lodge in 1914. Passersby are welcome to look around the lobby, restored to reflect its original Victorian splendor. Linger on the porch over coffee or a drink, if you like, before pressing on to the **Chatham Fish Pier,** about a quarter-mile farther along Shore Road (© **508/945-5177**). If you've timed your visit right (from noon on), the trawlers should just now be bringing in the catch of the day: You can observe the haul from an observation deck. Also have a look at *The Provider,* an intriguing outdoor sculpture by Woods Hole artist Sig Purwin.

WINDING DOWN When you've had enough, or the insects insist that you head on home, go back to Main Street down Seaview Street, past the Chatham Seaside Links golf course. One long block later (about 1/2 mile), you're back in the center of town. You can relax and unwind at the **Chatham Wayside Inn ★** at 512 Main St. (© **508/945-5550**). Secure a table on the greenery-curtained patio and watch the world go by, as you fortify yourself with regionally inspired snacks and sweets on the large screened porch.

BEACHES & RECREATIONAL PURSUITS

BEACHES Chatham has an unusual array of beach styles, from the peaceful shores of the Nantucket Sound to the treacherous, shifting shoals along the Atlantic. For information on beach stickers ($15 per day, $60 per week), call the **Permit Department** on George Ryder Road in West Chatham (© **508/945-5180**).

- **Chatham Light Beach ★★:** Located directly below the lighthouse parking lot (where stopovers are limited to 30 min.), this narrow stretch of sand is easy to get to: Just walk down the stairs. Currents here can be tricky and swift, though, so swimming is discouraged.
- **Cockle Cove Beach, Ridgevale Beach,** and **Hardings Beach ★★:** Lined up along the sound, each at the end of its namesake road south of Route 28, these family-pleasing beaches offer gentle surf suitable for all ages, as well as full facilities, including lifeguards. Parking stickers are required.
- **Forest Beach ★:** No longer an officially recognized town beach (there's no lifeguard), this sound landing near the Harwich border is still popular, especially among surfboarders.
- **North Beach ★★:** Extending all the way south from Orleans, this 5-mile barrier beach is accessible from Chatham only by boat; if you don't have your own, you can take the **Beachcomber,** a water taxi, which leaves from Chatham fish pier on Shore Road. Call © **508/945-5265** (www.sealwatch.com) to schedule your trip, though reservations are not necessary. Round-trip costs $25 for adults, and $21 for children 12 and under. The water taxi makes the trip from 10am to 5pm daily in season on sunny days. Inquire about other possible drop-off points if you'd like to beach around.
- **Oyster Pond Beach,** off Route 28: Only a block from Chatham's Main Street, this sheltered saltwater pond (with restrooms) swarms with children. It's free to park here and there is a lifeguard.
- **South Beach ★★:** A former island jutting out slightly to the south of the Chatham Light, this glorified sandbar can be dangerous, so heed posted warnings and content yourself with strolling or, at most, wading. A sticker is not required to park here.

BICYCLING Though Chatham has no separate recreational paths per se, a demarcated bike/blading lane makes a scenic, 8-mile circuit of town, heading south onto "The Neck," east to the Chatham Light, up Shore Road all the way to North Chatham, and back to the center of town. A descriptive brochure prepared by the **Chatham Chamber**

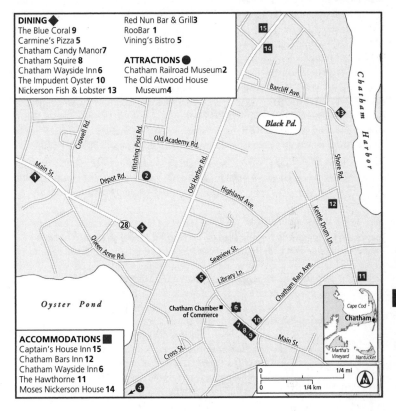

DINING ◆
The Blue Coral **9**
Carmine's Pizza **5**
Chatham Candy Manor **7**
Chatham Squire **8**
Chatham Wayside Inn **6**
The Impudent Oyster **10**
Nickerson Fish & Lobster **13**

Red Nun Bar & Grill **3**
RooBar **1**
Vining's Bistro **5**

ATTRACTIONS ●
Chatham Railroad Museum **2**
The Old Atwood House
    Museum **4**

ACCOMMODATIONS ■
Captain's House Inn **15**
Chatham Bars Inn **12**
Chatham Wayside Inn **6**
The Hawthorne **11**
Moses Nickerson House **14**

of Commerce (© **800/715-5567** or 508/945-5199) shows the suggested route, and there are lots of lightly trafficked detours worth taking.

BIRD-WATCHING In summer, the Wellfleet Bay Wildlife chapter of the **Audubon Society** (© **508/349-2615**) offers bird-watching trips to the **Monomoy National Wildlife Refuge** ★★ on North Monomoy Island (monomoy.fws.gov). On the tour of North Monomoy, after a 15-minute boat ride from Chatham, you'll embark on a 4-hour guided tour, where you'll encounter a variety of species—from herring gulls and sandpipers to black-bellied plovers and willets. Tours cost around $35 adults, $30 children 12 and under, and are recommended not just for avid bird-watchers, but for anyone who enjoys the outdoors. Reservations are required.

BOATING You can rent a kayak (see below) and paddle down the Oyster River, past Hardings Beach, and over to Morris Island. You can also explore Pleasant Bay, the Cape's largest, and reach the inside shore of the Outer Beach. For those with sufficient experience, Pleasant Bay is the best place to sail; if the winds don't go your way, try Forest Beach on the South Chatham shore.

NautiJane's Boat Rental at 337 Rte. 28 in Harwich Port (© **508/430-6893**) also offers kayak and sailboat rentals at the Wequassett Inn on Pleasant Bay and on Ridgevale

Beach in Chatham (© **508/432-4339**): Available crafts include kayaks, Sunfish, surf bikes, and sailboats up to 16 feet. Kayaks rent for $25 per hour or $42 for 2 hours; sailboats rent for $65 to $99 for two hours or $115 to $185 for half-day.

FISHING   Chatham has five ponds and lakes that permit fishing; Goose Pond off Fisherman's Landing is among the top spots. For saltwater fishing sans boat, try the fishing bridge on Bridge Street at the southern end of Mill Pond. First, though, get a license at **Town Hall** at 549 Main St. in Harwich (© **508/430-7553**) or at Goose Hummock in Orleans (© 508/255-2620). If you hear the deep sea calling, sign on with *The Head-hunter* (© **508/430-2312;** www.capecodfishingcharters.com), a 33-foot sportfishing boat, or the 31-foot *Banshee* (© **508/945-0403**), both berthed in Stage Harbor. Sport-fishing rates average around $650 for 5 hours. Shellfishing licenses are available at the **Permit Department** on George Ryder Road in West Chatham (© **508/945-5180**).

GOLF   Once part of the Chatham Bars Inn property and now owned by the town, the scenic 9-hole, par-34 **Chatham Seaside Links** at 209 Seaview St. in Chatham (© **508/945-4774**) isn't very challenging but is fun for neophytes; inquire about instruction. A 9-hole round costs $19.

NATURE & WILDLIFE AREAS   Heading southeast from the Hardings Beach parking lot, the 2-mile round-trip **Seaside Trail** offers beautiful parallel panoramas of Nantucket Sound and Oyster Pond River; keep an eye out for nesting pairs of horned lark. Access to 40-acre Morris Island, southwest of the Chatham Light, is easy: You can walk or drive across and start right in on a marked .75-mile trail. Heed the high tides, as advised, though—they can come in surprisingly quickly, leaving you stranded.

Chatham's natural bonanza lies southward: The uninhabited **Monomoy Islands ★★**, 2,750 acres of brush-covered sand favored by some 285 species of migrating birds, is the perfect pit stop along the Atlantic Flyway. Harbor and gray seals are catching on, too: Hundreds now carpet the coastline from late November through May. If you go out during that time, you won't have any trouble seeing them—they're practically unavoid-able. **Wellfleet Bay Wildlife Sanctuary,** operated by the Audubon Society (© **508/349-2615**), offers guided trips. The Audubon's 3-, 4-, or 7-hour trips take place April through November, and they cost $30 to $60 per person. The boat to Monomoy leaves from Chatham, and the trip includes a naturalist-guided nature hike.

SEAL-WATCHING   The **Beachcomber ★★** (© 508/945-5265; www.sealwatch.com) runs **seal-watching cruises** out of Stage Harbor from mid-May to late September daily in season and weekends in the shoulder seasons. Parking is on Crowell Road at Chatham Boat Company near the bakery. The 90-minute cruises cost $25 for adults, $23 for seniors, $21 for children 3 to 15, and free for children 2 and under.

Outermost Adventures (© **508/945-5858;** www.outermostharbor.com) runs boat shuttle service to South Beach. The ride takes 10 minutes and once on the beach, pas-sengers can walk for two minutes to the far side of the spit to see seals gathered along the coast. The shuttle beginning at 8am goes every 20 minutes and is first come, first served. The last pick-up is at 4:30pm. The cost is $20 adults, $10 children 12 and under. Trips run from Memorial Day to Columbus Day.

The Wellfleet Bay Wildlife chapter of the **Audubon Society** (© **508/349-2615**) also runs family seal trips to South Beach during the summer for $45 for adults, $40 for children.

TENNIS   Free public courts are located near the Railroad Museum on Depot Street and at Chatham High School on Crowell Road; for details contact the **Chatham Recreation**

CHATHAM HISTORICAL SIGHTS

Chatham Railroad Museum ★ (Kids)   Even if you're not a railroad fanatic, it's worth visiting this beautiful 1887 depot to imagine the sights that would greet a Victorian visitor. To begin, the building itself is a "Railroad Gothic" work of wooden art, topped by a tapering turret. Inside you'll find volunteers dispensing lore and explaining the many displays. The museum's major holding is lined up in back: a "walk-through" 1918 New York caboose.

153 Depot Rd. (off Main St., 1 block north of the rotary). No phone. Donations accepted. Mid-June to mid-Sept Tues–Sat 10am–4pm. Closed mid-Sept to mid-June.

The Old Atwood House Museum ★   For further glimpses of Chatham's past, visit this gambrel-roofed 1752 homestead, divided (rather awkwardly) into assorted wings celebrating different phases and products of the local culture. The house harbors all sorts of odd collections, from seashells to the complete works of early-20th-century author Joseph C. Lincoln, a renowned Cape writer whose hokey books are avidly collected by locals. One room definitely worth a visit is the New Gallery, featuring admirably direct portraits of crusty sea-goers by local artist Frederick Stallknecht Wight. His work, unfortunately, was always overshadowed by the *oeuvre* of his mother, Alice Stallknecht Wight, who executed pretend-primitive murals of villagers enacting religious scenes (a contemporary Christ-as-fisherman, for instance, celebrating the Last Supper). Her work occupies an adjoining barn; see if you think she deserves it. By far, the most enchanting exhibit on hand is an entire 1947 fishing "camp"—a one-room old boys' club salvaged, complete with shabby furnishings, from the onslaught of the winter storms that brought about the "break" of 1987.

347 Stage Harbor Rd. (about ²/₃ mile south of Main St.). © **508/945-2493.** Admission $5 adults, $3 students. Mid-June to Oct Tues–Sat 10am–4pm. Closed Nov to mid-June.

BASEBALL

The Chatham Athletics (or "A's"), part of the **Cape Cod Baseball League,** play at Veterans Field off Depot Street. Admission is free, though donations are requested. For a schedule, contact the **Chatham Chamber of Commerce** (© 800/715-5567 or 508/945-5199), the **Chatham Recreation Center** (© **508/945-5175**), or the **League** (© **508/432-6909**).

KID STUFF

The **Play-a-Round Park ★★** on Depot Street (see "A Stroll Around Chatham," above) will suffice to keep kids entertained for hours on end. Treat them to lunch at the quirkily casual Breakaway Cafe at the Chatham airport (perhaps followed by a sightseeing flight?). The weekly **band concerts ★★** (© 508/945-5199) at Kate Gould Park, held Friday nights in summer, are perfectly gauged for underage enjoyment: There's usually a bunny-hop at some point in the evening. Junior connoisseurs get a chance, once a year in late July, to enjoy some really fine music, when the Monomoy Chamber Ensemble puts on a free morning children's performance at the **Monomoy Theatre** (© 508/945-1589), and musicals there are always fun.

Chatham's tree-shaded Main Street, lined with specialty stores, offers a terrific opportunity to shop and stroll. The goods tend to be on the conservative side, but every so often, you'll happen upon a hedonistic delight.

ARTS & CRAFTS   Headed for such prestigious outlets as Neiman Marcus, the hand-blown glassworks of James Holmes originate at **Chatham Glass Company,** 758 Main St., just west of the Chatham rotary (☎ **508/945-5547**), where you can literally look over their shoulders as the pieces take shape. Luscious colors are their hallmark; the intense hues, combined with a purity of form at once traditional and cutting-edge contemporary, add up to objects that demand to be coveted.

At **Chatham Pottery,** 2058 Rte. 28, east of the intersection with Route 137 (☎ **508/430-2191**), striking graphics characterize the collaborative work of Gill Wilson (potter) and Margaret Wilson-Grey (glazer). Their work consists primarily of blue block print-style designs set against off-white stoneware. The most popular design may be the etched pair of swimming fish, based on sketches over 100 years old. It's a look that's somewhat addictive. Luckily, it's available in everything from platters and bowls to lamps and tiles.

BOOKS   **Yellow Umbrella Bookstore,** 501 Main St., in the center of town (☎ **508/945-0144**), offers both new and used books (from rare volumes to paperbacks perfect for a disposable beach read). This full-service, all-ages bookstore invites protracted browsing.

FASHION   Catering to fashionable parents and their kids, ages newborn well into the teens, **The Children's Shop,** 515 Main St., in the center of town (☎ **508/945-0234**), is the best children's clothing store in a 100-mile radius. While according a nod to doting grannies with such classics as hand-smocked party dresses, Ginny Nickerson also stays up-to-speed on what kids themselves prefer.

The flagship store of **Puritan Clothing Company** is at 573 Main St., Chatham (☎ **508/945-0326**). This venerable institution, with stores all over the Cape, has updated its clothing considerably in the last 10 years. You'll find a wide range of quality men's and women's wear, including Polo, Nautica, Eileen Fisher, and Teva, at good prices.

WHERE TO STAY

Chatham's lodging choices tend to be more expensive than those of neighboring towns because it's considered a chichi place to vacation. But for those allergic to fussy, fancy B&Bs and inns, Chatham has several good motel options.

Practically across the street from the Chatham Bars Inn, **The Hawthorne ★**, 196 Shore Rd. (☎ **508/945-0372;** www.thehawthorne.com), is a motel with one of the best locations in town: right on the water, with striking views of Chatham Harbor, Pleasant Bay, and the Atlantic Ocean. An additional perk here is free phone calls (local and long distance) and Internet access. Rates for the 26 rooms are $230 to $290 double. The more expensive rooms are efficiencies with kitchenettes. Closed mid-October to mid-May.

Chatham Seafarer, 2079 Rte. 28 (about ¹/₂ mile east of Rte. 137), West Chatham (☎ **800/786-2772** or 508/432-1739; www.chathamseafarer.com), is a lovely, personable, well-run motel on Route 28. It's only about a half-mile from Ridgevale Beach, but there is also a pool here. Rates are $155 to $175 double, $195 efficiencies.

The least expensive option is **The Chatham Motel,** 1487 Main St./Rte. 28, Chatham (☎ **800/770-5545** or 508/945-2630; www.chathammotel.com), 1¹/₂ miles from Hardings Beach. Look for the shingled motel with yellow shutters. There's an outdoor pool, shuffleboard, and plenty of barbecue grills. Summer rates in the 32 rooms are $165 double, $225 suite.

Very Expensive

Chatham Bars Inn ★★★ (Kids)   The grand old Chatham Bars Inn, overlooking a barrier beach and the Atlantic Ocean is one of the premier properties on Cape Cod. The main inn building is surrounded by 26 shingled cottages on 25 acres. Most rooms are tastefully up-to-date, and many have private balconies with views of the beach or the prettily landscaped grounds. A deluxe spa and 12 new spa rooms completed recently have luxurious amenities, including Jacuzzi tubs and in-room saunas.

Shore Rd. (off Seaview St., about 1/2 mile northwest of the town center), Chatham, MA 02633. © **800/ 527-4884** or 508/945-0096. Fax 508/945-5491. www.chathambarsinn.com. 205 units. Summer $455–$655 double; $925–$1,050 1-bedroom suite; $790–$1,700 2-bedroom suite. AE, DC, MC, V. **Amenities:** 4 restaurants (the formal Main Dining Room, the Chef's Table & Wine Cellar, the Tavern, and the seasonal Beach House Grill located on the beach); outdoor heated pool; putting green (Seaside Links, a 9-hole course open to the public, adjoins the resort; guests play for $18 fee); 3 all-weather tennis courts ($15 an hour); Wellness Center offering spa and massage services and fitness equipment; complimentary children's program for ages 4 and up, available morning–night in summer; concierge; room service; babysitting. *In room:* A/C, TV/VCR/DVD, Wi-Fi, fridge, hair dryer, iron, safe.

Expensive

Captain's House Inn ★★★ (Finds)   This 1839 Greek Revival house—along with a cottage and a carriage house—set on 2 meticulously maintained acres is a shining example of its era and style. The hospitality and amenities here make this one of the top B&Bs on Cape Cod. The inn provides a wonderful array of extras, like robes, bottled water, newspapers, early-morning coffee, and room service. The breakfast room is also the site of a traditional tea. Be sure to book your room well in advance.

369–377 Old Harbor Rd. (about 1/2 mile north of the rotary), Chatham, MA 02633. © **800/315-0728** or 508/945-0127. Fax 508/945-0866. www.captainshouseinn.com. 16 units, 14 with tub/shower, 2 with shower only. Summer $250–$475 double. Rates include full breakfast and afternoon tea. AE, DISC, MC, V. **Amenities:** Outdoor heated pool; exercise room; room service. *In room:* A/C, TV/VCR, coffeemaker, hair dryer, iron.

Chatham Wayside Inn ★★   Centrally located on Chatham's Main Street, this former stagecoach stop, dating from 1860, has undergone a thoroughly modern renovation. Don't expect any musty antique trappings: It's all lush carpeting, a warehouse worth of Waverly fabrics, and polished reproduction furnishings, including four-posters. There's an outdoor heated pool in the back. This is one of the few inns on the Cape with rooms and a restaurant fully accessible to travelers with disabilities.

512 Main St. (in the center of town), Chatham, MA 02633. © **800/391-5734** or 508/945-5550. Fax 508/945-3407. www.waysideinn.com. 56 units. Summer $265–$365 double, $345–$495 suite; off-season packages available. DISC, MC, V. **Amenities:** Restaurant/bar (see review below); outdoor heated pool. *In room:* A/C, TV/VCR, hair dryer, iron.

Pleasant Bay Village ★★   Across the street from Pleasant Bay, a few minutes' walk from Pleasant Bay beach, this is one fancy motel (with prices set accordingly). The six-acre complex has an array of rooms and cottages, done in restful pastels. Many bathrooms feature marble countertops and stone floors. In summer, you can order lunch from the grill without having to leave your place at the heated pool.

1191 Orleans Rd./Rte. 28 (about 3 miles north of Chatham center), Chatham Port, MA 02633. © **800/ 547-1011** or 508/945-1133. Fax 508/945-9701. www.pleasantbayvillage.com. 58 units. Summer $185–$265 double; $395–$525 1- or 2-bedroom suite (for 4 occupants). AE, MC, V. Closed Nov–Apr.

Amenities: Restaurant (breakfast May–Oct; lunch and dinner July and August only); heated pool; 8-person hot tub; game room. *In room:* A/C, TV, fridge, hair dryer, iron.

Moderate

Moses Nickerson House ★ (Value) Your host George "I am not Moses" Watts and his wife, Linda, run this gem of a B&B with a sense of humor mixed with gracious hospitality. A grand captain's home in the classicist style, this 1839 manse's every inch is devoted to stylish comfort.

364 Old Harbor Rd. (about ½ mile north of Main St.), Chatham, MA 02633. © **800/628-6972** or 508/945-5859. Fax 508/945-7087. www.mosesnickersonhouse.com. 7 units, 1 with tub/shower, 6 with shower only. Summer $199–$239 double. Rates include full breakfast and afternoon tea. AE, DISC, MC, V. *In room:* A/C, TV, hair dryer.

WHERE TO DINE
Expensive

The Blue Coral ★ NEW AMERICAN "Seaside cuisine" starts on an outdoor courtyard just off Main Street. Specialties include the 3-pound lobster dinner with all the fixins' and sushi-grade bluefin tuna pan-seared with balsamic *demiglace.* One of the most popular dishes is the lobster ravioli served with a brandy cream sauce. There's live entertainment in the form of jazz and blues on Thursday through Sunday nights in season. This place gets a big crowd on clear nights, so come early or late.

483 Main St. © **508/348-0485.** Reservations accepted. Main courses $18–$40. AE, DISC, MC, V. Early June to early Sept daily 11:30am–4pm and 5:30–10pm. Closed mid-Sept to early June.

RooBar ★★ NEW AMERICAN Like its sister restaurant in Hyannis, the RooBar in Chatham is the place to see and be seen. A former Friendly's Restaurant is now a sleek and stylish venue that features a garden patio area as well as a welcoming bar. The food and service here are top-notch. The menu offers a wide range of options, from seafood specialties like seafood jambalaya to fine meat dishes like herb-grilled Delmonico. You may also opt for a brick-oven pizza like the spicy prawn or the barbecue chicken. The only downside to this restaurant is it's not on Chatham's main drag with all the other shops and restaurants. It's a short drive (about a mile) away.

907 Main St. © **508/945-9988.** Reservations accepted for parties of 6 or more. Main courses $17–$28. AE, MC, V. Daily 5–10pm. Open year-round.

Moderate

Chatham Squire ★★ (Finds) AMERICAN The Chatham Squire is the unofficial center of Chatham where generations of summer residents mix with the year-rounders: fishermen and landed gentry. The surprise is that this quintessential Cape Cod pub has the best clam chowder in these parts. It turns out the Squire gets its clams from the elite clam beds off Monomoy, cultivated in pristine water and considered the freshest around. The menu also features pasta (zebra ravioli is filled with lobster meat) and barbecued baby back ribs (with the Squire's secret sauce), among other dishes.

487 Main St. (in the center of town). © **508/945-0945.** Main courses $11–$23. AE, DISC, MC, V. Sun–Thurs 11:30am–10pm; Fri–Sat 11:30am–10:30pm; call for off-season hours (Nov–Apr).

Chatham Wayside Inn ★ NEW AMERICAN The Wayside's central location on Main Street makes it a good spot for a reasonably priced meal in Chatham. Diners have several seating choices depending on their mood (and the weather): the clubby tavern with gleaming wood tables surrounded by comfy Windsor chairs, the front room with cozy booths, or the large screened terrace, perfect during summer's dog days. More

important, perhaps, is what's on the plate. Wayside specialties include crab cakes, or entrees like rack of lamb and pesto cod. For something a little different, try the chowder; it's prepared Portuguese-style with double-smoked bacon, fresh quahogs, and red bliss potatoes. Whether it's summer or winter, you'll want to end your meal with the apple-and-cranberry crisp; the secret is the oatmeal-and-brown-sugar crust. The Wayside is an even better choice at lunchtime, when the terrace is the perfect spot to watch Main Street's parade of shoppers.

512 Main St. (in the center of town). ☏ **508/945-5550.** Reservations accepted. Main courses $16–$26. DISC, MC, V. May–Oct daily 8–11am, 11:30am–4pm, and 5–10pm; Nov–Dec and Feb–Apr Tues–Sun 8–11am, 11:30am–4pm, and 5–9pm. Closed Jan.

The Impudent Oyster ★ INTERNATIONAL   All but hidden off the main drag, this perennially popular 1970s-era eatery—complete with decorative stained glass—continues to cook up fabulous fish in exotic guises, ranging from Mexican to Szechuan, but mostly Continental. The flavorful specialties of the house are the sole piccata (native sole with lemon, fresh herb, and caper butter sauce), the steak au poivre, and the *pesca fra diavolo* (local littlenecks, lobster, and other seafood simmered in a spicy sauce over fettuccine). A tavern menu is served at the bar from 3 to 5pm with soup, salads, raw bar, chicken fingers, and burgers. There is also a children's menu. This place is very busy in the summer, so make a reservation.

15 Chatham Bars Ave. (off Main St., in the center of town). ☏ **508/945-3545.** Reservations recommended. Main courses $14–$20. AE, MC, V. Mon–Sat 11:30am–3pm and 5–9:30pm; Sun noon–3pm and 5–9:30pm.

Vining's Bistro ★★ (Finds) FUSION   If you're looking for cutting-edge cuisine in a sophisticated setting, venture upstairs at Chatham's innocuous-looking minimall and into this ineffably cool cafe. The film-noirish wall murals suggest a certain bohemian abandon, but the food is up-to-the-minute and priced to suit young people. The menu offers compelling juxtapositions such as the warm lobster tacos with salsa *fresca* and crème fraîche, or the spit-roasted chicken suffused with *achiote*-lime marinade and sided with a salad of oranges and jicama.

595 Main St. (in the center of town). ☏ **508/945-5033.** Reservations not accepted. Main courses $16–$24. AE, DC, MC, V. June to mid-Oct daily 5:30–9:30pm; call for off-season hours. Closed Jan–Mar.

Inexpensive

Carmine's Pizza ★ ITALIAN   A new-wave pizzeria that pays homage to the old ways with checkered tablecloths and soda-parlor chairs, this little eatery takes a bold approach to toppings—for example, pineapple, jalapeños, and pesto. A favorite is the Californian, with garlic, feta cheese, spinach, sautéed mushrooms and onions, plum tomato, artichoke, and Kalamata olives. Cool down with creamy gelato.

595 Main St. (in the center of town). ☏ **508/945-5300.** Pizzas $10–$19. MC, V. May–Sept daily 10am–11pm; call for off-season hours. Closed Jan–Mar.

Red Nun Bar & Grill (Value) DINER   There used to be lots of casual little hole-in-the-wall places like this on the Cape. Now there are precious few. With just five tables and some bar seats, this is a good place to go early, late, or off season. They serve comfort food, like Mama's meatloaf, cheeseburgers, and a fish sandwich made from this morning's catch that was probably brought in by one of the guys bellied up to the bar. A good selection of beers is on tap, too.

746 Main St. (near Monomoy Theatre and Veterans Field). ✆ **508/348-0469.** Under $11. MC, V. May–Sept daily 11:30am–10pm; call for off-season hours. Closed Jan 15–Apr 1.

A Pie Shop

Marion's Pie Shop ★ (Finds) Nearly a half-century's worth of summer visitors have come to depend on this bakery for dinner and dessert pies, from sea clam to lemon meringue. Load up on the fruit breads and sweet rolls, and you can pretend you're having a four-course B&B breakfast—on the beach.

2022 Rte. 28 (about 1/2 mile east of Rte. 137). ✆ **508/432-9439.** Tues–Sat 8am–6pm; Sun 8am–4pm.

Fresh Seafood

Nickerson Fish & Lobster ★ The fish have to travel all of 50 yards from the boat, so you can imagine how fresh they are. And you don't need a kitchen to partake: They sell homemade quahog (giant clam) chowder and precooked frozen entrees to go.

Chatham Fish Pier, Shore Rd. ✆ **508/945-0145.** Daily 9am–8pm. Closed mid-Oct to late May.

Sweets

Chatham Candy Manor ★ (Kids) Normally, I cross the street to avoid this type of temptation, but Naomi Turner's hand-dipped chocolates (her mother opened the shop in the 1940s) are just too good to pass up. Surely there can't be anything too terribly harmful in an occasional "cranberry cordial" or chocolate-dipped strawberry, right? But once you start perusing the old-fashioned oak cases, it can be very hard to stop. Turtles, truffles, and the homemade fudge are tops. Children line up to watch them make candy canes here at Christmas time.

484 Main St. (in the center of town). ✆ **508/945-0825.** June–Aug daily 9am–10pm; Sept–May daily 9am–6pm.

CHATHAM AFTER DARK

Although most towns boast some comparable event, Chatham's free **band concerts**—40 players strong—are arguably the best on the Cape and attract crowds in the thousands. This is small-town America at its most nostalgic, as the band, made up mostly of local folks, plays those standards of yesteryear that never go out of style. Held in Kate Gould Park (off Chatham Bars Ave., in the center of town) from July to early September, it kicks off at 8pm every Friday. Better come early to claim your square of lawn (it's already a checkerboard of blankets by late afternoon), and be prepared to sing—or dance—along. Call ✆ **508/945-5199** for information.

Performance Arts

Monomoy Theatre Every summer since 1958, the Ohio University Players have commuted to this jewel box of a 1930s theater to put on a challenging play a week, from musicals to Shakespeare. In late July, they take a well-earned week off to cede the stage to the highly accomplished Monomoy Chamber Ensemble. Performances take place mid-June to August, Tuesday to Saturday at 8pm and Thursday matinee at 2pm. Closed September to mid-June. 776 Rte. 28 (about 1/4 mile west of the rotary). ✆ **508/945-1589.** Tickets $17–$23.

Bars & Live Music

The Chatham Squire A great leveler, this local institution attracts patrons from all the social strata in town. CEOs, seafarers, and college students alike convene to kibitz over the roar of a jukebox or band (Fri–Sat off season only) and their own hubbub. Good pub grub, too (see "Where to Dine," above). 487 Main St. (in the center of town). ✆ **508/945-0945.**

4 ORLEANS ★★

31 miles E of Sandwich; 25 miles S of Provincetown

Orleans is where the *Narrow Land* (the early Algonquin name for the Cape) starts to get very narrow indeed: From here on up—or "down," in paradoxical local parlance—it's never more than a few miles wide from coast to coast, and in some spots it's as little as 1 mile. All three main roads (rtes. 6, 6A, and 28) converge here, too, so on summer weekends, traffic can be fierce.

But this is also where the oceanside beaches open up into a glorious expanse some 40 miles long, framed by dramatic dunes and blessed—from a swimmer's or boarder's perspective—with serious surf. The thousands of ship crews who crashed on these shoals over the past 4 centuries could hardly be expected to assume so sanguine a view. Shipwrecks may sound like the stuff of romance, but in these frigid waters, hitting a sandbar usually spelled a death sentence for all involved. So enamored were local inhabitants by the opportunity to salvage that some improved their odds by becoming "mooncussers"— praying for cloudy skies and luring ships toward shore by tying a lantern to the tail of a donkey, so as to simulate the listing of a ship at sea.

Such dark deeds seem very far removed from the Orleans of today, a sedate town that shadows Hyannis as a year-round center of commerce. Lacking the cohesiveness of smaller towns, and somewhat chopped up by the roadways coursing through, it's not the most ideal town to hang out in, despite some appealing restaurants and shops. The village of East Orleans, however, is fast emerging as a sweet little off-beach town with allure for both families and singles. About 2 miles east is seemingly endless (nearly 10 miles long) Nauset Beach, the southernmost stretch of the Cape Cod National Seashore preserve and a magnet for the young and the buff.

ESSENTIALS

GETTING THERE After crossing the Sagamore Bridge (see "Getting There," in chapter 3), head east on Route 6 or 6A, which converges with Route 28 in Orleans. Or fly into Hyannis (see "Getting There," in chapter 3).

VISITOR INFORMATION Contact the **Orleans Chamber of Commerce,** 44 Main St. (P.O. Box 153), Orleans, MA 02653 (© **800/865-1386** or 508/255-1386; www. capecod-orleans.com), open year-round Monday through Friday from 10am to 6pm; or the **Cape Cod Chamber of Commerce** (see "Visitor Information," in the "Brewster" section, earlier in this chapter). There's an **information booth** at the corner of Route 6A and Eldredge Parkway (© **508/240-2484**). Its hours are mid-May to mid-October, Monday through Saturday from 10am to 6pm and Sunday from 11am to 3pm. Closed mid-October to mid-May.

BEACHES & RECREATIONAL PURSUITS

BEACHES From here on up, on the eastern side you're dealing with the wild and whimsical Atlantic, which can be kittenish one day and tigerish the next. While storms may whip up surf you can actually take a board to, less confident swimmers should definitely wait a few days until the turmoil and riptides subside. In any case, current conditions are clearly posted at the entrance. Weeklong parking permits ($50 for renters) may be obtained from **Town Hall** on School Road (© **508/240-3775**). Day-trippers who arrive early enough—better make that before 10am on weekends in July and August—can pay at the gate (© **508/240-3780**).

- **Crystal Lake ★**, off Monument Road about ³/₄ mile south of Main Street: Parking—if you can find a space—is free, but there are no facilities.
- **Nauset Beach ★★★**, in East Orleans (© **508/240-3780**): Stretching southward all the way past Chatham, this 10-mile-long barrier beach, which is part of the Cape Cod National Seashore but is managed by the town, has long been one of the Cape's gonzo beach scenes—good surf, big crowds, lots of young people. Full facilities, including a snack bar serving terrific fried fish, can be found within the 1,000-car parking lot; the in-season fee is $15 per car, which is also good for same-day parking at Skaket Beach (see below). Substantial waves make for good surfing in the special section reserved for that purpose, and boogie boards are ubiquitous. In July and August, there are concerts from 7 to 9pm in the gazebo.
- **Pilgrim Lake ★**, off Monument Road about 1 mile south of Main Street: A beach parking sticker is necessary for this small freshwater beach, which has lifeguards.
- **Skaket Beach ★**, off Skaket Beach Road to the west of town: This peaceful bay beach is a better choice for families with young children. When the tide recedes (as much as a mile), little kids will enjoy splashing about in the tide pools left behind. Parking costs $15, and you'd better turn up early.

BICYCLING Orleans presents the one slight gap in the 25-mile off-road **Cape Cod Rail Trail ★★★** (© **508/896-3491**): Just east of the Brewster border, the trail merges with town roads for about 1¹/₂ miles. The best way to avoid vehicular aggravation and fumes is to zigzag west to scenic Rock Harbor. Bike rentals are available at **Orleans Cycle** at 26 Main St. in the center of town (© **508/255-9115**), which charges $22 for a 24-hour rental, and there are several good places (see "Takeout & Picnic Fare," later in this chapter) to grab some snacks.

BOATING You can rent a canoe (see below) and paddle around Town Cove, Little Pleasant Bay (to Sampson, Hog, and Pochet islands), and the body of water called simply The River. Experienced paddlers can paddle through Pleasant Bay to the inside shore of the Outer Beach.

Arey's Pond Sailing School, off Route 28 in South Orleans (© **508/255-7900;** www. areyspondboatyard.com), offers sailing lessons on Daysailers, Catboats, and Rhode 19s in season on Little Pleasant Bay. Individual lessons are $65 per hour; weekly group lessons are around $189. The **Goose Hummock Outdoor Center** at 15 Rte. 6A, south of the rotary (© **508/255-2620;** www.goose.com), rents out canoes, kayaks, and more, and the northern half of Pleasant Bay is the place to use them; inquire about guided excursions. Canoe and kayak rentals are $50 to $75 per day.

FISHING Fishing is allowed in Baker Pond, Pilgrim Lake, and Crystal Lake; the latter is a likely spot to reel in trout and perch. For details and a license, visit **Town Hall** at Post Office Square in the center of town (© **508/240-3700**, ext. 305) or **Goose Hummock** (see "Boating," above). Surf-casting—no license needed—is permitted on Nauset Beach South, off Beach Road. **Rock Harbor ★★**, a former packet landing on the bay (about 1¹/₄ miles northwest of the town center), shelters New England's largest sportfishing fleet: some 18 boats at last count. One call (© **508/255-9757**) will get you information on them all. Or go look them over. Rock Harbor charter prices range from $550 for 4 hours to $750 for 8 hours. Individual prices are also available ($140 per person for 4 hr.; $150 per person for 8 hr.).

Fun Facts   **Rock Harbor**

Yes, those are trees in the middle of the harbor at Rock Harbor; and no, they are not live trees. For decades, dead trees have been erected in the harbor in order to mark the channel. At sunset, the row of narrow trees silhouetted against the horizon makes a pretty photo, like the one in the color insert, at the front of this guide.

FITNESS   If you're here for a while and need a place to stay in shape on rainy days, check out **Willy's Gym, Fitness, and Wellness Center** at 21 Old Colony Way at Orleans Marketplace (© **508/255-6826**). The Cape's biggest (21,000 sq. ft.) exercise facility is air-conditioned and open year-round. Dozens of classes are offered weekly, from basic aerobics to tai chi and Indonesian martial arts. Willy's also provides child care. Day passes are $17.

HORSEBACK RIDING   The small farm **Black Sand Stable** at 36 Bakers Pond Rd. (© **508/255-7185**) is one of the only places still offering horseback riding in the area. Trail rides through Nickerson State Park take 1 to 1¹/₂ hours and cost $50. Pony rides, hayrides, and carriage rides are also available.

ICE-SKATING   Orleans boasts a massive municipal rink, the **Charles Moore Arena** on O'Connor Way, off Eldredge Park Way, about 1 mile southwest of the town center (© **508/255-2971**). In season, it's open to the public Monday to Friday from 11am to 1pm. From September through March, it's open to the public Monday and Wednesday from 11am to 1pm, Thursday from 3:30 to 5pm, and Sunday from 2 to 4pm. Friday night is "Rock Nite" for party animals ages 9 through 14. The cost is $5 adults, $4 children 12 and under; skate rentals run $2.

NATURE & WILDLIFE AREAS   Inland there's not much, but on the Atlantic shore is a biggie: **Nauset Beach.** Once you get past the swarms of people near the parking lot, you'll have about 9 miles of beach mostly to yourself. You'll see lots of birds (take a field guide) and perhaps some harbor seals off season.

TENNIS   Hard-surface public courts are located at the Nauset Middle School in Eldredge Park on a first-come, first-served basis; for details, contact the **Orleans Recreation Department** (© **508/240-3785**).

WATERSPORTS   The **Pump House Surf Co.** at 9 Cranberry Hwy./Rte. 6A (© **508/240-2226**) rents and sells wet suits, body boards, and surfboards, while providing up-to-date reports on where to find the best waves. Surfboards rent for $20 to $30 a day. **Nauset Sports** at Jeremiah Square, Route 6A at the rotary (© **508/255-4742**), also rents surfboards, boogie boards, skim boards, kayaks, and wet suits.

HISTORICAL MUSEUMS
French Transatlantic Cable Station Museum ★
This ordinary-looking house was, from 1890 to 1940, a nexus of intercontinental communications. Connected to France via a huge cable laid across the ocean floor, local operators bore the responsibility of relaying stock-market data, keeping tabs on World War I troops, and receiving the joyous news of Lindbergh's 1927 crossing. Service was discontinued with the German invasion of France in 1940, and resumed briefly between 1952 and 1959, when newer,

automated technologies rendered the facility obsolete. The exhibits, prepared with the assistance of the Smithsonian, are a bit technical for nonscientists, but docents on hand will patiently fill in the blanks.

41 Rte. 28 (corner of Cove Rd., north of Main St.). © **508/240-1735.** Free admission. July–Aug Thurs–Sun 1–4pm; June and Sept Fri–Sun 1–4pm. Closed Oct–May.

Jonathan Young Windmill (Kids)   The majestic old windmill in Cove Park (next to Town Cove) has been authentically restored and is open for guided tours in season. Though it is no longer grinding corn and barley, the mill's works are fully operable. Most mills on the Cape have been moved many times from town to town, and the Orleans mill has certainly seen more than its share of relocations. The mill was built in the early 1700s in South Orleans. In 1839, it was moved to Orleans center and then to Hyannisport. In 1983, it was moved back to Orleans and donated to the Orleans Historical Society. Some of the guides at the mill are actual millers, who give visitors an entertaining spiel about the millwrights (the men who built the mills and kept the gears in working order) and millers (who ground the corn) who have worked at this mill over the centuries.

Rte. 6A (just south of the rotary). © **508/240-1329.** Free admission; donations accepted. Late June to Aug daily 11am–4pm; call for off-season hours.

Orleans Historical Society at The Meeting House Museum ★   Other towns may have fancier facilities to house their historical societies, but few have quite so colorful a history as Orleans—the only town on the Cape with a non-English, non-native name. Upon separating from Eastham in 1797, Orleans assumed the name of an honored guest: future king Louis-Philippe de Bourbon, duke of Orleans, who safely sat out the Revolution abroad, earning his living as a French tutor. Not that all remained quiet on these shores either: Orleans suffered British naval attacks during the War of 1812 and German submarine fire in 1918. You'll find a great many mementos in this 1833 Greek Revival church, along with assorted artifacts—from arrowheads to hand-hewn farm tools—and a thinly veiled terrorist threat, dated 1814, from a British captain offering to spare the town's saltworks in Rock Harbor for a paltry $1,000. The townspeople balked, a warship struck, and the home team triumphed in the Battle of Orleans. Though the displays are far from jazzy, a great many have interesting stories attached and could spark an urge to learn more. Head over to Rock Harbor to see a gold-medal, award-winning Coast Guard rescue boat. Shipwreck items from the wreck of the *Pendleton* tanker in 1952 were installed by the Historical Society as an additional exhibit.

3 River Rd. (at Main St., about 1 mile east of the town center). © **508/240-1329.** Donation $2. July–Aug Thurs–Sat 10am–1pm; off season by appointment.

BASEBALL

The Orleans Cardinals, the easternmost team in the **Cape Cod Baseball League,** play at Eldredge Park (off Eldredge Park Way between rtes. 6A and 28). For a schedule, call the **Orleans Chamber of Commerce** (© **800/865-1386** or 508/255-1386), the **Orleans Recreation Department** (© **508/240-3785**), or the **League** (© **508/432-6909**).

KID STUFF

The **Charles Moore Arena** (see "Ice-Skating," above) offers respite from a rainy day. Young skaters—and anxious parents—might be interested to know that the Nauset Regional Middle School in Eldredge Park has its own **skateboard park,** with four ramps and a "fun box"; helmets are required.

Though shops are somewhat scattered, Orleans is full of great finds for browsers and grazers.

ANTIQUES/COLLECTIBLES   Got an old house in need of illumination, or a new one in want of some style? You'll find some 400 vintage light fixtures at **Continuum Antiques,** 7 S. Orleans Rd./Rte 28, south of the junction with Route 6A (© **508/255-8513**), from Victorian on down, along with a smattering of old advertising signs and venerable duck decoys.

ARTS & CRAFTS   Stop by **Kemp Pottery,** 9 Cranberry Hwy./Rte. 6A, about ¼ mile south of the rotary (© **508/255-5853**), and check out Steve Kemp's turned and slab-built creations. From soup tureens to fanciful sculptures, they're remarkably colorful and one of a kind.

   Tree's Place, Route 6A at the intersection of Route 28, Orleans (© **888/255-1330** or 508/255-1330), is considered the premier gallery for contemporary realist work in the region. There is also an extensive fine-crafts, gift, and tile shop here.

BOOKS   In the Skaket Corners shopping center on Route 6A is a branch of the large retailer **Booksmith/Musicsmith** (© **508/255-4590**).

FASHION   **Karol Richardson,** 47 Main St., in the center of town (© **508/255-3944**), is a preview of Richardson's main showroom in Wellfleet; stop in to see the latest from this gifted ex-Londoner.

GIFTS   Birders will go batty over **Bird Watcher's General Store,** 36 Rte. 6A, south of the rotary (© **800/562-1512** or 508/255-6974). The brainchild of local aficionado Mike O'Connor, who'd like everyone to share his passion, it stocks virtually every bird-watching accessory under the sun, from basic binoculars to costly telescopes, modest birdhouses to birdbaths fit for a tiny Roman emperor; there's also a good selection of CDs and field guides.

   For something a little different, check out **Weekend** (217 Main St., East Orleans; © **508/255-9300**), a new boutique opened by former set designer Mari Pocari in a historic building that used to be a general store. It sells one-of-a-kind colorful jewelry, art, women's fashions, baby apparel, home design and spa products.

WHERE TO STAY
Expensive
A Little Inn on Pleasant Bay ★★ (Finds)   Set back from a winding road that follows the coast between Orleans and Chatham, A Little Inn on Pleasant Bay sits on a hill next to a cranberry bog and overlooks the water (Pleasant Bay, naturally). The four rooms in the peaceful main house, which dates to 1798, have been completely renovated in warm tiles, light woods, and subtle colors that reflect a sort of Zen–Pottery Barn aesthetic. An adjacent building has three additional rooms. There is also a carriage house with two rooms.

654 S. Orleans Rd., South Orleans, MA 02662. © **888/332-3351** or 508/255-0780. www.alittleinnon pleasantbay.com. 9 units. $230–$300 double. Extra person $30 per night. Rates include continental breakfast and evening sherry. AE, MC, V. No children under 10 accepted. *In room:* A/C, hair dryer, no phone.

The Cove ★   This well-camouflaged motel complex on busy Route 28 also fronts placid Town Cove, where guests are offered a free minicruise in season. The interiors are adequate, if not dazzling, and a small heated pool and restful gazebo overlook the waterfront. Some rooms have kitchenettes (complete with microwave). Be sure to request one with a balcony and a cove view.

13 S. Orleans Rd. (Rte. 28, north of Main St.), Orleans, MA 02653. ✆ **800/343-2233** or 508/255-1203. Fax 508/255-7736. www.thecoveorleans.com. 47 units. Summer $145–$234 double; $165–$226 suite or efficiency. AE, DC, DISC, MC, V. Open year-round. **Amenities:** Small heated pool. *In room:* A/C, TV/VCR, fridge, coffeemaker, hair dryer.

Nauset Knoll Motor Lodge ★★ (Value)   Overlooking Nauset Beach, one of Cape Cod's most popular beaches, this nothing-fancy motel with picture windows will suit beach lovers to a T. The simple, clean rooms are well maintained, and by staying here, you'll save on daily parking charges at Nauset Beach. The whole complex is owned by Uncle Sam and is under the supervision of the National Park Service.

237 Beach Rd. (at Nauset Beach, about 2 miles east of the town center), East Orleans, MA 02643. ✆ **508/255-2364.** www.capecodtravel.com/nausetknoll. 12 units, all with tub/shower. Summer $185 double. MC, V. Closed late Oct to early Apr. *In room:* TV, no phone.

The Orleans Inn ★   You can't miss this mansard-roofed beauty, perched right on the edge of Town Cove. Absolutely, get one of the rooms facing the water. Built in 1875, the inn has been lovingly restored and maintains its central place in the community. The simple rooms, some with twin beds or sleeper sofas, are cheerful with modern amenities and extra touches like a box of chocolates on the bureau. Downstairs is a bar and restaurant with wonderful views of the cove.

Rte. 6A (P.O. Box 188, just south of the Orleans rotary), Orleans, MA 02653. ✆ **508/255-2222.** Fax 508/255-6722. www.orleansinn.com. 11 units. Summer $175–$225 double; $250–$300 suite. Rates include continental breakfast. AE, MC, V. Dogs allowed. **Amenities:** Restaurant/bar. *In room:* TV, fridge.

Ship's Knees Inn   The rooms here aren't fancy—more like "homey" with quilts and nautical decor—but the proximity to Nauset Beach (a 5-minute walk from the inn) makes this restored sea captain's home a fine choice for those interested primarily in hitting the beach.

186 Beach Rd., East Orleans, MA 02643 ✆ **888/744-7756** or 508/255-1312. Fax 508/240-1351. www.shipskneesinn.com. 16 units, 2 with shared bathroom. Summer $115–$120 shared bathroom; $170–$225 double. Rates include continental breakfast. AE, MC, V. **Amenities:** Pool. *In room:* A/C, TV, Wi-Fi, fridge.

Inexpensive

Nauset House Inn ★★ (Value)   Just a half-mile from Nauset Beach, this reasonably priced country inn is a cozy setting for those seeking a quiet retreat. Several of the rooms in greenery-draped outbuildings feature such romantic extras as a sunken bath or private deck. The most romantic hideaway here, though, is a 1907 conservatory appended to the 1810 farmhouse inn.

143 Beach Rd. (P.O. Box 774, about 1 mile east of the town center), East Orleans, MA 02643. ✆ **800/771-5508** or 508/255-2195. Fax 508/240-6276. www.nausethouseinn.com. 14 units, 6 with shared bathroom, 4 with tub/shower, 4 with shower only. Summer $75 single; $85 double with shared bathroom; $115–$175 double with private bathroom. Rates include full breakfast. DISC, MC, V. Closed Nov–Mar. No children under 12. *In room:* No phone.

The Parsonage Inn ★ (Value)   Blessed with charming British innkeepers, this 1770 full Cape—whose name describes its original function—offers a unique, personalized experience. Elizabeth Browne is an accomplished pianist who might, if the evening mood is right, take flight in a Chopin mazurka or Mozart sonata, as her husband, Ian, treats guests to a glass of wine.

202 Main St. (P.O. Box 1501), East Orleans, MA 02643. ✆ **888/422-8217** or 508/255-8217. Fax 508/255-8216. www.parsonageinn.com. 8 units, 3 with tub/shower, 5 with shower only. Summer $135–$180 double. Rates include full breakfast. AE, MC, V. Open year-round. *In room:* A/C, TV, coffeemaker, hair dryer, iron, no phone.

WHERE TO DINE
Expensive
Abba ★★★ INTERNATIONAL   Abba, a local favorite, is a fresh take on fine dining in the Lower Cape. Tables are closely packed inside, so we prefer the covered outdoor dining area behind the restaurant. Chef/co-owner Erez Pinhas of Israel creates what can be described only as fusion cuisine, a little Middle Eastern, a little European, a little New American, plus some Thai and New England thrown in. Where else can you start with a falafel, and then try a steaming plate of shrimp pad thai, and end with chilled melon soup?

West Rd. and Old Colony Way (2 blocks from Main St., toward Skaket Beach). ✆ **508/255-8144.** Reservations recommended. Main courses $18–$27. AE, MC, V. June–Aug daily 5–10pm; call for off-season hours. Open year-round.

Moderate
Joe's Beach Road Bar & Grille ★ NEW AMERICAN   This 1857 captain's house with adjoining tavern is a favorite with locals. While the front room has a more traditional ambience, the tavern space features a huge fieldstone fireplace and World War II posters. With denim tablecloths and bandannas serving as napkins, the atmosphere is casual. The 28-foot mahogany bar is a popular meeting place. The menu varies from fancy dishes such as grilled Atlantic salmon filet with a red-pepper *coulis* and basil vinaigrette to Joe's pizza (with goat cheese, roasted peppers, and spinach) or high-falutin' fish and chips—beer-battered, with saffron aioli.

At The Barley Neck Inn, 5 Beach Rd. (about ¹⁄₂ mile east of the town center), East Orleans. ✆ **508/255-0212.** www.barleyneck.com. Reservations accepted. Main courses $10–$25. AE, DC, MC, V. June to early Sept daily 5–10pm; call for off-season hours. Open year-round.

The Lobster Claw Restaurant ★ SEAFOOD   This family-owned and operated business has been serving up quality seafood for almost 30 years. There's plenty of room for everyone in this sprawling restaurant, where booths spill over with boisterous families, and the usual flotsam and jetsam hang artfully from the ceiling. Get the baked stuffed lobster here with all the fixings. There's a children's menu, as well as early-bird specials served daily from 4 to 5:30pm.

Rte. 6A (just south of the rotary). ✆ **508/255-1800.** Reservations not accepted. Main courses $10–$19. AE, DC, DISC, MC, V. Apr–Oct daily 11:30am–9pm. Closed Nov–Mar.

Mahoney's Atlantic Bar & Grill ★ NEW AMERICAN   Seafood is the specialty at this casual bar/restaurant on Main Street. Dishes like tuna sashimi, grilled sea bass, and pan-seared lobster explain why you came to Cape Cod. The menu also offers poultry, meat, pasta, and vegetarian dishes. Sixteen wines are available by the glass for those who like to sample. Grab a booth and stay awhile. Thursday and Saturday nights in season, there's live jazz and blues with no cover.

28 Main St. (in the center of town). ✆ 508/255-5505. www.mahoneysatlantic.com. Reservations not accepted. Main courses $16–$25. AE, MC, V. May–Sept daily 5–10pm; Oct–Apr Tues–Sun 5–10pm.

Inexpensive

Cap't Cass Rock Harbor Seafood ★ SEAFOOD   Most tourists figure that a silvered shack sporting this many salvaged lobster buoys has an inside track on the freshest of seafood. The supposition makes sense, but the stuff here is about par for the area and the preparations are plain. Nevertheless, it's fun to eat in a joint left untouched for decades as time—and dining fads—marched on.

117 Rock Harbor Rd. (on the harbor, about 1½ miles northwest of the town center). No phone. Most main courses under $12. No credit cards. Late June to mid-Oct Tues–Sun 11am–2pm and 5–9pm. Closed mid-Oct to late June.

Land Ho! ★★ AMERICAN   A longtime hit with the locals (who call it, affectionately, "the Ho"), this rough-and-tumble pub attracts its share of knowledgeable tourists as well, drawn by the good prices and relaxed feeling. The food may be nothing to write home about, but it's satisfying and easy on the budget. Light fare, like soup, pizza, and burgers, is served until midnight. Just being there (provided you can find the door; it's around back) will make you feel like an insider.

38 Main St. (at Rte. 6A, in the center of town). ✆ 508/255-5165. Reservations not accepted. Main courses $9–$22. AE, DISC, MC, V. Mon–Sat 11:30am–10pm; Sun noon–10pm. Open year-round.

The Yardarm ★ PUB GRUB   This rowdy joint serves the best chowder in town. It's a delectable seafood concoction that comes in three sizes: little predicament, big predicament, and huge dilemma. Locals also flock to Prime Rib Night (Mon and Thurs), Mexican Night (Tues–Wed), and Steak Night (Fri–Sat). But you'll go to watch the colorful characters bellying up to the bar for a burger and a brew.

48 Rte. 28 (just east of Main St.). ✆ 508/255-4840. Most items under $15. AE, DC, MC, V. Daily 11:30am–3pm and 5:30–9:30pm. Open year-round.

Takeout & Picnic Fare

Fancy's Farm ★   Rarely are vegetables rendered so appealing, and many of them are grown locally. The charming barnlike setting contributes to this place's appeal, as do the extras—fresh breads, pastries, juices, sandwiches, and exotic salads and soups to go. This is a great stop on the way to Nauset Beach for picnic supplies.

199 Main St., East Orleans. ✆ 508/255-1949. July–Aug Mon–Sat 6am–8pm, Sun 6am–6pm; Sept–June Mon–Sat 7am–6pm, Sun 6:30am–7pm. Closed Feb.

Nauset Fish & Lobster Pool ★   The area's premier spot for fresh seafood; the selection is extensive and bountiful.

Just south of the rotary on Rte. 6A in Orleans. ✆ 508/255-1019. July–Aug daily 9am–8pm; call for off-season hours. Open year-round.

Orleans Whole Food   The largest health-food store on the Cape, this bright and cheerful porch-fronted grocery offers all sorts of freshly made snacks and sandwiches to take out—or to tear into during an impromptu picnic in the adjoining garden.

46 Main St. (in the center of town). ✆ 508/255-6540. Mon–Sat 8:30am–8pm; Sun 9am–6pm. Open year-round.

Cottage Street Bakery ★   One of the Cape's best bakeries, this one specializes in homemade breads, cookies, and Danish. There are also homemade soups and tasty sandwiches.

5 Cottage St. ☏ **508/255-2821.** Wed–Mon 6am–4pm; call for off-season hours. Closed Tues.

The Hot Chocolate Sparrow ★★   This is the place to come for coffee and treats in Orleans. Real fudge flavors the hot chocolate and all mocha derivatives thereof. Frozen hot chocolate and frozen mochas are summer specialties. It's a good place to stop in, casually check the posters announcing local happenings, and then dive in for a remorseless pig-out.

6 Old Colony Way. ☏ **508/240-2230.** Apr–May and Sept–Oct daily 6:30am–10pm; June–Aug daily 6:30am–11pm; Nov–Mar Sun–Thurs 6:30am–9pm, Fri–Sat 6:30am–11pm.

Sundae School ★   A smaller branch of the local chain (also in Dennis Port and Harwich Port), this little ice-cream shop offers some mighty sophisticated flavors.

210 Main St., East Orleans. ☏ **508/255-5473.** Mid-May to early Oct daily 11am–10:30pm. Closed early Oct to mid-May.

ORLEANS AFTER DARK

Joe's Beach Road Bar & Grille (☏ **508/255-0212;** see "Where to Dine," above) is a big old barn of a bar that might as well be town hall: It's where you'll find all the locals exchanging juicy gossip and jokes. Live music ranges from jazz to rock to blues. There's never a cover charge.

There's often live music at the **Land Ho!** (☏ **508/255-5165;** see "Where to Dine," above), the best pub in town. Performers are on the bill on Monday and Tuesday nights in season, and Thursday and Saturdays off season. There's usually no cover charge.

The Academy Playhouse, 120 Main St., about ³/₄ mile southeast of the town center (☏ **508/255-1963;** www.apa1.org), makes a fine platform for local talent in the form of musicals and drama, recitals, and poetry readings. The 162-seat arena-style stage is housed in the town's old town hall (built in 1873). Tickets are $20. Shows take place July through August Monday to Saturday at 8:30pm; call for off-season hours. A children's theater series runs from late June to early September on Friday and Saturday mornings. Cost is $10.

8

The Outer Cape

The rest of the Cape may have its civilized enticements, but it's only on the Outer Cape that the landscape and even the air feel really beachy. You can smell the seashore just over the horizon—in fact, you can smell it everywhere you go because you're never more than a mile or two away from sand and surf.

You won't find any high-rise hotels along the shoreline here. No tacky amusement arcades either. Just miles of pristine beaches and dune grass rippling in the wind. You'll also see the occasional cottage inhabited by some lucky soul who managed to get his or her hands on it before the coastline became the federally protected Cape Cod National Seashore in the early 1960s.

Henry David Thoreau witnessed virtually the same peaceful panorama when he roamed here in the 1850s. With luck and determination on the part of current inhabitants and visitors, the landscape will remain intact. The Outer Cape, after all, is a place to play—in the sand, and in the delightful, unconventional towns that have flourished here, far from the rest of civilization.

While they share the majestic National Seashore, Outer Cape towns are quite diverse. Eastham, as the official gateway to the National Seashore, certainly gets its share of visitors, yet there is also a sleepy quality to this town, which used to have the distinction of being the turnip capital of the country. Grab a stool at a locals' joint like Flemings Donut Shop on Route 6 for a taste of Olde Cape Cod before there was ever any talk of a National Seashore.

Wellfleet, called the art-gallery town, is in my view one of the nicest towns on Cape Cod. The very strollable Main Street is lined with intriguing shops in historic buildings. Commercial Street, which leads to the harbor, has the art galleries, filled with work by mainly local artists inspired by this region. Wellfleet was for years one of the premier fishing villages on Cape Cod, and it still has a bustling and picturesque harbor. There are also freshwater ponds and National Seashore beaches; some of Cape Cod's finest swimming holes and most spectacular beaches line the coast of Wellfleet.

Tiny Truro is the least developed of the Cape's towns; it has the smallest population and the highest proportion of acreage reserved for the National Seashore. The center of town is one of those blink-and-you-miss-it affairs, though the fact that Truro has four libraries should tell you something about its residents.

Provincetown is a former Portuguese fishing village turned into an internationally famous art and gay colony with a flamboyant nightlife. The main drag (so to speak) is Commercial Street, with the best shopping on Cape Cod. Families come for the strolling, museums, and whale-watching; bon vivants for the restaurants, cafes, and entertainment; and gays for the camaraderie. And the beaches? Seemingly endless.

1 EASTHAM

35 miles E of Sandwich; 21 miles S of Provincetown

Despite its optimal waterside location (the distance from bay to ocean is as little as 1 mile in spots), Eastham is one of the least pretentious locales on the Cape—and yet highly popular as the gateway to the magnificent Cape Cod National Seashore.

The downside—or upside, depending on how you look at it—is that there aren't many shops or attractions worth checking out. Even Eastham's colorful history, as the site of the Pilgrims' first encounter with hostile natives, has faded with time. A mock-1680s windmill in the center of town serves as a reminder of the days when, according to Cape historian Arthur Wilson Tarbell, Eastham served as "the granary of eastern Massachusetts." Few take the trouble to track down the graves of three "First Comers" in the Old Cove Burying Ground, on Route 6, a mile past the Orleans rotary on the right (park at Corliss Way).

Mostly, though, this is a place to kick back and let the sun, surf, and sand dictate your day.

ESSENTIALS

GETTING THERE After crossing the Sagamore Bridge, head east on Route 6. Once you pass straight through the Orleans rotary, you are in Eastham. Or fly into Hyannis or Provincetown (see "Getting There & Getting Around," in chapter 3).

VISITOR INFORMATION An information booth run by the town of Eastham is located on Route 6 at Governor Prence Road (© **508/255-3444**) and is open Memorial Day to late September daily from 9am to 7pm with reduced hours in the shoulder season. Call or write the **Eastham Chamber of Commerce** for an informational brochure: P.O. Box 1329, Eastham, MA 02642 (© **508/240-7211;** www.easthamchamber.com). You may also contact the **Cape Cod Chamber of Commerce,** routes 6 and 132, Hyannis, MA 02601 (© **888/332-2732** or 508/362-3225; www.capecodchamber.org), open year-round Monday to Saturday from 9am to 5pm and Sunday and holidays from 10am to 4pm.

BEACHES & RECREATIONAL PURSUITS

BEACHES From here on up, the Atlantic beaches are best reserved for strong swimmers: Waves are big (often taller than you), and the undertow can be treacherous. The flat, nearly placid bay beaches, on the other hand, are just right for families with young children. The sand slopes so gradually that you won't have to worry about them slipping in over their heads. When the tide recedes (twice daily), it leaves a mile-wide playground of rippled sand full of fascinating creatures, including horseshoe and hermit crabs. Stickers for town beaches can be purchased ($50 for a weeklong pass) at the Department of Public Works office on Old Orchard Road near the town dump. A day pass for $15 can be purchased at most town beaches and at the ocean-side National Seashore beaches.

- **Coast Guard & Nauset Light** ★★★, off Ocean View Drive: Connected to outlying parking lots by a free shuttle, these pristine National Seashore beaches have lifeguards and restrooms. Coast Guard Beach consistently ranks as one of the best beaches in the U.S. in national surveys. Though National Seashore beaches can be chilly (this is the Atlantic Ocean, after all), the water is clean and clear. Similar to all National Seashore beaches, the vistas are lovely (just 30 miles of beach). At Coast Guard Beach, the old white Coast Guard building is scenically perched on a bluff. At Nauset Light Beach, the red-striped lighthouse, having moved back from its oceanfront perch, looks over the parking lot. A short walk away are the Three Sisters Lighthouses, three squat structures that have been set in a parklike enclave. Parking is $15 per day, $45 per season.

- **First Encounter, Campground & Sunken Meadow ★★**: These town-operated bay beaches generally charge $15 a day; permits ($50 per week) can be obtained from the Highway Department on Old Orchard Road in North Eastham (𝄐 **508/240-5900**).
- **Great Pond & Wiley Park ★**: These two town-run freshwater beaches are also open to the public, on the same terms as the bay beaches.

BICYCLING With plenty of free parking available at the **Cape Cod National Seashore's Salt Pond Visitor Center ★★** (𝄐 **508/255-3421**), Eastham makes a convenient access point for the **Cape Cod Rail Trail ★★** (𝄐 **508/896-3491**). Northward, it's about 5 wildflower-lined miles to Wellfleet, where the trail ends; Dennis is about 20 miles southwest. A 1.5-mile spur trail, winding through locust and apple groves, links the visitor center with glorious Coast Guard Beach: It's for bikes only (no blades). Rentals are available at the **Little Capistrano Bike Shop** (𝄐 **508/255-6515**), on Salt Pond Road just west of Route 6 and across the street from the Salt Pond Visitor Center. Bikes rent for about $23 per day. The best trail-side eatery—fried clams, lobster, and the like—is **Arnold's** (𝄐 **508/255-2575**), located on Route 6 about 1 mile north of the visitor center.

BOATING The best way to experience Nauset Marsh is by kayak or canoe. Rentals are available in neighboring towns: The closest source would be the **Goose Hummock Outdoor Center** at 15 Rte. 6A in Orleans (𝄐 **508/255-2620**).

Jack's Boat Rentals (𝄐 **508/349-9808**) is located on Route 6 next to Cumberland Farms in Wellfleet. Canoes rent for $50 a day, kayaks for $45 to $55 a day. Jack's also rents Sunfish sailboats and paddleboats. If you rent for 2 days, the third day is free. They have a seasonal outlet from mid-June to early September on **Wellfleet's Gull Pond** (𝄐 **508/349-7553**). Kayak and canoe rentals at Gull Pond cost $20 to $25 for a half-hour and $10 to $15 for each additional hour. After 3 hours, the fourth hour is free.

FISHING Eastham has four ponds open to fishing; Herring Pond is stocked. Freshwater-fishing licenses can be purchased at **Goose Hummock,** Route 6A, Orleans (𝄐 **508/255-0455**), or from the town clerk at Town Hall, Route 6 (𝄐 **508/240-5900**). For a shellfishing license, visit the **Natural Resources Department** at 555 Old Orchard Rd. (𝄐 **508/240-5972**). Surf-casting is permitted at Nauset Beach North (off Doane Rd.) and Nauset Light Beach (off Cable Rd.).

FITNESS **Willy's Gym, Fitness and Wellness Center,** 4730 Rte. 6, North Eastham (𝄐 **508/255-6370**), offers racket sports, plus Nautilus and free weights, various classes, an Olympic pool, saunas, steam rooms, and whirlpools. Nonmembers pay $20 a day.

NATURE TRAILS There are five self-guided nature trails with descriptive markers—for walkers only—within this portion of the Cape Cod National Seashore. The 1.5-mile **Fort Hill Trail** off Fort Hill Road (off Rte. 6, about 1 mile south of the town center) takes off from a free parking lot just past the **Captain Edward Penniman House ★**, a fancy multicolored 1868 Second Empire manse maintained by rangers from the Cape Cod National Seashore. Seashore rangers lead occasional tours of the house's interior in

⏱ **Tips**   **Drive with Caution**

There have been many serious accidents on Route 6 in Eastham, and as a result, the speed limit here declines rather abruptly from 55 to 40 mph. Eastham police are vigilant about enforcement.

season. You can visit the house in July and August, Tuesday to Friday from 1 to 4pm. Call the visitor center at ✆ 508/255-3421. But the exterior far outshines the interior, and more interesting sights await outside. Check out the huge whale-jawbone gate before walking across the street to the trail. Following the trail markers, you'll pass "Indian Rock" (bearing the marks of untold generations who used it to sharpen their tools) and enjoy scenic vantage points overlooking the channel-carved marsh—keep an eye out for egrets and great blue herons—and out to sea. The Fort Hill Trail hooks up with the half-mile **Red Cedar Swamp Trail,** offering boardwalk views of an ecology otherwise inaccessible.

Three relatively short trails fan out from the Cape Cod National Seashore's Salt Pond Visitor Center by Eastham. The most unusual is the quarter-mile **Buttonbush Trail ★,** specially adapted for the sight-impaired, with a guide rope and descriptive plaques in both oversize type and Braille. The **Doane Loop Trail ★,** a half-mile woodland circuit about 1 mile east of the visitor center, is graded to allow access to wheelchairs and strollers. The 1-mile **Nauset Marsh Trail ★** skirts Salt Pond to cross the marsh (via boardwalk) and open fields before returning by way of a recovering forest. Look both ways for bike crossings!

SURFING   Hitting the surf is a popular pastime at the National Seashore beaches like Cahoon's Hollow on the Outer Cape. For surfing, windsurfing and kitesurfing lessons, contact Eric Gustafson of Funseekers (✆ **508/349-1429;** www.funseekers.org), which charges $120 for a 2-hour surfing lesson for one person. A 2-hour lesson for two people is $180 and for three people, it's $240. Kitesurfing lessons are $250 for three hours.

TENNIS   Five public courts are located at the **Nauset Regional High School** in North Eastham and can be used on a first-come, first-served basis; for details, contact the Nauset Regional High School (✆ **508/255-1505**). **Willy's Gym,** 4730 Rte. 6, North Eastham (✆ **508/255-6370**), offers six indoor courts at a fee of $20 per person.

TWO MUSEUMS
The 1869 Schoolhouse Museum   Run by the volunteers of the Eastham Historical Society, this former one-room schoolhouse—with separate entrances for boys and girls—encapsulates the town's accomplishments. Exhibits range from early Native American tools to mementos of author Henry Beston's yearlong stay on Coast Guard Beach, which resulted in *The Outermost House,* as compelling a read today as it was back in 1928. And in case you were wondering—yes, that strange garden gate is in fact the washed-up jawbones of a rather large whale.

Nauset Rd. (off Rte. 6, opposite the Salt Pond Visitor Center). ✆ **508/255-0788.** Free admission. July–Aug Mon–Fri 1–4pm; Sept Sat 1–4pm. Closed Oct–June.

Salt Pond Visitor Center at the Cape Cod National Seashore ★★   Begin your exploration of the seashore by taking a look at the center's excellent exhibits about this unique environment. After all, since you're undoubtedly going to spend a fair amount of time on the beach, you might as well find out how it came to be, what other creatures you'll be sharing it with, and how not to harm it or them.

Occupying more than half the landmass north of Orleans and covering the entire 30-mile oceanfront, the 44,000-acre Cape Cod National Seashore is a free gift from legislators who had the foresight to set it aside as a sanctuary in 1961. Take advantage of the excellent educational exhibits and continuous film loops offered here; particularly fascinating is a video about the 1990 discovery of an 11,000-year-old campsite amid the storm-ravaged dunes of Coast Guard Beach, which was about 5 miles inland when these early settlers spent their summers here. After absorbing some of the local history, be sure to take time to venture out—on your own or with a ranger guide—to the surrounding trails (see "Nature Trails," above).

Note: For more information about the Cape Cod National Seashore, journey up to Race Point in Provincetown, where another visitor center is tucked into the dunes.

Salt Pond Rd. (east of Rte. 6). © **508/255-3421.** www.nps.gov/caco. Free admission. Late May to mid-Oct daily 9am–5pm; mid-Oct to late May daily 9am–4:30pm.

KID STUFF

No one will look askance if you let your kids try the **Buttonbush Trail** ★ (see "Nature Trails," above) in a blindfold: In fact, it's encouraged, not only as a good way to foster empathy for the blind but also to heighten multisensory awareness. You'll find more pastimes, such as miniature golf, along Route 6, and, of course, at the beaches.

WHERE TO STAY

Expensive

Fort Hill Bed and Breakfast ★★ Overlooking Nauset Marsh in the scenic Fort Hill area is the delightfully sophisticated Fort Hill Bed and Breakfast. Built in the Greek Revival style of the mid-1800s, this former farmhouse-turned-B&B offers three suites, all of which have queen-size beds. The spacious and pleasant Emma suite includes a living area complete with a piano and a library of excellent books. The bathroom is plenty roomy and has a large bay window. The Nantucket cottage is perfect for those looking for that extra bit of privacy or space, and the separate kitchen and large living area with working fireplace make for comfortable digs for a longer stay. The warm and amiable innkeepers, Jean and Gordon Avery, serve up a creative and delicious breakfast.

75 Fort Hill Rd., Eastham, MA 02642. © **508/240-2870.** www.forthillbedandbreakfast.com. 3 units. Memorial Day–Columbus Day $270–$325. Rates include full breakfast. Ask about weekly discounts for the Nantucket cottage. No credit cards. Closed Thanksgiving and Christmas. **Amenities:** Wi-Fi in main living area. *In room:* A/C, TV/VCR, kitchen (Nantucket cottage only), hair dryer, iron and board available on request, no phone.

The Whalewalk Inn & Spa ★★ (Finds) This is where you stay if you are looking for a deluxe B&B in the Outer Cape. Regularly hailed as one of the Cape's prettiest inns, this 1830 Greek Revival manse fully deserves its reputation. Located in a quiet residential area just a few blocks off the Rail Trail, the inn is decorated in a tasteful, mostly pastel, palette. A six-room carriage house sports deluxe rooms with antique four-poster beds, fireplaces, and private decks, and several have whirlpool baths for two. A new spa makes this inn even more noteworthy.

220 Bridge Rd. (about ³/₄ mile west of the Orleans rotary), Eastham, MA 02642. © **800/440-1281** or 508/255-0617. Fax 508/240-0017. www.whalewalkinn.com. 16 units, 11 with tub/shower, 5 with shower only. Summer $220–$365 double; $290–$420 suite. Rates include full breakfast. AE, DISC, MC, V. No children

11 and under. Closed Jan–Feb. **Amenities:** Resistance pool; weight machines; spa w/massage; hot tub;
sauna. *In room:* A/C, TV/DVD/VCR, hair dryer, iron.

Moderate

Inn at the Oaks ★ This 1869 Queen Anne Victorian, across the street from the Salt
Pond Visitor Center and about a mile from Coast Guard Beach, is one of the few bed-
and-breakfasts on Cape Cod with a billiard room. The large, colorful house is set well
back from the road on a woodsy property. Rooms range from cozy to spacious; some have
brass beds and claw-foot tubs. The carriage house in back has three large family suites.

3085 County Rd./Rte. 6 (opposite Salt Pond Visitor Center), Eastham, MA 02642. © **877/255-1886** or
508/255-1886. Fax 508/240-0345. www.innattheoaks.com. 10 units, 7 with tub/shower, 3 with shower
only. Summer $155–$210 double; $210–$270 suite. Rates include full breakfast and afternoon tea. AE,
DISC, MC, V. Open year-round. Pets allowed in certain suites. **Amenities:** Spa room w/massage services
and 2-person hot tub; billiard room. *In room:* A/C, TV/DVD, Wi-Fi, hair dryer.

The Penny House Inn & Spa Whizzing past on Route 6, you'd scarcely suspect
there's a peaceful inn tucked away behind a massive hedge. The rooms vary widely in size
and price. Many rooms have fireplaces; a couple have whirlpool tubs. Five deluxe rooms
are equipped with bathrobes, phones, TVs, and minifridges.

4885 Rte. 6, Eastham, MA 02651. © **800/554-1751** or 508/255-6632. Fax 508/255-4893. www.penny
houseinn.com. 12 units, 8 with tub/shower, 4 with shower only. Summer $215–$325 double; $335–$375
suite. Rates include full breakfast. AE, DISC, MC, V. **Amenities:** Heated outdoor pool; day spa w/hydro tub
and massage. *In room:* A/C, TV/VCR (in some), fridge (in some), hair dryer, no phone (in some).

Inexpensive

Beach Plum Motor Lodge (Value) Look for the riot of flowers that Gloria Moll
cultivates each year around her tiny front-yard pool, which is just big enough for a cool
dip and fragrant sunning. The rooms—in classic little cabins out back—are also smallish,
but they're more than adequate for most people's needs and very generously priced,
especially when you take into account the home-baked breakfast treats.

2555 Rte. 6 (about ¼ mile north of the town center), Eastham, MA 02642. © **508/255-7668.** www.
beachplummotorlodge.com. 5 units, 2 with shared bathroom, showers only. Summer $76–$82 double.
Rates include continental breakfast. AE, MC, V. Closed Nov–Apr. **Amenities:** Small outdoor pool. *In room:*
No phone.

HI-Mid Cape Eastham Hostel (Value) Though nowhere near as picturesque as the
Hostelling International–Truro 14 miles north (see "Where to Stay," in Truro), this
inland cluster of cabins makes a good stopover along the almost adjacent Rail Trail, and
the bay is a quick glide away.

75 Goody Hallet Dr. (off Bridge Rd., about ½ mile west of the Orleans rotary), Eastham, MA 02642.
© **508/255-2785.** www.capecodhostels.org. 50 beds. $32–$35 per bunk for members; $35–$38 per
bunk for nonmembers; $90 private cabins. MC, V. Closed mid-Sept to mid-May. *In room:* No phone.

WHERE TO DINE

Moderate

Arnold's Lobster & Clam Bar ★★ (Finds) (Kids) AMERICAN Some consider this
the best clam shack on the Cape for its fresh fish, hearty portions, and reasonable prices.
Offering a takeout window on the Rail Trail and a picnic grove for those who hate to
waste vacation hours sitting indoors, this popular eatery dishes out all the usual seashore
standards, from rich and crunchy fried clams (cognoscenti know to order whole clams,
not strips) to foot-long chili dogs. There's a good kids menu too.

188 3580 Rte. 6 (about 1¼ miles north of the town center). ✆ **508/255-2575.** www.arnoldsrestaurant.com.
Main courses $3–$34. No credit cards. Mid-June to mid-Sept daily 11:30am–9pm; late May to mid-June
call for hours. Closed mid-Sept to late May.

Take-Out & Picnic Fare

Box Lunch ★ (Finds) This is yet another source of the popular, Cape-invented pita
"rollwiches."

4205 Rte. 6, North Eastham. ✆ **508/255-0799.** May–Oct daily 9am–3pm; call for off-season hours.
Closed Jan.

Sweets

Ben & Jerry's Scoop Shop ★ (Kids) This premium ice-cream parlor is just about all
most Eastham residents need in the way of evening entertainment.

50 Brackett Rd. (at Rte. 6), North Eastham. ✆ **508/255-2817.** July–Aug 8am–10:30pm; call for off-season
hours. Closed Nov–Apr.

Hole-in-One Donut Shop Old-timers convene at the counter of this shop to pon-
der the state of the world. You can join in, or scurry home with your haul of hand-cut
donuts and fresh-baked muffins and bagels.

4295 Rte. 6 (about ¼ mile south of the town center). ✆ **508/255-9446.** Daily 5am–noon. Open year-
round.

EASTHAM AFTER DARK

Most Saturday nights in season (the schedule is somewhat erratic), the **First Encounter
Coffee House,** Chapel in the Pines, 220 Samoset Rd. (off Rte. 6, ¼ mile west of town
center; no phone; www.firstencounter.org), a tiny 1899 church in Eastham, hosts some
very big names on the folk/rock circuit, such as Livingston Taylor and Patty Larkin.
Tickets are $15 to $20; call for a schedule. Closed May and September.

The **Salt Pond Visitor Center,** on Salt Pond Road in Eastham (east of Rte. 6; ✆ **508/
255-3421**), puts on a varying schedule of entertainment, including concerts and guest
presentations, in season. A nominal fee ($2–$3) may apply. Call for a schedule.

2 WELLFLEET ★★★

42 miles NE of Sandwich; 14 miles S of Provincetown

Wellfleet—with the well-tended look of a classic New England village—is the favored
destination of artists, writers, off-duty psychiatrists, and other contemplative types. Distinguished literati such as Edna St. Vincent Millay and Edmund Wilson put the rural
village on the map in the 1920s, when Provincetown's bohemian heyday was fading. In
her brief and tumultuous tenure as Wilson's wife, Mary McCarthy pilloried the pretensions of the summer population in her novel, *A Charmed Life,* but had to concede that
the region possesses natural beauty: "steel-blue freshwater ponds and pine forests and
mushrooms and white bluffs dropping to a strangely pebbled beach."

To this day, Wellfleet remains remarkably unspoiled. Once you depart from Route 6,
commercialism is kept to a minimum, though the town boasts plenty of appealing
shops—including a number of distinguished galleries—and a couple of excellent New
American restaurants. It's hard to imagine any other community on the Cape supporting
so sophisticated an undertaking as the Wellfleet Harbor Actors' Theatre, or hosting such

a wholesome event as public square dancing on the Town Pier. And where else could you find, right next door to an outstanding nature preserve (the Wellfleet Bay Wildlife Sanctuary), a thriving drive-in movie theater?

ESSENTIALS

GETTING THERE After crossing the Sagamore Bridge, head east on Route 6. Pass through the Orleans rotary, and continue on Route 6 to Wellfleet. Or fly into Provincetown or Hyannis (see "Getting There," in chapter 3).

VISITOR INFORMATION Contact the **Wellfleet Chamber of Commerce** (off Rte. 6), P.O. Box 571, Wellfleet, MA 02663 (𝒞 **508/349-2510;** fax 508/349-3740; www. wellfleetchamber.com), or the **Cape Cod Chamber of Commerce** (see "Visitor Information," in the "Eastham" section, earlier in this chapter). The Wellfleet information center is open mid-June to mid-September 9am to 6pm daily. Call for off-season hours.

BEACHES & RECREATIONAL PURSUITS

BEACHES Though the distinctions are far from hard and fast, Wellfleet's fabulous ocean beaches tend to sort themselves demographically: LeCount Hollow is popular with families, Newcomb Hollow with high-schoolers, White Crest with the college crowd (including surfers and off-hour hang gliders), and Cahoon Hollow with 30-somethings. Only the latter two beaches permit parking by nonresidents ($15 per day). To enjoy the other two, as well as Burton Baker Beach on the harbor and Duck Harbor on the bay, plus three freshwater ponds, you'll have to walk or bike in, or see if you qualify for a sticker ($30 for 3 consecutive days, $60 per week). Bring proof of residency to the seasonal Beach Sticker Booth on the Town Pier, or call the **Wellfleet Recreation Department** (𝒞 **508/349-9818**). Parking is free at all beaches and ponds after 4pm.

- **Marconi Beach** ★★, off Marconi Beach Road in South Wellfleet: A National Seashore property, this cliff-lined beach (with restrooms) charges an entry fee of $15 per day, or only $45 for the season. *Note:* The bluffs are so high that the beach lies in shadow by late afternoon.
- **Mayo Beach,** Kendrick Avenue (near the Town Pier): Right by the harbor, facing south, this warm, shallow bay beach (with restrooms) is hardly secluded but will please young waders and splashers. And the price is right; parking is free. Make sure you go at high tide; at low tide, oyster farmers take over. You could grab a bite (and a paperback) at The Bookstore Restaurant across the street, which serves three meals a day and sells used books around back.
- **White Crest & Cahoon Hollow Beaches** ★★★, off Ocean View Drive in Wellfleet: These two town-run ocean beaches—big with surfers—are open to all. Both have snack bars and restrooms. Parking costs $15 per day.

BICYCLING The end (to date) of the 25-mile (and growing) **Cape Cod Rail Trail** ★★★ (𝒞 **508/896-3491**), Wellfleet is also among its more desirable destinations: A country road off the bike path leads right to LeCount Hollow Beach. Located near the bike path terminus, **South Wellfleet General Store** (𝒞 **508/349-2335**) can see to your snacking needs and also rents bikes for $26 per day.

BOATING Jack's Boat Rentals, located on Gull Pond off Gull Pond Road, about a half-mile south of the Truro border (𝒞 **508/349-9808**), rents out canoes, kayaks, sailboards, and Sunfish, as well as sea cycles and surf bikes. Gull Pond connects to Higgins Pond by way of a placid, narrow channel lined with red maples and choked with yellow

Cape Cod National Seashore

No trip to Cape Cod would be complete without a visit to **the Cape Cod National Seashore** on the Outer Cape and an afternoon barefoot stroll along "The Great Beach," where you see exactly why the Cape attracts artists and poets. On August 7, 1961, Pres. John F. Kennedy signed a bill designating 27,000 acres in the 40 miles from Chatham to Provincetown as the Cape Cod National Seashore, a new national park. Unusual in a national park, the Seashore includes 500 private residences, the owners of which lease land from the park service. Convincing residents that a National Seashore would be a good thing for Cape Cod was an arduous task back then, and Provincetown still grapples with Seashore officials over town land issues.

The Seashore's claim to fame is its spectacular beaches—in reality, one long beach—with dunes 50 to 150 feet high. This is the Atlantic Ocean, so the surf is rough (and cold), but a number of the beaches have lifeguards. Seashore beaches include **Coast Guard** and **Nauset Light** beaches in Eastham, **Marconi Beach** in Wellfleet, **Head of the Meadow Beach** in Truro, and Provincetown's **Race Point** and **Herring Cove** beaches. A $45 pass will get you into all of them for the season, or you can pay a daily rate of $15.

The Seashore also has a number of walking trails—all free, all picturesque, and all worth a trip. In Eastham, **Fort Hill** (off Rte. 6) has one of the best scenic views on Cape Cod and a popular boardwalk trail through a red-maple swamp. The **Nauset Marsh Trail** is accessed from the Salt Pond Visitor Center on Route 6 in Eastham. **Great Island** on the bay side in Wellfleet is surely one of the finest places to have a picnic; you could spend the day hiking the trails. On **Pamet Trail** off North Pamet Road in Truro, hikers pass the decrepit old cranberry-bog building (restoration is in the works) on the way to a trail through the dunes. Don't try the old boardwalk trail over the bogs here; it has flooded and is no longer in use. The **Atlantic White Cedar Swamp Trail** is located at the Marconi

water lilies. Needless to say, it's a great place to paddle. Renting a kayak or canoe at Gull Pond for a couple of hours costs about $50. If you'd like a canoe for a few days, you'll need to go to the Jack's Boat Rentals location on Route 6 in Wellfleet (next to the Cumberland Farms). There, a kayak rents for $50 for a single, and $65 for a tandem for 24 hours. Sunfish sailboats are $200 for three days. Rentals come with a roof rack if you need it. There are many wonderful places to canoe in Wellfleet—for example, a trip from Wellfleet's Town Pier across the harbor to Great Island.

For information about other excellent naturalist-guided tours, inquire about trips sponsored by the **Cape Cod Museum of Natural History** (© **800/479-3867** or 508/896-3867) and the **Wellfleet Bay Wildlife Sanctuary** (© **508/349-2615**).

The **Chequessett Yacht & Country Club** on Chequessett Neck Road in Wellfleet (© **508/349-0198**) offers group sailing lessons. Call for rates. For experienced sailors, **Wellfleet Marine Corp.**, on the Town Pier (© **508/349-2233**), rents 14- and 19-foot sailboats in season. The cost is $45 to $55 for the first hour, $16 to $19 for each additional hour, or $125 to $150 for the day. They also rent 14- to 16-foot motorboats for

Station site, **Small Swamp** and **Pilgrim Spring** trails are found at Pilgrim Heights Beach, and **Beech Forest Trail** is located at Race Point in Provincetown. The best bike path on Cape Cod is the Province Lands Trail, 5 swooping and invigorating miles, at Race Point Beach. If that's not enough in the way of sports, surf-casting is allowed from the ocean beaches—Race Point is a popular spot.

The Seashore also includes several historic buildings that tell their part of the region's history. At Race Point Beach in Provincetown, the **Old Harbor Lifesaving Station** serves as a museum of early lifesaving techniques. **Captain Edward Penniman's 1868 house** at Fort Hill in Eastham is a grandly ornate Second Empire home, and the 1730 **Atwood-Higgins House** in Wellfleet is a typical Cape-style home; both are open for tours. Five lighthouses dot the Seashore, including **Highland Light** in Truro and **Nauset Light** in Eastham, both of which have been moved back from precarious positions on the edges of dunes. Most of the Seashore beaches have large parking lots, but you'll need to get there early (before 10am) on busy summer weekends. If the beach you want to go to is full, try the one next door—most of the beaches are 5 to 10 miles apart. Don't forget your beach umbrella; the sun exposure here can get intense.

Getting There: Take Route 6, the Mid-Cape Highway, to Eastham (about 50 miles). Pick up a map at the Cape Cod National Seashore's **Salt Pond Visitor Center** in Eastham (© **508/255-3421;** www.nps.gov/caco). Another visitor center is at **Race Point.** Both centers have ranger activities, maps, gift shops, and restrooms. Seashore beaches are all off Route 6 and are clearly marked. Additional beaches along this stretch are run by individual towns, and you must have a sticker or pay a fee.

$45 to $70 for the first hour and $16 to $30 for each additional hour, plus a 20% fuel surcharge on all rentals.

FISHING For a license to fish at Long Pond, Great Pond, or Gull Pond (all stocked with trout and full of native perch, pickerel, and sunfish), visit **Town Hall** at 300 Main St. (© **508/349-0301**). Massachusetts residents pay $14 for a 3-day pass or $29 for a season pass; nonresidents pay $25 for a 3-day pass or $39 for a season pass. Surf-casting, which doesn't require a license, is permitted at the town beaches. Shellfishing licenses—Wellfleet's oysters are world-famous—can be obtained from the **Shellfish Department** on the Town Pier off Kendrick Avenue (© **508/349-0300**). Shellfish licenses are $40 per season for residents, $125 per season for nonresidents. Also heading out from here, in season, is the 60-foot party fishing boat *Navigator* (© **508/349-6003**), which charges $40 for adults, $35 for seniors, and $30 for children for a 4-hour trip, gear and bait provided. Charter boats include the *Erin-H* (© **508/349-9663;** www.virtualcapecod.com/erinh), charging about $650 for a half-day and $800 for a full day.

GOLF   Hugging a pretty cove, the **Chequessett Yacht & Country Club** on Chequessett Neck Road (© **508/349-3704**) has one of the loveliest 9-hole courses on the Cape; nonmembers need to reserve at least 3 days ahead. Greens fees are $32 for 9 holes, $46 for 18 holes; prices are lower in the afternoon.

NATURE & WILDLIFE AREAS   You'll find 6 miles of very scenic trails lined with lupines and bayberries—Goose Pond, Silver Spring, and Bay View—within the **Wellfleet Bay Wildlife Sanctuary** in South Wellfleet (see below). Right in town, the short, picturesque boardwalk known as **Uncle Tim's Bridge,** off East Commercial Street, crosses Duck Creek to access a tiny island crisscrossed by paths. The Cape Cod National Seashore maintains two spectacular self-guided trails. The 1.25-mile **Atlantic White Cedar Swamp Trail,** off the parking area for the Marconi Wireless Station (see "Wellfleet Historical Sights," below), shelters a rare stand of the lightweight species of cedars prized by Native Americans as wood for canoes; red maples are slowly crowding out the cedars, but meanwhile the tea-tinted, moss-choked swamp is a magical place, refreshingly cool even at the height of summer. A boardwalk will see you over the muck (these peat bogs are 7 ft. deep in places), but the return trip does entail a calf-testing half-mile trek through deep sand. Consider it a warm-up for magnificent **Great Island,** jutting 4 miles into the bay (off the western end of Chequessett Neck Rd.) to cup Wellfleet Harbor. Before attaching itself to the mainland in 1831, Great Island harbored a busy whaling post; a 1970 dig turned up the foundations of an early-18th-century tavern. These days the "island" is quite uninhabited and a true refuge for those strong enough to go the distance. Just be sure to cover up, wear sturdy shoes, bring water, and venture to Jeremy Point—the very tip—only if you're sure the tide is going out.

A spiffy, eco-friendly visitor center serves as both introduction and gateway to the **Wellfleet Bay Wildlife Sanctuary,** off Route 6, a couple hundred yards north of the Eastham border, in South Wellfleet (© **508/349-2615;** fax 508/349-2632; www.wellfleetbay.org), a 1,000-acre refuge maintained by the Massachusetts Audubon Society. Passive solar heat and composting toilets are just a few of the waste-cutting elements incorporated into the seemingly simple $1.6-million building, which nestles in its wooded site like well-camouflaged wildlife. You'll see plenty of the latter—especially lyrical red-winged blackbirds and circling osprey—as you follow 5 miles of looping trails through pine forests, salt marsh, and moors. To hone your observation skills, avail yourself of the naturalist-guided tours offered during the day and sometimes at night (see "Wellfleet After Dark," later in this chapter): You'll see and learn much more. Also inquire about special workshops for children (some, like the Japanese "fish-printing" session, are truly ingenious), and about canoeing, birding, and seal-watching excursions. **Seal-watching trips** are $45 for adults, $40 for children for a 1½-hour tour by boat. Canoe trips for experienced paddlers (over age 12) are scheduled in season throughout the Lower Cape. The cost is $25 to $35. A listing of all Wellfleet Bay Wildlife Sanctuary events with dates and times is posted in the main building.

Trail use is free for Massachusetts Audubon Society members; the trail fee for nonmembers is $5 for adults and $3 for seniors and children. Trails are open July through August from 8am to 8pm, and September through June from 8am to dusk. The visitor center is open Memorial Day to Columbus Day daily from 8:30am to 5pm; during the off season, it's closed Monday.

Note: It's worth joining the Massachusetts Audubon Society just for the chance—afforded only to members—to camp out here.

TENNIS   Public courts are located at Mayo Beach on Kendrick Avenue near the harbor; for details and exact fees, contact the **Wellfleet Recreation Department** (© 508/349-0330). Also for a fee, book one of the five clay courts at the **Chequessett Yacht & Country Club** on Chequessett Neck Road (© 508/349-3704) or one of the eight at **Oliver's Clay Courts** at 2183 Rte. 6, about 1 mile south of town (© 508/349-3330). At both venues, 1 hour of singles play on clay courts costs $22, doubles $26.

WATERSPORTS   Surfing is restricted to White Crest Beach, and sailboarding to Burton Baker Beach at Indian Neck during certain tide conditions; ask for a copy of the regulations at the Beach Sticker Booth on the Town Pier.

   Eric Gustafson (© 508/349-1429; www.funseekers.org) offers windsurfing and surfing lessons ($120 for 2 hr.), and, for the most adventurous, kite boarding ($250 for 3 hr.).

WELLFLEET HISTORICAL SIGHTS

Marconi Wireless Station   It's from this bleak spot that Italian inventor Guglielmo Marconi broadcast, via a complex of 210-foot cable towers, the world's first wireless communiqué: "Cordial greetings from President Theadore [sic] Roosevelt to King Edward VII in Poldhu, Wales." It was also here that news of the troubled *Titanic* first reached these shores. There's scarcely a trace left of this extraordinary feat of technology (the station was dismantled in 1920); still, the displays convey the leap of imagination that was required.

Marconi Site Rd. (off Rte. 6, about ¾ mile south of the town center). © 508/349-3785. www.nps.gov/caco. Free parking and admission. Open dawn–dusk, year-round.

Wellfleet Historical Society Museum   Every last bit of spare Wellfleet memorabilia seems to have been crammed into this old storefront. The volunteer curators have taken pains to arrange the surfeit of artifacts so that visitors can follow up on a particular interest—the United Fruit Company (now Chiquita Brands International, Inc.), say, which got its start here in 1870 when one of Lorenzo Dow Baker's swift clipper ships delivered a cargo of exotic bananas, or Marconi's mysterious transoceanic experiments. Even restless children are likely to find something of interest, particularly among the antique toys in the attic. The museum hosts fascinating speakers and sponsors a chowder supper once a summer. Historical walking tours around town take 1¼ hours, cost $3, and leave at 10:15am.

266 Main St. (in the center of town). © 508/349-9157. www.wellfleethistoricalsociety.com. Free admission. Late June to early Sept Tues and Fri 10am–4pm, Wed, Thurs and Sat 1–4pm. Closed early Sept to late June.

KID STUFF

No conceivable nocturnal treat beats an outing to the **Wellfleet Drive-In Theater**—unless it's a double feature prefaced by a game of on-site minigolf while you're waiting for the sky to darken. The restaurant on-site is the **Dairy Bar and Grill** (© 508/349-0278), which specializes in fried seafood and is open from 11:30am to 10pm daily in season. There's minigolf next to the restaurant. During the day, check out what's up at the Wellfleet Bay Wildlife Sanctuary. (See "Beaches & Recreational Pursuits," above.)

SHOPPING

Boasting more than a dozen arts emporia, Wellfleet has begun hailing itself as "the art-gallery town." Though it may lag behind Provincetown in terms of quantity, the quality does achieve comparable heights. Crafts make a strong showing, too, as do contemporary women's clothing and eclectic home furnishings. There's just one drawback: Unlike Provincetown, which has something to offer virtually year-round, Wellfleet pretty much closes up come Columbus Day, so buy while the getting's good.

ANTIQUES/COLLECTIBLES Wheeler-dealers should head for the **Wellfleet Flea Market,** 51 Rte. 6, north of the Eastham-Wellfleet border (© **800/696-3532** or 508/349-2520). A few days a week in summer and during the shoulder seasons, the parking lot of the Wellfleet Drive-In Theater "daylights" as an outdoor bazaar featuring as many as 300 booths. Though a great many vendors stock discount surplus, there are usually enough collectibles dealers on hand to warrant a browse through. An added bonus: Kids can kick loose in the little playground or grab a quick bite at the snack bar. Lookers are charged $1 to $2 per carload. Open weekends and Monday holidays, from mid-April through June, September, and October, from 8am to 4pm; Wednesdays, Thursdays, weekends, and Monday holidays in July and August from 8am to 4pm.

Farmhouse Antiques, Route 6 at Village Lane, South Wellfleet (© **508/349-1708**), is a large storehouse filled with a variety of goods, including a wide array of furniture, stacks of books and ephemera, and the antique chandeliers that didn't fit in the Orleans shop, Continuum (Farmhouse is a dealer for Continuum's wares).

ARTS & CRAFTS **Cherrystone Gallery,** 70 E. Commercial St., about ¼ mile south of East Main Street (© **508/349-3026**), is slightly off the main arts drag and intentionally out of step, but this tiny gallery is probably more influential than all the others put together. It got a head start by opening in 1972 and showing such luminaries as Rauschenberg, Motherwell, and, more recently, Wellfleet resident Helen Miranda Wilson. Closed late September to mid-June.

One of the more distinguished galleries in town, the smallish **Cove Gallery,** 15 Commercial St., by Duck Creek (© **508/349-2530**)—with a waterside sculpture garden—carries the paintings and prints of many well-known artists, including Barry Moser and Leonard Baskin. John Grillo's work astounds every summer during his annual show, which has featured boldly painted tango-themed paintings, watercolors, and prints. Alan Nyiri, whose dazzling color photographs are collected in the coffee-table book *Cape Cod,* shows regularly, as does Carla Golembe, whose lively Caribbean-influenced tableaux have graced several children's books. Closed mid-October through April.

Crafts make a stronger stand than art at **Left Bank Gallery,** 25 Commercial St., by Duck Creek (© **508/349-9451**). A 1933 American Legion Hall, it's an optimal display space. Whereas the paintings occupying the former auditorium sometimes verge on hackneyed, the "Potter's Room" overlooking the cove is packed with sturdy, handsome, useful vessels, along with compatible textiles. Also worth hunting out are the curious collages of Kim Victoria Kettler. The **Left Bank Small Works & Jewelry Gallery,** 3 W. Main St., in the center of town (© **508/349-7939**), features the spillover from the Left Bank Gallery, and in some ways, it's superior. There's also an irresistible sampling of new-wave jewelry designs, collected from over 100 noted artisans across the nation and arrayed in clever thematic displays.

FASHION At **Hannah,** 234 Main St. (© **508/349-9884**), Susan Hannah shows her own private label in this nicely rehabbed house, along with other designers' works. The emphasis is on flowing lines and relaxed fabrics—slinky rayon, soft cotton jersey, and nubby linen. Closed mid-September to late May.

Slightly more citified is **Off Center,** 354 Main St. (© **508/349-3634**), where the clothes are neither traditional nor trendy, but right-on, go-anywhere chic. Closed January through March.

Somewhat to the left of—and across the street from—its parent shop, Off Center, is Eccentricity, 361 Main St., in the center of town (© **508/349-7554**), which lives up to its name with dramatic antique kimonos and artifacts from Japan, India, and Africa. Closed January through March.

Karol Richardson, 11 W. Main St. (© **508/349-6378**), is owned and operated by its namesake, an alumna of the London College of Fashion and a refugee from the New York rag trade. She has a feel for sensual fabrics and a knack for fashions that, in her own words, are "wonderfully comfortable but sophisticated at the same time and very flattering to the less-than-perfect body." The lovely clothes that are seasonally displayed in this barn showroom, and slavered over by several generations, bear out the claim. Closed mid-October through April.

GIFTS **Jules Besch Stationers,** 15 Bank St. (© **508/349-1231**), specializes in stationery products, including papers, ribbon, gift cards, handmade journals and albums, desktop pen sets, guest books, and unusual gift items. This is an exquisite store in a mansard-roofed former bank building and is certainly worth a browse. Closed January through March.

WHERE TO STAY
Moderate
Aunt Sukie's Bayside Bed & Breakfast ★
Sue and Dan Hamar's house is perched on a bluff in an exclusive residential neighborhood overlooking Cape Cod Bay. Behind the house, a boardwalk path leads to a private bay beach. The Nickerson Suite is in the old part of the house and has wide-board wood floors and a fireplace. The Chequessett and Billingsgate rooms are more contemporary, as befits the addition completed in 1993. All rooms have sweeping bay views. In the back is a large deck where guests eat breakfast and can sunbathe during the day.

525 Chequessett Neck Rd., Wellfleet, MA 02667. © **800/420-9999** or 508/349-2804. www.auntsukies. com. 3 units, 1 with tub/shower, 2 with shower only, 1 cottage. Summer $270 double; cottage $1,600 per week. Room rates include continental breakfast. MC, V. Closed mid-Oct to mid-May. *In room:* Fridge.

Even'tide ★ (Kids)
Set back from the road in its own roomy compound, complete with playground, this motel on the main highway of the outer Cape feels more like a friendly village centered around a 60-foot, heated indoor pool—a godsend in inclement weather and a rarity in this part of the Cape. Besides the main motel building, there are seven cottages on the property with one, two, and three bedrooms. The Rail Trail goes right by the motel, and a 1-mile footpath through the woods leads to Marconi Beach.

650 Rte. 6 (about 1 mile north of the Eastham border), South Wellfleet, MA 02663. © **800/368-0007** in Mass. only, or 508/349-3410. Fax 508/349-7804. www.eventidemotel.com. 40 units, 39 with tub/shower, 1 with shower only. Summer $145–$180 double; $185–$220 efficiency. There is a $25 surcharge here on weekends for a 1-night stay. AE, DISC, MC, V. Closed Dec to mid-Apr. **Amenities:** Large heated indoor pool; playground; self-service laundromat. *In room:* A/C, TV, fridge, coffeemaker.

Surf Side Cottages ★★ (Kids)
This is where you want to be: smack dab on a spectacular beach with 50-foot dunes, within biking distance of Wellfleet Center, and a short drive from Provincetown for dinner. These cottages, fun and modern in a 1960s way, have one, two, or three bedrooms. All cottages have kitchens including microwaves, as well as fireplaces, barbecues, outdoor showers, and screened porches. Some have dishwashers and (most important) roof decks. From mid-May to mid-October, the cottages rent weekly. It's best to bring your own sheets and towels; renting a set costs $10 per person. Reserve early.

Ocean View Dr. (at LeCount Hollow Rd.; P.O. Box 937), South Wellfleet, MA 02663. ✆/fax **508/349-3959.** www.surfsidecottages.com. 18 cottages, showers only. Summer $1,150–$2,500 weekly; off season $95–$175 per day. MC, V. Closed mid-Nov to early Apr. Pets allowed off season. *In room:* Fridge, coffeemaker.

Inexpensive

The Inn at Duck Creeke ⓥⓐⓛⓤⓔ   This historic complex consists of four buildings set on 5 woodsy acres overlooking a tidal creek and salt marsh. Three lodging buildings include the main building, an 1880s captain's house with charming but basic rooms, many with shared bathrooms; the carriage house with cabin-style rooms; and the 1715 saltworks building with smaller, cottage-type rooms with antique decor. In the main building, the shared bathrooms adjoin two rooms, so there's an intimacy here those in search of privacy might not desire. There's definitely a no-frills quality to this lodging option—towels are thin, and so are walls. There are two restaurants (see "Where to Dine," below) on-site: Sweet Seasons, the more expensive, and the Duck Creeke Tavern, with a publike atmosphere and live entertainment in season.

70 Main St. (P.O. Box 364), Wellfleet, MA 02667. ✆ **508/349-9333.** Fax 508/349-0234. www.innatduck creeke.com. 26 units, 8 with shared bathroom, 13 with tub/shower, 5 with shower only. Summer $90–$95 double with shared bathroom; $115–$135 double with private bathroom. Rates include continental breakfast. AE, MC, V. Closed Nov–Apr. **Amenities:** 2 restaurants (seafood restaurant and tavern). *In room:* No phone.

WHERE TO DINE
Expensive

Sweet Seasons Restaurant/Duck Creeke Tavern ★ NEW AMERICAN   Chef/owner Judith Pihl's Mediterranean-influenced fare is still appealing after 20-plus years, as is this mullion-windowed dining room's peaceful pond view. Some of the dishes can be a bit heavy by contemporary standards, but there's usually a healthy alternative: Wellfleet littlenecks and mussels in a golden, aromatic tomato-and-cumin broth, for instance, as opposed to Russian oysters with smoked salmon, vodka, and sour cream. Specialties of the house include creamy sage-and-asparagus ravioli, swordfish with artichoke tapenade, and Seasons shrimp with feta and ouzo. Lighter fare is served in the adjoining Duck Creeke Tavern, with main courses costing $9 to $17.

At the Inn at Duck Creeke, 70 Main St. (about ¼ mile west of Rte. 6). ✆ **508/349-6535.** Reservations recommended. Main courses $17–$30. AE, MC, V. July–Sept Tues–Sun 5:30–10pm. Closed Oct–June.

Moderate

The Lighthouse ⓚⓘⓓⓢ AMERICAN   Nothing special in and of itself, this bustling, nearly year-round institution on Main Street is an off-season haven for locals and a beacon to passing tourists year-round. The casual, bustling atmosphere means it's a good place to bring kids. People might not notice right away that they are misbehaving. Except on Thursday's Mexican Night, the menu is all-American normal, from the steak-and-eggs breakfast to the native seafood dinners. Appreciative patrons usually keep up a dull roar throughout the day, revving up to a deafening roar as the Bass and Guinness flow from the tap.

317 Main St. (in the center of town). ✆ **508/349-3681.** Main courses $10–$25. DISC, MC, V. May–Oct daily 7am–10pm; call for off-season hours. Closed Mar.

The Wicked Oyster ★★ NEW AMERICAN   This old warehouse-style building on the way to Wellfleet Center has been converted into a cool and casual year-round restaurant. Several restaurants have come and gone from this spot, but this one looks like a keeper. There are several sections of the restaurant: an enclosed front porch, an ample dining room, and a large bar area. With a busy to-go area for coffee and pastries, this place definitely has a bustling atmosphere. You'll see families with small children, 20-something couples, and older folks enjoying this comfortable and convenient restaurant. Breakfast is popular here and features a multitude of omelets plus very strong coffee. For lunch, sandwiches and fried fish are on the menu. Dinner choices range from burgers to more refined options, like pan-fried sole with lemon caper butter; spring risotto with mushrooms and asparagus; or, for large appetites, grilled Angus tenderloin.

50 Main St. (just off Rte. 6, close to Wellfleet Center). ✆ **508/349-3455.** Reservations recommended. Main courses $16–$26. MC, V. June–Aug Thurs–Tues 7am–noon and 5–10:30pm; call for off-season hours. Open year-round.

Winslow's Tavern ★★ BISTRO   This upscale bistro offers summertime treats such as grilled lobster along with bistro classics like steak frites. Of course they have Wellfleet oysters, the town's world-famous bivalve. But they also have wonderful salads and light meals. With an alert waitstaff and contemporary setting, this is a very pleasant dining experience. On sunny afternoons, sit out on the front lawn here, the perfect perch for people-watching on Wellfleet's Main Street.

316 Main St. (in the center of town). ✆ **508/349-6450.** Reservations for parties of 6 or more only. Main courses $13–$23. AE, MC, V. Mid-June to Aug daily noon–3pm and 5:30–9:30pm; call for off-season hours. Closed late Oct to mid-May.

Inexpensive

Mac's Shack ★ Kids SEAFOOD   Mac and Alex Hay are brothers on a mission: They want to run the best darn clam shack on Cape Cod. In 2006 they rehabbed the landmark Lobster Hutt building (it's the large building with the boat and fisherman on the roof) and opened to the raves of the summer crowd. Come here for Wellfleet's world-famous oysters from an expert shucker at the extensive raw bar. Standard clam-shack fare, such as lobster dinners and fried clams, is served, and there's a sushi bar. The large picnic tables and paper plates make this an indestructible place to bring kids.

91 Commercial St. (a few blocks north of Wellfleet Center). ✆ **508/349-6333.** www.macsseafood.com. Reservations not accepted. Main courses $8–$20. MC, V. Mid-June to early Sept daily 4:30–9:30pm; call for off-season hours. Closed mid-Oct to mid-May.

Moby Dick's Restaurant ★ Kids SEAFOOD   This is your typical clam shack, with the requisite netting and buoys hanging from the ceiling. Order your meal at the register, sit at a picnic table, and a cheerful college student brings it to you. During your meal, one of the owners, Todd or Mignon Barry, will usually come by to ask how you're doing. Fried fish, clams, scallops, and shrimp are all good here; try the Moby's Seafood Special— a heaping platter of all of the above, plus coleslaw and fries. Then there's the clambake special with lobster, steamers, and corn on the cob. The lobster bisque is quite popular. There's also a kids' menu. Portions are huge; bring the family and chow down.

Rte. 6. ✆ **508/349-9795.** www.mobydicksrestaurant.com. Reservations not accepted. Main courses $8–$20. MC, V. Mid-June to early Sept daily 11:30am–10pm; call for off-season hours. Closed mid-Oct to Apr.

Takeout & Picnic Fare

Box Lunch ★   With a porch usually hemmed in by bicycles, this is the original source of the Cape's signature "rollwiches": rolled pita sandwiches with unusual fillings, like stuffing included in the turkey sandwich.

50 Briar Lane (north of Main St. in the town center). ✆ **508/349-2178.** Mid-June to mid-Sept daily 7am–4pm; mid-Sept to mid-June daily 7am–2:30pm.

Hatch's Fish & Produce Market (Finds)

This former fishing shack is the unofficial heart of Wellfleet. You'll find the best of local bounty, from fresh-picked corn and fruit-juice Popsicles to steaming lobsters and home-smoked local mussels and pâté. Virtually no one passes through without picking up a little something, along with the latest talk of the town.

310 Main St. (behind Town Hall). ✆ **508/349-2810** (fish) or 508/349-6734 (produce). June to mid-Sept 9am–7pm. Closed mid-Sept to May.

Mac's Seafood Market and Harbor Grill Restaurant ★ (Finds) (Kids)

Located on the town pier, this takeout shack with picnic tables features fresh local seafood unloaded from the boats just steps away. Besides grilled fish dinners, there are homemade chowders, seafood salads, sushi, and a raw bar. Perfect for families, you can sit on the picnic tables overlooking the harbor or take your meal over to Mayo Beach next door.

Wellfleet Town Pier. ✆ **508/349-9611.** Daily 11am–9pm. Closed Oct to late May.

Sweets

The Chocolate Sparrow ★

This closet-size outlet of a local chocolatier is hard to pass by once you've happened upon it. There's also a room full of penny candy.

326 Main St. (in the center of town). ✆ **508/349-1333.** Daily 10:30am–9:30pm. Closed early Sept to late May.

A Nice Cream Stop (Kids)

This is Wellfleet's premier premium ice-cream parlor, scooping Emack & Bolio's, a luscious Boston boutique brand.

326 Main St. (in the center of town). ✆ **508/349-2210.** Mid-June to early Sept daily 11am–10pm. Closed early Sept to mid-June.

WELLFLEET AFTER DARK

Clubs & Watering Holes

The Beachcomber ★ Arguably the best dance club on Cape Cod, the 'Comber—housed in an 1897 lifesaving station—is definitely the most scenic, and not just in terms of the youthful clientele. It's right on Cahoon Hollow Beach—so close, in fact, that late beachgoers on summer weekends can count on a free concert: reggae, perhaps, or the homegrown Toots and the Maytalls. Other nights, you might run into blues, ska, or rock, and often some very big names playing mostly for the fun of it. Parking is tricky here because the restaurant is on a busy beach where parking costs $15. If you park in the Beachcomber lot before 5pm, the $15 cost can be put toward food or a T-shirt at the restaurant. After 5pm, parking is free. Open late June to early September daily noon to 1am; call for off-season hours. Closed early September to late May. 1220 Old Cahoon Hollow Rd. (off Ocean View Dr. at Cahoon Hollow Beach). ✆ **508/349-6055.** www.beachcomber.com. Cover varies $10–$25.

Duck Creeke Tavern Live music featuring local talent—jazz, pop, folk, blues, and various hybrids—is on the bill Thursday through Sunday nights in the summer. A good light-fare menu is also available. Check out the bar itself, fashioned from old doors. There is usually no cover. Closed mid-October to late May. At the Inn at Duck Creeke, 70 Main St. (about ¼ mile west of Rte. 6). ✆ **508/349-7369.**

The **First Congregational Church of Wellfleet**, 200 Main St., about ¹/₄ mile west of Route 6 (© **508/349-6877**), hosts organ concerts Sundays at 8pm during July and August on its elaborate 1873 instrument. They're a good excuse to stop in and take a look around—the soaring 1850 Greek Revival church has the world's only bell tower ringing ship's time (an innovation introduced in 1952). Admission is free.

Wednesday nights in July and August, Wellfleet's workaday fishing pier (off Kendrick Ave.) resounds to the footfalls of avid amateur **square dancers** of every age. Call the Wellfleet Recreation Department at © **508/349-0330** for more information.

How about a night hike or bat walk? Both are offered at the **Wellfleet Bay Wildlife Sanctuary** (© **508/349-2615;** see "Beaches & Recreational Pursuits," earlier in this chapter). Rates vary; call for schedule and reservations. Just don't take in any vampire movies at the drive-in beforehand.

The **Wellfleet Drive-In Theater,** 51 Rte. 6, just north of the Eastham border (© **800/696-3532** or 508/349-2520), clearly deserves National Landmark status: Built in 1957, it's the only drive-in left on Cape Cod and one of a scant half-dozen surviving in the state. The rituals are unbending and every bit as endearing as ever: the playtime preceding the cartoons, the countdown plugging the allures of the snack bar, and finally, two full first-run features. The drive-in is open daily from late May through mid-September; show time is at dusk. Call for off-season hours. Admission is $7.50 for adults and $4.50 for seniors and children 5 to 11.

The principals behind the **Wellfleet Harbor Actors' Theatre (WHAT),** 2357 Rte. 6 (next to the post office) or 1 Kendrick Ave. (next to the town pier) (© **508/349-6835;** www.what.org), aim to provoke—and usually succeed, even amid this very sophisticated, seen-it-all summer colony. WHAT's new 200-seat space, the Julie Harris Stage, which opened in June 2007 on Route 6, is up and running. Smaller shows are still shown in the 90-seat harbor theatre. WHAT for Kids shows are performed in a tent on the Route 6 property. What makes this theatre stand out is that they go to great lengths to secure original work, some local and some by playwrights of considerable renown, with the result that the repertory rarely suffers a dull moment. Performances at the harbor and on the Julie Harris Stage are given Wednesday to Sunday with afternoon and evening shows from late May through October; call or check their website for a schedule. Tickets are $32. WHAT for Kids performances cost $9 for open seating in the tent Mondays through Thursdays at 7:30pm.

3 TRURO ★★

46 miles E of Sandwich; 10 miles S of Provincetown

Although Truro is one of those blink-and-you'll-miss-it towns, the location is great: a tranquil village between charming Wellfleet and rowdy Provincetown. With only 1,600 year-round residents (fewer than in 1840, when Pamet Harbor was a whaling and ship-building port), the town amounts to little more than a smattering of stores and public buildings, and lots of low-profile houses hidden away in the woods and dunes. As in Wellfleet, writers, artists, and vacationing psychotherapists are drawn to the quiet and calm. Painter Edward Hopper lived in contented isolation in a South Truro cottage for nearly 4 decades.

The natives manage to entertain themselves with get-togethers at the Truro Center for the Arts or, more simply, among themselves. A lot of money may be circulating in this rusticated community, but inconspicuous consumption is the rule of the day. The culmination of the social season, tellingly enough, is the late-September "dump dance" held at Truro's recycling center. For bigger kinds of excitement or cultural stimulation, Provincetown is only a 10-minute drive away (you'll know you're getting close when you spot the wall-to-wall tourist cabins lining the bay in North Truro).

ESSENTIALS

GETTING THERE   After crossing the Sagamore Bridge, head east on Route 6 or 6A to Orleans and north on Route 6. Or fly into Provincetown (see "Getting There," in chapter 3).

VISITOR INFORMATION   Contact the **Truro Chamber of Commerce,** Route 6A (at Head of the Meadow Rd.), Truro, MA 02666 (© **508/487-1288;** www.trurochamberof commerce.com); or the **Cape Cod Chamber of Commerce** (see "Visitor Information," in the "Eastham" section, earlier in this chapter). The Truro Chamber office is open Monday through Friday 10am to 4pm in season.

BEACHES & RECREATIONAL PURSUITS

BEACHES   Parking at all of Truro's exquisite Atlantic beaches, except for one Cape Cod National Seashore access point, is reserved for residents and renters. To obtain a sticker ($30 per week), inquire at the beach-sticker office next to the North Truro Post Office (© **508/487-6983**). Walkers and bikers are welcome to visit such natural wonders as Ballston Beach, where all you'll see is silky sand and grass-etched dunes. Parking is free at all beaches after 4pm.

- **Corn Hill Beach ★★**, off Corn Hill Road: Offering restrooms, this bay beach—near the hill where the Pilgrims found the seed corn that ensured their survival—is open to nonresidents for a parking fee of $10 per day.
- **Head of the Meadow ★★★**, off Head of the Meadow Road: Among the more remote National Seashore beaches, this spot (equipped with restrooms) is known for its excellent surf. A parking lot connected by a short boardwalk to the beach makes this beach more easily accessible than other National Seashore beaches. It is also connected by a short bike path to Pilgrim Heights (see "Bicycling," below). Parking costs $10 per day or $30 per season in the town section of the lot, $15 per day or $45 per season in the National Seashore section of the lot.

BICYCLING   Although it has yet to be linked up to the Cape Cod Rail Trail, Truro does have a stunning 2-mile bike path of its own: the **Head of the Meadow Trail ★**, off the road of the same name (look for a right-hand turn about ¹/₂-mile north of where rtes. 6 and 6A intersect). Part of the old 1850 road toward Provincetown—Thoreau traveled this same route—skirts the bluffs, passing Pilgrim Heights (where the Pilgrims found their first drinking water) and ending at High Head Road. Being fairly flat as well as short, this stretch should suit youngsters and beginners. You can rent a bike in Provincetown or Wellfleet.

BOATING   The inlets of Pamet Harbor are great for canoeing and kayaking; when planning an excursion, study the tides so you won't be working against them. The closest rentals are in Wellfleet at **Jack's Boat Rentals** (© **508/349-9808**) on Route 6, next to the Cumberland Farms.

FISHING   Great Pond, Horseleech Pond, and Pilgrim Lake—flanked by parabolic dunes carved by the wind—are all fishable; for a freshwater fishing license, visit **Town Hall** on Town Hall Road (② **508/349-7004**). You can also call town hall for a shellfishing license. Surf-casting is permitted at Highland Light Beach, off Highland Road.

GOLF   North Truro boasts the most scenic—and historic—9-hole course on the Cape. Created in 1892, the minimally groomed, Scottish-style **Highland Links** at 10 Lighthouse Rd., off South Highland Road (② **508/487-9201;** www.truro-ma.gov), shares a lofty bluff with the 1853 Highland Light, where Thoreau used to stay during his Outer Cape expeditions. Greens fees at the federally owned, town-run Highland Links are reasonable ($30 for 9 holes, $50 for 18 holes).

NATURE TRAILS   The Cape Cod National Seashore, comprising 70% of Truro's land, offers three self-guided nature trails. The .5-mile **Pamet Trail ★** off North Pamet Road leads you past an old cranberry-bog building and bogs that have reverted to marshland. Park in the lot to the left of the Hostelling International–Truro (see "Where to Stay," below) and walk back to the fire-road entrance about 500 feet down North Pamet Road. The **Pilgrim Spring Trail ★** and **Small Swamp Trail ★** (each a .75-mile loop) head out from the National Seashore parking lot just east of Pilgrim Lake. Pilgrim Spring is where the parched colonists sipped their first fresh water in months. Small Swamp is named for Thomas Small, a rather overly optimistic 19th-century farmer who tried to cultivate fruit trees in soil more suited to salt hay. Both paths overlook Salt Meadow, a freshwater marsh favored by hawks and osprey.

TENNIS   Courts are available at the **Pamet Harbor Yacht and Tennis Club** on Depot Road (② **508/349-3772**). Hourly fees are $20 singles and $30 doubles.

A MUSEUM & AN ARTS CENTER

Highland House Museum and Highland Lighthouse   Built as a hotel in 1907, the Highland House is a perfect repository of the odds and ends collected by the Truro Historical Society: ship's models, harpoons, primitive toys, a pirate's chest, and so on. Be sure to visit the second floor, set up as if still occupied by 19th-century tourists. In 1996, Highland Lighthouse was moved back from its perilous perch above a rapidly eroding dune. Now the lighthouse is within 800 feet of the museum and is also operated by the Truro Historical Society. Seasonal lighthouse tours run May through October. There is a 48-inch height requirement, so little ones can't climb up the tower.

27 Highland Light Rd. (off S. Highland Rd., 2 miles north of the town center on Rte. 6). ② **508/487-1121.** Admission to both museum and lighthouse $5 adults, free for children 12 and under; admission to lighthouse $4 for all with height requirement of 48 in. Museum June–Sept daily 10am–4:30pm (last ticket sold at 3:30pm); lighthouse May–Oct daily 10am–6pm. Closed Nov–Apr.

Truro Center for the Arts at Castle Hill   Send ahead for a brochure, and you could work some learning into your vacation. A great many celebrated writers and artists—from poet Alan Dugan to painter Edith Vonnegut—emerge from their summer hideaways to offer courses, lectures, and exhibits at this bustling little complex, an 1880s horse barn with windmill (now home to the administrative offices). The roster changes slightly from year to year, but you can rest assured that the stellar instructors will be at the top of their form in this stimulating environment. The center also offers lots of children's workshops for artists age 7 and up. Castle Hill Evenings, which are $10 lectures and readings, take place Tuesdays in July and August at 8pm at the Wellfleet Library.

10 Meetinghouse Rd. (at Castle Rd., about ³/₄ mile northwest of the town center). ② **508/349-7511.** www.castlehill.org. Admission varies. Call for schedule. Closed Oct–May.

The Susan Baker Memorial Museum, 46 Shore Rd./Rte 6A, a quarter-mile northwest of Route 6 (© 508/487-2557), showcases Ms. Baker's creative output, from fanciful/functional papier-mâché objets to brightly colored European landscapes. Despite the place's name, Baker has not passed on; it seems that she herself has exaggerated rumors of her death so as to rate her own museum without actually croaking. You might guess that she is definitely a character, as original as her work. Her main stock in trade—here, and at her Provincetown outlet—is humor displayed in various media, from artist's books to very atypical T-shirts (among the more popular slogans in Provincetown: "Too Mean to Marry"). Open June to September daily 10am to 5pm. Call ahead October through May.

A VINEYARD IN THE DUNES ★

Truro Vineyards of Cape Cod, 11 Shore Rd./Rte. 6A, North Truro (© 508/487-6200), is one of the last working farms in the Outer Cape and the site of an honest-to-goodness vineyard. The vineyard uncorked its first homegrown chardonnay and cabernet franc in the fall of 1996, the Muscadet in 1997, the merlot in 1998. Inside the main house on this pastoral property, the living room, with its exposed beams, is decorated with interesting oenological artifacts. Late May through October, free wine tastings are held Monday to Saturday from 11am to 5pm, Sunday noon to 5pm. Guided tours of the property take place at 1 and 3pm.

WHERE TO STAY
Moderate

Days' Cottages ★ (Value These are the famous tiny cottages you always see in local paintings and photos. Lined up along the bay beach in North Truro, these absolutely identical cottages—named after flowers—are all white clapboard with sea-foam-green shutters. Although lacking frills, each has a living room, two small bedrooms, a kitchen, and a bathroom. The downside is that these accommodations are somewhat rough: The bedrooms are minuscule, and in some of the cottages, the fireplace has about 10 years' worth of graffiti written on the brick chimney. There is also the noise of passing cars on this busy stretch of road to contend with. The upside is miles of bay beach for walking and swimming with views of Provincetown's quirky skyline in the distance. In season, beginning June 1, the cottages are rented only by the week, and they usually book up far in advance.

Rte. 6A (a couple miles south of the Provincetown border), North Truro, MA 02652. © 508/487-1062. Fax 508/487-5595. www.dayscottages.com. 23 cottages, all shower only. Summer $1,250 weekly. No credit cards. Closed mid-Oct to Apr. In room: Kitchen.

Kalmar Village ★★ (Value (Kids Spiffier than many of the motels and cottages along this spit of sand, this 1940s complex has little white cottages with black shutters. Cottages have picnic tables, grills, and daily maid service. Some cottages have air-conditioning. The clientele—mostly families—can splash the day away in the 60-foot freshwater pool or on the 400-foot private beach. This place books up early and by the week only in July and August.

674 Shore Rd. (Rte. 6A, about ¼ mile south of the Provincetown border), North Truro, MA 02652. © 508/487-0585. Fax 508/487-5827. www.kalmarvillage.com. 16 units, 40 cottages. Summer $125–$300 double; $655–$1,065 efficiencies weekly; $1,485–$2,600 cottages weekly. DISC, MC, V. Closed mid-Oct to mid-May. **Amenities:** Outdoor pool; coin-op laundry. In room: TV, fridge.

Outer Reach Resort Value This motel set high on a bluff on Route 6 (the Mid Cape Hwy.) is where you stay if you are looking for a cheap, no-frills motel room and you don't plan to spend much time there. Rooms are clean and surprisingly spacious, some with king-size beds. Many rooms have distant ocean views, and some have balconies and views of Provincetown. But the complex is a bit run-down in places, and the staff is unusually surly (even by Cape Cod standards). In addition to the outdoor pool and tennis court, there's a basketball hoop and shuffleboard. The ocean is 1 mile east. There's a mediocre restaurant, Adrian's, within the complex. You're better off driving to Provincetown for dinner.

535 Rte. 6 (midway between North Truro center and the Provincetown border), North Truro, MA 02652. © **800/942-5388** or 508/487-9090. Fax 508/487-9007. www.outerreachresort.com. 58 units. Summer $139–$189 double. MC, V. Closed late Oct to mid-May. Dogs allowed in some rooms for a fee. **Amenities:** Restaurant; outdoor pool; concrete tennis court. *In room:* A/C, TV, fridge, no phone.

Inexpensive

Hostelling International–Truro Value By far the most scenic of the youth hostels on the Cape, this Hopperesque house on a lonely bluff a short stroll from Ballston Beach was once a Coast Guard station; these days, it winters as an environmental-studies center. During the summer, it's a magnet for hikers, cyclists, and surfers.

111 N. Pamet Rd. (1¹⁄₄ miles east of Rte. 6), Truro, MA 02666. © **508/349-3889.** www.capecodhostels.org. 42 beds. $35 members; $38 nonmembers. MC, V. Closed early Sept to late June.

WHERE TO DINE

Babe's Mediterranean Bistro ★ MIDDLE EASTERN Formerly a humble little breakfast diner a stone's throw from the dunes of the Outer Cape, Babe's is now the Outer Cape's newest place for ethnic cuisine. Chef/owner Peter Thrasher takes his inspiration from the Eastern Mediterranean and North Africa in preparing his cuisine. The menu, which uses vegetables from the chef's garden, changes often. Flavors taste wonderfully different, making this a perfect place for diners unafraid to explore. Dishes to try include *Muhammara,* a hummus-like spread served as an appetizer with special bread; chickpea and asparagus soup; Turkish lamb kabobs; *Izmiri Krofte,* a type of meatball dish with figs and peppers; and Moroccan chicken served in a clay pot.

69 Shore Rd. (Rte. 6A), North Truro. © **508/487-9955.** www.babestruro.com. Reservations recommended. Main courses $14–$20. MC, V. June–Sept daily 5:30–10pm. Closed Oct–May.

Terra Luna ★ BREAKFAST/FUSION People come from miles around to sample the outstanding breakfasts at this modest restaurant. The muffins and scones emerge fresh from the oven, and entrees such as the breakfast burrito or strawberry mascarpone-cheese pancakes call for a hearty appetite. You can start in again in the evening, on well-priced Pacific Rim and/or neo-Italian fare, such as penne prosciutto sautéed with garlic, black pepper, and a splash of vodka. Main courses include local seafood and lobster dishes, like lobster risotto with asparagus and saffron. There's even a creative children's menu here.

104 Shore Rd. (Rte. 6A), North Truro. © **508/487-1019.** Reservations recommended. Main courses $14–$20. AE, MC, V. Late May to mid-Oct daily 5:30–10pm. Closed mid-Oct to late May.

SWEETS & TAKEOUT

Jams Finds Seeing as this deli/bakery/grocery is basically the whole enchilada in terms of downtown Truro, and seasonal to boot, it's good that it's so delightful. It's full of tantalizing aromas: fresh, creative pizzas; rotisserie fowl sizzling on the spit; or cookies straight from the oven. The pastry and deli selections deserve their own four-star restaurant, but they are all the more savory as part of a picnic.

14 Truro Center Rd. (off Rte. 6, in the center of town). ☎ **508/349-1616.** July–Aug 6:30am–6pm; call for off-season hours. Closed early Sept to late May.

4 PROVINCETOWN ★★★

56 miles NE of Sandwich; 42 miles NE of Hyannis

You made it all the way to the end of the Cape: one of the most interesting, rewarding spots on the eastern seaboard. Throughout history, the place has thrilled just about everyone who's come here. Explorer Bartholomew Gosnold was surely pleased in 1602, when he and his crew happened upon a "great stoare of codfysshes" here (it wasn't quite the gold they were seeking but valuable enough to warrant changing the peninsula's name). The Pilgrims, of course, were overjoyed when they slogged into the harbor 18 years later: Never mind that they'd landed several hundred miles off course—it was a miracle they'd made it around the treacherous Outer Cape at all. Portuguese fishing and whaling crews from the Azores came here on purpose, found the sea generous, and built a life.

The painter Charles Hawthorne "discovered" the near-derelict fishing town in the late 1890s. Besotted by the "jumble of color in the intense sunlight accentuated by the brilliant blue of the harbor," he introduced the place to New York City's Greenwich Village intelligentsia. He'd probably be aghast at the commercial circus that rolls into town each summer, but he'd no doubt be proud that the Provincetown Art Association & Museum, which he helped found in 1914, is still going strong.

Every so often Provincetown has had an off year or dull stretch, but the town is wholeheartedly dedicated to creative expression, both visual and verbal, and right now, it's on a roll. Some would ascribe the inspiration to the quality of the light (and it is particularly lovely—soft and diffuse) or the solitude afforded by long, lonely winters. But the general atmosphere of open-mindedness plays at least as pivotal a role, allowing a very varied assortment of individuals to pull together in pushing the cultural envelope. That same warm embrace of different lifestyles accounts for Provincetown's ascendancy as a gay and lesbian resort. During peak season, Provincetown's streets are a celebration of individual freedom and of the right to be as out as imagination allows.

The very traditional, devout Portuguese-American community still plies the maritime trades in Provincetown, and you might think that such a conservative culture would clash with free-spirited gays and artists. In fact, "family values" enjoy a very broad definition in this isolated settlement founded by the adventurous. Those who have chosen Provincetown (affectionately referred to as "P-town") know they live in a very special place, and in that, they have something precious in common.

ESSENTIALS

GETTING THERE   After crossing the Sagamore Bridge (see "Getting There," in chapter 3), head east on Route 6 or 6A to Orleans, and then north on Route 6.

If you plan to spend your entire vacation in Provincetown, you don't need a car because everything is within walking or biking distance. And since parking is a hassle in this tiny town, consider leaving your car at home and taking a boat from Boston or Plymouth. Another advantage is that you'll get to skip the horrendous Sagamore Bridge traffic jams and arrive like the Pilgrims did.

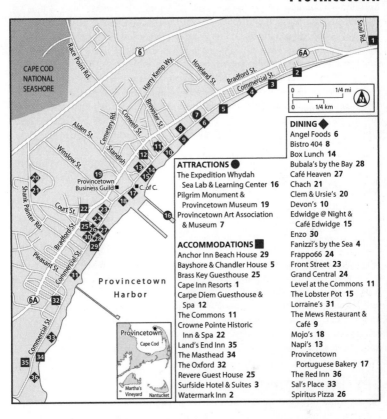

DINING ◆
Angel Foods **6**
Bistro 404 **8**
Box Lunch **14**
Bubala's by the Bay **28**
Café Heaven **27**
Chach **21**
Clem & Ursie's **20**
Devon's **10**
Edwidge @ Night &
  Café Edwidge **15**
Enzo **30**
Fanizzi's by the Sea **4**
Frappo66 **24**
Front Street **23**
Grand Central **24**
Level at the Commons **11**
The Lobster Pot **15**
Lorraine's **31**
The Mews Restaurant &
  Café **9**
Mojo's **18**
Napi's **13**
Provincetown
  Portuguese Bakery **17**
The Red Inn **36**
Sal's Place **33**
Spiritus Pizza **26**

ATTRACTIONS ●
The Expedition Whydah
  Sea Lab & Learning Center **16**
Pilgrim Monument &
  Provincetown Museum **19**
Provincetown Art Association
  & Museum **7**

ACCOMMODATIONS ■
Anchor Inn Beach House **29**
Bayshore & Chandler House **5**
Brass Key Guesthouse **25**
Cape Inn Resorts **1**
Carpe Diem Guesthouse &
  Spa **12**
The Commons **11**
Crowne Pointe Historic
  Inn & Spa **22**
Land's End Inn **35**
The Masthead **34**
The Oxford **32**
Revere Guest House **25**
Surfside Hotel & Suites **3**
Watermark Inn **2**

THE OUTER CAPE

8

PROVINCETOWN

Bay State Cruises (© **617/748-1428;** www.provincetownfastferry.com) makes round-trips from Boston, daily from May to early October.

The high-speed *Provincetown Express* boat takes 90 minutes and makes three round-trips daily. It leaves Commonwealth Pier at Boston's World Trade Center at 8am, 1pm, and 5:30pm. On the return trip, it leaves Provincetown at 10am, 3pm, and 7:30pm. Tickets on the high-speed boat cost $49 one-way, $79 round-trip for adults. Seniors are $43 one-way and $73 round-trip. Children 4 to 11 are $31 one-way, $58 round-trip. Reservations are recommended.

The regular 3-hour boat, called *Provincetown II,* leaves Boston's Commonwealth Pier on Saturdays and Sundays at 9:30am and arrives in Provincetown at 12:30pm. At 3:30pm, the boat leaves Provincetown, arriving in Boston at 6:30pm. It runs daily late June through Labor Day and on weekends in May and mid- to late September. On the slow boat, round-trip fare is $41 for adults and free for children 3 to 12.

Boston Harbor Cruises (© **617/227-4321;** www.bostonharborcruises.com) runs fast ferries from Long Wharf in Boston to Provincetown's MacMillan Wharf. It's a 90-minute trip. In high season, there are two or three round-trips a day from Boston, leaving at 9am and 2pm, with an additional 6:30pm trip Thursdays to Sundays. The boat leaves from Provincetown at 11am and 4pm, with an additional 8:30pm trip on Thursdays through Sundays. In the shoulder season, beginning in late May to mid-June and from early September to mid-October, there are one or two trips a day. Ferry tickets cost $49 one-way, $77 round-trip for adults. Tickets for seniors cost $43 one-way, $71 round-trip; and tickets for children cost $37 one-way, $66 round-trip. Bikes cost $5 each way. Reservations are a must on this popular boat.

Capt. John Boats (© 508/747-2400; www.provincetownferry.com) connects Plymouth and Provincetown daily, weather permitting, mid-June through Labor Day; Tuesday, Wednesday, Saturday, and Sunday in September; and weekends only from late May to mid-June. The 90-minute boat ride leaves the state pier in Plymouth at 10am; it leaves Provincetown at 4:30pm. The adult round-trip fare is $37, seniors $32, children 11 and under $27; bikes are $5 extra.

You can also fly into Provincetown (see "Getting There," in chapter 3). Cape Air/ Nantucket Air (© 800/352-0714; www.flycapeair.com) offers flights from Boston in season. The trip takes about 25 minutes and costs $200 to $250 round-trip.

As far as getting around once you're settled, you can enjoy the vintage fleet of the Mercedes Cab Company (© 508/487-3333). There's also Judy's Taxi (© 508/487-0265). They charge only $6 per person to take passengers from MacMillan Pier to just about anywhere in town.

VISITOR INFORMATION   Contact the Provincetown Chamber of Commerce, 307 Commercial St., Provincetown, MA 02657 (© 508/487-3424; fax 508/487-8966; www.ptownchamber.com), open late May to mid-September daily from 9am to 5pm (call for off-season hours); the gay-oriented Provincetown Business Guild, 115 Bradford St., P.O. Box 421, Provincetown, MA 02657 (© 508/487-2313; fax 508/487-1252; www.ptown.org), open Monday to Friday from 9am to noon and 12:30 to 2pm; or the Cape Cod Chamber of Commerce (see "Visitor Information," in the "Eastham" section, earlier in this chapter).

GETTING AROUND

Parking is at a premium in Provincetown. Illegally parked cars are ticketed (even on Sun), and repeat offenders will be towed. If your inn provides parking, you may want to keep your car there and get around on foot, bicycle, or shuttle. Provincetown's Summer Shuttle (© 800/352-7155) loops through town daily every 20 minutes late June to mid-September from 7am to 12:30am, traveling all along Bradford Street, to MacMillan Wharf off Commercial Street, and all the way to North Truro. The beach loop travels to Herring Cove every 20 minutes from 9am to 7pm. Riders may flag down the bus at any intersection on Bradford Street. Service continues through October in Provincetown only, without the Truro stops. All rides cost $1 for adults, 50¢ for seniors and kids 6 to 17.

BEACHES & RECREATIONAL PURSUITS

BEACHES   With nine-tenths of its territory (basically, all but the "downtown" area) protected by the Cape Cod National Seashore (CCNS), Provincetown has miles of beaches. The 3-mile bay beach that lines the harbor, though certainly swimmable, is not all that inviting compared to the magnificent ocean beaches overseen by the National Seashore. The two official access areas (see below) tend to be crowded; however, you can always find a less densely populated stretch if you're willing to hike.

Note: Local beachgoer activists have been lobbying for "clothing-optional" beaches for years, but the rangers, fearful of voyeurs trampling the dune grass, are firmly opposed and routinely issue tickets, so stand forewarned (and fully clothed).

- **Herring Cove ★★★** and **Race Point ★★★**: Both National Seashore beaches are
  spectacular, with long stretches of pristine sand, and they are very popular. Herring
  Cove, facing west, is known for its spectacular sunsets; observers often applaud. Race
  Point, on the ocean side, is rougher, and you might actually spot whales en route to
  Stellwagen Bank. Calmer Herring Cove is a haven for same-sex couples, who tend to
  sort themselves by gender. Parking costs $15 per day, $45 per season.
- **Long Point:** Trek out over the breakwater and beyond by catching a water shuttle to
  visit this very last spit of land, capped by an 1827 lighthouse. Locals call it "the end
  of the Earth." Shuttles run hourly from 9am to 5pm in July and August—$8 one-way,
  $12 round-trip, hourly in season or by demand off season—from Flyer's Boat Rental
  (see "Boating," below), located at slip 2 on MacMillan Wharf.

BICYCLING   North of town, nestled amid the Cape Cod National Seashore preserve,
is one of the more spectacular bike paths in New England, the 7-mile **Province
Lands Trail ★★**, a heady swirl of steep dunes (watch out for sand drifts on the path)
anchored by wind-stunted scrub pines. With its free parking, the **Province Lands Visitor
Center ★** (© **508/487-1256**) is a good place to start: You can survey the landscape from
the observation tower to try to get your bearings before setting off amid the dizzy-
ing maze. Signs point to spur paths leading to Race Point or Herring Cove beaches.
Bike rentals are offered May through October at **Gale Force Bikes** at 144 Bradford St.
(© **508/487-4849**) in the West End. The Province Lands Trail begins nearby. The Beach
Market, on-site at Gale Force Bikes, offers delicious sandwiches and wraps (think
Thanksgiving dinner—complete with roast turkey, stuffing, and fresh cranberries—in a
wrap) and other picnic fare for your ride. It's also an easy jaunt from town, where you'll
find plenty of good bike shops—such as the centrally located **Ptown Bikes** at 42 Bradford
St. (© **508/487-8735;** reserve several days in advance)—as well as all the picnic fixings
you could possibly desire. Bike rentals cost $20 for 24 hours.

BOATING   In addition to operating a Long Point shuttle from its own dock (see
"Beaches," above), **Flyer's Boat Rental** at 131 Commercial St. in the West End (© **508/
487-0898**)—established in 1945—offers all sorts of crafts, from kayaks ($30–$50 half-
day for singles and tandems) to various sailboats ($40–$75 for a half-day).

FISHING   Surf-casting is permitted at Herring Cove Beach (off Rte. 6) and Race Point
Beach (near the Race Point Coast Guard Station); many people drop a hand-line or light
tackle right off the West End breakwater. For low-cost deep-sea fishing via party boat,
board the *Cee Jay* (© **508/487-4330**); it makes two 4-hour trips a day and costs $35 for
adults and $25 for children. Both depart from MacMillan Wharf.

FITNESS   For days when the weather forces your workouts indoors, the **Provincetown
Gym** at 81 Shank Painter Rd. (© **508/487-2776**) has the usual equipment and promises
a non-intimidating atmosphere. Day passes cost $15. The **Mussel Beach Health Club,**
35 Bradford St. (© **508/487-0001**), attracts a rather buff clientele. Day passes are $20.
For post-workout pampering, book a massage or herbal wrap at the **West End Salon &
Spa,** 155 Commercial St. (© **508/487-1872**).

NATURE TRAILS   Within the Province Lands (off Race Point Rd., ¹/₂ mile north of
Rte. 6), the **Cape Cod National Seashore** maintains the 1-mile, self-guided **Beech Forest Trail ★**, a shaded path that circles a shallow freshwater pond blanketed with water
lilies (also look for sunning turtles) before heading into the woods. You can see the shifting dunes (much of this terrain is soft sand) gradually encroaching on the forest.

A walk along the **West End breakwater** ★★ and out to the end of **Long Point,** about 5 miles round-trip, is for hearty hikers. Walking just to the end of the wide breakwater, located at the end of Commercial Street next to the Provincetown Inn, is quite popular and takes about 30 minutes each way. You'll see all ages maneuvering the layered boulders. If you want to continue to Long Point, the very tip of Cape Cod, it's about an hour and a half across soft sand to the end of the point. At low tide, the distance can be shortened by cutting across the salt flats. **Wood End Lighthouse** is directly across the spit of sand near the breakwater. **Long Point Lighthouse** is at the end of the point. Hikers determined to reach the end of Long Point will want to bring a hat, water, and sunscreen for this intense trek along the beach. The outside of the arm, where you look out on Cape Cod Bay, tends to be the more scenic route for contemplative hikers; the inside of the arm has views of Provincetown and Provincetown Harbor and a couple of shipwrecks. The **Long Point Shuttle** runs from Flyer's Boat Rental in the West End across to Long Point for $15 round-trip. Service is continuous in season.

TENNIS Three public courts are located at Motta Memorial Field at the top of Winslow Street (near the Provincetown Monument); for details, contact the **Provincetown Recreation Department** (✆ **508/487-7097**). Open mid-May to mid-October, the **Provincetown Tennis Club** at 186 Bradford St. (✆ **508/487-9574**) has seven courts—two asphalt, five clay—tucked amid tall trees. Court time is $24 to $34 an hour. If you plan to visit the courts several times during your stay, it may pay to get the season pass, $80 per person for unlimited play.

ORGANIZED TOURS

Art's Dune Tours ★★ In 1946, Art Costa started driving sightseers out to ogle the decrepit "dune shacks" where such transient luminaries as Eugene O'Neill, Jack Kerouac, and Jackson Pollock found their respective muses; in one such hovel, Tennessee Williams cooked up the steamy *A Streetcar Named Desire.* The park service wanted to raze these eyesores, but luckily saner heads prevailed: They're now National Historic Landmarks. The tours conducted by Art's son and others, via Chevy Suburban, typically take about 1 to 1½ hours and are filled with wonderful stories of local literati and other characters. Don't forget your camera for the views of this totally unique landscape. Additional tours offered include a sunset clambake dune tour ($85) and a barbecue tour ($75).

At the corner of Commercial and Standish sts. (in the center of town). ✆ **800/894-1951** or 508/487-1950. www.artsdunetours.com. Tickets $25 adults, $17 children 6–11. Sunset tours $35 adults, $24 children. Call for schedule and reservations.

Bay Lady II ★ In sightseeing aboard this 73-foot reproduction gaff-rigged Grand Banks schooner, you'll actually add to the scenery for onlookers onshore. The sunset trip is especially spectacular.

MacMillan Wharf (in the center of town). ✆ **508/487-9308.** www.sailcapecod.com. Tickets $20–$25 adults, $12–$20 children 12 and under. Mid-May to mid-Oct, 4 2-hr. sails daily at 10am, 12:30pm, 3:30pm, and 7pm; call for reservations. Closed mid-Oct to mid-May.

PROVINCETOWN MUSEUMS

The Expedition Whydah Sea Lab & Learning Center (Overrated) Though the subject matter here is fascinating, this site is a bit of a tourist trap. Cape Cod native Barry Clifford made headlines in 1984 when he tracked down the wreck of the 17th-century pirate ship *Whydah* (pronounced *Wid*-dah, like Yankee for "widow") 1,500 feet off the coast of Wellfleet, where it had lain undisturbed since 1717. Only 10% excavated to date,

Whale-Watching

In 1975, 4 years after the U.S. government—fearing the species' extinction—called an official halt to whaling, fisherman Al Avellar noticed that they seemed to be making a comeback in the Stellwagen Bank feeding area, 8 miles off Provincetown. Together with marine biologist Charles "Stormy" Mayo of the Center for Coastal Studies, he came up with the notion of a new kind of hunt, spearheaded by tourists bearing cameras. An immediate success, their **Dolphin Fleet/Portuguese Princess** ★★, which works with the Center for Coastal Studies and uses their naturalists on the trips, on MacMillan Wharf (© **800/826-9300** or 508/349-1900), was widely copied up and down the coast. These are still the prime feeding grounds, however, which is why all the whale-watching fleets can confidently "guarantee" sightings—they offer a rain check should the cetaceans fail to surface. Prices for whale-watching trips are $37 for adults, $34 for seniors, $29 for children 5 to 12, and free for children 4 and under. Discounts are available for AAA memberships and by using coupons available at the chamber of commerce.

Another good Cape Cod whale-watch organization is **Capt. John Boats,** which operates daily 4-hour trips in season out of Plymouth Harbor in Plymouth, about 20 miles north of the Sagamore Bridge (© **800/242-2469** or 508/746-2643). Prices are $41 for adults, $35 for seniors, and $29 for children 12 and under.

On most cruises, running commentary is provided by naturalists with various qualifications. The naturalists aboard the *Portuguese Princess* are Center for Coastal Studies scientists who do research crucial to the whales' survival. Part of the *Princess'* tourist proceeds go to the center's efforts. Serious whale aficionados can take a daylong trip to the Great South Channel, where humpbacks and finbacks are likely to be found by the dozen.

Some tips for first-timers: Dress very warmly, in layers (it's cold out on the water), and definitely take along a windbreaker, waterproof if possible. The weather is capricious, and if you stand in the bow of the boat, the best viewing point, you can count on getting drenched. Veteran whale-watchers know to bring a spare set of dry clothes, as well as binoculars—although if the whales seem to be feeling friendly and frisky, as they often are, they'll play practically within reach of the boat. And last but not least, if you're prone to seasickness, bring along some motion-sickness pills: It can get pretty rough out there.

THE OUTER CAPE

8

PROVINCETOWN

it has already yielded over 100,000 artifacts, including 10,000 gold and silver coins, plus its namesake bell, proving its authenticity. In this museum/lab, visitors can supposedly observe the reclamation work involving electrolytic reduction, though it's unusual to see scientists or scholars actually at work removing barnacles. Some of the loot, like a surprisingly small man's boot, is displayed in cases.

MacMillan Wharf (just past the whale-watching fleet). © **508/487-8899.** www.whydah.com. Admission $10 adults, $8 senior and children 6–12. June–Sept daily 10am–7pm; Oct–Dec and mid-Apr to May weekends only 10am–5pm. Closed Jan to mid-Apr.

Old Harbor Life-Saving Museum ★ (Moments) One of 13 lifesaving stations mandated by Congress in the late 19th century, this shingled shelter with a lookout tower was part of a network responsible for saving some 100,000 lives. Before the U.S. Life-Saving Service was founded in 1872 (it became part of the Coast Guard in 1915, once the Cape Cod Canal was in place), shipwreck victims lucky enough to be washed ashore were still doomed unless they could find a "charity shed"—a hut supplied with firewood—maintained by the Massachusetts Humane Society. The six valiant "Surfmen" manning each lifesaving station took a more active approach, patrolling the beach at all hours, sending up flares at the first sign of a ship in distress and rowing out into the surf to save all they could. When the breakers were too high to breach, they'd use a Lyle gun to shoot a line to be secured to the ship's mast, and over this, one by one, the crew would be pulled to shore astride a "breeches buoy"—like a lifesaving ring fitted out with canvas BVDs. All the old equipment is on view at this museum, and Thursday evenings at 6pm in season, rangers reenact a breeches-buoy rescue.

Race Point Beach (off Race Point Rd., about 2 miles northwest of the town center). ⓒ **508/487-1256.** Free admission; parking fee for Race Point is $15. July–Sept daily 2:30–5pm; call for off-season hours. Closed Nov–Apr.

Pilgrim Monument & Provincetown Museum ★★ You can't miss it: Anywhere you go in town, this granite tower looms, ever ready to restore your bearings. Climb up the 60 gradual ramps interspersed with 116 steps—a surprisingly easy lope—and you'll get a gargoyle's-eye view of the spiraling coast and, in the distance, Boston against a backdrop of New Hampshire's mountains. Definitely devote some time to the curious exhibits in the museum at the monument's foot, chronicling P-town's checkered past as both fishing port and arts nexus. Among the memorabilia, you'll find polar bears brought back from MacMillan expeditions and early programs for the Provincetown Players. The museum now also houses the collection of the former Provincetown Heritage Museum, which includes a replica dune shack, furniture made by artist Peter Hunt, and paintings by Provincetown artists.

High Pole Hill Rd. (off Winslow St., north of Bradford St.). ⓒ **508/487-1310.** www.pilgrim-monument. org. Admission $7 adults, $5 seniors and students, $3.50 children 4–14. July–Aug daily 9am–7pm; off season daily 9am–5pm. Last admission 45 min. before closing. Closed Dec–Mar.

Province Lands Visitor Center of the Cape Cod National Seashore ★ Though much smaller than the Salt Pond Visitor Center, this satellite also does a good job of explicating this special environment, where plant life must fight a fierce battle to maintain its hold amid shifting sands buffeted by salty winds. After perusing the exhibits, be sure to circle the observation deck for great views of the parabolic dunes. A variety of ranger-guided tours and programs is offered daily in July and August, and frequently during the shoulder seasons. Inquire about special events, such as family campfires (reservations required). There are also canoe programs ($15 adults, $9 children) and surf-casting programs ($12), both with equipment provided.

Race Point Rd. (about 1½ miles northwest of the town center). ⓒ **508/487-1256.** Free admission. Mid-Apr to late Nov daily 9am–5pm. Closed late Nov to mid-Apr.

Provincetown Art Association & Museum ★★ (Moments) This extraordinary cache of 20th-century American art began with five paintings donated by local artists, including Charles Hawthorne, the charismatic teacher who first "discovered" this picturesque outpost. Founded in 1914, only a year after New York's revolutionary Armory Show, the museum was the site of innumerable "space wars," as classicists and modernists

vied for square footage; an uneasy truce was finally struck in 1927, when each camp was **211**
accorded its own show. In today's less competitive atmosphere, it's not unusual to see an
acknowledged master sharing space with a less skilled upstart. Juried members' shows
usually accompany the in-depth retrospectives, so there are always new discoveries to be
made. Nor is there a hard and firm wall between creators and onlookers. Fulfilling its
charter to promote "social intercourse between artists and laymen," the museum sponsors
a full schedule of concerts, lectures, readings, and classes, in such disciplines as dance,
yoga, and life drawing.

460 Commercial St. (in the East End). ℂ **508/487-1750.** www.paam.org. Admission $5. July–Aug Mon–Thurs 11am–8pm, Fri 11am–10pm, Sat–Sun 11am–5pm; call for off-season hours. Open year-round.

KID STUFF

Kids love going out on whale-watching trips, where sightings are guaranteed. To really
tire them out, climb the **Provincetown Monument,** which is located just a couple blocks
from Commercial Street, just north of town hall in the center of town. Toddlers will also
enjoy the story hour held Wednesday and Saturday at 10:30am in the newly renovated
Provincetown Public Library (ℂ **508/487-7094**) at 356 Commercial St. Kids will
marvel at how the second-floor children's room is built around a 66^1/$_2$-foot-long half-
scale replica of the *Rose Dorothea* schooner, which captured the Lipton Cup in 1907 in
the famous sailboat race from Boston to Gloucester.

SHOPPING

If you want to stay one step ahead of the fashion-victims' pack, you have come to the right
place. Many mavens visit off season just to stock up on markdowns that are still well ahead
of the curve. Of the several dozen art galleries in town, quite a few (noted below) are reliably
worthwhile. For the largest concentration of galleries, wander down to the east end of town.
(For in-depth coverage of the local arts scene, look to *Provincetown Arts,* a glossy annual sold
at the Provincetown Art Association & Museum shop.) In season, most of the galleries and
even some of the shops open around 11am, and then take a supper-time siesta from around
5 to 7pm, reopening and greeting visitors up to as late as 10 or 11pm. Shows usually open
Friday evening, prompting a "stroll" tradition spanning the many receptions.

Antiques/Collectibles

Remembrances of Things Past, 376 Commercial St. (ℂ **508/487-9443**), is a kitsch-
fest with a jumble of 20th-century nostalgia ranging from Bakelite bangles to neon
advertising art to vintage *True Confessions.*

At **Small Pleasures,** 359 Commercial St. (ℂ **508/487-3712**), proprietor Virginia
McKenna (also known as "Ginny Jewels") stocks fine estate jewelry, ranging from romantic Victorian settings to sleek silver for the 1920s-era male.

Art Galleries

Showing the work of Provincetown's past and current luminaries, **Albert Merola Gallery,**
424 Commercial St. in the East End (ℂ **508/487-4424**), is simply one of the best galleries in town. Each summer, such respected figures as Michael Mazur *(Dante's Inferno)*
and Helen Miranda Wilson deliver their latest musings. Closed mid-October to March.

Berta Walker is a force to be reckoned with, having nurtured many top artists through
her association with the Fine Arts Work Center before opening her own gallery in 1990.
At **Berta Walker Gallery,** 208 Bradford St. in the East End (ℂ **508/487-6411**), the
historic holdings span Charles Hawthorne, Milton Avery, and Robert Motherwell.

Whoever has Berta's current attention, such as figurative sculptor Romolo Del Deo, warrants watching. Closed late October to late May.

Founded in 1994 by artist and publishing scion Nick Lawrence, **DNA (Definitive New Art) Gallery,** 288 Bradford St. above the Provincetown Tennis Club in the East End (© **508/487-7700**), has risen to the top tier. It has attracted such talents as photographer Joel Meyerowitz, Provincetown's favorite portraitist, known for such tomes as *Cape Light;* sculptor Conrad Malicoat, whose free-form brick chimneys and hearths can be seen and admired about town; and painter Tabitha Vevers, who devises woman-centered shrines and "shields" out of goatskin vellum and gold leaf. Another contributor is local conceptualist/provocateur Jay Critchley. It's a very lively bunch, appropriately grouped under the rubric "definitive new art," and readings by cutting-edge authors add to the buzz. Closed mid-October to late May.

The **Fine Arts Works Center** displays weekly shows that are always worth checking out in its **Hudson D. Walker Gallery,** 24 Pearl St. in the center of town (© **508/487-9960;** www.fawc.org). The center is the heart of creativity in town, since it supports a crew of creative artists and writers on fellowships in residence every year.

Julie Heller started collecting early P-town paintings as a child—and a tourist at that. She chose so incredibly well, her roster at **Julie Heller Gallery,** 2 Gosnold St. on the beach in the center of town (© **508/487-2169**), reads like a who's who of local art. Hawthorne, Avery, Hofmann, Lazzell, Hensche—all the big names from Provincetown's past are here, as well as some contemporary artists. Closed weekdays January to April. Open winter weekends by chance or appointment.

The work of Anne Packard and her daughters Cynthia and Leslie are displayed in **The Packard Gallery,** 418 Commercial St. in the East End (© **508/487-4690**), a majestic former church. Anne Packard's large canvases tend to depict emotive land- and seascapes with the horizon as a focus. Cynthia's colorful figurative work has Fauvist elements, and Leslie's watercolors capture Provincetown landscapes. Closed mid-October to mid-June.

At **Rice/Polak Gallery,** 430 Commercial St. in the East End (© **508/487-1052**), you'll find art with a decorative bent, which is not to say that it will match anyone's sofa, only that it has a certain stylish snap. Several gallery artists have fun with dimensions—such as painter Tom Seghi with his mammoth pears, and sculptor Larry Calkins with his assemblages of undersize, antique-looking dresses. Peter Plamondon's oil paintings capture still lifes with exquisite clarity. Closed December to April.

Schoolhouse Gallery, 494 Commercial St. in the East End (© **508/487-4800**), is an impressive setup with two galleries, studios, arts programs, and an events series. The Driskel Gallery features photography and fine objects, while the Silas-Kenyon Gallery shows contemporary fine arts.

William-Scott Gallery, 439 Commercial St. in the East End (© **508/487-4040**), can be counted on to showcase the work of local emerging artists, as well as several who seem to have made it. In the latter category is John Dowd. Still quite young, his patrons include the Schiffenhaus brothers, who inherited the Hoppers' Truro house. Other selections, such as John DiMestico's Cape landscapes on paper, Dan Rupe's bold portraits in oil, and Will Klemm's lush and mysterious pastel landscapes, augur well for an influential future. Closed December to late May.

Books

Now Voyager, 357 Commercial St. in the East End (© **508/487-0848**), offers both new and collectible gay and lesbian books and serves as an informal social center. There is also a large section of mystery and suspense books.

Provincetown Bookshop, 246 Commercial St. (© **508/487-0964**), has the most complete selection in town. You'll find all the bestsellers, as well as books about the region and local lore.

Discount Shopping

Marine Specialties, 235 Commercial St. in the center of town (© **508/487-1730**), is packed to the rafters with useful stuff, from discounted Doc Martens to cut-rate Swiss Army knives and all sorts of odd nautical surplus whose uses will suggest themselves to you eventually. Be sure to look up: Hanging from the ceiling are some real antiques, including several carillons' worth of ships' bells.

Erotica

The dirtiest (and I don't mean dusty) store in Provincetown is **Shop Therapy,** 346 Commercial St. (© **508/487-9387**), a store with wild murals (or is it graffiti?) that are filled with all manner of erotica. You'll want to wander in just for the sheer outrageousness of it all. Tall people beware; there's stuff hanging from the low ceiling that you might not want near your face.

Fashion

Giardelli/Antonelli Studio Showroom, 417 Commercial St. in the East End (© **508/487-3016**), is filled with Jerry Giardelli's unstructured clothing elements—shells, shifts, and palazzo pants—in vibrant colors and inviting textures. They demand to be mixed, matched, and perhaps offset by Diana Antonelli's statement jewelry.

Want to try on new identities? **Mad as a Hatter,** 360 Commercial St. (© **508/487-4063**), may be your best bet, with hats to suit every style and inclination, from folksy to downright diva-esque. Closed January to mid-February.

Moda Fina, 349 Commercial St. (© **508/487-6632**), specializes in women's clothing and accessories, including shoes and lingerie, and a variety of unique summer dresses.

Silk & Feathers, 377 Commercial St. in the East End (© **508/487-2057**), has seasonal styles, and the lingerie they sell is almost too pretty to cover up. Other indulgences include seaweed soaps and statement jewelry.

Gifts/Home Decor

A breath of fresh contemporary design, **Utilities,** 393 Commercial St. in the center of town (© **508/487-6800**), is a kitchenware/tabletop shop that features sleek and colorful essentials.

A study in beiges and blacks, **Wa,** 184 Commercial St. in the West End (© **508/487-6355**), is a minimalist shop—its name means "harmony" in Japanese—specializing in decorative home accessories that embrace a Zen aesthetic. This might mean a trickling stone fountain or Chinese calligraphy stones.

Toys

Take advantage of the Cape's strong winds and wide-open beaches by shopping at **Outer Cape Kites,** 277A Commercial St. at Ryder Street Extension, near MacMillan Wharf (© **508/487-6133**). Closed mid-October to March.

WHERE TO STAY
Very Expensive

Brass Key Guesthouse ★★★ Brass Key Guesthouse, a compound of six buildings, is *the* place to stay in Provincetown. With Ritz-Carlton–style amenities and service in mind, the innkeepers have created a paean to luxury. They are the kinds of innkeepers who think of everything: goose-down pillows (choose yours from the pillow menu), showers with wall jets, and gratis iced tea and lemonade delivered poolside in season. Although all rooms share top-notch amenities like Bose radios, decorative styles vary according to the building. In the center is the extensively landscaped multilevel patio area with outdoor heated pool and large (17-ft.) whirlpool. The inn has partnered with a local spa to offer in-room massages and other body treatments. There are two wheelchair-accessible rooms. In high season, the clientele here is primarily gay men, though all are made to feel welcome.

67 Bradford St. (in the center of town), Provincetown, MA 02657. (C) **800/842-9858** or 508/487-9005. Fax 508/487-9020. www.brasskey.com. 42 units. Summer $400–$500 double. Rates include continental breakfast and afternoon wine-and-cheese hour. AE, DISC, MC, V. Closed late Nov to early Apr. No children under 16. **Amenities:** Outdoor heated pool; 17-ft. hot tub. *In room:* A/C, TV/DVD, Wi-Fi, fridge, hair dryer, safe.

Crowne Pointe Historic Inn and Spa ★★ This property—an inn, restaurant, and spa—perched high on Bradford Street is a welcome addition to Provincetown's high-end lodging choices. Rooms are spacious and some of the deluxe rooms and suites have fireplaces, wet bars, and whirlpool spas. All rooms have luxuries like down pillows, 300-count linens, thick cotton robes, and gourmet chocolates. A hearty buffet breakfast is served in the large living room. The in-house spa has full-service treatment rooms for massages, facials, manicures, and pedicures, as well as a steam room, mineral soaking tub, and sauna. The restaurant, the Bistro at Crowne Pointe, which is open nightly in season, offers a light menu, as well as fine-dining choices with suggestions on wine pairings. One of this inn's unique services is complimentary airport, ferry, or bus pickup.

82 Bradford St. (in the center of town), Provincetown, MA 02657. (C) **877/CROWNE1** (877/276-9631) or 508/487-6767. Fax 508/487-5554. www.crownepointe.com. 35 units. Summer $299–$529 double. Rates include full breakfast, afternoon tea and cookies, and wine-and-cheese hour. AE, MC, V. Open year-round. **Amenities:** Restaurant (bistro dinner only); heated outdoor pool; spa, w/steam room, mineral soaking tub, and sauna; 2 10-person outdoor Jacuzzis. *In room:* A/C, TV/DVD/VCR, CD player, Wi-Fi, fridge, coffeemaker, hair dryer, iron.

Expensive

Anchor Inn Beach House ★★ This waterfront property centrally located on Commercial Street is exquisitely decorated with fine furniture and deluxe amenities. Each guest room has a wet bar with sink and fridge, as well as luxury bathroom amenities, including a robe. Many of the rooms feature deluxe showers, whirlpool baths, and fireplaces. Sixteen rooms have balconies overlooking the harbor. Four rooms have separate entrances through private porches complete with wicker furniture.

175 Commercial St. (in the center of town), Provincetown, MA 02657. (C) **800/858-2657** or 508/487-0432. Fax 508/487-6280. www.anchorinnbeachhouse.com. 23 units. Summer $260–$385 double; $400 suite. Rates include continental breakfast. AE, MC, V. Closed Jan–Feb. *In room:* A/C, TV/VCR, CD player, fridge, hair dryer.

Land's End Inn ★★★ (Finds Enjoying a prime 1-acre perch atop Gull Hill in the far west end of Commercial Street, this magical, whimsical 1907 bungalow is bursting with rare and often outlandish antiques. The two-bedroom loft suite, entered through an armoire (very *Narnia*) must be one of the most unusual and spectacular lodging spaces on the Cape. There's also a wonderful octagonal tower room with windows wrapping halfway around, bay-view decks on two sides, and a cobalt glass turret. Though the inn is predominantly gay, cosmopolitan visitors will feel welcome. The staff is top-notch here and the breakfast, an elaborate continental spread, features fresh fruits and homemade baked goods.

22 Commercial St. (in the West End), Provincetown, MA 02657. © **800/276-7088** or 508/487-0706. Fax 508/487-0755. www.landsendinn.com. 16 units. Summer $295–$420 double; $385–$560 tower rooms. Rates include continental breakfast and wine-and-cheese hour. AE, MC, V. Closed Nov to late May. *In room:* A/C, no phone.

The Oxford ★ (Value)   British innkeepers Stephen Mascilo and Trevor Pinker run this 1853 house in the far West End. All rooms have upscale amenities like down comforters, bathrobes, phones with voice mail and dataport, and radio/CD players. An extensive continental breakfast is served in the morning, when the inn fills with the scrumptious aroma of home-baked breads and coffeecake. You may want to take your coffee outside on the veranda overlooking the courtyard's fountain and pond.

8 Cottage St. (in the West End), Provincetown, MA 02657. © **888/456-9103** or 508/487-9103. www. oxfordguesthouse.com. 7 units, 2 with shared bathroom, shower only. Summer $185 double with shared bathroom; $260–$310 double with private bathroom. Rates include continental breakfast. AE, DC, DISC, MC, V. *In room:* A/C, TV/DVD, CD player, fridge, hair dryer, iron.

Watermark Inn ★★ (Kids)   If you'd like to experience P-town without being stuck in the thick of it (the carnival atmosphere can get tiring at times), this contemporary inn at the peaceful edge of town is the perfect choice. Resident innkeeper/architect Kevin Shea carved this beachfront manor into 10 dazzling suites: The prize ones, on the top floor, have peaked picture windows and sweeping water views from their decks. All have kitchenettes that include dishwashers. This inn is a favorite with families.

603 Commercial St. (in the East End), Provincetown, MA 02657. © **508/487-0165.** Fax 508/487-2383. www.watermark-inn.com. 10 units. Summer $205–$405 suite; weekly $1,310–$2,580. AE, MC, V. Open year-round. *In room:* TV, kitchenette, coffeemaker.

Moderate

Bayshore and Chandler House ★★   This cherished beachfront complex in the far east end of town continues to be a popular lodging choice. It's a short walk to the center of P-town, but being in the East End means quiet nights. An additional property at 77 Commercial St. on the far west end of town has two additional one-bedroom units. All of the apartments have improvised charm, such as a few select antiques and salvaged architectural details. Rooms have private entrances and kitchenettes, including microwave ovens and dishwashers. The prize rooms at the east-side property surround a flower-lined lawn, with pride of place going to a cathedral-ceilinged loft right over the water. From late June to early September, rooms are available on a weekly basis only.

493 Commercial St. (in the East End), Provincetown, MA 02657. ©/fax **508/487-9133.** www.bayshore chandler.com. 25 units, 20 with tub/shower, 5 with shower. Summer $1,400 weekly studio, $2,100–$2,150 weekly 1-bedroom, $2,550 weekly 2-bedroom; shoulder season daily $140 studio, $140–$199 1-bedroom, $240–$275 2-bedroom. AE, DISC, MC, V. Open year-round. Dogs allowed with advance notice. *In room:* A/C (some units), TV/VCR, kitchenette, coffeemaker, iron.

Cape Inn Resort ★   Formerly a Holiday Inn, this waterfront motel is a good choice for first-timers not quite sure what they're getting into. It's a no-surprises motel with a pool at the far eastern edge of town. Guests in waterfront rooms get a nice view. There are free movies in the restaurant/lounge shown on a 100-foot screen in season. Though this motel is a bit of a hike from the town's center, an in-season town shuttle will whisk you down Commercial Street or to the beaches for a minimal cost.

698 Commercial St. (at Rte. 6A, in the East End), Provincetown, MA 02657. © **800/422-4224** or 508/487-1711. Fax 508/487-3929. www.capeinn.com. 78 units. Summer $155–$195 double. Rates include continental breakfast. AE, DC, DISC, MC, V. Closed Nov–Apr. Dogs allowed. **Amenities:** Restaurant; outdoor pool. *In room:* A/C, TV, fridge, coffeemaker, hair dryer, iron.

Carpe Diem Guesthouse and Spa ★★★   This guesthouse has always been top shelf but in recent years it has been transformed by its three owners, a trio of hip German men, into one of the finest boutique hotels in Provincetown. With the addition of a new building, there are also four new suites and new common rooms and patios. The state-of-the-art Namaste spa here has to be one of the most deluxe in town, with a large hydrojet spa tub, Finnish dry sauna, Provincetown's largest steam room and massage rooms. The full breakfast prepared by the inn's French manager features homemade French-influenced pastries.

12-14 Johnson St. (in the center of town), Provincetown, MA 02657. ☎ **800/487-0132** or 508/487-4242 (also fax). www.carpediemguesthouse.com. 18 units. Summer $225–$245 double; $305–$365 suites; $385–$425 cottage. Rates include full breakfast and wine-and-cheese hour. AE, DISC, MC, V. Open year-round. **Amenities:** 6-person hot tub; guest office. *In room:* A/C, TV/DVD, fridge (in most).

The Commons ★★   Right in the thick of town, but removed from the hurly-burly by a street-side bistro and peaceful brick patio is this venerable old guesthouse. The parlor is basic but comfortable; the bedrooms, with their marble-look bathrooms and (in most cases) bay views, are stylish and spacious. Two suites have private balconies with views of Provincetown Harbor and pull-out sofas that allow an extra person. All the delights of Provincetown are easily within reach, including—on-site—one of Provincetown's best up-and-coming restaurants, Level at The Commons (see "Where to Dine," below).

386 Commercial St. (in the center of town), Provincetown, MA 02657. ☎ **800/487-0784** or 508/487-7800. Fax 508/487-6114. www.ptcommons.com. 14 units, 3 with tub/shower, 11 with shower only. Summer $165–$195 double; $275 suite. Rates include continental breakfast. AE, DISC, MC, V. Closed Dec–Mar. Pets allowed. **Amenities:** Restaurant (bistro). *In room:* A/C, TV, iron.

The Masthead ★★ Ⓥalue Ⓚids   This is the best-priced waterfront lodging option in Provincetown. The cottages are fun, some with net stair railings, wicker furniture, and hand-painted antique furniture by Peter Hunt, as well as full (if tiny) kitchens, which include microwave ovens. Two rooms are accessible to travelers with disabilities. In season, the cottage units rent weekly, but the rather generic motel units rent nightly. In some water-view rooms, with their 7-foot picture windows overlooking the bay and Long Point, you may feel like you're onboard a ship.

31–41 Commercial St. (in the West End), Provincetown, MA 02657. ☎ **800/395-5095** or 508/487-0523. Fax 508/487-9251. www.themasthead.com. 21 units, 2 with shared bathroom, 3 with tub/shower, 16 with shower; 4 cottages. Summer $99 double with shared bathroom; $125–$286 double; $213–$333 efficiency and 1-bedroom; $489 2-bedroom apt; $2,324–$2,926 cottage weekly. AE, DC, DISC, MC, V. Open year-round. *In room:* A/C, TV, fridge, coffeemaker.

Revere Guest House ★★   Nineteenth century charm plus modern amenities prevail at this recently updated guesthouse on a quiet side street between Commercial and Bradford streets. Owner Gary Palochko has created a restful place from the back garden blooming with lilacs and roses, to the multi-jet Jacuzzi on the patio and the outdoor shower, that classic summertime amenity. The rooftop deck has a 360 degree view of P-town. Rooms range from small ones that share bathrooms to large suites with whirlpool tubs.

14 Court St., Provincetown, MA 02657. ☎ **508/487-2292.** www.reverehouse.com. 10 units. Summer $175, with shared bath; $195–$295 double; $280–$345 suite. Rates include continental breakfast. MC, V. Open year-round. **Amenities:** 5-person spa. *In room:* A/C, TV/DVD, Wi-Fi, minifridge.

Surfside Hotel and Suites ★   This motel on the far east end of Commercial Street, with one building on the water side and one across the street, has recently undergone a freshening up in decor that brings it up a level in comfort. But the reasonable prices make it a good bet for inexpensive lodging, particularly for busy weekends when more stylish options are booked. The beds and bedding are top-notch. Rooms with views of the waterfront are prized, and second best are the ones facing the rear for quiet nights. Ones facing the street/pool can be noisy.

543 Commercial St. (in the East End), Provincetown, MA 02657. ✆ **860/757-8616.** Fax 508/487-6556. www.surfsideinn.cc. 88 units. Summer $114–$169 double; $450 suite. AE, DC, DISC, MC, V. Open year-round. Pet-friendly. **Amenities:** Outdoor pool. *In room:* A/C, TV, fridge, coffeemaker, hair dryer, iron.

WHERE TO DINE
Very Expensive
Bistro 404 ★★ NEW AMERICAN   The buzz is good on this expensive restaurant that replaced Chester on the east end of town. Come to this restaurant expecting fine-dining, with prices and service to match. Expect to wait a bit between courses, the better to appreciate the flavors. The menu changes nightly but among the highlights are the nicoise salad with lobster. Look for the fresh fish specialty prepared in a creative style; you can't go wrong.

404 Commercial St. ✆ **508/487-5404.** Reservations required. Main courses $31–$41. AE, DC, DISC, MC, V. Mid-June to early Sept daily 5:30–9:30pm; call for off-season hours.

The Red Inn ★★ NEW AMERICAN   Nothing beats the view from the floor to ceiling windows of this restaurant seemingly at the end of the earth, the far east end of Provincetown. This is the type of place where you might feel like beginning your meal with a glass of champagne and ending it with a soufflé. It's fine dining on the calorie-rich side, with entrees like grilled thick pork chops with tomatillo salsa and pepper-crusted filet mignon with truffle mashed potatoes and Jack Daniel's sauce. Fresh fish and vegetarian main courses are always on the menu also.

15 Commercial St. ✆ **508/487-7334.** www.theredinn.com. Reservations required. Main courses $21–$38. AE, DC, DISC, MC, V. Mid-June to early Sept daily 5:30–9:30pm, Thurs–Sun 10am–2:30pm; call for off-season hours.

Expensive
Devon's ★★★ NEW AMERICAN   You can tell which one is Devon. He's seating people, acting as line cook, busing tables, taking reservations, and chatting with customers. The restaurant itself, a former boat shack, is tiny with fewer than 10 tables inside—all next to the open kitchen. In good weather, the choice seats are on the patio out front. Service is professional here. The food is elegantly prepared and presented with special touches. The menu changes often but features wonderful fish, steak, chicken, and vegetarian preparations. One night we were there patrons were raving over the sole that was prepared with a wonderfully simple beurre blanc sauce. This is a romantic option, but you definitely need a reservation. It's also a good choice for breakfast for those staying in the far east end of town.

401½ Commercial St. (in the East End). ✆ **508/487-4773.** Reservations recommended. Main courses $18–$25. DISC, MC, V. June–Sept Thurs–Tues 8am–1pm and 6–10pm; call for off-season hours. Closed Nov–Apr.

Edwidge @ Night and Café Edwidge ★★ NEW AMERICAN   Dinner and breakfast are run by two different teams at this second-floor restaurant, long a favorite with locals. For seating, you have a choice: inside where wooden booths, rafters, and close-set tables provide a casual feel, or outside on a narrow, breezy patio that offers more private dining. Outstanding menu items include tuna tartare or lobster dumplings as appetizers, and for the main course, filet mignon with a blue cheese fritter or *moqueca,* a Brazilian seafood dish. Breakfast here is a favorite with locals and visitors alike, so arrive early if you expect to get a table.

333 Commercial St. (☎ **508/487-4020.** Reservations recommended. Main courses $18–$29. MC, V. June–Sept daily 8–11am, Wed to Mon 6–10pm; call for off-season hours.

Front Street ★★ MEDITERRANEAN FUSION/ITALIAN   For years, this restaurant has delivered consistently high-quality food and service, and locals consider it a favorite, dependable locale. Located in a below-ground space on Commercial Street in the center of town, this cozy restaurant feels most comfortable in the chilly days of spring and summer. The decor is very romantic with antique booths and low lighting. Chef Donna Aliperti is constantly improving her menu, inspired by trips to Italy and southern France. The fusion menu, available in season, has creative items like soft-shell crabs with corn-studded risotto and Chinese five-spice grilled duckling. There is also a traditional Italian menu with pastas available every night.

230 Commercial St. (☎ **508/487-9715.** www.frontstreetrestaurant.com. Reservations recommended. Main courses $18–$25. DISC, MC, V. June–Sept Wed–Mon 5:30–10pm; call for off-season hours.

Lorraine's ★★ (Finds) MEXICAN/NEW AMERICAN   Located in the far west end of Commercial Street, Lorraine's has long been considered one of the town's top dining spots. Even those who shy away from Mexican restaurants should try Lorraine's; chef/owner Lorraine Najar brings a certain daring to bear on the cuisine she learned at her grandmother's knee. Abandon all caution and begin with *chile relleno de queso,* which is fresh chile peppers stuffed with the chef's choice nightly, rolled in cornmeal and corn flour, and lightly fried. Maryland soft-shell crabs are lightly dusted in flour with Chimayo chile powder and pan-sautéed and served with a jalapeño aioli. For a main course, consider *viere verde*—sea scallops sautéed with tomatillos, flambéed in tequila, and cloaked in a green-chile sauce. For a treat, check out the extensive tequila menu; shots are served with a wonderful tomato-juice-based chaser.

133 Commercial St. (in the West End). (☎ **508/487-6074.** Reservations suggested. Main courses $17–$26. DISC, MC, V. June–Sept daily 6–10pm; call for off-season hours. Open year-round.

The Mews Restaurant & Cafe ★★ INTERNATIONAL/AMERICAN FUSION   Bank on fine food and suave service at this beachfront restaurant, an enduring favorite since 1961. Upstairs is the cafe with its century-old carved mahogany bar. The dining room downstairs sits right on the beach—and is practically of the beach, with its sand-toned walls warmed by toffee-colored Tiffany table lamps. The best soup in the region is the Mews' scrumptious summertime special, chilled cucumber miso bisque with curry shrimp timbale. Perennial pleasures include the Marsala-marinated portobello mushrooms and a mixed-seafood carpaccio. Among the showier entrees is "captured scallops": prime Wellfleet specimens enclosed with a shrimp-and-crab mousse in a crisp wonton pouch and served atop a petite filet mignon with chipotle aioli. Desserts and coffees—you might take them upstairs in the cafe to the accompaniment of soft-jazz piano—are delectable. Awash in sea blues that blend with the view, Cafe Mews offers a lighter, less expensive menu and serves as an elegantly informal community clubhouse year-round.

429 Commercial St. (☎ **508/487-1500.** www.mews.com. Reservations recommended. Main courses $18–$29. AE, DC, DISC, MC, V. Mid-June to early Sept daily 6–10pm, Sun 11am–2:30pm; early Dec to mid-Feb daily 6–10pm; call for off-season hours. Open year-round.

Moderate

Bubala's by the Bay ★ ECLECTIC   This trendy bistro—with a gaudy yellow paint job and Picasso-esque wall murals—promises "serious food at sensible prices." And that's what it delivers: from buttermilk waffles with real maple syrup to lobster tarragon salad to creative focaccia sandwiches to fajitas, Cajun calamari, and pad thai. This is a big operation for Provincetown, and the huge outdoor patio facing Commercial Street means it's popular, particularly for breakfast. This is the only place on Cape Cod that serves ostrich. They're raised in Pennsylvania and served with a grilled pepper crust and a caramelized-onion-and-balsamic glaze. In season, there's entertainment nightly from 10pm to 1am.

183 Commercial St. (in the West End). ✆ **508/487-0773.** Main courses $10–$21. AE, DISC, MC, V. Mid-Apr to late Oct daily 11am–11pm. Closed late Oct to mid-Apr.

Enzo ★ NORTHERN ITALIAN   Run by the owners of the popular Bubala's (see above) across the street, this West End restaurant is one of the newer places on the Provincetown scene. Named after Enzo Ferrari, it has a sleek look that brings to mind modern Italian style. The menu features Italian classics such as *osso buco* and *linguini con l'araguota*, a favorite dish of linguini with lobster. Inside are several serene dining rooms and a bar area; outside, two levels of patio seating are perfect for people-watching. Still working to build a clientele, Enzo is a good choice in the crowded summer months, when it is a challenge to secure a table at many Provincetown hot spots. The downstairs bar, Grotta, offers live entertainment most nights in season, and an upstairs inn has five recently restored rooms.

186 Commercial St. (in the West End). ✆ **508/487-7555.** Reservations not accepted. Most items $12–$28. AE, DISC, MC, V. July–Aug daily 6–10pm; call for off-season hours. Closed Feb–May.

Fanizzi's By The Sea ★ ITALIAN/SEAFOOD   This waterfront restaurant in the far east end of town is the perfect place to get away from all the hustle and bustle in the center of town. The beauty of this casual restaurant is that you can have a burger and fries, enjoy comfort food like Mom's best meatloaf, or splurge on shrimp scampi, and it's all very reasonably priced. The view seen here through large wraparound plate-glass windows is among the best in town. The $13 buffet brunch, served 'til 2pm on Sundays, is a good deal.

539 Commercial St. (in the far east end of town). ✆ **508/487-1964.** Reservations accepted. Main courses $9–$21. AE, MC, V. Mid-June to mid-Sept Mon–Sat 11:30am–10pm, Sun 10am–9pm; call for off-season hours. Open year-round.

Frappo66 ★ CAFETERIA   It's a new dining concept: the fine-dining cafeteria. And it works. Tucked into the lobby of the Art House theatre, this is the place to go for a reasonably priced gourmet meal where you save time and money by serving yourself. Besides soups, salads and sandwiches, there is always a special, like filet of sole with lobster mushroom stuffing, and you get to choose three "sides," like broccoli with tofu or pasta salad for example. This is the perfect place to go for a light meal after a show.

214 Commercial St. (in the center of town). ✆ **508/487-9066.** Reservations not accepted. Main courses $9–$21. MC, V. Mid-June to mid-Sept daily 8am–10pm, call for off-season hours. Open year-round.

Grand Central (Finds) AMERICAN   Grand Central, which is a few steps off the beaten path of Commercial Street, is a great place to go for a light bite when you're not in the mood for fine dining. The menu is small but varied. You could have an 8-ounce Angus burger with onion relish or vegetarian pad thai. To find this restaurant, look for the narrow street, Masonic Lane. The restaurant is very funky looking, cobbled together with driftwood and folk-art fragments. There's also an outdoor patio and a cozy bar area upstairs.

5 Masonic Place (off Commercial St., in the center of town). ✆ **508/487-7599.** Reservations not accepted. Main courses $9–$19. MC, V. Early May to mid-Oct daily 5–10pm; closed mid-Oct to early May.

Level at The Commons ★ ECLECTIC/FRENCH BISTRO   Where to sit? The sidewalk cafe is optimal for studying P-town's inimitable street life, but the garden enclave promises privacy and romance. A second-floor terrace takes in views of the harbor, and the dining room smolders with red walls and bold artwork. Then there's the bar, extra-inviting with sliding glass doors open to the street. Whatever your perch, you're in for a treat at the reincarnation of The Commons, a longtime P-town favorite. The menu has a little something for everyone: inexpensive burgers; gourmet pizzas from the only wood-fired oven in town; and fresh, creatively prepared dishes.

386 Commercial St. (see "Where to Stay," earlier in this chapter). ✆ **508/487-7800.** Reservations recommended. Main courses $10–$34. AE, MC, V. Mid-June to mid-Sept daily 8am–4pm and 5:30pm–midnight; call for off-season hours. Closed January.

The Lobster Pot ★ SEAFOOD   Snobbish foodies might turn their noses up at a venue so flagrantly Olde Cape Coddish, but for Provincetown regulars, no season seems complete without at least one pilgrimage. You may feel like a long-suffering pilgrim waiting to get in: The line, which starts near the aromatic, albeit frantic, kitchen, often snakes into the street. While waiting, check out the hand-painted bar stools, which provide an architectural history of Provincetown. A lucky few will make it all the way to the outdoor deck; however, most tables, indoors and out, afford nice views of MacMillan Wharf. Spring for a jumbo lobster—boiled or broiled, sauced or simple. And definitely start off with the chowder, a perennial award-winner.

321 Commercial St. (in the center of town). ✆ **508/487-0842.** www.ptownlobsterpot.com. Reservations not accepted. Main courses $15–$25. AE, DC, DISC, MC, V. Mid-June to mid-Sept daily 11:30am–10:30pm; mid-Apr to mid-June and mid-Sept to Dec daily 11:30am–9:30pm. Closed Jan to mid-Apr.

Napi's ★★ INTERNATIONAL   Restaurateur Napi Van Dereck can be credited with bringing P-town's restaurant scene up to speed—back in the early 1970s. His namesake restaurant still reflects that zeitgeist, with its rococo-hippie carpentry, select outtakes from his sideline in antiques, and some rather outstanding art, including a crazy quilt of a brick wall by local sculptor Conrad Malicoat. The food is truly international, with dumplings from China; falafel from Syria; and, from Greece, shrimp feta flambéed with the Greek liquors ouzo and *Metaxa*. The lower-priced tavern menu available on weeknights ranges from $5 to $11. Unusual in Provincetown, this restaurant has its own parking lot (around back).

7 Freeman St. (at Bradford St.). ✆ **800/571-6274** or 508/487-1145. Reservations recommended. Main courses $14–$26. DISC, MC, V. May to mid-Sept daily 5–10pm; mid-Sept to Apr daily 11:30am–4pm and 5–9pm.

Sal's Place ★ (Finds) SOUTHERN ITALIAN   Sit in the front room close to the street in this authentic Italian restaurant. With its red-checkered tablecloths, chianti basket bottles hanging from the ceiling, and vintage photos on the walls, it feels like a place in Boston's North End. There is also an open-air deck in the rear with a harbor view, a good spot to sit on very hot nights. There is nothing subtle about this hearty Italian food, huge portions of traditional pasta dishes like homemade manicotti, eggplant parmigiana, and spaghettini with sausage.

99 Commercial St. (in the West End). ✆ **508/487-1279.** Reservations recommended. Main courses $13–$23. MC, V. Apr–Oct daily 5:30–10pm; call for off-season hours.

Cafe Heaven ★ AMERICAN   Prized for its leisurely country breakfasts (served 'til mid-afternoon, for reluctant risers), this modern storefront—adorned with big, bold paintings by acclaimed Wellfleet artist John Grillo—also turns out substantial sandwiches, such as avocado and goat cheese on a French baguette. The salads are appealing as well—especially the "special shrimp," lightly doused with dilled sour cream and tossed with tomatoes and grapes. This casual cafe is a popular place in the evenings, especially late night when a limited light dinner menu, including hamburgers and a wonderful grilled ahi tuna sandwich, is served until 11pm.

199 Commercial St. (in the West End). ✆ **508/487-9639.** Reservations not accepted. Most items $8–$15. No credit cards. July–Aug daily 8am–2:30pm and 6–10pm; call for off-season hours. Closed Feb–May.

Chach ★ (Finds) DINER   A diner run by a chef, instead of a cook, means the omelets are divine, the BLTs are heavenly, and all kinds of little surprises are on the menu. It's a little off the beaten track, but it's worth seeking out Chach's for reasonably priced dining without the crowds you find on Commercial Street.

73 Shankpainter Rd. (off Bradford St., a few blocks south of town). ✆ **508/487-1530.** Most items under $10. No credit cards. Apr–Feb Thurs–Tues 8am–2:30pm. Closed Mar.

Clem and Ursie's ★ (Finds) (Kids) SEAFOOD/BARBECUE   This is a great choice for a big family dinner on picnic tables. Make it a shoreman's dinner or a clambake. The menu is heavy on fried seafood, as well as barbecue chicken, ribs, and seafood. There are also more elaborate choices like bouillabaisse, *fra diavolo* (fish and shellfish in a spicy tomato sauce), and Japanese *udon* (fish, shellfish, and vegetables in a *dashi* broth over noodles). A full sushi bar is on-site. On the children's menu, it's $5 for your choice of six entrees with french fries, drink, dessert, and a surprise. Takeout is popular here, as is the separate ice-cream section.

85 Shankpainter Rd. (off Bradford St., a few blocks south of town). ✆ **508/487-2333.** Main courses $6–$17. MC, V. Apr to mid-Oct daily 7am–10pm. Closed mid-Oct to Mar.

Mojo's (Kids) SEAFOOD   This fried-seafood shack is known for its lightly breaded fried fish. French fries are hand-cut daily. There are also kid-friendly hot dogs and hamburgers, subs, veggie burgers, burritos, pizza, and chicken tenders. Eat at one of the six picnic tables on the patio or take it to the beach.

5 Ryder St. Extension (near Fisherman's Wharf). ✆ **508/487-3140.** All items under $15. No credit cards. Early May to mid-Oct daily 11am–10pm; closed mid-Oct to early May.

Spiritus Pizza PIZZA/ICE CREAM   A local landmark, Spiritus is an extravagant pizza parlor known for post-last-call cruising: It's open until 2am. The pizza's good, as are the fruit drinks, specialty coffees, and four brands of premium ice cream, from Emack & Bolio's to Coconut Joe's. For a peaceful morning repast—and perhaps a relaxed round of boccie—check out the little garden in back.

190 Commercial St. (in the center of town). ✆ **508/487-2808.** All items under $15. No credit cards. Apr–Oct daily 11:30am–2am. Closed Nov–Mar.

Ice Cream

Not only a good spot to satisfy any ice-cream cravings (how about a 20-scoop "Vermonster"?), **Ben & Jerry's Scoop Shop** ★, 258 Commercial St., in the center of town (✆ **508/487-3360**), is also handy for refueling mid-stroll with a fresh-fruit drink.

Angel Foods, 467 Commercial St., in the East End (© **508/487-6666**), is a gourmet takeout shop offering Italian specialties and other scrumptious prepared foods to go.

The rollwiches—pita bread packed with a wide range of fillings—at **Box Lunch,** 353 Commercial St., in the center of town (© **508/487-6026**), are ideal for a strolling lunch.

One thing you absolutely have to do while in town is peruse the cases of pasties (meat pies) and pastries at **Provincetown Portuguese Bakery,** 299 Commercial St., in the center of town (© **508/487-1803**). Point to a few and take your surprise package out on the pier for delectation. Though perhaps not the wisest course for the whale-watch-bound, it's the best way to sample the scrumptious international output of this beloved institution. Closed November to early April.

CYBERCAFE

To check your e-mail, surf online, or just hang out with techies, stop by **Cyber Cove,** an Internet lounge on the second floor of Whalers' Wharf at 237 Commercial St. (© **508/487-7778**). It's open Monday to Saturday 9am to 6pm.

PROVINCETOWN AFTER DARK
The Club Scene

The Atlantic House The "A-house"—the nation's premier gay bar—also welcomes straights of both sexes, except in the leather-oriented Macho Bar upstairs. Late in the evening, there's usually plenty going on in the Big Room dance bar. In the little bar downstairs—warm up at the fireplace—check out the Tennessee Williams memorabilia, including a portrait *au naturel;* there's more across the street in the restaurant, Grand Central. Open year-round. 6 Masonic Place (off Commercial St., 2 blocks west of town hall). © 508/487-3821. Cover for the Big Room $5–$10.

Crown & Anchor The specialty bars at the large complex span leather ("The Vault"), disco, comedy, drag shows, and cabaret. Facilities include a pool bar and game room. Call for schedule. Closed November to April. 247 Commercial St. (in the center of town). © 508/487-1430. Admission to shows $18–$22.

Post Office Café and Cabaret One of P-town's top clubs, the Post Office, despite its cramped space, can be depended on for amusing drag and comedy shows. In recent years, the B-Girlz (Hard Kora, Barbie-Q, and Belle Bottom) have been the featured act. Call for schedule. Closed November to April. 303 Commercial St. (in the center of town). © 508/487-3892. Cover $25.

Vixen This chic women's bar occupies the lower floors of a former hotel. On the roster are jazz, blues, and comedy acts. There are also pool tables. Call for schedule. Closed November to April. Pilgrim House, 336 Commercial St. (in the center of town). © 508/487-6424. Cover $20 for shows.

The Bar Scene

Cafe Mews This venue, with its bay view and vintage mahogany bar, is one of the few nightspots in town to lend itself well to the art of conversation. The jazz piano enhances rather than intrudes. A light cafe menu, in addition to the dining-room menu, is available. At The Mews (see "Where to Dine," earlier in this chapter). © 508/487-1500.

Governor Bradford   It's a good old bar, featuring pool tables, drag karaoke (summer **223**
nights at 9:30pm), and disco. Call for a schedule. 312 Commercial St. (in the center of
town). ℂ 508/487-2781.

Patio   A large outdoor seating area right on Commercial Street makes this a terrific
place to sip summer cocktails and people-watch. A favorite for decades as Café Blasé, the
renamed, remade watering hole now serves tasty appetizers, desserts, light fare, and even
whole dinners. The updated interior holds a sleek, attractive bar. 328 Commercial St. (in
the center of town). ℂ 508/487-9465.

Performance

Art House   This theater in a former cinema mounts avant-garde productions, like a
drag *Romeo and Juliet,* presenting four shows a night in season. While you wait for the
show to begin, you can sip a latte and order main courses and yummy dessert crepes from
the café's large menu. Performances are offered mid-May to mid-September from 7 to
10pm. Closed mid-September to mid-May. 214 Commercial St. (in the center of town).
ℂ 508/487-9222. Tickets $25-$35.

Meetinghouse Theatre and Concert Hall   In season, this glorious space is given
over to a wide range of performances, from plays to opera to cabaret. Upstairs is an
acoustically superb concert hall with a restored 1929 Steinway concert grand piano.
Downstairs is an intimate theater. The season is usually capped off by a series of concerts
by the Flirtations, a gay a cappella ensemble. A highlight in season is the Sunday at 5
Music Series with a variety of performers, costing $10. At the Unitarian-Universalist Meet-
inghouse, 236 Commercial St. (in the center of town). ℂ 508/487-9344. Ticket prices vary.

The Provincetown Theater   With both Eugene O'Neill and Tennessee Williams as
one-time residents, Provincetown went far too long without a state-of-the-art theater.
The town had no dedicated theater from 1977, when the venerable Playhouse on the
Wharf was destroyed by fire, until 2004, when this 200-seat venue was completed. The
home of two local acting troupes, Provincetown Theatre Company and Provincetown
Repertory Theater, the building also serves as a concert hall, dance studio, cinema, and
meetinghouse. Credit cards are accepted at the theater, which is open year-round. Tickets
can be purchased from Ptown Tix (located at 209 Commercial St. at the Aquarium
Marketplace), at the box office, or online. 238 Bradford St. (2 blocks east of Howland St.).
ℂ 508/487-7487 (800/791-7487 or 508/487-9793 for box office). www.provincetowntheater.com
(www.ptowntix.com for box office). Ticket prices vary.

Low-Key Evenings

Fine Arts Work Center   Drawing on its roster of visiting artists and scholars, FAWC
offers exceptional readings and talks (some serve as fundraisers) year-round. Call for a
schedule. 24 Pearl St. (off Bradford St. in the center of town). ℂ 508/487-9960. www.fawc.org.
Most events free.

Provincetown Art Association & Museum   Concerts, lectures, and readings
attract an intellectually inclined after-hours crowd. Call for a schedule. 460 Commercial
St. (in the East End). ℂ 508/487-1750. Cover varies.

9

Nantucket

In his classic novel, Moby Dick, Herman Melville wrote, "Nantucket! Take out your map and look at it. See what a real corner of the world it occupies; how it stands there, away off shore . . ." More than 100 years later, this tiny island 30 miles off the coast of Cape Cod still defines itself, in part, by its isolation. At only 3½ by 14 miles in size, Nantucket is smaller and more insular than Martha's Vineyard. But charm-wise, Nantucket stands alone—all the creature comforts of the 21st century wrapped in an elegant 19th-century package.

The island has long appealed to wealthy visitors, and the ultrarich are more visible than ever. Locals shake their heads over the changing demographics. "If they can't get a reservation at a restaurant, they buy the restaurant," one islander said. Nevertheless, this is still a terrific spot for a family vacation or a romantic retreat. After all, window-shopping at the island's exclusive boutiques and soaking up the sunshine on the pristine beaches are both free of charge.

The Nantucket we see today is the result of a dramatic boom and bust that took place in the 1800s. The whaling capital of the world, the Nantucket of Melville's time was a bustling international port whose wealth and sophistication belied its size. But the discovery of crude oil spelled doom for the whale-oil industry. Nantucket sank into a severe economic depression until the tourism industry revived it at the end of the 19th century. Stringent regulations have preserved the 19th-century character of Nantucket

Town, and today 36% of the island (and counting) is maintained as conservation land.

Nantucket Island's one town, also called Nantucket, hugs the yacht-filled harbor. This sophisticated burg bursts with bountiful stores, quaint inns, cobblestone streets, interesting historic sites, and pristine beaches. Scores of shops and galleries occupy wharf shacks on the harbor. The rest of the island is mainly residential, but for a couple of notable villages. Siasconset (nicknamed 'Sconset), on the east side of the island, is a tranquil community with picturesque, rose-covered cottages and a handful of businesses, including a pricey French restaurant. Sunset aficionados head to Madaket, on the west coast of the island, for the evening spectacular.

The lay of the land on Nantucket is rolling moors, heaths, cranberry bogs, and miles of exquisite public beaches. The vistas are honeymoon-romantic: an operating windmill, three lighthouses, and a skyline dotted with church steeples. Although July and August are still the most popular times to visit the island, Nantucket's tourist season has been lengthened considerably by several popular festivals: the Daffodil Festival in April, Nantucket Harvest Weekend in October, and the month-long Nantucket Noel, the granddaddy of all holiday celebrations in the region. Off season, a vacation can be more tranquil, and certainly less expensive. The "Grey Lady's" infamous fog is liable to swallow you whole, but you may well learn to relish the moody, atmospheric weather.

1 ESSENTIALS

GETTING THERE

BY FERRY The two companies that offer ferry service from Hyannis to Nantucket are the Steamship Authority and Hy-Line Cruises. Their terminals are on opposite sides of Hyannis Harbor.

From the South Street Dock in Hyannis, the **Steamship Authority** (✆ **508/477-8600,** or 508/228-3274 in Nantucket; www.steamshipauthority.com) operates year-round ferry service (including cars, passengers, and bicycles) to Steamboat Wharf in Nantucket using both **high-speed** ferries—which get you there in one hour—and **conventional** ferries, which take two hours and 15 minutes and cost about half the price.

Only the conventional ferries have space for cars, but there is no need to bring a vehicle to the island.

The Steamship Authority's **fast ferry to Nantucket, MV *Iyanough*** (✆ **508/495-3278**), is for passengers only (no cars). It takes 1 hour and runs five to six times a day in season. It is more than $10 cheaper than the Hy-Line ferry (see below), the other ferry company that makes the trip from Hyannis. Tickets in season cost $33 one-way ($65 round-trip) for adults, $25 one-way ($49 round-trip) for children 5 to 12, and it is free for children 4 and under. Parking costs $10 to $15 per day. Passenger reservations are highly recommended.

Bringing a car to Nantucket: If you must bring a car, to the island you need to reserve *months in advance* to secure a spot on the conventional ferry since only six boats make the trip daily in season (three boats daily off season). Before you call, have alternative departure dates. When bringing a car to the island, remember to arrive at least 1 hour before departure to avoid your space being released to standbys. If you arrive without a reservation and plan to wait in the standby line, there is no guarantee you will get to the island that day. There is a $10 processing fee for canceling reservations. No advance reservations are required for passengers traveling without cars.

A round-trip fare if you are bringing a car costs a whopping $380 to $430 from mid-May to mid-October; and off season, $260 to $300 from mid-October to mid-May. (Do you get the impression they don't want you to bring a car?)

Note: The Steamship Authority now charges different rates for different length cars. You will need to specify the make and model of your car when you place your reservation.

Car rates do not include drivers or passengers; you must get tickets for each person going to the island. For passengers, a one-way ticket on the Steamship Authority for passengers traveling on the conventional ferry (with or without cars) is $17 ($33 round-trip) for adults, $8.50 one-way ($17 round-trip) for children 5 to 12, and $12 extra round-trip for bikes. Remember that Steamship Authority parking costs $10 to $15 per day; you do not need to make parking reservations.

Also from Hyannis, passenger ferries to Nantucket's Straight Wharf are operated by **Hy-Line Cruises,** Ocean Street Dock (✆ **888/778-1132** or 508/778-2600; for high-speed ferry reservations, call ✆ **800/492-8082** or 508/778-0404; www.hy-linecruises.com). Hy-Line offers year-round service with its high-speed passenger catamaran, the ***Grey Lady,*** which makes five to six hourly trips per day. The cost of a one-way fare is $42 for adults ($77 round-trip), $32 for children 5 to 12 ($56 round-trip), and $6 extra for bicycles ($12 round-trip). It's best to reserve in advance for your ferry ticket and for a parking space. Pets are allowed on the *Grey Lady.*

ⓘ Tips Parking

You don't need a car on Nantucket, so plan to park your car in Hyannis before boarding a ferry to the island. For all **Hy-Line** ferry services, Ocean Street Dock (© 888/778-1132 or 508/778-2602), in July and August it's a good idea not only to reserve ferry tickets in advance, but also to reserve a parking spot ahead of time. The all-day parking fee is $17 per calendar day in season. If the Hy-Line lot is full, there are two competing lots next to the Hyannis Harbor Motel. **Note:** Choose the one where the attendants are wearing yellow shirts (not yellow jackets!)—they have the more reliable rates. Travelers on **Steamship Authority** (© 508/477-8600) vessels do not need a parking reservation. Be sure to arrive at least 1 hour before sailing time to allow for parking. Parking at the Steamship Authority lots costs $10 to $15 per day. When the nearby lot across from Cape Cod Hospital is full, there are parking lots several blocks away on Yarmouth Road, Lewis Bay Road and Brooks Road. From the outlying lots, you access the ferry terminal via a free shuttle bus. In season, watch signs on Route 6 or tune in to radio station 1610 AM for up-to-the-minute ferry parking information.

Hint: It pays to buy a round-trip ticket on the Hy-Line fast ferry. It's cheaper than buying two one-way tickets.

From early May through October, Hy-Line's standard 1-hour-and-50-minute ferry service is also offered. Round-trip tickets are $45 for adults, $26 for children ages 5 to 12, and $12 extra for bikes. On busy holiday weekends, you may want to order tickets in advance; otherwise, be sure to buy your tickets at least a half-hour before your boat leaves the dock.

The standard ferry also has a **first-class section** with a private lounge, bathrooms, a bar, and a snack bar; a continental breakfast or afternoon cheese and crackers is also served onboard. No pets are allowed on the *Great Point* ferry in the first-class section. Tickets in the first-class section are $52, round-trip for all ages.

Note: Hy-Line reserves the right to add a fuel surcharge onto all of its tickets. In the summer of 2008, the fuel surcharge was $6 per round-trip ticket.

Hy-Line's **Around the Sound** cruise is a 1-day round-trip excursion from Hyannis with stops in Nantucket and Martha's Vineyard that runs from mid-June to mid-September. The price is $89 for adults, $59 for children 5 to 12, and $15 extra for bikes.

Hy-Line runs three passenger-only high-speed ferries **from Oak Bluffs** on Martha's Vineyard to Nantucket from early June to mid-September (there is no car-ferry service between the islands). The trip time from Oak Bluffs is 1 hour and 10 minutes. The one-way fare is $28 for adults, $16 for children 5 to 12, and $5 extra for bikes.

From Harwich Port, you can avoid the summer crowds in Hyannis and board one of **Freedom Cruise Line**'s (702 Rte. 28 in Harwich Port, across from Brax Landing; © 508/432-8999; www.nantucketislandferry.com) passenger-only ferries to Nantucket. From mid-May to early October, boats leave from Saquatucket Harbor in Harwich Port. They make two or three trips a day in season and one trip per day in the shoulder season. The trip takes 1 hour and 10 minutes. A round-trip ticket is $68 for adults, $55 for children ages 2 to 11, $6 for children 1 and under, and $10 extra for bikes. Parking is free for day-trippers; it's $15 per night. Advance reservations are highly recommended.

BY AIR You can also fly into **Nantucket Memorial Airport** (© 508/325-5300), which is about 3 miles south of Nantucket Road on Old South Road. The flight to Nantucket takes about 30 to 40 minutes from Boston, 20 minutes from Hyannis, and a little more than an hour from New York City airports. Keep in mind, there is frequent shuttle bus service from Nantucket Airport terminal to town for $2.

Airlines providing service to Nantucket include: **Cape Air/Nantucket Airlines** (© 800/352-0714 or 508/771-6944; www.flycapeair.com) year-round from Hyannis ($109 round-trip), Boston (about $271 round-trip), Martha's Vineyard ($86 round-trip), and New Bedford ($157 round-trip); **Continental Express** (© 800/525-0280; www.continental.com) seasonally from Newark (about $520 round-trip); **Island Airlines** (© 800/248-7779 or 508/775-6606; www.islandair.net) year-round from Hyannis ($94 round-trip); and **Colgan/US Airways Express** (© 800/428-4322; www.colganair.com) year-round from Boston ($383 round-trip) and New York ($479 and up round-trip).

Island Airlines and Nantucket Airlines both offer year-round charter service to the island. Another recommended charter company is **Ocean Wings** (© 800/253-5039; www.flyoceanwings.com).

Nantucket is easily navigated on bike, moped, or foot, and also by shuttle bus or taxi. If you're staying outside of Nantucket Town, however, or if you simply prefer to explore by car, you might want to bring your own car or rent one when you arrive. Adventure-minded travelers may even want to rent a jeep or other four-wheel-drive vehicle, which you can take out on the sand—a unique island experience—on certain sections of the coast (a permit is required—see "By Car & Jeep," below). Keep in mind that if you do opt to travel by car, in-town traffic can reach gridlock in the peak season, and parking can be a nightmare.

BY BIKE & MOPED   When I head to Nantucket for a few days, biking is my preferred mode of transportation. The island itself is relatively flat, and paved bike paths abound— they'll get you from Nantucket Town to Siasconset, Surfside, and Madaket. There are also many unpaved back roads to explore, which make mountain bikes a wise choice when pedaling around Nantucket.

A word of warning to bikers: One-way street signs and all other traffic rules apply to you, too! This law is enforced in Nantucket Town, and don't be surprised if a tanned but stern island policeman requests that you get off your bike and walk. Helmets are required for children 15 and under. Bikers should also remember not to ride on the sidewalks in town, which are busy with pedestrians strolling and exiting shops.

Mopeds and scooters are also prevalent, but watch out for sand on the roads. Be aware that local rules and regulations are strictly enforced. Mopeds are not allowed on sidewalks or bike paths. You'll need a driver's license to rent a moped, and state law requires that you wear a helmet. The following shops rent bikes and scooters; all are within walking distance of the ferries: **Cook's Cycle Shop, Inc.,** 6 S. Beach St. (© **508/228-0800**); **Nantucket Bike Shops,** at Steamboat and Straight wharves (© **508/228-1999**); and **Young's Bicycle Shop,** at Steamboat Wharf (© **508/228-1151**), which also does repairs. Cook's has the lowest bike rental rates. Bike rentals average $20 to $30 for a full day. Scooters cost $70 for a one-seater or $90 for a two-seater for 24 hours.

BY SHUTTLE BUS   Inexpensive shuttle buses, with bike racks and accessibility for those with disabilities, make frequent loops through Nantucket Town, beaches and to outlying spots. For routes and stops, contact the **Nantucket Regional Transit Authority** (© **508/228-7025**) or pick up a map and schedule at the visitor center on Federal Street or the chamber of commerce office on Main Street (see "Visitor Information," below). The shuttle permits you to bring your clean, dry dog along, too. There's room for two bikes on a first-come, first-served basis. The cost is $1 to $2, and exact change is required. A 3-day pass can be purchased at the visitor center for $10.

Shuttle routes and fares are pretty simple. Downtown shuttle stops are located on the corner of Salem and Washington streets (for South, Miacomet, and the Airport loops), on Broad Street in front of the Foulger Museum (for Madaket Loop and Beach Express), and on Washington Street at the corner of Main Street (for 'Sconset loops).

- **Airport Loop** services Nantucket Airport to the center of town at Washington Street; every 30 minutes, on the hour and half-hour from 7am to 11:30pm; $2.
- **South Loop** services the Surfside Beach, Hooper Farm Road, and Pleasant Street areas; every 15 minutes from 7am to 11:30pm; $1.
- **Miacomet Loop** services the Fairgrounds Road, Bartlett Road, and Hummock Pond areas; every 30 minutes from 7am to 11:30pm; $1.
- **Madaket Route** services Madaket (from Broad St. downtown) via Cliff Road and New Lane; every 30 minutes from 7:30am to 11:30pm; $2 each way.

- **'Sconset Route 1** services 'Sconset via Polpis Road; every 30 minutes from 8:20am to 11pm; $2 each way.
- **'Sconset Route 2** services 'Sconset via Old South/Nobadeer Farm and Milestone roads; every 30 minutes from 7:40am to 10:30pm; $2 each way.
- **Beach Express** services Surfside and Jetties beaches (the in-town stop is on Broad St.); every 30 minutes for Jetties Beach and every hour for Surfside Beach from 10:15am to 5:45pm; $2 each way to Surfside, $1 each way to Jetties.

BY CAR & JEEP   I recommend a car if you'll be here for more than a week or if you're staying outside Nantucket Town. However, there are no in-town parking lots; parking, although free, is limited to Nantucket's handful of narrow streets, which can be a problem in the busy summer months. Also, gas is much more expensive on Nantucket than it is on the mainland.

Four-wheel-drive vehicles are your best bet, since many beaches and nature areas are off sandy paths; be sure to reserve at least a month in advance if you're coming in summer. If you plan on doing any four-wheeling in the sand, you need to get an **Over-Sand Permit** ($100) from the **Nantucket Police Department** (© 508/228-1212). To drive in the **Coskata–Coatue** nature area, you need a separate permit from the **Trustees of Reservations,** at the gatehouse (© 508/228-0006), which costs about $125 for a season pass, or a $25 gate fee for a day-rental four-wheel-drive that comes with the Over-Sand Permit. Dogs are not allowed, even in a car.

The following on-island rental agencies offer cars, jeeps, and other four-wheel-drive vehicles: **Affordable Rentals of Nantucket,** 6 S. Beach Rd. (© 508/228-3501); **Hertz,** at the airport (© 800/654-3131 or 508/228-9421); **Nantucket Windmill Auto Rental,** at the airport (© 800/228-1227 or 508/228-1227); and **Young's 4×4 & Car Rental,** Steamboat Wharf (© 508/228-1151). A standard car costs about $95 to $129 per day in season; a four-wheel-drive rental is about $200 to $249 per day (including an Over-Sand Permit).

BY TAXI   You'll find taxis (many are vans that can accommodate large groups or those traveling with bikes) waiting at the airport and at all ferry ports. During the busy summer months, I recommend reserving a taxi in advance to avoid a long wait upon arrival. Rates are flat fees, based on one person riding before 1am, with surcharges for additional passengers, bikes, and dogs. The most centrally located taxi stand is at the bottom of Main Street in front of The Club Car restaurant. A taxi from the airport to Nantucket Town will cost about $15, plus $1 for each additional person. Reliable cab companies on the island include **A-1 Taxi** (© 508/228-3330), **Chief's Taxi** (© 508/284-8497), **Milestone Taxi** (© 508/325-5511), **Lisa's Taxi** (© 508/228-2223), and **Val's Cab Service** (© 508/228-9410).

VISITOR INFORMATION

For information contact the **Nantucket Island Chamber of Commerce** at 48 Main St., Nantucket, MA 02554 (© 508/228-1700; www.nantucketchamber.org).

When you arrive, you should also stop by the **Nantucket Visitors Service and Information Bureau** in Nantucket Town at 25 Federal St. (© 508/228-0925), which is open daily from June to September, and Monday to Saturday from October to May, 10am to 5pm. Visitor Services is where to call if you are having trouble finding an available room. They have the most up-to-date accommodations availability listings. They can also help with 1-night stays and special event listings.

There are also information booths at Steamboat and Straight wharves. Always check the island's newspapers, *The Inquirer & Mirror* (www.ack.net) and *The Nantucket Independent* (www.nantucketindependent.com), for information on current events and activities around town.

Nantucket Accommodations, P.O. Box 217, Nantucket, MA 02554 (© **508/228-9559;** fax 508/325-7009; www.nantucketaccommodation.com), a fee-based private service, can arrange advance reservations for 95% of the island's lodgings. Last-minute travelers can use the **Nantucket Visitors Service and Information Bureau** (© **508/228-0925**), a daily referral service rather than a booking service. It always has the most updated list of available accommodations.

Automated teller machines (ATMs) can be difficult to locate on Nantucket. **Nantucket Bank** (© **508/228-0580**) has five locations: 2 Orange St., 104 Pleasant St., Amelia Street, the Hub on Main Street, and the airport lobby, all open 24 hours. **Pacific National Bank** has four locations: the A&P Supermarket (next to the wharves), the Stop & Shop (open 24 hr. seasonally), the Steamship Wharf Terminal, and Pacific National Bank lobby (open during bank hours only).

In case of a **medical emergency,** the **Nantucket Cottage Hospital,** 57 Prospect St. (© **508/228-1200**), is open 24 hours.

---

2 BEACHES & RECREATIONAL PURSUITS

BEACHES   In distinct contrast to Martha's Vineyard, virtually all of Nantucket's 110-mile coastline is free and open to the public. Though the pressure to keep people out is sometimes intense (especially when four-wheel-drivers insist on their right to go anywhere, anytime), islanders are proud that they've managed to keep the shoreline in the public domain.

Each of the following areas tends to attract a different crowd.

- **Children's Beach ★:** This small beach is a protected cove just west of busy Steamship Wharf. Appealing to families, it has a park, a playground, restrooms, lifeguards, a snack bar (the beloved Downy Flake, famous for its homemade doughnuts), and even a bandstand for free weekend concerts.
- **Cisco Beach ★★:** About 4 miles from town, in the southwestern quadrant of the island (from Main St., turn onto Milk St., which becomes Hummock Pond Rd.), Cisco enjoys vigorous waves—great for the surfers who flock here, not so great for the waterfront homeowners. Restrooms are available and lifeguards are on duty.
- **Coatue ★:** This fishhook-shaped barrier beach, on the northeastern side of the island at Wauwinet, is Nantucket's outback, accessible only by four-wheel-drive vehicles, watercraft, or the very strong-legged. Swimming is strongly discouraged because of fierce tides.
- **Dionis Beach ★★★:** About 3 miles out of town (take the Madaket bike path to Eel Point Rd.) is Dionis, which enjoys the gentle sound surf and steep, picturesque bluffs. It's a great spot for swimming, picnicking, and shelling, and you'll find fewer children than at Jetties or Children's beaches. Stick to the established paths to prevent further erosion. Lifeguards patrol here, and restrooms are available.
- **Jetties Beach ★★★:** Located about a half-mile west of Children's Beach on North Beach Street, Jetties is about a 20-minute walk, or an even shorter bike ride, shuttle

bus ride, or drive, from town (there's a large parking lot, but it fills up early on summer weekends). It's another family favorite, for its mild waves, lifeguards, bathhouse, and restrooms. Facilities include the town tennis courts, volleyball nets, a skate park, and a playground; watersports equipment and chairs are also available to rent. There is also The Jetties, an upscale concession stand complete with bar, serving lunch and dinner. The Fourth of July fireworks are held here. Every August, Jetties hosts an intense sand-castle competition.

- **Madaket Beach ★★★**: Accessible by Madaket Road, the 6-mile bike path that runs parallel to it, and by shuttle bus, this westerly beach is narrow and subject to pounding surf and sometimes serious crosscurrents. Unless it's a fairly tame day, you might content yourself with wading. It's the best spot on the island for admiring the sunset. Facilities include restrooms, lifeguards, and mobile food service.

- **Siasconset ('Sconset) Beach ★★**: The eastern coast of 'Sconset is as pretty as the town itself and rarely, if ever, crowded, perhaps because of the water's strong sideways tow. You can reach it by car, by shuttle bus, or by a less scenic and somewhat hilly (at least for Nantucket) 7-mile bike path. Lifeguards are usually on duty, but the closest facilities (restrooms, grocery store, and cafe) are back in the center of the village.

- **Surfside Beach ★★★**: Three miles south of town via a popular bike/skate path, broad Surfside—equipped with lifeguards, restrooms, and a surprisingly accomplished little snack bar—is appropriately named and commensurately popular. It draws thousands of visitors a day in high season, from college students to families, but the free parking lot can fit only about 60 cars—you do the math, or better yet, ride your bike or take the shuttle bus.

BICYCLING   Several lovely, paved bike paths radiate from the center of town to outlying beaches. The **bike paths** run about 6¼ miles west to Madaket, 3½ miles south to Surfside, and 8¼ miles east to Siasconset. To avoid backtracking from Siasconset, continue north through the charming village and return on the Polpis Road bike path. Strong riders could do a whole circuit of the island in a day. Picnic benches and water fountains stand at strategic points along all the paths.

For a free map of the island's bike paths (it also lists Nantucket's bicycle rules), stop by **Young's Bicycle Shop,** at Steamboat Wharf (© **508/228-1151**). It's definitely the best place for bike rentals, from basic three-speeds to high-tech suspension models. In operation since 1931—check out the vintage vehicles on display—they also deliver to your door. See "Getting Around," above, for more bike-rental shops.

FISHING   For shellfishing, you'll need a permit from the **harbormaster's office** at 34 Washington St. (© **508/228-7261**), which costs $100 for nonresidents for the season. You'll see surf-casters all over the island (no permit is required); for a guided trip, try Mike Monte of **Surf & Fly Fishing Trips** (© **508/228-0529**), who charges $140 per person for a 3-hour guided trip in the early fall. Deep-sea charters heading out of Straight Wharf include Capt. Bob DeCosta's *The Albacore* (© **508/228-5074**), Capt. Josh Eldridge's *Monomoy* (© **508/228-6867**), and Capt. David Martin's *Absolute* (© **508/ 325-4000**). On the *Monomoy* and the *Absolute,* 5-hour trips for bass for up to 8 people cost $1,100.

FITNESS   **Nantucket Health Club** at 10 Youngs Way (© **508/228-4750**) offers all the usual equipment and classes. Nonmembers pay $25 a day.

GOLF Two pretty courses are open to the public: the 18-hole **Miacomet Golf Club,** 12 W. Miacomet Rd. (© **508/325-0333**), and the 9-hole **Siasconset Golf Club,** off Milestone Road (© **508/257-6596**). You'll pay $105 for 18 holes at Miacomet. At Siasconset, playing 9 holes costs $35.

NATURE TRAILS Through preservationist foresight, about one-third of Nantucket's 42 square miles are protected from development. Contact the **Nantucket Conservation Foundation** at 118 Cliff Rd. (© **508/228-2884**) for a map of their holdings ($4), which include the 205-acre **Windswept Cranberry Bog** (off Polpis Rd.), where bogs are interspersed amid hardwood forests; and a portion of the 1,100-acre **Coskata–Coatue Wildlife Refuge,** comprising the barrier beaches beyond Wauwinet (see "Organized Tours," below). **The Maria Mitchell Association** (see "Museums & Historic Landmarks," below) sponsors guided birding and wildflower walks in season.

TENNIS The town courts are located next to Jetties Beach, a short walk west of town; call the **Nantucket Park and Recreation Commission** (© **508/325-5334**) for information. The town courts cost $20 an hour for singles and $25 an hour for doubles. Nine clay courts are available for rent nearby at the **Nantucket Tennis and Swim Club,** on North Beach Street (© **508/228-3700**), for $46 an hour. Though it's not generally open to the public, the grand, turn-of-the-19th-century **Siasconset Casino,** New Street, Siasconset (© **508/257-6585**), occasionally has courts available for rent for nonmembers from 1 to 3pm for $40 an hour.

WATERSPORTS **Nantucket Community Sailing** manages the concession at **Jetties Beach** (© **508/228-5358**), which offers lessons and rents out kayaks, sailboards, sailboats, and more. Rental rates for single kayaks are $20 to $25 per hour; windsurfers $20 to $25 per hour; and Sunfish $35 per hour. **Sea Nantucket,** on tiny Francis Street Beach off Washington Street (© **508/228-7499**), also rents kayaks; it's a quick sprint across the harbor to beautiful Coatue. Single kayaks rent for $40 and tandems rent for $70 for 4$^1/_2$ hours. **Nantucket Island Community Sailing** (© **508/228-6600**) gives relatively low-cost private and group lessons from the Jetties pier for adults (16 and up) and children; a seasonal adult membership covering open-sail privileges costs $250 for 4 weeks. One 2-hour private lesson costs $125.

Gear for scuba-diving, fishing, and snorkeling is readily available at the souvenir shop **Sunken Ship** on South Water and Broad streets near Steamboat Wharf (© **508/228-9226**). Fishing costs $30 per day, snorkeling gear costs $25 per day, and scuba-diving gear costs $50 to $70 per day. Scuba-diving lessons are $550.

3 MUSEUMS & HISTORIC LANDMARKS

Hadwen House ★★ During Nantucket's most prosperous years, whaling merchant Joseph Starbuck built the "Three Bricks" (nos. 93, 95, and 97 Main St.) for his three sons. His daughter married successful businessman William Hadwen, owner of the candle factory that is now the Whaling Museum, and Hadwen built this grand Greek Revival home across the street from his brothers-in-law in 1845. Although locals (mostly Quakers) were scandalized by the opulence, the local outrage spurred Hadwen on, and he decided to make the home even grander than he had first intended. The home soon became a showplace for entertaining the Hadwens' many wealthy friends. The Historical Association has done a magnificent job of restoring the home and furnishing it with period furniture, fabrics, porcelains, wallpapers, and other decorative accessories thought

to be original. The gardens are maintained in period style by the Nantucket Garden **233**
Club.

96 Main St. (at Pleasant St., a few blocks southwest of the town center). ℂ **508/228-1894.** www.nha.org. Admission included in Nantucket Historical Association's History Ticket ($18 adults, $9 children; admission for historic sites only [not Whaling Museum] $6 adults, $3 children). June–Sept Mon–Sat 10am–5pm, Sun noon–5pm; call for off-season hours. Closed Dec–Mar.

Jethro Coffin House ★★   Built around 1686, this saltbox is the oldest building left on the island. A National Historical Landmark, the brick design on its central chimney has earned it the nickname "The Horseshoe House." It was struck by lightning and severely damaged (in fact, nearly cut in two) in 1987, prompting a long-overdue restoration. Dimly lit by leaded-glass diamond-pane windows, it's filled with period furniture such as lathed ladder-back chairs and a clever trundle bed on wooden wheels. Nantucket Historical Association docents will fill you in on all the related lore.

Sunset Hill Rd. (off W. Chester Rd., about ¹/₂ mile northwest of the town center). ℂ **508/228-1894.** www. nha.org. Admission included in Nantucket Historical Association's History Ticket ($18 adults, $9 children; admission for historic sites only [not the Whaling Museum], $6 adults, $3 children). Late May to mid-Oct Mon–Sat 10am–5pm, Sun noon–5pm. Closed mid-Oct to late May.

Maria Mitchell Association ★★ (Kids)   This is a group of six buildings organized and maintained in honor of distinguished astronomer and Nantucket native Maria Mitchell (1818–89). The science center consists of astronomical observatories, with a lecture series, children's science seminars, and stellar observation opportunities (when the sky is clear) from the **Loines Observatory** at 59 Milk St. Extension (ℂ **508/228-9273**). The Loines Observatory is open July and August Monday, Wednesday, and Friday at 9pm; September to June it's open Friday at 8pm. There is no opportunity for viewing at the older **Vestal Street Observatory** at 3 Vestal St. (ℂ **508/228-9273**), which is open June to September Tuesday through Saturday at 11am for a 1-hour lecture about the association's history in the field of astronomy.

The **Hinchman House Natural Science Museum** (ℂ **508/228-0898**) at 7 Milk St. (at Vestal St.) houses a visitor center and offers evening lectures, bird-watching, wildflower and nature walks, and discovery classes for children and adults. The **Mitchell House** (ℂ **508/228-2896**) at 1 Vestal St., the astronomer's birthplace, features a children's history series and adult-artisan seminars, and it has wildflower and herb gardens. The **Science Library** (ℂ **508/228-9219**) is at 2 Vestal St., and the tiny, child-oriented **aquarium** (ℂ **508/228-5387**) is at 28 Washington St. and is open Monday to Saturday, 9am to 4pm.

4 Vestal St. (at Milk St., about ¹/₂ mile southwest of the town center). ℂ **508/228-9198.** www.mmo.org. Admission to each site $6 adults, $5 children. Museum pass (for birthplace, aquarium, science museum, and Vestal St. Observatory) $10 adults, $8 children ages 6–12. Early June to late Aug Tues–Sat 10am–4pm; call for off-season hours.

Nantucket Shipwreck and Life-Saving Museum ★★ (Finds)   Housed in a replica of the Nantucket Life-Saving Station (the original serves as the island's youth hostel), the museum, which has recently been renovated, has loads of interesting exhibits, including historic photos and newspaper clippings, as well as one of the last remaining Massachusetts Humane Society surf boats and its horse-drawn carriage. Two-hour children's programs (ages 6–10) are offered in the summer for $20, with one offering demonstrations of the breaches buoy lifesaving technique.

158 Polpis Rd. (3 miles east of town). ℂ **508/228-1885.** Admission $5 adults, $3 children. Mid-June to mid-Oct daily 10am–4pm.

Whaling Museum ★★★ (Kids) Reopened after a grand multimillion-dollar renovation, this museum is a showpiece in the region. Appropriately, it is housed in a former spermaceti-candle factory (candles used to be made from a waxy fluid extracted from sperm whales). Kids will love the awe-inspiring skeleton of a 43-foot finback whale (stranded in the 1960s), and adults will be fascinated by the exceptional collections of scrimshaw and nautical art. (Check out the action painting, *Ship Spermo of Nantucket in a Heavy Thunder-Squall on the Coast of California 1876,* executed by a captain who survived the storm.) A wall-size map depicts the around-the-world meanderings of the *Alpha,* accompanied by related journal entries. The admission price includes daily lectures on the brief and colorful history of the industry, like the beachside "whalebecue" feasts that natives and settlers once enjoyed. Don't miss the gift shop on the way out.

13 Broad St. (in the center of town). ✆ **508/228-1894.** www.nha.org. Admission $15 adults, $8 children 5–14; admission also included in the Nantucket Historical Association's History Ticket ($18 adults, $9 children). Apr–Nov Mon–Wed and Fri–Sat 10am–5pm, Thurs 10am–8pm, Sun noon–5pm. Closed Dec–Mar.

4 ORGANIZED TOURS

Coskata–Coatue Wildlife Refuge Natural History Tour ★★★ (Kids) The Trustees of the Reservations, a private statewide conservation organization that oversees the bulk of the Coskata–Coatue Wildlife Refuge, offers a 3-hour naturalist-guided tour twice a day. The trip is over sand dunes via Ford Expedition out to the **Great Point Lighthouse,** a partly solar-powered replica of the 1818 original. Those interested can also tour the inside of the lighthouse. During the trip through this rare habitat, you might spot snowy egrets, ospreys, terns, and oystercatchers. Call to make a reservation and meet the group at the Wauwinet parking lot at 120 Wauwinet Rd.

✆ **508/228-6799.** $40 adults, $15 children 12 and under. Call for reservations. Mid-May to mid-Oct daily 9:30am and 1:30pm. Closed mid-Oct to mid-May.

Endeavor Sailing Excursions ★★ (Moments) The *Endeavor* is a spirited 31-foot replica Friendship sloop, ideal for jaunts across the harbor into Nantucket Sound. Skipper James Genthner will gladly drop you off at one of the beaches for a bit of sunbathing or beachcombing.

Slip 15, Straight Wharf. ✆ **508/228-5585.** www.endeavorsailing.com. Reservations recommended. Rates $25–$35 for a 1¹⁄₂-hr. sail (highest rates July–Aug). Closed Nov–Apr.

Gail's Tours ★★ (Value) If you want to get some dirt on the island's colorful residents, Gail Nickerson Johnson—a seventh-generation native whose mother started a tour business back in the 1940s—has the inside track, and the charm, to keep a captive vanload rapt throughout a 1¹⁄₂-hour circuit of island highlights, including lots of celebrity info.

Departs from the Nantucket Information Bureau at 25 Federal St. and from prearranged pickup sites. ✆ **508/257-6557.** Reservations required. Rates $25 adults, free for children 3 and under. July–Aug departures at 10am, 1pm, and 3pm; call for off-season hours.

Nantucket Historical Association Guided Walking Tours ★ Stroll along downtown's cobblestone streets on this Historical Association tour that spotlights the history and architecture of Nantucket. The tours are led by Nantucket Historical Association docents trained in Nantucket history.

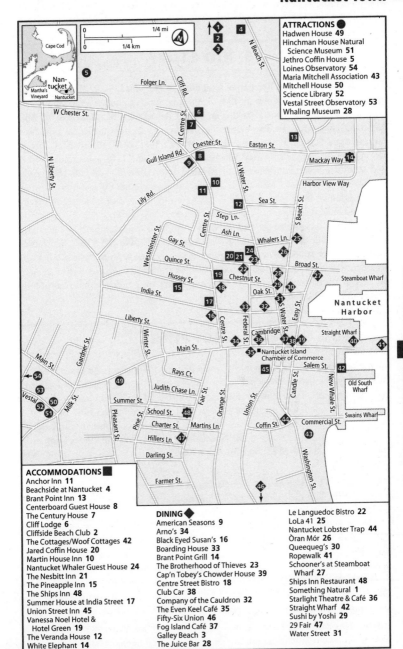

ATTRACTIONS ●
Hadwen House **49**
Hinchman House Natural
 Science Museum **51**
Jethro Coffin House **5**
Loines Observatory **54**
Maria Mitchell Association **43**
Mitchell House **50**
Science Library **52**
Vestal Street Observatory **53**
Whaling Museum **28**

ACCOMMODATIONS ■
Anchor Inn **11**
Beachside at Nantucket **4**
Brant Point Inn **13**
Centerboard Guest House **8**
The Century House **7**
Cliff Lodge **6**
Cliffside Beach Club **2**
The Cottages/Woof Cottages **42**
Jared Coffin House **20**
Martin House Inn **10**
Nantucket Whaler Guest House **24**
The Nesbitt Inn **21**
The Pineapple Inn **15**
The Ships Inn **48**
Summer House at India Street **17**
Union Street Inn **45**
Vanessa Noel Hotel &
 Hotel Green **19**
The Veranda House **12**
White Elephant **14**

DINING ◆
American Seasons **9**
Arno's **34**
Black Eyed Susan's **16**
Boarding House **33**
Brant Point Grill **14**
The Brotherhood of Thieves **23**
Cap'n Tobey's Chowder House **39**
Centre Street Bistro **18**
Club Car **38**
Company of the Cauldron **32**
The Even Keel Café **35**
Fifty-Six Union **46**
Fog Island Café **37**
Galley Beach **3**
The Juice Bar **28**

Le Languedoc Bistro **22**
LoLa 41 **25**
Nantucket Lobster Trap **44**
Òran Mór **26**
Queequeg's **30**
Ropewalk **41**
Schooner's at Steamboat
 Wharf **27**
Ships Inn Restaurant **48**
Something Natural **1**
Starlight Theatre & Café **36**
Straight Wharf **42**
Sushi by Yoshi **29**
29 Fair **47**
Water Street **31**

Sign up for tour at the Whaling Museum at 13 Broad St. (in the center of town). ☎ **508/228-1894.** www. nha.org. Admission included with Historical Association's History Ticket (adults $18, children $9). Apr–Nov Mon–Sat 10:15am and 2:15pm. Closed Dec–Mar.

---

5 KID STUFF

The **Nantucket Park and Recreation Commission** (☎ 508/228-7213) organizes various free and low-cost activities for kids, like tennis clinics, a concert series, and tie-dye workshops (bring your own T-shirt). The **Artists' Association of Nantucket** (☎ 508/325-5251) sponsors a variety of classes for children in different media, and the **Nantucket Island School of Design and the Arts** (☎ 508/228-9248) offers all sorts of summer courses. The **Nantucket Atheneum** (☎ 508/228-1110) holds readings in its spiffy children's wing. The **Nantucket Historical Association** (☎ 508/228-1894) sponsors **Living History for Children,** 3- to 4-day camp adventures for ages 6 to 12, which include grinding flour at the Old Mill, baking bread at the Oldest House, and trying your hand at knots and sailors' valentines. The cost is $120 to $140.

Little kids might like to get their hands on (and into) the touch tanks at the modest little **Maria Mitchell Aquarium** at 28 Washington St. (☎ 508/228-5387), which overlooks the harbor from whence the creatures came; the cost is $6 for adults and $5 for children. It's open June through mid-October Tuesday to Saturday from 10am to 4pm. For a real seafaring adventure, consider embarking on a treasure hunt aboard the *Endeavor* (☎ 508/228-5585).

---

6 SHOPPING

Nantucket shopping is so phenomenal you'll be tempted to rent a U-Haul. It's as if all the best big-city buyers, from Bendel's to Brooks Brothers, got together and gathered their favorite stuff. True, some tourist dreck has managed to drift in, but most of what you'll find for sale is as high in quality as it is in price—everything from $6 boxes of chocolate-covered dried cranberries to $900 cashmere sweaters. There are also bargains, like lightly-used designer togs at **the Nantucket Cottage Hospital Thrift Shop** at 17 India St. (☎ 508/228-1125) and **Murray's Warehouse** outlet at 7 New St. (☎ 508/228-3584).

ART & CRAFTS   The **Artists' Association of Nantucket** has the widest selection of work by locals, and the gallery at 19 Washington St. (☎ 508/228-0294) is impressive. In February and March it's open by appointment only.

The celebrated sculptor **David L. Hostetler** exhibits his work in one of the little galleries along Old South Wharf, 2 Old South Wharf (☎ 508/228-5152). Private viewing appointments are also available in his large showroom. His work in various media appears as spiritual icons expressed in the female form.

Exquisite art-glass pieces, as well as ceramics, jewelry, and basketry, can be found at **Dane Gallery,** 28 Centre St. (☎ 508/228-7779), where owners Robert and Jayne Dane show top-quality work. You'll be amazed at the colors and shapes of the glassware.

BOOKS   At **Mitchell's Book Corner,** 54 Main St. (☎ 508/228-1080), Mimi Beman handpicks her stock, with an astute sampling of general-interest books and an entire room dedicated to regional and maritime titles. **Nantucket Bookworks,** 25 Broad St.

(© **508/228-4000**), is a charming bookstore, strong on customer service and with a central location.

FASHION **Current Vintage** (4 Easy St.; © **508/228-5073**) is one of the most original shops to open in recent years. Beth English, who is known on the island for exquisite taste, sells gorgeous vintage gowns and accessories like antique bags and jewelry, as well as special wines from small wineries.

Martha's Vineyard may have spawned "Black Dog" fever, but this island boasts the inimitable "Nantucket reds"—cotton clothing that starts out tomato-red and washes out to salmon-pink. The fashion originated at **Murray's Toggery Shop,** 62 Main St. (© **800/ 368-2134** or 508/228-0437). Legend has it that the original duds were colored with an inferior dye that washed out almost immediately. However, customers so liked the thick cottons and instant aged look that the proprietor was forced to search high and low for more of the same fabric. Roland Hussey Macy, founder of Macy's, got his start here in the 1830s. Today's management also keeps up with current trends.

Preppy patterns and bright colors are back! You'll find **Lilly Pulitzer's In The Pink,** which has sensational minidresses, at 5 S. Water St. (© **508/228-0569**).

Ralph Lauren's store at 16 Main St. (© **508/228-9451**) scandalized Nantucketers when it first opened (there are no chains here, not even upscale ones), but now everyone is used to it. The store is stocked with high-end resort ware.

Zero Main, at 0 Main St. (© **508/228-4401**), has a limited but fine selection of elegant yet casual women's clothes, shoes, and accessories.

GIFTS/HOME DECOR **Nantucket Looms** at 16 Federal St. (© **508/228-1908**) is the place to ogle exquisite brushed mohair chaise throws, and other handmade woven items. The weaving studio is upstairs, where they also make blankets and sweaters of cotton and cashmere.

A casual counterpart to its Madison Avenue boutique, **Erica Wilson Needle Works,** 25–27 Main St. (© **508/228-9881**), features the designs of its namesake, an islander since 1958 and author of more than two dozen books on needlepoint. The shop offers hands-on guidance for hundreds of grateful adepts, as well as kits and handiwork of other noteworthy designers.

The also eponymous **Claire Murray,** 11 S. Water St. (© **508/228-1913**), is famous for its elaborate hand-hooked rugs. As a New York transplant running a Nantucket B&B in the late 1970s, Murray took up the traditional art of hooking rugs to see her through the slow season. She now runs a retail company grossing millions a year and is so busy creating new collections that she has hundreds of "hookers" (probably an old profession, but not the oldest) working for her around the world. Do-it-yourself kits ($100–$500) are sold in the shop here for about two-thirds the price of the finished rugs and come with complimentary lessons.

JEWELRY **Diana Kim England, Goldsmiths,** 56 Main St. (© **508/228-3766**), is a team of five goldsmiths that have almost 70 years of combined experience in making jewelry. You'll find gold baskets and pearls, as well as unique custom pieces.

NEWSSTAND **The Hub,** 31 Main St. (© **508/325-0200**), offers a selection of newspapers, magazines, and books, as well as greeting cards by local artists.

SEAFOOD **Sayle's Seafood,** Washington Street Extension (© **508/228-4599**), sells fresh seafood from Nantucket waters and a menu of takeout seafood platters. This is a great place to get a huge, steaming plate of fried clams to go.

TOYS **The Toy Boat,** 41 Straight Wharf (© **508/228-4552**), is keen on creative toys that are also educational. In addition to the top commercial lines, owner Loren Brock stocks lots of locally crafted, hand-carved playthings, such as "rainbow fleet" sailboats, part of the Harbor Series that includes docks, lighthouses, boats, and everything your child needs to create his or her own Nantucket Harbor. There are also stackable lighthouse puzzles replicating Nantucket's beams.

7 WHERE TO STAY

Most visitors to Nantucket will wish to stay in the center of town. There's no need for a car here; in fact, parking can be a real problem in season. Everything is within walking distance, including beaches, restaurants, and the finest shopping in the region. Unless otherwise stated, hotels are open year-round.

VERY EXPENSIVE

Cliffside Beach Club ★★★ (Finds)   Right on the beach and within walking distance (about 1 mile) of town, this is the premier lodging on the island. There's a sublime beachy-ness to the whole setup, from the simply decorated rooms, the cheerful, youthful staff, the sea of antique wicker in the clubhouse, and of course, the blue, yellow, and green umbrellas lined up on the beach. All rooms have such luxuries as French milled soaps and exceptional linens. A very good continental breakfast is served in the large clubhouse room, its beamed ceilings draped with colorful quilts.

46 Jefferson Ave. (about 1 mile from town center), Nantucket, MA 02554. © **800/932-9645** or 508/228-0618. Fax 508/325-4735. www.cliffsidebeach.com. 25 units, 1 cottage. Summer $450–$710 double; $875–$1,085 suite; $905 3-bedroom apt; $1,080 cottage. There is a 5.3% service charge in addition to taxes. Rates include continental breakfast. AE. Closed mid-Oct to late May. **Amenities:** Restaurant (The Galley, see review below); exercise facility (Cybex equipment and a trainer on staff); indoor hydrotherapy spa; steam saunas; concierge; babysitting. *In room:* A/C, TV/VCR, fridge, coffeemaker, hair dryer.

Nantucket Whaler Guest House ★★   This lodging option, an 1850s Greek Revival sea captain's house, is unique in that all of the rooms are suites with their own entrance and kitchen facilities. Compared to other B&Bs on the island, this one has a particularly private feel, almost like having your own apartment. Many of the rooms have decks or patios. All rooms are comfortably outfitted with cottage-y furnishings including overstuffed couches and stacks of games and books. Those guests who would prefer not to whip up their own breakfast and want to eat in can order up a customized continental breakfast basket for $40 per person.

8 N. Water St. (in the center of town), Nantucket, MA 02554. © **508/228-6597.** Fax 508/228-6291. www.nantucketwhaler.com. 12 units, 8 with tub/shower, 4 with shower only. Summer $350–$495 double; $650–$825 2-bedroom. AE, DC, MC, V. Closed mid-Dec to late Apr. No children under age 12. *In room:* A/C, TV/VCR, CD player, hair dryer, iron.

Vanessa Noel Hotel (VNH) and Hotel Green (Overrated)   Shoe designer Vanessa Noel has two centrally-located inns side by side. VNH has eight rooms with boutique hotel features like Philippe Starck fixtures, queen-size feather beds with custom Frette linens, Bulgari toiletries, robes, slippers, 15-inch flatscreen plasma televisions, and mini-bars stocked with the hotel's bottled water. But most of the rooms in this historic building are tiny, though there are two, including an attic space, that are comfortably spacious. **Vanessa Noel Hotel Green,** 33 Center St. (© **508/228-5300**), which has an ecological

theme, uses organic cottons on the bedding and eco-friendly toiletries. **The Café V Bar**
(𝒞 **508/228-8133**), a caviar and champagne bar on the first floor, serves breakfast fare, like a lobster omelet, as well as light dinner fare nightly.

5 Chestnut St. (in the center of town), Nantucket, MA 02554. 𝒞 **508/228-5300.** Fax 508/228-8995. www. vanessanoelhotel.com. 16 units. Summer VNH $300–$480 double; Green Hotel $250–$900 double. AE, DISC, MC, V. Open year-round. **Amenities:** Caviar bar. *In room:* A/C, TV, minibar, hair dryer.

The Wauwinet ★★ This ultradeluxe beachfront retreat is Nantucket's only Relais & Châteaux property. The inn is at the tip of a wildlife sanctuary and is nestled between the Atlantic Ocean and Nantucket Bay. All the rooms—some are on the small side—have pine armoires, Audubon prints, handsome fabrics, and an array of antique accessories. Extras include Egyptian cotton bathrobes and bottled water. Additional perks include a personalized set of engraved notecards. It's fun and romantic to order breakfast in your room here; the steward sets it up with a snowy white tablecloth and fine china. There is complimentary van service in to town (12 trips daily).

120 Wauwinet Rd. (P.O. Box 2580, about 8 miles east of Nantucket center), Nantucket, MA 02554. 𝒞 **800/ 426-8718** or 508/228-0145. Fax 508/325-0657. www.wauwinet.com. 25 units, 10 cottages, all with tub/ shower. Summer $800–$900 double; $1,000–$1,220 1- and 2-bedroom cottages. Rates include full breakfast and afternoon wine and cheese. AE, DC, MC, V. Closed mid-Oct to mid-May. **Amenities:** Fine-dining restaurant, Topper's at The Wauwinet (see "Where to Dine," below); 2 clay tennis courts w/pro shop and teaching pro; spa; rowboats, sailboats, sea kayaks on loan; mountain bikes on loan; croquet lawn; boccie ball on loan; concierge; room service. *In room:* A/C, TV/DVD and movie library, CD player, hair dryer, iron.

White Elephant ★★★ This luxury property, right on the harbor, is the ultimate in-town lodging. Rooms are big and airy (the most spacious rooms on Nantucket), with country-chic decor and most with harbor views. Rooms are in the main hotel building as well as in 12 smaller "cottages," some of which contain two or three units. About half the rooms have working fireplaces. The hotel has pleasant commons rooms including a cozy library with a large fireplace.

50 Easton St. (P.O. Box 1139), Nantucket, MA 02554. 𝒞 **800/445-6574** or 508/228-2500. Fax 508/325-1195. www.whiteelephanthotel.com. 52 units, 11 cottages, 61 with tub/shower, 2 with shower only. Summer $580–$680 double; $680 1-bedroom cottage; $1,700 2-bedroom cottage; $1,430 3-bedroom cottage. Rates include full breakfast. AE, DC, DISC, MC, V. Closed Nov–Mar. **Amenities:** Restaurant (lobster and steakhouse serving lunch and dinner daily plus an afternoon raw bar); exercise room; concierge; business lounge; full room service; fee-based laundry service; dry cleaning. *In room:* A/C, TV/DVD and movie library, fridge, hair dryer, iron, safe.

EXPENSIVE

Beachside at Nantucket ★ No ordinary motel, the Beachside's 90 air-conditioned bedrooms and lobby have been lavished with Provençal prints and handsome rattan and wicker furniture; the patios and decks overlooking the central courtyard with its heated pool have been prettified with French doors and latticework. This place has very inexpensive deals in the shoulder season, with rooms as cheap as $110 per night!

30 N. Beach St. (about ³/₄ mile west of the town center), Nantucket, MA 02554. 𝒞 **800/322-4433** or 508/228-2241. Fax 508/228-8901. www.thebeachside.com. 90 units, all with tub/shower. Summer $380–$420 double; $800 suite. Rates include continental breakfast. AE, DC, DISC, MC, V. Closed late Oct to late Apr. **Amenities:** Heated outdoor pool. *In room:* A/C, TV, Wi-Fi, fridge, hair dryer.

The Cottages/Woof Cottages ★★ These small apartments have the best location on the island, stacked up on a wharf that juts out into Nantucket Harbor. If you are looking for a place on Nantucket where you can bring your pooch, these one- and two-bedroom cottages are the perfect choice. All cottages are fresh and sparkling—floors polished, walls painted—and each has an eat-in kitchen and cozy living room area. Dogs get a welcome basket of treats and a Nantucket bandana. Guests have privileges at the White Elephant spa at a sister property.

One Old South Wharf (in the center of town), Nantucket, MA 02554. (© **866/838-9253** or 508/325-1499. Fax 508/325-1173. www.harborviewcottages.com. 33 units (all with tub/shower). Summer $490–$720 studio and 1-bedroom; $590–$1,090 2-bedroom; $990–$1,200 3-bedroom. AE, MC, V. Closed mid-Oct to May. Pet-friendly. *In room:* TV/VCR/CD, Wi-Fi (fee), kitchenette, hair dryer.

The Pineapple Inn ★★   The graceful Quaker entrance of the 1838 home bespeaks the hospitality to come. Rooms are spacious and decorated in a Colonial style with fine reproductions and antiques, including handmade Oriental rugs, marble bathrooms, and many four-poster canopy beds. Five large king bedrooms feature tiger maple beds. The smaller, less expensive rooms are on the third floor. The garden patio with climbing roses is a fine place to enjoy an afternoon cocktail and contemplate dinner plans. This inn is owned by the same owners as the Summer House and guests can take a jitney ride to 'Sconset to enjoy the pool at that oceanfront property.

10 Hussey St. (in the center of town), Nantucket, MA 02554. (© **508/228-9992.** Fax 508/325-6051. www. pineappleinn.com. 12 units, 8 with tub/shower, 4 with shower only. Summer $215–$295 double. Rates include continental breakfast. AE, MC, V. Closed early Dec to mid-Apr. No children under age 8. *In room:* A/C, TV, hair dryer, iron.

Summer House at India Street ★   There are five Summer House properties, four in town and the original property, the Summer House cottages, in 'Sconset. The India Street property is the most centrally located and is a handsome, restored historic house with top-notch amenities. Rooms are equipped with robes and deluxe toiletries. Most of the rooms are on the small side; bathrooms are former closets. Guests have access to complimentary jitney service to the Summer House beachfront property in 'Sconset and use of the pool there.

31 India St. (in the center of town), Nantucket, MA 02554. (© **508/257-4577.** Fax 508/257-4590. www. thesummerhouse.com. 10 units. Summer $335–$395 double. Rates include continental breakfast. AE, MC, V. Closed Jan–Apr. *In room:* A/C, TV, hair dryer.

Union Street Inn ★★ (Finds)   Sophisticated innkeepers Deborah and Ken Withrow have a terrific location for their historic 1770s property, just steps from Main Street yet in a quiet, residential section. Many rooms have canopied or four-poster beds; half have working wood-burning fireplaces. The comfortable beds are made up with Egyptian cotton linens. Bathrooms are equipped with piqué-woven bathrobes and large terry bath towels.

7 Union St. (in the center of town), Nantucket, MA 02554. (© **800/225-5116** or 508/228-9222. Fax 508/325-0848. www.unioninn.com. 12 units, 1 with tub/shower, 11 with shower only. Summer $425–$525 double; $550 suite. Rates include full breakfast. AE, MC, V. Closed Nov–Mar. *In room:* A/C, TV, Wi-Fi, hair dryer, no phone.

The Veranda House ★★ (Finds)   This stylish boutique inn is located in a quiet neighborhood a short walk from the center of town. It is perched on a hill, so rooms on the third floor have distant harbor views. Some of the more deluxe rooms have private balconies. All rooms have extras like robes; beds are made with Frette linens and goose-down comforters. Breakfast, which features hot delicacies like quiches and frittatas, is served with great hospitality on the ample front porch.

3 Step Lane (a few blocks from town center), Nantucket, MA 02554. ℂ **508/228-0695.** Fax 508/374-
0406. www.theverandahouse.com. 20 units, 7 with shared bathroom. Summer $309–$409 double; $489
suite. Rates include continental breakfast. AE, MC, V. Closed mid-Oct to late May. *In room:* A/C, Wi-Fi, hair
dryer.

MODERATE

Anchor Inn ★ (**Value**)   Innkeepers Ann and Charles Balas have a historic gem in this
1806 sea captain's home located next to the Old North Church. Also part of the inn is
72 Centre St., three doors down from the main inn. Authentic details can be found
throughout both houses, in the antique hardware and paneling, wide-board floors, and
period furnishings. The five rooms in the 72 Centre St. house are a particularly good
value; they are larger and less expensive. Guests enjoy a continental breakfast with home-
baked muffins at individual tables on the sunny enclosed porch or in the garden.

66 Centre St. (P.O. Box 387, in the center of town), Nantucket, MA 02554. ℂ **508/228-0072.** www.anchor-
inn.net. 16 units, 2 with tub/shower, 13 with shower only, 1 with tub only. Summer $225–$325 double;
$250–$280 suite. Rates include continental breakfast. AE, MC, V. Closed Jan–Feb. *In room:* A/C, TV, hair
dryer.

Brant Point Inn ★ (**Value**)   Thea and Pete Kaiser's two inn buildings, Brant Point and
Atlantic Mainstap next door, offer relatively affordable accommodations in a good location, in between town and Jetties Beach. The inns are traditional post and beam style
with country furnishings, like quilts on the beds. The guest living room has exposed oak
beams and a massive Belgian block fireplace. Pete is an experienced fishermen and guests
can arrange for fishing trips.

6 North Beach St. (a few blocks west of town), Nantucket, MA 02554. ℂ **508/228-5442.** Fax 508/228-
8498. www.brantpointinn.com. 8 units. Summer $165–$245 double; $225-$325 suite. Rates include
continental breakfast. AE, MC, V. Closed Nov–Apr. *In room:* TV.

Centerboard Guest House ★ (**Value**)   This 1886 home is replete with parquet
floors, Oriental rugs, lavish fabrics, plush feather mattresses, and lace-trimmed linens.
The overall look is light, airy, and less cluttered than the original Victorian look. Of the
inn's seven bedrooms, the first-floor suite is perhaps the most romantic, with a green-
marble Jacuzzi and a private living room with fireplace. Other rooms and bathrooms are
small, but all have bathrobes and minifridges.

8 Chester St. (in the center of town), Nantucket, MA 02554. ℂ **508/228-9696.** Fax 508/325-4798. www.
centerboardguesthouse.com. 7 units. Summer $295–$450 double; $435 suite. Rates include continental
breakfast. AE, MC, V. Closed Nov–Apr. *In room:* A/C, TV, fridge, hair dryer.

Cliff Lodge ★ (**Finds**)   A few blocks from the center of town, this charming 1771
whaling captain's house maintains its fresh, cozy-casual style. The cheerful guest rooms
feature colorful quilts and splatter-painted floors. Rooms range from a first-floor beauty
with king-size bed, paneled walls, and fireplace to the tiny third-floor rooms tucked into
the eaves. The spacious apartment in the rear of the house is a sunny delight. Climb up
to the widow's walk for a bird's-eye view of the town and harbor.

9 Cliff Rd. (a few blocks from the center of town), Nantucket, MA 02554. ℂ **508/228-9480.** Fax 508/228-
6308. www.clifflodgenantucket.com. 12 units. Summer $195 single; $210–$310 double; $395 apt. Rates
include continental breakfast. AE, MC, V. Open year-round. No children under 10. *In room:* A/C, TV.

Jared Coffin House ★ (**Kids**)   A little down on its heels, this grand brick manse in the
center of town was built in 1845 to the specs of the social-climbing Mrs. Coffin, who
abandoned Nantucket for the big city after 2 years and left the house to boarders. The

several buildings in the complex are awaiting a renovation by new owners, who also own the White Elephant on the harbor. The central location does have a drawback: The front rooms can be quite noisy.

29 Broad St. (at Centre St.), Nantucket, MA 02554. ✆ **800/248-2405** or 508/228-2400. Fax 508/228-8549. www.jaredcoffinhouse.com. 60 units, 52 with tub/shower, 8 with shower only. Summer $109 single; $260–$380 double. AE, DC, DISC, MC, V. Open year-round. **Amenities:** Restaurant (Chinese); in-room spa treatments; concierge. *In room:* TV, fridge, coffeemaker, hair dryer, iron.

Martin House Inn ★ (Value) This is one of the lower-priced B&Bs in town but also one of the most stylish, with a formal parlor, dining rooms, and a spacious side porch. This historic 1803 mariner's home is kept shipshape; and since your innkeeper is an expert baker, it always smells yummy here. The four garret rooms with a shared bathroom are a bargain. Higher-priced rooms have four-posters and working fireplaces. The suite has extras like a flatscreen TV, DVD player, and CD player.

61 Centre St. (between Broad and Chester sts., a couple blocks from town center), Nantucket, MA 02554. ✆ **508/228-0678.** Fax 508/325-4798. www.martinhouseinn.net. 13 units, 4 with shared bathroom, 4 with tub/shower, 5 with shower only. Summer $120 single (shared bathroom); $195 double (shared bathroom); $210–$315 double; $375 suite. Rates include continental breakfast. AE, MC, V. Open year-round. *In room:* A/C, no phone.

The Ships Inn ★ (Value) This pretty, historic inn is on a quiet side street, just slightly removed—3 blocks—from Nantucket's center. Rooms are comfortable, spacious, and charming, and offer a good variety of bed arrangements like single rooms and twin beds. The restaurant downstairs holds its own (see "Where to Dine," below).

13 Fair St. (a few blocks from town center), Nantucket, MA 02554. ✆ **888/872-4052** or 508/228-0040. Fax 508/228-6524. www.shipsinnnantucket.com. 12 units, 2 with shared bathroom. Summer $125 single with shared bathroom; $250 double. Rates include continental breakfast. AE, DISC, MC, V. Closed late Oct to mid-May. **Amenities:** Fine-dining restaurant located in the basement. *In room:* A/C, TV, fridge, hair dryer, iron.

INEXPENSIVE

The Nesbitt Inn (Value) The owners of this Victorian-style inn, one of the last of the old guesthouses with shared bathrooms, are slowly renovating the property, which has a great location in the center of town. Instead of having all rooms that share bathrooms, some of the rooms will now have private bathrooms. The place still has an old-fashioned feel and is still a bargain. It is spotlessly clean and actually quite charming.

21 Broad St., Nantucket, MA 02554. ✆ **508/228-0156** or 228-2446. 15 units, 13 with shared bathroom. Summer $125 double with shared bathroom; $170 queen with private bathroom; $240/night, $1,600/ week apt (with bathroom). Rates include continental breakfast. MC, V. Open year-round. *In room:* No phone.

Robert B. Johnson Memorial Hostel (Value) This youth hostel enjoys an almost perfect location. Set right beside Surfside Beach, the former "Star of the Sea" is an authentic 1873 lifesaving station, Nantucket's first. Where seven Surfmen once stood ready to save shipwrecked sailors, 49 backpackers now enjoy gender-segregated bunk rooms; the women's quarters, upstairs, still contain a climb-up lookout post. The usual hostel lockout (10am–5pm) and curfew (11pm) rules prevail.

31 Western Ave. (on Surfside Beach, about 3 miles south of Nantucket Town), Surfside, MA 02554. ✆ **508/228-0433.** Fax 508/228-5672. www.capecodhostels.org. 49 beds. $32 to $35 for members; $35 to $38 for nonmembers. MC, V. Closed mid-Oct to mid-Apr.

Nantucket is filled with outrageously priced restaurants, in which star chefs create dazzling meals served in high style. Obviously, you don't need this kind of treatment every night, but you'll probably want to try at least one deluxe place. Many of the best restaurants serve terrific lunches at half the price of their dinners. Thankfully, there are also a number of cafes scattered around town that serve reasonably priced lunches and dinners. Nantucket also has an old-fashioned drugstore soda fountain, **Island Pharmacy,** serving breakfast and lunch on upper Main Street, as well as the best smoothie on the island. It's really the best deli in town. If you dine in town, you may enjoy an evening stroll afterward, since many stores stay open late.

VERY EXPENSIVE

Brant Point Grill ★★ NEW AMERICAN   Recent renovations to the entire White Elephant complex on the harbor have converted this pretty dining room into a lobster, steak, and chops house. Many of the signature dishes, like the cedar-planked Atlantic salmon and rotisserie of prime rib, are prepared on the Fire Cone grill, a 21st-century interpretation of a Native American technique that cooks food by radiant heat and imparts it with a smoky mesquite flavor. If you can't sit on the terrace, try to snag a seat near one of the windows where you can watch the twilight fade over the harbor. The candlelight and white, airy dining room make for a perfectly romantic setting. Dinner at this establishment is an expensive proposition. However, the raw bar is open July through Labor Day from 4 to 7pm for light snacks, and a limited and less expensive all-day menu is served from 2:30 to 11pm. You may want to consider having lunch here, a perfect idea for a rainy day, when prices are more reasonable.

At the White Elephant Hotel (Easton and Willard sts.). ✆ **508/325-1320.** Reservations strongly recommended. Collared shirt and long pants requested for gentlemen. Main courses $26–$39. AE, DISC, MC, V. Mid-Apr to early Dec daily 7–11am breakfast, 11:30am–3pm lunch, and 5:30–10pm dinner; all-day menu 2:30–11pm. Closed early Dec to mid-Apr.

Club Car ★ CONTINENTAL   For decades one of the top restaurants on Nantucket, this venue is coasting a bit on its reputation these days. Prices are sky-high, but quality is not as top-shelf as other venues in town. But this is still a fine place to come for lunch or, even better, the late night piano bar scene, both of which are in the antique first-class rail car. The menu at dinner has classic French influences with the type of dishes, like sautéed calf's brains and duck foie gras, that are rarely seen on the Cape and islands. The signature dish is roast rack of lamb Club Car (with fresh herbs, honey-mustard glaze, and minted Madeira sauce).

1 Main St. ✆ **508/228-1101.** Reservations recommended. Main courses $24–$45. AE, MC, V. July–Aug daily 11am–3pm and 6–9:30pm; call for off-season hours. Closed late Oct to Apr.

Galley Beach ★★★ ⓘMoments NEW AMERICAN   This beachfront restaurant with the coolest bar decor on the island is where you go if you want to feel like you are in a *Travel + Leisure* fashion spread. Given the setting, it's no surprise that the Galley specializes in seafood caught locally by island fishermen. Produce comes from the restaurant's own organic garden. The menu changes often, but noteworthy menu options include the restaurant's signature New England clam chowder with smoked bacon or the shrimp tempura served with Asian slaw. As a main course, there might be a luscious lobster risotto, native halibut with forest-mushroom strudel, Black Angus filet, or simply a 2-pound lobster with all the fixings. Desserts are made on-site by one of the island's finest pastry chefs. The Galley is also a good choice for lunch, when you can enjoy this delicious gourmet food at lower prices.

54 Jefferson Ave. (?) **508/228-9641.** Reservations required for dinner. Main courses $29–$39. AE, MC, V. Summer daily 11:30am–2pm and 6–10pm; call for off-season hours. Closed late Sept to late May.

Ship's Inn Restaurant ★★ NEW AMERICAN   In the brick-walled basement of a 12-room inn, this cozy hideaway is a short walk from Main Street down a quiet side street. Professional and entertaining waitstaff make dining in the candlelit alcoves a real treat. The menu features a variety of fresh fish, meat, and pasta dishes, including several lighter options made without butter or cream. A flavorful starter is the Roquefort and walnut terrine with Asian pear. Popular main courses include the pan-roasted Muscovy duck breast and the grilled yellowtail flounder. For a festive dessert, there's always the Grand Marnier soufflé. The lengthy wine list, with a number of well-priced options, has won awards.

13 Fair St. (?) **508/228-0040.** Reservations recommended. Main courses $28–$38. AE, DISC, MC, V. July–Sept Wed–Mon 5:30–9:30pm; call for off-season hours. Closed Nov to mid-May.

Straight Wharf ★★★ NEW AMERICAN   New chef/owners, Amanda Lydon and Gabriel Frasca, have turned long-established Straight Wharf into the must-get reservation on the island. This is fine dining on the waterfront in the center of town. Make your reservation for 8pm on the outside deck so you can watch the sun set over the harbor. Straight Wharf has long been known for its creative cuisine, and also as the place where the island's top chefs hang out after their shifts. While the menu changes to reflect the best available ingredients, one special item to look for is the watermelon gazpacho, which may be the perfect chilled summer treat. Everyone loves Straight Wharf's "clambake," which includes corn pudding, littlenecks, and lobster. In fact, you can't go wrong with seafood here (or just about anything else on the menu), including the cherished smoked bluefish pâté.

6 Harbor Sq. (on Straight Wharf). (?) **508/228-4499.** Reservations recommended. Main courses $34–$39. AE, MC, V. July–Aug daily noon–2pm and 5:30–10pm; call for off-season hours. Closed late Sept to late May.

The Summer House ★★ (Finds) NEW AMERICAN   Old-school Nantucket atmosphere, 'Sconset-style, distinguishes this fine-dining experience from others on the island: wicker and wrought iron, roses and honeysuckle. A pianist plays nightly—often Gershwin standards. The pounding Atlantic Ocean is just over the bluff. Service is wonderful, and the food is excellent, though expensive. Specialties of the house include fresh, locally caught seafood with island vegetables delicately prepared and stylishly presented. Tempting appetizers include the grilled portobello mushrooms served with a pungent Stilton-basil terrine, and the house-smoked salmon *frisée* with avocado salsa. The distinctive main courses are roast saddle of lamb with rosemary caponatina port and feta mashed potatoes; the unusual and tasty lobster cutlets with coconut-jasmine risotto timbale and mint-tomato relish; and the grilled rib-eye with wild mushrooms, foie gras, and cabernet. Desserts are bountiful. Order the blueberry pie if it's in season. The Summer House also operates a **Beachside Bistro** next to its pool across the street with views of the ocean. At lunch and dinner the bistro serves light fare like salads, specialty pizzas, burgers, and sushi. The bistro is open 11:30am to 8pm in the summer.

17 Ocean Ave., Siasconset. ℓ **508/257-9976.** Reservations recommended. Main courses $33–$39. AE, **245**
MC, V. July–Aug daily 6–10pm; May–June and Sept to mid-Oct Wed–Sun 6–10pm. Closed mid-Oct to
Apr.

Topper's at The Wauwinet ★★★ REGIONAL/NEW AMERICAN   This 1850
restaurant—part of a secluded resort—is tastefully subdued, with wicker armchairs,
splashes of chintz, and a two-tailed mermaid to oversee a chill-chasing fire. Try to sit at
one of the cozy banquettes if you can. The menu features the finest regional cuisine:
Lobster is a major event (it's often sautéed with champagne beurre blanc), and be on the
lookout for unusual delicacies such as arctic char. Those are Gruyère-and-chive biscuits
in the breadbasket, and you must try one. Other recommendable house specialties
include the lobster-and-crab-cakes appetizer and the roasted Muscovy duck breast. Desserts are fanciful and fabulous: Consider the toasted brioche with poached pears and
caramel sauce. The Wauwinet runs a complimentary launch service from mid-June to
mid-September to the restaurant for lunch and dinner; it leaves from Straight Wharf at
11am and 5pm, takes 1 hour, and also makes the return trip.

120 Wauwinet Rd. (off Squam Rd.), Wauwinet. ℓ **508/228-8768.** Reservations required for dinner and
the launch ride over. Jacket requested for men. Main courses $34–$56. AE, DC, MC, V. May–Oct daily
noon–2pm and 6–9:30pm. Closed Nov–Apr.

Water Street ★ NEW AMERICAN   This two-level restaurant has an ultramodern,
urban-style bar upstairs. Prices on the menu, which focuses on organic, local ingredients,
suggest the offerings are precious indeed. One way or another, the $44 rib-eye steak will
make you swoon.

21 S. Water St. ℓ **508/228-7080.** Reservations recommended. Main courses $28–$44. AE, DISC, MC, V.
July–Sept daily 5:30–10pm; call for off-season hours. Closed Jan–Apr.

EXPENSIVE
American Seasons ★★ REGIONAL AMERICAN   This romantic little restaurant
has a great theme: Choose your region (New England, Pacific Coast, Wild West, or
Down South) and select creative offerings. You can mix or match your appetizers and
main courses. For instance, begin with the Louisiana crawfish risotto with fire-roasted
onion and fried parsnips in a sweet corn purée from Down South; then from the Pacific
Coast, try an aged beef sirloin with caramelized shallot and Yukon potato hash served
with an Oregon blue-cheese salad with white-truffle oil and fried onions. A lighter *tapas*
menu is available throughout the evening.

80 Centre St. (2 blocks from the center of town). ℓ **508/228-7111.** Reservations recommended. Main
courses $24–$30. AE, MC, V. Mid-Apr to Nov daily 6–9:30pm; call for off-season hours. Closed early Dec to
mid-Apr.

Boarding House ★★ NEW AMERICAN   This centrally located fine-dining restaurant doubles as one of the most popular bars in town. You can dine in the romantic
lower-level dining room or upstairs in the hopping bar area. But on clear summer nights,
you'll want to get one of the tables outside on the patio. The menu has definite Asian
and Mediterranean influences in dishes like the seared yellowfin tuna with sesame sushi
rice cake and wasabi aioli. One of the best soups on Nantucket is the luxe double lobster
chowder with fresh corn and truffle mousseline. But the signature dish is the classic
grilled lobster tails with grilled asparagus, mashed potatoes, and champagne beurre blanc.
The award-winning wine list offers a range of prices.

12 Federal St. ℓ **508/228-9622.** Reservations recommended. Main courses $24–$35. AE, MC, V. July–
Aug daily 5:30–10pm; call for off-season hours. Open year-round.

The Chanticleer ★★ FRENCH   The Chanticleer in the signature rose-covered cottage in 'Sconset has the atmosphere of a private club and beautiful garden seating. Owners Susan Handy and chef Jeff Worster, who also own Black Eyed Susan's (see below), run this charming place as a "brasserie moderne." Wonderful inventions like cod beignets and traditional appetizers like moules frites share the menu with creative versions of steak au poivre and seared Nantucket sea scallops. Tart au citron is among the stellar desserts, but you can also end your meal with a plats fromage with three types of succulent cheeses. How French!

9 New St., Siasconset (on the south side of the island). ✆ 508/257-4499. Reservations recommended. Main courses $24–$43. AE, MC, V. June–Aug Tues–Sun noon–2pm and 6–9:30pm; call for off-season hours. Closed mid-Oct to May.

Cinco Restaurant and Bar ★ TAPAS   This exquisite restaurant specializes in *tapas*, those popular little Spanish-style plates of food. This is not the place to come with a big appetite, but it's a great spot for a light meal and lively atmosphere. About two dozen tapas are on the menu; three or four per person would make a small meal, but you'll want to pass them around and share. The preparations and flavors are unusual and sophisticated. There are cured meats, marinated vegetables, grilled fish, and other delicacies, like cornmeal-crusted soft-shell crab and Nantucket fluke ceviche.

5 Amelia Dr. (¼ mile from the rotary, just off South Rd.). ✆ 508/325-5151. Reservations recommended. Tapas $5–$20; main courses $24–$31. AE, MC, V. Mid-June to Sept daily 6–10:30pm; call for off-season hours. Closed Jan–Mar.

Company of the Cauldron ★★★ CONTINENTAL   This is one of the island's most romantic restaurants, run by one of the island's most creative chefs, Al Kovalencik. What is unusual here is the chef offers one distinctive three- to four-course fixed-price meal each night, so check the menu out front or by telephone before booking. In the candlelit dining room, classic American and Continental influences predominate; don't miss the soft-shell crab appetizer when it's offered. The main course could be a special swordfish preparation, rack of lamb, or beef Wellington. For dessert, there's always something exceptional, like a chocolate soufflé cake. Because the fixed price includes three courses—an appetizer, main course, and dessert—and large portions, this restaurant is actually a fine-dining bargain on Nantucket. Several nights a week in season, a harpist serenades diners.

5 India St. (between Federal and Centre sts.). ✆ 508/228-4016. www.companyofthecauldron.com. Reservations required. Fixed-price dinner $55. MC, V. Early July to early Sept Tues–Sun 2 seatings 6:45 and 8:45pm, Mon 7pm seating only; call for off-season hours. Closed mid-Oct to mid-Apr, except Thanksgiving weekend and the first 2 weeks of Dec.

Fifty-Six Union ★★ NEW AMERICAN   This understated restaurant offers fine dining without pretensions: just good service, a pleasing contemporary atmosphere, and wonderful food. Diners can sit in the bar area, which tends to be loud and lively, or the quieter Garden Room or outdoor patio. Intriguing appetizers include a salad with prosciutto and grilled fig, and a crabmeat spring roll with a pepper *coulis*. Main-course choices could include anything from Javanese fried rice to risotto with wild mushrooms to a rack of Colorado lamb.

56 Union St. (½ mile from Main St.). ✆ 508/228-6135. www.fiftysixunion.com. Reservations suggested. Main courses $23–$32. AE, MC, V. Early July to early Sept daily 5:30–10pm; call for off-season hours. Open year-round.

Le Languedoc Bistro ★★ NEW AMERICAN/FRENCH   This is Nantucket's most authentic French cafe. The atmosphere in this historic building is wonderful and the prices are reasonable. There's also an expensive dining room upstairs, but locals prefer the casual bistro atmosphere downstairs and out on the terrace. There's a clubby feel here as diners come and go, greeting each other and enjoying themselves. Soups are superb, as are the Angus-steak burgers—which some call the best burgers in the world—with garlic french fries. More elaborate dishes include the roasted tenderloin of pork stuffed with figs and pancetta; *berlotti* bean stew; and the napoleon of grilled tuna, tapenade, and roasted vegetables with pesto sauce. Save room for classic French desserts, like chocolate *pot du crème* and crème brûlée.

24 Broad St. ✆ 508/228-2552. www.lelanguedoc.com. Reservations not accepted for cafe; reservations recommended for dining room. Main courses $24–$44 (half portions $15-$22). AE, MC, V. June–Sept Tues–Sun 5:30–9:30pm; call for off-season hours. Closed mid-Dec to mid-May.

Òran Mór ★★★ Finds INTERNATIONAL   This second-floor waterfront venue is one of the premier restaurants on the island. The menu changes nightly, and there are always surprising and unusual choices. Appetizer standouts are the Jonah crab and hearts of palm; and the braised rabbit ravioli with truffle butter sauce. Hearty entrees include grilled Wolf Neck Farm steak with cottage potatoes; and sautéed fluke with soft polenta. An excellent sommelier is on hand to assist wine lovers.

2 S. Beach St. (in the center of town). ✆ 508/228-8655. Reservations recommended. Main courses $22–$34. AE, MC, V. June to mid-Oct daily 6–9:30pm; mid-Oct to mid-Dec and mid-Apr to May Thurs–Tues 6–9pm. Closed mid-Dec to mid-Apr.

Ropewalk ★ SEAFOOD   This open-air restaurant on the harbor is Nantucket's only outdoor raw bar, and it's where the yachting crowd hangs out after a day on the boat. While the food is a bit overpriced, the location is prime. The raw bar, serving littlenecks, oysters, and shrimp, is open daily from 3 to 10pm in high season and it attracts a crowd. This is a good place to enjoy a light meal or appetizers, such as fried calamari, crab cakes, or fried oysters. The dinner menu includes grilled swordfish with ratatouille and grilled breast of chicken with roasted garlic and rosemary *jus*.

1 Straight Wharf. ✆ 508/228-8886. Reservations not accepted. Main courses $23–$33. AE, MC, V. May to mid-Oct daily 11am–10pm. Closed mid-Oct to Apr.

29 Fair ★★ FRENCH BISTRO   One of the island's most historic restaurant venues, the 1702 building's atmosphere, with its low-beamed ceilings and wide pine floors, transports you to the era of the whaling captains. The small dining rooms are decorated with antique tables, Oriental rugs, and bone china. There are innovative offerings like a slowly cooked crispy salmon filet with lavender honey glaze, and specialties like French onion soup and beef Wellington.

29 Fair St. ✆ 508/228-7800. Main courses $22–$32. AE, MC, V. Late Mar to early Jan Tues–Sun 6:30–9pm. Closed early Jan to late Mar.

MODERATE

Black Eyed Susan's ★★ Finds ETHNIC ECLECTIC   This is supremely exciting food in a funky bistro atmosphere. The place is small, popular with locals, and packed. Reservations are accepted for the 6pm seating only, and they go fast. Others must line up outside the restaurant (the line starts forming around 5:30pm), and the hostess will assign you a time to dine. If you don't mind sitting at the counter, you'll have a better choice. Inside, it may seem a bit too cozy, but that's all part of the charm. I always enjoy the spicy Thai fish cake when that is on the menu, and also the tandoori chicken with green mango chutney. There's usually a Southwestern touch like the Dos Equis beer-battered catfish quesadilla with mango slaw, hoppin' johns, and jalapeño. You'll mop up the sauce with the delectable organic sourdough bread. There's no liquor license, but you can BYOB. The corking fee is $1 per person.

10 India St. (in the center of town). ✆ **508/325-0308.** Reservations accepted for 6pm seating only. Main courses $12–$25. No credit cards. Apr–Oct daily 7am–1pm, Mon–Sat 6–10pm. Closed Nov–Mar.

Cap'n Tobey's Chowder House ★ SEAFOOD

This convenient eatery close to the harbor specializes in seafood obtained daily from local fishermen. Diners can choose between halibut, yellowfin tuna, Atlantic sea scallops, swordfish, and salmon, and have it grilled, baked, or blackened. Lobster is always on the menu. The raw bar features oysters, littlenecks, and shrimp. There is also a less expensive fried-fish menu, a good choice for families. Upstairs, called Off Shore at Cap'n Tobey's, there's live music in season.

20 Straight Wharf. ✆ **508/228-0836.** Reservations accepted. Main courses $17–$27. AE, DC, DISC, MC, V. Late June to Sept daily 11am–10pm; call for off-season hours. Closed Jan–Apr.

Centre Street Bistro ★★★ NEW AMERICAN

This tiny fine-dining restaurant in the center of Nantucket town is owned and operated by Ruth and Tim Pitts, who are considered top chefs on the island. The dining room has only about eight tables and a few bar seats, though in the summer there is extra seating on the front patio. This cozy place features wonderful, creative cuisine at reasonable prices, especially compared to other island fine-dining restaurants. The menu is in constant flux, but high points have included the warm goat-cheese tart to start, and the Long Island duck breast with pumpkin and butternut-squash risotto as a main course. If the sautéed Nantucket Bay scallops are on the menu, you won't want to miss whatever clever preparations the Pitts have dreamed up. One dish featured these world-famous local scallops with wontons and a citrus-soy-and-spice glaze.

29 Centre St. ✆ **508/228-8470.** www.nantucketbistro.com. Reservations not accepted. Main courses $19–$25. No credit cards. Mon and Wed–Fri 11:30am–2pm and 6–9:30pm; Sat–Sun 8am–1pm and 6–9pm; call for off-season hours. Open year-round.

LoLa 41 ★ GLOBAL BISTRO

Sushi is the highlight at Lola's, one of Nantucket's newest restaurants and a place to see and be seen. This is a fun place, with attitude, dominated by a bar that pours colorful and uncommon specialty concoctions at $10 to $12 a pop. The theme is "neoglobal" cuisine: pasta and *osso bucco* from Italy, bacalao (salt cod with polenta and caviar) from Barcelona, and Asian-inspired green and black tea-glazed chicken breast with Buddha's rice. There are even fried clams and calamari—both very good—on the appetizer list. But most people are here for the impressive sushi bar, where you can gorge on *nigiri* and sashimi to your heart's content. The only thing that might give you pause are the prices; sushi rolls are $15 to $17 apiece.

15 South Beach St. ✆ **508/325-4001.** Reservations accepted for same-day seating. Main courses $18–$30. AE, MC, V. June–Sept daily 5:30–11pm; call for off-season hours. Closed Jan–Apr.

Nantucket Lobster Trap SEAFOOD

When only a bowl of chowder and a giant lobster roll will do, bring the whole family to this quintessential clam shack where the big game is usually on the TV behind the bar. Seating is on large picnic tables, and lobsters come straight from local waters. The mussels and clams served here are also from local waters, as are the world-renowned Nantucket bay scallops. The prices are kept relatively affordable. There's also a kids' menu.

Queequeg's ★★ NEW AMERICAN A cozy bistro atmosphere and good value are the hallmarks of this small restaurant, which is tucked along a side street behind the Atheneum. Outside seating is available in good weather. As befits the Moby Dick reference in the name, the specialty here is seafood. The menu offers a range from basics to fancier fare. For example, as an appetizer, you could have the New England clam chowder or tuna tartare. The rich and flavorful pan-seared halibut with Parmesan risotto is a favorite with locals. Meat-lovers may enjoy chargrilled New Zealand lamb or New York strip sirloin. Vegetarians also have options.

6 Oak St. ℂ **508/325-0992.** Reservations recommended. Main courses $18–$25. MC, V. June–Sept daily 6–9:30pm; call for off-season hours. Closed late Nov to late Apr.

Schooner's at Steamboat Wharf AMERICAN This casual family-friendly restaurant near the Steamship Authority dock is noteworthy for the outdoor dining on the screened-in porch. Diners who sit on the second floor have views of the harbor. Prices are reasonable and portions are generous in this casual pub. The most popular dishes are the fajitas, fried clams, fish and chips, and the lobster salad. There is a lively late-night bar scene here with live acoustic music some nights in season.

31 Easy St. ℂ **508/228-5824.** Reservations accepted. Main courses $18–$24. AE, MC, V. Apr–Dec daily 11am–10pm. Closed Jan–Mar.

Trattoria Sfoglia ★★★ NORTHERN ITALIAN This rustic Italian eatery ranks near the top of many people's "my favorite" lists for Nantucket. Quirky and homespun, its style runs to mismatched glasses and fresh flowers in mason jars. The menu combinations are unusual in a familiar way—how about an antipasto of clams, salami, tomato, and fennel? There is a corn risotto with lobster and zucchini, and a roasted sausage accompanied by a plateful of *contorni* (tasty preparations of farm-fresh vegetables). Light eaters can ask for a half-order of pasta, which is enough to satisfy the average appetite. The kitchen turns out home-baked bread that some call the island's best, as well as desserts such as a fruit tart. They also make their own gelato. The only catch is that the restaurant is not in the center of town; you have to take a taxi.

130 Pleasant St. (across from the Stop and Shop). ℂ **508/325-4500.** Reservations accepted. Main courses $16–$26. No credit cards. Apr to mid-Oct Mon–Sat 6–10pm; call for off-season hours. Open year-round.

INEXPENSIVE

Arno's (Kids) ECLECTIC A storefront facing the passing parade of Main Street, this casual restaurant packs surprising style between its bare-brick walls. It also has a wine bar, offering close to 30 vintages by the glass and an extensive appetizer menu. The internationally influenced menu yields tasty, bountiful platters for breakfast, lunch, and dinner. Specialties include grilled sirloin steaks and fresh grilled fish. Generous servings of specialty pasta dishes like shrimp and scallop scampi Florentine are featured nightly. The central location and relatively low prices make this a good choice for families.

41 Main St. ℂ **508/228-7001.** Reservations recommended. Main courses $9–$17. AE, DC, DISC, MC, V. Apr–Dec daily 8am–10pm. Closed Jan–Mar.

The Brotherhood of Thieves ★ PUB This classic whaling bar housed in an early-19th-century brick building in the center of town is a Nantucket institution, though a recent renovation after a fire removed a lot of its former charm. In July and August, tourists line up for a table in the dark tavern downstairs to chow on burgers and hand-cut curly fries. An elaborate renovation added an upstairs dining room; there is also seating outside on a raised terrace. In the fall and winter, locals sit beside the cozy brick hearth to enjoy decently priced dinner offerings like chicken teriyaki and fried Cajun shrimp. This place serves food later than anywhere else in town; you can order off the late-night menu 'til midnight.

23 Broad St. ✆ **508/228-2551.** Reservations not accepted. Main courses $9–$18. No credit cards. Mar–Jan Mon–Sat 11:30am–midnight, Sun noon–10pm. Closed Feb.

The Even Keel Café AMERICAN   This low-key cafe in the heart of town serves breakfast, lunch, and dinner both indoors and outside on the patio in the back. You'll find reasonable prices and nonexotic fare here, like burgers and sandwiches. There are always vegetarian choices as well as meat and fish dishes, everything from a cheeseburger to grilled salmon to veal *osso buco*. There's also a kids' menu, as well as high-speed Internet access. This place has lots of off-season dining deals, like half-price weekday breakfasts and two-for-one dinners. On Sundays, they serve a hearty brunch. There is no alcohol for sale here but you can BYOB.

40 Main St. ✆ **508/228-1979.** Reservations not accepted. Main courses $10–$25. AE, MC, V. July–Aug daily 7am–9:30pm; call for off-season hours. Open year-round.

Fog Island Cafe ★ NEW AMERICAN   You'll be wowed by the creative breakfasts and lunches at this sassy cafe; they're reasonably priced, with super-fresh ingredients. Homemade soups and salads are healthy and delicious.

7 S. Water St. ✆ **508/228-1818.** Reservations not accepted. All items under $15. MC, V. July–Aug Mon–Sat 7am–2pm, Sun 7am–1pm; call for off-season hours. Open year-round.

Starlight Theatre and Cafe ★ (Finds) (Kids) AMERICAN   This small cafe/movie theater is a convenient place to come either with kids or on a dinner date for a quick bite before or after a film. It's simple fare like salads, sandwiches, and burgers. For something a little different, try the lobster macaroni and cheese.

1 N. Union St. ✆ **508/228-4479.** Reservations not accepted. All items under $15. AE, MC, V. July–Aug Mon–Thurs 11:30am–9pm, Fri–Sat 11:30am–11pm, Sun 9am–9pm; call for off-season hours. Open year-round.

TAKEOUT & PICNIC FARE

Broad Street, located just steps from Steamboat Wharf, is the place to go for cheap takeout eats any time. Good choices are **Walters Deli** (10 Broad St., ✆ **508/228-0010**) for sandwiches and **Stubby's** (8 Broad St., ✆ **508/228-0028**) for burgers.

Bartlett's Farm ★★   You can get fresh-picked produce (in season, the tomatoes are incomparable) right in town from Bartlett's traveling market, or head out to this seventh-generation farm where, in June, you might get to pick your own strawberries. They also sell sandwiches, quiches, pastries, pies, and more. Nearby are Cisco Brewery and East Coast Seafood, to round out your picnic purchases.

33 Bartlett Farm Rd. ✆ **508/228-9403.** www.bartlettsfarm.com. Apr–Dec daily 7:30am–7pm. Truck parked on Main St. in season.

Something Natural ★★   A local institution and a terrific value, Something Natural turns out gigantic sandwiches, with fresh ingredients piled atop fabulous bread. Plan on sharing, so you'll have room for their addictive chocolate-chip cookies. It's a great place to stock up for a day at the beach, or you can eat your lunch at picnic tables on the grounds. This sandwich shop is a bit too far from town to walk to, unless you're in the mood for a hike. It's a great stop on a bike ride, though.

50 Cliff Rd. ✆ **508/228-0504.** Apr to mid-Oct daily 8am–6:30pm. Closed mid-Oct to Mar.

Sushi by Yoshi ★★ This tiny place is Nantucket's best source of great sushi. The incredibly fresh local fish is artfully presented by chef Yoshihisa Mabuchi, who also dishes up such healthy, affordable staples as miso or *udon* (noodle) soup. This is a busy place; in season, allow an hour for takeout.

2 E. Chestnut St. ✆ **508/228-1801.** May to mid-Oct Sun–Thurs 11:30am–10pm, Fri–Sat 11:30am–10:30pm; mid-Oct to Apr Thurs–Sat 11:30am–9pm, Sun–Wed 5–9pm.

SWEETS

The Juice Bar ★★ This humble hole-in-the-wall scoops up some of the best home-made ice cream and frozen yogurt around, complemented by superb homemade hot fudge. Waffle cones are homemade, too. And, yes, you can also get juice—from refreshing lime rickeys to healthful carrot cocktails.

12 Broad St. ✆ **508/228-5799.** June–Aug Sun–Thurs 10am–11:30pm, Fri–Sat 10am–2am; mid-Apr to May and Sept to mid-Oct 11am–9pm daily. Closed mid-Oct to mid-Apr.

---

9 NANTUCKET AFTER DARK

Nantucket usually has an attractive crowd of barhoppers making the scene around town. The best part is, everything is within walking distance, so you don't have to worry about driving back to your inn. You'll find good singles scenes at the **Boarding House** and the **Club Car,** which are reviewed above as restaurants, or **Slip 14 on South Wharf** (✆ **508/228-2033**). Live music comes in many guises on Nantucket, and there are a number of good itinerant performers who play at different venues. Meanwhile, it may be Reggae Night at **The Chicken Box,** when the median age of this rocking venue rises by a decade or two. For a fun, not-too-fancy bar in town, try **Rose and Crown.**

MOVIES

Nantucket has one first-run movie theater: **Starlight Theatre & Cafe,** 1 N. Union St. (✆ **508/228-4435**). The **Siasconset Casino,** 10 New St., Siasconset (✆ **508/257-6661**), shows films Tuesday, Thursday, and Sunday in season for $5.

NANTUCKET LITERATI

Nantucket Atheneum Continuing a 160-year tradition, the Nantucket Atheneum offers readings and lectures for general edification year-round, with such local literati as Frank Conroy, and Nathaniel Philbrick filling in for the likes of Henry David Thoreau and Herman Melville. The summer events are often followed by a charming garden reception. The library is open Monday through Saturday from 9:30am to 5pm, until 8pm on Tuesday and Thursday. Call for an event schedule. Lower India St. ✆ **508/228-1110.** www.nantucketatheneum.org. Free admission.

Martha's Vineyard

New England sea captains' houses, white picket fences, and ice-cream shops trim an authentic fishing village. Lighthouses pierce the fog with their signals. A Native American community preserves its identity amid miles of pristine beaches and rolling farmland. Martha's Vineyard is a picturesque island indeed.

Visit the Vineyard to bicycle the shaded paths that hug the coastline. Admire the regal mariners' homes in Edgartown and stop by the Edgartown Scrimshaw Gallery for a memento of the sea. Stroll down Circuit Avenue in Oak Bluffs with a Mad Martha's ice-cream cone and then ride the Flying Horses Carousel, said to be the oldest working carousel in the country. Don't miss the cheerful "gingerbread" cottages behind Circuit Avenue, where you can almost hear the echoes of 19th-century revival meetings in the imposing Tabernacle. Travel the country roads of West Tisbury and Chilmark, stopping at Allen Farm for sweaters made from the wool of their flock of over 200 sheep. Buy bread at the Scottish Bakehouse in North Tisbury and a lobster roll in the fishing village of Menemsha.

Unlike much of New England, Martha's Vineyard has long been a melting pot. In the tiny town of Aquinnah, the Wampanoag tribe is the only Native American tribe in the region to have official status in Washington, D.C. Once known as Gay Head, the red-clay cliffs of Aquinnah are a National Historic Landmark. The Wampanoags, 12th-generation Vineyarders, farm the land in Chilmark, and at Cronig's Market they rub shoulders with posh Yankees from Edgartown.

In the late 19th century, the religious retreat community of Oak Bluffs was one of the first vacation spots for African Americans of means. Today this community includes such notables as film director Spike Lee and Washington power broker Vernon Jordan.

Unfortunately, Martha's Vineyard has been discovered, in a big way. When the former First Family, the Clintons, chose to vacation on the island several years in a row, it only increased the worldwide fascination with this popular place. In fact, the island is loaded with luminaries, but you are unlikely to see them, as they prefer private house parties. But don't come to this island on a star search: It's considered impolite to gawk and, like jaded New Yorkers, Vineyarders barely seem to notice the VIPs in their midst. Year-round locals and seasonal celebrity residents coexist in an almost effortless comfort, united in their protective attitude toward the island, their disapproval of traffic, and their criticism of the Steamship Authority.

There's always a lot of "hurry up and wait" involved in ferry travel to and from the Vineyard, so a weekend may not be enough time for a visit. If you're traveling from New York, take an extra day off, allowing a minimum of 3 days for this trip. Four days will feel more comfortable. One great way to shorten the journey from New York is to take the ferry from Rhode Island or New Bedford and avoid Cape traffic.

From Boston, a couple of days are fine (the drive from Boston to Woods Hole takes $1^{1}/_{2}$ hr. with no traffic), but beware of summer weekend bottlenecks (never aim for the last ferry). You really don't need to bring a car to get around this small island, but if you absolutely must be accompanied by four wheels, you'll need a car reservation for the ferry (see "Getting There," below, for details).

(Fun Facts   Going Native on Martha's Vineyard

Down-island: If you must buy a Black Dog T-shirt, wait until you get home to wear it. Don't loiter at the Charlotte Inn. Have cocktails on the porch of the Harbor View Hotel. In Oak Bluffs, don't ask when Illumination Night is. (It's a secret.) Experience Edgartown on a snowy winter weekend or in spring when the lilacs are in bloom. Up-island: When in doubt, don't wear shoes. Sail a boat to a remote beach for a picnic. Don't view the rolling farmlands from a tour bus. By all means, bike. Kayak. Rent a cottage for a week or two. Don't be a day-tripper.

Try to savor the 45-minute ferry ride to and from this pastoral place. The Vineyard's pace is decidedly laid-back—try to blend in with the ultracool attitude. The six towns on Martha's Vineyard have distinct identities, but they are either "down-island," referring to Vineyard Haven (officially called Tisbury), Edgartown, and Oak Bluffs; or "up-island," the towns of West Tisbury, Chilmark, and Aquinnah (formerly Gay Head).

If you can survive the hassles of getting to Martha's Vineyard, and can cope with the crowds and traffic once you arrive, you may just have the perfect vacation. Better yet, visit the island off season, in May or October, when the weather is often mild and the crowds have cleared out.

1 ESSENTIALS

GETTING THERE

BY FERRY   Most visitors take the ferry service connecting the Vineyard and the mainland. If you're traveling via car or bus, you will most likely catch the ferry from Woods Hole in the town of Falmouth on Cape Cod; however, boats do run from Falmouth Inner Harbor, Hyannis, New Bedford, Rhode Island, and Nantucket. On weekends in season, the Steamship Authority ferries make over 25 trips a day to Martha's Vineyard from Woods Hole (2 other companies provide an additional 12 passenger ferries a day from Falmouth Inner Harbor). Schedules are available from the **Martha's Vineyard Chamber of Commerce** (© **508/693-0085;** fax 508/693-7589; www.mvy.com) or the Steamship Authority (see below).

The state-run **Steamship Authority** (www.steamshipauthority.com) runs the show in Woods Hole (© **508/477-8600** early Apr to early Sept daily 8am–5pm; or 508/693-9130 daily 8am–5pm) and operates every day, year-round (weather permitting). It maintains the only ferries to Martha's Vineyard that accommodate cars, in addition to passengers, and makes about 20 crossings a day in season. The large ferries make the 45-minute trip to Vineyard Haven throughout the year; some boats go to Oak Bluffs from late May to late October (call for seasonal schedules). During the summer, you'll need a reservation to bring your car to the island, and you must reserve *months in advance* to secure a spot. If you plan to bring your car over to the island, plan to get to the Woods Hole terminal at least 30 minutes before your scheduled departure.

Reservations-Only Policy for Car Passage to Martha's Vineyard

Vehicle reservations are required to bring your car to Martha's Vineyard Friday through Monday from mid-June to mid-September. During these times, standby is in effect only on Tuesday through Thursday. Vehicle reservations are also required to bring your car to Martha's Vineyard on Memorial Day weekend. Technically, vehicle reservations can be made up to 1 hour in advance of ferry departure, but ferries in season are almost always filled with cars, and you cannot depend on a cancellation during the summer months. Also be aware that your space may be forfeited if you have not checked into the ferry terminal 30 minutes prior to sailing time. Reservations may be changed to another date and time with at least 24 hours' notice; otherwise, you will have to pay for an additional ticket for your vehicle.

If you arrive without a reservation on a day that allows standby in the summer, come early and be prepared to wait in the standby line for hours. The Steamship Authority guarantees your passage if you're in line by 2pm on designated standby days only. For up-to-date **Steamship Authority** information, check out its website (www.steamshipauthority.com).

Many people prefer to leave their cars on the mainland, take the ferry (often with their bikes), and then rent a car, jeep, or bicycle on the island. You can park your car at the Woods Hole lot (always full in the summer) or at one of the many lots in Falmouth and Bourne that absorb the overflow of cars during the summer months; parking is $10 to $12 per day. Plan to arrive at the parking lots in Falmouth at least an hour before sailing time to allow for parking, taking the free shuttle bus to the ferry terminal, and buying your ferry ticket. Free shuttle buses (some equipped for bikes) run regularly from the outlying lots to the Woods Hole ferry terminal.

The cost of a round-trip passenger ticket on the ferry to Martha's Vineyard is $15 for adults and $8 for children 5 to 12. (Kids 4 and under ride free.) If you bring your bike along, it's an extra $6 round-trip, year-round. You do not need a reservation on the ferry if you're traveling without a car, and no reservations are needed for parking. The cost of a round-trip car passage from April through October is $135 to $155; in the off season it drops to $85 to $105. Car rates do not include drivers or passengers; you must buy tickets for each person going to the island.

Note: The Steamship Authority now charges different rates for different length cars. You will need to specify the make and model of your car when you place your reservation.

Once you are aboard the ferry, you have won the right to feel relieved and relaxed. Now your vacation can begin. Ferries are equipped with bathrooms and snack bars. Your fellow passengers will be a gaggle of kids, dogs, and happy-looking travelers.

From Falmouth, you can board the ***Island Queen*** at Falmouth Inner Harbor (© **508/548-4800;** www.islandqueen.com) for a 35-minute cruise to Oak Bluffs (passengers only). The boat runs from late May to mid-October; round-trip fare is $18 for adults, $9 for children under 12 and under, and an extra $6 for bikes. There are seven

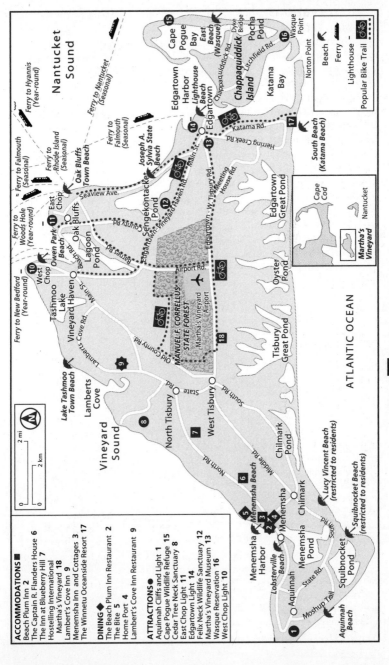

ACCOMMODATIONS ■
Beach Plum Inn 2
The Captain R. Flanders House 6
The Inn at Blueberry Hill 7
Hostelling International
    Martha's Vineyard 18
Lambert's Cove Inn 9
Menemsha Inn and Cottages 3
The Winnetu Oceanside Resort 17

DINING ◆
The Beach Plum Inn Restaurant 2
The Bite 5
Home Port 4
Lambert's Cove Inn Restaurant 9

ATTRACTIONS ●
Aquinnah Cliffs and Light 1
Cape Pogue Wildlife Refuge 15
Cedar Tree Neck Sanctuary 8
East Chop Light 11
Edgartown Light 14
Felix Neck Wildlife Sanctuary 12
Martha's Vineyard Museum 13
Wasque Reservation 16
West Chop Light 10

Beach
Ferry
Lighthouse
Popular Bike Trail

Nantucket
Sound

Cape
Pogue
Bay

East
Beach
(Wasque)

Dyke
Bridge

Pocha
Pond

Wasque
Point

Chappaquiddick
Island

Katama
Bay

Edgartown
Harbor

Edgartown
Lighthouse
Beach

Edgartown

Norton Point

South Beach
(Katama Beach)

Edgartown
Great Pond

Cape
Cod

Nantucket

Martha's
Vineyard

Ferry to Nantucket
(Year-round)

Ferry to Hyannis
(Year-round)

Ferry to Nantucket
(Seasonal)

Ferry to
Falmouth
(Seasonal)

Ferry to
Rhode Island
(Seasonal)

Ferry to Falmouth
(Seasonal)

Ferry to
Woods Hole
(Year-round)

Ferry to New Bedford
(Year-round)

Joseph A.
Sylvia State
Beach

Oak Bluffs
Town Beach

Seaview Ave.

East
Chop

Owen Park
Beach

West
Chop

Oak Bluffs

Lagoon
Pond

Tashmoo
Lake

Vineyard Haven

Sengekontacket
Pond

County Rd.

Main St.

Edgartown-Vineyard Haven Rd.

Katama Rd.

Herring Creek Rd.

Edgartown-W. Tisbury Rd.

Meeting House Rd.

Airport Rd.

Martha's Vineyard
Airport

Oyster
Pond

MANUEL F.
CORREILUS
STATE FOREST

Lambert's Cove Rd.

Old County Rd.

State Rd.

North Tisbury

West Tisbury

South Rd.

North Rd.

Middle Rd.

Chilmark
Pond

Tisbury
Great Pond

Edgartown-W. Tisbury Rd.

Lake Tashmoo
Town Beach

Lamberts
Cove

Vineyard
Sound

Menemsha
Beach

Menemsha

Chilmark

Lucy Vincent Beach
(restricted to residents)

Squibnocket Beach
(restricted to residents)

Menemsha
Harbor

Lobsterville
Beach

Aquinnah

Menemsha
Pond

Squibnocket
Pond

State Rd.

South Rd.

Moshup Trail

Aquinnah
Beach

ATLANTIC OCEAN

2 mi

2 km

crossings a day in season (8 on Fri and Sun), and no reservations are needed. Parking will run you $15 a day. Credit cards are not accepted.

The **Falmouth–Edgartown Ferry Service,** 278 Scranton Ave. (© **508/548-9400;** www.falmouthferry.com), operates a 1-hour passenger ferry, called the *Pied Piper,* from Falmouth Harbor to Edgartown. The boat runs from late May to mid-October, and reservations are required. In season, there are five crossings a day (6 on Fri). Round-trip fares are $50 for adults and $30 for children 6 to 12. Bicycles are $10 round-trip. Parking is $25 per day.

From Hyannis, you can take the **Hy-Line,** Ocean Street Dock (© **508/778-2600;** www.hy-linecruises.com), to Oak Bluffs, early June through late September. They run three trips a day, and trip time is about 1 hour and 45 minutes; round-trip costs $32 for adults and $17 for children 5 to 12 ($10 extra for bikes).

Hy-Line also operates a year-round **fast ferry** from Hyannis to Martha's Vineyard. It departs five times daily in season and takes 55 minutes. Round-trip tickets cost $69 for adults, $45 for children.

From Nantucket, Hy-Line runs three passenger-only ferries to Oak Bluffs on Martha's Vineyard from early June to mid-September (there is no car-ferry service between the islands). The trip time is 2 hours and 15 minutes. The round-trip fare is $33 for adults, $17 for children 5 to 12, and $5 extra for bikes.

From New Bedford, Massachusetts, the fast ferry MV *Whaling City Express* travels to Martha's Vineyard in 1 hour. It makes six trips a day in season and is in service year-round, 7 days a week. A ticket costs $36 one-way and $72 round-trip for adults, $32 one-way and $64 round-trip for seniors; and $21 one-way and $42 round-trip for children 12 and under. Contact **New England Fast Ferry** for details (© **866/453-6800;** www.nefastferry.com).

Tip: Traveling to Martha's Vineyard from New Bedford is a great way to avoid Cape traffic and enjoy a scenic ocean cruise.

From **North Kingstown, Rhode Island,** to Oak Bluffs, Vineyard Fast Ferry runs its high-speed catamaran, *Millennium,* two to three round-trips daily from mid-June through October. The trip takes 90 minutes. The ferry leaves from Quonset Point, about 10 minutes from Route I-95, 15 minutes from T.F. Green Airport in Providence, and 20 minutes from the Amtrak station in Kingston. There is dockside parking. Rates are $52 one-way, $75 round-trip for adults; $47 one-way, $52 round-trip for children 4 to 12; and $12 round-trip for bikes. Parking next to the ferry port is $10 per day. Reservations can be made by calling © **401/295-4040** or by visiting www.vineyardfastferry.com.

BY AIR You can fly into **Martha's Vineyard Airport,** also known as Dukes County Airport (© **508/693-7022**), in West Tisbury, about 5 miles outside Edgartown.

Airlines serving the Vineyard include **Cape Air/Nantucket Airlines** (© **800/352-0714** or 508/771-6944; www.flycapeair.com), which connects the island year-round with Boston (trip time 34 min., hourly shuttle service in summer about $240 round-trip); Hyannis (trip time 20 min., cost $109); Nantucket (15 min., $95); Providence, Rhode Island (25 min., $173); and New Bedford (20 min., $100); and **US Airways** (© **800/428-4322;** www.usairways.com), which flies from Boston for about $215 round-trip and also has seasonal weekend service from LaGuardia (trip time $1^1/_4$ hr.), which costs approximately $400 round-trip.

The only company offering year-round charter service is **Direct Flight** (© **508/693-6688;** flydirect@vineyard.net).

BY BUS **Peter Pan Bus Lines** (© 888/751-8800 or 508/548-7588; www.peterpan
bus.com) connects the Woods Hole ferry port with South Station and Logan Airport in
Boston, as well as with New York City and Providence, Rhode Island. The trip from
South Station takes about 1 hour and 35 minutes and costs about $26 one-way, $50
round-trip; from Boston's Logan Airport, the cost is $27 one-way, $47 round-trip; from
Providence, the 2½-hr trip to Woods Hole costs $29 one-way or $56 round-trip; from
New York, the bus trip to Woods Hole takes about 6 hours and costs approximately $73
one-way or $121 round-trip.

BY LIMO **King's Coach** (© 800/235-5669 or 508/563-5669) will pick you up at
Boston's Logan Airport and take you to meet your ferry in Woods Hole (or anywhere else
in the Upper Cape area). The trip takes about 90 minutes depending on traffic and costs
about $135 to $165 one-way plus a gratuity for a carload or a vanload of people. You'll
need to book the service a few days in advance. **Falmouth Taxi** (© 508/548-3100) also
runs limo service from Boston and the airport. It charges $185 plus gratuity.

GETTING AROUND

The down-island towns of Vineyard Haven, Oak Bluffs, and Edgartown are fairly compact, and if your inn is located in the heart of one of these small towns, you will be within
walking distance of shopping, beaches, and attractions in town. Frequent shuttle buses
can whisk you to the other down-island towns and beaches in 5 to 15 minutes. To
explore the up-island towns, you will need to bike; it's possible to tour the entire island—
60-some odd miles—in 1 day. In season, you can also take the shuttle bus up-island.
Otherwise, you will have to take a cab.

BY BICYCLE & MOPED You shouldn't leave without exploring the Vineyard on two
wheels, even if only for a couple of hours. There's a little of everything for cyclists, from
paved paths to hilly country roads (see "Beaches & Recreational Pursuits," below, for
details on where to ride), and you don't have to be an expert rider to enjoy yourself. Plus,
biking is a relatively hassle-free way to get around the island.

Mopeds are also a way to navigate Vineyard roads, but the number of accidents involving mopeds seems to rise every year, and many islanders are opposed to these vehicles. If
you rent one, be aware they are considered quite dangerous on the island's busy, narrow,
winding and sandy roads. Moped renting is banned in Edgartown.

Bike-rental shops are clustered throughout all three down-island towns. Mopeds and
scooters can be rented in Oak Bluffs and Vineyard Haven only and you will need a
driver's license. Bike rentals cost about $18 to $25 a day, mopeds cost $90 a day. For bike
rentals in Vineyard Haven, try **Martha's Bikes,** at Five Corners (© 508/693-0782), or
Martha's Bike Rentals, Lagoon Pond Road (© 508/693-6593). For mopeds, try
Adventure Rentals, Beach Road (© 508/693-1959). In Oak Bluffs, there's **Anderson's,**
Circuit Avenue Extension (© 508/693-9346), which rents bikes only; and **Sun 'n' Fun,**
Lake Avenue (© 508/693-5457), which also rents mopeds. In Edgartown, you'll find
bike rentals only at **R. W. Cutler Bike,** 1 Main St. (© 508/627-4052); and **Wheel
Happy,** 204 Upper Main St. and 8 S. Water St. (© 508/627-5928).

BY CAR If you're coming to the Vineyard for a few days and you're going to stick to
the down-island towns, it's best to leave your car at home, since traffic and parking on
the island can be brutal in summer. Also, it's easy to take the shuttle buses (see below)
from town to town, or you can simply bike your way around. If you're staying for a
longer period of time or you want to do some exploring up-island, you should bring your

car or rent one on the island—my favorite way to tour the Vineyard is by jeep. Keep in mind that car-rental rates can soar during peak season, and gas is much more expensive on the island. Off-road driving on the beaches is a major topic of debate on the Vineyard, and the most popular spots may be closed for nesting Piping Plovers at the height of the season. If you plan to do some off-road exploration, check with the chamber of commerce to see if the trails are open to vehicles before you rent. To drive off-road at Cape Pogue or Cape Wasque on Chappaquiddick, you'll need to purchase a permit from the **Trustees of Reservations** (© 508/627-7260); the cost is $190 for the car and $3 per person. Keep in mind, if you drive a rental car off-road without permission from the rental company, you could be subjected to a $500 fine.

There are representatives of the national car-rental chains at the airport and in Vineyard Haven and Oak Bluffs. Local agencies also operate out of all three port towns, and many of them also rent jeeps, mopeds, and bikes. The national chains include **Budget** (© 800/527-0700 or 508/693-1911), **Hertz** (© 800/654-3131), and **Thrifty** (© 800/874-4389).

In Vineyard Haven, you'll find **Adventure Rentals,** Beach Road (© 508/693-1959), where a jeep will run you about $160 per day in season and a regular car costs about $79 to $109 per day. In Edgartown, try **AAA Island Rentals,** 141 Main St. (© 508/627-6800; also at Five Corners in Vineyard Haven, © 508/696-5300).

BY SHUTTLE BUS & TROLLEY In season, shuttle buses run often enough to make them a practical means of getting around. They are also cheap, dependable, and easy.

The **Martha's Vineyard Regional Transit Authority** (© 508/693-9440; www.vineyardtransit.com) operates shuttle buses year-round on about a dozen routes around the island. The buses, which are white with purple logos, cost about $2 to $5 depending on distance. The formula is $1 per town. For example, Vineyard Haven to Oak Bluffs is $2, but Vineyard Haven to Edgartown (passing through Oak Bluffs) is $3. A 1-day pass is $6; a 3-day pass is $15. The Edgartown Downtown Shuttle and the South Beach buses circle throughout town or out to South Beach every 20 minutes in season. They also stop at the free parking lots just north of the town center—this is a great way to avoid circling the streets in search of a vacant spot on busy weekends. The main down-island stops are Vineyard Haven (near the ferry terminal), Oak Bluffs (near the Civil War statue in Ocean Park), and Edgartown (Church St., near the Old Whaling Church). From late June to early September, they run more frequently—from 6am to midnight every 15 minutes or half-hour. Hours are reduced in spring and fall. Buses also go out to Aquinnah (via the airport, West Tisbury, and Chilmark), leaving every couple of hours from down-island towns and looping about every hour through up-island towns.

For bus tours of the island, call **Island Transport** (© 508/693-0058) or hop on one of the Island Transport buses that are stationed at the ferry terminals in Vineyard Haven and Oak Bluffs in the summer.

BY TAXI Upon arrival, you'll find taxis at all ferry terminals and at the airport, and there are permanent taxi stands in Oak Bluffs (at the Flying Horses Carousel) and Edgartown (next to the Town Wharf). Most taxi outfits operate cars as well as vans for larger groups and travelers with bikes. Cab companies on the island include **Adam Cab** (© 800/281-4462 or 508/693-3332), **Accurate Cab** (© 888/557-9798 or 508/627-9798; the only 24-hr. service), **All Island Taxi** (© 508/693-3705), **Vineyard Taxi** (© 508/693-8660), **Patti's Taxi** (© 508/693-1663), and **Atlantic Taxi** (© 508/693-7110). Rates from town to town in summer are generally flat fees based on where you're headed and the number of passengers on board. A trip from Vineyard Haven to

Edgartown would probably cost around $17 for two people. Late-night revelers should keep in mind that rates double after midnight until 7am.

THE CHAPPAQUIDDICK FERRY The **On-Time ferry** (© 508/627-9427) runs the 5-minute trip from Memorial Wharf on Dock Street in Edgartown to Chappaquiddick Island from June to mid-October daily, every 5 minutes from 7am to midnight. Passengers, bikes, mopeds, dogs, and cars (3 at a time) are all welcome. A round trip is $3 per person, $10 for one car/one driver, $6 for one bike/one person.

VISITOR INFORMATION

Contact the **Martha's Vineyard Chamber of Commerce** at Beach Road, Vineyard Haven, MA 02568 (© **508/693-0085;** fax 508/693-7589), or visit their website at **www.mvy.com.** Their office is just 2 blocks up from the ferry terminal in Vineyard Haven and is open Monday to Friday 9am to 5pm year-round plus weekends in season. There are also information booths at the ferry terminal in Vineyard Haven, across from the Flying Horses Carousel in Oak Bluffs, and on Church Street in Edgartown. You'll want to poke your head into these offices to pick up free maps, tourist handbooks, and flyers on tours and events or to get answers to any questions you might have. Most inns also have tourist handbooks and maps available for guests.

Always check the two local newspapers, the *Vineyard Gazette* (www.mvgazette.com) and the free *Martha's Vineyard Times* (www.mvtimes.com), for information on current events.

In case of an **emergency,** call © 911 and/or head for the **Martha's Vineyard Hospital,** Linton Lane, Oak Bluffs (© **508/693-0410**), which has a 24-hour emergency room.

---

2 A STROLL AROUND EDGARTOWN

A good way to acclimate yourself to the pace and flavor of the Vineyard is to walk the streets of Edgartown. This walk starts at the Dr. Daniel Fisher House and meanders along for about a mile; depending on how long you linger at each stop, it should take about 2 to 3 hours.

If you're driving, park at the free lots at the edge of town (you'll see signs on the roads from Vineyard Haven and West Tisbury), and bike or take the shuttle bus (it costs only 50¢) to the Edgartown Visitor Center on Church Street. Around the corner are three local landmarks: the Dr. Daniel Fisher House, Vincent House Museum, and Old Whaling Church.

The **Dr. Daniel Fisher House,** 99 Main St. (© **508/627-8017**), is a prime example of Edgartown's trademark Greek Revival opulence. A key player in the 19th-century whaling trade, Dr. Fisher amassed a fortune sufficient to found the Martha's Vineyard National Bank. Built in 1840, his prosperous and proud mansion boasts such classical elements as colonnaded porticos, as well as a delicate roof walk. The only way to view the interior (now headquarters for the Martha's Vineyard Preservation Trust) is with a guided **Vineyard Historic Walking Tour** (© 508/627-8619). This tour originates next door at the **Vincent House Museum,** off Main Street between Planting Field Way and Church Street. The transplanted 1672 full Cape is considered the oldest surviving dwelling on the island. Plexiglass-covered cutaways permit a view of traditional building techniques, and three rooms have been refurbished to encapsulate the decorative styles of 3 centuries,

A STROLL AROUND EDGARTOWN

from bare-bones Colonial to elegant Federal. The tour also takes in the neighboring **Old Whaling Church,** 89 Main St., a magnificent 1843 Greek Revival edifice designed by local architect Frederick Baylies, Jr., and built as a whaling boat would have been, out of massive pine beams. With its 27-foot windows and 92-foot tower, this is a building that knows its place in the community (central). Maintained by the Preservation Trust and still supporting a Methodist parish, the building is now primarily used as a performance site.

Continuing down Main Street and turning right onto School Street, you'll pass another Baylies monument, the 1839 **Baptist Church,** which, having lost its spire, was converted into a private home with a rather grand, column-fronted facade. Two blocks farther, on your left, is the **Vineyard Museum,** 59 School St. (© **508/627-4441**), a fascinating complex assembled by the Dukes County Historical Society. An absorbing display of island history, this cluster of buildings contains exhibits of early Native American crafts; an entire 1765 house; an extraordinary array of maritime art, from whalers' logs to WPA-era studies by Thomas Hart Benton; a carriage house to catch odds and ends; and the Gay Head Light Tower's decommissioned Fresnel lens.

Give yourself enough time to explore the museum's curiosities before heading south 1 block on Cooke Street. Cater-cornered across South Summer Street, you'll spot the first of Baylies's impressive endeavors, the 1828 **Federated Church.** One block left are the offices of the *Vineyard Gazette,* 34 S. Summer St. (© **508/627-4311**). Operating out of a 1760 house, this exemplary small-town newspaper has been going strong since 1846; its 14,000 subscribers span the globe. If you are wandering by on a Thursday afternoon, you might catch a press run in progress.

Now, head down Main Street toward the water, stopping in at any of the inviting shops along the way. Veer left on Dock Street to reach the **Old Sculpin Gallery,** 58 Dock St. (© **508/627-4881**; open late June to mid-Sept). The output of the Martha's Vineyard Art Association displayed here tends to be amateurish, but you might happen upon a find. The real draw is the stark old building itself, which started out as a granary (part of Dr. Fisher's vast holdings) and spent the better part of the 20th century as a boat-building shop. Keep an eye out for vintage beauties when you cross the street to survey the harbor from the deck at Town Wharf. It's from here that the tiny On-Time ferry makes its 5-minute crossing to **Chappaquiddick Island,** hauling three cars at a time and a great many more sightseers—not that there's much to see on the other side. However, the island does offer great stretches of conservation land that will reward the hearty hiker or mountain biker.

Mere strollers might want to remain in town to admire the many formidable captains' homes lining **North Water Street,** some of which have been converted into inns. Each has a tale to tell. The 1750 **Daggett House** (no. 59), for instance, expanded upon a 1660 tavern, and the original beehive oven is flanked by a secret passageway. Formerly an inn, the Daggett House is now a private home. Nathaniel Hawthorne holed up at the **Edgartown Inn** (no. 56) for nearly a year in 1789 while writing *Twice Told Tales*—and, it is rumored, romancing a local maiden who inspired *The Scarlet Letter.* On your way back to Main Street, you'll pass the **Gardner–Colby Gallery** (no. 27), filled with beautiful island-inspired paintings.

WINDING DOWN   After all that walking, you may need a refreshment. **The Newes from America,** at The Kelley House, 23 Kelley St. (just off N. Water St.; © **508/627-4397**), is a classic old-world tavern with specialty beers and the best French onion soup on the island.

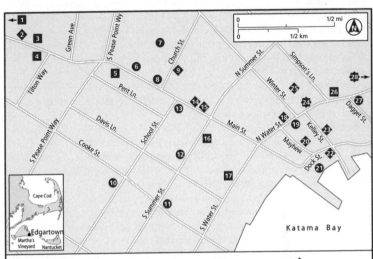

ATTRACTIONS ●
Baptist Church **13**
Dr. Daniel Fisher House **6**
Federated Church **11**
Gardner-Colby Gallery **19**
Martha's Vineyard Museum **10**
North Water Street
    captains' homes **27**
Old Sculpin Gallery **21**
Old Whaling Church **8**
Vincent House Museum **7**
Vineyard Gazette **12**

ACCOMMODATIONS ■
The Arbor Inn **1**
Ashley Inn **3**
Charlotte Inn **16**
Colonial Inn of
    Martha's Vineyard **24**
Edgartown Inn **26**
Harbor View Hotel &
    Resort **28**
The Hob Knob **4**
The Jonathan Munroe House **5**
The Victorian Inn **17**

DINING ◆
Alchemy **14**
Among the Flowers Cafe **20**
Atria **2**
Chesca's **24**
Détente **25**
L'etoile **18**
Lure **29**
Main Street Diner **15**
The Newes from America **23**
Seafood Shanty **22**
Water Street **28**

3 BEACHES & RECREATIONAL PURSUITS

BEACHES   Most down-island beaches in Vineyard Haven, Oak Bluffs, and Edgartown are open to the public and just a walk or a short bike ride from town. In season, shuttle buses make stops at **State Beach** between Oak Bluffs and Edgartown. Most of the Vineyard's magnificent up-island shoreline, alas, is privately owned or restricted to residents, and thus off limits to transient visitors. Renters in up-island communities, however, can obtain a beach sticker (around $35–$50 for a season sticker) for those private beaches by applying with a lease at the relevant **town hall:** West Tisbury, ✆ **508/696-0147;** Chilmark, ✆ **508/645-2100;** or Aquinnah, ✆ **508/645-2300.** Also, many up-island inns offer the perk of temporary passes to residents-only beaches such as Lucy Vincent Beach (see below). In addition to the public beaches listed below, you might also track down a few hidden coves by requesting a map of conservation properties from the **Martha's Vineyard Land Bank** (✆ **508/627-7141**). Below is a list of visitor-friendly beaches.

• **Aquinnah Beach** ★★★ (Moshup Beach), off Moshup Trail: Parking costs $15 a day (in season) at this peaceful half-mile beach just east (Atlantic side) of the colorful cliffs. Go early, since the lot is small and a bit of a hike from the beach. I suggest that all but one person get off at the wooden boardwalk along the road with towels, toys, lunches, and so on, while the remaining person heads back up to park. In season, you can also take the shuttle buses from down-island to the parking lot at the Aquinnah (formerly Gay Head) cliffs and walk to the beach. Although it is against the law, nudists tend to gravitate here. Remember that climbing the cliffs or stealing clay for a souvenir here is against the law for environmental reasons: The cliffs are suffering from rapid erosion. Restrooms are near the parking lot.

- **East Beach** ★★, Wasque (pronounced *Way*-squee) Reservation, Chappaquiddick: Relatively few people bother biking or hiking (or four-wheel-driving) this far, so this beach remains one of the Vineyard's best-kept secrets (and an ideal spot for bird-watching). You should be able to find all the privacy you crave. If you're staying in Edgartown, the Chappy ferry is probably minutes by bike from your inn. Biking on Chappaquiddick is one of the great Vineyard experiences, but the roads can be sandy and are best suited for a mountain bike. You may have to dismount during the 5-mile ride to Wasque. Because of its exposure on the east shore of the island, the surf here is rough. Pack a picnic and make this an afternoon adventure. Sorry, no facilities. The area is owned by the Trustees of Reservations. It costs $180 for a season pass for non-members to drive a four-wheel-drive vehicle out to the beach. Most people park their car near the Dyke Bridge and walk the couple hundred yards out to the beach. Admission is $3 per person.

- **Joseph A. Sylvia State Beach** ★★★, midway between Oak Bluffs and Edgartown: Stretching a mile and flanked by a paved bike path, this placid beach has views of Cape Cod and Nantucket Sound and is prized for its gentle and (relatively) warm waves, which make it perfect for swimming. The wooden drawbridge is a local landmark, and visitors and islanders alike have been jumping off it for years. Be aware that State Beach is one of the Vineyard's most popular; come midsummer, it's packed. The shuttle bus stops here, and roadside parking is also available—but it fills up fast, so stake your claim early. Located on the eastern shore of the island, this is a Nantucket Sound beach, so waters are shallow and rarely rough. There are no restrooms, and only the Edgartown end of the beach, known as Bend-in-the-Road Beach, has lifeguards.

- **Lake Tashmoo Town Beach** ★, off Herring Creek Road, Vineyard Haven: The only spot on the island where lake meets ocean, this tiny strip of sand is good for swimming and surf-casting but is somewhat marred by limited parking and often brackish waters. Nonetheless, this is a popular spot, as beachgoers enjoy a choice between the Vineyard Sound beach with mild surf or the placid lake beach. Bikers will have no problem reaching this beach from Vineyard Haven; otherwise, you have to use a car to get to this beach.

- **Lobsterville Beach** ★★, at the end of Lobsterville Road in Aquinnah (formerly Gay Head; restricted): This 2-mile beauty on Menemsha Pond boasts calm, shallow waters, which are ideal for children. It's also a prime spot for birding—just past the dunes are nesting areas for terns and gulls. Surf-casters tend to gravitate here, too. The only drawback is that parking is for residents only. This is a great beach for bikers to hit on their way back from Aquinnah and before taking the bike ferry over to Menemsha.

- **Menemsha Beach** ★★, next to Dutchers Dock in Menemsha Harbor: Despite its rough surface, this small but well-trafficked strand, with lifeguards and restrooms, is popular with families. In season, it's virtually wall-to-wall colorful umbrellas and beach toys. Nearby food vendors in Menemsha—selling everything from ice cream and hot dogs to steamers and shrimp cocktails—are a plus here. *Tip:* This beach is the ideal place to watch a sunset. Get a lobster dinner to go at the famous **Home Port restaurant** right next to the beach in Menemsha, grab a blanket and a bottle of wine, and picnic here for a spectacular evening. If you are staying at an up-island inn, Menemsha is a fun bike ride downhill. Energetic bikers can make it from down-island towns; plan to make it part of an entire day of scenic biking. Otherwise, you'll need a car to get here.

- **Oak Bluffs Town Beach,** Seaview Avenue: This sandy strip extends from both sides of the ferry wharf, which makes it a convenient place to linger while you wait for the next boat. This is an in-town beach, within walking distance for visitors staying in Oak Bluffs. The surf is consistently calm and the sand smooth, so it's also ideal for families with small children. Public restrooms are available at the ferry dock, but there are no lifeguards.

- **Owen Park Beach,** off Main Street in Vineyard Haven: A tiny strip of harborside beach adjoining a town green with swings and a bandstand will suffice for young children, who, by the way, get lifeguard supervision. There are no restrooms, but this is an in-town beach, which is a quick walk from most Vineyard Haven inns.

- **South Beach ★★★** (Katama Beach), about 4 miles south of Edgartown on Katama Road: If you have time for only one trip to the beach and you can't get up-island, go with this popular, 3-mile barrier strand that boasts heavy wave action (check with lifeguards for swimming conditions), sweeping dunes, and, most important, relatively ample parking space. It's also accessible by bike path or shuttle. Lifeguards patrol some sections of the beach, and there are sparsely scattered toilet facilities. The rough surf here is popular with surfers. *Tip:* Families tend to head to the left, college kids to the right.

- **Wasque Beach ★★,** Wasque Reservation, Chappaquiddick: Surprisingly easy to get to (via the On-Time ferry and a bike or car), this half-mile-long beach has all the amenities—lifeguards, parking, restrooms—without the crowds. Wasque Beach is a Trustees of Reservations property, and if you are not a member of this land-preservation organization, you must pay at the gatehouse (© **508/627-7260**). To park your car here and go to the beach, it is $3 per car plus $3 per person. To drive your car on to the beach, it's $30 for a day pass, plus $3 per person. For a season pass to drive on to the other beaches on Chappaquiddick, it's $100 for Norton Point and $180 for Cape Pogue.

BICYCLING What's unique about biking on Martha's Vineyard is that you'll find not only the smooth, well-maintained paths indigenous to the Cape, but also long stretches of road with virtually no traffic that, while rough in spots, traverse breathtaking country landscapes with sweeping ocean views. Serious cyclists will want to do a 1-day **circle-the-island tour** through the up-island towns and out to Aquinnah, stopping in Menemsha before heading back down-island. You'll pass through all six Vineyard towns and encounter some unique off-the-beaten-track businesses.

For much of the trek, you'll travel country roads, so beware of sandy shoulders and blind curves. Avoid tour buses by taking routes outlined below, such as the Moshup Trail to Aquinnah or the triangle of paved bike paths between the down-island towns. These bike paths, roughly 8 miles to a side, link the down-island towns of Oak Bluffs, Edgartown, and Vineyard Haven (the sound portion along Beach Rd., flanked by water on both sides, is especially scenic). From Edgartown, you can also follow the bike path to

South Beach (also known as Katama Beach). The bike paths are accessible off Edgartown–West Tisbury Road in Oak Bluffs, West Tisbury, and Edgartown.

The up-island roads leading to West Tisbury, Chilmark, Menemsha, and Aquinnah are a cyclist's paradise, with sprawling, unspoiled pastureland, old farmhouses, and brilliant sea views reminiscent of Ireland's countryside. But the terrain is often hilly, and the roads are narrow and a little rough around the edges. Try **South Road** from the town of West Tisbury to Chilmark Center (about 5 miles). En route, you'll pass stone walls rolling over moors, clumps of pine and wildflowers, verdant marshes and tide pools, and, every once in a while, an old Vineyard farmhouse. About halfway, you'll notice the road becoming hillier as you approach a summit, **Abel's Hill,** home to the **Chilmark Cemetery,** where comedian John Belushi is buried. A mile farther, don't miss the view of **Allen Farm,** an operating sheep farm amidst picturesque pastureland. **Middle Road** is another lovely ride with a country feel and will also get you from West Tisbury to Chilmark. (It's usually less trafficked, too.)

My favorite up-island route is the 6-mile stretch from Chilmark Center out to Aquinnah via **State Road** and **Moshup Trail** ★. The ocean views along this route are spectacular. Don't miss the **Quitsa Pond Lookout,** about 2 miles down State Road, which provides a panoramic vista of Nashaquitsa and Menemsha ponds, beyond which you can see Menemsha, the Vineyard Sound, and the Elizabeth Islands—it's an amazing place to watch the sunset on a clear evening. A bit farther, just over the Aquinnah town line, is the Aquinnah spring, a roadside iron pipe where you can refill your water bottle with the freshest and coldest water on the island. At the fork after the spring, turn left on Moshup Trail—in fact, a regular road—and follow the coast, which offers gorgeous views of the water and the sweeping sand dunes. You'll soon wind up in Aquinnah, where you can explore the red-clay cliffs and pristine beaches. On the return trip, you can take the handy bike ferry ($7 round-trip) from Aquinnah to Menemsha. It runs daily in summer and weekends in May.

A word about Aquinnah: Almost every visitor to the Vineyard finds his or her way to the cliffs, and with all the tour buses lined up in the huge parking lot and the rows of tacky concession stands and gift shops, this can seem like a rather outrageous tourist trap. You're right; it's not the Grand Canyon. But the observation deck, with its view of the colorful cliffs, the adorable brick lighthouse, and the Elizabeth Islands beyond, will make you glad you bothered. Instead of rushing away, stop for a cool drink and a clam roll at the snack bar with the deck overlooking the ocean.

The adventurous **mountain biker** will want to head to the eight miles of trails in the **Manuel F. Correllus State Forest** (© 508/693-2540), a vast spread of scrub oak and pine smack-dab in the middle of the island that also boasts paved paths and hiking and horseback-riding trails. For those seeking an escape from the multitudes, the trails are so extensive that even during peak summer season it is possible to not see another soul for hours. On most of the conservation land on the Vineyard, however, mountain biking is prohibited for environmental reasons.

Bike-rental operations are ubiquitous near the ferry landings in Vineyard Haven and Oak Bluffs, and there are also a few outfits in Edgartown. For information on bike-rental shops, see "Getting Around," earlier in this chapter.

A very good outfit out of Boston called **Bike Riders** (© 800/473-7040; www.bike riderstours.com) runs 6-day island-hopping tours of Martha's Vineyard and Nantucket. The cost is $1,395 per person plus $60 if you borrow one of their bikes. It's a perfect way to experience both islands.

The chamber of commerce has a great bike map available at its office on Beach Road in Vineyard Haven (see "Visitor Information," earlier in this chapter).

BIRD-WATCHING Felix Neck Wildlife Sanctuary, Edgartown–Vineyard Haven Road, Edgartown (✆ **508/627-4850**), is an easy 2-mile bike ride from Edgartown. A Massachusetts Audubon Property, it has a complete visitor center staffed by naturalists who lead bird-watching walks, among other activities. You'll see osprey nests on your right on the way to the center. Pick up a trail map at the center before heading out. Several of the trails pass Sengekontacket Pond, and the orange trail leads to Waterfowl Pond, which has an observation deck with bird-sighting information. While managed by the conservation group Sheriff's Meadow Foundation, the 300-acre **Cedar Tree Neck Sanctuary** ★★★ (State Rd., follow to Indian Hill Rd., then to Obed Daggett Rd. and follow signs), Tisbury (see "Nature Trails," below), was acquired with the assistance of Massachusetts Audubon Society. There are several trails, but you'll eventually arrive out on a picturesque bluff overlooking Vineyard Sound and the Elizabeth Islands. Check out the map posted at the parking lot for an overview of the property. The range of terrain here—ponds, fields, woods, and bog—provides diverse opportunities for sightings. **Wasque Reservation** ★★★ on Chappaquiddick (see "Nature Trails," below), a sanctuary owned by the Trustees of Reservations and located on the easternmost reaches of the island, can be accessed by bike or four-wheel-drive vehicle (see "Getting Around," earlier in this chapter). The hundreds of untouched acres here draw flocks of nesting shorebirds, including egrets, herons, terns, and plovers.

FISHING For shellfishing, you'll need to get information and a permit from the appropriate town hall (for the telephone numbers, see "Beaches," above). Popular spots for surf-casting include **Wasque Point** (Wasque Reservation) on Chappaquiddick (see "Nature Trails," below). Deep-sea excursions can be arranged aboard **Summer's Lease** (✆ **508/693-2880**) out of Oak Bluffs. Up-island, there are **North Shore Charters** (✆ **508/645-2993**; www.bassnblue.com) and **Flashy Lady Fishing Charters** (✆ **508/645-2462**; www.flashyladycharters.com) out of Menemsha, locus of the island's commercial fishing fleet (you may recognize this weathered port from *Jaws*). Flashy Lady guarantees striped bass catches; their motto is "you don't catch, you don't pay." Charter costs are about $650 for a half-day for five people and $1,300 for a full day.

Cooper Gilkes III, proprietor of **Coop's Bait & Tackle** at 147 W. Tisbury Rd. in Edgartown (✆ **508/627-3909**), which offers rentals as well as supplies, is another acknowledged authority. He's available as an instructor or charter guide and is even amenable to sharing hard-won pointers on local hot spots.

FITNESS Gym addicts can get their workout fix at the **Health Club at the Mansion House Inn** on Main Street in Vineyard Haven (✆ **508/693-7400**), which accepts visitors for a $16 fee.

GOLF The 9-hole **Mink Meadows Golf Course** off Franklin Street in Vineyard Haven (✆ **508/693-0600**), despite occupying a top-dollar chunk of real estate, is open to the general public. There is also the semiprivate, championship-level 18-hole **Farm Neck Golf Club** off Farm Neck Road in Oak Bluffs (✆ **508/693-3057**). The Cafe at Farm Neck serves a wonderful lunch overlooking their manicured greens. In season, greens fees at Mink Meadows are $50 for 9 holes and $75 for 18 holes. In season, greens fees at Farm Neck are $145 (including cart) for 18 holes.

ICE-SKATING   The **Martha's Vineyard Ice Arena** on Edgartown–Vineyard Haven Road, Oak Bluffs (☎ 508/693-4438), offers public skating for $4 from mid-July to mid-April; call for details.

NATURE TRAILS   About a fifth of the Vineyard's landmass has been set aside for conservation, and much of it is accessible to energetic bikers and hikers. The **West Chop Woods,** off Franklin Street in Vineyard Haven, comprise 85 acres with marked walking trails. Midway between Vineyard Haven and Edgartown, the **Felix Neck Wildlife Sanctuary** (see "Bird-Watching," above) includes a 6-mile network of trails over varying terrain, from woodland to beach. Accessible by ferry from Edgartown, quiet Chappaquiddick is home to two sizable preserves. The **Cape Pogue Wildlife Refuge ★★★** and **Wasque Reservation ★★★** (gatehouse ☎ 508/627-7260), covering much of the island's eastern barrier beach, have 709 acres that draw flocks of nesting or resting shorebirds. Also on the island, 3 miles east on Dyke Road, is another Trustees of Reservations property, the distinctly poetic and alluring **Mytoi,** a 14-acre Japanese garden that is an oasis of textures and flora and fauna.

The 633-acre **Long Point Wildlife Refuge ★★★** off Waldron's Bottom Road in West Tisbury (gatehouse ☎ 508/693-7392) offers heath and dunes, freshwater ponds, a popular family-oriented beach, and interpretive nature walks for children. In season, the Trustees of Reservations charge a $10 parking fee, plus $3 per adult over age 16. The 4,000-acre **Manuel F. Correllus Vineyard State Forest** occupies a sizable, if not especially scenic, chunk mid-island; it's riddled with mountain-bike paths and riding trails. This sanctuary was created in 1908 to try to save the endangered heath hen, a species now extinct. In season, there are free interpretive and birding walks.

Up-island, along the sound, the **Menemsha Hills Reservation** off North Road in Chilmark (☎ 508/693-7662) encompasses 210 acres of rocks and bluffs, with steep paths, lovely views, and even a public beach. The **Cedar Tree Neck Sanctuary,** off Indian Hill Road southwest of Vineyard Haven (☎ 508/693-5207), offers some 300 forested acres that end in a stony beach (alas, swimming and sunbathing are prohibited). It's still a refreshing retreat.

Some remarkable botanical surprises can be found at the 20-acre **Polly Hill Arboretum,** 8809 State Rd., West Tisbury (☎ 508/693-9426). Horticulturist Polly Hill developed this property over the past 40 years and allows the public to wander the grounds Thursday to Tuesday from sunrise until sunset. There are guided tours at 2pm. The visitor's center and plant sale is open 9:30am to 4pm. This is a magical place, particularly mid-June to July when the Dogwood Allee is in bloom. Wanderers will pass old stone walls on the way to The Tunnel of Love, an arbor of bleached hornbeam. There are also witch hazels, camellias, magnolias, and rhododendrons. To get there from Vineyard Haven, go south on State Road, bearing left at the junction of North Road. The arboretum entrance is about a half-mile down, on the right. There is a requested donation of $5 for adults.

TENNIS   Public courts typically charge a small fee and can be reserved in person a day in advance. You'll find clay courts on **Church Street** in Vineyard Haven and non-clay in Oak Bluffs' **Niantic Park,** West Tisbury's **grammar school** on Old County Road, and the **Chilmark Community Center** on South Road. Three public courts—plus a basketball court, softball field, and children's playground—are located at the **Edgartown Recreation Area** on Robinson Road. You can also book a court (1 day in advance only) at two semiprivate clubs in Oak Bluffs: the **Farm Neck Tennis Club** (☎ 508/693-9728)

WATERSPORTS Wind's Up, 199 Beach Rd., Vineyard Haven ((✆ **508/693-4252**), rents out canoes, kayaks, and various sailing craft, including windsurfers, and offers instruction on-site, on a placid pond; it also rents surfboards and boogie boards. Canoes and kayaks rent for $25 per hour, $45 for a half-day, and $65 for a full day.

4 MUSEUMS & HISTORIC LANDMARKS

Cottage Museum ★   Oak Bluffs' famous "Camp Meeting Grounds," a 34-acre circle with more than 300 multicolored, elaborately trimmed carpenter's Gothic cottages, looks very much the way it might have more than a hundred years ago. These adorable little houses, loosely modeled on the revivalists' canvas tents that inspired them, have been handed down through the generations. Unless you happen to know a lucky camper, your best chance of getting inside one is to visit this homey little museum, which embodies the late-19th-century zeitgeist and displays representative artifacts: bulky black bathing costumes and a melodeon (a 19th-century organ) used for informal hymnal singalongs.

The compact architecture is at once practical and symbolic. The Gothic-arched French doors off the peak-roofed second-story bedroom, for instance, lead to a tiny balcony used for keeping tabs on community doings. The daily schedule was, in fact, rather hectic. In 1867, when this cottage was built, campers typically attended three lengthy prayer services daily. Today's denizens tend to blend in with the visiting tourists, though opportunities for worship remain at the 1878 Trinity Methodist Church within the park or, just outside, on Samoset Avenue, at the nonsectarian 1870 Union Chapel, a magnificent octagonal structure with superb acoustics (posted signs give the lineup of guest preachers and musicians).

At the very center of the Camp Meeting Grounds is the striking **Trinity Park Tabernacle ★★**. Built in 1879, the open-sided chapel is the largest wrought-iron structure in the country. Thousands can be accommodated on its long wooden benches, which are usually filled to capacity for the Sunday-morning services in summer, as well as for community sings (Wed in July and Aug) and occasional concerts. (See "Martha's Vineyard After Dark," later in this chapter.)

1 Trinity Park (within the Camp Meeting Grounds), Oak Bluffs. (✆ **508/693-7784.** Admission $1.50 (donation). Mid-June to Sept Mon–Sat 10am–4pm. Closed Oct to mid-June.

Flying Horses Carousel ★★ (Kids)   You don't have to be a kid to enjoy the colorful mounts adorning what is considered to be the oldest working carousel in the country. Built in 1876 at Coney Island, this National Historic Landmark maintained by the Martha's Vineyard Preservation Trust predates the era of horses that "gallop." Lacking the necessary gears, these merely glide smoothly in place to the joyful strains of a calliope. The challenge lies in going for the brass ring that entitles the lucky winner to a free ride. Some regulars, adults included, have grown rather adept—you'll see them scoop up several in a single pass. In between rides, take a moment to admire the intricate hand-carving and real horsehair manes, and gaze into the horses' glass eyes for a surprise: tiny animal charms glinting within.

33 Circuit Ave. (at Lake Ave.), Oak Bluffs. (✆ **508/693-9481.** Tickets $1.50 per ride, or 8 rides for $10. Late May to early Sept daily 10am–10pm; call for off-season hours. Closed mid-Oct to mid-Apr.

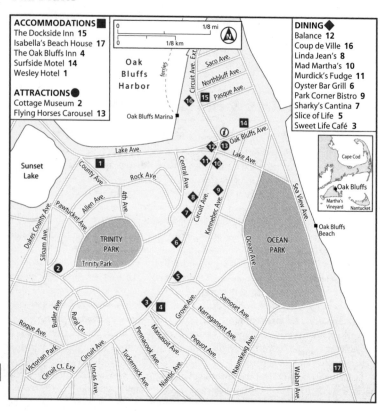

ACCOMMODATIONS ■
The Dockside Inn **15**
Isabella's Beach House **17**
The Oak Bluffs Inn **4**
Surfside Motel **14**
Wesley Hotel **1**

ATTRACTIONS ●
Cottage Museum **2**
Flying Horses Carousel **13**

DINING ◆
Balance **12**
Coup de Ville **16**
Linda Jean's **8**
Mad Martha's **10**
Murdick's Fudge **11**
Oyster Bar Grill **6**
Park Corner Bistro **9**
Sharky's Cantina **7**
Slice of Life **5**
Sweet Life Café **3**

Martha's Vineyard Historical Society ★ All of Martha's Vineyard's colorful history is captured here, in a compound of historic buildings. To acclimate yourself chronologically, start with the pre-Colonial artifacts—from arrowheads to colorful Gay Head clay pottery—displayed in the 1845 **Captain Francis Pease House;** there's also an oral history exhibit, a gift shop, and a gallery to showcase local students' work.

The **Gale Huntington Reference Library** houses rare documentation of the island's history, from genealogical records to whaling-ship logs. The recorded history of Martha's Vineyard (the name has been attributed, variously, to a Dutch seaman named Martin Wyngaard, and to the daughter and/or mother-in-law of early explorer Bartholomew Gosnold) begins in 1642 with the arrival of missionary Thomas Mayhew, Jr., whose father bought the whole chain of islands, from Nantucket through the Elizabeths, for £40, as a speculative venture. Mayhew, Jr. had loftier goals in mind, and it is a tribute to his methodology that long after he was lost at sea in 1657, the Wampanoags whom he had converted to Christianity continued to mourn him (a stone monument to his memory still survives by the roadside opposite the airport). In his relatively brief sojourn on-island, Mayhew helped to found what would become, in 1671, Edgartown (named for the British heir apparent). The library's holdings on this epoch are extensive, and some extraordinary memorabilia, including scrimshaw and portraiture, are on view in the adjoining **Francis Foster Maritime Gallery.** Outside, a reproduction "tryworks" shows how whale blubber was reduced to precious oil.

To get a sense of daily life during the era when the waters of the East Coast were the equivalent of a modern highway, visit the **Thomas Cooke House,** a shipwright-built Colonial, built in 1765, where the Customs collector lived and worked. A few of the house's 10 rooms are decorated as they might have been at the height of the maritime trade; others are devoted to special exhibits on other fascinating aspects of island history, such as the revivalist fever that enveloped Oak Bluffs. Further curiosities are stored in the nearby Carriage Shed. Among the vintage 19th-century vehicles are a painted peddler's cart, a whaling boat, a hearse, and a fire engine.

The Fresnel lens on display outside the museum was lifted from the Gay Head Lighthouse in 1952, after nearly a century of service. Though it no longer serves to warn ships of dangerous shoals (that light is automated now), it still lights up the night every evening in summer, just for show.

59 School St. (corner of Cooke St., 2 blocks southwest of Main St.), Edgartown. ✆ **508/627-4441.** www. marthasvineyardhistory.org. Admission $7 adults, $4 children 6–15. Mid-June to mid-Oct Mon–Sat 10am–5pm; mid-Oct to late Dec and mid-Mar to mid-June Wed–Fri 1–4pm, Sat 10am–4pm; early Jan to mid-Mar Wed–Fri by appointment, Sat 10am–4pm.

5 ORGANIZED TOURS

Ghosts, Gossip, and Downright Scandal Walking Tours ★★   Laced with local lore and often led by the entertaining local historian Liz Villard, this 75-minute walking tour of Edgartown by the Vineyard History Tours organization gives a fun look at town history. Other tours provide access to the interiors of the 1672 Vincent House (the island's oldest surviving dwelling), the 1840 Dr. Daniel Fisher House (an elegant Greek Revival mansion), and the splendid Old Whaling Church, a town showpiece built in 1843. There are also a variety of other van and walking tours, including "A-Whaling We Will Go" in Edgartown and "Cottages, Campgrounds, and Flying Horses" in Oak Bluffs (which includes admission to the Cottage Museum and a ride on the Flying Horses).

From the Vincent House Museum, behind 99 Main St., Edgartown. ✆ **508/627-8619.** Also from the Cottage Museum, 1 Trinity Park, Oak Bluffs, and at the Steamship Authority kiosk in Vineyard Haven. $8–$10 adults, free for children 12 and under. June–Sept Mon–Sat noon–3pm; call for off-season hours. Closed Nov–Apr.

Trustees of Reservations Natural History Tours ★★★   The Trustees, a statewide land-conservation group, offers several fascinating 2^1/$_2$-hour tours by safari vehicle or canoe around this idyllic nature preserve. The Natural History kayak tour on Poucha Pond and Cape Poge Bay is designed for all levels. It costs $40 for adults and $18 for children. There's also a tour of the Cape Poge lighthouse at 10am, noon, and 2pm. The cost is $25 for adults and $12 for children 15 and under. The trustees also offer 1^1/$_2$-hour kayak tours around Long Point for $20 for adults and $10 for children. Call ✆ **508/693-7392** for details.

Cape Pogue, Chappaquiddick Island. ✆ **508/627-3599.** www.ttor.org. In season Mon–Fri 8:30am and 3pm. Call for reservations. Meet at Mytoi on Chappaquiddick. Closed mid-Oct to May.

6 KID STUFF

A must for tots to preteens is the unique **Flying Horses Carousel** in the center of Oak Bluffs (see "Museums & Historic Landmarks," above). For an atmospheric minigolf course, visit **Island Cove Mini Golf,** on State Road outside Vineyard Haven (© 508/ 693-2611), a family-friendly setup with a snack bar serving Mad Martha's ice cream, an island favorite. A round costs $9 for adults, $8 for children. A climbing wall costs $5. Island Cove is closed October through March. On Tuesday to Sunday, from 10am to 3pm, children might enjoy visiting the **World of Reptiles and Birds** off Edgartown– Vineyard Haven Road on Bachelder Avenue, Edgartown (© 508/627-5634), where they'll meet various snakes, including a 21-foot python, turtles, and even an alligator. There's also a bird park. Admission is $5. Call for hours. World of Reptiles is closed October through March. Nearby, the **Felix Neck Wildlife Sanctuary** (see "Beaches & Recreational Pursuits," earlier in this chapter; © 508/627-4850), on Edgartown–Vineyard Haven Road, is always a popular destination with its exhibit room and self-guided trails. On Sundays in season, there are natural-history talks and activities geared to children. **Native Earth Teaching Farm** (94 North Rd., Chilmark; © 508/645-3304) features rare ducks and other animals, and children can participate in the "chore of the day." It's open Wednesday, Saturday and Sunday 10am to 6pm. Many families plan their vacations around the **Agricultural Society Annual Livestock Show and Fair** (© 508/ 693-9549) in West Tisbury in mid-August. It's an old-fashioned country fair with animals, food, and entertainment. An island event that your kids will always remember is **Illumination Night** in Oak Bluffs, when all the cottages in the campground are lit up with Japanese lanterns. The exact date is a secret, but it's usually a Wednesday evening at 7:30pm in late August.

7 SHOPPING

ANTIQUES/COLLECTIBLES For exquisite Asian furniture, lamps, porcelains, and jewelry, visit **All Things Oriental** at 123 Beach Rd. in Vineyard Haven (© 508/693-8375). The treasures on sale here are handpicked in China by owner Shirley Seaton.

ARTS & CRAFTS A new little art gallery cluster in Oak Bluffs, just beyond the "ginger bread" cottage colony, is worth a visit. On Dukes County Avenue, there are six interesting shops: **Periwinkle Studio,** an intriguing gallery; **Alison Shaw Gallery,** featuring the exquisite photographs of this artist; **Pik Nik,** a funky array of crafts, gifts, and clothing; **Dragonfly Gallery,** showing a range of mediums; **Red Mannequin,** with clothing, gifts and artwork; and **Lucinda's Enamels,** with fine art jewelry.

No visit to Edgartown would be complete without a peek at the wares of scrimshander Thomas J. DeMont, Jr., at **Edgartown Scrimshaw Gallery** at 43 Main St. (© 508/627-9439). In addition to DeMont's work, the shop carries the work of a number of the country's top scrimshaw artists. All the scrimshaw in the gallery is hand-carved using ancient mammoth ivory or antique fossil ivory.

The **Chilmark Pottery,** off State Road (about 4 miles southwest of Vineyard Haven), West Tisbury (© 508/693-6476), features tableware fashioned to suit its setting. Geoffrey Borr takes his palette from the sea and sky and produces serviceable stoneware with clean lines and a long life span. Summer pottery classes are available.

MARTHA'S VINEYARD

10

SHOPPING

The Field Gallery, State Road (in the center of town), West Tisbury (© 508/693- **271**

5595), set in a rural pasture, is where Marc Chagall meets Henry Moore and where Tom Maley's playful figures have enchanted locals and passersby for decades. You'll also find paintings by Albert Alcalay and drawings and cartoons by Jules Feiffer. The Sunday-evening openings are high points of the summer social season. Closed mid-October to mid-May.

Don't miss the **Granary Gallery at the Red Barn,** Old County Road (off Edgartown–West Tisbury Rd., about ¹/₄ mile north of the intersection), West Tisbury (© **508/ 693-0455**), which displays astounding prints by the late longtime summerer Alfred Eisenstaedt, dazzling color photos by local luminary Alison Shaw, and a changing roster of fine artists—some just emerging, some long since "discovered." A fine selection of country and provincial antiques is also sold here. Open April to December, and by appointment only January through March.

Another unique local artisans' venue is **Martha's Vineyard Glass Works,** State Road, North Tisbury (© **508/693-6026**). World-renowned master glass blowers sometimes lend a hand at this handsome rural studio/shop just for the fun of it. The three resident artists—Andrew Magdanz, Susan Shapiro, and Mark Weiner—are no slouches themselves, having shown nationwide to considerable acclaim. Their output is decidedly avant-garde and may not suit all tastes, but it's an eye-opening array and all the more fascinating once you've witnessed a work in progress.

Etherington Fine Art, 71 Main St., second floor, Vineyard Haven (© **508/693-9696**), features estimable work like Vineyard- and Venice-inspired paintings by Rez Williams, nature collages by Lucy Mitchell, pastels and oils by Wolf Kahn, and the colorful iconographic sculptures by Sam Milstein that grace the front yard. Gallery owner Mary Etherington's selection is a giant step up from the usual seascapes and lighthouses offered by other Vineyard galleries.

BOOKS **Edgartown Books,** Main Street (in the center of town), Edgartown (© **508/ 627-8463**), has a lively presentation of timely titles highlighting local endeavors; inquire about readings and signings. Closed January to March.

FASHION **The Great Put On,** Dock Street (in the center of town), Edgartown (© **508/627-5495**), dates back to 1969, but always keeps up with the latest styles, including lines by Vivienne Tam, Moschino, and BCBG. **Dream Weaver** at 1 S. Water St., Edgartown (© **508/627-9683**), has a very fine collection of contemporary women's apparel. **Sheila Allen Styles** at 41A Main St., Edgartown (© **508/627-8868),** is a fun store that sells accessories—matching handbags, jewelry, and scarves in a range of colors—all for $25 or less. **Saffron** at 65 Main St., Edgartown (© **508/627-7088**), offers a hip selection of island ware. **Katydid** is another high-fashion option at 38 Main St. in Edgartown (© **508/627-1232**).

GIFTS/HOME DECOR The owners of **Bramhall & Dunn,** 23 Main St., Vineyard Haven (© **508/693-6437**), have a great eye for the kind of chunky, eclectic extras that lend character to country homes. Expect to find the requisite rag rugs, rustic pottery, English country antiques, bed linens, and a large selection of sweaters.

My favorite place for gifts in Oak Bluffs is **Craftworks,** 149 Circuit Ave. (© **508/693-7463**), which is filled to the rafters with whimsical, colorful contemporary American crafts, some by local artisans.

Carly Simon owns a shop called **Midnight Farm,** 18 Water-Cromwell Lane, Vineyard Haven (© **508/693-1997**), named after her popular children's book. This home store offers a world of high-end, carefully selected, and imaginative gift items starting with

MARTHA'S VINEYARD

10

SHOPPING

soaps and candles and including children's clothes and toys, rugs, furniture, books, clothes, and glassware.

Third World Trading Co., 52 Circuit Ave., Oak Bluffs (© **508/693-5550**), features well-priced clothing, accessories, and home accents gathered from around the globe.

JEWELRY   Stop by **C. B. Stark Jewelers,** 53A Main St., Vineyard Haven (© **508/693-2284**), where proprietor Cheryl Stark started fashioning island-motif charms back in 1966.

SEAFOOD   Feel like whipping up your own lobster feast? For the freshest and biggest crustaceans on the island, head to **The Net Result,** 79 Beach Rd., Vineyard Haven (© **508/693-6071**). Run by the Larsen family, you'll find everything from shrimp, scallops, and swordfish to bluefish and tuna. If you're up-island, stop by **Larsen's Fish Market,** right on the docks at Menemsha Harbor.

8 WHERE TO STAY

When deciding where to stay on Martha's Vineyard, you'll need to consider the type of vacation you prefer. The down-island towns of Vineyard Haven, Oak Bluffs, and Edgartown provide shops, restaurants, beaches, and harbors within walking distance, and frequent shuttles to get you all over the island. But all three can be overly crowded on busy summer weekends. Vineyard Haven is the gateway for most of the ferry traffic; Oak Bluffs is a raucous town with most of the Vineyard's bars and nightclubs; and many visitors make a beeline to Edgartown's manicured Main Street. Up-island inns provide more peace and quiet, but you'll probably need a car to get around, including going to the beach. Nevertheless, there are some wonderful places to stay on the Vineyard, and all of the following choices have something special to offer.

EDGARTOWN
Very Expensive
Charlotte Inn ★★   Owners Gery and Paula Conover have been tirelessly fine-tuning this cluster of 18th- and 19th-century houses (5 in all, counting the carriage house, a replica) since 1971. Linked by formal gardens, each house has a distinctive look and feel, though the predominant mode is English country, with fascinating antiques, hunting prints, and quirky decorative accents. Bathrooms are luxurious, and some are enormous (bigger than most hotel rooms). This is one of only two Relais & Châteaux properties on the Cape and Islands (the second is The Wauwinet, on Nantucket; p. 239)—a world-class distinction that designates excellence in hospitality. On-site is The Terrace, a fine-dining restaurant.

27 S. Summer St. (in the center of town), Edgartown, MA 02539. © **508/627-4151.** Fax 508/627-4652. www.relaischateaux.com/charlotte. 25 units, all with tub/shower. Summer $350–$695 double; $850–$950 suite. Rates include continental breakfast; full breakfast offered for extra charge ($15). AE, MC, V. Open year-round. No children 13 and under. **Amenities:** Restaurant. *In room:* A/C, TV, hair dryer.

Harbor View Hotel & Resort ★★   This grand 19th-century hotel is in the midst of a multi-year renovation, estimated to cost $77 million. Among the changes, 21 smaller hotel rooms will be converted into 13 luxury suites, some with private gardens and outdoor showers. Parts of the hotel will remain open during the renovation. The shingle-style complex started out as two Gilded Age waterfront hotels, later joined by a 300-foot veranda that overlooks Edgartown Harbor and the lighthouse. Behind the hotel, there's a large pool. A new spa and fitness center opened this year. The hotel is just far enough from "downtown" Edgartown to avoid the traffic, but close enough for a pleasant walk past regal captain's houses. **Water Street** (p. 280) serves three meals in an elegant setting, and **Henry's** is a cozy barroom.

131 N. Water St. (about 1/2 mile northwest of Main St.), Edgartown, MA 02539. ℂ **800/225-6005** or 508/627-7000. Fax 508/627-8417. www.harbor-view.com. 124 units (all with tub/shower). Summer $350–$625 double; $775 one-bedroom suite; $825 two-bedroom suite; $1,250 three-bedroom suite. AE, DC, MC, V. Open year-round. **Amenities:** 2 restaurants (fine-dining; more casual bar open daily for lunch and dinner); heated outdoor pool; 2 tennis courts; concierge; room service (seasonal only: breakfast, lunch, and dinner); babysitting; same-day laundry. *In room:* A/C, TV, Wi-Fi, fridge, hair dryer, iron, safe.

The Hob Knob ★★★   Owner Maggie White has reinvented this 19th-century building as an exquisite destination now vying for top honors as one of the Vineyard's premier luxury boutique hotels. She also wants to stay eco-friendly and that ideal extends to all aspects of the inn, from recycling and composting to an organic menu. All rooms are equipped with plush bathrobes and fine Aveda toiletries, as well as flatscreen TVs. Maggie and her attentive staff will pack a splendid picnic basket ($20/person), or plan a charter fishing trip on Maggie's 27-foot Boston Whaler or organize windsurfing lessons. The full farm breakfast is a delight and is served at beautifully appointed individual tables in the sunny, brightly painted dining rooms or outside on the terrace.

128 Main St. (on upper Main St., in the center of town), Edgartown, MA 02539. ℂ **800/696-2723** or 508/627-9510. Fax 508/627-4560. www.hobknob.com. 17 units, 3-bedroom and 4-bedroom cottage. Summer $350–$625 double. Rates include full breakfast and afternoon tea. AE, MC, V. Open year-round. No children 6 and under. **Amenities:** Exercise room; spa; rental bikes ($20 per day); room service; business center. *In room:* A/C, TV/DVD, Wi-Fi, minifridge, hair dryer.

The Winnetu Oceanside Resort ★★★   One of the island's most full-service resorts, this large luxury hotel sits on 11 acres overlooking South Beach in Katama. Guests can walk down a 250-yard path to get to the private beach. A 3-mile bike path links the inn to Edgartown. Most rooms are two- and three-bedroom suites with kitchenettes. Some have ocean views and conveniences like a washer/dryer. Many have private decks or patios. The rooms are decorated in a cozy beach-house style. The inn offers a number of amenities at an extra charge, including rental of beach cabanas, bicycle delivery service, grocery delivery service, and Wednesday-evening family-style clambakes in season. With giant chess pieces, outdoor Ping-Pong, foosball, the pool, and the putting green, there are many on-site amusements for kids. For active guests, the inn staff arranges day trips that include fishing, kayaking, and beach-buggy rides. The inn's finedining restaurant, Lure, is top-notch (see "Where to Dine," later in this chapter). Several wheelchair-accessible rooms are available.

South Beach, Edgartown, MA 02539. ℂ **866/335-1133** (reservations line), or 508/310-1733. www.winnetu.com. 48 units. Summer $320 double; $770–$1,200 1-bedroom suite; $920 2-bedroom suite; $1,600 3-bedroom suite. AE, MC, V. Closed Dec to mid-Apr. **Amenities:** Fine-dining restaurant; outdoor heated pool; putting green; tennis courts with pro (6 Har-Tru, 4 all-weather); fitness room; children's program (late June to early Sept complimentary 9am–noon; fee in evenings for 3-year-olds through preteens); concierge; laundry facilities; general store. *In room:* A/C, TV/VCR, fridge, coffeemaker, iron, microwave.

Expensive

Ashley Inn ★ ⓥⓐⓛⓤⓔ   Located on Upper Main Street in Edgartown, this attractive B&B is just a short walk to the many shops and restaurants on Main Street and the picturesque Edgartown Harbor. Innkeepers Fred and Janet Hurley have decorated the bedrooms in the 1860 captain's house with period antiques and quilts, and some rooms have canopy or four-poster beds. There are thoughtful extras at this B&B, like a little box of Chilmark Chocolates left on your pillow. There's also a carriage house offering suites with a kitchen and whirlpool bath. In the morning, breakfast is served at individual tables in the dining room.

129 Main St., Edgartown, MA 02539. © **508/627-9655.** Fax 508/627-6629. www.ashleyinn.net. 10 units. Summer $225–$325 double. Rates include full breakfast. MC, V. Open year-round. *In room:* A/C, TV.

Colonial Inn of Martha's Vineyard ★★ (Kids)   Built in 1911, this four-story inn in the center of Edgartown has been kept up-to-date, making it a fine modern hotel. Its lobby serves as a conduit to the Nevins Square shops beyond, and two good restaurants are also on the premises. The 28 rooms, decorated in soothing, contemporary tones (with pine furniture, crisp fabrics, hardwood floors, wainscoting, and four-poster beds), offer all you could want in the way of "affordable luxury." Guests whose rooms lack harbor views can wander onto one of the four common harbor-view decks to have a cocktail and enjoy the scenery. Two rooms are accessible to guests with disabilities.

38 N. Water St., Edgartown, MA 02539. © **800/627-4701** or 508/627-4711. Fax 508/627-5904. www.colonialinnmvy.com. 28 units. Summer $250–$460 double; $410–$495 suite or efficiency. Rates include continental breakfast. AE, MC, V. Closed Dec–Mar. Pets allowed in designated rooms for $30 per day. **Amenities:** 2 restaurants (including Chesca's; see "Where to Dine," below); fitness room; spa; shopping arcade. *In room:* A/C, TV, hair dryer, iron.

The Victorian Inn ★★   In the center of Edgartown, the Victorian Inn is a freshened-up version of those old-style hotels that used to exist in the center of every New England town. There are enough rooms here so you don't feel like you are trespassing in someone's home, yet there's a personal touch. Several rooms have canopy beds and a balcony with a harbor view. Each year innkeepers Stephen and Karen Caliri improve and refine the inn, and they are always quick to dispense helpful advice with good humor.

24 S. Water St. (in the center of town), Edgartown, MA 02539. © **508/627-4784.** www.thevic.com. 14 units, 2 with tub/shower, 12 with shower only. Summer $225–$425 double. Rates include full breakfast and afternoon tea. MC, V. Closed Nov–Mar. *In room:* A/C, TV, hair dryer, no phone.

Moderate

The Arbor Inn ★ (Value)   This 1880 farmhouse is at the far end of town, but it is still within walking distance from the center. The inn has a lovely cathedral-ceilinged living room with lots of comfortable seating for guests. Rooms range from tiny to spacious, but all are nicely appointed with antiques and reproductions. In the morning, baked goods are served in the dining room or outside in the garden. The rates are quite reasonable here compared to other Edgartown B&Bs.

222 Main St., Edgartown, MA 02539. © **888/748-4383** or 508/627-8137. Fax 508/627-9104. www.arborinn.net. 10 units, 2 with shared bathroom. Summer $140 shared bath; $175–$225 double. Rates include continental breakfast. MC, V. Closed Dec–Apr. *In room:* A/C, TV, no phone.

Edgartown Inn ★ (Value)   This centrally located historic inn offers perhaps the best value on the island. Nathaniel Hawthorne holed up here for nearly a year, and Daniel Webster also spent time here. Rooms are no-frills but pleasantly traditional; some have TVs. Breakfast, which is open to the public, is available in the dining room for an extra charge of $5.50 to $8.50. Some rooms in the front of the house have harbor views and

two have private balconies. Modernists may prefer the two cathedral-ceilinged quarters **275**
in the annex out back, which offer lovely light and a sense of seclusion.

56 N. Water St., Edgartown, MA 02539. ⓒ **508/627-4794**. Fax 508/627-9420. www.edgartowninn.com.
20 units, 4 with shared bathroom. Summer $125 shared bathroom; $125–$275 double. No credit cards.
Closed Nov–Mar. No children 6 and under. *In room:* A/C, TV (some units), no phone.

The Jonathan Munroe House ★★ ⓕinds   With its graceful wraparound and colonnaded front porch, the Jonathan Munroe House stands out from the other inns and
captain's homes on this stretch of upper Main Street. Guest rooms are immaculate,
antiques-filled, and dotted with clever details. Many rooms have fireplaces and baths
with whirlpool jets. At breakfast, don't miss the homemade waffles and pancakes, served
on the sunny porch. Wine and cheese are served in the evening. Request the garden cottage, with its flowering window boxes, if you are in a honeymooning mood.

100 Main St., Edgartown, MA 02539. ⓒ **877/468-6763** or 508/627-5536. Fax 508/627-5536. 7 units, 1
cottage. Summer $215–$225 double; $300 cottage. Rates include full breakfast and wine-and-cheese
hour. AE, MC, V. Open year-round. No children 11 and under. *In room:* A/C, hair dryer.

OAK BLUFFS

If you're looking for a basic motel with a central location, you'll want to stay at **Surfside
Motel** across from the ferry dock on Oak Bluffs Avenue in Oak Bluffs (ⓒ **800/537-3007**
or 508/693-2500; www.mvsurfside.com). Summer rates are $195 double, $245–$305 for
suites. Rooms are equipped with air-conditioning, TVs, minifridges, and phones. Open
year-round. Well-behaved pets allowed.

Expensive

Isabelle's Beach House ★   This grand 19th-century home across the street from the
ocean in Oak Bluffs has been recently renovated. Some of the rooms are on the small size
but they are light and airy, with crisp bedding. You'll love sitting out on the veranda,
rocking away as the sea breeze cools the air.

83 Seaview Ave. (on the sound), Oak Bluffs, MA 02557. ⓒ **800/674-3129** or 508/693-3955. www.
isabellesbeachhouse.com. 11 units. Summer $250–$275 double; $295–$395 suite. Rates include continental breakfast. AE, DISC, MC, V. Closed late Oct to early May. *In room:* A/C, TV, minifridge, hair dryer.

The Oak Bluffs Inn ★   This homey Victorian inn has a fun location at the top of
Circuit Avenue, Oak Bluff's main drag. The inn stands out with its whimsical, colorful
Victorian paint scheme and its prominent cupola, from which guests can enjoy a
360-degree view of Oak Bluffs. As is typical in a house of this vintage, some of the rooms
are a tad on the small side, but others are spacious and even have comfortable seating
areas. All rooms have ceiling fans.

64 Circuit Ave. (at the corner of Pequot Ave.), Oak Bluffs, MA 02557. ⓒ **800/955-6235** or 508/693-7171.
Fax 508/693-8787. www.oakbluffsinn.com. 9 units. Summer $250–$345 double. Rates include continental breakfast. AE, MC, V. Closed Nov–Apr. *In room:* A/C, hair dryer, no phone.

Moderate

The Dockside Inn ★ ⓚids   Set close to the harbor, the Dockside is perfectly located
for exploring the town of Oak Bluffs and is geared toward families. A number of the
apartments and suites have kitchenettes, allowing you to prepare your own meals and
save money. Most of the standard-size rooms have either a garden or harbor view; they're
decorated cheerfully in pinks and greens. Besides kitchenettes, some of the suites and
apartments have private decks. There are two wheelchair-accessible rooms.

MARTHA'S VINEYARD

10

WHERE TO STAY

9 Circuit Ave. Extension (P.O. Box 1206), Oak Bluffs, MA 02557. ✆ **800/245-5979** or 508/693-2966. Fax 508/696-7293. www.vineyardinns.com. 22 units. Summer $185–$225 double; $295–$400 suite. Rates include continental breakfast. AE, DISC, MC, V. Closed late Oct to early Apr. **Amenities:** 6-seat hot tub; free access to computer w/Internet. *In room:* A/C, TV, hair dryer, iron.

Wesley Hotel ★ (Value)   Formerly one of the grand hotels of Martha's Vineyard, this imposing 1879 property, right on the harbor, is now a solid entry in the good-value category. The only drawback here can be the noise from revelers on the boats in the harbor or traffic on busy Lake Avenue. Most of the rooms are fairly compact and basic. Many have easy access to the wraparound decks on all three floors of the inn. The Wesley Arms, behind the main building, contains 33 air-conditioned rooms. Five rooms are equipped for travelers with disabilities. *Note:* Reserve early to specify harbor views, which do not cost more than regular rooms. This is also one of the few Vineyard hotels that does not require a minimum stay in season.

70 Lake Ave. (on the harbor), Oak Bluffs, MA 02557. ✆ **800/638-9027** or 508/693-6611. Fax 508/693-5389. www.wesleyhotel.com. 95 units, all with shower only. Summer $220–$260 double; $310 suite. AE, DC, MC, V. Closed late Oct–Apr. *In room:* A/C, TV, no phone.

VINEYARD HAVEN (TISBURY)
Expensive
The Mansion House Inn ★★ (Finds)   After a fire burned down the 200-year-old Tisbury Inn several years ago, the owners decided to rebuild, making this one of the island's most full-service inns. The building, occupying a prominent corner location in Vineyard Haven, is now a community hub, with a restaurant, health club, and shops. The rooms range in size from cozy to spacious, and prices vary accordingly. Many have kitchenettes, plasma-screen televisions, and extra-large bathtubs. Some have harbor views and gas fireplaces. One of the most unique features of the inn is the 75-foot mineral spring (no chlorine) swimming pool in the inn's basement. A full gourmet breakfast is served buffet-style at Zephrus, the hotel's restaurant.

9 Main St., Vineyard Haven, MA 02568. ✆ **800/332-4112** or 508/693-2200. Fax 508/693-4095. www.mvmansionhouse.com. 32 units. $289–$299 double; $399–$559 suite. Rates include full buffet breakfast. AE, MC, V. Open year-round. **Amenities:** Restaurant (Zephrus, a fine-dining New American–style restaurant; see "Where to Dine," below); health club; spa w/75-ft. pool; room service. *In room:* A/C, TV, Wi-Fi (additional charge), fridge, hair dryer, iron.

CHILMARK (INCLUDING MENEMSHA), WEST TISBURY & AQUINNAH
Very Expensive
Beach Plum Inn ★★ (Finds)   This 8-acre property is tucked away in Menemsha yet is within walking distance of the harbor. There's a croquet course and Nova Grass tennis court on the grounds, plus bikes to take exploring (extra charge). The well-kept rooms are in the main inn and in four cottages, which contain six additional rooms. The room decor is predominantly cottage-y, though some rooms lean toward elegance. Linens are exceptional. Half the rooms have whirlpool baths. Most have decks or patios, some with views of Menemsha Harbor. One room is wheelchair-accessible. Inn guests get beach passes to the private up-island beaches. The inn's restaurant is one of the best fine-dining spots on the island (see "Where to Dine," below).

Beach Plum Lane (off North Rd., ¹/₂ mile northeast of the harbor), Menemsha, MA 02552. ⓒ **877/645-** **277**
7398 or 508/645-9454. Fax 508/645-2801. www.beachpluminn.com. 11 units, all with tub/shower. Summer $275–$450 double or cottage. Rates include full breakfast in season, continental off season. AE, DC, DISC, MC, V. Closed Jan–Apr. **Amenities:** Restaurant; tennis court; croquet court; in-room massage; babysitting by arrangement; laundry service for a charge; private beach passes. *In room:* A/C, TV, fridge, hair dryer, iron.

Expensive

The Inn at Blueberry Hill ★★ ⓕinds This bucolic property is set on 56 acres in the up-island town of Chilmark. Book a room at this inn if you want a secluded vacation in the country, far away from the tourist crowds. The comfortable rooms and suites are spread out in six buildings. The serene rooms feature white cotton linens, ceiling fans, and hand-painted furniture. Many rooms have private balconies or porches. There are exercise and spa services, as well as a lap pool and a tennis court. Also on-site is Theo's, an attractive fine-dining restaurant. Guests are given passes and offered shuttle service to the private beaches, Lucy Vincent and Squibnocket, which are about 4 miles away.

74 North Rd., Chilmark, MA 02535. ⓒ **800/356-3322** or 508/645-3322. Fax 508/645-3799. www.blueberryinn.com. 25 units. Summer $335–$288 double; $380–$774 suite and cottage. Rates include continental breakfast. AE, MC, V. Closed Nov–Apr. **Amenities:** Restaurant (New American fine dining); 25-yd. (75-ft.) lap pool; tennis court; exercise room; spa (facials, body treatments for extra charge); Jacuzzi; massage (extra charge); private beach passes. *In room:* A/C, TV (available on request), hair dryer.

Lambert's Cove Inn ★★ Set far off the main road and surrounded by apple trees and lilacs, this secluded estate suggests an age when time was measured in generations. Rooms have been recently updated and are exceedingly comfortable. You'll find an all-weather tennis court on the grounds, and the namesake beach 1 mile away. The inn's restaurant is known for New American dinners prepared by one of the island's best chefs.

Lambert's Cove Rd. (off State Rd., about 5 miles west of Vineyard Haven), West Tisbury, MA 02568. ⓒ **508/693-2298.** Fax 508/693-7890. www.lambertscoveinn.com. 15 units. Summer $225–$355 double. Rates include full breakfast. AE, MC, V. Closed early Dec to mid-Mar. **Amenities:** Restaurant (dinner only; see "Where to Dine," below); tennis court; private beach passes. *In room:* A/C, TV/DVD, CD player, hair dryer, iron.

Menemsha Inn & Cottages ★★ This 11-acre compound is about a half-mile walk through a wooded path to the beach at Menemsha Harbor. There's no restaurant—just a restful breakfast room. There are regular rooms, suites, and cottages, which have outdoor showers, barbecue grills, and kitchenettes. Guests have access to complimentary passes and shuttle-bus service to the Lucy Vincent and Squibnocket private beaches.

Off North Rd. (about ¹/₂ mile northeast of the harbor), Menemsha, MA 02552. ⓒ **508/645-2521.** Fax 508/645-9500. www.menemshainn.com. 15 units, 12 cottages. Summer $270–$340 double; $475 suite; $575 2-bedroom cottage; $550–$700/night, $3,800–$4,200/week 3-bedroom cottage. Rates include continental breakfast for rooms and suites. MC, V. Closed Dec to mid-Apr. **Amenities:** Tennis court; fitness room (step machine, treadmill, exercise bike, and free weights); beach passes. *In room:* TV/DVD, hair dryers.

Moderate

The Captain R. Flanders House ★ ⓕinds Set amid 60 acres of rolling meadows crisscrossed by stone walls, this late-18th-century farmhouse, built by a whaling captain, has remained much the same for 2 centuries. This is a working farm, so there's no time for posing. Two countrified modern cottages overlooking the pond have living rooms but not kitchenettes. After fortifying yourself with homemade muffins, island-made honey, and jam at breakfast, you are free to fritter the day away. The owners will provide you with a coveted pass to nearby Lucy Vincent Beach, or perhaps you'd prefer a long country walk.

North Rd. (about ¹/₂ mile northeast of Menemsha), Chilmark, MA 02535. ✆ **508/645-3123.** www.captain flandersinn.com. 5 units, 3 with shared bathroom; 2 cottages. Summer $80 single with shared bathroom; $175 double with shared bathroom; $195 double with private bathroom; $275 cottage. Rates include continental breakfast. AE, MC, V. Closed Nov to early May. **Amenities:** Private beach pass; shuttle bus to beach. *In room:* No phone.

Inexpensive
Hostelling International Martha's Vineyard   The first "purpose-built" youth hostel in the United States, this homey cedar-shake saltbox set at the edge of a vast state forest is still a front-runner. The hallways are plastered with notices of local attractions (some stores offer discounts to hostelers), and the check-in desk also serves as a tourist information booth. Outside, there's a volleyball court and a sheltered bike rack. By bike, the hostel is a little more than 7 miles from the Vineyard Haven ferry terminal; shuttle buses also make the rounds in summer. You'll have no trouble at all finding enjoyable ways to spend the 10am-to-5pm lockout; just don't forget the 11pm curfew.

525 Edgartown–West Tisbury Rd. (about 1 mile east of the town center), West Tisbury, MA 02575. ✆ 508/ 693-2665. Fax 508/693-2699. www.usahostels.org. 76 beds, 1 family room. $32 for members; $35 for nonmembers. MC, V. Closed mid-Oct to Mar. *In room:* No phone.

9 WHERE TO DINE

Restaurants tend to be expensive on the Vineyard, but the stiff competition has produced a bevy of places that offer excellent service, evocative settings, and creative cuisine. *A note on spirits:* Outside Oak Bluffs and Edgartown, all of Martha's Vineyard is "dry," including Vineyard Haven, so bring your own bottle; some restaurants charge a small fee for uncorking. **Great Harbour Gourmet & Spirits,** 40 Main St., Edgartown (✆ 508/627-4390), has a very good wine selection. There's also **Jim's Package Store** on Circuit Avenue Extension in Oak Bluffs (✆ 508/693-0236).

EDGARTOWN
Very Expensive
Atria ★★ NEW AMERICAN   This fine-dining restaurant set in an 18th-century sea captain's house on Upper Main Street in Edgartown gets rave reviews for its gourmet cuisine and high-caliber service. Pronounced with the emphasis on the second syllable (ah-*tre*-ah), the name refers to the brightest of three stars forming the Southern Triangle constellation. You can sit in the elegant dining room, the rose-covered wraparound porch, or the brick cellar bar downstairs for more casual dining. Chef/owner Christian Thornton's menu offers a variety of creative dishes with influences from around the country and around the world, with stops in the Mediterranean, Middle East, and Asia. It features organic island-grown produce, off-the-boat seafood, local shellfish, and aged prime meats. Popular starters include miso soup with steamed crab dumplings or Thai lemon-grass mussels. Unusual main courses include wok-fried Martha's Vineyard lobster or cracklin' pork shank with southern collard greens. There is live entertainment in the bar on weekends.

Main courses $30–$48. AE, MC, V. June–Aug daily 5:30–10pm; call for off-season hours. Open year-round.

L'étoile ★★★ CONTEMPORARY FRENCH   Chef Michael Brisson, one of the Vineyard's most acclaimed chefs, creates an ever-evolving menu devoted to local produce and seafood, along with delicacies flown in from the four corners of the earth. Sevruga usually makes an appearance—perhaps as a garnish for chilled leek soup. An étouffée of lobster with lobster, cognac, and chervil sauce might come with littlenecks, bay scallops, and roasted corn fritters; or roasted pheasant breast in a cider, apple-brandy, and thyme sauce may be accompanied by apple, sun-dried cherry, and mascarpone-filled wild-rice crepes.

22 N. Water St. (off Main St.). ℂ **508/627-5187.** Reservations recommended. Main courses $36–$49; Chef's Tasting Menu $115. AE, MC, V. July–Aug 6–10pm; call for off-season hours. Closed Dec to April.

Expensive
Alchemy ★★ FRENCH BISTRO   Chef/owners Scott Caskey and Michael Presnol serve up a little slice of Paris on Edgartown's Main Street. Such esoteric choices as oyster brie soup and Burgundy Vintners salad share the bill with escargot-and-chanterelle fricassee and *lapin moutarde spatzle* (yes, that's rabbit). As befits a true bistro, there's a large selection of cocktails, liqueurs, and wines. In addition to lunch and dinner, a bar menu is served from 2:30 to 11pm. This choice isn't for everyone, but sophisticated diners will enjoy the Continental flair.

71 Main St. (in the center of town). ℂ **508/627-9999.** Reservations accepted. Main courses $22–$33. AE, MC, V. June–Nov Mon–Sat noon–2:30pm lunch, daily 5:30–10pm dinner, daily 2:30–11pm bar menu; call for off-season hours. Open year-round.

Chesca's ★★ (Finds) ITALIAN   This modern-decor restaurant at the Colonial Inn is a solid entry, with yummy food at reasonable prices. You're sure to find favorites like paella (with roasted lobster and other choice seafood), risotto (with roasted vegetables), and ravioli (with portobello mushrooms and asparagus). Smaller appetites can fill up on homemade soup and salad.

At the Colonial Inn, 38 N. Water St. ℂ **508/627-1234.** Reservations accepted for parties with 6 or more only. Main courses $22–$36. AE, MC, V. Late June to early Sept daily 5:30–10pm; call for off-season hours. Closed Nov–Mar.

Detente ★★ NEW AMERICAN   In high season, it's difficult to get a reservation at this small restaurant. There's very good buzz on this intimate and cozy spot, which takes its name from the French word for relaxation and good relations. The theme for the menu here is seasonal specials featuring foods from local farms and markets. For starters, you can go light, with a spring watercress and spiced pecan salad, or heavy, with island lobster ravioli. The main courses are similarly varied, from pesto-marinated rack of lamb to orange curry-crusted monkfish. The wine list is extensive with numerous intriguing choices available by the glass.

Off Winter St. (in Nevin Sq. behind the Colonial Inn). ℂ **508/627-8810.** Reservations recommended. Main courses $29–$35. AE, MC, V. June–Aug daily 6–10pm; call for off-season hours. Closed Feb–Mar.

Lure ★★★ NEW AMERICAN   This elegant restaurant on the second floor of the Winnetu Resort in Katama is making a name for itself as a wonderful place for dinner. Those fortunate to get a window seat or a spot on the deck in good weather can watch the sun set as they enjoy the fine cuisine and professional service. Menu selections make the most of local produce and seafood. You might begin with local Katama oysters or seared foie gras. For a main course, there are unique choices like poached lobster with pea ravioli or wild king salmon with crabmeat-and-artichoke risotto. Homemade desserts like the caramelized apple charlotte are inspired. A restaurant for families with children, **Minnows,** is also on-site.

At the Winnetu Oceanside Resort, Katama (South Beach). ✆ **508/627-3663.** Reservations recommended. Main courses $24–$37. AE, MC, V. July–Aug daily 6:30–9:30pm; call for off-season hours. Closed Dec to mid-Apr.

Water Street ★★ NEW AMERICAN   This is a terrific place to have a drink or to dine, with its exquisite view of Edgartown Harbor and the lighthouse. The long and elegant bar is particularly smashing. The menu is simple but stylish. To start, there's soft-shell crab with arugula and teardrop tomatoes. As a main course, try the caramelized sea scallops with a salad of Asian pear and apple. Service is excellent; these are trained waiters, not your usual college surfer dudes. At the end of your meal, you may want to sit on the rockers on the Harbor View Hotel's wraparound porch and watch the lights twinkling in the harbor.

At the Harbor View Hotel (see "Where to Stay," earlier in this chapter), 131 N. Water St. ✆ **508/627-3761.** Reservations recommended. Main courses $22–$30. AE, MC, V. June–Aug daily 7–11am, noon–2pm and 6–10pm; call for off-season hours. Open year-round.

Moderate

Among the Flowers Cafe ★★ (Value) AMERICAN   Everything's fresh and appealing at this small outdoor cafe near the dock. Sit under the awning, and you'll just catch a glimpse of the harbor. The breakfasts are the best around, and all the crepes, waffles, and eggs are also available at lunch. The comfort-food dinners (chicken-and-black-pepper sauté over pasta; butter-and-crumb-crusted baked haddock with a sautéed lobster-and-shallot-butter cream) are among the most affordable options in this pricey town. There's almost always a wait, not just because it's so picturesque, but because the food is homey, hearty, and kind on the wallet.

Mayhew Lane. ✆ **508/627-3233.** Main courses $10–$18. AE, DC, DISC, MC, V. July–Aug daily 8am–9:30pm; May–June and Sept–Oct daily 8am–4pm. Closed Nov–Apr.

Seafood Shanty ★ (Finds) SEAFOOD   This casual restaurant overlooking Edgartown Harbor features outdoor dining and cheerful service by college kids. This is a great place for lunch with a water view. Good lunch choices are the lobster roll or the cold poached salmon. For dinner, options include a classic bouillabaisse-seafood stew or a prime-rib plate. There is also a children's menu. The restaurant has a convenient walk-up counter in a shack on Dock Street in front of the restaurant where virtually the entire menu is available to go.

31 Dock St. ✆ **508/627-8622.** Reservations recommended. Lunch $9–$17; dinner $17–$35. AE, MC, V. June–Aug daily 11am–10pm; call for off-season hours. Closed Nov to mid-May.

Inexpensive

Main Street Diner (Kids) AMERICAN   It's a little kitschy-cute, what with cartoon wallpaper decorated with vintage doodads, but tony Edgartown could use a place geared to folks not out to bust the budget. Kids and adults alike will enjoy this ersatz diner, where the food, as well as the trimmings, harken back to the 1950s. A one-egg breakfast with home fries and a buttermilk biscuit will set you back only $2; the burgers and sandwiches (including a classic open-face hot turkey with gravy, potatoes, and cranberry

sauce) less than $6. Grab a grilled cheese or BLT, and wash it down with a cherry
Coke.

Old Post Office Sq. (off Main St. in the center of town). C 508/627-9337. Most items under $15. AE, MC, V. Daily 8am–10pm year-round.

The Newes from America ★★ (Finds) PUB GRUB   The food is better than average at this subterranean tavern, built in 1742. The decor may be more Edwardian than Colonial, but those who come to quaff don't seem to care. Locals love the French onion soup. Beers are a specialty here. Try a rack of five esoteric brews, or let your choice of food—from a wood-smoked oyster "Island Poor Boy" sandwich with linguiça relish to an 18-ounce porterhouse steak—dictate your draft; the menu comes handily annotated with recommendations. Don't miss their seasoned fries, accompanied by a savory Southwestern dipping sauce.

At The Kelley House, 23 Kelley St. C 508/627-4397. Reservations not accepted. Main courses $7–$10. AE, MC, V. Daily 11:30am–11pm. Open year-round.

OAK BLUFFS
Expensive
Balance ★★ NEW AMERICAN   Ben DeForest is one talented and innovative chef. For a treat, try things here you're not accustomed to ordering, like the green beans tempura or the creamy gazpacho. The space features a long bar and rows of tables in front of an open kitchen. The bar attracts a hip-hop crowd late night.

67 Circuit Ave., Oak Bluffs. C 508/696-3000. Reservations recommended. Main courses $21–$39. AE, MC, V. May–Nov daily 5–11pm; call for off-season hours. Open year-round.

Oyster Bar Grill ★★ STEAK/SEAFOOD   Occupying a large space on Circuit Avenue, this restaurant with a huge oak bar is a hip venue for the 30-something crowd. Specializing in seafood and—unusual for Martha's Vineyard—steak, this place serves wonderful food, including a variety of its namesake oysters. Staff are particularly knowledgeable about food here. In season, there is live music and a hopping scene.

57 Circuit Ave., Oak Bluffs. C 508/693-6600. Reservations recommended. Main courses $19–$39. AE, MC, V. May–Nov daily 5–11pm; call for off-season hours. Open year-round.

Park Corner Bistro ★★★ (Finds) NEW AMERICAN   This superb restaurant in the center of Oak Bluffs is an intimate and cozy bistro that has a definite European aura. With just 10 tables, it's a romantic space for casual fine dining. Owner Josh Aronie and his partner chef Jesse Martin serve up creative offerings, and locals and visitors keep the place packed all summer. Favorite appetizers are the beet salad and the Parmesan gnocchi, which is sautéed with chanterelle and black trumpet mushrooms. The best main courses are the Australian lamb loin with sweet corn flan and champagne-corn emulsion; and the Black Angus steak with arugula, Yukon Gold whipped potatoes, and Vidalia onion compote. For dessert, don't miss the warm fruit cobbler with vanilla ice cream. A jazz trio performs here several nights a week.

20 Kennebec Ave. (off Circuit Ave., across from the OB Post Office). C 508/696-9922. Reservations suggested. Main courses $25–$37. AE, MC, V. July–Aug Tues–Sat 6–9:30pm, Sun noon–3pm and 6–9:30pm; call for off-season hours. Open year-round.

Sweet Life Cafe ★★★ FRENCH/AMERICAN   Locals are crazy about this pearl of a restaurant, set in a restored Victorian house on upper Circuit Avenue. In season, the most popular seating is outside in the garden. Fresh island produce is featured, with seafood specials an enticing draw. The menu changes often, and everything is terrific. Expect yummy soups like vegetable white-bean pistou and main courses like roast lamb loin with ratatouille. There are also always vegetarian entrees on the menu.

63 Circuit Ave. © **508/696-0200.** Reservations recommended. Main courses $32–$44. AE, DISC, MC, V. Mid-May to Aug daily 5:30–9:30pm; Apr to mid-May and Sept–Oct Thurs–Mon 5:30–9:30pm. Closed Nov–Mar.

Inexpensive

Coup de Ville ★ SEAFOOD Of the several open-air harborfront choices in Oak Bluffs, this one has the best service and food. This outdoor fried-seafood shack serves up tasty beer-battered shrimp, grilled swordfish, lobster salad, and "world-famous" chicken wings. Wing connoisseurs can choose from mild to suicide to Three Mile Island, as well as Cajun, mango, and Maryland style, among others. It's a fun place to people-watch on sunny summer days as boaters cruise around the harbor.

Dockside Market Place, Oak Bluffs Harbor. © **508/693-3420.** Most items $9–$20. MC, V. June–Aug daily 11am–10pm; call for off-season hours. Closed mid-Oct to Apr.

Linda Jean's ★ DINER A great place to bring kids or just to have a low-key meal with no pretensions, Linda Jean's has excellent breakfast, lunch and even dinner selections on their all-American-type menu of omelets, salads, sandwiches, and burgers. At breakfast, the line starts forming early here.

25 Circuit Ave., Oak Bluffs. © **508/693-4093.** Most items under $15. MC, V. June–Aug daily 8am–8pm; call for off-season hours. Open year-round.

Sharky's Cantina ★ MEXICAN A swinging Mexican joint right on Circuit Avenue is the new hot spot in Oak Bluffs. Stretching from one end of the restaurant to the other, the large bar is packed five deep (with mostly young people) in the summer. It's within yelling distance of the dining area, where the margaritas wash down a standard array of quesadillas, tacos, enchiladas, and burritos. Although typical for a Mexican restaurant, the menu is an inexpensive rarity on the Vineyard. This well-run establishment is a solid entry on the Oak Bluffs scene.

31 Circuit Ave. © **508/693-7501.** Reservations accepted. Main courses $6–$15. MC, V. June–Aug daily 8am–10pm; call for off-season hours. Open year-round.

Slice of Life (Finds) DELI This deli at the upper end of Circuit Avenue is the place to head for gourmet sandwiches, salads, and soups. There are just a handful of tables inside and more out on the screened porch in front. The eclectic menu includes burgers and pizza. Sandwiches are made with bread baked on-site. Wine, beer, and specialty coffees are served.

50 Circuit Ave. © **508/693-3838.** Reservations not accepted. Most items under $10. MC, V. June–Aug daily 8am–10pm; call for off-season hours. Open year-round.

Sweets

Mad Martha's ★ Vineyarders are mad for this locally made ice cream, which comes in two dozen enticing flavors. You could opt for a restrained mango sorbet, which isn't to say you shouldn't go for a hot-fudge sundae.

117 Circuit Ave. (in the center of town). © **508/693-9151.** Branches at 7 N. Water St., Edgartown. © **508/627-8761.** Daily 10am–1am. Closed Oct–Apr.

Murdick's Fudge Since 1887, the Murdick family has been serving up homemade fudge, brittle, clusters, and bark. Bring the kids and watch the candy-makers.

5 Circuit Ave. and 21 N. Water St., Edgartown. ✆ **508/627-8047.** Summer daily 9:30am–11pm; call for off-season hours.

VINEYARD HAVEN (TISBURY)
Expensive
Le Grenier ★★ FRENCH If Paris is the heart of France, Lyons is its belly—and that's where chef/owner Jean Dupon grew up on his *Maman's* hearty cuisine. Dupon has the Continental moves down, as evidenced by such classics as steak au poivre, calves' brains Grenobloise with *beurre noir* and capers, and lobster Normande flambéed with Calvados, apples, and cream. Despite the fact that Le Grenier means (and, in fact, is housed in) an attic, the restaurant is quite romantic, especially when aglow with hurricane lamps. *Remember:* You must BYOB here.

96 Main St. (in the center of town). ✆ **508/693-4906.** Reservations suggested. Main courses $22–$32. AE, DC, DISC, MC, V. Daily 5:30–9pm. Open year-round.

Zephrus at the Mansion House Inn ★★ INTERNATIONAL This hip restaurant at the Mansion House Inn in the center of Vineyard Haven is a great place to go for casual fine-dining. Seating is at the sidewalk cafe on Main Street or inside by the hearth in view of the open kitchen. Menu items are creative at this high-energy venue, and portions are generous. For starters you might try the snow crab cakes or the spicy mussels. Main-course winners are pan-roasted pork tenderloin served with sweet tater tots; and shrimp and *farfalle* pasta. Though the menu is in constant flux, there is always a good vegetarian choice like the delicious vegetable risotto with truffle vinaigrette. Since the restaurant is in BYOB Vineyard Haven, you'll want to bring your favorite wine to complement this winning cuisine. The corkage fee is $5 per table.

9 Main St. ✆ **508/693-3416.** Reservations recommended. Main courses $20–$28. AE, DC, DISC, MC, V. July–Aug Mon–Sat 11:30am–3pm and 5:30–10pm, Sun 5:30–9:30pm; call for off-season hours. Open year-round.

Moderate
Black Dog Tavern ★ NEW AMERICAN How does a humble harbor shack come to be a national icon? Location helps. So do cool T-shirts. Soon after *Shenandoah* captain Robert Douglas decided, in 1971, that this hardworking port could use a good restaurant, influential vacationers stuck waiting for the ferry began to wander into this saltbox to tide themselves over with a bit of "blackout cake" or peanut-butter pie. The rest is history, as smart marketing moves extrapolated on word of mouth. The smartest of these moves was the invention of the signature "Martha's Vineyard whitefoot," a black Lab whose stalwart profile now adorns everything from babies' overalls to doggy bandannas, golf balls, and needlepoint kits. Originally the symbol signaled Vineyard ties to fellow insiders; now it merely bespeaks an acquaintance with mail-order catalogs.

Still, tourists love this rough-hewn tavern, though it's mostly hype that keeps them happy. The food is heavy on the seafood, of course (including grilled swordfish with banana, basil, and lime; and bluefish with mustard-soufflé sauce)—and the blackout cake has lost none of its appeal.

Beach St. Extension (on the harbor). ✆ **508/693-9223.** Reservations not accepted. Main courses $14–$27. AE, MC, V. June to early Sept Mon–Sat 7–11am, noon–4pm, and 5–10pm; Sun 7am–noon, 1–4pm, and 5–10pm; call for off-season hours. Open year-round.

Art Cliff Diner ★★ ECLECTIC DINER   Expect the best food you've ever had at a diner at this quirky establishment. It's a short walk from the center of Vineyard Haven. Be aware that the hours are a little unreliable and you should call to be sure it is open before making the trek. The food here is scrumptious, whether you are having the fish of the day that has just been caught that morning served with herbs from the chef's garden, or a simple burger that is cooked just right. Desserts are homemade, of course.

39 Beach Rd. (a short walk from Main St.). ✆ **508/693-1224.** Reservations not accepted. Main courses all under $15. No credit cards. July–Aug Thurs–Tues 7am–2pm, closed Wed; call for off-season hours. Closed Nov–Apr.

Takeout & Picnic Fare

Black Dog Bakery ★   In need of a snack at 5:30am? That's when the doors to this fabled bakery open; from mid-morning on, it's elbow room only. The selection of freshly baked breads, muffins, and desserts can't be beat. Don't forget homemade doggie biscuits for your pooch.

Water St. (near the harbor). ✆ **508/693-4786.** Summer daily 5:30am–8pm; winter daily 5:30am–5pm.

CHILMARK (INCLUDING MENEMSHA) & WEST TISBURY
Very Expensive

The Beach Plum Inn Restaurant ★★★ INTERNATIONAL   This jewel of a restaurant is located in an inn that sits on a bluff overlooking the fishing village of Menemsha. Extensive renovations and attention to quality have made this one of the island's top dining venues. Guests can dine inside in the spare, but elegant, dining room, or outside on the tiled patio. Either way, diners enjoy sunset views of the harbor. Most popular dishes include hazelnut-encrusted halibut with Marsala wine beurre-blanc sauce and Alaskan king salmon, grilled over Peruvian blue mashed potatoes with a morel mushroom sauce and crabmeat timbale. For dessert, you'll flip for the chocolate quadruple-layer cake made with white and dark chocolate mousse and Chambord.

At the Beach Plum Inn, 50 Beach Plum Lane (off North Rd.), Menemsha. ✆ **508/645-9454.** Reservations required. Main courses $32–$40; 4-course fixed-price menu $68; off-season-only fixed-priced menu $50. AE, MC, V. Mid-June to early Sept daily seatings 5:30–6:45pm and 8–9:30pm; call for off-season hours. Closed Dec–Apr.

Expensive

Home Port ★★ SEAFOOD   When the basics—a lobster and a sunset—are what you crave, head to this favorite of locals and visitors alike. At first glance, prices for the dinners may seem a bit high, but note that they include an appetizer of your choice (go with the stuffed quahog), salad, amazing fresh-baked breads, a nonalcoholic beverage (remember, it's BYOB in these parts), and dessert. Locals not keen on summer crowds prefer to order their lobster dinners for pickup (less than half price) at the restaurant door, then head down to Menemsha Beach for a private sunset supper.

North Rd., Menemsha. ✆ **508/645-2679.** Reservations suggested. Complete dinners $30–$50. MC, V. July–Aug daily 5–9pm; call for off-season hours. Closed Labor Day to mid-May.

Lambert's Cove Inn Restaurant ★★ (Finds) NEW AMERICAN   One of the Vineyard's favorite chefs, Joe Silva, runs the kitchen at this romantic country inn. If you are staying in one of the down-island towns such as Edgartown or Oak Bluffs, driving through the wooded countryside to this secluded inn feels like an expedition to an earlier time. The interior of the restaurant is set up with crisp white tablecloths and antique furniture. In good weather, you can dine alfresco on a deck surrounded by flowering trees and shrubs. The menu features fresh seafood and island produce and meats. You might start with a crab and asparagus Napoleon, or simply a luscious cream of mushroom soup. Special dinner entrees include grilled marinated duck-breast casserole baked in a sherry lobster cream sauce. Desserts are homemade delicacies. Don't forget: The town of West Tisbury is "dry," so you must bring your own alcoholic beverages.

Lamberts Cove Rd. (off State Rd., about 3 miles west of Vineyard Haven), West Tisbury. ✆ **508/693-2298.** Reservations suggested. Main courses $24–$32. AE, MC, V. July–Aug daily 6–9pm; call for off-season hours. Open year-round.

Moderate
The Bite ★★ ⟨Finds⟩ SEAFOOD   It's places like The Bite that you crave when you think of New England. This is your quintessential "chowdah" and clam shack, flanked by picnic tables. Run by two sisters using their grandmother's recipes, The Bite makes superlative chowder, potato salad, fried fish, and so forth. The food comes in graduated containers, with a jumbo portion of shrimp topping out at around $26.

Basin Rd. (off North Rd., about 1/4 mile northeast of the harbor), Menemsha. ✆ **508/645-9239.** Main courses $18–$30. No credit cards. July–Aug daily 11am–8pm; call for off-season hours. Closed late Sept to Apr.

Takeout & Picnic Fare
Alley's General Store ⟨Finds⟩   That endangered rarity, a true New England general store, Alley's—in business since 1858—nearly foundered in the profit-mad 1980s. Luckily the Martha's Vineyard Preservation Trust interceded to give it a new lease on life, along with a much-needed structural overhaul. The stock is still the same, though: basically, everything you could possibly need, from scrub brushes to fresh-made salsa. Best of all, the no-longer-sagging front porch still supports a popular bank of benches, along with a blizzard of bulletin-board notices. For a local's-eye view of noteworthy activities and events, this is the first place to check.

State Rd. (in the center of town), West Tisbury. ✆ **508/693-0088.** Summer daily 7am–7pm; winter Mon–Sat 7am–6pm, Sun 8am–5pm.

West Tisbury Farmer's Market ⟨Finds⟩   This seasonal outdoor market, open Wednesday from 2:30 to 5:30pm and Saturday from 9am to noon, is among the biggest and best in New England, and certainly the most rarefied, with local celebrities loading up on prize produce and snacking on pesto bread and other international goodies. The fun starts in June and runs for 18 Saturdays and 10 Wednesdays.

Old Agricultural Hall, West Tisbury. No phone.

10 MARTHA'S VINEYARD AFTER DARK

PUBS, BARS, DANCE CLUBS & LIVE MUSIC
The Lampost/Rare Duck   Young and loud are the watchwords at this pair of clubs; the larger features live bands or DJs and a dance floor, the smaller (down in the basement), acoustic acts. This is where the young folk go, and the performers could be playing blues, reggae, R&B, or '80s. Call for a schedule. Closed November to March. 111 Circuit Ave. (in the center of town), Oak Bluffs. ✆ **508/696-9352.** Cover $1–$5.

Lola's With a large dance floor for the over-30 set, Lola's always has a hip and fun-loving crowd. There's live music 7 nights a week from June to Labor Day. Off season, bands play on Thursday, Friday, and Saturday nights. Call for a schedule. Open year-round. At the Island Inn, Beach Rd., Oak Bluffs. ✆ 508/693-5007.

Offshore Ale Company (Finds) In 1602, the first barley in the New World was grown on Martha's Vineyard. A few years ago, the Vineyard's first and only brew pub opened, featuring eight locally made beers on tap ($2.75–$5). It's an attractively rustic place, with high ceilings, oak booths lining the walls, and peanut shells strewn on the floor. There's a raw bar, and late-night munchies are served 'til 10pm, featuring pizza and hamburgers, among other offerings. Local acoustic performers entertain 6 nights a week in season. Open June to September daily noon to midnight; call for off-season hours. 30 Kennebec Ave., Oak Bluffs. ✆ 508/693-2626. Cover $2–$3.

Outerland The dance club at the airport features top musicians, comedy, theme nights, and teen nights. Doors open on show nights at 7pm. Food is served until 11pm. Open April to mid-January. At Martha's Vineyard Airport (take West Tisbury/Edgartown Rd. to the airport). ✆ 508/693-1137. Tickets $10–$30.

The Ritz Cafe Locals and visitors alike flock to this down-and-dirty hole-in-the-wall that features live music every night in season and on weekends year-round. The crowd—a boozing, brawling lot—enjoy the pool tables in the back. Call for a schedule. On the dock, Oak Bluffs. ✆ 508/693-9851. Cover $3.

The Sand Bar & Grille This cool cat bar is the place to hang out in Oak Bluffs near the harbor to listen to the latest local bands. 1 Circuit Ave. (in the center of town), Oak Bluffs. ✆ 508/693-7111.

LOW-KEY EVENINGS

Old Whaling Church This magnificent 1843 Greek Revival church functions primarily as a 500-seat performing-arts center offering lectures and symposiums, films, plays, and concerts. Such Vineyard luminaries as the actress Patricia Neal have taken their place at the pulpit, not to mention Livingston Taylor and Andre Previn, whose annual gigs always sell out. It's also the Edgartown United Methodist Church, with a 9am service on Sundays. Call for a schedule. 89 Main St. (in the center of town), Edgartown. ✆ 508/627-4442. Ticket prices vary.

THEATER & DANCE

Vineyard Playhouse In an intimate (112-seat) black-box theater, carved out of an 1833 church-turned-Masonic lodge, Equity professionals put on a rich season of favorites and challenging new work, followed, on summer weekends, by musical or comedic cabaret in the gallery/lounge. Children's theater selections are performed on Saturdays at 10am. Townspeople often get involved in the outdoor Shakespeare production, a 3-week run starting in mid-July at the Tashmoo Overlook Amphitheatre about 1 mile west of town, where tickets for the 5pm performances Tuesday to Sunday run only $5 to $10. MasterCard and Visa are accepted. Open June to September Tuesday to Saturday at 8pm, Sunday at 7pm; call for off-season hours. 24 Church St. (in the center of town), Vineyard Haven. ✆ 508/696-6300 or 693-6450. www.vineyardplayhouse.org. Tickets $15–$30.

MOVIES

The **Entertainment Cinemas** at 65 Main St. (© **508/627-8008**) in Edgartown has two screens. There are also vintage Art Deco movie theaters: **Island Theater,** at the bottom of Circuit Avenue, Oak Bluffs; the **Capawock** in Vineyard Haven, and **The Strand,** Oak Bluffs Avenue Extension, Oak Bluffs. Call © **508/627-6689** for movie times.

ONLY ON THE VINEYARD

Gay Head Lighthouse   Though generally closed to the public, this 1856 lighthouse opens its doors on summer-weekend evenings to afford an awe-inspiring view of the sunset over the Devil's Bridge shoals. The light has been automated since 1952 (the original lens lights up the night sky in Edgartown), but the experience continues to be romantic. Tour time varies nightly. It begins an hour and a half before sunset and ends a half-hour past sunset. Open late June to late September Friday to Sunday 7 to 9pm. Off State Rd., Aquinnah. © **508/645-2211.** Admission $2 adults, free for children 11 and under.

Trinity Park Tabernacle   Designed by architect J. W. Hoyt of Springfield, Massachusetts, and built in 1879 for just over $7,000, this open-air church, now on the National Register of Historic Places, is the largest wrought-iron-and-wood structure in America. Its conical crown is ringed with a geometric pattern of amber, carmine, and midnight-blue stained glass. Old-fashioned community sings take place Wednesday at 8pm, and concerts are scheduled irregularly on weekends. James Taylor and Bonnie Raitt have regaled the faithful here, but usually the acts are more homespun. Open July to August on Wednesdays at 8pm and occasional weekend evenings. Call for a schedule. Trinity Park (within the Camp Meeting Grounds), Oak Bluffs. © **508/693-0525.** Free admission and $20 community tours.

Fast Facts, Toll-Free Numbers & Websites

1 FAST FACTS: CAPE COD & THE ISLANDS

AMERICAN EXPRESS The **American Express Travel Service** office is at 1600 Falmouth Rd. in Centerville (© **800/937-1255** or 508/778-2310) and is open Monday to Friday from 9am to 5:30pm.

AREA CODES The telephone area code for the Cape and islands is **508.** You must always dial © 1 and this area code first, even if you are making a call within the same town.

ATM NETWORKS See "Money & Costs," p. 49.

AUTOMOBILE ORGANIZATIONS Auto clubs will supply maps, suggested routes, guidebooks, accident and bail-bond insurance, and emergency road service. The **American Automobile Association (AAA)** is the major auto club in the United States. If you belong to an auto club in your home country, inquire about AAA reciprocity before you leave. You may be able to join AAA even if you're not a member of a reciprocal club; to inquire, call AAA (© **800/222-4357**). AAA is actually an organization of regional auto clubs, so look under "AAA Automobile Club" in the White Pages of the telephone directory. AAA has a nationwide emergency road service telephone number (© **800/AAA-HELP** [800/222-4357]).

BUSINESS HOURS Business hours in public and private offices are usually Monday to Friday from 8 or 9am to 5pm. Most stores are open Monday to Saturday from 9:30 or 10am to 5:30 or 6pm; many are

also open on Sunday from noon to 5pm or earlier. The exception is Provincetown, where many stores are open until 10 or 11pm. Virtually every town has some kind of convenience store carrying food, beverages, newspapers, and household basics; and the larger communities have supermarkets, which generally stay open as late as 10 or 11pm or even 24 hours.

CAR RENTALS See "Getting There & Getting Around," p. 41.

CURRENCY For information see "Money & Costs," p. 49.

DRINKING LAWS The legal age for purchase and consumption of alcoholic beverages is 21; proof of age is required and often requested at bars, nightclubs, and restaurants, so it's always a good idea to bring ID when you go out.

Bars are allowed to stay open until 1am every day, with last call at 12:30am. Beer and wine are sold at grocery as well as package stores, hard liquor at package stores only. A few towns on Martha's Vineyard are dry by choice or tradition (no alcohol can be sold or served), but at most establishments lacking a liquor license, you're welcome to bring your own wine or beer; if in doubt, call ahead.

Do not carry open containers of alcohol in your car or in any public area that isn't zoned for alcohol consumption. The police can fine you on the spot. And nothing will ruin your trip faster than getting a citation for DUI ("driving under the influence"), so don't even think about driving while intoxicated.

DRIVING RULES See "Getting There & Getting Around," p. 41.

ELECTRICITY Like Canada, the United States uses 110 to 120 volts AC (60 cycles), compared to 220 to 240 volts AC (50 cycles) in most of Europe, Australia, and New Zealand. Downward converters that change 220–240 volts to 110–120 volts are difficult to find in the United States, so bring one with you. Wherever you go, bring a **connection kit** of the right power and phone adapters, a spare phone cord, and a spare Ethernet network cable—or find out whether your hotel supplies them to guests.

EMBASSIES & CONSULATES All embassies are located in the nation's capital, Washington, D.C. Some consulates are located in major U.S. cities, and most nations have a mission to the United Nations in New York City. If your country isn't listed below, call for directory information in Washington, D.C. (© **202/555-1212**) or log on to **www.embassy.org/embassies**.

The embassy of **Australia** is at 1601 Massachusetts Ave. NW, Washington, DC 20036 (© **202/797-3000**; www.austemb. org). There are consulates in New York, Honolulu, Houston, Los Angeles, and San Francisco.

The embassy of **Canada** is at 501 Pennsylvania Ave. NW, Washington, DC 20001 (© **202/682-1740**; www.canadian embassy.org). Other Canadian consulates are in Buffalo (New York), Detroit, Los Angeles, New York, and Seattle.

The embassy of **Ireland** is at 2234 Massachusetts Ave. NW, Washington, DC 20008 (© **202/462-3939**; www.ireland emb.org). Irish consulates are in Boston, Chicago, New York, San Francisco, and other cities. See website for complete listing.

The embassy of **New Zealand** is at 37 Observatory Circle NW, Washington, DC 20008 (© **202/328-4800**; www.nzembassy. com). New Zealand consulates are in Los Angeles, Salt Lake City, San Francisco, and Seattle.

The embassy of the **United Kingdom** is at 3100 Massachusetts Ave. NW, Washington, DC 20008 (© **202/588-7800**; www.britainusa.com). Other British consulates are in Atlanta, Boston, Chicago, Cleveland, Houston, Los Angeles, New York, San Francisco, and Seattle.

EMERGENCIES In an emergency, call © **911.**

GASOLINE (PETROL) At press time, the cost of U.S. gasoline (also known as gas, but never petrol), has been varying widely for months. Cape Cod has some of the highest prices in the country, averaging at about $3 per gallon, with the islands of Martha's Vineyard and Nantucket even higher. Taxes are already included in the posted price. One U.S. gallon equals 3.8 liters or .85 imperial gallons. Fill-up locations are known as gas or service stations.

HOLIDAYS Banks, government offices, post offices, and many stores, restaurants, and museums are closed on the following legal national holidays: January 1 (New Year's Day), the third Monday in January (Martin Luther King, Jr., Day), the third Monday in February (Presidents' Day), the last Monday in May (Memorial Day), July 4 (Independence Day), the first Monday in September (Labor Day), the second Monday in October (Columbus Day), November 11 (Veterans' Day/Armistice Day), the fourth Thursday in November (Thanksgiving Day), and December 25 (Christmas). The Tuesday after the first Monday in November is Election Day, a federal government holiday in presidential-election years (held every 4 years, most recently in 2008).

For more information on holidays see "Calendar of Events" in chapter 3.

HOSPITALS The **Cape Cod Hospital** at 27 Park St., Hyannis (© **508/771-1800**, ext. 5235), offers 24-hour emergency medical service and consultation, as does the **Falmouth Hospital** at 100 Ter Heun Dr. (© **508/457-3524**). On the islands, contact the **Martha's Vineyard Hospital** on Linton Lane in Oak Bluffs (© **508/693-0410**) or **Nantucket Cottage Hospital** on South Prospect Street (© 508/228-1200).

INSURANCE One thing to keep in mind when visiting the Cape and islands is that there are no refunds for bad weather. Fortunately, there are a number of things to do when you are stuck with a run of cloudy or rainy days. Most hotels and inns in the region give details about their cancellation policies when you book. Some will refund your money if you cancel more than a month before the trip and they are able to rebook the room. Some people would rather rely on travel insurance.

Medical Insurance: Although it's not required of travelers, health insurance is highly recommended. Most health insurance policies cover you if you get sick away from home—but check your coverage before you leave.

International visitors to the U.S. should note that unlike many European countries, the United States does not usually offer free or low-cost medical care to its citizens or visitors. Doctors and hospitals are expensive, and in most cases will require advance payment or proof of coverage before they render their services. Good policies will cover the costs of an accident, repatriation, or death. Packages such as **Europ Assistance's "Worldwide Healthcare Plan"** are sold by European automobile clubs and travel agencies at attractive rates. **Worldwide Assistance Services, Inc.** (© 800/777-8710; www. worldwideassistance.com) is the agent for Europ Assistance in the United States.

Though lack of health insurance may prevent you from being admitted to a hospital in nonemergencies, don't worry about being left on a street corner to die: The American way is to fix you now and bill the daylights out of you later.

If you're ever hospitalized more than 150 miles from home, **MedjetAssist** (© **800/527-7478**; www.medjetassistance.com) will pick you up and fly you to the hospital of your choice in a medically equipped and staffed aircraft 24 hours day, 7 days a week. Annual memberships are $225 individual, $350 family; you can also purchase short-term memberships.

Canadians should check with their provincial health plan offices or call **Health Canada** (© 866/225-0709; www.hc-sc. gc.ca) to find out the extent of their coverage and what documentation and receipts they must take home in case they are treated in the United States.

Travelers from the U.K. should carry their European Health Insurance Card (EHIC), which replaced the E111 form as proof of entitlement to free/reduced cost medical treatment abroad (© **0845 606 2030;** www. ehic.org.uk). Note, however, that the EHIC only covers "necessary medical treatment," and for repatriation costs, lost money, baggage, or cancellation, travel insurance from a reputable company should always be sought (www.travelinsuranceweb.com).

Travel Insurance: The cost of travel insurance varies widely, depending on the destination, the cost and length of your trip, your age and health, and the type of trip you're taking, but expect to pay between 5% and 8% of the vacation itself. You can get estimates from various providers through **InsureMyTrip.com**. Enter your trip cost and dates, your age, and other information, for prices from more than a dozen companies.

U.K. citizens and their families who make more than one trip abroad per year may find an annual travel insurance policy works out cheaper. Check **www.money supermarket.com**, which compares prices across a wide range of providers for single- and multi-trip policies.

Most big travel agents offer their own insurance and will probably try to sell you their package when you book a holiday. Think before you sign. **Britain's Consumers' Association** recommends that you insist on seeing the policy and reading the fine print before buying travel insurance. **The Association of British Insurers** (© 020/7600-3333; www.abi.org.uk) gives advice by phone and publishes Holiday Insurance, a free guide to policy provisions and prices. You might also shop around for better deals: Try **Columbus Direct** (© 0870/033-9988; www.columbusdirect.net).

Trip Cancellation Insurance: Trip cancellation insurance will help retrieve your money if you have to back out of a trip or depart early, or if your travel supplier goes bankrupt. Trip cancellation traditionally covers such events as sickness, natural disasters, and State Department advisories. The latest news in trip-cancellation insurance is the availability of **expanded hurricane coverage** and the **"any-reason"** cancellation coverage—which costs more but covers cancellations made for any reason. You won't get back 100% of your prepaid trip cost, but you'll be refunded a substantial portion. **TravelSafe** (© 888/885-7233; www.travelsafe.com) offers both types of coverage. Expedia also offers any-reason cancellation coverage for its air-hotel packages. For details, contact one of the following recommended insurers: **Access America** (© 866/807-3982; www.accessamerica.com); **Travel Guard International** (© 800/826-4919; www.travelguard.com); **Travel Insured International** (© 800/243-3174; www.travelinsured.com); and **Travelex Insurance Services** (© 888/457-4602; www.travelex-insurance.com).

INTERNET ACCESS Most Cape and island towns have at least one cybercafe; check with your innkeeper or the local chamber of commerce to find the closest one. In addition, almost all libraries have free Internet access.

LEGAL AID If you are "pulled over" for a minor infraction (such as speeding), never attempt to pay the fine directly to a police officer; this could be construed as attempted bribery, a much more serious crime. Pay fines by mail, or directly into the hands of the clerk of the court. If accused of a more serious offense, say and do nothing before consulting a lawyer. Here the burden is on the state to prove a person's guilt beyond a reasonable doubt, and everyone has the right to remain silent, whether he or she is suspected of a crime or actually arrested. Once arrested, a person can make one telephone call to a party of his or her choice. International visitors should call their embassy or consulate.

LOST & FOUND Be sure to tell all of your credit card companies the minute you discover your wallet has been lost or stolen and file a report at the nearest police precinct. Your credit card company or insurer may require a police report number or record of the loss. Most credit card companies have an emergency toll-free number to call if your card is lost or stolen; they may be able to wire you a cash advance immediately or deliver an emergency credit card in a day or two. Visa's U.S. emergency number is © 800/847-2911 or 410/581-9994. American Express cardholders and traveler's check holders should call © 800/221-7282. MasterCard holders should call © 800/307-7309 or 636/722-7111. For other credit cards, call the toll-free number directory at © 800/555-1212.

If you need emergency cash over the weekend when all banks and American Express offices are closed, you can have money wired to you via **Western Union** (© 800/325-6000; www.westernunion.com).

MAIL At press time, domestic postage rates were 27¢ for a postcard and 42¢ for a letter. For international mail, a first-class letter of up to 1 ounce costs 94¢ (72¢ to

Canada and Mexico); a first-class postcard costs 94¢ (72¢ to Canada and Mexico). For more information go to **www.usps. com** and click on "Calculate Postage."

If you aren't sure what your address will be in the United States, mail can be sent to you, in your name, c/o General Delivery at the main post office of the city or region where you expect to be. (Call © 800/275-8777 for information on the nearest post office.) The addressee must pick up mail in person and must produce proof of identity (driver's license, passport, and so on). Most post offices will hold your mail for up to 1 month, and are open Monday to Friday from 8am to 6pm and Saturday from 9am to 3pm.

Always include zip codes when mailing items in the U.S. If you don't know your zip code, visit www.usps.com/zip4.

MEASUREMENTS   See the chart on the inside front cover of this book for details on converting metric measurements to nonmetric equivalents.

MEDICAL CONDITIONS   If you have a medical condition that requires **syringe-administered medications,** carry a valid signed prescription from your physician; syringes in carry-on baggage will be inspected. Insulin in any form should have the proper pharmaceutical documentation. If you have a disease that requires treatment with **narcotics,** you should also carry documented proof with you—smuggling narcotics aboard a plane carries severe penalties in the U.S.

For **HIV-positive visitors,** requirements for entering the United States are somewhat vague and change frequently. For up-to-the-minute information, contact **AIDSinfo** (© **800/448-0440** or 301/519-6616 outside the U.S.; www.aidsinfo. nih.gov) or the **Gay Men's Health Crisis** (© **212/367-1000;** www.gmhc.org).

NEWSPAPERS & MAGAZINES   The Enterprise Newspaper Group publishes the *Falmouth Enterprise, Bourne Enterprise,*

Sandwich Enterprise and *Mashpee Enterprise,* good resources for travelers visiting those towns. *The Cape Cod Times* is published daily and runs regular supplements on arts and antiques, events and entertainment, and restaurants. In addition, several other towns have their own weekly local paper. Martha's Vineyard has two weekly papers, *The Martha's Vineyard Times* and the *Vineyard Gazette,* each offering insight into regional issues. Nantucket also has one: *The Nantucket Inquirer and Mirror* (nicknamed "the Inky"). *Cape Cod Life* is a glossy bimonthly with beautiful photography of the area. Each island has its own glossy. *Provincetown Arts,* published yearly, is a must for those interested in local arts and letters. In addition, a great many summer-guide magazines are available (don't expect much new information), and free booklets with discount coupons are ubiquitous; the nicest of these, with a friendly tone and a lot of useful information, is the *Cape Cod Guide.*

PASSPORTS   The websites listed provide downloadable passport applications as well as the current fees for processing applications. For an up-to-date, country-by-country listing of passport requirements around the world, go to the "International Travel" tab of the U.S. State Department at **http://travel.state.gov.** International visitors to the U.S. can obtain a visa application at the same website. *Note:* Children are required to present a passport when entering the United States at airports. More information on obtaining a passport for a minor can be found at http://travel.state.gov. Allow plenty of time before your trip to apply for a passport; processing normally takes 4–6 weeks (3 weeks for expedited service) but can take longer during busy periods (especially spring). And keep in mind that if you need a passport in a hurry, you'll pay a higher processing fee.

For Residents of Australia: You can pick up an application from your local post office or any branch of Passports Australia, but you must schedule an interview at the passport office to present your application materials. Call the **Australian Passport Information Service** at (℗ **131-232,** or visit the government website at www.passports.gov.au.

For Residents of Canada: Passport applications are available at travel agencies throughout Canada or from the central **Passport Office,** Department of Foreign Affairs and International Trade, Ottawa, ON K1A 0G3 (℗ **800/567-6868;** www. ppt.gc.ca). *Note:* Canadian children who travel must have their own passport. However, if you hold a valid Canadian passport issued before December 11, 2001, that bears the name of your child, the passport remains valid for you and your child until it expires.

For Residents of Ireland: You can apply for a 10-year passport at the **Passport Office,** Setanta Centre, Molesworth Street, Dublin 2 (℗ **01/671-1633;** www. irlgov.ie/iveagh). Those age 17 and under must apply for a 5-year passport. You can also apply at 1A South Mall, Cork (℗ **21/494-4700**) or at most main post offices.

For Residents of New Zealand: You can pick up a passport application at any New Zealand Passports Office or download it from their website. Contact the **Passports Office** at (℗ **0800/225-050** in New Zealand or 04/474-8100, or log on to www.passports.govt.nz.

For Residents of the United Kingdom: To pick up an application for a standard 10-year passport (5-yr. passport for children 16 and under), visit your nearest passport office, major post office, or travel agency or contact the **United Kingdom Passport Service** at (℗ **0870/521-0410** or search its website at www. ukpa.gov.uk.

POLICE   For police emergencies, call (℗ **911.**

SMOKING   In the past few years, 14 out of 15 Cape Cod towns have gone "smoke-free" to some extent. The towns of Falmouth, Barnstable, Yarmouth, Dennis, Brewster, Chatham, Orleans, Eastham, Wellfleet, Truro, and Provincetown, and the islands of Martha's Vineyard and Nantucket, have all passed some variation on laws forbidding smoking in public places as a way to protect nonsmokers from secondhand smoke. This means that in the majority of restaurants and even bars in these towns, you cannot light up. A few bars have installed a ventilation system and/or a separate area where smoking is allowed, but these are few and far between. While some large hotels set aside rooms for smokers, the vast majority of lodging establishments on Cape Cod are non-smoking. There is one establishment in Barnstable where smoking is currently allowed. At **Puff the Magic,** 649 Main St., Hyannis (℗ **508/771-9090**), a cigar bar where no food is served, you can smoke to your heart's discontent.

On Martha's Vineyard, all restaurants are smoke-free except those in Oak Bluffs and Edgartown that have separately enclosed and ventilated bar areas. Since the other four towns on the Vineyard are "dry," meaning no alcohol can be sold, there are no bars in those towns and therefore no smoking at all in restaurants. There is also no smoking allowed in the common areas of inns on the Vineyard. There may be some inns where certain rooms are designated for smokers, and visitors wishing to smoke should inquire when they book their rooms.

TAXES   In Massachusetts, the state sales tax is 5%. This tax applies to restaurant meals (but not to food bought in stores) and all goods, with the exception of clothing items priced lower than $175. The hotel tax varies from town to town; the maximum, including state tax, is 9.7%. The United States has no value-added tax

(VAT) or other indirect tax at the national level. Every state, county, and city may levy its own local tax on all purchases, including hotel and restaurant checks and airline tickets. These taxes will not appear on price tags.

TELEPHONES Many convenience groceries and packaging services sell **prepaid calling cards** in denominations up to $50; for international visitors these can be the least expensive way to call home. Many public pay phones at airports now accept American Express, MasterCard, and Visa credit cards. **Local calls** made from pay phones in most locales cost either 25¢ or 35¢ (no pennies, please). Most long-distance and international calls can be dialed directly from any phone. **For calls within the United States and to Canada,** dial 1 followed by the area code and the seven-digit number. **For other international calls,** dial 011 followed by the country code, city code, and the number you are calling.

Calls to area codes **800, 888, 877,** and **866** are toll-free. However, calls to area codes **700** and **900** (chat lines, bulletin boards, "dating" services, and so on) can be very expensive—usually a charge of 95¢ to $3 or more per minute, and they sometimes have minimum charges that can run as high as $15 or more.

For **reversed-charge or collect calls,** and for person-to-person calls, dial the number 0 then the area code and number; an operator will come on the line, and you should specify whether you are calling collect, person-to-person, or both. If your operator-assisted call is international, ask for the overseas operator.

For **local directory assistance** ("information"), dial ⓒ 411; for long-distance information, dial 1, then the appropriate area code and ⓒ 555-1212.

TELEGRAPH, TELEX & FAX Telegraph and telex services are provided primarily by **Western Union** (ⓒ **800/325-6000;** www.westernunion.com). You can telegraph (wire) money, or have it telegraphed to you, very quickly over the Western Union system, but this service can cost as much as 15% to 20% of the amount sent.

Most hotels have **fax machines** available for guest use (be sure to ask about the charge to use it). Many hotel rooms are wired for guests' fax machines. A less expensive way to send and receive faxes may be at stores such as **The UPS Store.**

TIME Cape Cod and the islands are in the Eastern Standard time zone. The continental United States is divided into **four time zones:** Eastern Standard Time (EST), Central Standard Time (CST), Mountain Standard Time (MST), and Pacific Standard Time (PST). Alaska and Hawaii have their own zones. For example, when it's 9am in Los Angeles (PST), it's 7am in Honolulu (HST), 10am in Denver (MST), 11am in Chicago (CST), noon in New York City (EST), 5pm in London (GMT), and 2am the next day in Sydney.

Daylight saving time is in effect from 1am on the second Sunday in March to 1am on the first Sunday in November, except in Arizona, Hawaii, the U.S. Virgin Islands, and Puerto Rico. Daylight saving time moves the clock 1 hour ahead of standard time.

TIPPING Tips are a very important part of certain workers' income, and gratuities are the standard way of showing appreciation for services provided. (Tipping is certainly not compulsory if the service is poor!) In hotels, tip **bellhops** at least $1 per bag ($2–$3 if you have a lot of luggage) and tip the **chamber staff** $1 to $2 per day (more if you've left a disaster area for him or her to clean up). Tip the **doorman** or **concierge** only if he or she has provided you with some specific service (for example, calling a cab for you or obtaining difficult-to-get theater tickets). Tip the **valet-parking attendant** $1 every time you get your car.

In restaurants, bars, and nightclubs, tip **service staff** 15% to 20% of the check, tip **bartenders** 10% to 15%, tip **checkroom attendants** $1 per garment, and tip **valet-parking attendants** $1 per vehicle.

As for other service personnel, tip **cab drivers** 15% of the fare; tip **skycaps** at airports at least $1 per bag ($2–$3 if you have a lot of luggage); and tip **hairdressers** and **barbers** 15% to 20%.

TOILETS You won't find public toilets or "restrooms" on the streets in most U.S. cities but they can be found in hotel lobbies, bars, restaurants, museums, department stores, railway and bus stations, and service stations. Large hotels and fast-food restaurants are often the best bet for clean facilities. Restaurants and bars in resorts or heavily visited areas may reserve their restrooms for patrons.

USEFUL PHONE NUMBERS U.S. **Dept. of State Travel Advisory** 𝄞 202/647-5225 (manned 24 hrs.). **U.S. Passport Agency** 𝄞 202/647-0518. **U.S. Centers for Disease Control International Traveler's Hotline** 𝄞 404/332-4559.

VISAS For information about U.S. visas go to **http://travel.state.gov** and click on "Visas." Or go to one of the following websites:

Australian citizens can obtain up-to-date visa information from the **U.S. Embassy Canberra,** Moonah Place, Yarralumla, ACT 2600 (𝄞 **02/6214-5600**) or by checking the U.S. Diplomatic Mission's website at **http://usembassy-australia. state.gov/consular**.

British subjects can obtain up-to-date visa information by calling the **U.S. Embassy Visa Information Line** (𝄞 **0891/ 200-290**) or by visiting the "Visas to the U.S." section of the American Embassy London's website at **www.usembassy. org.uk**.

Irish citizens can obtain up-to-date visa information through the **Embassy of the USA Dublin,** 42 Elgin Rd., Dublin 4, Ireland (𝄞 **353/1-668-8777;** or by checking the "Consular Services" section of the website at **http://dublin.usembassy.gov**.

Citizens of **New Zealand** can obtain up-to-date visa information by contacting the **U.S. Embassy New Zealand,** 29 Fitzherbert Terrace, Thorndon, Wellington (𝄞 **644/472-2068**), or get the information directly from the website at **http:// wellington.usembassy.gov**.

---

2 TOLL-FREE NUMBERS & WEBSITES

MAJOR U.S. AIRLINES

(*flies internationally as well)

American Airlines*
𝄞 800/433-7300 (in U.S. or Canada)
𝄞 020/7365-0777 (in U.K.)
www.aa.com

Cape Air
𝄞 800/352-0714
www.flycapeair.com

Continental Airlines*
𝄞 800/523-3273 (in U.S. or Canada)
𝄞 084/5607-6760 (in U.K.)
www.continental.com

Delta Air Lines*
𝄞 800/221-1212 (in U.S. or Canada)
𝄞 084/5600-0950 (in U.K.)
www.delta.com

Frontier Airlines
𝄞 800/432-1359
www.frontierairlines.com

JetBlue Airways
𝄞 800/538-2583 (in U.S.)
𝄞 801/365-2525 (in U.K. or Canada)
www.jetblue.com

Midwest Airlines
℡ 800/452-2022
www.midwestairlines.com

North American Airlines*
℡ 800/371-6297
www.flynaa.com

Nantucket Airlines
℡ 800/635-8787
www.nantucketairlines.com

Northwest Airlines
℡ 800/225-2525 (in U.S.)
℡ 870/0507-4074 (in U.K.)
www.flynaa.com

PenAir (The Spirit of Alaska)
℡ 800/448-4226 (in U.S.)
www.penair.com

United Airlines*
℡ 800/864-8331 (in U.S. and Canada)
℡ 084/5844-4777 in U.K.
www.united.com

US Airways*
℡ 800/428-4322 (in U.S. and Canada)
℡ 084/5600-3300 (in U.K.)
www.usairways.com

Virgin America*
℡ 877/359-8474
www.virginamerica.com

MAJOR INTERNATIONAL AIRLINES

Aeroméxico
℡ 800/237-6639 (in U.S.)
℡ 020/7801-6234 (in U.K.,
   information only)
www.aeromexico.com

Air France
℡ 800/237-2747 (in U.S.)
℡ 800/375-8723 (U.S. and Canada)
℡ 087/0142-4343 (in U.K.)
www.airfrance.com

Air New Zealand
℡ 800/262-1234 (in U.S.)
℡ 800/663-5494 (in Canada)
℡ 0800/028-4149 (in U.K.)
www.airnewzealand.com

Alitalia
℡ 800/223-5730 (in U.S.)
℡ 800/361-8336 (in Canada)
℡ 087/0608-6003 (in U.K.)
www.alitalia.com

British Airways
℡ 800/247-9297 (in U.S. and Canada)
℡ 087/0850-9850 (in U.K.)
www.british-airways.com

Lufthansa
℡ 800/399-5838 (in U.S.)
℡ 800/563-5954 (in Canada)
℡ 087/0837-7747 (in U.K.)
www.lufthansa.com

Virgin Atlantic Airways
℡ 800/821-5438 (in U.S. and Canada)
℡ 087/0574-7747 (in U.K.)
www.virgin-atlantic.com

BUDGET AIRLINES

AirTran Airways
℡ 800/247-8726
www.airtran.com

Frontier Airlines
℡ 800/432-1359
www.frontierairlines.com

Southwest Airlines
℡ 800/435-9792 (in U.S., U.K.
   and Canada)
www.southwest.com

Spirit Airlines
℡ 800/772-7117
www.spiritair.com

Ted (part of United Airlines)
℡ 800/225-5561
www.flyted.com

CAR RENTAL AGENCIES

Advantage
✆ 800/777-5500 (in U.S.)
✆ 021/0344-4712 (outside of U.S.)
www.advantagerentacar.com

Alamo
✆ 800/GO-ALAMO (800/462-5266)
www.alamo.com

Avis
✆ 800/331-1212 (in U.S. and Canada)
✆ 084/4581-8181 (in U.K.)
www.avis.com

Budget
✆ 800/527-0700 (in U.S.)
✆ 800/268-8900 (in Canada)
✆ 087/0156-5656 (in U.K.)
www.budget.com

Dollar
✆ 800/800-4000 (in U.S.)
✆ 800/848-8268 (in Canada)
✆ 080/8234-7524 (in U.K.)
www.dollar.com

Enterprise
✆ 800/261-7331 (in U.S.)
✆ 514/355-4028 (in Canada)
✆ 012/9360-9090 (in U.K.)
www.enterprise.com

Hertz
✆ 800/645-3131
✆ 800/654-3001 (for international reservations)
www.hertz.com

National
✆ 800/CAR-RENT (800/227-7368)
www.nationalcar.com

Payless
✆ 800/PAYLESS (800/729-5377)
www.paylesscarrental.com

Rent-A-Wreck
✆ 800/535-1391
www.rentawreck.com

Thrifty
✆ 800/367-2277
✆ 918/669-2168 (international)
www.thrifty.com

MAJOR HOTEL & MOTEL CHAINS

Best Western International
✆ 800/780-7234 (in U.S. and Canada)
✆ 0800/393-130 (in U.K.)
www.bestwestern.com

Clarion Hotels
✆ 800/CLARION (800/252-7566) or 877/424-6423 (in U.S. and Canada)
✆ 0800/444-444 (in U.K.)
www.choicehotels.com

Comfort Inns
✆ 800/228-5150
✆ 0800/444-444 (in U.K.)
www.comfortinn.com

Courtyard by Marriott
✆ 888/236-2427 (in U.S.)
✆ 0800/221-222 (in U.K.)
www.marriott.com/courtyard

Crowne Plaza Hotels
✆ 888/303-1746
www.ichotelsgroup.com/crowneplaza

Days Inn
✆ 800/329-7466 (in U.S.)
✆ 0800/280-400 (in U.K.)
www.daysinn.com

Doubletree Hotels
✆ 800/222-TREE (800/222-8733) (in U.S. and Canada)
✆ 087/0590-9090 (in U.K.)
www.doubletree.com

Econo Lodges
✆ 800/55-ECONO (800/552-3666)
www.choicehotels.com

Embassy Suites
✆ 800/EMBASSY (800/362-2779)
www.embassysuites.com

Fairfield Inn by Marriott
☎ 800/228-2800 (in U.S. and Canada)
☎ 0800/221-222 (in U.K.)
www.marriott.com/fairfieldinn

Four Seasons
☎ 800/819-5053 (in U.S. and Canada)
www.fourseasons.com

Hampton Inn
☎ 800/HAMPTON (800/426-4766)
www.hamptoninn.com

Hilton Hotels
☎ 800/HILTONS (800/445-8667)
   (in U.S. and Canada)
☎ 087/0590-9090 (in U.K.)
www.hilton.com

Holiday Inn
☎ 800/315-2621 (in U.S. and Canada)
☎ 0800/405-060 (in U.K.)
www.holidayinn.com

Hyatt
☎ 888/591-1234 (in U.S. and Canada)
☎ 084/5888-1234 (in U.K.)
www.hyatt.com

InterContinental Hotels & Resorts
☎ 800/424-6835 (in U.S. and Canada)
☎ 0800/1800-1800 (in U.K.)
www.ichotelsgroup.com

Marriott
☎ 877/236-2427 (in U.S. and Canada)
☎ 0800/221-222 (in U.K.)
www.marriott.com

Motel 6
☎ 800/4MOTEL6 (800/466-8356)
www.motel6.com

Quality
☎ 877/424-6423 (in U.S. and Canada)
☎ 0800/444-444 (in U.K.)
www.QualityInn.ChoiceHotels.com

Ramada Worldwide
☎ 888/2-RAMADA (888/272-6232)
   (in U.S. and Canada)
☎ 080/8100-0783 (in U.K.)
www.ramada.com

Red Carpet Inns
☎ 800/251-1962
www.bookroomsnow.com

Red Lion Hotels
☎ 800/RED-LION (800/733-5466)
www.redlion.rdln.com

Red Roof Inns
☎ 866/686-4335 (in U.S. and Canada)
☎ 614/601-4075 (international)
www.redroof.com

Residence Inn by Marriott
☎ 800/331-3131
☎ 800/221-222 (in U.K.)
www.marriott.com/residenceinn

Sheraton Hotels & Resorts
☎ 800/325-3535 (in U.S.)
☎ 800/543-4300 (in Canada)
☎ 0800/3253-5353 (in U.K.)
www.starwoodhotels.com/sheraton

Super 8 Motels
☎ 800/800-8000
www.super8.com

Travelodge
☎ 800/578-7878
www.travelodge.com

Westin Hotels & Resorts
☎ 800/937-8461 (in U.S. and Canada)
☎ 0800/3259-5959 (in U.K.)
www.starwoodhotels.com/westin

Wyndham Hotels & Resorts
☎ 877/999-3223 (in U.S. and Canada)
☎ 050/6638-4899 (in U.K.)
www.wyndham.com

INDEX

See also Accommodations and Restaurant indexes, below.

FROMMER'S® COMPLETE TRAVEL GUIDES

Alaska
Amalfi Coast
American Southwest
Amsterdam
Argentina
Arizona
Atlanta
Australia
Austria
Bahamas
Barcelona
Beijing
Belgium· Holland & Luxembourg
Belize
Bermuda
Boston
Brazil
British Columbia & the Canadian
    Rockies
Brussels & Bruges
Budapest & the Best of Hungary
Buenos Aires
Calgary
California
Canada
Cancún· Cozumel & the Yucatán
Cape Cod· Nantucket & Martha's
    Vineyard
Caribbean
Caribbean Ports of Call
Carolinas & Georgia
Chicago
Chile & Easter Island
China
Colorado
Costa Rica
Croatia
Cuba
Denmark
Denver· Boulder & Colorado Springs
Eastern Europe
Ecuador & the Galapagos Islands
Edinburgh & Glasgow
England
Europe
Europe by Rail

Florence· Tuscany & Umbria
Florida
France
Germany
Greece
Greek Islands
Guatemala
Hawaii
Hong Kong
Honolulu· Waikiki & Oahu
India
Ireland
Israel
Italy
Jamaica
Japan
Kauai
Las Vegas
London
Los Angeles
Los Cabos & Baja
Madrid
Maine Coast
Maryland & Delaware
Maui
Mexico
Montana & Wyoming
Montréal & Québec City
Morocco
Moscow & St· Petersburg
Munich & the Bavarian Alps
Nashville & Memphis
New England
Newfoundland & Labrador
New Mexico
New Orleans
New York City
New York State
New Zealand
Northern Italy
Norway
Nova Scotia· New Brunswick &
    Prince Edward Island
Oregon
Paris
Peru

Philadelphia & the Amish Country
Portugal
Prague & the Best of the Czech
    Republic
Provence & the Riviera
Puerto Rico
Rome
San Antonio & Austin
San Diego
San Francisco
Santa Fe· Taos & Albuquerque
Scandinavia
Scotland
Seattle
Seville· Granada & the Best of
    Andalusia
Shanghai
Sicily
Singapore & Malaysia
South Africa
South America
South Florida
South Korea
South Pacific
Southeast Asia
Spain
Sweden
Switzerland
Tahiti & French Polynesia
Texas
Thailand
Tokyo
Toronto
Turkey
USA
Utah
Vancouver & Victoria
Vermont· New Hampshire & Maine
Vienna & the Danube Valley
Vietnam
Virgin Islands
Virginia
Walt Disney World* & Orlando
Washington· D·C·
Washington State

FROMMER'S® DAY BY DAY GUIDES

Amsterdam
Barcelona
Beijing
Boston
Cancun & the Yucatan
Chicago
Florence & Tuscany

Hong Kong
Honolulu & Oahu
London
Maui
Montréal
Napa & Sonoma
New York City

Paris
Provence & the Riviera
Rome
San Francisco
Venice
Washington D·C·

PAULINE FROMMER'S GUIDES: SEE MORE. SPEND LESS.

Alaska
Hawaii
Italy

Las Vegas
London
New York City

Paris
Walt Disney World*
Washington D·C·

FROMMER'S® PORTABLE GUIDES

Acapulco, Ixtapa & Zihuatanejo
Amsterdam
Aruba, Bonaire & Curacao
Australia's Great Barrier Reef
Bahamas
Big Island of Hawaii
Boston
California Wine Country
Cancún
Cayman Islands
Charleston
Chicago
Dominican Republic

Florence
Las Vegas
Las Vegas for Non-Gamblers
London
Maui
Nantucket & Martha's Vineyard
New Orleans
New York City
Paris
Portland
Puerto Rico
Puerto Vallarta, Manzanillo & Guadalajara

Rio de Janeiro
San Diego
San Francisco
Savannah
St. Martin, Sint Maarten, Anguila & St. Bart's
Turks & Caicos
Vancouver
Venice
Virgin Islands
Washington, D.C.
Whistler

FROMMER'S® CRUISE GUIDES

Alaska Cruises & Ports of Call

Cruises & Ports of Call

European Cruises & Ports of Call

FROMMER'S® NATIONAL PARK GUIDES

Algonquin Provincial Park
Banff & Jasper
Grand Canyon

National Parks of the American West
Rocky Mountain
Yellowstone & Grand Teton

Yosemite and Sequoia & Kings Canyon
Zion & Bryce Canyon

FROMMER'S® WITH KIDS GUIDES

Chicago
Hawaii
Las Vegas
London

National Parks
New York City
San Francisco

Toronto
Walt Disney World® & Orlando
Washington, D.C.

FROMMER'S® PHRASEFINDER DICTIONARY GUIDES

Chinese
French

German
Italian

Japanese
Spanish

SUZY GERSHMAN'S BORN TO SHOP GUIDES

France
Hong Kong, Shanghai & Beijing
Italy

London
New York
Paris

San Francisco
Where to Buy the Best of Everything.

FROMMER'S® BEST-LOVED DRIVING TOURS

Britain
California
France
Germany

Ireland
Italy
New England
Northern Italy

Scotland
Spain
Tuscany & Umbria

THE UNOFFICIAL GUIDES®

Adventure Travel in Alaska
Beyond Disney
California with Kids
Central Italy
Chicago
Cruises
Disneyland®
England
Hawaii

Ireland
Las Vegas
London
Maui
Mexico's Best Beach Resorts
Mini Mickey
New Orleans
New York City
Paris

San Francisco
South Florida including Miami & the Keys
Walt Disney World®
Walt Disney World® for Grown-ups
Walt Disney World® with Kids
Washington, D.C.

SPECIAL-INTEREST TITLES

Athens Past & Present
Best Places to Raise Your Family
Cities Ranked & Rated
500 Places to Take Your Kids Before They Grow Up
Frommer's Best Day Trips from London
Frommer's Best RV & Tent Campgrounds in the U.S.A.

Frommer's Exploring America by RV
Frommer's NYC Free & Dirt Cheap
Frommer's Road Atlas Europe
Frommer's Road Atlas Ireland
Retirement Places Rated